Anonymous

The American Almanac and Repository of Useful Knowledge for the Year 1860

Anonymous

The American Almanac and Repository of Useful Knowledge for the Year 1860

ISBN/EAN: 9783337217327

Printed in Europe, USA, Canada, Australia, Japan

THE

AMERICAN ALMANAC

AND

REPOSITORY

OF

USEFUL KNOWLEDGE,

FOR THE YEAR

1860.

BOSTON:
CROSBY, NICHOLS, AND COMPANY.
LONDON:
TRÜBNER AND CO., 60 PATERNOSTER ROW.
PARIS: HECTOR BOSSANGE.
For sale by all Booksellers in the United States and Canadas.

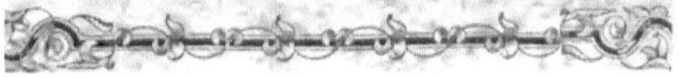

THE

AMERICAN ALMANAC

AND

REPOSITORY

OF

USEFUL KNOWLEDGE,

FOR THE YEAR

1860.

BOSTON:
CROSBY, NICHOLS, AND COMPANY.
LONDON:
TRÜBNER & CO., 60 PATERNOSTER ROW.
PARIS: HECTOR BOSSANGE.
1860.

PREFACE.

The thirty-first volume of the American Almanac, being the *First* volume of the *Fourth Series*, is now offered to the public. Unwearied pains has been taken to collect full, authentic, and varied information concerning the complex affairs of the general and State governments; and a mass of official documents and private correspondence has been digested relating to the government, finances, legislation, public institutions, internal improvements, and resources of the United States, and of the several States. It is hoped that the present volume will be found equal to its predecessors in fulness and accuracy, and that it will sustain the high character of the American Almanac as a trustworthy manual for reference and a full repository of useful knowledge.

The Astronomical Department has been prepared by Mr. George P. Bond, Assistant Observer at the Cambridge Observatory. There are interesting papers upon Donati's Comet of 1858, the Law of Storms, and the Aurora Borealis and Australis. The Table of Occultations, the Eclipses of Jupiter's Satellites, the Ephemeris of the Sun, the True Apparent Places of the Pole Star and the Principal Fixed Stars, Dr. Young's Table of Refractions, and the Sun's Parallax in Altitude, are not given, and it is proposed hereafter to omit them, as the reasons originally making their publication desirable are not now so pressing, and the space heretofore occupied by them can be better filled.

In the Second Part of the volume will be found full lists of the Executive and Judiciary of the General Government, including the chief officers and clerks of the several Departments, and of the Court of Claims; of Collectors of Customs, of Postmasters in the principal places, of Army and Navy Pension Agents, and of the Indian Superintendents and Agents; of the Inspectors of Steamboats and their Districts; of the Army, and the various Military Departments and Posts under the new organization; of the Navy, the public vessels, and the Marine Corps; of our Ministers and Consuls in Foreign Countries, and of Foreign Ministers and Consuls in the United States. These lists have been corrected from official sources to the latest dates possible for publication. Later changes are noted in the "Additions and Corrections," at the end of the volume. The titles, Commerce and Navigation, and Revenue and Expenditure, published each year in the Almanac, are full and complete abstracts of the public documents of the same name, and the tables connected therewith, and with the Post-Office, Mint, and Public Lands, show the receipts and expenditures of the Government under their several heads, the public debt, the imports, exports, tonnage, coinage, sales of land, and the operations of the Post-Office Department, for each year since the adoption of the Federal Constitution. The rates of postage, with the inland and foreign mail service, are believed to be complete and correct. The Titles and Abstracts of the Public Laws and Joint Resolutions have been carefully prepared, and are sufficiently full, except for professional use. Among those this year of special interest are the Acts relative to the lien law in the District of Columbia; the keeping and distributing of Public Documents; the admission of Oregon; the incorporation of the Washington National Monument Society; to carry into effect the convention between the United States and China; the care and preservation of the Washington Water-Works; and the resolution in relation to the restrictions on the Tobacco trade. Tables of Railroads in this country and in Canada, and of the surveyed routes to the Pacific; of Telegraphs and Submarine Telegraphs; of Colleges and Professional Schools in the United States; of the Population of the several States at the decennial periods; of the Debts, Property, and Expenses of the States; of the Times of the State Elections and the Meetings of the State Legislatures, and of the Votes at the different Presidential Elections, are given.

The alphabetical arrangement of the Individual States has, for obvious reasons, been substituted for the geographical. The information concerning the Individual States is as full as in former years. It is believed that nowhere else can be found collected such full details respecting the Executive and Judiciary, the finances, schools, charitable institutions, and pauperism and crime, of the several States. Should any one note inaccuracies or deficiencies therein, he is urgently requested to correct them. The European part of the work, revised from the best authority to the latest dates, gives the several States of Europe, with their form of government, the name, title, and date of accession of the reigning sovereigns, the area and population of the several countries. It also gives the Royal Family, the Ministry, and the Judiciary of England, and the Ministry of France. The Obituary Notices and Chronicle of Events have been prepared with care. The space is so limited, that many names and events which otherwise would be given are necessarily omitted.

The thanks of the Editor are particularly due to the Heads of Departments at Washington, and to his many contributors and correspondents, to whom the work is indebted for a great part of its value. A continuance of their favors is respectfully solicited. A work embracing such a multitude of facts must necessarily contain errors; persons who may detect any are earnestly requested to communicate them to the Editor. It is particularly desirable that these communications should not be anonymous. It is frequently a source of regret to the Editor, that he cannot suitably acknowledge the valuable hints and assistance of anonymous correspondents. It is a matter of some public interest, that a periodical which circulates so widely, both in Europe and America, and which is so universally trusted as a manual for reference, should be rendered as accurate as possible; and this end can be obtained only by the co-operation of many individuals. Communications should be addressed to the "Editor of the American Almanac," Boston.

Boston, Mass., December, 1859.

CONTENTS.

PART I.

Calendar and Celestial Phenomena for the Year 1860.

PART II.

United States.

Individual States.

American States.

Europe.

INDEX.

THE

AMERICAN ALMANAC,

FOR

1860.

PART I.

1

THE

AMERICAN ALMANAC,

FOR THE YEAR

1860,

Being the latter part of the 84th, and the beginning of the 85th year of the Independence of the United States of America;

" the 6573d year of the Julian Period;

" the latter part of the 5620th, and the beginning of the 5621st
" year since the creation of the world, according to the Jews;

" the 2613th year (according to Varro) since the foundation of Rome;

" the 2607th year since the era of Nabonassar, which has been assigned to Wednesday, the 26th of February, of the 3967th year of the Julian Period, which corresponds, according to the chronologists, to the 747th, and, according to the astronomers, to the 746th year before the birth of Christ;

" the 2636th year of the Olympiads, or the fourth year of the 659th Olympiad, beginning in July, 1857, if we fix the era of the Olympiads at 775½ years before Christ, or at or about the beginning of July of the year 3938 of the Julian Period;

" the latter part of the 1276th, and the beginning of the 1277th year (of twelve lunations) since the Hegira, or flight of Mahomet, which, as is generally supposed, took place on the 16th of July, in the year 622 of the Christian era.

I. CALENDAR AND CELESTIAL PHENOMENA FOR THE YEAR.

SIGNS OF THE PLANETS, &c.

☉ The Sun.	♂ Mars.	♃ Jupiter.
⊕ The Earth.	⚶ Vesta.	♄ Saturn.
● ☽ ○ ☾ The Moon.	⚵ Juno.	♅ Herschel or Uranus.
☿ Mercury.	⚴ Pallas.	♆ Neptune.
♀ Venus.	⚳ Ceres.	✱ A fixed star.

☌ Conjunction, or having the same Longitude or Right Ascension.
□ Quadrature, or differing 90° in " " "
☍ Opposition, or differing 180° in " " "
☊ The ascending, ☋ the descending node.

The sign + is prefixed to the latitude, or declination, of the Sun, or other heavenly body, when *north*, and the sign — when *south*.

The letters *M. A.*, *m. a.*, denote *Morning* and *Afternoon*.

CHRONOLOGICAL CYCLES.

Dominical Letters, . . .	A G	Solar Cycle, ...	21
Epact, ...	7	Roman Indiction, ...	3
Lunar Cycle, or Golden Number,	18	Julian Period, ...	6573

SIGNS OF THE ZODIAC.

Spring signs.	1. ♈ Aries. 2. ♉ Taurus. 3. ♊ Gemini.	Autumn signs.	7. ♎ Libra. 8. ♏ Scorpio. 9. ♐ Sagittarius.
Summer signs.	4. ♋ Cancer. 5. ♌ Leo. 6. ♍ Virgo.	Winter signs.	10. ♑ Capricornus. 11. ♒ Aquarius. 12. ♓ Pisces.

BEGINNING AND LENGTH OF THE SEASONS.

			h. m.	
Sun enters ♑	(Winter begins)	1859, Dec. 22d,	2 55 M.	Mean Time at Washington Observatory.
" " ♈	(Spring ")	1860, March 20th,	3 57 M.	
" " ♋	(Summer ")	" June 21st,	0 35 M.	
" " ♎	(Autumn ")	" Sept. 22d,	2 44 A.	
" " ♑	(Winter ")	" Dec. 21st,	8 43 M.	

	d.	h.	m.
Sun in the Winter signs, ...	89	1	2
" " Spring "	92	20	38
" " Summer "	93	14	9
" " Autumn "	89	17	59
" north of Equator, (Spring and Summer,)	186	10	47
" south of " (Winter and Autumn,)	178	19	1
Length of the tropical year, commencing at the winter solstice, 1859, and terminating at the winter solstice, 1860, ...	365	5	48
Mean or average length of the tropical year,	365	5	49

MOVABLE FESTIVALS OF THE CHURCH IN 1860.

Septuagesima Sunday,	Feb. 5th	Rogation Sunday,	May 13th
Quinq. or Shrove Sunday,	Feb. 19th	Ascen. Day, or Holy Th.,	May 17th
Ash Wed., Lent begins,	Feb. 22d	Whitsunday, or Pentecost,	May 27th
First Sunday in Lent,	Feb. 26th	Trinity Sunday,	June 3d
Palm Sunday,	April 1st	Corpus Christi Day, } Fête Dieu, }	June 7th
EASTER SUNDAY,	April 8th		
Low Sunday,	April 15th	1st Sunday in Advent,	Dec. 2d

JEWISH CALENDAR.

[The anniversaries marked with an asterisk (*) are to be strictly observed.]

Year.	Names of the Months.	
5620	Thebet begins,	Dec. 27, 1859
"	" 10th, Fast for the Siege of Jerusalem,	Jan. 5, 1860
"	Sebat begins,	Jan. 25, "
"	Adar begins,	Feb. 24, "
"	" 13th, Fast of Esther,	Mar. 7, "
"	" 14th, Purim,	Mar. 8, "
"	" 15th, Schuscan Purim,	Mar. 9, "
"	Nisan begins,	Mar. 24, "
"	" 15th, *Beginning of the Passover,	Apr. 7, "
"	" 16th, *Second Feast, or Morrow of the Passover,	Apr. 8, "
"	" 21st, *Seventh Feast,	Apr. 13, "
"	" 22d, *End of the Passover,	Apr. 14, "
"	Ijar begins,	Apr. 23, "
"	" 18th, Lag Beomer,	May 10, "
"	Sivan begins,	May 22, "
"	" 6th, *Feast of Weeks, or Pentecost,	May 27, "
"	" 7th, *Second Feast,	May 28, "
"	Thammuz begins,	June 21, "
"	" 18th, Fast for the taking of the Temple,	July 8, "
"	Ab begins,	July 20, "
"	" 10th, *Fast for the burning of the Temple,	July 29, "
"	" Elul begins,	Aug. 19, "
5621	Tisri begins, *Feast for the New Year,	Sept. 17, "
"	" 2d, *Second Feast for the New Year,	Sept. 18, "
"	" 3d, Fast of Gedaljah,	Sept. 19, "
"	" 10th, *Fast of the Reconciliation or Atonement,	Sept. 26, "
"	" 15th, *Feast of the Huts or Tabernacles,	Oct. 1, "
"	" 16th, *Second Feast of the Huts,	Oct. 2, "

Year.	Names of the Months.	
5621	Tisri 21st, Feast of Palms or Branches,	Oct. 7, 1860
"	" 22d, *End of the Hut or Congregation Feast,	Oct. 8, "
"	" 23d, *Rejoicing for the Discovery of the Law,	Oct. 9, "
"	Marchesvan begins,	Oct. 17, "
"	Chisleu begins,	Nov. 15, "
"	" 25th, Consecration of the Temple,	Dec. 9, "
"	Thebet begins,	Dec. 14, "
"	" 10th, Fast for the Siege of Jerusalem,	Dec. 23, "
"	Sebat begins,	Jan. 12, 1861

The Jewish year generally contains 354 days, or 12 lunations of the Moon; but in a cycle of 19 years, an intercalary month (Veadar) is 7 times introduced, for the purpose of rendering the average duration of the year nearly or quite correct.

MAHOMETAN CALENDAR.

Year.	Names of the Months.			
1276	Jomadhi II.	begins,		Dec. 29, 1859
"	Redjeb	"		Jan. 24, 1860
"	Chaban	"		Feb. 23, "
"	Ramadan	"	(Month of Fasting,)	Mar. 23, "
"	Schewall	"	(Bairam,)	Apr. 22, "
"	Dsu'l-kadah	"		May 21, "
"	Dsu'l-hejjah	"		June 20, "
1277	Muharrem	"		July 20, "
"	Saphar	"		Aug. 19, "
"	Rabia I.	"		Sept. 17, "
"	Rabia II.	"		Oct. 17, "
"	Jomadhi I.	"		Nov. 15, "
"	Jomadhi II.	"		Dec. 15, "
"	Redjeb,	"		Jan. 13, 1861

The Mahometan Era dates from the flight of Mahomet to Medina, July 16th, A. D. 622.

The Mahometan year is purely lunar; it consists of 12 synodical periods of the Moon, or of 354 days 19 times in a cycle of 30 years, and of 355 days 11 times. The average length of this year is therefore $354\frac{11}{30}$ days, which differs only *thirty-three seconds* from the truth; a degree of exactness that could only have been attained by a long series of observations. But as no allowance is made for the excess of 11 days in the length of a tropical year over the time of 12 revolutions of the Moon, it is obvious that once in about 33 years the above months will correspond to every season and every part of the Gregorian year.

HEIGHT OF THE GREATEST OR SPRING TIDES IN 1860.

Computed by the Formula of La Place (Mécanique Céleste, Vol. II. pp. 289, *Paris ed., and* [2858] *Bowd. ed.*).

Washington Mean Time of New or Full Moon.				Height of the Tide.	Washington Mean Time of New or Full Moon.				Height of the Tide.
		d.	h.				d.	h.	
Full Moon,	Jan.	8,	10 M.	0.93	New Moon,	July	18,	9 M.	0.96
New "		22,	7 A.	0.77	Full "	Aug.	1,	0 A.	0.82
Full "	Feb.	6,	9 A.	1.09	New "		16,	5 A.	1.08
New "		21,	2 A.	0.83	Full "		31,	4 M.	0.85
Full "	Mar.	7,	8 M.	1.15	New "	Sept.	15,	1 M.	1.15
New "		22,	9 M.	0.88	Full "		29,	9 A.	0.85
Full "	April	5,	5 A.	1.10	New "	Oct.	14,	9 M.	1.10
New "		21,	1 M.	0.86	Full "		29,	2 A.	0.81
Full "	May	5,	2 M.	0.95	New "	Nov.	12,	7 A.	0.96
New "		20,	2 A.	0.81	Full "		28,	6 M.	0.78
Full "	June	3,	0 A.	0.82	New "	Dec.	12,	8 M.	0.86
New "		19,	0 M.	0.84	Full "		27,	10 A.	0.83
Full "	July	2,	11 A.	0.79					

The unit of altitude at any place is the height at that place of that tide which arrives *about a day and a half* after the time of New or Full Moon, when the Sun and Moon, at the moment of conjunction or opposition, are at their mean distance from the Earth, and in the plane of the celestial equator.

This unit of altitude, which must be derived from observation for each place, multiplied by the quantities in the above table, gives the height of the spring tides at that place during the present year.

By the above table it appears that the highest tides of 1860 will be those of Feb. 6, March 7, April 5, Aug. 16, Sept. 15, and Oct. 14.

The actual rise of the tide, however, depends so much on the strength and direction of the wind, that it not unfrequently happens that a tide, which would, independently of these, have been small, is higher than another, otherwise much greater. But when a tide, which arrives when the Sun and Moon are in a favorable position for producing a great elevation, is still further increased by a very strong wind, the rise of the water will be uncommonly great.

The formula from which these tides were computed is, however, strictly true only for Brest and its vicinity, and must be regarded as a very uncertain approximation for the coast of the United States.

Twilight begins and ends. Mean Time.

	1st day.		7th day.		13th day.		19th day.		25th day.	
	Begins. h. m.	Ends. h. m.	Begins. h. m.	Ends. h. m.	Begins. h. m.	Ends. h. m.	Begins. h. m.	Ends. h. m.	Begins. h. m.	Ends. h. m.
Boston, .	5 48m	6 20a	5 48m	6 24a	5 48m	6 29a	5 47m	6 35a	5 44m	6 42a
N. York,	5 46	6 22	5 46	6 26	5 46	6 31	5 45	6 37	5 42	6 44
Wash'n,	5 43	6 25	5 44	6 29	5 44	6 34	5 43	6 39	5 41	6 45
Charles.,	5 35	6 33	5 36	6 37	5 37	6 41	5 36	6 46	5 35	6 51
N. Orl's,	5 31	6 37	5 33	6 40	5 34	6 44	5 33	6 49	5 32	6 54
S. Fran.,	5 42	6 26	5 43	6 30	5 43	6 35	5 42	6 40	5 40	6 46

PHASES, AND PERIGEE AND APOGEE, OF THE MOON.

Full Moon, 8th day, 10h. 15m. M. | New Moon, 22d day, 7h. 8m. A.
Last Quarter, 15th " 1 50 M. | First Quarter, 30th " 12 2 M.
Perigee, 9th day, 10h. A. | Apogee, 25th day, 0h. A.

Sun's *upper* limb rises and sets (cor. for refr.) Mean Time.

Days of Month.	Days of Week.	Boston, &c. rises. h. m.	Boston, &c. sets. h. m.	New York, &c. rises. h. m.	New York, &c. sets. h. m.	Washington, &c. rises. h. m.	Washington, &c. sets. h. m.	Charleston, &c. rises. h. m.	Charleston, &c. sets. h. m.	N. Orleans, &c. rises. h. m.	N. Orleans, &c. sets. h. m.	San Francisco, &c. rises. h. m.	San Francisco, &c. sets. h. m.	Moon Souths. Mean Time. h. m.
1	*Su.*	7 30	4 39	7 25	4 43	7 19	4 48	7 3	5 5	6 56	5 11	7 16	4 51	6 11a
2	M.	30	39	25	44	19	49	3	6	56	12	16	52	6 55
3	Tu.	30	40	25	45	19	50	3	6	56	13	16	53	7 44
4	W.	30	41	25	46	19	51	3	7	57	14	16	54	8 37
5	Th.	30	42	25	47	19	52	3	8	57	14	16	55	9 35
6	F.	30	43	25	48	19	53	4	9	57	15	16	56	10 38
7	S.	30	44	25	49	19	54	4	10	57	16	16	57	11 41a
8	*Su.*	7 29	4 45	7 25	4 50	7 19	4 55	7 4	5 10	6 57	5 17	7 16	4 58	☍
9	M.	29	46	24	51	19	56	4	11	57	17	16	59	0 44m
10	Tu.	29	47	24	52	19	57	4	12	57	18	16	5 0	1 42
11	W.	29	48	24	53	19	58	4	13	57	19	16	1	2 37
12	Th.	28	49	24	54	18	59	3	14	57	20	15	2	3 28
13	F.	28	50	23	55	18	5 0	3	15	57	21	15	3	4 17
14	S.	28	51	23	56	18	1	3	16	57	22	15	4	5 6
15	*Su.*	7 27	4 53	7 23	4 57	7 18	5 2	7 3	5 16	6 57	5 23	7 15	5 5	5 55
16	M.	27	54	22	58	17	3	3	17	57	23	14	6	6 45
17	Tu.	26	55	22	59	17	4	3	18	57	24	14	7	7 38
18	W.	26	56	21	5 1	16	5	2	19	57	25	13	8	8 21
19	Th.	25	57	21	2	16	6	2	20	56	26	13	9	9 25
20	F.	25	59	20	3	15	7	2	21	56	27	12	10	10 19
21	S.	24	5 0	20	4	15	8	1	22	56	28	12	11	11 11
22	*Su.*	7 23	5 1	7 19	5 5	7 14	5 10	7 1	5 23	6 55	5 28	7 11	5 13	11 59m
23	M.	23	2	18	6	14	11	1	24	55	29	11	14	0 45a
24	T.	22	3	17	8	13	12	0	25	55	30	10	15	1 28
25	W.	21	5	17	9	13	13	0	26	54	31	10	16	2 8
26	Th.	21	6	16	10	12	14	6 59	27	54	32	9	17	2 48
27	F.	20	7	15	11	11	15	59	28	53	33	8	18	3 27
28	S.	19	8	14	12	10	16	58	29	53	34	7	19	4 7
29	*Su.*	7 18	5 10	7 14	5 14	7 10	5 17	6 58	5 30	6 52	5 35	7 7	5 20	4 49
30	M.	17	11	13	15	9	19	57	31	52	36	6	22	5 34
31	T.	16	13	12	16	8	20	56	32	52	36	5	23	6 24a

Passage of the Meridian (mean time) and Declination of the Planets at Transit.

	1st day.		7th day.		13th day.		19th day.		25th day.	
	souths.	Dec.	*souths.*	Dec.	*souths.*	Dec.	*souths.*	Dec.	*souths.*	Dec.
	h. m.	° ′	h. m.	° ′	h. m.	° ′	h. m.	° ′	h. m.	° ′
☿	10 26m	—20 47	10 28m	—22 5	10 38m	—23 4	10 50m	—23 30	11 5m	—23 13
♀	1 45a	—20 48	1 52a	—18 54	1 58a	—16 41	2 4a	—14 12	2 8a	—11 29
♂	7 57m	—14 27	7 48m	—15 35	7 39m	—16 40	7 30m	—17 40	7 21m	—18 36
♃	0 53	+22 1	0 26	+22 9	11 54a	+22 19	11 27a	+22 26	11 00a	+22 33
♄	3 12	+14 15	2 47	+14 22	2 22m	+14 30	1 57m	+14 39	1 28m	+14 50
♅	9 26a	+20 56	9 1a	+20 54	8 37a	+20 53	8 13a	+20 51	7 49a	+20 50
♆	4 59	— 3 20	4 36	— 3 17	4 13	— 3 14	3 49	— 3 11	3 26	— 3 7

Days of Month.	Moon rises or sets. Mean Time.						High Water. Mean Time.			
	Boston, &c.	New York, &c.	Washington, &c.	Charleston, &c.	N. Orleans, &c.	San Francisco, &c.	Boston, &c.	New York, &c.	Charleston, &c.	San Francisco (North Beach).
	sets. h. m.	*sets.* h. m.	*sets.* h. m.	*sets.* h. m.	*sets.* h. m.	*sets.* h. m.	h. m.	h. m.	h. m.	h. m.
S.	0 3m	0 2m	0 1m	. . .	. . .	0 8m	4 38m	1 26m	0 29m	5 41m
2	1 8	1 6	1 3	0 55m	0 53m	1 10	5 25	2 12	1 13	6 32
3	2 15	2 11	2 8	1 56	1 52	2 14	6 18	3 5	2 4	7 25
4	3 23	3 18	3 13	2 58	2 53	3 18	7 18	4 4	3 7	8 22
5	4 33	4 27	4 21	4 03	3 56	4 26	8 20	5 5	4 14	9 21
6	5 42	5 35	5 29	5 09	5 2	5 33	9 23	6 9	5 21	10 14
7	6 45	6 38	6 31	6 12	6 5	6 35	10 25	7 11	6 26	11 6
S.	7 37m	7 31m	7 25m	7 7m	7 0m	7 29m	11 21m	8 5	7 21	11 54m
9	*rises.*	*rises.*	*rises.*	*rises.*	*rises.*	*rises.*	0 13a	9 0	8 15	0 45a
10	7 34a	7 38a	7 41a	7 50a	7 56a	7 51a	1 4	9 50	9 2	1 32
11	8 54	8 56	8 58	9 1	9 5	9 8	1 51	10 36	9 40	2 18
12	10 11	10 11	10 11	10 11	10 12	10 21	2 37	11 20m	10 31	3 8
13	11 25	11 24	11 22	11 17	11 17	11 31	3 22	0 9a	11 16m	4 7
14	. . .	. . .	. . .	. . .	. . .	. . .	4 12	1 0	0 42	5 11
S.	0 38m	0 35m	0 32m	0 23m	0 21m	0 40m	5 6	1 13	0 55	6 12
16	1 50	1 46	1 42	1 29	1 25	1 49	6 6	2 53	1 52	7 12
17	3 3	2 58	2 52	3 36	3 30	2 57	7 9	3 55	2 58	8 14
18	4 8	4 2	3 55	4 36	4 30	4 00	8 13	4 58	4 7	9 15
19	5 10	5 3	4 57	4 36	4 30	5 00	9 12	5 58	5 9	10 6
20	6 1	5 54	5 47	5 27	5 20	5 50	10 6	6 53	5 7	10 50
21	6 45	6 39	6 33	6 14	6 8	6 35	10 56	7 40	6 56	11 31a
S.	7 21m	7 16m	7 11m	6 54m	6 49m	7 12m	11 36a	8 19	7 37	. . .
23	*sets.*	*sets.*	*sets.*	*sets.*	*sets.*	*sets.*	. . .	9 2	8 16	0 9m
24	6 49a	6 53a	6 56a	7 5a	7 11a	7 5a	0 15m	9 38	8 50	0 46
25	7 50	7 52	7 52	7 59	8 2	8 2	0 51	10 12	9 22	1 20
26	8 52	8 53	8 54	8 55	8 57	9 1	1 26	10 45	9 56	1 53
27	9 51	9 50	9 52	9 48	9 48	9 57	2 1	11 19	10 30	2 28
28	10 55	10 53	10 51	10 44	10 43	10 57	2 36	11 59a	11 6	3 7
S.	11 58a	11 55a	11 52a	11 41a	11 38a	11 58a	3 13	. . .	11 47a	3 55
30	. . .	. . .	. . .	. . .	. . .	. . .	3 54	0 42m	. . .	4 49
31	1 4m	1 00m	0 55m	0 42m	0 37m	1 1m	4 42m	1 30m	0 33m	5 46m

Twilight begins and ends. Mean Time.

	1st day.		7th day.		13th day.		19th day.		25th day.	
	Begins.	Ends.	Begins.	Ends.	Begins.	Ends.	Begins.	Ends	Begins.	Ends
	h. m.	h. m.	h. m.	h. m.	h. m.	h. m.	h. m.	h. m.	h. m.	h. m.
Boston,	5 38m	6 50a	5 32m	6 56a	5 26m	7 3a	5 18m	7 10a	5 9m	7 17a
N. York,	5 37	6 51	5 31	6 57	5 25	7 4	5 18	7 10	5 10	7 16
Wash'n,	5 36	6 52	5 31	6 58	5 25	7 4	5 18	7 10	5 10	7 16
Charles.,	5 31	6 57	5 27	7 1	5 23	7 6	5 17	7 11	5 10	7 16
N. Orl's,	5 29	6 59	5 25	7 3	5 21	7 8	5 16	7 12	5 11	7 15
S. Fran.,	5 35	6 53	5 36	6 59	5 25	7 4	5 18	7 10	5 10	7 16

PHASES, AND PERIGEE AND APOGEE, OF THE MOON.

Full Moon,	6th day,	9h. 27m.	A.	New Moon,	21st day,	2h. 30m.	A.
Last Quarter,	13th "	1 43	A.	First Quarter,	29th "	2 47	A.

Perigee, 7th day, 8h. M. | Apogee, 21st day, 4h. A.

Sun's *upper* limb rises and sets (cor. for refr.) Mean Time.

Days of Month.	Days of Week.	Boston, &c. rises	Boston, &c. sets	New York, &c. rises	New York, &c. sets	Washington, &c. rises	Washington, &c. sets	Charleston, &c. rises	Charleston, &c. sets	N. Orleans, &c. rises	N. Orleans, &c. sets	San Francisco, &c. rises	San Francisco, &c. sets	Moon Souths. Mean Time.
		h. m.	h. m.	h. m.	h. m.	h. m.	h. m.	h. m.	h. m.	h. m.	h. m.	h. m.	h. m.	h. m.
1	W.	7 15	5 14	7 11	5 17	7 7	5 21	6 56	5 33	6 51	5 37	7 4	5 24	7 18a
2	Th.	14	15	10	18	6	22	55	34	50	38	3	25	8 17
3	F.	13	16	9	20	5	23	54	34	50	39	2	26	9 19
4	S.	11	18	8	21	5	24	54	35	49	40	2	27	10 22
5	*Su.*	7 10	5 19	7 7	5 22	7 4	5 26	6 53	5 36	6 49	5 40	7 1	5 29	11 22a
6	M.	9	20	6	23	3	27	52	37	48	41	0	30	&
7	Tu.	8	21	5	25	2	28	51	38	47	42	6 59	31	0 20m
8	W.	7	23	4	26	1	29	50	39	46	43	58	32	1 15
9	Th.	6	24	2	27	6 59	30	50	40	46	44	56	33	2 7
10	F.	4	25	1	28	58	31	49	41	45	45	55	34	2 57
11	S.	3	27	0	29	57	32	48	42	44	45	54	35	3 48
12	*Su.*	7 2	5 28	6 59	5 31	6 56	5 34	6 47	5 43	6 43	5 46	6 53	5 37	4 40
13	M.	0	29	58	32	55	35	46	44	42	47	52	38	5 32
14	Tu.	6 58	31	56	33	54	36	45	44	41	48	51	39	6 27
15	W.	58	32	55	34	52	37	44	45	41	49	49	40	7 21
16	Th.	56	33	53	36	51	38	43	46	40	49	48	41	8 15
17	F.	55	34	53	37	50	39	42	47	39	50	47	42	9 7
18	S.	54	36	51	38	49	40	41	48	38	51	46	43	9 57
19	*Su.*	6 52	5 37	6 50	5 39	6 47	5 42	6 40	5 49	6 37	5 52	6 44	5 45	10 43
20	M.	51	38	48	40	46	43	39	50	36	53	43	46	11 26m
21	Tu.	49	39	47	42	45	44	38	50	35	53	42	47	0 7a
22	W.	48	41	45	43	43	45	37	51	34	54	40	48	0 47
23	Th.	46	42	44	44	42	46	36	52	33	55	39	49	1 26
24	F.	45	43	43	45	41	47	35	53	32	55	38	50	2 6
25	S.	43	44	41	46	39	48	34	54	31	56	36	51	2 47
26	*Su.*	6 42	5 46	6 40	5 48	6 38	5 49	6 32	5 55	6 30	5 57	6 35	5 52	3 31
27	M.	40	47	38	49	37	50	31	55	29	58	34	53	4 18
28	Tu.	38	48	37	50	35	51	30	56	28	58	33	53	5 9
29	W.	37	49	35	51	34	52	29	57	27	59	32	54	6 43

Passage of the Meridian (mean time) and Declination of the Planets at Transit.

	1st day.		7th day.		13th day.		19th day.		25th day.	
	souths.	Dec.	*souths.*	Dec.	*souths.*	Dec.	*souths.*	Dec.	*souths.*	Dec.
	h. m.	° ′	h. m.	° ′	h. m.	° ′	h. m.	° ′	h. m.	° ′
☿	11 24m	−21 53	11 41m	−19 50	11 59m	−16 55	0 17a	−13 8	0 35a	−8 31
♀	2 13a	−8 5	2 16a	−5 3	2 19a	−1 56	2 22	+1 13	2 25	+4 22
♂	7 11m	−19 36	7 2m	−20 22	6 54m	−21 3	6 45m	−21 39	6 36m	−22 11
♃	10 30a	+22 41	10 3a	+22 46	9 37a	+22 50	9 12a	+22 54	8 47a	+22 57
♄	1 3m	+16 0	0 37m	+16 10	0 12m	+16 20	11 42	+16 31	11 17	+16 41
♅	7 21a	+20 49	6 57a	+20 49	6 34a	+20 49	6 10	+20 50	5 47	+20 51
♆	3 0	−3 2	2 37	−2 58	2 14	−2 53	1 51	−2 48	1 28	−2 43

Days of Month.	Moon rises or sets. Mean Time.						High Water. Mean Time.			
	Boston, &c.	New York, &c.	Washington, &c.	Charleston, &c.	N. Orleans, &c.	San Francisco, &c.	Boston, &c.	New York, &c.	Charleston, &c.	San Francisco (North Beach).
	sets. h. m.	*sets.* h. m.	*sets.* h. m.	*sets.* h. m.	*sets.* h. m.	*sets.* h. m.	h. m.	h. m.	h. m.	h. m.
1	2 12m	2 6m	2 0m	1 43m	1 37m	2 5m	5 41m	2 28m	1 27m	6 47m
2	3 21	3 15	3 8	2 49	2 43	3 13	6 46	3 33	2 23	7 53
3	4 25	4 18	4 12	3 52	3 45	4 15	7 56	4 42	3 50	9 0
4	5 22	5 16	5 9	4 50	4 42	5 12	9 6	5 52	4 53	10 0
S.	6 10m	6 4m	5 59m	5 42m	5 35m	6 1m	10 9	6 56	6 10	10 53
6	6 48	6 44	6 40	6 26	6 23	6 41	11 5	7 49	7 5	11 38m
7	*rises.*	*rises.*	*rises.*	*rises.*	*rises.*	*rises.*	11 54m	8 39	7 55	0 26a
8	7 46a	7 47a	7 48a	7 49a	7 51a	7 57a	0 40a	9 28	8 40	1 10
9	9 4	9 4	9 3	9 0	9 1	9 12	1 25	10 12	9 22	1 52
10	10 22	10 20	10 18	10 10	10 6	10 26	2 9	10 53	10 4	2 36
11	11 37	11 33	11 30	11 18	11 14	11 37	2 25	11 40m	10 49	3 22
S.	. . .	. . .	. . .	. . .	. . .	. . .	3 45	0 32a	11 36m	4 37
13	0 54m	0 49m	0 44m	0 28m	0 23m	0 49m	4 40	1 28	0 31a	5 43
14	2 1	1 55	0 49	0 31	0 24	1 54	5 44	2 31	1 31	6 50
15	3 4	2 57	2 51	2 30	2 24	2 54	6 49	3 36	2 37	7 56
16	3 58	3 51	3 44	3 24	3 17	3 47	7 54	4 39	3 47	8 57
17	4 44	4 38	4 31	4 12	4 5	4 33	8 54	5 38	4 50	9 49
18	5 23	5 18	5 12	4 55	4 50	5 13	9 44	6 31	5 44	10 32
S.	5 52m	5 47m	5 43m	5 29m	5 25m	5 44m	10 30	7 16	6 31	11 9
20	6 18	6 15	6 11	6 1	5 57	6 12	11 8	7 52	7 8	11 41a
21	6 39	6 37	6 34	6 27	6 25	6 36	11 43a	8 27	7 44	. . .
22	*sets.*	*sets.*	*sets.*	*sets.*	*sets.*	*sets.*	. . .	9 3	8 18	0 16m
23	7 44a	7 44a	7 44a	7 43a	7 44a	7 51a	0 16m	9 37	8 49	0 48
24	8 46	8 44	8 43	8 38	8 38	8 50	0 49	10 11	9 21	1 29
25	9 49	9 46	9 43	9 34	9 32	9 50	1 25	10 45	9 56	1 51
S.	10 54a	10 50a	10 46a	10 33a	10 29a	10 51a	2 0	11 23a	10 34	2 27
27	. . .	11 55	11 49	11 32	11 26	11 54	2 40	. . .	11 17a	3 12
28	0 0	. . .	. . .	. . .	. . .	. . .	3 23	0 10m	. . .	4 8
29	1 6m	1 0m	0 54m	0 35m	0 29m	0 50m	4 15m	1 3m	0 7m	5 15m

Twilight begins and ends. Mean Time.

	1st day.		7th day.		13th day.		19th day.		25th day.	
	Begins. h. m.	Ends. h. m.	Begins. h. m.	Ends. h. m.	Begins. h. m.	Ends. h. m.	Begins. h. m.	Ends. h. m.	Begins. h. m.	Ends. h. m.
Boston,	5 3m	7 23a	4 53m	7 29a	4 43m	7 37a	4 32m	7 45a	4 20m	7 52a
N. York,	5 4	7 22	4 54	7 28	4 44	7 35	4 34	7 42	4 23	7 49
Wash'n,	5 5	7 21	4 55	7 27	4 46	7 34	4 36	7 40	4 26	7 46
Charles.,	5 7	7 19	4 59	7 24	4 51	7 29	4 43	7 33	4 34	7 38
N. Orl's,	5 7	7 19	5 0	7 23	4 53	7 27	4 45	7 31	4 37	7 35
S. Fran.,	5 5	7 21	4 56	7 26	4 47	7 33	4 37	7 39	4 27	7 45

PHASES, AND PERIGEE AND APOGEE, OF THE MOON.

Full Moon, 7th day, 7h. 36m. M. | New Moon, 22d day, 8h. 47m. M.
Last Quarter, 14th " 4 0 M. | First Quarter, 30th " 1 45 M.

Perigee. 6th day, 11h. A. | Apogee, 19th day, 8h. A.

Sun's *upper* limb rises and sets (cor. for refr.) Mean Time.

Days of Month.	Days of Week.	Boston, &c. rises. h. m.	Boston, &c. sets. h. m.	New York, &c. rises. h. m.	New York, &c. sets. h. m.	Washington, &c. rises. h. m.	Washington, &c. sets. h. m.	Charleston, &c. rises. h. m.	Charleston, &c. sets. h. m.	N. Orleans, &c. rises. h. m.	N. Orleans, &c. sets. h. m.	San Francisco, &c. rises. h. m.	San Francisco, &c. sets. h. m.	Moon Souths. Mean Time. h. m.
1	Th.	6 35	5 51	6 34	5 52	6 32	5 53	6 28	5 58	6 26	5 59	6 30	5 55	7 3a
2	F.	34	52	32	53	31	54	27	59	25	6 0	29	56	8 3
3	S.	32	53	31	54	29	55	25	59	24	1	27	57	9 3
4	*Su.*	6 30	5 54	6 29	5 55	6 28	5 56	6 24	6 0	6 22	6 2	6 26	5 58	10 1
5	M.	28	55	28	56	27	57	23	1	21	2	25	59	10 56
6	Tu.	27	57	26	57	25	58	22	2	20	3	23	6 0	11 50a
7	W.	25	58	24	59	24	59	20	2	19	4	22	1	☍
8	Th.	24	59	23	6 0	22	6 1	19	3	18	4	20	3	0 42m
9	F.	22	6 0	21	1	21	2	18	4	17	5	19	4	1 34
10	S.	20	1	19	2	19	3	16	5	15	6	17	5	2 27
11	*Su.*	6 18	6 2	6 18	6 3	6 17	6 4	6 15	6 5	6 14	6 6	6 15	6 6	3 22
12	M.	17	4	16	4	16	5	14	6	13	7	14	7	4 17
13	Tu.	15	5	15	5	14	6	13	7	12	7	12	8	5 14
14	W.	13	6	13	6	13	7	11	8	11	8	11	9	6 9
15	Th.	12	7	11	7	11	8	10	8	10	9	9	10	7 3
16	F.	10	8	10	8	10	9	9	9	9	9	8	11	7 53
17	S.	8	9	8	9	8	10	7	10	7	10	6	12	8 40
18	*Su.*	6 6	6 10	6 6	6 11	6 6	6 10	6 6	6 11	6 6	6 11	6 4	6 12	9 25
19	M.	5	12	5	12	5	11	5	11	5	11	3	13	10 6
20	Tu.	3	13	3	13	3	12	4	12	4	12	2	13	10 46
21	W.	1	14	1	14	2	13	2	13	3	12	1	14	11 26m
22	Th.	5 59	15	0	15	0	14	1	13	1	13	5 59	15	0 53a
23	F.	58	16	5 58	16	5 58	15	0	14	0	14	57	16	0 47
24	S.	56	17	56	17	57	16	5 58	15	5 58	14	56	17	1 30
25	*Su.*	5 54	6 18	5 55	6 18	5 55	6 17	5 57	6 15	5 57	6 15	5 54	6 18	2 16
26	M.	52	19	53	19	54	18	56	16	56	15	53	19	3 6
27	Tu.	51	20	51	20	52	19	54	17	55	16	51	20	3 59
28	W.	49	22	50	21	51	20	53	18	54	17	50	21	4 56
29	Th.	47	23	48	22	49	21	52	18	52	17	48	22	5 54
30	F.	45	24	46	23	47	22	50	19	51	18	46	23	6 51
31	S.	44	25	45	24	46	23	49	20	50	18	45	24	7 48a

Passage of the Meridian (mean time) and Declination of the Planets at Transit.

	1st day.		7th day.		13th day.		19th day.		25th day.	
	souths.	Dec.	*souths.*	Dec.	*souths.*	Dec.	*souths.*	Dec.	*souths.*	Dec.
	h. m.	° ′	h. m.	° ′	h. m.	° ′	h. m.	° ′	h. m.	° ′
☿	0 50a	— 4 10	1 5a	+ 1 12	1 13a	+ 6 4	1 8a	+ 9 18	0 8a	+10 14
♀	2 27	+ 6 56	2 29	+ 9 57	2 33	+12 40	2 36	+15 31	2 39	+18 0
♂	6 29m	—22 33	6 20m	—22 55	6 11m	—23 12	6 2m	—23 25	5 53m	—23 34
♃	8 26a	+22 56	8 2a	+22 59	7 39a	+23 0	7 16a	+22 59	6 53a	+22 56
♄	10 55	+15 48	10 30	+15 56	10 5	+16 4	9 40	+16 10	9 15	+16 16
♅	5 28	+20 51	5 5	+20 53	4 42	+20 55	4 19	+20 57	3 56	+20 58
♆	1 9	— 2 38	0 46	— 2 33	0 24	— 2 28	0 1	— 2 22	11 38m	— 2 17

Days of Month.	Moon rises or sets. Mean time. Boston, &c.	New York, &c.	Washington, &c.	Charleston, &c.	N. Orleans, &c.	San Francisco, &c.	High Water. Mean Time. Boston, &c.	New York, &c.	Charleston, &c.	San Francisco (North Beach).
	sets. h. m.	*sets.* h. m.	*sets.* h. m.	*sets.* h. m.	*sets.* h. m.	*sets.* h. m.	h. m.	h. m.	h. m.	h. m.
1	2 9m	2 2m	1 56m	1 36m	1 29m	1 59m	5 16m	2 4m	1 5m	6 24m
2	3 9	3 2	2 56	2 35	2 29	2 58	6 27	3 15	2 14	7 35
3	3 59	3 53	3 47	3 29	3 22	3 50	7 40	4 26	3 32	8 44
S.	4 41m	4 36m	4 31m	4 17m	4 11m	4 34m	8 49	5 35	4 45	9 45
5	5 16	5 12	5 9	4 58	4 54	5 11	9 49	6 36	5 49	10 36
6	5 42	5 40	5 38	5 31	5 30	5 41	10 43	7 28	6 43	11 19m
7	6 10	6 10	6 9	6 7	6 8	6 13	11 29m	8 1	7 29	0 1a
8	*rises.*	*rises.*	*rises.*	*rises.*	*rises.*	*rises.*	0 12a	8 59	8 13	0 44
9	9 12a	9 9a	9 6a	8 56a	8 53a	9 49a	0 57	9 43	8 55	1 25
10	10 29	10 25	10 20	10 6	10 3	10 27	1 42	10 27	9 38	2 9
S.	11 43a	11 37a	11 31a	11 14a	11 8a	11 38a	2 32	11 15m	10 27	3 5
12	. . .	. . .	. . .	. . .	. . .	. . .	3 22	0 9a	11 16m	4 8
13	0 52m	0 46m	0 39m	0 20m	0 14m	0 43m	4 21	1 4	0 12a	5 21
14	1 52	1 45	1 39	1 18	1 12	1 41	5 23	2 10	1 11	6 30
15	2 43	2 37	2 30	2 11	2 3	2 31	6 28	3 15	2 14	7 35
16	3 23	3 17	3 11	2 54	2 48	3 12	7 29	4 15	3 19	8 33
17	3 55	3 50	3 45	3 31	3 26	3 47	8 23	5 9	4 18	9 24
S.	4 22m	4 16m	4 14m	4 8m	3 59m	4 15m	9 11	5 57	5 8	10 5
19	4 45	4 42	4 40	4 32	4 29	4 41	9 54	6 41	5 54	10 40
20	5 6	5 5	5 3	4 59	4 58	5 6	10 32	7 18	6 33	11 11
21	5 25	5 25	5 25	5 24	5 24	5 26	11 8	7 52	7 8	11 41a
22	5 44	5 44	5 44	5 42	5 42	5 45	11 42a	8 26	7 43	. . .
23	*sets.*	*sets.*	*sets.*	*sets.*	*sets.*	*sets.*	. . .	9 3	8 18	0 16m
24	8 45a	8 41a	8 38a	8 26a	8 22a	8 44a	0 16m	9 40	8 52	0 48
S.	9 50a	9 45a	9 41a	9 26a	9 21a	9 48a	0 53	10 19	9 29	1 23
26	10 57	10 51	10 45	10 27	10 21	10 50	1 33	11 0	10 12	2 0
27	. . .	11 55	11 48	11 28	11 22	11 52	2 17	11 51a	10 59	2 45
28	0 1m	. . .	. . .	. . .	. . .	. . .	3 5	. . .	11 54a	3 45
29	1 0	0 53m	0 47m	0 27m	0 20m	0 49m	4 1	0 49m	. . .	4 58
30	1 51	1 45	1 38	1 19	1 13	1 41	5 5	1 52	0 54m	6 11
31	2 36	2 30	2 25	2 9	2 3	2 27	6 13m	3 0m	1 59m	7 20m

Twilight begins and ends. Mean Time.

	1st day.		7th day.		13th day.		19th day.		25th day.	
	Begins. h. m.	Ends. h. m.	Begins. h. m.	Ends. h. m.	Begins. h. m.	Ends. h. m.	Begins. h. m.	Ends. h. m.	Begins. h. m.	Ends. h. m.
Boston,	4 7m	8 1a	3 55m	8 9a	3 43m	8 18a	3 31m	8 27a	3 19m	8 37a
N. York,	4 11	7 57	3 59	8 5	3 48	8 14	3 37	8 22	3 26	8 30
Wash'n,	4 15	7 53	4 4	8 1	3 53	8 9	3 43	8 17	3 33	8 25
Charles.,	4 25	7 43	4 16	7 49	4 7	7 55	3 59	8 0	3 51	8 5
N. Orl's,	4 29	7 39	4 21	7 44	4 13	7 49	4 5	7 53	3 58	7 58
S.-Fran.,	4 17	7 51	4 6	7 9	3 55	8 7	3 46	8 14	3 38	8 22

PHASES, AND PERIGEE AND APOGEE, OF THE MOON.

Full Moon, 5th day, 4h. 52m. A. | New Moon, 21st day, 0h. 37m. M.
Last Quarter, 12th " 8 26 A. | First Quarter, 28th " 9 28 M.
Perigee, 4th day, 6h. M. | Apogee, 16th day, 9h. M.

Sun's *upper* limb rises and sets (cor. for refr.) Mean Time.

Days of Month.	Days of Week.	Boston, &c. rises. h. m.	Boston, &c. sets. h. m.	New York, &c. rises. h. m.	New York, &c. sets. h. m.	Washington, &c. rises. h. m.	Washington, &c. sets. h. m.	Charleston, &c. rises. h. m.	Charleston, &c. sets. h. m.	N. Orleans, &c. rises. h. m.	N. Orleans, &c. sets. h. m.	San Francisco, &c. rises. h. m.	San Francisco, &c. sets. h. m.	Moon Souths. Mean Time. h. m.
1	*Su.*	5 42	6 26	5 43	6 25	5 44	6 24	5 48	6 20	5 49	6 19	5 43	6 25	8 42a
2	M.	40	27	41	26	43	25	46	21	48	20	42	26	9 35
3	Tu.	39	28	40	27	41	26	45	22	47	20	40	27	10 27
4	W.	37	30	38	28	40	27	44	22	46	21	39	28	11 18a
5	Th.	35	31	36	29	38	28	42	23	44	21	37	29	☍
6	F.	33	32	35	30	37	29	41	24	43	22	36	30	0 11m
7	S.	32	33	33	31	35	30	40	25	42	23	34	31	1 5
8	*Su.*	5 30	6 34	5 32	6 32	5 34	6 31	5 39	6 25	5 41	6 23	5 33	6 32	2 2
9	M.	28	35	30	33	32	32	37	26	39	24	31	33	3 0
10	Tu.	27	36	28	34	30	33	36	27	38	24	29	34	3 58
11	W.	25	37	27	36	29	33	35	27	37	25	28	34	4 54
12	Th.	23	38	25	37	27	34	34	28	36	26	27	34	5 46
13	F.	22	40	24	38	26	35	32	29	35	26	26	35	6 36
14	S.	20	41	22	39	24	36	31	29	34	27	24	36	7 21
15	*Su.*	5 19	6 42	5 21	6 40	5 23	6 37	5 30	6 30	5 33	6 27	5 23	6 37	8 4
16	M.	17	43	19	41	22	38	29	31	32	28	22	38	8 45
17	Tu.	16	44	18	42	20	39	28	32	31	29	20	39	9 24
18	W.	14	45	16	43	19	40	26	32	30	29	19	40	10 4
19	Th.	12	46	15	44	17	41	25	33	29	30	17	41	10 45
20	F.	11	47	13	45	16	42	24	34	27	30	16	42	11 27m
21	S.	9	48	12	46	15	43	23	35	26	31	15	43	0 13a
22	*Su.*	5 8	6 50	5 10	6 47	5 13	6 44	5 22	6 35	5 25	6 32	5 13	6 44	1 2
23	M.	6	51	9	48	12	45	21	36	24	32	12	45	1 55
24	Tu.	5	52	8	49	11	46	20	36	23	33	11	46	2 51
25	W.	3	53	6	50	9	47	19	37	22	34	9	47	3 49
26	Th.	2	54	5	51	8	48	18	38	22	34	8	48	4 46
27	F.	0	55	3	52	7	49	17	39	21	35	8	48	5 42
28	S.	4 59	56	2	53	6	50	16	40	20	35	7	49	6 36
29	*Su.*	4 58	6 57	5 1	6 54	5 4	6 51	5 15	6 41	5 19	6 36	5 5	6 50	7 27
30	M.	56	59	4 59	55	3	52	14	41	18	36	4	51	8 17a

Passage of the Meridian (mean time) and Declination of the Planets at Transit.

	1st day.		7th day.		13th day.		19th day.		25th day.	
	souths.	Dec.	*souths.*	Dec.	*souths.*	Dec.	*souths.*	Dec.	*souths.*	Dec.
	h. m.	° ′	h. m.	° ′	h. m.	° ′	h. m.	° ′	h. m.	° ′
☿	0 7a	+ 8 20	11 29m	+ 5 17	10 57m	+ 2 38	10 36m	+ 1 22	10 24m	+ 1 37
♀	2 44	+20 34	2 46a	+22 28	2 53a	+24 1	2 57a	+25 14	3 2a	+26 4
♂	5 40m	—23 40	5 31m	—23 40	5 21m	—23 38	5 10m	—23 34	4 58m	—23 29
♃	6 27a	+22 55	6 6a	+22 52	5 44a	+22 48	5 24a	+22 43	5 3a	+22 38
♄	8 47	+16 20	8 23	+16 23	7 59	+16 25	7 35	+16 25	7 11	+16 24
♅	3 30	+21 2	3 7	+21 5	2 45	+21 8	2 22	+21 11	2 0	+21 14
♆	11 12m	— 2 11	10 49m	— 2 6	10 26m	— 2 1	10 3m	— 1 56	9 40m	— 1 52

Days of Month.	Moon rises or sets. Mean Time.						High Water. Mean Time.			
	Boston, &c.	New York, &c.	Washington, &c.	Charleston, &c.	N. Orleans, &c.	San Francisco, &c.	Boston, &c.	New York, &c.	Charleston, &c.	San Francisco (North Beach).
	sets. h. m.	*sets.* h. m.	*sets.* h. m.	*sets.* h. m.	*sets.* h. m.	*sets.* h. m.	h. m.	h. m.	h. m.	h. m.
S.	3 15m	3 11m	3 7m	2 54m	2 50m	3 9m	7 23m	4 9m	3 12m	8 27m
2	3 43	3 40	3 37	3 28	3 25	3 40	8 25	5 11	4 20	9 26
3	4 11	4 10	4 9	4 5	4 4	4 11	9 21	6 9	5 20	10 14
4	4 35	4 36	4 36	4 36	4 37	4 40	10 14	7 1	6 15	10 57
5	5 0	5 2	5 4	5 9	5 12	5 9	11 1	7 45	7 1	11 36m
6	*rises.*	*rises.*	*rises.*	*rises.*	*rises.*	*rises.*	11 46m	8 31	7 48	0 19a
7	9 19a	9 14a	9 9a	8 53a	8 49a	9 15a	0 32a	9 19	8 32	1 2
S.	10 33a	10 27a	10 21a	10 3a	9 57a	10 26a	1 21	10 8	9 18	1 48
9	11 39	11 32	11 26	11 6	11 0	11 29	2 12	10 55	10 7	2 39
10	. . .	. . .	. . .	. . .	11 54	. . .	3 3	11 49m	10 57	3 42
11	0 31m	0 27m	0 20m	0 1m	. . .	0 23m	3 58	0 46a	11 51m	4 54
12	1 20	1 14	1 6	0 49	0 43m	1 10	4 56	1 44	0 46a	6 1
13	1 55	1 50	1 45	1 29	1 24	1 46	5 58	2 41	1 40	7 0
14	2 24	2 20	2 16	2 20	1 59	2 17	6 49	3 36	2 38	7 56
S.	2 49m	2 46m	2 43m	2 34m	2 31m	2 44m	7 41	4 27	3 33	8 45
16	3 9	3 7	3 5	3 0	2 58	3 7	8 29	5 14	4 24	9 29
17	3 30	3 30	3 29	3 27	3 27	3 31	9 11	5 57	5 8	10 5
18	3 49	3 50	3 50	3 52	3 53	3 54	9 52	6 39	5 52	10 38
19	4 8	4 10	4 12	4 18	4 19	4 16	10 32	7 18	6 33	11 11
20	4 30	4 33	4 36	4 45	4 49	4 41	11 9	7 53	7 9	11 42a
21	*sets.*	*sets.*	*sets.*	*sets.*	*sets.*	*sets.*	11 48a	8 33	7 49	. . .
S.	8 48a	8 43a	8 37a	8 21a	8 15a	8 42a	. . .	9 17	8 30	0 20m
23	9 54	9 48	9 41	9 23	9 16	9 46	0 29m	10 2	9 12	1 0
24	10 56	10 49	10 43	10 23	10 17	10 46	1 15	10 48	9 59	1 42
25	11 49	11 43	11 36	11 17	11 0	11 39	2 4	11 41a	10 50	2 31
26	. . .	. . .	. . .	. . .	. . .	. . .	2 56	. . .	11 44a	3 33
27	0 36m	0 30m	0 24m	0 7m	0 1m	0 26m	3 51	0 39m	. . .	4 45
28	1 13	1 8	1 4	0 50	0 46	1 5	4 51	1 39	0 42m	5 57
S.	1 43m	1 40m	1 36m	1 26m	1 23m	1 39m	5 55	2 42	1 41	7 1
30	2 11	2 9	2 7	2 1	2 0	2 10	6 57m	3 43m	2 45m	8 3m

Twilight begins and ends. Mean Time.

	1st day.		7th day.		13th day.		19th day.		25th day.	
	Begins. h. m.	Ends. h. m.	Begins. h. m.	Ends. h. m.	Begins. h. m.	Ends. h. m.	Begins. h. m.	Ends. h. m.	Begins. h. m.	Ends. h. m.
Boston,	3 7m	8 47a	2 56m	8 57a	2 45m	9 7a	2 35m	9 17a	2 25m	9 28a
N. York,	3 14	8 40	3 4	8 49	2 54	8 58	2 45	9 8	2 36	9 18
Wash'n,	3 22	8 32	3 13	8 40	3 4	8 48	2 55	8 57	2 47	9 7
Charles.,	3 43	8 11	3 36	8 17	3 28	8 24	3 22	8 30	3 17	8 37
N. Orl's,	3 51	8 3	3 45	8 8	3 38	8 14	3 33	8 20	3 28	8 26
S. Fran.,	3 26	8 28	3 17	8 36	3 8	8 44	2 59	8 52	2 52	9 2

PHASES, AND PERIGEE AND APOGEE, OF THE MOON.

Full Moon,	5th day, 1h. 54m. M.	New Moon,	20th day, 1h. 38m. A.
Last Quarter,	12th " 2 8 A.	First Quarter,	27th " 2 57 A.

Perigee, 2d day, 6h. M. | Apogee, 14th day, 3h. A. | Perigee, 28th day, 10h. A.

Sun's *upper* limb rises and sets (cor. for refr.) Mean Time.

Days of Month.	Days of Week.	Boston, &c. rises. h. m.	Boston, &c. sets. h. m.	New York, &c. rises. h. m.	New York, &c. sets. h. m.	Washington, &c. rises. h. m.	Washington, &c. sets. h. m.	Charleston, &c. rises. h. m.	Charleston, &c. sets. h. m.	N. Orleans, &c. rises. h. m.	N. Orleans, &c. sets. h. m.	San Francisco, &c. rises. h. m.	San Francisco, &c. sets. h. m.	Moon Souths. Mean Time. h. m.
1	Tu.	4 55	6 59	4 58	6 56	5 2	6 52	5 13	6 42	5 17	6 37	5 3	6 51	9 7a
2	W.	53	7 1	57	57	1	53	12	42	16	38	2	52	9 58
3	Th.	52	2	56	58	4 59	54	11	43	15	38	0	53	10 50
4	F.	51	3	54	59	58	55	10	44	14	39	4 59	54	11 45a
5	S.	49	4	53	7 0	57	56	9	45	13	40	58	55	☍
6	*Su.*	4 48	7 5	4 52	7 2	4 56	6 57	5 8	6 45	5 12	6 40	4 57	6 56	0 43m
7	M.	47	6	51	3	55	58	7	46	11	41	56	57	1 42
8	Tu.	46	7	50	4	54	59	6	47	11	42	55	58	2 40
9	W.	45	8	49	5	53	7 0	5	47	10	42	54	59	3 35
10	Th.	43	9	47	6	52	1	4	48	10	43	53	7 0	4 27
11	F.	42	10	46	7	51	2	4	49	9	44	52	1	5 15
12	S.	41	12	45	8	50	3	3	50	8	44	52	1	5 59
13	*Su.*	4 40	7 13	4 44	7 9	4 49	7 4	5 2	6 50	5 7	6 45	4 51	7 2	6 41
14	M.	39	14	43	9	48	5	1	51	7	46	50	3	7 21
15	Tu.	38	15	42	10	47	6	1	52	6	46	49	4	8 1
16	W.	37	16	42	11	46	7	0	53	5	47	48	5	8 41
17	Th.	36	17	41	12	45	7	4 59	53	5	47	47	5	9 23
18	F.	35	18	40	13	44	8	59	54	5	48	46	6	10 7
19	S.	34	19	39	14	44	9	58	55	4	49	46	7	10 56
20	*Su.*	4 33	7 20	4 38	7 15	4 43	7 10	4 58	6 55	5 4	6 49	4 45	7 8	11 48m
21	M.	32	21	37	16	42	11	57	56	3	50	44	9	0 44a
22	Tu.	32	22	36	17	41	12	56	57	3	51	43	10	1 42
23	W.	31	23	36	18	41	13	56	57	2	51	43	11	2 41
24	Th.	30	24	35	18	40	13	55	58	2	52	42	11	3 38
25	F.	29	24	34	19	40	14	55	59	2	52	42	12	4 32
26	S.	28	25	34	20	39	15	55	59	1	53	41	13	5 24
27	*Su.*	4 28	7 26	4 33	7 21	4 38	7 16	4 54	7 0	5 1	6 53	4 40	7 14	6 14
28	M.	28	27	33	22	38	16	54	1	0	54	40	14	7 2
29	Tu.	27	28	32	23	37	17	54	1	0	54	40	15	7 51
30	W.	26	29	32	23	37	18	53	2	0	55	39	15	8 41
31	Th.	26	30	31	24	36	19	53	2	4 59	55	39	16	9 34a

Passage of the Meridian (mean time) and Declination of the Planets at Transit.

	1st day.		7th day.		13th day.		19th day.		25th day.	
	souths.	Dec.	*souths.*	Dec.	*souths.*	Dec.	*souths.*	Dec.	*souths.*	Dec.
	h. m.	° ′	h. m.	° ′	h. m.	° ′	h. m.	° ′	h. m.	° ′
☿	10 20m	+ 3 7	10 22m	+ 5 38	10 29m	+ 8 54	10 42m	+12 42	11 1m	+16 44
♀	3 6a	+26 33	3 9a	+26 39	3 11a	+26 25	3 11a	+25 52	3 10a	+25 3
♂	4 46m	−23 23	4 33m	−23 18	4 18m	−23 13	4 3m	−23 12	3 47m	−23 14
♃	4 43a	+22 31	4 23a	+22 24	4 4a	+22 16	3 44a	+22 6	3 25a	+21 56
♄	6 48	+16 22	6 25	+16 18	6 2	+16 14	5 40	+16 8	5 18	+16 2
♅	1 38	+21 18	1 16	+21 21	0 53	+21 25	0 31	+21 28	0 9	+21 32
♆	9 17m	− 1 47	8 54m	− 1 43	8 31m	− 1 40	8 8m	− 1 37	7 45m	− 1 34

Days of Month.	Moon rises or sets. Mean Time.						High Water. Mean Time.			
	Boston, &c.	New York, &c.	Washington, &c.	Charleston, &c.	N. Orleans, &c.	San Francisco, &c.	Boston, &c.	New York, &c.	Charleston, &c.	San Francisco (North Beach).
	sets. h. m.	*sets.* h. m.	*sets.* h. m.	*sets.* h. m.	*sets.* h. m.	*sets.* h. m.	h. m.	h. m.	h. m.	h. m.
1	2 36m	2 36m	2 35m	2 34m	2 35m	2 39m	7 56m	4 42m	3 50m	9 0m
2	3 0	3 1	3 2	3 5	3 7	3 7	8 54	5 38	4 50	9 49
3	3 27	3 30	3 33	3 41	3 45	3 38	9 46	6 33	5 46	10 33
4	3 56	4 0	4 5	4 17	4 23	4 12	10 36	7 22	6 37	11 14
5	*rises.*	*rises.*	*rises.*	*rises.*	*rises.*	*rises.*	11 24m	8 8	7 24	11 57m
S.	9 19a	9 13a	9 6a	8 47a	8 41a	9 11a	0 13a	9 0	8 14	0 44a
7	10 21	10 14	10 7	9 48	9 41	10 10	1 4	9 50	9 1	1 31
8	11 11	11 5	10 58	10 39	10 33	10 50	1 54	10 39	9 50	2 21
9	11 51	11 46	11 40	11 23	11 18	11 41	2 43	11 27m	10 37	3 16
10	. . .	. . .	. . .	. . .	11 56	. . .	3 32	0 9a	11 25m	4 20
11	0 23m	0 18m	0 14m	0 1m	. . .	0 16m	4 22	1 10	0 14a	5 23
12	0 50	0 46	0 43	0 33	0 29m	0 44	5 11	1 58	1 0	6 18
S.	1 11m	1 9m	1 7m	0 59m	0 57m	1 8m	6 1	2 48	1 47	7 7
14	1 33	1 32	1 31	1 28	1 26	1 34	6 49	3 36	2 37	7 56
15	1 52	1 52	1 52	1 53	1 54	1 56	7 38	4 24	3 29	8 42
16	2 12	2 13	2 15	2 18	2 21	2 18	8 24	5 10	4 19	9 25
17	2 33	2 35	2 36	2 45	2 49	2 42	9 10	5 56	5 7	10 4
18	2 57	3 1	3 5	3 16	3 21	3 11	9 55	6 42	5 55	10 41
19	3 26	3 31	3 37	3 50	3 57	3 44	10 42	7 27	6 42	11 18
S.	4 0m	4 6m	4 13m	4 30m	4 39m	4 21m	11 27a	8 10	7 27	11 59a
21	*sets.*	*sets.*	*sets.*	*sets.*	*sets.*	*sets.*	. . .	9 1	8 15	. . .
22	9 44a	9 38a	9 31a	9 12a	9 6a	9 34a	0 14m	9 50	9 2	0 45m
23	10 34	10 28	10 22	10 5	9 58	10 24	1 4	10 40	9 51	1 32
24	11 14	11 9	11 4	10 50	10 45	11 6	1 55	11 30a	10 40	2 22
25	11 46	11 42	11 39	11 28	11 24	11 41	2 46	. . .	11 30a	3 20
26	. . .	. . .	. . .	. . .	. . .	. . .	3 37	0 24m	. . .	4 26
S.	0 14m	0 12m	0 10m	0 8m	0 1m	0 13m	4 31	1 19	0 22m	5 34
28	0 40	0 39	0 39	0 36	0 36	0 41	5 29	2 16	1 16	6 35
29	1 2	1 3	1 3	1 5	1 6	1 8	6 26	3 13	2 12	7 33
30	1 28	1 30	1 33	1 39	1 42	1 38	7 26	4 12	3 16	8 30
31	1 55	1 59	2 8	2 13	2 18	2 9	8 24m	5 10m	4 19m	9 25m

Twilight begins and ends. Mean Time.

	1st day. Begins. h. m.	1st day. Ends. h. m.	7th day. Begins. h. m.	7th day. Ends. h. m.	13th day. Begins. h. m.	13th day. Ends. h. m.	19th day. Begins. h. m.	19th day. Ends. h. m.	25th day. Begins. h. m.	25th day. Ends. h. m.
Boston,	2 17m	9 37a	2 12m	9 44a	2 9m	9 50a	2 8m	9 54a	2 9m	9 55a
N. York,	2 29	9 25	2 25	9 31	2 23	9 37	2 22	9 40	2 23	9 41
Wash'n,	2 41	9 13	2 37	9 19	2 36	9 24	2 35	9 27	2 36	9 28
Charles.,	3 13	8 41	3 10	8 46	3 10	8 50	3 10	8 52	3 11	8 53
N. Orl's,	3 24	8 30	3 22	8 34	3 22	8 38	3 22	8 40	3 23	8 41
S. Fran.,	2 46	9 8	2 43	9 13	2 42	9 16	2 41	9 21	2 42	9 22

PHASES, AND PERIGEE AND APOGEE, OF THE MOON.

Full Moon,	3d day,	11h.	33m.	M.	New Moon,	19th day,	0h.	16m.	M.
Last Quarter,	11th "	7	56	M.	First Quarter,	25th "	7	28	A.

Apogee, 10th day, 10h. A. | Perigee, 23d day, 4h. M.

Sun's *upper* limb rises and sets (cor. for refr.) Mean Time.

Days of Month.	Days of Week.	Boston, &c. *rises.* h. m.	Boston, &c. *sets.* h. m.	New York, &c. *rises.* h. m.	New York, &c. *sets.* h. m.	Washington, &c. *rises.* h. m.	Washington, &c. *sets.* h. m.	Charleston, &c. *rises.* h. m.	Charleston, &c. *sets.* h. m.	N. Orleans, &c. *rises.* h. m.	N. Orleans, &c. *sets.* h. m.	San Francisco, &c. *rises.* h. m.	San Francisco, &c. *sets.* h. m.	Moon Souths. Mean Time. h. m.
1	F.	4 25	7 30	4 31	7 25	4 36	7 19	4 53	7 3	4 59	6 56	4 39	7 16	10 30a
2	S.	25	31	30	26	36	20	52	3	59	57	39	17	11 27a
3	*Su.*	4 25	7 32	4 30	7 26	4 35	7 21	4 52	7 4	4 59	6 57	4 38	7 17	☍
4	M.	24	32	29	27	35	21	52	4	59	58	38	18	0 26m
5	Tu.	24	33	29	28	35	22	52	5	59	58	38	19	1 23
6	W.	23	34	29	28	34	23	52	5	58	59	37	19	2 17
7	Th.	23	34	29	29	34	23	51	6	58	59	37	20	3 7
8	F.	23	35	28	29	34	24	51	6	58	7 0	37	20	3 53
9	S.	23	35	28	30	34	24	51	7	58	0	37	21	4 38
10	*Su.*	4 22	7 36	4 28	7 30	4 34	7 25	4 51	7 7	4 58	7 1	4 37	7 21	5 17
11	M.	22	36	28	31	34	25	51	8	58	1	37	22	5 56
12	Tu.	22	37	28	31	34	26	51	8	58	1	37	22	6 36
13	W.	22	37	28	32	34	26	51	8	58	2	37	23	7 17
14	Th.	22	38	28	32	34	26	51	9	58	2	37	23	8 0
15	F.	22	38	28	33	34	27	51	9	58	2	37	24	8 47
16	S.	22	38	28	33	34	27	51	10	58	3	37	24	9 37
17	*Su.*	4 22	7 39	4 28	7 33	4 34	7 27	4 51	7 10	4 58	7 3	4 37	7 24	10 32
18	M.	23	39	28	34	34	28	51	10	59	3	38	25	11 30m
19	Tu.	23	40	28	34	34	28	52	11	59	3	38	25	0 30a
20	W.	23	40	28	34	34	28	52	11	59	3	38	25	1 29
21	Th.	23	40	29	34	34	28	52	11	59	4	38	25	2 26
22	F.	23	40	29	35	35	29	52	11	59	4	39	26	3 20
23	S.	24	40	29	35	35	29	53	11	5 0	4	39	26	4 11
24	*Su.*	4 24	7 40	4 29	7 35	4 35	7 29	4 53	7 11	5 0	7 4	4 39	7 26	5 0
25	M.	24	40	30	35	36	29	53	11	0	4	40	26	5 49
26	Tu.	25	40	30	35	36	29	53	12	1	4	40	26	6 38
27	W.	25	40	31	35	36	29	54	12	1	5	40	26	7 29
28	Th.	25	40	31	35	37	29	54	12	1	5	41	26	8 22
29	F.	26	40	31	35	37	29	54	12	1	5	41	26	9 18
30	S.	26	40	32	35	38	29	55	12	2	5	42	26	10 16a

Passage of the Meridian (mean time) and Declination of the Planets at Transit.

	1st day.		7th day.		13th day.		19th day.		25th day.	
	souths.	Dec.	*souths.*	Dec.	*souths.*	Dec.	*souths.*	Dec.	*souths.*	Dec.
	h. m.	° ′	h. m.	° ′	h. m.	° ′	h. m.	° ′	h. m.	° ′
☿	11 32m	+21 8	0 4a	+23 54	0 37a	+25 7	1 6a	+24 44	1 29a	+23 4
♀	3 5a	+23 48	2 56	+22 34	2 47	+21 15	2 31	+19 51	2 11	+18 37
♂	3 26m	—23 22	3 7m	—23 35	2 46m	—23 54	2 23m	—24 20	1 58m	—24 52
♃	3 3a	+21 43	2 44a	+21 30	2 26a	+21 17	2 7a	+21 3	1 49a	+20 48
♄	4 52	+15 53	4 30	+15 44	4 8	+15 34	3 47	+15 23	3 25	+15 12
♅	11 43m	+21 36	11 21m	+21 39	10 59m	+21 42	10 37m	+21 46	10 15m	+21 49
♆	7 18	— 1 31	6 55	— 1 29	6 32	— 1 28	6 8	— 1 27	5 45	— 1 27

Days of Month.	Moon rises or sets. Mean Time.						High Water. Mean Time.			
	Boston, &c.	New York, &c.	Washington, &c.	Charleston, &c.	N. Orleans, &c.	San Francisco, &c.	Boston, &c.	New York, &c.	Charleston, &c.	San Francisco (North Beach).
	sets. h. m.	*sets.* h. m.	*sets.* h. m.	*sets.* h. m.	*sets.* h. m.	*sets.* h. m.	h. m.	h. m.	h. m.	h. m.
1	2 26m	2 31m	2 37m	2 50m	2 57m	2 44m	9 21m	6 6m	5 19m	10 13m
2	3 3	3 10	3 16	3 33	3 42	3 24	10 17	7 4	6 16	10 59
S.	3 49m	3 56m	4 4m	4 23m	4 33m	4 12m	11 9	7 53	7 9	11 42m
4	*rises.*	*rises.*	*rises.*	*rises.*	*rises.*	*rises.*	11 59m	8 45	8 0	0 31a
5	9 46a	9 40a	9 34a	9 17a	9 11a	9 36a	0 47a	9 35	8 46	1 16
6	10 22	10 17	10 12	9 58	9 53	10 15	1 34	10 20	9 30	2 1
7	10 51	10 47	10 43	10 32	10 28	10 45	2 17	11 0	10 12	2 45
8	11 16	11 13	11 11	11 3	11 0	11 12	3 0	11 45m	10 54	3 38
9	11 36	11 35	11 33	11 29	11 27	11 36	3 41	0 28a	11 34m	4 31
S.	11 54a	11 54a	11 54a	11 53a	11 53a	11 56a	4 24	1 12	0 16a	5 25
11	. . .	. . .	. . .	. . .	. . .	. . .	5 7	1 55	0 57	6 14
12	0 15m	0 16m	0 17m	0 19m	0 21m	0 20m	5 55	2 42	1 41	7 1
13	0 36	0 28	0 41	0 47	0 50	0 45	6 44	3 31	2 34	7 51
14	0 57	1 1	1 4	1 14	1 18	1 10	7 37	4 23	3 28	8 41
15	1 24	1 29	1 34	1 46	1 53	1 40	8 30	5 16	4 25	9 29
16	1 55	2 1	2 7	2 22	2 31	2 15	9 25	6 11	5 23	10 16
S.	2 35m	2 42m	2 49m	3 6m	3 17m	2 58m	10 19	7 6	6 20	11 1
18	3 25	3 31	3 40	4 0	4 10	3 51	11 12a	7 55	7 12	11 44a
19	*sets.*	*sets.*	*sets.*	*sets.*	*sets.*	*sets.*	. . .	8 48	8 4	. . .
20	9 11a	9 6a	9 1a	8 45a	8 39a	9 3a	0 2m	9 39	8 51	0 34m
21	9 46	9 42	9 38	9 26	9 21	9 40	0 52	10 27	9 38	1 21
22	10 17	10 14	10 12	10 3	10 1	10 14	1 41	11 14a	10 25	2 8
23	10 42	10 41	10 40	10 36	10 36	10 43	2 30	. . .	11 10	3 0
S.	11 8a	11 9a	11 9a	11 9a	11 10a	11 12a	3 17	0 3m	11 58a	4 0
25	11 31	11 33	11 35	11 39	11 42	11 40	4 5	0 53	. . .	5 3
26	11 58	. . .	. . .	. . .	. . .	. . .	4 59	1 47	0 49m	6 5
27	. . .	0 1m	0 5m	0 14m	0 19m	0 11m	5 58	2 45	1 44	7 4
28	0 27m	0 32	0 37	0 49	0 56	0 44	7 0	3 46	2 48	8 5
29	1 1	1 7	1 13	1 29	1 38	1 21	8 2	4 47	3 56	9 5
30	1 48	1 50	1 57	2 15	2 25	2 6	9 5m	5 51m	5 2m	9 59m

Twilight begins and ends. Mean Time.

	1st day.		7th day.		13th day.		19th day.		25th day.	
	Begins. h. m.	Ends. h. m.	Begins. h. m.	Ends. h. m.	Begins. h. m.	Ends. h. m.	Begins. h. m.	Ends. h. m.	Begins. h. m.	Ends. h. m.
Boston,	2 12m	9 54a	2 19m	9 49a	2 26m	9 44a	2 35m	9 37a	2 44m	9 28a
N. York,	2 26	9 40	2 32	9 36	2 39	9 31	2 46	9 25	2 54	9 18
Wash'n,	2 39	9 27	2 44	9 24	2 51	9 19	2 58	9 14	3 5	9 7
Charles.,	3 13	8 53	3 17	8 51	3 22	8 48	3 27	8 45	3 32	8 40
N. Orl's,	3 25	8 41	3 29	8 39	3 33	8 37	3 37	8 34	3 42	8 30
S. Fran.,	2 45	9 21	2 49	9 19	2 56	9 14	3 3	9 9	3 10	9 2

PHASES, AND APOGEE AND PERIGEE, OF THE MOON.

Full Moon,	2d day,	10h.	59m.	A.	New Moon,	18th day,	9h.	12m.	M.
Last Quarter,	11th "	0	50	M.	First Quarter,	25th "	0	32	M.
Apogee, 8th day, 4h. A.					Perigee, 20th day, 2h. A.				

Sun's *upper* limb rises and sets (cor. for refr.) Mean Time.

Days of Month.	Days of Week.	Boston, &c. rises. h. m.	Boston, &c. sets. h. m.	New York, &c. rises. h. m.	New York, &c. sets. h. m.	Washington, &c. rises. h. m.	Washington, &c. sets. h. m.	Charleston, &c. rises. h. m.	Charleston, &c. sets. h. m.	N. Orleans, &c. rises. h. m.	N. Orleans, &c. sets. h. m.	San Francisco, &c. rises. h. m.	San Francisco, &c. sets. h. m.	Moon Souths. Mean Time. h. m.
1	*Su.*	4 27	7 40	4 32	7 35	4 38	7 29	4 55	7 12	5 2	7 5	4 42	7 26	7 12a
2	M.	27	40	33	34	39	29	56	12	3	5	43	26	☍
3	Tu.	28	40	33	34	39	29	56	12	3	5	43	26	0 7m
4	W.	28	40	34	34	40	28	57	11	4	5	44	25	0 58
5	Th.	29	39	35	34	40	28	57	11	4	5	44	25	1 46
6	F.	29	39	35	33	41	28	58	11	4	4	45	25	2 31
7	S.	30	39	36	33	41	28	58	11	5	4	45	25	3 12
8	*Su.*	4 31	7 38	4 37	7 33	4 42	7 27	4 58	7 11	5 5	7 4	4 46	7 24	3 53
9	M.	32	38	38	32	43	27	59	10	6	4	47	24	4 32
10	Tu.	33	37	38	32	43	27	59	10	6	4	47	24	5 12
11	W.	33	37	39	32	44	26	5 0	10	7	4	48	23	5 54
12	Th.	34	36	39	31	45	26	1	9	7	3	49	23	6 38
13	F.	35	36	40	31	45	25	1	9	8	3	49	22	7 26
14	S.	36	35	41	30	46	24	2	9	8	2	50	21	8 18
15	*Su.*	4 36	7 34	4 41	7 30	4 47	7 24	5 2	7 8	5 9	7 2	4 51	7 21	9 16
16	M.	37	34	42	29	47	24	3	8	10	2	51	21	10 14
17	Tu.	38	33	43	28	48	23	4	8	10	1	52	20	11 14m
18	W.	39	32	44	28	49	22	4	7	11	1	53	19	0 13a
19	Th.	40	32	45	27	50	22	5	7	11	1	54	19	1 10
20	F.	41	31	45	26	51	21	6	6	12	0	55	18	2 4
21	S.	42	30	46	25	51	20	6	6	12	6 59	55	17	2 55
22	*Su.*	4 43	7 29	4 47	7 25	4 52	7 20	5 7	7 5	5 13	6 59	4 56	7 17	3 45
23	M.	44	28	48	24	53	19	8	4	13	59	57	16	4 35
24	Tu.	44	28	49	23	54	18	8	4	14	58	58	15	5 26
25	W.	45	27	50	22	55	17	9	3	14	57	59	14	6 19
26	Th.	46	26	51	21	56	16	10	2	15	57	5 0	13	7 18
27	F.	47	25	52	20	56	16	10	2	16	56	0	13	8 10
28	S.	48	23	53	19	57	15	11	1	16	56	1	12	9 6
29	*Su.*	4 49	7 22	4 54	7 18	4 58	7 14	5 11	7 0	5 17	6 55	5 2	7 11	10 1
30	M.	50	21	55	17	59	13	12	0	17	54	3	10	10 53
31	Tu.	51	20	56	16	5 0	12	13	6 59	18	54	4	9	11 41a

Passage of the Meridian (mean time) and Declination of the Planets at Transit.

	1st day.		7th day.		13th day.		19th day.		25th day.	
	souths.	Dec.	souths.	Dec.	souths.	Dec.	souths.	Dec.	souths.	Dec.
	h. m.	° ′	h. m.	° ′	h. m.	° ′	h. m.	° ′	h. m.	° ′
☿	1 45a	+20 36	1 53a	+17 48	1 54a	+14 47	1 46a	+12 8	1 29a	+10 11
♀	1 45	+17 25	1 13	+16 31	0 36	+15 47	11 57m	+15 19	11 19m	+15 7
♂	1 31m	−25 28	1 3m	−26 6	0 33m	−26 43	0 2	−27 16	11 26a	−27 45
♃	1 31a	+20 33	1 13a	+20 16	0 54a	+19 59	0 36a	+19 40	0 18	+19 22
♄	3 4	+15 0	2 43	+14 47	2 22	+14 34	2 1	+14 20	1 40	+14 5
♅	9 53m	+21 52	9 30m	+21 54	9 6m	+21 57	8 46m	+21 59	8 23m	+22 2
♆	5 21	— 1 27	4 58	— 1 27	4 34	— 1 28	4 10	— 1 29	3 46	— 1 31

Days of Month.	Moon rises or sets. Mean Time.						High Water. Mean Time.			
	Boston, &c.	New York, &c.	Washington, &c.	Charleston, &c.	N. Orleans, &c.	San Francisco, &c.	Boston, &c.	New York, &c.	Charleston, &c.	San Francisco (North Beach).
	sets. h. m.	sets. h. m.	sets. h. m.	sets. h. m.	sets. h. m.	sets. h. m.	h. m.	h. m.	h. m.	h. m.
S.	2 33m	2 40m	2 48m	3 6m	3 19m	2 59m	10 3m	6 50m	6 3m	10 47m
2	3 32	3 40	3 47	4 7	4 19	3 59	10 57	7 41	6 57	11 31m
3	*rises.*	*rises.*	*rises.*	*rises.*	*rises.*	*rises.*	11 48m	8 27	7 44	0 16a
4	8 50a	8 46a	8 41a	8 29a	8 21a	8 43a	0 5a	9 13	8 26	0 56
5	9 17	9 14	9 11	9 2	8 59	9 12	1 7	9 53	9 5	1 35
6	9 39	9 37	9 35	9 29	9 27	9 37	1 46	10 31	9 42	2 13
7	9 57	9 57	9 56	9 55	9 55	9 59	2 23	11 6	10 18	2 51
S.	10 18a	10 19a	10 19a	10 20a	10 21a	10 22a	3 0	11 45m	10 54	3 37
9	10 39	10 41	10 43	10 47	10 50	10 47	3 37	0 24a	11 30m	4 27
10	11 0	11 3	11 6	11 14	11 19	11 11	4 18	1 6	0 10a	5 19
11	11 23	11 27	11 31	11 43	11 49	11 37a	5 5	1 52	0 54	6 11
12	11 52	11 57	. . .	. . .	. . .	. . .	5 58	2 45	1 44	7 5
13	. . .	. . .	0 3m	0 17m	0 24m	0 10m	6 56	3 42	2 44	8 2
14	0 26m	0 23m	0 39	0 56	1 6	0 49	7 58	4 43	3 51	9 1
S.	1 13m	1 20m	1 28m	1 48m	1 58m	1 38m	9 2	5 47	4 58	9 57
16	2 8	2 15	2 23	2 43	2 53	2 35	10 2	6 49	6 2	10 48
17	3 15	3 22	3 29	3 49	3 59	3 42	10 58	7 42	6 56	11 32a
18	4 29	4 35	4 41	4 58	5 7	4 53	11 48a	8 33	7 49	. . .
19	*sets.*	*sets.*	*sets.*	*sets.*	*sets.*	*sets.*	. . .	9 23	8 36	0 20m
20	8 44a	8 42a	8 41a	8 35a	8 34a	8 44a	0 36m	10 9	9 19	1 6
21	9 11	9 11	9 11	9 10	9 11	9 14	1 23	10 55	10 2	1 50
S.	9 36a	9 37a	9 39a	9 42a	9 44a	9 43a	2 8	11 37a	10 47	2 34
23	10 2	10 5	10 8	10 16	10 20	10 13	2 53	. . .	11 33a	3 28
24	10 31	10 35	10 40	10 52	10 58	10 47	3 40	0 27m	. . .	4 31
25	11 3	10 9	11 14	11 30	11 38	11 22	4 34	1 22	0 25m	5 36
26	11 42	11 49	11 56	. . .	. . .	. . .	5 35	2 22	1 22	6 41
27	. . .	. . .	. . .	0 14m	0 23m	0 5m	6 40	3 27	2 27	7 47
28	0 30m	0 37m	0 45m	1 5	1 15	0 55	7 48	4 34	3 41	8 52
S.	1 25m	1 33m	1 41m	2 1m	2 12m	1 51m	8 53	5 31	4 49	9 48
30	2 26	2 33	2 41	3 0	3 10	2 52	9 49	6 36	5 49	10 36
31	3 31	3 37	3 44	4 1	4 10	3 55	10 39m	7 25m	6 40m	11 16m

Twilight begins and ends. Mean Time.

	1st day.		7th day.		13th day.		19th day.		25th day.	
	Begins. h. m.	Ends. h. m.	Begins. h. m.	Ends. h. m.	Begins. h. m.	Ends. h. m.	Begins. h. m.	Ends. h. m.	Begins. h. m.	Ends. h. m.
Boston,	2 55m	9 17a	3 5m	9 5a	3 16m	8 53a	3 24m	8 42a	3 34m	8 30a
N. York,	3 4	9 6	3 14	8 56	3 23	8 45	3 32	8 34	3 40	8 24
Wash'n,	3 14	8 58	3 22	8 48	3 30	8 38	3 38	8 28	3 46	8 18
Charles.,	3 39	8 33	3 45	8 25	3 50	8 18	3 56	8 10	4 2	8 2
N. Orl's,	3 48	8 24	3 54	8 16	3 59	8 9	4 4	8 2	4 8	7 56
S. Fran.,	3 18	8 54	3 26	8 44	3 33	8 35	3 41	8 25	3 49	8 15

PHASES, AND APOGEE AND PERIGEE, OF THE MOON.

Full Moon,	1st day,	0h.	25m.	A.
Last Quarter,	9th "	4	15	A.
New Moon,	16th day,	5h.	12m.	A.
First Quarter,	23d "	7	42	M.
Full Moon,	31st "	3	49	M.

Apogee, 5th day, 9h. M. Perigee, 17th day, 6h. A.

Sun's upper limb rises and sets (cor. for refr.) Mean Time.

Days of Month.	Days of Week.	Boston, &c. rises. h. m.	Boston, &c. sets. h. m.	New York, &c. rises. h. m.	New York, &c. sets. h. m.	Washington, &c. rises. h. m.	Washington, &c. sets. h. m.	Charleston, &c. rises. h. m.	Charleston, &c. sets. h. m.	N. Orleans, &c. rises. h. m.	N. Orleans, &c. sets. h. m.	San Francisco, &c. rises. h. m.	San Francisco, &c. sets. h. m.	Moon Souths. Mean Time. h. m.
1	W.	4 52	7 19	4 57	7 15	5 1	7 11	5 14	6 58	5 19	6 53	5 5	7 7	☋
2	Th.	53	18	58	14	2	10	14	57	19	52	6	6	0 27m
3	F.	54	17	58	13	3	9	15	56	20	51	7	5	1 9
4	S.	55	15	59	12	4	8	16	55	20	51	8	4	1 50
5	*Su.*	4 57	7 14	5 0	7 10	5 4	7 6	5 16	6 55	5 21	6 50	5 8	7 2	2 30
6	M.	58	13	1	9	5	5	17	54	22	49	9	1	3 9
7	Tu.	59	12	2	8	6	4	18	53	22	48	9	1	3 50
8	W.	5 0	10	3	7	7	3	18	52	23	47	10	0	4 33
9	Th.	1	9	4	5	8	2	19	51	24	46	11	6 59	5 18
10	F.	2	8	5	4	9	1	20	50	24	45	12	58	6 7
11	S.	3	6	6	3	10	6 59	21	49	25	44	13	56	7 1
12	*Su.*	5 4	7 5	5 7	7 1	5 11	6 58	5 21	6 48	5 26	6 43	5 14	6 55	7 57
13	M.	5	3	8	0	12	57	22	47	26	43	15	54	8 56
14	Tu.	6	2	9	6 59	13	55	23	46	27	42	16	52	9 56
15	W.	7	0	10	58	13	54	23	45	27	41	16	51	10 54
16	Th.	8	6 59	11	56	14	53	24	43	28	40	17	50	11 50m
17	F.	9	57	12	54	15	52	25	42	28	39	18	49	0 43a
18	S.	10	56	13	53	16	50	25	41	29	38	19	47	1 35
19	*Su.*	5 11	6 54	5 14	6 52	5 17	6 49	5 26	6 40	5 30	6 37	5 20	6 46	2 27
20	M.	13	53	15	50	18	48	26	39	30	36	21	45	3 19
21	Tu.	14	51	16	49	19	46	27	38	31	34	22	43	4 13
22	W.	15	50	17	47	20	45	28	37	31	33	23	42	5 8
23	Th.	16	48	18	46	21	43	29	35	32	32	24	40	6 5
24	F.	17	47	19	44	22	42	29	34	33	31	25	39	7 1
25	S.	18	45	20	43	23	40	30	33	33	30	26	37	7 57
26	*Su.*	5 19	6 43	5 21	6 41	5 24	6 39	5 31	6 32	5 34	6 29	5 27	6 36	8 49
27	M.	20	42	22	40	24	38	31	31	34	28	27	35	9 39
28	Tu.	21	40	23	38	25	36	32	29	35	27	28	33	10 25
29	W.	22	39	24	37	26	34	33	28	35	26	29	31	11 8
30	Th.	23	37	25	35	27	33	33	27	36	24	30	30	11 49a
31	F.	24	35	26	33	28	31	34	26	36	23	31	28	☋

Passage of the Meridian (mean time) and Declination of the Planets at Transit.

	1st day.		7th day.		13th day.		19th day.		25th day.	
	souths.	Dec.	*souths.*	Dec.	*souths.*	Dec.	*souths.*	Dec.	*souths.*	Dec.
	h. m.	° ′	h. m.	° ′	h. m.	° ′	h. m.	° ′	h. m.	° ′
☿	0 56a	+ 9 22	0 17a	+10 16	11 36m	+12 18	11 5m	+14 28	10 51m	+15 37
♀	10 39m	+15 10	10 10m	+15 24	9 48	+15 43	9 30	+16 2	9 18	+16 16
♂	10 52a	—28 2	10 23a	—28 6	9 57a	—28 1	9 33a	—27 48	9 11a	—27 28
♃	11 57m	+19 59	11 39m	+18 39	11 20m	+18 19	11 2m	+17 58	11 44m	+17 37
♄	1 16a	+13 48	0 55a	+13 33	0 35a	+13 18	0 14a	+13 2	11 53	+12 46
♅	7 57m	+22 4	7 34m	+22 6	7 11m	+22 7	6 48m	+22 9	6 25	+22 10
♆	3 18	— 1 34	2 54	— 1 36	2 30	— 1 39	2 6	— 1 42	1 42	— 1 46

Days of Month.	Moon rises or sets. Mean Time. Boston, &c.	New York, &c.	Washington, &c.	Charleston, &c.	N. Orleans, &c.	San Francisco, &c.	High Water. Mean Time. Boston, &c.	New York, &c.	Charleston, &c.	San Francisco (North Beach).
	sets. h. m.	*sets.* h. m.	*sets.* h. m.	*sets.* h. m.	*sets.* h. m.	*sets.* h. m.	h. m.	h. m.	h. m.	h. m.
1	4 38m	4 43m	4 49m	5 3m	5 10m	5 0m	11 21m	8 5m	7 21m	11 54m
2	*rises.*	*rises.*	*rises.*	*rises.*	*rises.*	*rises.*	11 59m	8 45	8 1	0 32a
3	8 4a	8 3a	8 2a	7 58a	7 56a	8 4a	0 35a	9 22	8 35	1 5
4	8 23	8 23	8 23	8 23	8 23	8 26	1 10	9 57	9 8	1 38
S.	8 43a	8 44a	8 46a	8 49a	8 51a	8 49a	1 45	10 30	9 41	2 12
6	9 4	9 7	9 9	9 16	9 19	9 14	2 20	11 3	10 15	2 48
7	9 26	9 30	9 34	9 44	9 49	9 39	2 57	11 42m	10 51	3 34
8	9 52	9 57	10 2	10 15	10 22	10 7	3 37	0 4a	11 30m	4 27
9	10 24	10 30	10 37	10 53	11 1	10 45	4 25	1 13	0 17a	5 26
10	11 3	11 10	11 17	11 36	11 45	11 26	5 20	2 7	1 9	6 27
11	11 52	11 59	. . .	. . .	. . .	. . .	6 25	3 12	2 11	7 34
S.	. . .	. . .	0 7m	0 29m	0 37m	0 19m	7 33	4 19	3 24	8 37
13	0 53m	1 0m	1 8	1 28	1 38	1 20	8 42	5 27	4 37	9 38
14	2 3	2 10	2 17	2 35	2 44	2 29	9 44	6 31	5 44	10 21
15	3 20	3 25	3 31	3 45	3 53	3 43	10 40	7 25	6 40	11 17a
16	4 38	4 42	4 46	4 56	5 2	4 56	11 28a	8 10	7 28	. . .
17	*sets.*	*sets.*	*sets.*	*sets.*	*sets.*	*sets.*	. . .	9 0	8 14	0 0m
18	7 38a	7 39a	7 39a	7 41a	7 42a	7 44a	0 13m	9 44	8 56	0 44
S.	8 5a	8 7a	8 10a	8 16a	8 19a	8 15a	0 58	10 28	9 39	1 26
20	8 32	8 36	8 40	8 50	8 55	8 46	1 42	11 12a	10 14	2 9
21	9 4	9 9	9 13	9 28	9 35	9 22	2 29	. . .	11 12a	2 59
22	9 42	9 48	9 56	10 12	10 21	10 5	3 19	0 5m	. . .	4 3
23	10 27	10 34	10 42	11 1	11 11	10 52	4 14	1 2	0 6m	5 13
24	11 20	11 28	11 36	11 55	12 6	11 46	5 18	2 5	1 6	6 25
25	. . .	. . .	. . .	. . .	. . .	. . .	6 25	3 12	2 11	7·32
S.	0 20m	0 28m	0 36m	0 55m	1 5m	0 46m	7 33	4 19	3 24	8 37
27	1 22	1 29	1 35	1 53	2 3	1 47	8 34	5 19	4 29	9 32
28	2 2	2 33	2 38	2 53	3 1	2 49	9 27	6 12	5 25	10 17
29	3 32	3 37	3 39	3 53	3 59	3 51	10 12	6 59	6 13	10 54
30	4 34	4 37	4 41	4 48	4 53	4 49	10 53	7 37	6 53	11 28
31	5 36	5 38	5 42	5 45	5 48	5 49	11 28m	8 10m	7 28m	0 0m

Twilight begins and ends. Mean Time.

	1st day.		7th day.		13th day.		19th day.		25th day.	
	Begins. h. m.	Ends. h. m.	Begins. h. m.	Ends. h. m.	Begins. h. m.	Ends. h. m.	Begins. h. m.	Ends. h. m.	Begins. h. m.	Ends. h. m.
Boston,	3 44m	8 16a	3 51m	8 4a	3 59m	7 52a	4 7m	7 40a	4 16m	7 28a
N. York,	3 49	8 11	3 56	8 0	4 3	7 49	4 10	7 37	4 18	7 26
Wash'n,	3 54	8 6	4 0	7 56	4 7	7 45	4 14	7 34	4 21	7 23
Charles.,	4 8	7 52	4 12	7 43	4 17	7 34	4 22	7 25	4 28	7 16
N. Orl's,	4 14	7 46	4 17	7 39	4 21	7 31	4 25	7 22	4 30	7 14
S. Fran.,	3 56	8 4	4 2	7 54	4 9	7 43	4 15	7 33	4 22	7 22

PHASES, AND PERIGEE AND APOGEE, OF THE MOON.

Last Quarter,	8th day,	5h. 59m. M.	First Quarter,	21st day, 6h. 17m. A.
New Moon,	15th "	1 1 M.	Full Moon,	29th " 8 32 A.

Apogee, 1st day, 7h. A. | Perigee, 15th day, 3h. M. | Apogee, 28th day, 8h. A.

Days of Month.	Days of Week.	Sun's *upper* limb rises and sets (cor. for refr.) Mean Time. Boston, &c.		New York, &c.		Washington, &c.		Charleston, &c.		N. Orleans, &c.		San Francisco, &c.		Moon Souths. Mean Time.
		rises. h. m.	*sets.* h. m.	*rises.* h. m.	*sets.* h. m.	*rises.* h. m.	*sets.* h. m.	*rises.* h. m.	*sets.* h. m.	*rises.* h. m.	*sets.* h. m.	*rises.* h. m.	*sets.* h. m.	h. m.
1	S.	5 25	6 33	5 27	6 32	5 29	6 30	5 35	6 24	5 37	6 22	5 32	6 27	0 29m
2	*Su.*	5 26	6 32	5 28	6 30	5 30	6 28	5 35	6 23	5 37	6 21	5 32	6 26	1 8
3	M.	27	30	29	28	31	27	36	22	38	20	33	25	1 48
4	Tu.	28	28	30	27	32	25	36	20	38	18	34	23	2 30
5	W.	29	27	31	25	33	24	37	19	39	17	35	22	3 14
6	Th.	30	25	32	24	33	22	38	18	40	16	35	20	4 1
7	F.	32	23	33	22	34	20	38	16	40	15	36	18	4 52
8	S.	33	22	34	20	35	19	39	15	41	13	37	17	5 46
9	*Su.*	5 34	6 20	5 35	6 18	5 36	6 17	5 39	6 14	5 41	6 12	5 38	6 15	6 42
10	M.	35	18	36	17	37	16	40	12	42	11	39	14	7 40
11	Tu.	36	16	37	15	38	14	41	11	42	10	40	12	8 37
12	W.	37	14	38	14	39	13	42	10	43	9	41	11	9 33
13	Th.	38	13	39	12	40	11	42	8	43	7	42	9	10 27
14	F.	39	11	40	10	41	10	43	7	44	6	43	8	11 20m
15	S.	40	9	41	9	41	8	44	6	44	5	43	6	0 12a
16	*Su.*	5 41	6 7	5 42	6 7	5 42	6 6	5 44	6 4	5 45	6 4	5 44	6 4	1 6
17	M.	42	6	43	5	43	5	45	3	45	2	45	3	2 1
18	Tu.	43	4	44	4	44	3	46	2	46	1	46	1	2 58
19	W.	44	2	45	2	45	1	46	0	46	0	47	5 59	3 56
20	Th.	45	0	46	0	46	0	47	5 59	47	5 59	47	59	4 54
21	F.	46	5 59	47	5 59	47	5 58	48	58	48	58	48	57	5 51
22	S.	47	57	48	57	48	57	48	56	48	56	49	56	6 45
23	*Su.*	5 49	5 55	5 49	5 55	5 49	5 55	5 49	5 55	5 49	5 55	5 50	5 54	7 36
24	M.	50	53	50	54	50	53	49	54	49	54	51	52	8 23
25	Tu.	51	52	51	52	50	52	50	52	50	53	51	51	9 7
26	W.	52	50	52	50	51	50	51	51	50	51	52	49	9 48
27	Th.	53	48	53	48	52	49	51	50	51	50	53	48	10 28
28	F.	54	46	54	47	53	47	52	48	52	49	54	46	11 8
29	S.	55	45	55	45	54	45	53	47	52	48	55	44	11 48a
30	*Su.*	5 56	5 43	5 56	5 43	5 55	5 41	5 54	5 46	5 53	5 46	5 56	5 43	☌

Passage of the Meridian (mean time) and Declination of the Planets at Transit.

	1st day.		7th day.		13th day.		19th day.		25th day.	
	souths.	Dec.	*souths.*	Dec.	*souths.*	Dec.	*souths.*	Dec.	*souths.*	Dec.
	h. m.	° ′	h. m.	° ′	h. m.	° ′	h. m.	° ′	h. m.	° ′
☿	10 56m	+14 48	11 12m	+12 6	11 31m	+ 8 7	11 49m	+ 3 30	0 4a	− 1 14
♀	9 7	+16 21	9 2	+16 12	8 58	+15 48	8 56	+15 7	8 56m	+14 10
♂	8 47a	−26 57	8 29a	−26 25	8 13a	−25 48	7 59a	−25 5	7 45a	−24 18
♃	10 23m	+17 13	10 3m	+16 52	9 45m	+16 31	9 26m	+16 10	9 7m	+15 50
♄	11 29	+12 28	11 8	+12 12	10 48	+11 57	10 27	+11 42	10 6	+11 27
♅	5 58	+22 11	5 35	+22 11	5 12	+22 12	4 48	+22 12	4 34	+22 11
♆	1 14	− 1 50	0 50	− 1 54	0 26	− 1 58	11 58a	− 2 3	11 28a	− 2 7

Days of Month.	Moon rises or sets. Mean Time.						High Water. Mean Time.			
	Boston, &c.	New York, &c.	Washington, &c.	Charleston, &c.	N. Orleans, &c.	San Francisco, &c.	Boston, &c.	New York, &c.	Charleston, &c.	San Francisco (North Beach).
	rises. h. m.	*rises.* h. m.	*rises.* h. m.	*rises.* h. m.	*rises.* h. m.	*rises.* h. m.	h. m.	h. m.	h. m.	h. m.
1	6 50a	6 51a	6 53a	6 54a	6 55a	6 55a	0 1a	8 47m	8 8m	0 33a
S.	7 10a	7 12a	7 14a	7 20a	7 23a	7 18a	0 34	9 21	8 34	1 4
3	7 30	7 33	7 37	7 46	7 50	7 42	1 8	9 55	9 6	1 36
4	7 54	7 58	8 3	8 15	8 21	8 9	1 45	10 30	9 41	2 12
5	8 23	8 28	8 34	8 49	8 57	8 42	2 25	11 8	10 20	2 53
6	8 59	9 6	9 12	9 31	9 40	9 22	3 7	11 53m	11 1	3 47
7	9 44	9 51	9 59	10 18	10 28	10 9	3 57	0 45a	11 50m	4 53
8	10 37	10 44	10 52	11 12	11 22	11 3	4 56	1 44	0 46a	6 1
S.	11 41a	11 48a	11 56a	. . .	. . .	. . .	6 2	2 49	1 48	7 9
10	. . .	. . .	. . .	0 14m	0 24m	0 7m	7 13	3 59	3 2	8 17
11	0 53m	0 59m	1 5m	1 21	1 30	1 17	8 20	5 5	4 14	9 21
12	2 11	2 16	2 21	2 34	2 40	2 33	9 20	6 7	5 18	10 12
13	3 29	3 32	3 36	3 44	3 49	3 46	10 14	7 1	6 15	10 57
14	4 49	4 51	4 52	4 55	4 59	5 2	11 3	7 47	7 3	11 37a
15	*sets.*	*sets.*	*sets.*	*sets.*	*sets.*	*sets.*	11 47a	8 32	7 49	. . .
S.	6 31a	6 34a	6 37a	6 46a	6 50a	6 43a	. . .	9 20	8 33	0 20m
17	7 2	7 7	7 12	7 24	7 31	7 19	0 32m	10 7	9 17	1 3
18	7 38	7 44	7 50	8 6	8 14	7 59	1 20	10 53	10 5	1 47
19	8 22	8 29	7 36	8 54	9 4	8 45	2 10	11 48a	10 56	2 37
20	9 13	9 20	9 28	9 48	9 58	9 38	3 2	. . .	11 52a	3 41
21	10 12	10 20	10 27	10 47	10 58	10 39	3 59	0 47m	. . .	4 55
22	11 16	11 23	11 30	11 48	11 58	11 42	5 1	1 49	0 51m	6 8
S.	. . .	. . .	. . .	. . .	. . .	. . .	6 6	2 53	1 52	7 12
24	0 20m	0 26m	0 32m	0 47m	0 56m	0 43m	7 8	3 54	2 57	8 13
25	1 25	1 30	1 35	1 47	1 55	1 44	8 4	4 49	3 58	9 6
26	2 28	2 32	2 35	2 44	2 50	2 44	8 54	5 38	4 50	9 49
27	3 28	3 30	3 33	3 38	3 41	3 41	9 36	6 23	5 35	10 25
28	4 30	4 31	4 32	4 34	4 36	4 40	10 15	7 2	6 16	10 57
29	5 30	5 30	5 30	5 28	5 29	5 36	10 53	7 37	6 53	11 28
S.	6 28m	6 26m	6 25m	6 19m	6 19m	6 31m	11 27m	8 10m	7 27m	11 59m

Twilight begins and ends. Mean Time.

	1st day. Begins. h. m.	1st day. Ends. h. m.	7th day. Begins. h. m.	7th day. Ends. h. m.	13th day. Begins. h. m.	13th day. Ends. h. m.	19th day. Begins. h. m.	19th day. Ends. h. m.	25th day. Begins. h. m.	25th day. Ends. h. m.
Boston,	4 28m	7 17a	4 30m	7 6a	4 37m	6 55a	4 44m	6 46a	4 50m	6 38
N. York,	4 25	7 15	4 32	7 4	4 38	6 54	4 44	6 46	4 50	6 38
Wash'n,	4 27	7 13	4 33	7 3	4 38	6 54	4 44	6 46	4 50	6 38
Charles.,	4 32	7 8	4 36	7 0	4 40	6 52	4 45	6 45	4 49	6 39
N. Orl's,	4 34	7 6	4 37	6 56	4 41	6 51	4 45	6 45	4 48	6 40
S. Fran.,	4 28	7 12	4 34	7 2	4 38	6 54	4 44	6 46	4 50	6 38

PHASES, AND PERIGEE AND APOGEE, OF THE MOON.

Last Quarter, 7th day, 5h. 57m. A. | First Quarter, 21st day, 9h. 2m. M.
New Moon, 14th " 9 29 M. | Full Moon, 29th " 1 42 A.
Perigee, 13th day, 2h. A. | Apogee, 26th day, 2h. M.

Sun's *upper* limb rises and sets (cor. for refr.) Mean Time.

Days of Month.	Days of Week.	Boston, &c. rises. h. m.	Boston, &c. sets. h. m.	New York, &c. rises. h. m.	New York, &c. sets. h. m.	Washington, &c. rises. h. m.	Washington, &c. sets. h. m.	Charleston, &c. rises. h. m.	Charleston, &c. sets. h. m.	N. Orleans, &c. rises. h. m.	N. Orleans, &c. sets. h. m.	San Francisco, &c. rises. h. m.	San Francisco, &c. sets. h. m.	Moon Souths. Mean Time. h. m.
1	M.	5 57	5 41	5 57	5 42	5 56	5 42	5 54	5 44	5 53	5 45	5 57	5 41	0 29m
2	Tu.	58	39	58	40	57	41	55	43	53	44	58	40	1 13
3	W.	6 0	38	59	38	58	39	56	42	54	43	59	38	1 59
4	Th.	1	36	6 0	37	59	38	56	40	55	42	6 0	37	2 48
5	F.	2	34	1	35	6 0	36	57	39	56	40	1	35	3 40
6	S.	3	33	2	33	1	34	58	38	56	39	2	33	4 35
7	*Su.*	6 4	5 31	6 3	5 32	6 2	5 33	5 58	5 36	5 57	5 38	6 3	5 32	5 30
8	M.	5	29	4	30	3	32	59	35	57	37	4	31	6 25
9	Tu.	6	27	5	29	4	30	6 0	34	58	36	5	29	7 20
10	W.	8	26	6	27	5	29	1	33	59	34	6	28	8 13
11	Th.	9	24	7	26	6	27	1	32	59	33	7	26	9 5
12	F.	10	23	8	24	7	26	2	30	6 0	32	8	25	9 56
13	S.	11	21	9	22	8	24	3	29	1	31	8	24	10 49
14	*Su.*	6 12	5 19	6 10	5 21	6 9	5 23	6 4	5 28	6 1	5 30	6 9	5 23	11 43m
15	M.	14	18	11	19	10	21	4	27	2	29	10	21	0 40a
16	Tu.	15	16	13	18	11	20	5	26	3	28	11	20	1 39
17	W.	16	15	14	16	12	18	6	24	3	27	12	18	2 40
18	Th.	17	13	15	15	13	17	7	23	4	26	13	17	3 40
19	F.	18	11	16	13	14	16	7	22	5	25	14	16	4 37
20	S.	19	10	17	12	15	14	8	21	5	24	15	14	5 30
21	*Su.*	6 20	5 8	6 18	5 11	6 16	5 13	6 9	5 20	6 6	5 23	6 16	5 13	6 19
22	M.	22	7	19	9	17	12	10	19	7	22	17	12	7 4
23	Tu.	23	5	20	8	18	10	10	18	8	21	18	10	7 47
24	W.	24	4	21	6	19	9	11	17	8	20	19	9	8 27
25	Th.	25	3	23	5	20	8	12	16	9	19	20	8	9 7
26	F.	26	1	24	4	21	6	13	15	10	18	21	6	9 47
27	S.	28	0	25	2	22	5	14	14	10	17	22	5	10 28
28	*Su.*	6 29	4 58	6 26	5 1	6 23	5 4	6 15	5 13	6 11	5 16	6 22	5 5	11 11
29	M.	30	57	27	0	24	3	15	12	12	15	23	4	11 56a
30	Tu.	31	56	28	4 59	26	2	16	11	13	14	25	3	☋
31	W.	33	54	30	57	27	0	17	10	13	14	26	1	0 45m

Passage of the Meridian (mean time) and Declination of the Planets at Transit.

	1st day.		7th day.		13th day.		19th day.		25th day.	
	souths. h. m.	Dec. ° ′	*souths.* h. m.	Dec. ° ′	*souths.* h. m.	Dec. ° ′	*souths.* h. m.	Dec. ° ′	*souths.* h. m.	Dec. ° ′
☿	0 17a	— 5 49	0 29a	—10 7	0 40a	—14 3	0 51a	—17 31	1 1a	—20 27
♀	8 56m	+12 55	8 56m	+11 28	8 58m	+ 9 38	8 59m	+ 7 39	9 1m	+ 5 27
♂	7 33a	—23 25	7 21a	—22 28	7 10a	—21 25	7 0a	—20 17	6 50a	—19 3
♃	8 47m	+15 30	8 28m	+15 12	8 8m	+14 54	7 48m	+14 37	7 28m	+14 21
♄	9 45	+11 13	9 24	+10 59	9 3	+10 46	8 42	+10 34	8 20	+10 23
♅	4 0	+22 11	3 36	+22 10	3 12	+22 9	2 48	+22 8	2 24	+22 7
♆	11 9a	— 2 11	10 45a	— 2 14	10 21a	— 2 18	9 57a	— 2 21	9 33a	— 2 24

Days of Month.	Moon rises or sets. Mean Time.						High Water. Mean Time.			
	Boston, &c.	New York, &c.	Washington, &c.	Charleston, &c.	N. Orleans, &c.	San Francisco, &c.	Boston, &c.	New York, &c.	Charleston, &c.	San Francisco (North Beach).
	rises. h. m.	*rises.* h. m.	*rises.* h. m.	*rises.* h. m.	*rises.* h. m.	*rises.* h. m.	h. m.	h. m.	h. m.	h. m.
1	6 0a	6 4a	6 8a	6 20a	6 25a	6 14a	0 1a	8 47m	8 3m	0 3a
2	6 28	6 33	6 39	6 52	6 59	6 45	0 38	9 26	8 38	1 8
3	7 1	7 7	7 14	7 31	7 39	7 20	1 18	10 5	9 15	1 45
4	7 42	7 49	7 56	8 15	8 25	7 64	2 1	10 45	9 56	2 28
5	8 32	8 39	8 47	9 6	9 16	8 56	2 48	11 32m	10 42	3 22
6	9 30	9 37	9 44	10 4	10 14	9 55	3 40	0 27a	11 33m	4 30
S.	10 36a	10 42a	10 49a	11 7a	11 16a	11 0a	4 38	1 26	0 29a	5 41
8	11 50	11 55	. . .	. . .	. . .	. . .	5 43	2 30	1 30	6 49
9	. . .	. . .	0 1m	0 15m	0 22m	0 13m	6 48	3 35	2 36	7 55
10	1 4m	1 8m	1 12	1 22	1 28	1 23	7 52	4 37	3 45	8 55
11	2 21	2 23	2 26	2 31	2 36	2 36	8 51	5 37	4 47	9 47
12	3 39	3 40	3 41	3 42	3 44	3 50	9 44	6 31	5 44	10 32
13	4 56	4 58	4 57	4 54	4 54	4 56	10 35	7 21	6 36	11 13
S.	6 18m	6 16m	6 13m	6 5m	6 3m	6 21m	11 23a	8 6	7 23	11 55a
15	*sets.*	*sets.*	*sets.*	*sets.*	*sets.*	*sets.*	. . .	8 57	8 12	. . .
16	6 13a	6 19a	6 26a	6 43a	6 52a	6 36a	0 10m	9 47	8 59	0 42m
17	7 2	7 9	7 17	7 35	7 45	7 27	1 1	10 39	9 50	1 29
18	8 0	8 8	8 15	8 35	8 46	8 27	1 54	11 32a	10 42	2 21
19	9 3	9 10	9 18	9 36	9 46	9 29	2 48	. . .	11 35a	3 22
20	10 9	10 15	10 22	10 38	10 47	10 33	3 42	0 29m	. . .	4 33
S.	11 16a	11 21a	11 26a	11 40a	11 47a	11 36a	4 38	1 26	0 29m	5 41
22	. . .	. . .	. . .	. . .	. . .	. . .	5 35	2 22	1 12	6 41
23	0 19m	0 23m	0 27m	0 37m	0 53m	0 36m	6 29	3 16	2 15	7 36
24	1 22	1 25	1 28	1 34	1 38	1 36	7 21	4 7	3 11	8 25
25	2 20	2 21	2 23	2 25	2 28	2 30	8 8	4 53	4 2	9 11
26	3 21	3 21	3 21	3 20	3 22	3 29	8 54	5 38	4 50	9 49
27	4 25	4 24	4 23	4 18	4 18	4 29	9 35	6 22	5 34	10 24
S.	5 28m	5 26m	5 23m	5 15m	5 13m	5 29m	10 15	7 2	6 16	10 58
29	6 30	6 26	6 23	6 11	6 7	6 28	10 56	7 40	6 56	11 31m
30	*rises.*	*rises.*	*rises.*	*rises.*	*rises.*	*rises.*	11 34m	8 16	7 34	0 6a
31	5 41a	5 48a	5 55a	6 13a	6 22a	6 4a	0 15a	9 1m	8 16m	0 46a

Twilight begins and ends. Mean Time.

	1st day. Begins. h. m.	1st day. Ends. h. m.	7th day. Begins. h. m.	7th day. Ends. h. m.	13th day. Begins. h. m.	13th day. Ends. h. m.	19th day. Begins. h. m.	19th day. Ends. h. m.	25th day. Begins. h. m.	25th day. Ends. h. m.
Boston,	4 58m	6 30a	5 5m	6 23a	5 11m	6 18a	5 17m	6 14a	5 23m	6 11a
N. York,	4 57	6 31	5 4	6 24	5 10	6 19	5 15	6 16	5 21	6 13
Wash'n,	4 57	6 31	5 3	6 25	5 8	6 21	5 13	6 18	5 19	6 15
Charles.,	4 54	6 34	4 59	6 29	5 3	6 25	5 7	6 23	5 12	6 22
N. Orl's,	4 53	6 35	4 55	6 31	5 1	6 28	5 5	6 26	5 9	6 25
S. Fran.,	4 56	6 32	5 2	6 26	5 7	6 22	5 12	6 19	5 18	6 16

PHASES, AND PERIGEE AND APOGEE, OF THE MOON.

Last Quarter,	6th day,	4h. 9m.	M.	First Quarter,	20th day,	3h. 44m.	M.
New Moon,	12th "	7 28	A.	Full Moon,	28th "	6 30	M.

Perigee, 10th day, 10h. A. | Apogee, 22d day, 6h. A.

Sun's *upper* limb rises and sets (cor. for refr.) Mean Time.

Days of Month.	Days of Week.	Boston, &c. rises. h. m.	Boston, &c. sets. h. m.	New York, &c. rises. h. m.	New York, &c. sets. h. m.	Washington, &c. rises. h. m.	Washington, &c. sets. h. m.	Charleston, &c. rises. h. m.	Charleston, &c. sets. h. m.	N. Orleans, &c. rises. h. m.	N. Orleans, &c. sets. h. m.	San Francisco, &c. rises. h. m.	San Francisco, &c. sets. h. m.	Moon Souths. Mean Time. h. m.
1	Th.	6 34	4 53	6 31	4 56	6 28	4 59	6 18	5 9	6 14	5 13	6 27	5 0	1 37m
2	F.	35	52	32	55	29	58	19	8	15	12	28	4 59	2 31
3	S.	36	51	33	54	30	57	20	7	16	11	29	58	3 26
4	*Su.*	6 38	4 49	6 34	4 53	6 31	4 56	6 21	5 6	6 17	5 10	6 30	4 57	4 21
5	M.	39	48	36	52	32	55	22	6	17	10	31	56	5 14
6	Tu.	40	47	37	50	33	54	23	5	18	9	32	55	6 6
7	W.	41	46	38	49	34	53	24	4	19	8	33	54	6 56
8	Th.	43	45	39	48	36	52	24	3	20	8	35	53	7 45
9	F.	44	44	41	47	37	51	25	2	20	7	36	52	8 35
10	S.	45	43	42	46	38	50	26	2	21	7	37	51	9 38
11	*Su.*	6 46	4 42	6 43	4 45	6 39	4 49	6 27	5 1	6 22	5 6	6 38	4 50	10 22
12	M.	48	41	44	44	40	48	28	0	23	6	39	49	11 20m
13	Tu.	49	40	45	44	41	48	29	0	24	5	40	49	0 20a
14	W.	50	39	46	43	42	47	30	4 59	25	5	41	48	1 21
15	Th.	52	38	47	42	43	46	31	59	25	4	42	47	2 22
16	F.	53	37	49	41	44	45	32	58	26	4	43	46	3 18
17	S.	54	36	50	40	45	45	33	58	27	3	44	46	4 10
18	*Su.*	6 55	4 35	6 51	4 40	6 47	4 44	6 34	4 57	6 28	5 3	6 46	4 45	4 58
19	M.	56	35	52	39	48	44	34	57	29	2	47	45	5 42
20	Tu.	58	34	54	38	49	43	35	56	30	2	47	45	6 24
21	W.	59	33	55	38	50	42	36	56	31	2	48	44	7 4
22	Th.	7 0	33	56	37	51	42	37	56	31	1	49	44	7 44
23	F.	1	32	57	37	52	41	38	56	32	1	50	43	8 24
24	S.	2	32	58	36	53	41	39	55	33	1	51	43	9 6
25	*Su.*	7 4	4 31	6 59	4 36	6 54	4 40	6 40	4 55	6 34	5 1	6 52	4 42	9 51
26	M.	5	31	7 0	36	55	40	41	55	35	1	53	42	10 39
27	Tu.	6	30	1	35	56	39	42	54	36	1	54	41	11 31a
28	W.	7	30	2	35	57	39	42	54	36	0	55	41	☋
29	Th.	8	29	3	34	58	39	43	54	37	0	56	41	0 25m
30	F.	9	29	4	34	59	39	44	54	38	0	57	41	1 21m

Passage of the Meridian (mean time) and Declination of the Planets at Transit.

	1st day.		7th day.		13th day.		19th day.		25th day.	
	souths.	Dec.	*souths.*	Dec.	*souths.*	Dec.	*souths.*	Dec.	*souths.*	Dec.
	h. m.	° ′	h. m.	° ′	h. m.	° ′	h. m.	° ′	h. m.	° ′
☿	1 11a	—23 3	1 16a	—24 27	1 14a	—24 52	0 54a	—24 1	0 11a	—21 34
♀	9 4m	+ 2 41	9 6m	+ 0 11	9 8m	— 2 28	9 11m	— 5 59	9 14m	— 7 35
♂	6 38a	—17 32	6 29a	—16 22	6 20a	—14 41	6 11a	—13 10	6 2a	—11 36
♃	7 4m	+14 5	6 43m	+13 58	6 22m	+13 42	6 0m	+13 33	5 38m	+13 27
♄	7 55	+10 11	7 33	+10 2	7 11	+ 9 54	6 49	+ 9 47	6 26	+ 9 42
♅	1 56	+22 5	1 31	+22 4	1 6	+22 2	0 42	+22 0	0 17	+21 58
♆	9 5a	— 2 28	8 41a	— 2 30	8 17a	— 2 32	7 53a	— 2 33	7 29a	— 2 34

Days of Month.	Moon rises or sets. Mean Time. Boston, &c.	New York, &c.	Washington, &c.	Charleston, &c.	N. Orleans, &c.	San Francisco, &c.	High Water. Mean Time. Boston, &c.	New York, &c.	Charleston, &c.	San Francisco (North Beach).
	rises. h. m.	*rises.* h. m.	*rises.* h. m.	*rises.* h. m.	*rises.* h. m.	*rises.* h. m.	h. m.	h. m.	h. m.	h. m.
1	6 29a	6 36a	6 44a	7 3a	7 13a	6 53a	0 59a	9 46m	8 56m	1 28a
2	7 26	7 33	7 41	8 0	8 10	7 52	1 46	10 31	9 42	2 18
3	8 28	8 35	8 42	9 0	9 9	8 53	2 35	11 18m	10 30	3 6
S.	9 40a	9 46a	9 52a	10 6a	10 14a	10 2a	3 26	0 13a	11 20m	4 12
5	10 50	10 56	10 59	11 10	10 17	11 9	4 20	1 8	0 12a	5 21
6	. . .	. . .	. . .	. . .	. . .	. . .	5 18	2 5	1 6	6 25
7	0 4m	0 7m	0 10m	0 18m	0 20m	0 21m	6 19	3 6	2 5	7 26
8	1 18	1 19	1 21	1 23	1 27	1 30	7 19	4 5	3 6	8 21
9	2 32	2 33	2 32	2 31	2 33	2 23	8 15	5 3	4 12	9 19
10	3 50	3 48	3 47	3 41	3 40	3 55	9 14	6 0	5 12	10 7
S.	5 8m	5 5m	5 2m	4 51m	4 49m	5 10m	10 9	6 56	6 10	10 52
12	6 28	6 24	6 19	6 5	6 2	6 27	11 3	7 47	7 3	11 37a
13	*sets.*	*sets.*	*sets.*	*sets.*	*sets.*	*sets.*	11 54a	8 39	7 55	. . .
14	5 43a	5 50a	5 58a	6 17a	6 27a	6 9a	. . .	9 33	8 45	0 26m
15	6 46	6 53	7 1	7 20	7 31	7 13	0 45m	10 23	9 34	1 15
16	7 53	8 0	8 6	8 24	8 33	8 18	1 37	11 11a	10 23	2 4
17	9 0	9 6	9 11	9 26	9 34	9 22	2 28	. . .	11 9	2 56
S.	10 5	10 9a	10 14a	10 25a	10 32a	10 24a	3 16	0 2m	11 56a	3 50
19	11 9	11 12	11 15	11 23	11 28	11 25	4 3	0 51	. . .	5 1
20	. . .	. . .	. . .	. . .	. . .	. . .	4 51	1 39	0 42m	5 56
21	0 12m	0 14m	0 16m	0 19m	0 22m	0 23m	5 41	2 28	1 27	6 47
22	1 12	1 13	1 13	1 14	1 16	1 21	6 29	3 16	2 15	7 36
23	2 12	2 11	2 11	2 8	2 9	2 18	7 18	4 4	3 7	8 22
24	3 13	3 11	3 9	3 2	3 1	3 15	8 5	4 50	3 59	9 7
S.	4 15m	4 12m	4 9m	3 58m	3 55m	4 14m	8 53	5 37	4 49	9 48
26	5 18	5 14	5 9	4 56	4 52	5 14	9 39	6 26	5 38	10 28
27	6 23	6 18	6 12	5 56	5 50	6 17	10 26	7 12	6 27	11 6
28	*rises.*	*rises.*	*rises.*	*rises.*	*rises.*	*rises.*	11 12	7 58	7 12	11 44m
29	5 20a	5 27a	5 35a	5 54a	6 3a	5 46a	11 58m	8 44	8 0	0 20a
30	6 22	6 29	6 36	6 54	7 4	6 47	0 44a	9 32m	8 44m	1 14

Twilight begins and ends. Mean Time.

	1st day.		7th day.		13th day.		19th day.		25th day.	
	Begins. h. m.	Ends. h. m.	Begins. h. m.	Ends. h. m.	Begins h. m.	Ends. h. m.	Begins. h. m.	Ends. h. m.	Begins. h. m.	Ends. h. m.
Boston,	5 29m	6 9a	5 35m	6 9a	5 40m	6 16a	5 43m	6 10a	5 46m	6 14a
N. York,	5 27	6 11	5 33	6 11	5 37	6 11	5 41	6 13	5 44	6 16
Wash'n,	5 25	6 13	5 30	6 14	5 34	6 14	5 38	6 16	5 41	6 19
Charles.,	5 17	6 21	5 22	6 22	5 26	6 23	5 29	6 25	5 32	6 28
N. Orl's,	5 13	6 25	5 18	6 26	5 24	6 27	5 25	6 29	5 28	6 32
S. Fran.,	5 24	6 14	5 29	6 15	5 33	6 15	5 36	6 18	5 39	6 21

PHASES, AND PERIGEE AND APOGEE, OF THE MOON.

Last Quarter, 5th day, 0h. 53m. A. | First Quarter, 20th day, 1h. 2m. M.
New Moon, 12th " 7 40 M. | Full Moon, 27th " 10 9 A.
Perigee, 8th day, 3h. A. | Apogee, 20th day, 2h. A.

Sun's *upper* limb rises and sets (cor. for refr.) Mean Time.

Days of Month.	Days of Week.	Boston, &c. rises. h. m.	Boston, &c. sets. h. m.	New York, &c. rises. h. m.	New York, &c. sets. h. m.	Washington, &c. rises. h. m.	Washington, &c. sets. h. m.	Charleston, &c. rises. h. m.	Charleston, &c. sets. h. m.	N. Orleans, &c. rises. h. m	N. Orleans, &c. sets. h. m.	San Francisco, &c. rises. h. m.	San Francisco, &c. sets. h. m.	Moon Souths. Mean Time. h. m.
1	S.	7 10	4 29	7 5	4 34	7 0	4 39	6 45	4 54	6 39	5 0	6 58	4 41	2 16m
2	*Su.*	7 11	4 28	7 6	4 33	7 1	4 38	6 46	4 54	6 40	5 0	6 59	4 40	3 11
3	M.	12	28	7	33	2	38	46	54	41	0	7 0	40	4 3
4	Tu.	13	28	8	33	3	38	47	54	41	0	1	40	4 53
5	W.	14	28	9	33	4	38	48	54	42	1	2	40	5 42
6	Th.	15	28	10	33	5	38	49	54	43	1	3	40	6 30
7	F.	16	28	11	33	6	38	50	54	44	1	4	40	7 19
8	S.	17	28	12	33	7	38	51	54	44	1	5	40	8 11
9	*Su.*	7 18	4 28	7 13	4 33	7 7	4 38	6 51	4 54	6 45	5 1	7 5	4 40	9 5
10	M.	19	28	14	33	8	38	52	54	46	1	6	40	10 3
11	Tu.	20	28	15	33	9	39	53	55	46	1	7	41	11 3m
12	W.	20	28	15	33	10	39	54	55	47	2	8	41	0 4a
13	Th.	21	28	16	33	10	39	54	55	48	2	8	41	1 3
14	F.	22	29	17	34	11	39	55	55	48	2	9	41	1 56
15	S.	23	29	18	34	12	40	55	56	49	3	9	43	2 49
16	*Su.*	7 23	4 29	7 18	4 34	7 13	4 40	6 56	4 56	6 50	5 3	7 10	4 43	3 35
17	M.	24	29	19	35	13	40	57	57	50	3	10	43	4 18
18	Tu.	25	29	20	35	14	40	57	57	51	4	11	43	4 59
19	W.	25	30	20	35	14	41	58	58	51	4	11	44	5 39
20	Th.	26	31	21	36	15	41	58	58	52	5	12	44	6 19
21	F.	26	31	21	36	15	42	59	58	52	5	12	45	7 1
22	S.	27	32	21	37	16	42	59	59	52	6	13	45	7 43
23	*Su.*	7 27	4 32	7 22	4 38	7 16	4 43	7 0	5 0	6 53	5 6	7 13	4 46	8 30
24	M.	28	33	22	38	17	44	0	0	54	7	14	47	9 20
25	Tu.	28	33	23	39	17	44	1	1	54	7	14	47	10 14
26	W.	28	34	23	39	18	45	1	1	54	8	15	48	11 10a
27	Th.	29	35	23	40	18	45	1	2	55	9	15	48	[illegible]
28	F.	29	35	24	41	18	46	2	3	55	9	15	49	0 7m
29	S.	29	36	24	42	19	46	2	3	55	10	16	49	1 3
30	*Su.*	7 29	4 37	7 24	4 42	7 19	4 48	7 2	5 4	6 56	5 11	7 16	4 51	1 57
31	M.	30	38	24	43	19	48	3	5	56	12	16	51	2 49m

Passage of the Meridian (mean time) and Declination of the Planets at Transit.

	1st day.		7th day.		13th day.		19th day.		25th day.	
	souths.	Dec.	*souths.*	Dec.	*souths.*	Dec.	*souths*	Dec.	*souths.*	Dec.
	h. m.	° ′	h. m.	° ′	h. m.	° ′	h. m.	° ′	h. m.	° ′
☿	11 16m	—18 26	10 40m	—17 8	10 27m	—17 54	10 27m	—19 41	10 36m	—21 34
♀	9 18	—10 7	9 23	—12 34	9 27	—14 50	9 33	—16 55	9 40	—18 45
♂	5 53a	— 9 58	5 44a	—8 18	5 35a	— 6 36	5 26a	— 4 53	5 17a	— 3 8
♃	5 16m	+13 23	4 52m	+13 21	4 29m	+13 21	4 5m	+13 24	3 41m	+13 29
♄	6 4	+ 9 38	5 41	+ 9 35	5 17	+ 9 34	4 54	+ 9 35	4 30	+ 9 37
♅	11 48a	+21 55	11 24a	+21 53	10 59a	+21 51	10 34a	+21 49	10 10a	+21 47
♆	7 5	— 2 35	6 42	— 2 35	6 18	— 2 34	5 55	— 2 33	5 31	— 2 32

Days of Month.	Moon rises or sets. Mean Time.						High Water. Mean Time.			
	Boston, &c.	New York, &c.	Washington, &c.	Charleston, &c.	N. Orleans, &c.	San Francisco, &c.	Boston, &c.	New York, &c.	Charleston, &c.	San Francisco (North Beach).
	rises. h. m.	*rises.* h. m.	*rises.* h. m.	*rises.* h. m.	*rises.* h. m.	*rises.* h. m.	h. m.	h. m.	h. m.	h. m.
1	7 31a	7 37a	7 43a	7 59a	8 7a	7 56a	1 33a	10 19m	9 29m	2 0a
S.	8 42a	8 47a	8 51a	9 4a	9 9a	9 13a	2 21	11 5	10 16	2 51
3	9 55	9 58	10 2	10 10	10 15	10 12	3 9	11 55m	11 3	3 50
4	11 8	11 10	11 12	11 15	11 19	11 22	3 56	0 46a	11 51m	4 54
5	. . .	. . .	. . .	. . .	. . .	. . .	4 50	1 38	0 41a	5 55
6	0 19m	0 20m	0 20m	0 20m	0 22m	0 29m	5 48	2 35	1 34	6 54
7	1 33	1 32	1 31	1 26	1 27	1 40	6 47	3 34	2 35	7 54
8	2 48	2 46	2 43	2 34	2 32	2 50	7 49	4 35	3 42	8 53
S.	4 5m	4 1m	3 57m	3 45m	3 41m	3 54m	8 51	5 37	4 47	9 47
10	5 22	5 17	5 12	4 56	4 51	5 18	9 51	6 38	5 51	10 37
11	6 35	6 29	6 23	6 5	5 59	6 29	10 49	7 33	6 49	11 24a
12	7 41	7 35	7 28	7 9	7 3	7 33	11 40a	8 24	7 42	. . .
13	*sets.*	*sets.*	*sets.*	*sets.*	*sets.*	*sets.*	. . .	9 17	8 30	0 13m
14	6 41a	6 47a	6 53a	7 9a	7 18a	6 54a	0 40m	10 4	9 14	1 0
15	7 50	7 55	8 0	8 12	8 20	8 10	1 17	10 45	9 56	1 44
S.	8 56a	9 0a	9 3a	9 12a	9 18a	9 12a	2 1	11 27a	10 36	2 28
17	9 58	10 1	10 3	10 8	10 12	10 11	2 43	. . .	11 17	3 16
18	11 0	11 1	11 2	11 4	11 6	11 10	3 23	0 10m	11 57a	4 9
19	. . .	. . .	. . .	11 58	11 59	12 6	4 4	0 52	. . .	5 2
20	0 0m	0 0m	0 0m	. . .	. . .	. . .	4 48	1 36	0 39m	5 53
21	0 58	0 56	0 55	0 49m	0 49m	0 1m	5 35	2 22	1 22	6 41
22	2 1	1 58	1 55	1 46	1 44	2 1	6 25	3 12	2 11	7 32
S.	3 3m	2 59m	2 55m	2 43m	2 39m	3 0m	7 18	4 4	3 7	8 22
24	4 7	4 2	3 58	3 43	3 39	4 3	8 12	4 57	4 6	9 14
25	5 12	5 6	5 0	4 43	4 38	5 4	9 7	5 53	5 4	10 1
26	6 13	6 7	6 0	5 32	5 25	6 4	10 2	6 48	6 2	10 46
27	7 8	7 2	6 56	6 36	6 30	6 59	10 55	7 39	6 55	11 30m
28	*rises.*	*rises.*	*rises.*	*rises.*	*rises.*	*rises.*	11 43m	8 27	7 44	6 16a
29	6 30a	6 35a	6 40a	6 51a	7 1a	6 52a	0 30a	9 17	8 30	0 0
S.	7 44a	7 48a	7 52a	8 1a	8 7a	8 8a	1 16	10 3	9 14	1 44
31	8 59	9 1	9 4	9 9	9 13	9 14	2 2a	10 46m	9 57m	2 29a

EQUATION OF TIME FOR APPARENT NOON, WASHINGTON.

To be added to apparent time when the sign is +. To be subtracted from apparent time when the sign is —.

Day of Month.	January.	February.	March.	April.	May.	June.
	m. s.	m. s.	m. s.	m. s.	m. s.	m. s.
2	+ 4 11.18	+13 56.37	+12 14.04	+ 3 27.15	— 3 14.17	— 2 15.51
4	5 6.61	14 11.15	11 47.45	2 51.35	3 26.61	1 55.81
6	6 0.36	14 20.64	11 19.06	2 16.22	3 36.80	1 34.76
8	6 52.19	14 26.89	10 49.07	1 41.96	3 44.73	1 12.47
10	7 41.97	14 29.98	10 17.65	1 8.73	3 50.29	0 49.06
12	8 29.50	14 30.00	9 45.00	0 36.69	3 53.50	— 0 24.72
14	9 14.65	14 27.04	9 11.28	+ 0 5.02	3 54.32	+ 0 0.40
16	9 57.26	14 21.20	8 36.69	— 0 23.25	3 52.80	0 26.09
18	10 37.18	14 12.52	8 1.35	0 50.93	3 48.96	0 52.12
20	11 14.26	14 1.13	7 25.41	1 16.94	3 42.89	1 18.31
22	11 48.38	13 47.11	6 49.04	1 41.22	3 34.65	1 44.40
24	12 19.89	13 30.51	6 12.40	2 3.68	3 24.37	2 10.22
26	12 47.20	13 11.48	5 35.53	2 24.28	3 12.18	2 35.50
28	13 11.72	12 50.13	4 58.54	2 42.94	2 58.05	3 0.07
30	+13 32.90	+12 26.61	+ 4 21.74	— 2 59.60	— 2 42.24	+ 3 23.79

Day of Month.	July.	August.	September.	October.	November.	December.
	m. s.	m. s.	m. s.	m. s.	m. s.	m. s.
2	+ 3 46.50	+ 5 55.59	— 0 39.25	—10 50.96	—16 18.86	—10 7.71
4	4 8.04	5 45.27	1 18.32	11 27.56	16 17.23	9 19.22
6	4 28.28	5 32.50	1 58.26	12 2.66	16 12.23	8 28.42
8	4 47.04	5 17.82	2 38.96	12 36.07	16 3.85	7 35.52
10	5 4.45	5 0.41	3 20.16	13 7.65	15 52.00	6 40.77
12	5 20.10	4 41.00	4 1.83	13 37.24	15 36.69	5 44.44
14	5 33.95	4 19.45	4 43.78	14 4.72	15 17.99	4 46.78
16	5 45.68	3 55.83	5 25.88	14 29.96	14 55.91	3 48.11
18	5 55.74	3 30.14	6 8.02	14 52.68	14 30.83	2 48.72
20	6 3.46	3 2.43	6 50.04	15 13.36	14 1.96	1 48.92
22	6 8.90	2 32.80	7 31.80	15 31.27	13 30.25	— 0 48.96
24	6 11.98	2 1.39	8 13.16	15 46.53	12 55.46	+ 0 10.88
26	6 12.64	1 28.25	8 53.94	15 58.98	12 17.71	1 10.34
28	6 10.83	0 53.53	9 33.95	16 8.52	11 37.10	2 9.20
30	+ 6 6.56	+ 0 17.36	—10 13.02	—16 15.04	—10 53.72	+ 3 7.22

ECLIPSES IN 1860.

In the year 1860, there will be four eclipses; two of the Sun, and two of the Moon.

I. An annular eclipse of the Sun, January 22d, 1860, invisible at Washington.

Eclipse begins on the Earth, January 22d, 4h. 46.5m., Washington mean time, in longitude 183° 8′.1 West of Washington, and in latitude 49° 22′.8 South.

Central eclipse at noon, 6h. 43.1m., in longitude 277° 48′.0, and in latitude 89° 1′.0 South.

Central eclipse ends, 8h. 11.3m., in longitude 10° 59′.0, and in latitude 41° 52′.2 South.

Eclipse ends on the earth, 9h. 51.9m., in longitude 49° 30′.2, and in latitude 15° 7′.0 South.

This eclipse will be visible in the Southern Ocean, and at the southern extremity of South America.

II. A partial eclipse of the Moon, February 6th, 1860, visible at Washington.

Moon enters Shadow,	February 6th,		7h. 55.1m.	Washington Mean Time.
Greatest Eclipse,	"	"	9h. 21.3m.	
Moon leaves Shadow,	"	"	10h. 47.5m.	

	Eclipse begins. h. m.	Eclipse ends. h. m.
Halifax, N. S.,	8 48.8 A.	11 41.2 A.
Portland, Me.,	8 22.3	11 14.7
Boston, Mass.,	8 18.8	11 11.2
Quebec, C. E.,	8 18.5	11 10.9
Montreal, C. E.,	8 9.1	11 1.5
Albany, N. Y.,	8 8.3	11 0.7
New York, N. Y.,	8 7.3	10 59.7
Philadelphia, Pa.,	8 2.6	10 55.0
Baltimore, Md.,	7 56.9	10 49.3
Washington, D. C.,	7 55.1	10 47.5
Toronto, C. W.,	7 45.7	10 38.1
Charleston, S. C.,	7 43.6	10 36.0
Savannah,	7 38.9	10 31.3
Cincinnati,	7 25.5	10 17.9
Chicago,	7 12.8	10 5.2
New Orleans,	7 3.3	9 55.7
St. Louis,	7 2.3 A.	9 54.7 A.

III. A total eclipse of the Sun, July 17th (18th), 1860, visible as a partial one at Washington.

Eclipse begins on the Earth, July 17th, 18h. 46.4m., Washington mean time, in longitude 25° 28′.1 West of Washington, and in latitude 34° 40′.4 North.

Central eclipse begins, 19h. 49.8m., in longitude 48° 53′.8, and in latitude 45° 40′.0 North.

Central eclipse at noon, 21h. 0.7m., in longitude 313° 42′.2, and in latitude 56° 12′.4 North.

Central eclipse ends, 22h. 46.1m., in longitude 243° 52′.5, and in latitude 15° 48′.2 North.

Eclipse ends on the Earth, July 17th, 23h. 49.3m., in longitude 263° 16′.5, and in latitude 4° 8′.9 North.

This eclipse will be visible in North America, Europe, Africa, and Asia. The central line extends from the Western coast of North America, across that continent and the Atlantic Ocean, and over the northern part of Africa to the borders of the Red Sea.

The Sun will be totally eclipsed in Oregon near the mouth of the Columbia River, and thence over a narrow strip of country to Fort York on the shore of Hudson Bay, and to the northeastern point of Labrador (Cape Chidley), which will be the most favorable station on this continent for observing the total phase.

	Eclipse begins. h. m.	Eclipse ends. h. m.
Cape Hancock (Mouth of Columbia River),	Before Sunrise	5 35 M.
Portland, Oregon, ...	" "	5 39
Cumberland House, British America, .	5 17 M.	7 15
York Factory, British America, . . .	6 0	8 4
Toronto, C. W., ...	6 45	8 48
Montreal, C. E., ...	7 12	9 20
Portland, Me., ...	7 27	9 33
Boston, Mass., ...	7 23	9 29
Albany, N. Y., ...	7 11	9 16
New York, N. Y., ...	7 10	9 11
Philadelphia, Pa., ...	7 5	8 59
Baltimore, Md., ...	6 58	8 52
Washington, D. C., ...	6 56	8 50
Richmond, Va., ...	6 55	8 46
Ann Arbor, Mich., ...	6 24	8 23
Cincinnati, Ohio, ...	6 24	8 11
Charleston, S. C., ...	6 46	8 19
New Orleans, La., ...	6 1 M.	7 25 M.

IV. A partial eclipse of the Moon, July 31, and Aug. 1, 1860, invisible at Washington.

Moon enters Shadow,	July 31st,	23h. 0.6m.	Washington Mean Time.
Greatest Eclipse,	Aug. 1st,	0h. 16.6m.	
Moon leaves Shadow,	" "	1h. 32.6m.	

ELEMENTS OF THE ECLIPSES OF THE SUN.

1860.	January 22.	July 17.
	h. m. s.	h. m. s.
Washington Mean Time of ☌ in R. A.	6 43 4.3	21 0 44.4
☉ and ☾'s Right Ascension . .	20 18 6.66	7 52 20.37
	° ′ ″	° ′ ″
☾'s Declination	—21 31 40.7	+21 31 6.9
☉'s Declination	—19 40 22.6	+20 56 56.6
	s.	s.
☾'s Horary Motion in R. A. .	121.76	149.94
☉'s Horary Motion in R. A. . .	10.68	10.04
	′ ″	′ ″
☾'s Horary Motion in Declination	+ 9 24.4	— 9 53.2
☉'s Horary Motion in Declination .	+ 0 34.5	— 0 26.8
☾'s Equatorial Horizon. Parallax	54 19.6	59 48.8
☉'s Equatorial Horizon. Parallax .	8.7	8.7
☾'s True Semidiameter . .	14 47.5	16 19.5
☉'s True Semidiameter . . .	16 17.3	15 46.7

A Table showing the Illuminated Portions of the Discs of Venus and Mars.

The numbers in this table are the versed sines of that portion of the discs which, to an observer on the Earth, will appear to be illuminated; the apparent diameters of the planets at the time being considered as *unity*.

To a spectator on the Earth, Venus appears most brilliant when between her greatest elongation and her inferior conjunction; in which position she will be between May and September, 1860.

Mars is most brilliant about the time of his opposition to the Sun, being then also nearest to the Earth. The opposition will take place in July, 1860.

1860.		Venus.	Mars.	1860.		Venus.	Mars.
January	15	0.897	0.918	July	15	0.005	1.000
February	14	0.833	0.898	August	15	0.186	0.958
March	15	0.745	0.884	September	15	0.430	0.892
April	15	0.625	0.882	October	15	0.591	0.861
May	15	0.468	0.903	November	15	0.714	0.856
June	15	0.241	0.955	December	15	0.807	0.867

LATITUDE AND LONGITUDE OF THE PRINCIPAL AMERICAN OBSERVATORIES.

[The Longitudes are reckoned from Greenwich.]

Observatories.	Latitude.	Longitude in Time.
	° ′ ″	h. m. s.
Albany, ...	42 39 50 N.	4 54 58.6 W.
Ann Arbor, . . .	42 16 48	5 34 52.2
Cambridge, ...	42 22 48	4 44 30.7
Cincinnati, ...	39 5 54	5 37 58 0
Clinton, Hamilton College,	43 3 0	5 1 37.3
Georgetown, . . .	38 54 26 N.	5 8 17.4
Santiago, ...	33 26 25 S.	4 42 18.9
Toronto, ...	43 39 35 N.	5 17 33.4
Washington, . . .	38 53 39 N.	5 8 11.2

LATITUDE AND LONGITUDE OF THE PRINCIPAL FOREIGN OBSERVATORIES.

[The Longitudes are reckoned from Greenwich.]

Observatories.	Latitude.	Longitude in Time.
	° ′ ″	h. m. s.
Altona,	53 32 45 N.	0 39 46.2 E.
Armagh,	54 21 13 N.	0 26 35.5 W.
Berlin,	52 30 17 N.	0 53 35.5 E.
Brussels,	50 51 11 N.	0 17 27.6 E.
Cambridge,	52 12 52 N.	0 0 23.5 E.
Cape of Good Hope,	33 56 3 S.	1 13 56.0 E.
Dorpat,	58 22 47 N.	1 46 55 E.
Dublin,	53 23 13 N.	0 25 22 W.
Edinburgh,	55 57 23 N.	0 12 43.0 W.
Göttingen,	51 31 48 N.	0 39 46.1 E.
Greenwich,	51 28 38 N.	0 0 0.0
Königsberg,	54 42 50 N.	1 22 0.5 E.
Munich,	48 8 45 N.	0 46 26.5 E.
Paris,	48 50 13 N.	0 9 21.5 E.
Poulkova,	59 46 19 N.	2 1 18.7 E.
Rome,	41 53 54 N.	0 49 54.7 E.
Turin,	45 4 6 N.	0 30 48.4 E.
Vienna,	48 12 35 N.	1 5 32.5 E.

LATITUDE AND LONGITUDE OF THE PRINCIPAL PLACES IN THE UNITED STATES, ETC.*

[The Longitudes are reckoned from Greenwich.]

The Capitals (Seats of Government) of the States and Territories are designated by Italic Letters.

Place.		Latitude, North.	Longitude, West, in Degrees.	Longitude, West, in Time.	Dist. fr. Wash.
		° ′ ″	° ′ ″	h. m. s.	Miles.
Acapulco,	Mex.	16 50 19	99 49 9	6 39 16.6	
Albany (Dudley Observatory),	N. Y.	42 39 50	73 44 39	4 54 58.6	376
Alexandria,	Va.	38 49	77 4	5 8 16	6
Amherst (College Chapel),	Mass.	42 22 15.6	72 31 28	4 50 5.9	383
Annapolis (State-House),	Md.	38 58 40.2	76 29 9	5 5 56.6	37
Ann Arbor (Observatory),	Mich.	42 16 48	83 43 3	5 34 52.2	
Auburn,	N. Y.	42 55	76 28	5 5 52	339
Augusta,	Ga.	33 28	81 54	5 27 36	580
Augusta (State-House),	Me.	44 18 43	69 50	4 39 20	595
Austin,	Tex.	30 13 30	97 39	6 30 36	
Baker's Island (Lights),	Mass.	42 32 9.6	70 46 50	4 43 7.3	452
Baltimore (Washington Mon.),	Md.	39 17 47.8	76 36 39	5 6 26.6	38
Bangor (Court-House),	Me.	44 47 50	68 47	4 35 8	661
Barnstable (Cupola),	Mass.	41 42 13.1	70 18 42	4 41 14.8	466
Baton Rouge,	La.	30 26	91 18	6 5 12	
Benicia,	Cal.	38 3 21	122 7 13	8 8 28.9	

* The positions contained in this table have been derived from that given in the American Almanac for 1841; with additions and corrections from the determinations of the Coast Survey, and of the United States Topographical Engineers, and from other sources.

Place.		Latitude, North.	Longitude, West, in Degrees.	Longitude, West, in Time.	Dist. from Wash.
		° ′ ″	° ′ ″	h. m. s.	Miles.
Beaufort (Arsenal), . . .	S. C.	32 25 57	80 41 23	5 22 45.5	629
Bellevue, Am. Fur Co.'s trading post,		38 8 24	95 47 46	6 23 11.1	
Boston (State-House), . .	Mass.	42 21 27.6	71 3 30	4 44 14	432
Do. (Light), ...		42 19 38.8	70 53 5	4 43 32.3	
Brazos Santiago, ...	Tex.	26 6 0	97 12 0	6 28 48	
Brent's Fort, ...		38 2 38	103 33 15	6 54 13	
Bridgeport (South Spire), .	Conn.	41 10 30	73 11 4	4 52 44.3	284
Bristol (Court-House), .	R. I.	41 40 10.5	71 16 5	4 45 4.3	409
Brooklyn (Navy Yard), . .	N. Y.	40 42 2.4	73 58 31	4 55 54.1	227
Brunswick (College Chapel),	Me.	43 54 29	69 57 24	4 39 49.6	568
Buffalo, ...	N. Y.	42 53	78 55	5 15 40	376
Do. (Light-House), . .		42 50	78 59	5 15 56	
Burlington, ...	N. J.	40 4 51.6	74 52 37	4 59 30.5	156
Burlington, ...	Vt.	44 27	73 10	4 52 40	440
Cambridge (Observatory), .	Mass.	42 22 48.3	71 7 40	4 44 30.7	431
Camden, ...	S. C.	34 17	80 33	5 22 12	467
Canadian River, Head-waters of,		37 1 33	104 37 32	6 58 30.1	
Canandaigua, ...	N. Y.	42 54 9	77 17	5 9 8	336
Cape Ann, Thatcher's Island (North Light), .	Mass.	42 38 19.4	70 34 10	4 42 16.7	470
Do. (South Light), .		42 38 10.9	70 34 10	4 42 16.7	
Cape Cod (Long Point Light),	Mass.	42 1 57.1	70 9 47	4 40 39.1	507
Cape Elizabeth (Light-House),	Me.	43 33 36	70 11 36	4 40 46.4	
Cape Flattery, . . .	Wash. T.	48 22	124 45	8 19 0	
Do. (Light-House),		48 23 15	124 43 54	8 18 55.6	
Cape Hancock (Mouth of Columbia River), ...		46 16 35	124 1 45	8 16 7	
Cape Hatteras (Light-House),	N. C.	35 15	75 30	5 2 0	
Cape May (Light-House), .	N. J.	38 55 45	74 58 33	4 59 54.2	
Castine, ...	Me.	44 22 30	68 45	4 35	
Do. (Dice's Head Light-House),		44 23 12	68 49 30	4 35 18	
Cedar Keys, Depot Island, .		29 7 27	82 56 12	5 31 44.8	
Chapel Hill (University), .	N. C.	35 54 21	79 17 30	5 17 10	
Charleston (St. Mich.'s Ch.),	S. C.	32 46 33	79 55 38	5 19 42.5	544
Charlestown (Bun. Hill Mon.),	Mass.	42 22 33.1	71 3 20	4 44 13.3	433
Chagres (Centre of Plateau),	.	9 20	80 1 21	5 20 5.4	
Chicago (Roman Cath. Ch.),	Ill.	41 53 48	87 37 47	5 50 31.2	763
Cincinnati (Observatory), .	Ohio.	39 5 54	84 29 31	5 37 58	497
Cleveland (Light-House), .	Ohio.	41 31	81 51	5 27 24	
Columbia, ...	S. C.	33 57	81 7	5 24 28	500
Columbus, ...	Ohio.	39 57	83 3	5 32 12	396
Concord (State-House), . .	N. H.	43 12 29	71 29	4 45 56	474
Corpus Christi, ...	Tex.	27 47 17.8	97 27 2	6 29 48.1	
Council Bluffs, . . .	Neb. T.	41 30	95 48	6 23 12	
Dalles of the Columbia, Missionary Station, ...		45 35 55	120 55	8 3 40	
Dayton, ...	Ohio.	39 44	84 11	5 36 44	
Dedham (1st Cong. Ch.), .	Mass.	42 14 57	71 10 59	4 44 43.9	422
Depot Key, ...	Fa.	29 7 30	83 2 45	6 32 11	
Des Moines, ...	Io.	41 35	93 40	6 14 40	
Detroit (St. Paul's Ch.),	Mich.	42 19 45	83 2 30	5 32 10	526
Dorchester (Ast. Observ.), .	Mass.	42 19 10	71 4 19	4 44 17.3	432
Dover, ...	Del.	39 10	75 30	5 2 0	114
Dover, ...	N. H.	43 13	70 54	4 43 36	490

Place.		Latitude, North.	Longitude, West, in Degrees.	Longitude, West, in Time.	Dist. from Wash.
		° ' "	° ' "	h. m. s.	Miles.
Easton (Court-House), .	Md.	38 46 10	76 8	5 4 32	80
Eastport, ...	Me.	44 54	66 56	4 27 44	778
Edenton (Court-House), .	N. C.	36 3 27.4	76 35 48	5 6 23.2	284
Ewing Harbor, ...	Oreg.	42 44 21.7	124 28 52	8 17 55.5	
Exeter, ...	N. H.	42 58	70 55	4 43 40	474
Falls of St. Anthony, U. S. Cottage,		44 58 40	93 10 30	6 12 42	
Falls of the St. Croix, .		45 30 10	92 40	6 10 40	
False Dungeness Harbor,	Wash. T.	48 7 52	123 27 21	8 13 49.4	
False Washita, Head-waters of,		35 25 41	101 5	6 44 20	
Fort Boisée, ...	Oreg.	43 49 22	116 47 3	7 47 8.2	
Fort Gibson (old Block-House),		35 47 34.8	95 15 10	6 21 0.7	
Fort Gratiot (Light-House),	Mich.	42 55	82 22	5 29 28	
Fort Hall, ...		43 1 30	112 29 54	7 29 59.6	
Fort Laramie, ...	Neb. T.	42 12 10	104 47 43	6 59 10.9	
Fort Leavenworth (Landing),	Kan. T.	39 21 14	94 44	6 18 56	
Fort Nez Percé, ...	Oreg.	46 3 46			
Frankfort, ...	Ky.	38 14	84 40	5 38 40	551
Frederick, ...	Md.	39 24	77 18	5 9 12	43
Fredericksburg, ...	Va.	38 34	77 38	5 10 32	56
Frederickton, ...	N. B.	46 3	66 38 15	4 26 33	
Galveston (Court-House), .	Tex.	29 18 14.5	94 46 34	6 19 6.3	
Georgetown, ...	S. C.	33 21	79 17	5 17 8	482
Gloucester (Univ. Ch.), .	Mass.	42 36 45.8	70 39 30	4 42 38.6	462
Do. (E. Point Light),		42 34 47.2	70 39 33	4 42 38.2	466
Do. (Ten Pound Isl. Light),		42 36 4.8	70 39 36	4 42 38.4	463
Great Salt Lake, Island in,		41 10 42	112 21 5	7 29 24.3	
Greenfield (2d Cong. Ch.),	Mass.	42 35 16	72 36 32	4 50 26.1	396
Hagerstown, ...	Md.	39 37	77 35	5 10 20	68
Halifax, ...	N. S.	44 39 20	63 36 40	4 14 26.7	936
Hallowell, ...	Me.	44 17	69 50	4 39 20	593
Hanover (Dartmouth Coll.),	N. H.	43 43 30	72 18	4 49 12	
Harrisburg, ...	Pa.	40 16	76 50	5 7 20	110
Hartford (State-House), .	Conn.	41 45 59	72 40 45	4 50 43	335
High Plateau between waters of Atlantic and Gulf of Cal.,		42 2	107 3	7 8 12	
Holmes's Hole (Spire), .	Mass.	41 27 12.9	70 35 59	4 42 23.9	457
Hudson, ...	N. Y.	42 14	73 46	4 55 4	345
Hudson (West. Reserve Coll.),	Ohio.	41 14 42	81 25 19	5 25 41.3	
Huntsville, ...	Ala.	34 36	86 57	5 47 48	726
Indianapolis, ...	Ind.	39 55	86 5	5 44 20	573
Ipswich (Eastern Light), .	Mass.	42 41 5.7	70 45 39	4 43 2.6	462
Ipswich (Western Light), .	Mass.	42 41 4.9	70 45 46	4 43 3.1	
Jackson, ...	Miss.	32 23	90 8	6 0 32	1035
Jalapa, ...	Mex.	19 30 8	96 54 30	6 27 38	
Jefferson City, ...	Mo.	38 36	92 8	6 8 32	980
Kansas River, Mouth of, .		39 6 3	94 32 54	6 18 11.6	
Key West (S. W. Pt.), . .	Fa.	24 32	81 47 30	5 27 10	
Key West Light, . . .	Fa.	24 32 58	81 48 7	5 27 12.5	
Kingston, ...	C. W.	44 8	76 40	5 6 40	456
Do. (Court-House), .		44 8	76 28 37	5 5 54.5	
Knoxville, ...	Tenn.	35 59	83 54	5 35 36	516
Lancaster, ...	Pa.	40 2 36	76 20 33	5 5 22.2	109
Lansing, ...	Mich.	42 43	84 29	5 37 56	
La Vaca, ...	Tex.	28 37 0			

Place.		Latitude, North.	Longitude, West, in Degrees.	Longitude, West, in Time.	Dist. from Wash.
		° ′ ″	° ′ ″	h. m. s.	Miles.
Lexington,	Ky.	38 6	84 18	5 37 12	534
Little Rock,	Ark.	34 40	92 12	6 8 48	1068
Lockport,	N. Y.	43 11	78 46	5 15 4	403
Los Angeles,	Cal.	34 3 15	118 10 44	7 52 42.9	
Louisville,	Ky.	38 3	85 30	5 42 0	590
Lowell (St. Anne's Ch.),	Mass.	42 38 46	71 19 2	4 45 16.1	439
Lynchburg,	Va.	37 36	79 22	5 17 28	198
Lynn High Rock,	Mass.	42 28 3	70 56 28	4 43 45.9	441
Machias Bay,	Me.	44 33	67 22	4 29 28	
Madison (Dome of Capitol),	Wis.	43 4 31	89 23 16	5 57 33.1	
Marblehead (Black-top Ch.),	Mass.	42 30 23.7	70 50 32	4 43 22.1	450
Do. (Light),		42 30 14	70 50 39	4 43 22.6	448
Matagorda (E. end Island),	Texas.	28 20 48	96 23 57	6 25 35.8	
Mexico, City of,	Mex.	19 25 45	99 5 6	6 36 20.4	
Michigan City,	Io.	41 43 25	86 54 21	5 47 37.4	
Middletown (Wesl. Univ.),	Conn.	41 33 8	72 39	4 50 36	325
Milledgeville,	Ga.	33 7 20	83 19 45	5 33 19	642
Milwaukee (Spire Cath. Ch.),	Wisc.	43 2 33.9	87 54 22	5 51 37.5	
Missouri River, Mouth of,		38 51 36	90 0 40	6 0 2.7	
Mobile (Episcopal Ch.),	Ala.	30 41 26.2	88 1 29	5 52 5.9	1033
Monclova,	Mex.	26 54 0	101 39 18	6 46 37.2	
Monomoy Point Light,	Mass.	41 33 33	69 59 19	4 39 57.3	477
Monterey,	Mex.	25 40 13	100 25 36	6 41 42.4	
Monterey,	Cal.	36 36 24	121 52 25	8 7 29.7	
Montgomery,	Ala.	32 22	86 18	5 45 12	
Montpelier,	Vt.	44 17	72 36	4 50 24	524
Montreal,	C. E.	45 31	73 32 56	4 54 11.7	601
Nag's Head,	N. C.	35 55 43.7	75 35 59	5 2 23.9	
Nantucket (South Tower),	Mass.	41 16 54	70 5 36	4 40 22.4	490
Nashville (University),	Tenn.	36 9 33	86 49 3	5 47 16.2	714
Natchez (Fort Panmure),	Miss.	31 34	91 24 42	6 5 38.8	1146
Nebraska or Platte River, Junction of North and South Forks,		41 5 5	101 21 24	6 45 25.6	
Newark,	N. J.	40 45	74 10	4 56 40	215
New Bedford (Baptist Spire),	Mass.	41 38 10.2	70 55 16	4 43 41.1	429
Newbern,	N. C.	35 20	77 5	5 8 20	337
Newburg,	N. Y.	41 31	74 1	4 56 4	282
Newburyport (Harris St. Ch.),	Mass.	42 48 29.9	70 52 3	4 43 28.2	466
Do. (Plumb Isl. E. Light),		42 48 25	70 48 40	4 43 14.7	469
Newcastle (Spire Episc. Ch.),	Del.	39 39 36	75 33 27	5 2 13.8	103
New Haven (College),	Conn.	41 18 27.7	72 55 24	4 51 41.6	301
New London (Light-House),	Conn.	41 18 57.6	72 5 4	4 48 20.3	354
New Orleans (City Hall),	La.	29 57 30	90 0 0	6 0 0	1203
Newport (Spire),	R. I.	41 29 12.2	71 18 29	4 45 13.9	403
Newport (Light-House),		41 26 30	71 24 24	4 45 37.7	
New York (City Hall),	N. Y.	40 42 43	74 0 3	4 56 0.2	226
Nobsque Point Light,	Mass.	41 30 55	70 38 59	4 42 35.9	450
Norfolk (Farmers' Bank),	Va.	36 50 50	76 18 47	5 5 15.1	217
Northampton (1st Cong. Ch.),	Mass.	42 19 9	72 38 15	4 50 33	376
Norwich,	Conn.	41 33	72 7	4 48 28	362
Ocracoke Lighthouse,	N. C.	35 6 31.6	75 58 27	5 3 53.8	
Ogdensburg (Lighthouse),	N. Y.	44 45	75 30	5 2 0	
Olympia,	Wash. T.	47 3	122 55	8 11 40	6643
Omaha City,	Neb. T.	41 16	95 59	6 23 56.0	

Place.		Latitude, North.	Longitude, West, in Degrees.	Longitude, West, in Time.	Dist. from Wash.
		° ′ ″	° ′ ″	h. m. s.	Miles.
Ottawa, ...	C. W.		75 42 4	5 2 48.3	
Panama Cathedral, . .	Mex.	8 57 9	79 29 17	5 17 57.1	
Pass Washington, . . .		36 3 22	108 56	7 15 44	
Pensacola, ...	Fa.	30 24	87 10 12	5 48 40.8	1050
Perote, ...	Mex.	19 28 57	97 8 15	6 28 33	
Petersburg, ...	Va.	37 13 54	77 20	5 9 20	144
Philadelphia (Girard Coll.), .	Pa.	39 58 24	75 9 54	5 0 39.6	136
Do. (High School Obs.),		39 57 9	75 10 37	5 0 42.5	
Pittsburg, ...	Pa.	40 32	80 2	5 20 8	223
Pittsfield (1st Cong. Ch.), .	Mass.	42 26 55	73 15 36	4 53 2.4	380
Platte River, Mouth of,		41 3 13			
Do. Junc. of N. & S. Forks,		41 5 5	101 21 24	6 45 25.6	
Plattsburg, ...	N. Y.	44 42	73 26	4 53 44	539
Plymouth (Court-House), .	Mass.	41 57 23	70 39 47	4 42 39.1	439
Point Conception (C. S. Obs),	Cal.	34 26 56.3	120 25 33	8 1 42.2	
Point Hudson, . .	Wash. Ter.	48 7 3	122 44 33	8 10 58.2	
Point Loma (Light-House), .	Cal.	32 40 13	117 12 22	7 48 49.5	
Popocatapetl, ...	Mex.	18 59 47	98 32 51	6 34 11.4	
Portland (Mount Joy), . .	Me.	43 39 54	70 14 34	4 40 58.3	542
Do. (E. Light), . .		43 33 56	70 11 41	4 40 46.7	
Portland, ...	Oreg.	45 30	122 27 30	8 9 50	
Portsmouth (Unitarian Ch.),	N. H.	43 4 35	70 45 50	4 43 3.3	491
Do. (White Isl. Light),		42 58	70 37 45	4 42 31	
Poughkeepsie, . . .	N. Y.	41 41	73 55	4 55 40	301
Prairie du Chien (Am. Fur Co.'s House), . . .	Wis.	43 3 6	91 9 19	6 4 37.3	
Princeton (Nassau Hall), .	N. J.	40 20 41	74 39 30	4 58 38	177
Providence (College Hill), .	R. I.	41 50 17	71 23 40	4 45 34.7	394
Puebla de los Angeles, .	Mex.	19 0 15	98 2 21	6 32 9.4	
Punta de los Reyes (Sir F. Drake's Bay), ...	Cal.	37 59 34	122 57 40	8 11 50.7	
Quebec (Citadel), ...	C. E.	46 49 12	71 12 15	4 44 49.0	781
Racine (Dome of Court-House),	Wis.	42 43 45	87 47 4	5 51 8.3	
Raleigh, ...	N. C.	35 47	78 48	5 15 12	286
Remedios, Harbor de los, .		37 24 15	135 53 41	9 3 34.7	
Richmond (Capitol), . .	Va.	37 32 17	77 27 28	5 9 49.9	122
Rochester (Rochester House),	N. Y.	43 8 17	77 51	5 11 24	361
Sabine River, entrance of South or outer extremity of Bar,	Tex.	29 40 48	93 49 3	6 15 16.2	
Sable (Cape), ...	Fa.	24 50	81 15	5 25 0	
Sackett's Harbor, . .	N. Y.	43 55	75 57	5 3 48	407
Saco (Church), ...	Me.	43 30 1	70 26 14	4 41 44.9	527
Sacramento, ...	Cal.	38 34 41	121 27 44	8 5 51	
Saginaw Bay (Sand Point), .	Mich.	43 54 39.8	83 20 44	5 33 23.0	
St. Augustine, ...	Fa.	29 48 30	81 35	5 26 20	841
St. Croix River, Mouth of, .		44 45 30	92 45	6 11 0	
St. Joseph, ...		23 3 13	109 40 44	7 18 43	
St. Louis, ...	Mo.	38 37 28	90 15 16	6 1 1.1	856
St. Mark's Light, . .	Fa.	30 4 25	84 10 37	5 36 42.6	
St. Paul, ...	Min.	44 52 46	93 4 54	6 12 19.6	
Salem (tall Spire), . . .	Mass.	42 31 10	70 53 38	4 43 34.5	446
Salem, ...	Oreg.	44 56	123 1 30	8 12 6	6687
Saltillo, ...	Mex.	25 26 22	101 1 45	6 44 7	

Place.		Latitude, North.	Longitude, West, in Degrees.	Longitude, West, in Time.	Dist. from Wash.
		° ′ ″	° ′ ″	h. m. s.	Miles.
Salt Lake City,	Utah.	40 46 8	112 6 8	7 28 24.5	
San Antonio,	Tex.	29 25 22	98 29 15	6 33 57	
San Blas, Arsenal,		21 32 34	105 15 24	7 1 1.6	
San Diego, Public Square (C. S. Obs.),		32 41 58	117 13 22	7 48 53.5	
Sandusky (Light-House, Marble Head),	Ohio.	41 32 30	82 42 15	5 30 49	
Sandwich (1st Cong. Ch.),	Mass.	41 45 26	70 29 30	4 41 58.6	456
San Francisco (Presidio),	Cal.	37 47 35.6	122 26 48	8 9 47.2	
San Luis Obispo,		35 10 37.5	120 43 31	8 2 54.1	
San Pedro,		33 43 19.6	118 16.03	7 53 4.2	
Santa Barbara,		34 24 24.7	119 40 18	7 58 41.2	
Santa Cruz,		36 57 26.9	122 0 10	8 8 0.7	
Santa Fé,	N. M.	35 41 6	106 1 22	7 4 5.5	
Savannah (Exchange),	Ga.	32 4 53	81 5 14	5 24 20.9	662
Scarboro' Harbor,	Wash. Ter.	48 21 40	124 37 12	8 18 28.8	
Schenectady,	N. Y.	42 48	73 55	4 55 40	391
Snake River, above Amer. Falls,		42 47 5	112 40 13	7 30 40.9	
Springfield,	Ill.	39 48	89 33	5 58 12	801
Springfield (Court-House),	Mass.	42 6 4	72 35 45	4 50 23	357
Squam Harbor (Light),	Mass.	42 39 41	70 40 34	4 42 42.3	466
Straitsmouth Island (Light),	Mass.	42 39 42	70 34 58	4 42 19.9	471
Stratford Hill,	Conn.	41 13 6	73 8 51	4 52 35.4	287
Sweet-Water River, N. Fork of Platte River, Mouth of,		42 27 18	107 45 27	7 11 1.8	
Tallahassee,	Fa.	30 28	84 36	5 38 24	896
Tampico, Bar,	Mex.	22 15 30	97 51 51	6 31 27.4	
Taunton (Trin. Cong. Ch.),	Mass.	41 54 11	71 5 55	4 44 23.7	415
Tlamath Lake,		42 56 51			
Toronto or York (Observ.),	C. W.	43 39 35	79 23 21	5 17 33.4	500
Trenton,	N. J.	40 14	74 39	4 58 36	166
Trinidad Bay,	Cal.	41 5 40	124 5	8 16 20	
Troy,	N. Y.	42 44	73 40	4 54 40	383
Tuscaloosa,	Ala.	33 12	87 42	5 50 48	858
University of Virginia,	Va.	38 2 3	78 31 29	5 14 5.9	124
Utica (Dutch Church),	N. Y.	43 6 49	75 13	5 0 52	383
Vandalia,	Ill.	38 50	89 2	5 56 8	781
Vera Cruz,	Mex.	19 11 52	96 8 36	6 24 34.4	
Vevay,	Ind.	38 46	84 59	5 39 56	556
Victoria,	Tex.	28 46 57			
Vincennes,	Ind.	38 43	87 25	5 49 40	693
WASHINGTON (Capitol),	D. C.	38 53 20	77 0 15	5 8 1	
Do. (Observatory),		38 53 39.3	77 2 48	5 8 11.2	
Washington,	Miss.	31 36	91 20	6 5 20	1146
Waukegan,	Ill.	42 21 44	87 50 11	5 51 20.7	
West Point (Military Academy),	N. Y.	41 23 31.2	73 57 31	4 55 50.1	
Wheeling,	Va.	40 7	80 42	5 22 48	264
Williamstown (Cong. Ch.),	Mass.	42 42 49	73 13 10	4 52 52.7	406
Wilmington (Town-Hall),	Del.	39 44 27	75 32 42	5 2 10.8	111
Wilmington,	N. C.	34 11	78 10	5 12 40	416
Windsor,	C. W.		83 2 0	5 32 8.0	
Worcester (Ant. Hall),	Mass.	42 16 17	71 48 13	4 47 12.9	394
York,	Me.	43 10 0	70 40	4 42 40	500
York,	Pa.	39 58	76 40	5 6 40	87
Yorktown,	Va.	37 13	76 34	5 6 16	

COMETS, AND DONATI'S COMET OF 1858.*

The first characteristic presented in the physical aspect of comets is that they are mainly, and perhaps in most instances entirely, composed of an ill-defined gaseous or nebulous substance, endowed with properties so extraordinary that it can scarcely be classed with matter, in the ordinary acceptation of the term. Of its extreme attenuation and lightness, there can be no question. The planets, and among them our earth, must again and again have traversed unharmed the tails of comets. In October last, the *débris* of the magnificent train of the comet swept over the region occupied by the earth a few weeks earlier. Instances of more immediate proximity are of too common occurrence to allow us to suppose that we are always to escape an actual collision; but it is inconceivable that any disastrous consequences could ensue to our earth or its inhabitants therefrom, any more than from contact with sunlight, or with the ether of the planetary spaces.

A second characteristic is their internal condensation. All comets present this in a greater or less degree. Most of them have a minute stellar point, called the nucleus, which occupies the position of maximum density. There are others in which this latter feature is wholly wanting. But the number in which it cannot be detected with a powerful telescope is much smaller than has commonly been supposed. This centre of condensation, or brightest point, is, with rare exceptions, placed on the side which is nearest to the sun. It is always, however, very close to the centre of gravity, as is proved by the fact of its motion about the sun, in accordance with the law of gravitation.

The nucleus itself is a minute point compared with the immense volume of light-giving substance of which it is the controlling centre. Whether it is solid or not, is still undecided. As far as the eye alone is to be trusted, there are comets as truly solid as the planets or stars themselves. In size and weight, however, the true nuclei, apart from their surrounding nebulosity, are probably quite small, measured by the standard of the larger planets. Still, it is possible that there may have been instances in which the mass of these bodies has been comparable with that of the earth, and yet they may have completed their circuit around the sun, leaving no appreciable trace of their disturbing influence, — the only sure test by which their mass could be detected. The evidence from the fact that the smaller stars shine freely even through the most condensed portions of comets, adduced by astronomical writers in proof of their transparency, and, by inference, of their extreme tenuity, has a certain value when applied to the class of feeble telescopic comets, but is scarcely applicable to one like the comet of Donati, which overpowered all but the brighter stars in the neighborhood of the nucleus by its superior brilliancy.

The feature next in importance to the nucleus is the train, or tail, as it is usually called (although often preceding the nucleus in its motion), projected at an immense distance from it, and usually, although by no means invariably, in a direction opposite to that of the sun. The agency of the nucleus in the formation of the train, but still more in the subsequent control which it retains over it, is one of the most curious phenomena presented in nature. Often, several of these appendages are seen radiating at once from the same nucleus. The greatest variety in curvature of outline, length, brilliancy, and

* This article is the substance of a pamphlet entitled "An Account of Donati's Comet of 1858," by Mr. George P. Bond, and is printed by his permission. The account of the comet was prepared by Mr. Bond for the Mathematical Monthly. The pamphlet is illustrated by engravings and plates, which greatly aid the reader in understanding the condition, course, and appearance of the comet.

other peculiarities, is presented by different comets, or by the same one in different parts of its course. The portions near the axis are usually darker than the edges, giving at times the appearance of a division with a stream of light on either side. Ordinarily, the convex and brightest side of the tail is presented to the region towards which the comet is moving.

The larger bodies of this class exhibit a wonderful complication of phenomena in the region contiguous to the nucleus. Of these, the most prominent are the interposition between the nucleus and the sun of one or more well-defined and rounded screens, or caps of dense nebulosity, called envelopes, partially but not entirely surrounding the nucleus, and the emission of streams or jets of luminosity, bright sectors, &c., in a direction inclined or opposite to that of the tail. With great variety of detail in other respects, these have all a well-marked tendency to appear in the first instance on the side of the nucleus next the sun. The great comet of the present year undoubtedly takes a foremost rank in respect of the multiplied and most curious changes which it has exhibited, and especially in the complete illustration which it has afforded of the origin, construction, and final dissipation of a succession of envelopes. In these phenomena, the process of the formation of the tail, from the substance in immediate contact with the nucleus, is intimately concerned. The astronomer, night by night, sees the work of evolution going on with an amazing rapidity, and seemingly in defiance of the best established properties of matter, the laws of gravitation and of inertia. The results are evident to all, but the secret cause is a profound mystery, admirably calculated to stimulate speculation and intelligent investigation.

As regards the motion of comets in space, it is a well-established fact, so far as our present means of observation extend, that their nuclei alone move in obedience to the attractive force of the sun and planets. This property, which has been recognized with consistency and uniformity, is not the least singular peculiarity of their constitution. Immense volumes of matter, apparently of the identical substance of the nucleus, go to compose the enveloping nebulosity and the tail, but from the moment of leaving the central body their motion is perfectly inexplicable without assuming them to be under the influence of laws of force which greatly modify that of gravitation. The shape of the cometary orbits described about the sun is nearly that of a parabola, or of an elongated ellipse, with periods of revolution varying from a few years to many centuries. The point in the orbit which is nearest the sun is called the perihelion; the distance of this point from the sun, the perihelion distance; and the time of the comet's passing it, the perihelion passage.

Donati's Comet. — On the 2d of June, 1858, a faint nebulosity, slowly advancing towards the north, was descried by DONATI at Florence, near the star λ *Leonis*. This was the earliest observation of the great comet of 1858. Its distance from the sun was then about two hundred millions of miles, and from the earth it was more remote. Being, at first, inclined to question whether it might not be identical with another comet just before seen in the same quarter of the heavens (the third comet of 1858), he communicated the discovery with a suitable reserve, as "perhaps new;" and in a second despatch he said, "It is possible that this comet is the same as that discovered in America on the 2d of May." This conjecture, fortunately for Donati, did not prove true; although the apprehension of the Italian astronomer, from the rival zeal of his Transatlantic brethren, was not without reasonable foundation, for no sooner had the moon withdrawn from the evening sky so as to allow the comet to be seen, than it was detected almost simultaneously at three different points in America, each observer being at the time unaware of its previous discovery in Italy. It was seen by Mr. H. P. Tuttle on the evening of the 28th of June, and an accurate determination of its place was made on the same night at the Observatory of Harvard College. On the 29th, it was detected by H. M. Parkhurst, Esq., of Perth Amboy, N. J., and on the 1st of July, by Miss Mitchell, of Nantucket.

Three geocentric positions, obtained on the 7th, 11th, and 13th of June, furnished Donati with the means of computing approximate elements of the comet's motion, from which its interesting character was quickly recognized. There was considerable difficulty in fixing the precise time of perihelion passage, a most necessary condition in predicting its path as seen from the earth. While in other respects the results deduced by various computers were sufficiently accordant, they showed wide discrepancies in designating the place of the comet in the orbit. By the middle of August, however, its future course, and great increase of brightness in September and the early part of October, had been ascertained with entire certainty.

Up to this time it had remained a faint object, not even discernible by the unassisted eye. It was distinguished from ordinary telescopic comets only by the extreme slowness of its motion, in singular contrast with its subsequent career, and by the vivid light of the nucleus.

Traces of a tail were noticed on the 20th of August, and on the 29th it was seen with the naked eye as a hazy star. For a few weeks it occupied a position in the heavens where it rose before the sun and set after it, becoming thus a conspicuous object both in the morning and evening sky. This circumstance gave rise to the erroneous notion that two different comets had appeared. The statement, which was widely circulated, that this was the return of the comet of 1264 and of 1556, supposed by some to be identical, is equally incorrect. If it had ever before been seen by man, it must have been far back in history, since the most recent computations assign a time of revolution of about twenty-five hundred years.

On the 6th of September was first noticed the curvature of the tail, which subsequently, at the time of its greatest expansion, became one of its most impressive features. It is remarkable that this peculiarity should have been strongly enough exhibited to be distinguished at the above date, when the earth was close to the plane of the comet's orbit. The observation cannot, in fact, be reconciled with the commonly received opinion that the curvature of the tail lies in the plane of motion about the sun.

For the following details, relating to the appearance presented by the comet in the telescope or to the naked eye, use has been made principally of the manuscript records of the Observatory of Harvard College, the results of observations made elsewhere not being accessible through the ordinary channels of information at the time of writing.

There was a marked increase of brilliancy, accompanied by an equally perceptible lengthening of the tail, between the 10th and the 25th of September. Its sudden advance in size and splendor during the week following the latter date was in perfect keeping with the often repeated history of bodies of its class. On the 8th, the diameter of the nucleus was ascertained to be two thousand miles. In immediate contact with it was an intensely brilliant nebulosity, having a diameter of about three thousand miles, while the surrounding diffused light extended forty or fifty thousand miles towards the sun. Measured by ordinary standards, this latter distance appears large, but it was manifestly insignificant compared with the effusion of nebulosity in the direction of the tail. Indeed, the comparative absence of any considerable collection of diffuse light on the side nearest the sun, outside of the above radius, was so noticeable as to excite remark on several subsequent occasions. The fact of the position of the nucleus, precisely in the vertex of the train, must have been generally noticed. At this date the tail had acquired a length of sixteen millions of miles.

To ascertain the true dimensions of the nucleus, and to compare the intensity of its light with that of a star of equal brightness, the comet on the morning of the 9th was kept in the field of the great refractor by the clock-work motion, and the effect of the approach of daylight upon it carefully noted.

In the early twilight the nucleus resembled a star of the fifth magnitude, subtending an angle corresponding to a diameter of five thousand miles; but owing partly to atmospheric disturbances, and partly to the difficulty of distinguishing its precise border, this proved to be much too large, for it diminished to less than half that amount when the daylight had become sufficiently strong to obliterate all but the true centre, which continued in sight until twelve minutes before sunrise; the light, however, no longer retained the scintillating, starlike character which distinguished it when seen on the background of a dark sky. At this time, therefore, the nucleus must have been nearly of the size of our moon, and probably shone with somewhat inferior intrinsic brightness.

Sept. 12. "A rapid increase in brightness, and length of train, — the latter covers an arc of 6°. The intensity and the quantity of light emanating from the nucleus are the most distinctive features. To the naked eye, aided by the light of the envelope and contiguous part of the tail, it was as bright as a star of the third magnitude. In the telescope the light concentrated within a circle of 10″ diameter, or six thousand miles, resembles that of a star of the fifth or sixth magnitude diffused over an equal space." The view of the comet on the morning of the 13th was still more satisfactory. owing to its greater elevation and the absence of moonlight.

To the naked eye on the 17th, the head equalled a star of the second magnitude. Its southern side (on the left hand and below as seen in the evening) was decidedly the brightest. A similar contrast was noticeable through a considerable extent of the tail for several weeks following; the convex outline being both brighter and more clearly defined than the opposite side. Ultimately this distinction disappeared, or rather it was reversed; the change taking place gradually, and becoming most noticeable after the 6th of October.

The commencement of a most important epoch in the physical history of the comet dates in our records from the 20th of September. It is probable that symptoms of approaching changes, faintly indicated, may have appeared somewhat earlier; they were not, however, noticed on the 17th and 18th, on both of which occasions the comet was observed, though particular attention was not then given to the condition of the nucleus.

On the evening of the 20th, the train at its origin was plainly bifurcated, issuing from the head in two unequal streams forming its two sides, and leaving between them a dark space behind the nucleus. Their outline was a curve resembling an arc of the parabola or hyperbola. The southern stream was so much the more brilliant of the two, that in strong twilight this alone would have been seen as a short tail inclined by 30° or more to the true axis. "Between the nucleus and the sun is interposed an obscure crescent-shaped outline, within which the light is unequally distributed, and has a strangely confused, chaotic look; the details are too undecided for precise description. There is also an elongation of the nucleus, which is singularly brilliant, or perhaps a ray extending a few seconds from it on the following or upper side. The exact character of these phenomena cannot be made out, but they seem to indicate the presence of some internal disturbing force."

Sept. 23d. "A fine clear sky, with the moon nearly full. To the naked eye the head of the comet is as bright as a star of the first magnitude, and the train, notwithstanding the moonlight, is 6° or 8° long. It is already a brilliant object half an hour after sunset. The telescopic view is most extraordinary. The nucleus has diminished in size, being now only 3″, or 1300 miles, in diameter. Its light is exceedingly intense, and somewhat more concentrated than on the 20th. Outside of it is a bright envelope, with its vertex in the direction of the sun, and 15″, or 6,400 miles, distant. This is bounded on its outer margin by a dark band. The boundary of a second and less brilliant envelope is distant at its vertex about 30″, or 12,800 miles, from the nucleus, and is terminated by a similar dark arch, outside of which, again, is an atmosphere of faint, diffused nebulosity rapidly shaded off. The outlines can be distinguished through an arc of 220° or more, reckoned from the nucleus, but they extend considerably farther into the train on the following or bright side."

Sept. 24th. The train is 7° in length, and evidently curved. The telescopic view showed a decidedly dark axis to the tail, extending close up to the nucleus, which was elongated in a direction perpendicular to the axis. The inner envelope south of the nucleus was in part separated from it by a darker space, and was twice as bright as the one next outside of it, which in turn was much brighter than the exterior nebulosity.

On the 25th the nucleus presented itself under a new aspect, in the act, as it afterwards proved, of disengaging a new envelope, or rather in a stage preparatory to that event. This perhaps is the first instance where an envelope has been seen in embryo at the surface of the nucleus, and has been traced through successive stages to a full development. The same phenomenon was subsequently illustrated in the case of the present comet by several exhibitions of a similar nature; their history has a peculiar value, because it affords an insight into the mysterious processes by which the train is thrown out from the nucleus, under the stimulating influence of the sun's light and heat, or possibly of some unknown emanation from the same source. The following were the most conspicuous gradations of light recognized in its neighborhood. Commencing with the dark axis, we have, first, a narrow, well-defined dark stripe penetrating quite up to the central body. Next in order towards the sun is the nucleus, on the eve, as we may say, of an eruption. The expression is fully warranted by its subsequent history. When seen to best advantage, two little streams of luminous matter were observed issuing from it, one on each side, doubtless on their way to supply material to the tail now so rapidly expanding. Outside of the nucleus and of the nebulosity, apparently adhering to it, was a comparatively dark space, succeeded by envelopes, with intervening dark bands, and, lastly, over the whole a thin veil of diffuse light, the latter attaining a distance of seventy thousand miles. If we include the dark axis, and the dark background of the sky, we have nine alternations of light and shade, of various grades of intensity. At a distance of about three hundred thousand miles from its origin, the breadth of the tail was found to be one hundred and forty thousand miles. Its extreme length was 11°, and the breadth where widest 1°.

Sept. 27th. "The outline of a new envelope is clearly distinguished. In form and position it is a miniature of that which has hitherto been the innermost. Like the latter it sets awry, inclining to the right-hand side of the axis. The narrow dark stripe in the axis, having its vertex precisely at the nucleus, is a remarkable object;" its width near its origin was found to be 1,800 miles.

The tail had now attained a length of 13°, or eighteen millions of miles. A new appendage in the form of a long, narrow ray issuing from its convex side was seen, not following the curve of the tail proper, but projected nearly in a straight line from the sun. Its appearance simultaneously with the throwing off of a new envelope suggests the possibility of the two phenomena being in some way connected with each other; both, it will be noticed, lie on the same side of the axis. Supposing it to have started from the head of the comet on the 25th, its velocity must have reached eight or ten millions of miles daily. Other comets have exhibited similar rays. That of 1843 shot out its streamers to a much greater distance. One which appeared in 1744 is said to have had no less than six, spread out like a fan.

On the 28th, the image of the nucleus in the focus of the large refractor afforded distinct photographic action, but the surrounding luminosity was not intense enough to form a picture. "The dark opening in the axis of the tail occupies about one twelfth of its breadth at a distance of 1° from the nucleus; it may be traced distinctly one or two degrees. The head of the comet, seen with a small telescope in strong twilight which obliterates all but this brightest portion, is crescent-shaped. The tail is 19° long, or twenty-six millions of miles, with a streamer as on the 27th."

Sept. 29th. Between this date and the 30th, the comet passed its point of nearest approach to the sun, being distant about fifty millions of miles, and not quite seventy millions from the earth, which it was still rapidly approaching. "Marked changes have occurred since the 27th. The little half-moon envelope, then closely shrouding the nucleus, has elevated itself above it, and become the most conspicuous feature in the telescopic view. It is brightest near its outer edge," an indication that it was about to separate from the central nebulosity. There was also a general aspect of confusion, suggesting the idea of internal disturbances. It was afterwards observed, that, as the nebulous matter rose higher and higher above its origin, it became uniformly blended, as if, when relieved from the immediate neighborhood of the nucleus, it was disposed to an even and symmetrical arrangement.

Sept. 30th. "The edge of the envelope nearest the nucleus is very distinct, and may be traced through an angle of 270°, reckoned from the nucleus. The latter is truncated, as it has often before been seen on the side opposite to the sun, giving it a half-moon shape. The dark axis, which at its origin is almost black, and is of even breadth with the nucleus, completes the resemblance to a *phase* and *shadow*." There are objections to this explanation, although at first sight it is very plausible. Each new envelope as it emerges from the nucleus has the same phase-like form, while it is certainly everywhere permeated by the sunlight. A very small envelope still adhering to the nucleus would thus explain the peculiar form of the latter. The dark axis occupies a larger proportion of the whole breadth of the train at a distance of several degrees from the nucleus, than can with any probability be attributed to the defect of light intercepted by so small a body. It is moreover curved, which could not happen to a sensible amount in the shadow.

Perhaps two phenomena are here superimposed; a comparative deficiency of nebulosity towards the central regions of the tail, and an actual shadow perceptible a short distance only, close to the head of the comet, where at any rate we must assume the existence of a considerable collection of nebulous matter, sufficient to exhibit the outlines of a shadow cast upon it, if such really exists. This view receives some confirmation from a note of a later date. "The outlines of the axis-band are *straight lines* near the nucleus, but at a little distance they begin to blend with the general deficiency of light in the middle of the train." It seemed here to be conceivable that the shadow-margin and the outlines of the axis were distinct phenomena.

The tail to the naked eye was 22° long, or twenty-six millions of miles, and from 2° to 3° broad near its extremity, where also its rate of curvature was pretty suddenly increased. The upper outline was throughout brightest and best defined.

Oct. 2d. No new envelope had yet been formed, nor were any indications of its approach manifested, although they were carefully looked for, in the expectation that one would shortly appear. The nucleus, however, was unusually bright, and rounded on the side toward the sun. An increase of brilliancy in the nucleus was afterwards recognized as the precursor of a fresh eruption from its surface. Its diameter, perpendicular to the axis, was found to be less than 1,600 miles. There were three dark openings in the innermost envelope, between which it was intersected with bright rays. The breadth of the brightest part of the tail, at a distance of 144,000 miles from the nucleus, was 90,000 miles, and its extreme length 25° to 30°.

The date of the next observation was the 4th. Another envelope was then rising, having already attained a diameter of above nine thousand miles within forty-eight hours. The nucleus was smaller and less bright than on the 2d. The secondary tail was 35°, or thirty-four millions of miles long. On the 5th of October, the comet attained its greatest brilliancy. Its head was close to Arcturus, a star of the first magnitude, to which it was but little inferior in brightness, although the contrast in the *intensity* of their light was very evident. In Europe the two must have been seen still nearer to each other than they were in America, the nucleus passing a little to the south of the star, and the brightest part of the tail over it. The extremity of the train reached over Benetnasch and Mizar, the two southernmost stars in the tail of the Great Bear. It could be traced through an arc of 35°. Its breadth was 5° or 6°. With a little attention two additional streamers could be seen, one of which was between 50° and 60° long, or above fifty millions of miles, with a slight curvature.

The interest of the telescopic view, taking all the circumstances into account, — the size of the instrument, the perfect purity of the atmosphere, and the splendor of the object, — has rarely been surpassed. The nucleus and the outline of its nearest envelope were visible in full sunshine with the large telescope. The head of the comet could be seen with the naked eye at twenty minutes after sunset, at which time the second envelope was discernible with the telescope. It is most remarkable, that, with all this accession of brightness, the nucleus itself had now diminished to a diameter of only four or five hundred miles, scarcely one fifth of what it was on the morning of the 9th of September, by a very careful determination. Its volume had thus diminished to *one twentieth* part only. The remaining nineteen twentieths had, in the intervening period, expanded into the tail, or had gone to form the envelopes which now encircled it, by a process which had been fully illustrated in the preceding pages. But are we then to conclude that the nucleus, the focus of these mysterious operations, had in this way expended the greater part of its substance? To this inquiry the best reply is a consideration of its subsequent condition. After several more eruptions from its surface, similar to those above described, it receded from our view about the 20th of October, with an evident *increase* of size compared with its condition two weeks before, and still shining with its accustomed intensity.

Examined in the daytime on the 5th, with the highest powers which it would bear, no indication of a *phase* could be seen. The dark spot had expanded in about the same proportion with the whole envelope in which it was situated. From near the vertex, and from the sides of the latter, there seemed to be an escape of jets of luminous gas, which streamed off like light spray thrown up against an opposing wind and driven before it.

It will not be necessary to enter into the details of the history of other envelopes further than to indicate some of their leading features. Between the 2d and the 20th of October inclusive, four of them rose in succession from the nucleus; — one, which was first seen on the 4th as just described, one between the 8th and 9th, another on the 15th, and a fourth on the 20th.

A change in the relative proportion of light distributed on the two sides of the principal axis of the comet had been progressing up to about the 6th of October. At this date, although there may still have been a little more light on the right-hand side, the difference was not nearly so large as it had been. The diameter of the nucleus was then 800 miles. On the 8th, its diameter was 1100 miles. The envelopes were most distinct on the left-hand or preceding side. The change was a permanent one, and for the future this became the brightest half of the head of the comet. It is curious to observe a corresponding change in the inclination of the envelopes to the axis. They now inclined even more decidedly to the left hand than they had at first done to the opposite side. The last two, those of Oct. 15th and 20th, seem in fact in the first instance to have issued as luminous jets or streams from the side, rather than from the vertex of the nucleus. A similar reversal in the order of brightness was evident in the part of the train near the nucleus.

The tenth was the day of nearest approach to the earth, but the comet was manifestly on the wane, though expanded over a larger extent of the sky than before. Five envelopes, reckoning the exterior haze as one, could be traced through the whole or some part of their outline. The dark stripe of the axis was becoming less conspicuous, the central regions of the train being occupied with diffused light; on the 11th it was barely discernible. The last of the envelopes was thrown off on the 20th. The comet had now passed far to the south, and its low altitude prevented the continuance of the observations.

We must add a few words on the appearance presented by the tail between the 6th and the 10th of October. At the date first named, one of the supplementary rays attained a distance of 55°, or fifty millions of miles from the nucleus, somewhat exceeding that of the principal tail, and in a direction as usual, nearly in a line from the sun. Others less perfectly developed could be discerned near a point where the curvature of the main stream was pretty suddenly changed. On the 8th, five or six transverse bands could be distinguished in the tail half a degree or less in breadth, with clear, well-defined outlines, and perfectly resembling auroral streamers, excepting that they kept their position permanently, — that is, without motion sensible to the eye, they diverged from a point between the sun and the nucleus.

The train attained its largest apparent dimensions on the 10th, when the main stream of light could be distinguished through an arc of 60°, corresponding to a length of fifty-one millions of miles, or rather more than half the distance of our earth from the sun. The distribution of its light at a distance of 20° or 30° from the nucleus in parallel or slightly diverging bands, alternating with dark spaces, was strongly exhibited. They were 5° long, and 20′ or 30′ wide, and might aptly be compared either to the streamers which often break up the continuity of an auroral arch, or to a collection of five or six tails of small comets, forming from the remains of the large one. Whatever may have been their real nature, the impression to the eye involuntarily suggested the comparison. These bands were visible for one or two succeeding evenings, but were soon overpowered by the moonlight.

We will conclude with a review of some particulars relating to the comet which seem to deserve special attention. The dimensions of the tail, and of the nucleus and envelopes on the several dates of observation, are given below. Apparent variations in the size of the nucleus were sometimes caused by disturbances in our own atmosphere, but in most cases the changes were undoubtedly real ones. The presence of moonlight, or of the slightest haze in the sky, had a very perceptible effect in diminishing the arc through which the tail could be traced. This will sufficiently explain the irregularities noticed in comparing its proportions from night to night.

Date.			Length of tail.	Breadth at extremity.	Remarks.
1858.	Aug.	29	2° = 14,000,000 miles.		
"	Sept.	8 and 9	4 = 16,000,000 "		
"	"	12	6 = 19.000,000 "		
"	"	17	4 = 10,000,000 "		Moonlight.
"	"	23	7 = 12,000,000 "		"
"	"	24	7 = 12,000,000 "		"
"	"	25	11 = 17,000,000 "	1,500,000 miles.	
"	"	27	13 = 18,000,000 "		

5

Date.	Length of tail.	Breadth at extremity.	Remarks.
1858. Sept. 28	19° = 26,000,000 miles.		
" " 30	22 = 26,000,000 "	3,000,000 miles.	
" Oct. 2	25 = 27,000,000 "	5,000,000 "	
" " 5	35 = 33,000,000 "	5,000,000 "	
" " 6	50 = 45,000,000 "		
" " 8	50 = 43,000,000 "	7,000,000 "	
" " 10	60 = 51,000,000 "	10,000,000 "	
" " 12	45 = 39,000,000 "		
" " 15	15 = 14,000,000 "		Moonlight.

Date.	Length of "Streamers."	Breadth at extremity.
1858. Oct. 4	35° = 34,000,000 miles.	1,000,000 miles.
" " 5	55 = 53,000,000 "	" "
" " 6	55 = 50,000,000 "	" "

In computing the above, the curvature has not been regarded. It must be borne in mind that we have taken for the extremity of the tail the farthest point at which it was possible to detect a trace of it. It would scarcely have been noticed beyond 30° or 35°, even between the 5th and 10th of October, without a particular effort of the attention, and some training of the eye. The streamers, or additional rays, might easily have escaped notice altogether, from their faintness. In making a comparison of the size of this comet with others, it will be best to limit the extent of the tail to the arc over which it was plainly visible, which would give a length of about thirty-five millions of miles. The shortening of the tail between the 12th and the 17th of September is due entirely to the effect of moonlight. The more abrupt change between the 10th and 15th of October is partly due to the same cause, but there must also have been a great diminution in brilliancy.

For the nucleus we have the following measured diameters: — 1858, July 19. Diameter 5″ = 5600 miles. This probably includes the dense nebulosity immediately surrounding it, not distinguishable at the time from the true centre, on account of the low altitude of the comet.

Aug. 19. "Nucleus equals a star of the seventh magnitude." Aug. 29. Head of the comet visible to the unassisted eye as a star of the sixth magnitude. Aug. 30. Diameter 6″ = 4660 miles. This result perhaps includes more than the true nucleus.

Sept. 8, 9. Diameter 3″ = 1980 miles. Taken just before sunrise, when all of the comet, excepting the nebulosity next outside, which was 3300 miles in diameter, was obliterated. On a dark sky the apparent diameter was 5280 miles, and the light equivalent to that of a star of the fifth magnitude.

Sept. 12. To the naked eye the head of the comet appeared as a star of the third magnitude. On Sept. 17th, it equalled a star of the second magnitude. Sept. 23. "To the naked eye the head of the comet is brighter than a star of the first magnitude." Its brilliancy at this date (one week before its perihelion passage, and seventeen days before its nearest approach to the earth) had reached a maximum. It is interesting to remark, that between the 17th and 23d was first noticed the characteristic formation of envelopes, which plainly operated as a check upon the accumulation of brightness at the central point. The nucleus, during the remaining period of its visibility, went through a series of periodic changes, acquiring more light just before an eruption, and suddenly diminishing after it. The variations, although evident to the eye, could not be accurately measured on account of the smallness of the angle subtended, and its want of precise definition. Its diameter, which appeared to be less than usual, was 3″ = 1280 miles. Sept. 24. Diameter 2″.5 = 1030 miles.

Oct. 2. Diameter $5''.2 = 1560$ miles. Oct. 4. Nucleus evidently smaller than on the 2d. Oct. 5. Diameter $1''.5 = 400$ miles; "it is certainly less than $2'' = 540$ miles." This determination was made under most favorable conditions. Oct. 6. Diameter $3'' = 800$ miles. The head of the comet nearly equalled Arcturus. Oct. 8. Diameter $4''.4 = 1120$ miles. "The nucleus is decidedly brighter than on the 6th, and is preparing to throw off a new envelope." Oct. 9. The nucleus had diminished in size simultaneously with the appearance of a new envelope. Oct. 10. Diameter $2''.5 = 630$ miles. Oct. 11. Diameter $2'' = 510$ miles. Oct. 15. The head of the comet was as bright to the naked eye as a star of the third magnitude. Oct. 18. Diameter $3'' = 900$ miles. Oct. 19. Diameter $3 = 920$ miles. The nucleus was compared with three stars of the sixth magnitude at the same altitude, and found to be far brighter than either of them. It was probably at least as bright as a star of the fifth magnitude, while to the naked eye the head nearly equalled one of the third magnitude. Oct. 20. Diameter $2'' = 660$ miles. A new envelope was forming. As before remarked, the least observed diameter of the nucleus, 400 miles, occurred on October 5th, the evening when the comet reached its maximum of brightness.

In order to exhibit the progressive motion of the envelopes from their point of origin, we give below in one view the distances of their vertices from the nucleus at different dates. The distances were measured in the line from the nucleus towards the sun. The better to distinguish them, we will use the following notation :—

$a' =$ Vertex of envelope first seen on Sept. 20.
$b' =$ " " " " 23.
$c' =$ " " " " 27.
$d' =$ " " " Oct. 4.
$e' =$ " " " " 9.
$f' =$ " " " " 15.
$g' =$ " " " " 20.

Distances in miles from the nucleus (n) to the vertices of the envelopes a, b, and c :—

	na'	nb'	nc'	nd'	ne'	nf'
Sept. 23	* 13000	* 6400				
" 24	13400	5800				
" 25	* 18000	7100				
" 27		8400	3500			
" 29		10500	6000			
Oct. 2		13200	7500			
" 4			8900	3050		
" 5		14200	9550	4210		
" 6			10100	4270		
" 8			12400	7160		
" 9			13200	8650	1910	
" 10			14100	8780	2760	
" 11				* 10200	* 4200	
" 15				* 11400	8160	3200
" 18				* 14500	9950	4400
" 19					11200	5500

The vertex g' had barely left the surface of the nucleus on the 20th.

The comet of Donati, although surpassed by many others in size, has not often been equalled in the intensity of the light of the nucleus. The diameter of the surrounding nebulosity, on the other hand, was unusually small, never

* The numbers marked with an asterisk are less reliable than the others.

much exceeding one hundred thousand miles, while that of the great comet of 1811 was ten times larger, — its envelope attaining an elevation of more than three hundred thousand miles above the central body, exceeding by more than twenty times the largest of our measurements given above. Still it would be difficult to instance any one of its predecessors which has combined so many attractive features.

Its early discovery enabled astronomers, while it was yet scarcely distinguishable even with the telescope, to predict, some months in advance, the more prominent particulars of its approaching apparition, which was thus observed with all the advantage of previous preparation and anticipation. The perihelion passage occurred at a most favorable moment for presenting the comet to good advantage. Its situation in the latter part of its course afforded also a fair sight of the curvature of the train, which seems to have been exhibited with unusual distinctness, contributing greatly to the impressive effect of a full-length view. Frequent allusion has been made to the influence of the light of the moon on the visibility of the comet. Few readers will be aware how much of its splendor and vast dimensions, during the first ten days of October, we owe to the fortunate circumstance that, at this critical period, the moon was absent from our evening skies. The effect of the presence of a full moon, though simply optical, and due only to the force of contrast, would have been quite as prejudicial as if the comet had lost two thirds of its train, and as large a proportion of the brightness of the remaining third; above all, we must have lost those most singular phenomena, the supplementary rays, and the alternating bright and dark bands in the train; the latter seem to have been new in cometary history. Supposing the substance of the tail to be driven off into space, never again to return to its original source, the inquiry at once arises, What then becomes of it? The appearances in question show plainly enough a process of separation into distinct masses, and in each of these a tendency to condense about a central axis.

It is remarkable that the aggregation should have been around separate axes, rather than about one or more central points, and that the axes should have manifested a disposition to diverge from the sun. The increasing moonlight and low altitude of the comet would not allow their being followed to a more complete development.

The condition of the nucleus and neighboring region has received a large share of attention in the preceding pages, because it has afforded so ample an illustration of phenomena of which, up to the present time, very little has been certainly known. The comets of 1744 and of 1811 had well-formed envelopes, but the observations upon them were too imperfect and disconnected to afford much more than a basis for conjecture as to their origin and destination. That of Halley, at its apparition in 1835–36, furnishes an example more nearly parallel to the present one, but its phenomena were on a comparatively feeble scale.

The most recent intelligence leaves no room to doubt that the comet of Donati is periodical, having a time of revolution of about two thousand years. The following are the results arrived at by different computers: —

Watson,	2415 years.	Graham,	1620 years.
Bruhns,	2102 "	Brünnow,	2470 "
Löwy,	2495 "	Newcomb,	1854 "

The last two determinations are based upon longer intervals of observation than the others. The remaining uncertainty in the period will be materially reduced, when observations have been received from the southern hemisphere, where the comet was in sight after it had become invisible to us.

The subjoined table contains the distances of the comet from the sun and from the earth, and its hourly rate of motion: —

1858.	Distance from Sun in miles.	Distance from Earth in miles.	Hourly Velocity in miles.
June 2,	215,000,000	240,000,000	65,000
July 2,	173,000,000	240,000,000	72,000
Aug. 2,	127,000,000	220,000,000	84,000
Sept. 1,	82,000,000	160,000,000	105,000
" 11,	70,000,000	130,000,000	115,000
" 21,	60,000,000	95,000,000	124,000
Oct. 1,	56,000,000	66,000,000	128,000
" 11,	61,000,000	52,000,000	123,000
" 21,	71,000,000	67,000,000	114,000

Supposing its last perihelion passage to have occurred at the beginning of the Christian era, it must have passed its aphelion in the early part of the tenth century, at a distance of 14300 millions of miles from the sun, its velocity at that point being 480 miles an hour.

PROFESSOR LOOMIS'S GENERALIZATIONS AS TO THE LAWS OF STORMS.

At the Springfield Meeting of the American Association for the Promotion of Science, August, 1859, Professor Loomis, of New York, presented an elaborate investigation of a storm which was experienced in Europe about the 25th of December, 1836. This storm was selected for investigation, partly on account of its intrinsic interest, and partly on account of its supposed connection with a violent storm which had been experienced in the United States about the 20th of the same month. A thorough investigation of both storms has shown that the two were entirely independent of each other. The European storm evidently originated in Europe; and the American storm gradually wasted away, and probably could not be traced beyond the middle of the Atlantic.

The European storm of December 25 was remarkable for its superficial extent, for its duration, and for its violence. It covered nearly every portion of Europe, from Norway to Southern Italy, and from Spain to the Ural Mountains. It commenced on the 22d of December, and was not entirely concluded on the 28th. From the 24th to the 27th the storm was sensibly stationary in position, its centre being nearly over Mont Blanc, in Switzerland.

Throughout a considerable portion of Europe, this storm was one of great violence. In the southeastern part of England it was attended by one of the greatest falls of snow ever recorded in that country. The roads were so obstructed by the snow-drifts that for two whole days communication between London and the southern part of England was almost wholly interrupted.

By comparing the European storm of December 25th with the American storm of December 20th, and also the storms of February 4th and 16th, 1842, Professor Loomis has been led to the following generalizations. Some of these conclusions are substantially the same as given by Mr. Espy, in his Fourth Meteorological Report; but several of Mr. Espy's conclusions are only true when applied to American storms.

1. The area covered by a violent storm of rain or snow is sometimes nearly

circular in form; sometimes its form is very much elongated or elliptical, its length being two or three times its breadth; and frequently its form is very irregular. In the winter storms of the United States, the north and south diameter is generally very much greater than the east and west diameter.

2. When storms are circular in form, the area of rain or snow is sometimes fifteen hundred miles in diameter; when their form is elliptical, the area of rain or snow is sometimes one thousand miles wide, and two or three thousand miles long.

3. Violent storms sometimes remain sensibly stationary four or five days, but generally the centre of a storm has a progressive movement along the earth's surface. The rate of this progress has been observed to vary from zero to forty-four miles an hour. From our limited number of observations, it seems probable that American storms travel more rapidly than European storms.

4. Within the limits of prevalent westerly winds, when violent storms advance with considerable rapidity, the direction of progress is always from west to east. This direction is not absolutely uniform, but has been observed to vary from about due east to north fifty-four degrees east.

5. Great storms of rain and snow are accompanied by a depression of the barometer near the centre of the storm, and a rise of the barometer near the margin; but this rise is not generally uniform along the entire margin.

6. The depression of the barometer at the centre of a storm sometimes amounts to more than an inch *below* the mean height; and the rise along some portion of the margin sometimes amounts to more than an inch *above* the mean height.

7. Winter storms commence gradually, and generally attain their greatest violence only after a lapse of several days. After a time their violence gradually diminishes, and at length they disappear entirely. This succession of changes requires a period of several days, sometimes one or two weeks, and possibly even longer. Sometimes all these changes are experienced over the same country; that is, the storm makes no progress from place to place. More commonly, however, the storm travels along the earth's surface; and although the same storm may continue for one or two weeks, or even longer, its duration at any one place may not exceed one or two days.

8. For several hundred miles on each side of the centre of a violent storm, the wind inclines inward towards the area of least pressure, and at the same time circulates around the centre, in a direction contrary to the motion of the hands of a watch.

9. In Europe, as well as in the United States, on the north side of a great storm, the prevalent winds are from the northeast, while on the south side they are from the southwest.

10. The force of the wind is proportioned to the magnitude and suddenness of the depression of the barometer, but very near the centre of a violent storm there is often a calm.

11. On the borders of the storm, near the line of maximum pressure, the wind has but little force, and tends outwards from the line of greatest pressure.

12. The wind uniformly tends from an area of high barometer towards an area of low barometer; and this is probably the most important law regulating the movement of the wind.

13. In a great storm, the centre of the area of high thermometer frequently does not coincide with that of the area of low barometer, or with the centre of the area of rain and snow. In the United States, on the northeast side of a storm, at a distance of over five hundred miles from the area of rain and snow, the thermometer sometimes rises even twenty degrees above its mean height.

14. The storms of Europe are very much modified, and sometimes controlled, in a great measure, by the Alps of Switzerland. By the interposition

of these mountains, the air which sweeps over them is forced up to a great height, where it is suddenly cooled; its vapor is condensed; heat is accordingly liberated, by which the surrounding air is expanded, and rises above the usual limit of the atmosphere. It thence flows off laterally, leaving a diminished pressure beneath the cloud: that is, the barometer shows a diminished pressure in the neighborhood of the mountain. The mountain thus becomes the centre of a great storm, and the storm may continue stationary for several days, being apparently held in its place by the action of the mountain.

ON THE AURORA BOREALIS AND THE AURORA AUSTRALIS.

By Professor Joseph Lovering, of Harvard University.

The name of *Aurora Borealis* was given by Gassendi to an appearance in the heavens, now familiar, on the exhibition of it September 2, 1621. The phenomenon is called in the Shetland Islands "The Merry Dancers." The Indian thinks it the spirit of his fathers. Gmelen calls Siberia the birthplace of the aurora.

The various features of the aurora, a greater or smaller number of which may be detected in any aurora, are, 1. Auroral twilight. 2. Arches running nearly from east to west. 3. Streamers. 4. Crown around that point of the sky to which a perfectly free magnetized needle points. 5. Waves. 6. Auroral clouds. The late Professor Olmsted, after enumerating these specialities, remarks: "In different exhibitions of the aurora borealis the various forms above enumerated are sometimes seen single, but commonly more or less combined. In the most magnificent examples they are all seen in company. At first, usually at an early hour of the evening, appears the northern *twilight*, as though the sun, after he had set, was rising prematurely in the north. If a large bank of luminous vapor (which is so peculiar in its external properties, and so distinct from watery vapor, as to warrant the denomination of auroral vapor) rests on the northern horizon, we may expect to see the aurora put on, successively, more of its higher forms;—streamers will begin to shoot upwards; a dark, smoky front will cover the auroral vapor, exhibiting here and there changeable and transient white spots, which suddenly swell out, and often as suddenly disappear; then large columns of a clear, silvery lustre will form in the northwest and northeast, simultaneously, which will sometimes meet and span the heavens with an entire arch; suddenly the columns and clouds of auroral vapor will assume a crimson hue; next all the columns and streamers will rush towards a point a little southeast of the zenith, corresponding to the pole of the dipping-needle, and wreathe themselves around it in a splendid coronet,—and finally auroral waves will begin to flow upward from the horizon toward the same point in surprising undulations, which are often continued a great part of the night. Meanwhile the magnetic needle is violently agitated, and deflected from its normal position."*

Mr. Olmsted divides auroras into four classes. A first-class aurora displays corona, arch, brilliant crimson streamers and waves. A second-class aurora unites only two or three of these four most impressive characteristics; a third-rate aurora exhibits only one of them; a fourth-rate aurora, or an ordinary aurora, is distinguished by neither of these more dazzling peculiarities of the grandest displays.

* Smith. Contr., VIII. 5.

The distinguishing features of a rich aurora, notwithstanding the ten thousand varieties, can be recognized in the various descriptions they have received from the man of science, the poet, and the superstitious beholder. We have already given the words of science. This is the language of a poet, describing the aurora in Sweden: "And now the Northern Lights begin to burn, faintly at first, like sunbeams playing in the waters of the blue sea. Then a soft, crimson glow tinges the heavens. There is a blush on the cheek of night. The colors come and go, and change from crimson to gold, from gold to crimson. The snow is stained with rosy light. Twofold from the zenith, east and west, flames a fiery sword: and a broad band passes athwart the heavens, like a summer sunset. Soft purple clouds come sailing over the sky, and through their vapory folds the winking stars shine white as silver." *

Next follows the account, by Rev. Thomas Prince, of the Northern Lights *when first seen in England, in* 1716 :—

"There seemed to be a great stream of smoky light rising in the northeast, reaching from near the earth, ascending and waving like the light of a great house or bonfire in a dark evening about half a mile off, which we therefore thought it at first to be; but soon altered our minds when we saw it increasing in breadth, length, and brightness, and pushing forwards, retreating and advancing in the shape of a broad-sword, and like the shooting vibrations of a very high blaze, until it extended to the point over our heads. As it increased in bigness, so did it likewise in the swiftness and fury of its motion, and grew by degrees into a bluish, red and fiery color, almost like to that of the flame of brimstone. Both the color and figure continually changed, I know not how, till at length, on a sudden, it brake forth into the appearance of a raging and mighty torrent of bloody waters, that at first looked like the sudden giving way of a dam, and the sea bearing all irresistibly before it. Whereupon all that part of the heavens over us turned of an inconceivably bright rainbow color, and immediately run into an admirable, inexpressible confusion of an infinite variety of motions, that were amazingly quick and terrible to behold.

"I know not how to give you an idea of this part of the appearance; unless you may conceive something of it by the various and most violent motions that are in a great body of waters, when an higher stream happens to descend and impetuously rush into another. Sometimes they ran into circular forms, sometimes into ovals; sometimes the circles and ovals were variously comprest on their sides by their approaching nearer to one another, or the greater interflux of the nameless and unknown matter. Sometimes they ran winding within and hastily pursuing one another in the manner of whirlpools, and sometimes they ran round and crossed like an 8, and in numberless other different figures; that something resembled the various quick and confused rambles of flies in the midst of a room, or of spiders on the surface of a pond; or the perplexing contortions and turnings of a great heap of living eels just covered with water in the bottom of a boat; or as the little foldings and ridges at the tops and bottoms of the fingers; or to mention no more comparisons, like the figures it is probable you have seen of *Cartesius's vortices*.

"All this while, the brightness, bloodiness, and fieriness of the colors before mentioned, together with the swiftness of the motions, increased, insomuch as we could hardly trace them with our eyes; till at length almost all the whole heavens appeared as if they were set on a flame, which wrought and glimmered with flashes in a most dreadful and undescribable manner. It seemed to threaten us with an immediate descent and deluge of fire, filled the streets with loud and doleful outcries and lamentations, and frighted a

* Longfellow in N. A. Review, XLV. p. 157.

great many people into their houses: and we all began to think whether the Son of God was next to make his glorious and terrible appearance, or the conflagration of the world was now begun. For the elements seemed just as if they were melting with fervent heat, and the ethereal vault to be burning over us like the fierce agitations of the blaze in a furnace, or at the top of a fiery oven; and the glimmering light looked as if it proceeded from a more glorious body behind, that was approaching nearer and about to make its sudden appearance to our eyes.

"While we expected and wondered what would be the next alteration, and dreaded the consequence, all on a sudden the flaming body above us brake into innumerable spears of light, that at first darted every way and across one another; but in a little while they conformed to the same point of motion, and played in a regular and astonishing manner. At first it seemed as if the very frame of the world was a dissolving; but afterwards one would have thought that there was a furious battle of invisible spirits, that the powers and principalities of the air had broke out into a fierce contention, and that, transforming themselves into angels of light, they were converted into seraphic flames and figures that are said to resemble their natures.

"These distinct and various lights were in the shape of swords, and their several bodies did not appear entirely at the same time, but seemed to begin at one end and shoot a prodigious way to a sharp point in a moment like one continued blaze of a flying firebrand. As they continually appeared and streamed, so they continually vanished like the lucid path of a rocket, while others were incessantly making their appearance in different places round about. The motion of them all was now pointed upwards, and reached some a greater and some a lesser extent; but none above more than from about eight or ten degrees of the horizon to about six or eight from the zenith. For the most part they flashed unequally; but sometimes they seemed to begin, shoot and blaze all together, and made the earth almost as light as day. And then their appearance was like a thousand great swords or blazing stars shooting upwards from all sides of the hemisphere, but leaving, where their points ended, a vacant space in the centre of about ten or twelve degrees diameter, and sometimes of a roundish and sometimes of various multangular figures, directly over our heads. For there seemed to be a remarkable part of the heavens above us which they all violently pushed at, but could never enter.

"Thus they continued their exercise for about a quarter of an hour, but decreased by degrees both in number, quickness, and brightness, till they left the heavens as they were before, and indeed all the time of this amazing appearance almost as clear I think as ever I saw them. It was the more unaccountable and wonderful that there was no palpable cloud hung over us, but we saw the stars shining very plainly all the while in the intervals of the spears and in the very places where they were, as soon as ever they vanished; unless when the brightness of the apparition was so excessive as to drown their light."

I shall arrange what I have to say upon the aurora under these different heads. I. Periodicity, geographical extent, and locality of the aurora. II. The effects of the aurora, such as its light, sound, smell, magnetic and electrical properties. III. Its height and real configuration. IV. Its causes.

I. 1. It is said in Holmes's Annuals,* that the aurora was first seen in New England on December 17, 1719. The author refers to Dr. Trumbull's Century Sermon, preached at New Haven on January 1, 1801, in which occurs the following note:† "The aurora borealis, or northern light, is a

* I. p. 523. † Page 5.

new appearance, in the heavens, to this country, peculiar to the eighteenth century. It had been seen in Great Britain, especially in the north of Scotland, for many centuries past, but even in that country it had not appeared for eighty or an hundred years until March 6, 1716. Its first appearance in New England was on the 17th of December, 1719. It appears to have been a great light, and began about eight o'clock in the evening. It filled the country with the greatest alarm imaginable. It was the general opinion that it was the sign of the coming of the Son of man in the heavens, and that the judgment of the great day was about to commence. According to the accounts given by the ancient people who were spectators of it, there was little sleep in New England that night."

An anonymous account of this aurora by an eyewitness, dated December 15th, 1719, has been republished in the Collections of the Massachusetts Historical Society.* The author says in the first paragraph, "And I hope (though I believe I shall differ from some) I shall say nothing that shall be inconsistent either with Divinity or Philosophy." The aurora was seen from 8 o'clock in the evening, until an hour or two of daybreak the next morning. Its appearance at 11 o'clock "was somewhat dreadful: sometimes it looked of a flame, sometimes a blood-red color: and the whole N. E. horizon was very light, and looked as though the moon had been near her rising." The description ends in these words: "Thus I have given you the best account I am able of this meteor; which, though very unusual here, yet in northern countries more frequent, and seems to me to be what our modern philosophers call Aurora Borealis." He adds, after some attempt at an explanation, of less value than his observation, "As to prognostications from it, I utterly abhor and detest them all, and look upon these to be but the effect of ignorance and fancy: for I have not so learned philosophy or divinity, as to be dismayed at the signs of heaven: this would be to act the part of an heathen, not of a Christian philosopher." See Jer. x. 2.

I would suggest, in this connection, whether the following extracts do not indicate the appearance of an aurora in New England at a much earlier date than the one commonly assigned to its first appearance: —

"About midnight three men, coming in a boat to Boston, saw two lights arise out of the water near the north point of the town cove, in form like a man, and went at a small distance to the town, and to the south point, and there vanished away." "The like was seen by many, a week after." In the second case: "A light like the moon arose about the N. E. point in Boston, and met the former at Nottles Island, — and there they closed in one, and then parted, and closed and parted divers times, and so went over the hill in the island and vanished. Sometimes they shot out flames, and sometimes sparkles."† This was on the 11th and 18th of April, 1643.

The reader is, no doubt, surprised to learn that the aurora was observed for the first time, with the possible exceptions just mentioned, in New England in 1719. For the inference is that no good example of it had occurred since the settlement of the country. The people of New England were too much inclined to dwell upon unusual phenomena in the heavens to have overlooked or been silent in regard to so strange a spectacle as an aurora, had they had the opportunity of beholding one. That the aurora had been uncommon in old England during the preceding century appears from the fact that the great astronomer, Dr. Halley, was, as he says, dying to see one, and expected to die without seeing it. At last the opportunity came, on March 17, 1716, when Halley was sixty years old. In his description of it‡ he says: "This was the only one I had as yet seen, and of which I began to

* II. pp. 17–20.
† Winthrop's Hist. of New England, II. pp. 152, 153.
‡ Phil. Trans., XXIX. p. 416.

despair, since it is certain it hath not happened to any remarkable degree in this part of England since I was born." He adds that the like is not recorded in the English annals since 1574, or for 140 years. It was then seen two nights successively, on November 14th and 15th. It was not so uncommon in the reign of Queen Elizabeth. It was seen at London on January 30th, 1560, and on October 7th, 1564. It was seen twice at Brabant, in 1575. In Germany, in 1580, it was seen seven times in the space of twelve months. In 1621 it appeared in France, and was described by Gassendi under the name of Aurora Borealis. Though it was seen, on the last occasion, at Rouen and Paris, and in the northerly part of the horizon, it was not observed in England, so far as Halley knew. Since then, for eighty years, no account of it, at home or abroad, could be found by Halley, although the Philosophical Transactions had been published for half that period. Mairan's very laborious researches, however, have since accumulated 176 recorded appearances in Europe, between 1621 and 1716. But the same researches have collected 1,118 exhibitions for the thirty-five years following 1716, and only 98 for the thirty-five preceding years. Of these appearances, 116 were in a single year (1730), and 100 in another single year (1732). In the year 1699, which belongs to the period of infrequent auroras, there were 40, although for the few years preceding and following they were very rare.

Notwithstanding this infrequency of the aurora in England for a long period prior to 1716, John Huxham observed it at Plymouth in eighty-one instances between 1728 and 1748.* Celsius says that it was also rare in Sweden before 1716, although between 1716 and 1732 there are found 316 observations of it, and 224 independent appearances. Kirch has collected 106 appearances of the aurora at Berlin, between the years 1707 and 1735. Weidler has made a list of 95 appearances at Wittemberg, in Saxony, between 1730 and 1751. Delisle has furnished a record of 233 appearances at St. Petersburg between 1726 and 1737. Zanotti and Beccari have found 52 appearances in Bologna, or other parts of Italy, between the years 1727 and 1751, and 36 more of doubtful cases. Zanotti, in a description of an aurora which was seen in Italy, as well as in England, on December 5, 1737, remarks: "The Aurora Borealis which was formerly a rare phenomenon and almost unknown in this our climate (Italy), is now become very frequent. A great number have been observed for some years past."† In 1737 Thomas Short speaks of the current year as "having been the most irregularly constituted year of any in my time: not one month but what had the weather of all the seasons, and that not by gradual transitions, but by sudden jerks;" and then says: "I shall only add that our northern lights have been much seldomer and fainter both in appearance and motion than formerly: and whether they will dwindle away and vanish wholly for some years, or whether they have had their former periodic returns, is not certain."‡

This periodicity in the occurrence of the aurora, which seems to be indicated by what has gone before, was confirmed by the comprehensive review of the subject which Mairan took in his *Traité Physique et Historique de l'Aurore Boréale*, published by the French Academy, first in 1731, and a second edition in 1754. Mairan was incited to his great labor by the remarkable aurora of October 19, 1726. Mairan has collected 1,441 appearances, as has already been mentioned (2,137 recorded cases, of which some are duplicates), between the year 583 and the year 1751, and he makes out twenty-two unusual epochs of returning frequency in the course of that long interval.

---

* Amer. Journ. of Sci., XXXIII. p. 297. † Phil. Trans., XLI. p. 593.
‡ Ib. pp. 625–630.

I will now consider how the observations of the last hundred years bear upon this question of periodicity. Dalton has collected two hundred and twenty-seven appearances of the aurora in Kendall and Keswick, between the years 1787 and 1793, of which only twenty-nine are duplicates.* In Dalton's catalogue † of auroras observed in Great Britain and Ireland between 1793 and 1834, only sixty-five occurred before 1820, and one hundred and twenty between 1820 and 1834. If a comparison were made in regard to the numbers of *brilliant* auroras, the disparity is still more in favor of the latter period. Between 1806 and 1827, a remarkable aurora was observed only nineteen times, and not at all in the years 1807, 1809, 1810, 1811, 1812, 1813, 1815, 1822, 1823, and 1824. In 1817 and 1820 there were *brilliant* or *extensive* auroras. On the other hand, from 1827 to 1834, a much shorter period, the aurora was observed one hundred and eleven times, and thirty-two times in one year (1830). In this latter period eight are designated as *grand*, and many others as *fine*. Singer says, in his Elements of Electricity, published in 1814, that the aurora was then rarely visible in England. ‡

This, in fine, is the European history of the aurora for the last three centuries. For ten years in the neighborhood of 1560, it was common. Then an interval of forty years with scarcely any. About 1620 there were several. Then another intermission for eighty years. Next the eighteenth century abounds in them. In 1707 they were seen in Ireland, Copenhagen, and Berlin. In 1708 they were seen in London. In 1710 they were seen in Leeds. In 1716 they were seen in England, and then several times again before 1723, when they were visible even at Bologna. In 1726 there was an aurora which excited Mairan to his great undertaking. In 1736 Maupertuis saw one at Oswer Zornea, which he thus describes: "I saw a phenomenon of this kind that, in the midst of all the wonders to which I was now every day accustomed, excited my admiration. An extensive region towards the south appeared tinged of so lively a red that the constellation Orion seemed to be dyed in blood. This light was for some time fixed: but soon moved, and after having successively assumed all the tints of violet and blue, it formed a dance of which the summit nearly approached the zenith in the southwest. In this country, where there are lights of so many different colors, I never saw but two that were red, and such are always taken for presages of some great misfortune." In 1765 there was another red aurora. Another was seen in France and Pennsylvania in 1769. In 1814 an aurora with a bright arch was seen all over Great Britain. In 1825, 1827, 1828, 1831, 1833, 1835, 1836, 1837, 1839, 1843, 1847, and 1848, there were splendid auroras visible in Europe.§ It has been concluded, therefore, from European observations, that there is a *secular* periodicity to the aurora. "A period of this kind is comprised between 1707 and 1790: it attained its *maximum* about 1752; there was then a series of twenty years during which they were more rare, but from the year 1820 they have again become more common."‖ When, in September, 1827, a bright aurora was witnessed in Paris, it was stated, by Arago, that none had been seen there before for twenty years.

It may be interesting to inquire how the case stands in the western hemisphere. I have mentioned the surprise excited by the aurora of 1719 in New England. After that there are scattered accounts of the aurora during nearly the remainder of the century. Mr. Greenwood,¶ then Hollis Professor of Mathematics and Natural Philosophy at Harvard College, described one which was seen in 1730, at Cambridge. His successor, Professor John Winthrop,** records nine exhibitions of it between 1741 and 1757. Mr. Caleb Gannett has described an aurora, accompanied by the eastern and western

* Met. Ob. and Essays, p. 54. † Ib., p. 248. ‡ P. 253.
§ Thompson's Met., p. 350, &c. ‖ Kaemtz's Met., p. 458.
¶ Phil. Trans. Abridg., VI. p. 115. ** Amer. Journ. of Sci., XL. p. 204.

arch, which was seen at Cambridge on March 27, 1781.* Mr. Manasseh Cutler noticed the aurora repeatedly at Ipswich in 1781.† Auroras were seen at Salem, November 17 and 24, 1720, January 1, and October 2, 1728, and an extraordinary one October 22, 1730. On December 29, 1736 (probably), Dr. Holyoke saw an aurora of which he says: "The first aurora borealis I ever saw. The northern sky appeared suffused by a dark blood-red colored vapor, without any variety of different colored rays. I have never seen the like. Northern lights were then a great novelty, and excited great wonder and terror." On August 6, 1768, a bright streak of light extended from the west-northwest to the southeast, almost as bright as a rainbow. On July 19, 1769, there was an aurora of unusual brightness.‡ On April 21, 1750, the aurora was seen as far south as Charleston, S. C. "We had a most extraordinary appearance of the aurora borealis. One half of the sky seemed like a beautiful streaked liquid flame, so terrible to many of the female inhabitants that some of them were thrown into fits."§

It is well known that Dr. Holyoke, of Salem, kept a Meteorological Journal from 1754 to 1828. That part which relates to the weather has already been published in the Memoirs of the American Academy of Arts and Sciences in Boston. I have consulted the manuscript records of Dr. Holyoke, which he presented to the Academy, and have selected from them all the instances he has recorded of auroras observed by him. Unfortunately, the copy which the Academy possesses is not the original, until the year 1786; and, being prepared for a special purpose, does not contain any record of auroral appearances before 1786. But the Academy possesses the original manuscript Journal of Meteorology kept at Cambridge by Professor John Winthrop, from 1742 to 1779; and also that of Professor Edward Wigglesworth, kept at Cambridge from 1782 to 1793; and that of Dr. Enoch Hale, kept at Boston from 1818 to 1848. In all these Journals, except the last, the auroras are noted with great care; and all together cover more than a century, in which only two years are wanting, namely, 1780 and 1781. From this storehouse I have been able to collect 501 recorded examples of auroras, of which only 92 are duplicates, leaving 409 independent auroras, of which 400 have never before appeared in print. Professor Winthrop has recorded 116 exhibitions of the aurora, Professor Wigglesworth 123, and Dr. Holyoke 262. As these observations have been made at two places only a dozen miles apart, they are strictly comparable with each other, and furnish an almost uninterrupted record of the aurora for one hundred years in this immediate vicinity. The result of my discussion of these observations is, that during the thirty-three years from 1793 to 1827 there were only 17 recorded examples of the aurora. For the thirty-three years preceding 1793 there were 336; and in several instances, a single year of the latter epoch furnishes more cases than the whole of the former epoch; and in one year (1789) there are more than twice as many exhibitions of the aurora as in the whole thirty-three years next preceding 1827. Further details will appear in Volume VIII. of the Memoirs of the Academy.

Professor C. Dewey, then of Williams College, observed auroras, in 1818, on May 23 and 28; also from June 6th to 10th, on September 24 and 25, and October 6 and 7.‖

The examination of Dr. Holyoke's Journal furnishes *positive* testimony in favor of a conclusion which had been adopted already from *negative* evidence; the absence, that is, of any description of remarkable auroras during the present century before 1827, although the Memoirs of the American Academy and the Transactions of the Philosophical Society, and, after 1818, Silliman's

* Mem. Amer. Acad., II. p. 136.
† Ib., I. p. 368.
‡ Felt's Hist. of Salem, II. p. 137.
§ Gent. Mag., XX. p. 419, and XXI. p. 39.
‖ Mem. Amer. Acad., IV. p. 291.

Journal, were in existence, and would furnish a proper medium for any such description. Therefore, as Olmsted remarks, "the splendid arch and other striking accompaniments of the aurora of August, 1827, took us by surprise, and were viewed with wonder by nearly all the existing generation of the countries where it was visible." * Mr. Felt says it caused much apprehension lest the end of all things had come. The arch which signalized this aurora had been seen by Dr. Holyoke, who was then ninety-nine years old, only twice before, namely, in 1755 and 1769. The sight of a magnificent aurora was so unusual that in August, 1827, the bells were rung in Salem to call attention to it. On the contrary, for a period of seventeen years succeeding 1831, 780 auroras were visible in the State of New York, of which 10 were of the highest order, and 35 others only a little inferior. In the single year 1840, there were seen 75 auroras. In 1838, there were 42 in all, and 7 of a *high order*. This period of brilliant auroras still continues: there were four in 1847 and in 1848, three in September, 1851, one in February, 1852, two in 1853, and those of August 28 and 29, and of September 2, 1859.

The discussion of the American auroras leads to the same general conclusion as is suggested by the European observations: namely, that there is a *secular* periodicity, consisting of twenty years or more of abundant exhibitions, separated by intervals, equally long or longer, when the phenomenon, if not wholly wanting, is unaccompanied by any of its more striking characteristics. Though there is a general parallelism in the facts collected on the two continents, the correspondence is not probably so exact as to allow us to disregard in this discussion geographical locality altogether.

The question has also been entertained, whether there were indications of a *yearly* and *daily period* in the exhibitions of the aurora. Mairan states that out of the 1,441 appearances of the aurora which he collected between the years 583 and 1751, 972 were in the six months following October 1, and 469 in the remainder of the year. Olmsted states that of the 780 auroras observed during the seventeen years between 1832 and 1848 inclusive, 346 were in the winter half of the year and 434 in the summer half. Out of 386 auroras observed by Professor Winthrop and Dr. Holyoke at Cambridge or Salem between 1742 and 1827, the winter half of the year claims only 174 and the summer half 212.

Mr. Olmsted remarks: "In regard, however, to *intensity*, the balance has always been in favor of autumn, the greatest auroras having been most numerous in September and November, (August, also?) while they have never occurred in June; but in respect to number, the balance between the seasons of late years has been just the opposite of what it was a century ago, the minimum instead of the maximum number having of late occurred during the winter months; and this is the more remarkable, since the greater length of the winter nights would, of itself, lead us to expect a greater number of auroras at this season of the year." And *in a note:* "Great auroras about the middle of November in 1574, 1607, 1835, 1837, 1840, 1841, 1844, and 1848."

In regard to the *diurnal periodicity*, the general fact is observable, that, although grand auroras, as that for example of August 28, 1859, may last through the whole night, generally the aurora dies out before midnight; and even the best displays usually attain their maximum before 10 and 11 o'clock.

2. Next, as to the geographical relations of the aurora. And first, its area of visibility. The aurora of September 12, 1621, was seen in France, Venice, and Syria. The aurora of October 19, 1726, was seen at Moscow, Petersburg, Warsaw, Rome, Naples, Madrid, Lisbon, and perhaps Cadiz.† That of January 5, 1769, was seen in Pennsylvania and France.‡ The arch

* Smith. Contr., VIII. p. 4. † Dalton's Meteorology, p. 229. ‡ Kaemtz's Met., p. 456.

of August 28, 1827, was seen in New England and in Scotland. The auroras of 1830 and 1831 were common to Europe and America.* The aurora of November 7, 1835, was seen from Montreal to Mississippi, and from New England to Cincinnati. Those of January 7, 1831, February, 1837, and September 3, 1839, were visible in Europe and America. The splendid aurora of May 27, 1841, was seen at Cambridge, Philadelphia, New Haven, Toronto in Canada, and Greenwich in Great Britain. The aurora of November 17, 1848, was witnessed in Asia, Europe, and America; in Odessa in the east, and San Francisco in the west. Difference of latitude has more effect upon the appearance than difference of longitude. The auroral displays of August and September, 1859, were witnessed in England, Germany, Italy, as well as throughout the central and southern portions of North America. Humboldt remarks: "Many nights may be instanced in which the phenomenon has been simultaneously observed in England and in Pennsylvania, in Rome and in Pekin." †

Another circumstance to be mentioned in connection with the geographical characteristics of the aurora is, that it becomes more frequent as the magnetic latitude increases, and in Iceland, Greenland, Newfoundland, on the shores of the Slave Lake, and in Northern Canada, it is of nightly occurrence at certain seasons of the year. Lottin and his scientific associates observed, in the winter of 1838–39, in Finmark, in 70° north latitude, 151 displays in 201 nights. ‡ Scoresby says that in Iceland the aurora may be seen almost every clear night in winter. Franklin had 142 examples of it in six months in the Arctic sea.

As the frequency of the exhibition increases with the proximity of the observer to the *magnetic*, and not to the geographical pole, auroras abound (according to Scoresby, who observed there in 1822) between the parallels of 62° and 70°. It is not seen best in the very highest latitudes. As the longitude of the magnetic pole is about 97 W. from Greenwich, places in America are nearer to it than places in Europe on the same parallel. Accordingly the aurora is less frequently seen in Italy than in parts of the United States in the same latitude. Erman states that the aurora is not common at Tobolsk; he thinks the double magnetic pole affects the position of it. § The aurora is more frequent in New England than in Great Britain, though the latter is 10° farther north. The greatest number Dalton observed in England in one year was 30, in the year 1830. In Massachusetts there were 56 observed in the same year. ‖

3. At the beginning of the seventeenth century, Gassendi gave the name of *Aurora Borealis* to the appearances under consideration, because of the auroral light and the position of the meteor in the northern point of the horizon. Although the lights may begin at the north, they frequently extend round to the east and west and up to the zenith, and, continuing down to the south, inflame the whole firmament. Parry noticed that on one occasion the aurora was more remarkable at the south than at the opposite point of the horizon. Captain John Ross relates that, in 1818, while his ships were moving south from the parallel of 74° to 66°, he observed the aurora to be in the southern parts of the horizon; but when the ship was south of 66° then the aurora appeared in the northerly parts of the horizon. If the aurora borealis culminates at the magnetic pole, we might expect such a transition of the maximum splendor from the southern to the northern point of the horizon as Ross describes.

Corresponding to the *Aurora Borealis* in the northern hemisphere, there is the *Aurora Australis* in the southern hemisphere (*Südlichter* of the Germans). Forster, who accompanied Captain Cook ¶ to the South Seas, says

* Amer. Journ. Science, XXII. p. 143.
† Cosmos, I. p. 193.
‡ Voyages, &c., p. 543.
§ Travels in Siberia, I. p. 394 and p. 470.
‖ Amer. Journ. Science, XX. p. 272.
¶ Voyage, &c. Preface, lxv.

that no one before Captain Cook and himself had noticed it. They saw it in 1773, when between 58° and 60° of south latitude, on February 18, and again on six other nights between that date and March 16th. In 1745 it was seen off Cape Horn by Ulloa, and described to Mairan in a letter; possibly it was also seen in 1712.* The *Aurora Australis* was seen in 1820 by Simanoff, astronomer to Bellinghausen's expedition.† It was seen repeatedly by Commander James C. Ross‡ in his Antarctic expedition in the years 1839–43, and also by Captain Charles Wilkes in the United States Exploring Expedition."§ The *Aurora Australis* is better seen in the latitude of 68° than farther south. If no account can be found of an aurora australis comparable with the richer examples of aurora borealis, the want may be explained by the fact that observers approach the high latitudes of the southern hemisphere but seldom, and then only in the southern *summer*, the *short nights* of which are unfavorable for any grand display.

The *Aurora Australis* was observed by Dalton in England‖ and the *Aurora Borealis* has been seen as far south as Mexico and Peru.¶ On January 14, 1831, Lafonde, when in latitude of 45° south, and in the longitude of the centre of New Holland, saw a brilliant aurora in the northern part of the horizon, which he described to Arago.**

II. *Effects of the Aurora.* 1. The brightness of the auroral light may be judged from the fact that it is sometimes seen in the daytime. "Lowenörn, on June 29, 1786, recognized the coruscation of the polar light in bright sunshine."†† Parry saw the great arch of a northern light continue throughout the day.‡‡ Perhaps the arch seen at noon in England on September 9, 1827, was of the same kind, as an aurora followed it in the evening.§§ Richardson saw, near Bear Lake, the pulsations of the aurora before the end of daylight: during the day he had noticed clouds assuming the form of the auroral arches and columns. Graham, at Aberfoyle, in Perthshire, observed the same thing on February 10, 1799. He says, the coruscations were as instantaneous and as distinctly perceptible as in the night.‖‖ Ussher, after describing the aurora of May 24, 1788, adds, that on the next day he saw white rays ascend from all points of the horizon to the pole of dip, where they formed a crown similar to that of brilliant nocturnal auroras.¶¶ Col. Force, in his *Record of Auroral Phenomena* has adduced another example of an aurora seen in the daytime, about 1806. At 11 o'clock, observers were astonished to see the *streaks and flashes* of the aurora borealis, occupying the same place that they had done the night before.***

The observations made very near the magnetic poles do not indicate that the light is more intense or frequent there than at some distance from them. In Hudson's Bay the brightness of the northern lights is equal to that of a full moon, and in Lapland and Sweden they enliven and illuminate the path of the traveller. Kerguelen describes the night as being as brilliant as the day in north lat. 50°. The auroras are in *oriental* magnificence, "the heavens being on fire with flames of red and white light, changing to columns and arches, and at length confounded in a brilliant chaos of cones, pyramids, radii, sheaves, arrows, and globes of fire." On September 3, 1839, the aurora was so brilliant at New Orleans as to call out the firemen with their engines. Mr. Thompson, after describing the blood-colored aurora of March 26, 1847, the light of which was brilliant in London, says: "And such was the vigilance of the metropolitan firemen, that upon this, as on other occasions, they set out to extinguish the aurora."†††

* Mairan, p. 441.
† Edin. Journ. Science, I. p. 347.
‡ A Voyage, &c., I. pp. 166, 261, 265, 283, 311; II. 209, 214, 358, 368.
§ I. p. 151, and II. 322, 328, 360.
‖ Phil. Trans., No. 461. Ib., xliv.
¶ Humboldt's Cosmos. I. p. 192.
** Œuvres de Arago. — Notic. Sci., I. p. 600.
†† Humb. Cosmos, I. p. 190.
‡‡ Journ. of a Second Voyage, 1821-3, p. 156.
§§ Journ. R. Inst., 1828, p. 429.
‖‖ Trans. Soc. Roy. Edin., V.
¶¶ Trans. Irish Acad., II. p. 189.
*** Smith. Contr., VIII. p. 2.
††† Introd. to Met., p. 355.

To ascertain whether the light of the aurora is *direct* or *reflected* light, physicists have resorted to the test of polarization. Although Arago had found slight traces of polarization in an aurora, and Baudriment claimed the same result for the aurora of October 22, 1839, Arago still hesitated to say that the light was reflected, on account of the possibility of foreign light being mixed with it, or the auroral light itself being reflected after it left the aurora.* Biot attempted in vain to find traces of polarization in the light of the aurora seen by him at the Shetland Islands, August 27, 1817.† Brewster stated to the British Association in 1837 that the light of the aurora was not reflected. Henry,‡ in 1839, failed to find any evidence of polarization either with Savart's or Arago's polariscope. Rankine made a more decisive experiment of a positive character. Having failed to get any sign of polarization in the direct rays of the aurora, he next examined the auroral beams when reflected from the surface of water, and found that the light was bright enough to show traces of polarization.§ He used a Nicol's prism.

2. The aurora was first known simply by its light. In 1740, two Swedish observers, Celsius and Hiorter, observed at Upsal that, during the exhibition of the aurora, magnetic needles were agitated in a way not observed when the needles were made of any unmagnetic substance, as copper. Wargentin, in 1750, made a similar observation. Since then the same thing has been noticed by Van Swinden, Bergman, Biot, Gay-Lussac, Hansteen, Dalton, and too many others to be specially mentioned. Back observed, on one occasion, a change of 8° in the declination. These disturbances by the aurora are felt not in the *declination* only, but also in the *dip* and *intensity* of magnetic force. Examples of this association between the aurora and magnetism have been given in the Almanac for 1857, page 84. Dalton says, "I have never observed any considerable fluctuation of the needle in any evening but when there was an *aurora* visible, except once."‖ The large magnetic disturbances observed at Cambridge, U. S., in May and August, 1841, were accompanied with brilliant displays of the aurora.¶

Arago has studied this relation with great assiduity, and discovered, as early as 1819, that the influence of auroras upon the magnetic needle extends to places which their light does not reach; so that an aurora seen in the north of Europe, or even in the Southern Ocean, telegraphs itself *on invisible wires* to Paris. The fact that Foster, at Port Bowen, *living in the very beams of the aurora*, saw no agitation of the magnetic needle, is explained by the general irregularity of magnetism at that place, or by the disturbance being adapted there to act on *dip*, and not on declination.

3. The electrical effects of the auroral flashes are next to be mentioned. These are not of a *statical*, but a *dynamical* kind. The statical electrical state of the air has been examined, and generally nothing unusual has been found at the time of an aurora. However, on November 17, 1848, (during an aurora at Pisa,) Matteucci observed decided signs of statical positive electricity in the air. Cavallo informs us that the aurora did not affect his experiments with the electrical kite, but that Canton frequently collected electricity in a considerable degree, on such occasions, by means of an insulated rod.** But the flashing of the auroral beams produces the same electrical *current induction* in the telegraph wires as is produced by lightning, only more persistently and regularly, on account of the rapid succession of the flashes. This fact was observed in this country on March 19, 1847, also in September, 1851, and in February and April, 1852. The aurora of last August interfered with the telegraphic operators in Canada and New England so seriously as

* Œuvres, S. N., I. p. 603.
† Precis. Elemen. de Phys. Exp., II. p. 100.
‡ Amer. Journ. Sci., XXXIX. p. 368.
§ Phil. Mag., IV. p. 452.
‖ Met. Essays, p. 73.
¶ Mem. Amer. Acad., II. p. 54.
** Cavallo on Elec., I. 75 and II. 38.

to delay the transmission of the news by the steamer Indian. "On the wires between Portland and Boston the operators were enabled to hold conversations, and transmit and receive business, on the current induced by the auroral waves, the usual batteries being disconnected from the wires." Between the Cambridge Observatory and Congress Street, Boston, the wire of the Messrs. Bond was traversed by waves of a minute in duration. The effect was observed even in the daytime. The semi-weekly New York Evening Post of September 28, 1859, has the following paragraph: —

"The splendid auroral display of the night of Sunday, August 28th, was witnessed throughout Germany, where also, as well as in other parts of Europe, its peculiar freaks with the electric telegraph were observed. This was particularly the case at Olmutz, Vienna, Oldenburg, Parduwitz, Cracow, and Brussels. The operators at Antwerp were aroused from their slumbers by the ringing of the signal-bells. At Paris, London, and Berlin, communications were interrupted till 1.30 A. M., while the submarine line between Dover and Ostend remained undisturbed. The aurora was also seen at Rome and other parts of Italy."

The telegraphic engineer of the *London and North Western Railway* has commented upon a remarkable effect upon the telegraphic wires by the aurora of November 17, 1848. He says, "A telegraph passing through Watford Tunnel, (1,600 metres in length,) the wires of which extended out 400 metres at one end, and 800 at the other end, was put *hors de combat* for three hours." * He adds that such an action of the aurora is common; that it is sometimes manifested in the daytime when the aurora is not visible. On the same occasion (November, 1848) Matteucci states that the operators at the telegraph office in Pisa were surprised to find the armatures cling to the magnets of the registers on the line from Florence to Pisa; though the apparatus was in good order, no messages could be sent, even when the battery was increased. Occasionally the armature would drop and the pen would strike, but the manipulation was performed by the aurora.†

4. It has long been under discussion whether the aurora was *audible* as well as *visible*. All may not be satisfied with the satirical remark of Humboldt in his *Cosmos:* "Northern lights appear to have become less noisy since their occurrences have been more accurately recorded."‡ Some compare the noise to the rustling of silk stuff; others to the crack of the electric spark; and many to the noise of a roaring fire.

Gmelin, the botanist, describes the splendid exhibitions of aurora he had witnessed in Siberia as follows: "It begins with solitary pillars of light, rising in the north and almost at the same time in the northeast, which, gradually swelling, at last comprehend a large part of the firmament, rush about from place to place with incredible velocity, and finally cover the whole sky up to the zenith, and produce the impression of a vast tent hung in the heavens, and glittering with gold, rubies, and sapphire. A more beautiful spectacle cannot be imagined. But whoever should see such a northern light for the first time could not behold it without terror. So constantly accompanied is it, *as I have been informed by several intelligent persons*, with hissings and cracklings like those of fireworks. The hunters who go in search of the blue fox to the confines of the Frozen Ocean are frequently surprised by the unexpected appearance of this meteor; their dogs are frightened by it to such a degree that they fall to the ground and will not move till the noise has ceased."§ The inhabitants have a phrase to express this particular noise, which translated means, "The raging host is passing." Cavallo, referring to the aurora, says: "Sometimes these coruscations,

* Arago, Œuvres, Notic. Sci., I. p. 705.
† Rive, Elec., III. p. 286. Arago, N. S., I. 702.
‡ Cosmos, I. p. 194. § Voyage en Siberie, II. p. 31. Reise durch Siberien, III. p. 135.

when strong, are accompanied with a sort of crackling noise distinctly, as I remember to have heard it more than once."* In the Edinburgh Encyclopædia we read: "When the aurora appears low, a crack is heard like that of the electrical spark. The Greenlanders think that the souls of the dead are beating the air."† Edmonston, in an account of a remarkable aurora which he observed at Unst, on November 1, 1818, states as follows: "I am now in company with two credible persons who, on a voyage from London to the Shetland Islands, were driven by winds to the latitude of 63½°, near the northernmost extremity of the island. While they were in this latitude an aurora borealis appeared; the noise with which it was accompanied was such that the sailors were afraid to remain on deck."

Edmonston said to Biot that he had himself frequently heard the noise, and thought it most like that proceeding from a large fire. Belknap wrote in 1783, from Dover, N. H., to the Philosophical Society in Philadelphia as follows: "Did you ever, in observing the Aurora Borealis, perceive a sound? I own I once looked on the idea as frivolous and chimerical, having heard it at first from persons whose credulity I supposed exceeded their judgment." He adds, that two years before, while *listening* to the flashing of a luminous arch, he thought he "heard a faint rustling noise like the brushing of silk." Last Saturday evening, he adds, I had full auricular demonstration of the reality of this phenomenon. ‡

Murray says: we "can remember, in our boyish days, to have heard this sound most distinctly, while numbers in Scotland can attest the same thing, — a species of fanning sound, like a thin curtain waving in the breeze." § Ramm, inspector of the forests in Norway, wrote to Hansteen under date of 1825, that, "in the year 1766, 1767, or 1768, he heard the noise of the aurora borealis. Ramm, who was then only ten years old, remarked this effect while traversing a prairie in which there was no forest. The ground was covered with snow and hail. The noise always coincided with the appearance of the luminous jets."‖ Wargentin states that two of his pupils, Dr. Gisler and Hellant, who inhabited for a long time the north of Sweden, related to the Academy of Stockholm that "the matter of the aurora borealis descends so low sometimes as to touch the ground: on the summit of high mountains it produces on the body of the traveller an effect like that of the wind."

Dr. Gisler adds, "that he has frequently heard the noise of the aurora. The noise resembles that of a strong wind, or the noise that some chemical substances make in the act of decomposition." Olmsted states that on one occasion his pupils thought they detected a noise proceeding from an aurora, but he found that they heard the same sound on the next night, when there was no aurora. ¶ In 1737, and on several occasions since, it was urged that a *smell* could be perceived in the aurora.**

Besides this positive testimony, we have that of Parrot, Nairne, Abrahamson, Brooke, Dr. Henderson in Iceland, Jameson in Shetland and on the mainland of Scotland, and Hearne at the mouth of the Coppermine River. This sound is said to have been heard in Connecticut in 1781 or 1782,†† and in the fine display of aurora on August 28, 1827, it was mentioned as having been heard in Rochester and Utica, N. Y., and also in New Haven, Conn. ‡‡

Muschenbroek reports from the last century that the same fact is generally affirmed by sailors employed in the whale fishery on the coast of Greenland. Biot affirms that among the inhabitants of the Shetland Islands the testimony

* Elements of Nat. Phil., III. p. 445. † X. 468. ‡ Trans., II. p. 196.
§ A Treatise on Atmos. Elec., p. 41.
‖ Phil. Mag. for 1826, p. 177. Arago, Notic. Sci., p. 556.
¶ Smith. Contr., VIII. p. 30.
** Amer. Journ. Sci., VIII. p. 392. Arago, N. S., I. p. 558. Phil. Trans., XLI. p. 593.
†† Cited by Thompson. ‡‡ Silliman's Journ., XIV. 101.

was no less full and complete. Sir John Richardson, who accompanied Sir John Franklin to the Polar Seas, relates that the natives of these northern shores, Crees, Copper Indians and Esquimaux, with the older residents in that country, testified that sound was emitted during the display of auroral lights. Hansteen observes: "We have so many certain accounts of the noise attending the polar lights, that the negative experience of southern nations cannot be brought in opposition to our positive knowledge."* And Biot, in view of facts like these, observes: "I am well aware how little reliance is to be placed on common opinion under circumstances calculated to inspire terror, or when influenced by the frightful appearance of rapid and unexpected commotions: but the assertions thus made, like all others, possess a degree of credibility; and if it is unphilosophical to believe without proof, it is equally so to reject without examination;" and again: "If any one will inquire, without bias or prepossession, into the reality of the sounds alleged to proceed from the Aurora Borealis, I am persuaded that he will not hesitate to adopt the common opinion, so striking is the coincidence of testimony on this subject." And still again: "It seems probable, after this mass of testimony, that the meteor sometimes descends so low as to allow us to hear the noise proceeding from it."†

The alleged reality of these auroral sounds has been questioned on the following grounds: Arago quotes Patrin, who passed nine winters in different parts of Siberia, and saw very beautiful auroras without hearing any sound from them. Patrin remarks that, "neither Bishop Eggede, who lived fifteen years in Greenland, of which he has given the natural history and meteorology, nor the pastor Horrebow, who has described 116 auroræ boreales which he observed in Iceland, make any mention of these noises and cracklings."‡

Lieutenant Hood, who accompanied Franklin to the Arctic regions, observes: "We repeatedly heard a hissing noise, like that of a musket-bullet passing through the air, which seemed to proceed from the aurora, *but Dr. Wentzel assured us* that the noise was occasioned by severe cold succeeding mild weather, and acting upon the surface of the snow previously melted in the sun's rays. The temperature was then —35°, and on the two preceding days it had been above zero." The same sound was heard the next day, when there was no aurora.

Sir John Franklin himself relates that, at Cumberland House in latitude of 54° north, the aurora was displayed almost every evening, but no noise was heard even when it was most active. The residents at the factory, however, assured him that it was frequently attended by a rustling sound. But it is so natural to associate the idea of noise with that of a rapid motion, that observers might easily be carried away by the delusion. Captain Lyon has said: "It is impossible to observe the sudden apparition and the great motion of masses of light such as compose the aurora, without imagining that they are accompanied with a certain rustling: I am convinced, however, that the sound is an illusion. I have frequently remained upon the ice, far from our ships, for hours, with a view of verifying, without having heard anything."§

De la Rive has the following passage: "Necker, who has described a great number of auroras which he observed in 1839–40, in the Isle of Sky, in Scotland, never heard the noise. But he remarks that the noise has been heard very frequently by a person in charge of the meteorological observations at the lighthouse of Swenburghead (at the southern extremity of Shetland).‖ Siljeström one of the *Commission Scientifique du Nord*, says: "As to the pretended noise, I cannot deny it. But there is reason to suspect an illusion easily explained. In fact, seeing the whole heavens covered with

* See Thompson's Met.
† Precis. Element. de Phys. Exper., II.
‡ Bibl. Brit., XLV. p. 80. Arago, Œuvres, Notic. Sci., I. p. 559.
§ Private Journal, p. 100.
‖ Electricité, III. p. 285.

flames, as happens in the finest auroras, and beholding the changeable lights and the rays rapidly darting, it seems to me natural that the spectator (especially if not accustomed to precise observations upon nature) should be led into error, so that in the appearance of fire he should imagine the crackling, and thus refer to the ear what he has discovered by the eye. The illusion, once entertained, would spread rapidly.*

Martins adds: "On returning to France, through Lapland and Sweden, Bravais and myself inquired of all the intelligent persons that we met. To our question, Have you heard the noise of the auroræ boreales? their answer was almost always affirmative; but when we inquired what the nature of this noise was, we obtained the most contradictory replies. When we insisted on the possibility of confounding it with the noise of the wind, that of agitated trees, the rustling of snow swept before the wind, or the murmur of the waves of the sea, we arrived at the conviction that these observers were not on their guard against all such causes of error; these noises struck them in the silence of the night, and because they were concomitant with a brilliant phenomenon, which attracted their attention. Thus these persons themselves were finally led to share in our incredulity, and to confess that they had adopted the received opinion, but that their conviction was not the result of an attentive and faithful observation." †

Biot, though he favored the positive side of this question, nevertheless heard no sounds on occasion of the aurora which he beheld at Unst, in the Shetland Islands, in 1817. He explained the failure by the noise of the sea at the time. Scoresby, Back, Ross, Franklin, Richardson, never heard the noise in the north, nor Thienemann in Iceland, ‡ Gieseke in Greenland, Lottin, Bravais, &c., near the North Cape; neither Wrangel and Angin on the Siberian coast of the Polar Sea, though they were familiar with the scenes of greatest auroral display. Wrangel and Gieseke were convinced that the sound they heard was to be ascribed to the contraction of the ice and the crust of the snow, on the sudden cooling of the atmosphere.§

III. The height of the aurora above the earth's surface has been variously estimated. Mairan has given the estimated heights of twenty-three different auroras, seen between the year 1631 and the year 1750. These heights vary from 47 French leagues to 275. The average is 175.|| Bergman, of Sweden, calculated one seen in 1760 at 334 miles, and another seen in 1764 at 254 miles. Cavendish estimated the height of the auroral arch witnessed in 1784 at from 52 to 71 miles. Dalton¶ computed the height of an aurora in 1793 at 150 miles, and of that of 1826 at 100 miles. Potter calculated the height of one in 1828 at about 200 miles. Dr. Burney, in 1830, found the height between 99 and 134 miles. Airy made the height of two, seen in 1833, 60 and 80 miles. Chevallier has computed the height of an aurora in 1841 and of two others in 1847, at about 160, 175, and 106 miles respectively.** Bravais has worked up the observations collected in 1838–9 by the Scientific Commission of the North, and comes to the conclusion that the auroras there vary in height from about 60 to 100 miles (*between* 100 *and* 200 *kilometres.*) †† Twining calculated the height of an aurora seen in this country in 1835 at about 42 miles; and of two others in 1836 at 100 miles, and 144 miles. ‡‡ Lyman calculated the height of an aurora in 1852 at between 140 and 280 miles. §§

Some doubt has been thrown on these and similar results by the statement of Parry,|||| that on one occasion he observed "a bright ray of the aurora shoot

---

* Voyage, &c., p. 559. † Kaemtz's Met., p. 460. ‡ Edin. Phil. Journ., X. 367.
§ Cosmos, I. p. 195. || Mairan, pp. 433, 434.
¶ Met. Essays, pp. 68, 69. and p. 231. Phil. Trans., 1828.
** Thompson's Met., pp. 360, 361. †† Aurora Borealis, Lottin, &c., p. 542.
‡‡ Amer. Journ. Sci., XXXII. pp. 220, 227. §§ Ib., XV. p. 55.
|||| Third Voyage, p. 61.

suddenly downward from the general mass of light, and between us and the land, which was then distant only 3,000 yards." Parry adds: "Had I witnessed this phenomenon by myself, I should have been disposed to receive with caution the evidence even of my own senses, as to this last fact; but the appearance conveying precisely the same idea to three individuals at once, all intently engaged in looking toward the spot, I have no doubt that the ray of light actually passed within that distance of us."

Mr. Hardisty communicated to Capt. Lefroy this fact, in relation to the aurora of 1850: "It appeared between me and the trees on the opposite side of the river, which could not have been 40 feet above the level of the stream, the trees toward the top of the hill being high above it."* An account is given in the American Almanac† of a similar case observed in Vermont. "We had not viewed it long, before we observed the eastern part of it had settled so low as actually to be between us and the highland on the north side of White River, at the distance from us, perhaps, of about one mile and a half. The meteor (aurora borealis) we apprehended must have been nearly perpendicular to White River, and distant about half a mile."

Farquharson, of Scotland, has insisted upon the low elevation of the aurora, assigning it in one case a height of only 5693 feet.‡ Liais computed the height of an aurora seen at Cherbourg in 1853 at about 2½ miles.§ Hood and Richardson concluded, from a comparison of their observations, that the aurora was not more than six miles high. Thienemann, Wrangel, and Struve also assign to the aurora an inconsiderable elevation.‖

To reconcile results so widely at variance with each other, some suppose that the height of the aurora varies very much at different places or at different times. Dalton has criticised the statements of Farquharson and Parry, as inconsistent or insufficient. Humboldt, Forbes, and Thompson think the strange fact mentioned by Parry was an optical deception, explained by the *persistency of sensation in the eye* after the object is removed, as in the case of lightning flashes or fire-balls. Bravais remarks: "The aurora may give so strong an illumination to light clouds that these clouds may seem to disappear, and the aurora be thought between them and the ground. Also the rays may appear to extend down in front of a mountain, but the prolongation is caused by the reflection by the snow."¶

It is generally conceded, however, that the usual method of computing the height of inaccessible objects, namely, by the parallactic angle between the two directions in which two different observers see the same objects, is exposed to great difficulties in its special application to the aurora. The rule is worth nothing, unless the two observers can be sure that they are looking at the same objective reality, and at the same moment. Many of the phases of the aurora are effects of *celestial perspective*. As each observer has his own perspective, this picturesque part of the exhibition is not adapted for determining parallax; and hence distance. In regard to *objective realities*, they are so changeable and complex that there is difficulty in establishing the identity of any particular feature. Possibly the whole phenomenon may be *subjective* instead of *objective*. In this case, every observer has an aurora all to himself, as every man sees his own rainbow, and no one another's. This supposition would preclude all determination of parallax. Arago maintained this opinion, he says, many years ago, in his "Lessons on the Physics of the Globe," given to the Polytechnic School. He does not claim it as original with him, having found, in Memoirs 100 years old,** the idea advanced that

* Lefroy's Second Report, p. 14.

† For 1832, p. 109.

‡ Phil. Trans. for 1829, p. 103.

§ Compt. Rend.

‖ Kaemtz, p. 459.

¶ Aurora Borealis, Lottin, p. 531.

** Perhaps he refers to Halley, who says, in 1716: "Hence also it will be easily under-the aurora of one place is not the aurora of another place. Some have supposed that although the crown of the aurora could not be used for parallax, because it was a *perspective phenomenon*, the eastern and western bow might. On this subject Arago remarks: "*L'orientation magnétique* of the arc of the aurora proves nothing except that the exhibition is arranged symmetrically in regard to the magnetic axis of the earth. As to the *kind* of displacement which the centre of the *cupola* undergoes with the change in the observer's position, it cannot be explained by any *play of parallaxes*. This displacement is such, that an observer who goes from Paris towards the north magnetic pole sees the centre of the cupola, which is to the south of his zenith, rise higher and higher above the horizon. Now this is precisely the opposite to what would occur if the cupola was a radiating summit, and not a simple effect of perspective."* He adds, "As soon as it is established that one part of the appearance is a pure illusion, we do not see why we should suppose that the luminous *bow* of Paris is the same as that seen at Strasbourg," &c.

It has been noticed that the breadth of the same bow is greater at its highest point than at its feet. Bravais computed from this difference the height of the aurora, according to a method of Hansteen, and found it about 60 miles.† The method of Liais, which he practised in the case of the aurora of October 31, 1853, consists in measuring the different times which the arc of the aurora requires to run over the same angle, first near the horizon, and then near the zenith, on the assumption that the real velocity is constant.‡

IV. The explanations of the aurora have been various. Some may be passed over lightly; such as that of the ex-King of Sweden, who imagined the light was ground out by the friction of the earth on its great axle.§ The *savans* of the 17th century supposed that the beams of the aurora might be exhalations from the solid earth. Halley, whose interest in the subject, and late opportunity for witnessing the phenomenon, have already been recited, submitted the following explanation, suggested by Des Cartes's theory of magnetism, and the radiant lines assumed by the iron filings sprinkled around the pole of a magnet:—That a delicate substance issues from the north pole of the earth, which gave the planet its magnetic polarity, and, in certain degrees of intensity or velocity, becomes self-luminous and betrays itself to the eye in the aurora.‖ At a time when the arrangement of the auroral beams in parallelism with the local resultant of the earth's magnetic force, and the action of the auroral flashes upon the direction of a compass-needle, had not yet been noticed, there was a felicity in what Humboldt calls "the bold conjecture hazarded 128 years since by Halley," that the aurora borealis was a magnetic phenomenon. Did not Halley come near anticipating the geometrical conclusions of Cotes and Dalton, when he says: "Nor is it to be doubted but the pyramidal figure of these ascending beams is optical, since according to all likelihood they are parallel-sided, or rather tapering the other way."¶

Cotes, of whom Newton said, "If he had lived we should have known something," was a young contemporary of Halley, and after observing at Cambridge, in England, the aurora of 1620, he gave an exact description of it, which he accompanied with some generalizations upon the subject, of great value geometrically, though no improvement upon the physical view of Halley. Vapors, fermentation, winds, furnish the materials and the motion of the aurora. To Cotes belongs the great merit of seeing, with a geometrical eye, the actual framework of the machinery, and deducing its whole complicated

---

stood that this *corona* was not one and the same in all places, but was different in every differing horizon: exactly after the same manner as the rainbow seen in the same cloud is not the same bow, but different, to every several eye."—Phil. Trans., XXIX p. 425.

* Œuvres, Notic. Sci., I. p. 554.

† Aurora Borealis, par Lottin, &c., pp. 480, 481

‡ Compt. Rend., XXXIII. p. 302.

§ Amer. Journ. Sci., V. p. 178.

‖ Phil. Trans., XXIX. p. 422.

¶ Phil. Trans., XXIX. p. 425.

perspective from the foreshortening and projections of parallel columns upon the spherical background of the spectator's firmament.* Contemporary writers missed of the happy physical hint of Halley and the geometrical clearness of Cotes. They contrived mixtures of nitre and sulphur, which exhaled vapors of gunpowder. These, ascending high in the atmosphere, were inflamed by pressure or motion, causing the cloud, light, sound, and motions which characterize the exhibition.†

When Mairan published, in 1733,‡ the great work on the aurora, to which allusion has already been made, he discarded all the theories which had been broached, and advanced a cosmical theory of the aurora, elaborated with great care, and supported with an immense array of circumstantial evidence. The sphere of attraction of the earth, within which it exercises undisputed sway, extending to 186,000 miles, Mairan supposed that the zodiacal light, which in his view is the sun's atmosphere, is entered sometimes by the earth in its revolution round the sun, and that parts of it, becoming entangled in the earth's atmosphere, go to compose the aurora. This was not a lazy conjecture, but an hypothesis carefully examined and cross-examined from manifold points of view, in the defence and illustration of which the great height and the annual and secular periodicities of the aurora were turned to the best advantage.

We have seen when and why the aurora was associated with magnetism. It was also, in the latter half of the same century, associated with electricity. Dr. Priestley says: "That the Aurora Borealis is an electrical phenomenon, was, I believe, never disputed from the time that lightning was proved to be one."§ Cavallo also says: "The aurora borealis, or northern light, was soon attributed to electricity, on observing that by this that flaming light may be imitated, and that the aurora borealis, when very strong, has been known to disturb the magnetic needle, which is also an effect of electricity."‖

In 1779 (?) Franklin wrote this in a paper on the Aurora Borealis: "May not, then, the great quantity of electricity brought into the polar region, by the clouds, which are condensed there, and fall in snow, — which electricity would enter the earth, but cannot penetrate the ice, — may it not, I say, (*as a bottle overcharged*), break that low atmosphere, and run along in the vacuum over the air towards the equator, diverging as the degrees of longitude enlarge, strongly visible where densest, and becoming less visible as it more diverges; till it finds a passage to the earth in more temperate climates, or is mingled with the upper air? If such an operation of nature were really performed, would it not give all the appearances of an aurora borealis."¶ Mr. Rowell has recently attempted an explanation of the aurora, which is no improvement upon this of Franklin.**

Thienemann, who resided in Iceland in 1820, refers the aurora to electrical discharges in feathery clouds in regions where thunder is unknown. Singer expresses thus the association of the aurora with electricity: "When electricity passes through rarefied air, it exhibits a diffused luminous stream, which has all the characteristic appearances of the northern lights. There is the same variety of color and intensity, the same undulating motion and occasional coruscations; the streams exhibit the same diversity of character, at one moment minutely divided in ramifications and at another beaming forth in one body of light, or passing in distinct broad flashes; and when the rarefaction is considerable, various parts of the stream assume that peculiar

* Phil. Trans., No. 365. Abridged, VI. p. 83.
† Phil. Trans., No. 395. Abridged, VI. p. 94.
‡ Mairan, Traité Physique et Historique, pp. 4, &c.
§ Hist. of Electr., p. 376.
‖ Sparks's Edition, VI. p. 420.
¶ Cavallo on Elec., I. 75.
** Edin. Phil. Journ., XLII. p. 561.

glowing color which occasionally appears in the atmosphere and is regarded by the uninformed observer with astonishment and fear."*

In 1773, Dalton, after a careful study for six years of the appearances presented by auroras, published a theory which he supposed to be entirely original. He was no reader, and was not aware of the geometrical generalization of Cotes, though attention had recently been called to it by Cavendish,† or of the physical theory of Halley, which, crude as it was, nevertheless associated the aurora with magnetism. He, therefore, reasoned out *originally*, and by the laws of optics, the same conclusions as Cotes had published long before, namely, that the real beams were parallel, and that convergence of rays, crown, and bow were all the wonderful effects of celestial perspective. With such clear notions of geometrical optics, he was prepared to study the aurora of October 13, 1792, which first suggested to him (and, as he supposed, to any one) the relation between the aurora and magnetism. He says: "When the theodolite was adjusted without doors and the needle at rest, it was next to impossible not to notice the exactitude with which the needle pointed to the middle of the northern concentric arches; soon after, the grand dome being formed, it was divided so evidently into two similar parts, by the plane of the magnetic meridian, that the circumstances seemed extremely improbable to be fortuitous; and a line drawn to the vertex of the dome, being in direction of the *dipping-needle*, it followed, from what had been done before, *that the luminous beams at that time were all parallel to the dipping-needle*."‡ These facts, as well as the disturbance which the aurora had been observed to exert over the compass needle, led Dalton to the conclusion that the beams were guided and held in position, not by *gravity*, but by *terrestrial magnetism*. Before Dalton wrote the *Preface* to his Essays, he had discovered the views which Halley had published, of which he says: "The *light* of the *aurora* he is pretty much at a loss to account for, as electricity was then but imperfectly known."§ We may infer from this casual remark to what origin Dalton would look himself, for the *luminosity* of the auroral lines. In the appendix to the second edition of the Essays, published in 1834, he says expressly: "In fact, the light of the aurora exactly corresponds with that of the electric spark, when sent through a tube in which the air has been rarefied to as high a degree as can be effected by a good air-pump."‖

Two other questions now arise. 1. What *are* the auroral lines, to be influenced as they are by the earth's magnetism? and 2. Whence the electricity which runs over and illuminates them? This is, in substance, Biot's answer.¶ The atmosphere is filled, at times, with metallic (Dalton says, ferruginous) particles, highly pulverized. These particles are magnetized by the earth, and then arranged, like so many floating needles, in parallelism with the local resultant of the earth's magnetic forces. These files of needles make a favorable channel for the discharge of electricity between the higher and lower strata of the atmosphere. For these strata are known, by the kite experiment and otherwise, to be unequally charged with electricity.

As the columns of needles are broken, the passage of the electricity through them will be marked by light. In high magnetic latitudes the columns are nearly vertical, and connect strata of unequal elevation and intensity of charge. Near the magnetic equator the lines of needles will lie horizontal and wholly in the same stratum, and hence offer no facility for the electric discharge.

The theory of De La Rive, though based upon the laws of electricity and magnetism as well as the one which has just passed under consideration, combines these laws in a different way to reach the result. He says: "We

---

* Elements of Elec., p. 251.
† Phil. Trans., 1790, p. 103.
‡ Dalton, Met. Essays, p. 146.
§ Ib. Preface.
‖ P. 244.
¶ Précis Element. &c. Physique, II. p. 107, &c.

have seen that the atmosphere is constantly charged with positive electricity, furnished by the vapors which rise from the ocean, particularly within the tropics, and that the earth is left in a negative state of electricity. The recombination and neutralization of these separated electricities is effected through the instrumentality of the moisture diffused between the extreme layers of air or between the upper layer and the earth itself. But it is especially in the polar regions, where the eternal ice prevails, and where the aqueous vapors will be promptly condensed, that the electrical recomposition will take place. The heavily charged equatorial current, originally at a high elevation, approaches the surface of the earth as it approaches the pole. *There* must be the great centre of the electrical discharge, with the accompaniment of light when the charge is intense; if, as is always the case near the poles, and sometimes in the higher parts of the atmosphere, it meets in its path with the minute frozen particles which form fogs and very elevated clouds."* De La Rive adduces, in confirmation of his views, the experience of Bixio and Barral, who, ascending to a great height in a balloon through a serene and cloudless sky, found themselves suddenly in the midst of a transparent veil of small frozen needles, so minute as to be hardly visible. De La Rive goes on to say, that these columns of frozen particles, when employed as the carriers of electricity between the earth and clouds, must be acted upon by the magnetic poles of the earth in the same way as a powerful magnet (an electro-magnet, for example) acts upon a jet of artificial electricity directed upon its extremity. In this experiment, the electricity does not descend indiscriminately upon the end, but comes only to its circumference and forms a luminous ring about it. Moreover, the ring rotates in its own plane round the pole of the magnet. Bravais noticed a rotation of the auroral arch in the direction of west, south, and east. The absolute diameter of the ring must be greater as the distance of the magnetic pole from the surface of the earth *downward* increases. Only observers on the same magnetic meridian would have the same identical summit to their arch. De La Rive is at no loss to account for the noise and the smell which are said sometimes to attend upon the aurora, according to the analogy which he thinks to establish between the great case of nature and the artificial, experimental illustration. The lunar halos which often precede the aurora, and the fall of rain or snow in the high latitudes which precedes or follows the aurora, all these alleged facts De La Rive considers as favorable to his hypothesis.

The late Professor D. Olmsted of Yale College, who published, in 1856, a valuable contribution * on the "Recent Secular Period of the Aurora Borealis," favors the theory of Mairan to the extent of supposing the aurora to have a cosmical origin. He argues against the *telluric* origin and for the *cosmical* origin of the aurora: 1. Because of the great extent of country over which the same aurora is displayed. 2. Because the principal phases occur on *all meridians*, not at the same *absolute* instant, but at the same *local times*. 3. On account of the great velocity of the motions. 4. On account of the periodicity of the aurora, especially the secular period. Therefore the material of the aurora is foreign to the earth, being the zodiacal light, as Mairan supposed, or some other nebulous patch which the earth encounters in its motion round the sun. As the aurora is susceptible to the earth's magnetism, this matter is magnetic certainly, and perhaps ferruginous. It may be illuminated by electricity or by the friction of grinding against the earth's atmosphere. Its own motion and those of the earth are so accommodated to each other, that at one period the earth almost escapes it, at another period barely grazes it, and at still a third period cuts directly into this nebulous substance. Mr. Olmsted observes: "The occurrence of these exhibitions at certain hours of the night, that is, the *diurnal* periodicity, (a circum-

* Elec., III. p. 268.

* Smith. Contr., VIII.

stance which belongs to auroras of the polar regions, when it is continual night, as well as to lower latitudes,) plainly indicates that the phenomenon has *some* relation to the position of the sun, although, after much reflection, I have not been able to satisfy myself as to the precise nature of that relation. The most promising chance of solution of the case, which has suggested itself to my mind, is that which connects it with the zodiacal light, which is known to maintain a nearly constant position with respect to the sun." * As early as 1837, Mr. Olmsted published his opinion that the origin of the aurora "is to be sought for in a source extrinsic to the earth." † He does not think that the recent theory of Rev. George Jones, namely, that the zodiacal light is a ring around the earth, and not around the sun, will diminish its availability for supplying the auroral material.

Mr. Olmsted quotes the following passage from Humboldt, to show that the latter treated the cosmical origin of the aurora with some favor. "If we regard falling stars and meteoric stones as planetary asteroids, we may be allowed to conjecture that, in the streams of the so-called November phenomena, when, as in 1799, 1833, and 1834, myriads of falling stars traversed the vault of heaven, and the *northern lights* were simultaneously observed, our atmosphere may have received from the regions of space some elements foreign to it which were capable of exciting electro-magnetic processes. ‡

Whatever may be the origin of the material which composes the auroral beams, it is, during the time of action, so far within the earth's atmosphere as to be subject to the earth's rotation. Biot found, in September, 1817, that the aurora did not move to the west with the stars, but maintained the same position in the visible firmament. Bravais also concludes his discussion of the aurora as follows: "It seems to me to be the result of our observations, that the aurora borealis has its seat at heights generally more than 100,000 metres, near the limits of the atmosphere, and that it must be considered amenable to its general movements of rotation and translation. But it is impossible at present to declare the *nature* of the *matter* which generates it. The analogies which ally the aurora borealis to terrestrial magnetism, those which seem to associate it with the *cirrus cloud* of high regions of the air, and also to the shooting stars, may put us upon the track of new observations, but they are not sufficient to close this important problem." §

I would remark, in conclusion, that there is not, necessarily, any inconsistency in the terrestrial and cosmical theories. The *matter* may come from the zodiacal light. But after the earth has obtained possession of it, it may *arrange* and *illuminate* it in accordance with the laws of magnetism and electricity, as applied to the case by Dalton and Biot.

When Mairan resolved the aurora into the zodiacal light, he left its light to be explained as that of the zodiacal light itself may be: in any way possible. He also supposed that the tails of comets were streamers of the zodiacal light in which these strange bodies had arrayed themselves. Euler, ‖ on the contrary, thought to explain the zodiacal light, the aurora borealis, and the tails of comets, all upon one principle: the *impulse* of the sun's rays. This impulse, acting on the sun's atmosphere, repelled some of it in a zodiacal ring; acting upon the comet's atmosphere forced some of it to form a tail; and acting upon the earth's atmosphere carried it high enough above the earth to be outside of its shadow, and to be in sunshine even at night.

Sir William Herschel, in his remarkable paper on the solar spots, published in 1801, ¶ has thrown out the suggestion, that the same causes which, in intense activity, produce the light of the sun, operating on the earth upon a diminutive scale excite the light of the aurora. His language is, "But it

---

* Smith. Contr., VIII. pp. 50 - 51.
† Amer. Journ. Sci., VII. pp. 127 - 298.
‡ Cosmos, III. p. 50.
§ Aurora Boréales, par Lottin, Bravais, &c., p. 550.
‖ Acad. Berlin. 1746.
¶ Phil. Trans., XCI. p. 304.

should be remembered that, on account of the great compression, arising from the force of gravity, all the elastic solar gases must be much condensed; and that, consequently, phenomena in the sun's atmosphere, which in ours would be mere transitory coruscations, such as those of the *aurora borealis*, will be so compressed as to become much more efficacious and permanent." If the analogy here suggested is a real one, it cannot be said whether our knowledge of the origin of the aurora or of the sun's light will be the greater gainer by it.

Captain John Ross, in the Appendix to the account of his second voyage, published in 1833, attributes the aurora to the sun's rays reflected from the ice and snow round the poles. The effect on the magnetic needle he attributes to the heat of these rays, as the same effect, in his opinion, was produced when the rays of an artificial flame were condensed upon it Mr. Wharton had the same view as Ross, because the aurora came from a place in the same azimuth as the sun, and converged to the opposite point above. Ross derives the color of the aurora from the brilliant colors of the ice. In the southern hemisphere, the ice is not colored, (according to the statement of Captain Cook,) and the aurora is white.

METEOROLOGICAL INFORMATION.

I. METEOROLOGICAL TABLES FOR PORTLAND, ME.

For the Year ending December 31*st*, 1858. *By Henry Willis.*

Lat. 43° 39′ 24″.49 *N.*, *Long.* 70° 15′ 24″ *W.*

1. Barometer.

Barometer cistern with constant level, No. 1225, by J. Green, N. Y. Scale, English inches, reduced to 32° Fahr. Station 87.5 feet above the mean level of the sea.

Months.	Highest.					Lowest.					Monthly Mean for each Hour.			Mean for the Month.
	Day.	7 A. M.	2 P. M.	9 P. M.	Mean.	Day.	7 A. M.	2 P. M.	9 P. M.	Mean.	7 A. M.	2 P. M.	9 P. M.	
		inch.	inch.	inch.	inch.		inch	inch.	inch.	inch.	inch.	inch.	inch.	inch.
January,	23	30.73	30.66	30.56	30.65	4	29.55	29.29	29.31	29.38	30.000	29.939	29.952	29.956
February,	1	30.26	30.37	30.37	30.33	10	29.22	29.20	29.41	29.28	29.889	29.819	29.862	29.856
March,	20	30.29	30.16	29.97	30.14	9	28.99	28.97	29.18	29.05	29.754	29.671	29.761	29.721
April,	19	30.24	30.16	30.12	30.17	14	29.43	29.34	29.36	29.38	29.845	29.793	29.827	29.822
May,	3	30.41	30.29	30.25	30.32	24	29.44	29.32	29.55	29.44	29.946	29.912	29.973	29.944
June,	9	30.11	30.04	30.01	30.05	11	29.54	29.66	29.79	29.66	29.915	29.873	29.892	29.897
July,	6	30.25	30.18	30.05	30.16	22	29.62	29.67	29.67	29.64	29.914	29.886	29.892	29.897
August,	13	30.24	30.27	30.28	30.26	29	29.62	29.57	29.59	29.59	29.947	29.900	29.972	29.940
September,	19	30.34	30.33	30.35	30.34	16	29.70	29.75	29.15	29.55	29.994	29.935	29.970	29.967
October,	17	30.55	30.49	30.44	30.49	7	29.81	29.53	29.33	29.56	29.992	29.963	29.955	29.970
November,	2	30.35	30.33	30.38	30.35	24	29.50	29.44	29.47	29.47	29.817	29.777	29.804	29.799
December,	12	30.39	30.45	30.56	30.47	22	29.03	29.27	29.63	29.31	30.014	30.011	30.015	30.010
An. Mean,		30.35	30.31	30.28	30.31		29.45	29.41	29.46	29.44	29.918	29.873	29.907	29.898

Barometer highest, Jan. 23d, at 7 A. M., 30.73 in.; lowest, March 9th, at 2 P. M., 28.97 in.

2. Thermometer.

Housed as directed by the Smithsonian Institution.

Months.	Highest.					Lowest.					Monthly Mean for each Hour.			Mean for the Month.
	Day.	7 A. M.	2 P. M.	9 P. M.	Mean.	Day.	7 A. M.	2 P. M.	9 P. M.	Mean.	7 A. M.	2 P. M.	9 P. M.	
January,	26	36°.5	43°.0	41°.5	40°.33	8	3°.0	13°.0	7°.5	7°.83	22°.93	30°.60	26°.63	26°.72
February,	28	30.0	42.0	40.0	37.33	12	−6.0	13.0	8.0	5.00	12.54	24.05	19.15	18.56
March,	30	37.0	50.5	39.0	42.16	6	3.0	20.0	14.5	12.50	24.61	35.88	31.57	30.68
April,	3	41.0	65.0	45.0	50.33	7	27.0	34.0	32.0	31.00	37.30	47.50	39.18	41.31
May,	31	52.5	67.5	51.5	57.16	3	39.0	48.0	40.5	42.50	47.95	55.60	47.66	50.40
June,	18	65.0	87.0	72.0	74.66	15	49.0	50.0	49.5	49.50	61.45	69.60	60.73	63.62
July,	11	75.0	87.0	67.0	76.33	12	57.0	56.0	54.5	55.88	64.62	71.98	64.32	66.58
August,	6	70.0	79.0	65.0	71.33	24	49.5	74.0	64.5	62.66	61.92	69.58	62.11	64.56
September,	8	65.0	87.0	68.5	73.50	23	40.5	56.0	46.0	47.50	55.62	67.70	57.88	60.40
October,	4	57.0	68.0	53.0	59.33	26	31.5	48.5	41.0	40.83	44.94	55.16	47.87	49.32
November,	1	42.0	58.5	48.5	49.66	15	16.5	30.5	24.0	23.66	29.88	37.42	32.60	33.26
December,	15	39.0	35.0	37.0	37.00	30	−1.0	5.5	4.5	3.00	18.45	25.89	22.65	22.30
An. Mean,		50.8	64.1	52.3	55.76		25.8	37.4	32.2	31.78	40.18	49.25	42.70	44.04

Thermometer highest, June 18th, July 11th, and September 8th, at 2 P. M., 87°; lowest, February 12th, at 7 A. M., −6°.

3. Weather.

Months.	Number of Days				Water, in Inches.‡	Snow in Inches.	Winds.§ — Number of Days							
	Clear.*	Cloudy.†	Variable.	Rain or Snow.			North.	South.	East.	West.	Northeast.	Northwest.	Southeast.	Southwest.
January,	1	4	26	9	2.995	9.	21	4	6	22	9	12	0	19
February,	1	3	24	7	2.513	15.5	5	5	1	29	6	29	0	7
March,	2	5	24	10	1.665	8.	12	10	2	17	10	33	3	6
April,	2	6	22	11	3.830	5.	15	10	9	24	8	9	12	3
May,	4	5	22	9	3.679		9	17	18	8	12	8	8	11
June,	1	6	23	15	2.150		10	14	21	8	11	6	8	11
July,	2	6	23	19	5.583		9	19	12	7	11	15	8	8
August,	1	6	24	14	4.693		5	16	21	9	7	9	20	6
September,	1	3	26	7	3.815		11	17	6	15	7	16	3	11
October,	1	8	22	14	5.606		16	12	10	14	3	21	6	5
November,	0	6	24	8	1.975	8.5	25	2	1	20	15	22	1	4
December,	1	7	23	13	4.919	16.5	30	4	0	14	11	19	1	13
Total,	17	65	283	136	43.423	63.0	168	130	107	187	110	199	70	114

Remarks. Jan. 2d, 10 to 10.15 A. M., solar halo, with rainbow hues. Jan. 8th, 6 P. M., to 10 P. M., brilliant aurora from east to west. There were but five days' sleighing during the month of January. March 3d, 1 P. M., shock of an earthquake; 1.50 P. M., second shock of an earthquake, lasting from six to 10 seconds, commencing with a sudden report. March 4th, 4 A. M., another slight shock of an earthquake. March 12th, 10 P. M., till morning, March 13th and 14th, 7 P. M. to 12 P. M., aurora visible. April 1st, wild geese passing north. April 14th and 15th, brilliant aurora seen through the clouds each evening. April 23d, distant thunder from 2.15 P. M. to 2.40 P. M. April 28th, 9.30 P. M., two Paraselenæ or mock moons observed for two hours; last snow in the spring. May 7th, 8.30 P. M. to 9.45 P. M., aurora visible. May 29th, 30th, and 31st, white frost, A. M. August 24th, first frost this season. Oct. 19th, 27th, and 31st, aurora observed. Oct. 21st, large lunar halo. Oct. 26th, ice formed this A. M. for the first time this season. Nov. 4th, first snow, 12 M. Dec. 1st, Penobscot River closed with ice at Bangor. The coldest day in the year, on the average of three observations, was February 11th, 2°.33. The warmest day in the year, on the average of three observations, was July 8th, 78°.5.

* Entirely clear, no clouds to be seen at three daily observations.
† Entirely cloudy, no clear sky to be seen at three daily observations.
‡ Melted snow included. § Three daily observations, at 7 A. M., 2 P. M., and 9 P. M.

II. METEOROLOGICAL TABLES FOR CAMBRIDGE, Mass.

Summary of the Meteorological Observations made at the Observatory of Harvard College during the Year commencing January 1st, 1858, and ending December 31st, 1858. By William Cranch Bond.

Lat. 42° 22′ 48″ *N., Long.* 71° 7′ 40″ *W.*

1. Mean Barometric Pressure and External Temperature.

Months.	Mean Height of the Barometer.						External Thermometer.				
	7 A. M.	9 A. M.	Diff.	2 P. M.	9 P. M.	Monthly Mean.	7 A. M.	9 A. M.	2 P. M.	9 P. M.	Monthly Mean.
1858.	Inch.	Inch.	In.	Inch.	Inch.	Inch.	°	°	°	°	°
January,	30.056	30.068	.077	29.991	30.031	30.036	26.7	29.2	36.7	30.9	30.88
February,	29.958	29.958	.077	29.881	29.924	29.929	17.6	21.5	28.1	21.7	22.22
March,	29.853	29.828	.061	29.767	29.821	29.817	25.7	31.1	39.0	30.6	31.60
April,	29.885	29.859	.042	29.817	29.850	29.820	39.3	45.0	52.5	44.2	45.25
May,	29.971	29.971	.028	29.943	29.975	29.965	48.8	53.7	59.6	49.5	52.90
June,	29.952	29.948	.040	29.906	29.926	29.933	63.2	68.6	75.5	64.1	67.85
July,	29.952	29.943	.034	29.909	29.925	29.932	64.9	70.2	77.1	67.2	69.90
August,	29.969	29.974	.030	29.944	29.964	29.962	62.2	67.6	73.5	63.0	66.56
September,	30.045	30.033	.031	30.002	30.012	30.022	56.3	62.8	69.3	58.9	61.82
October,	30.041	30.041	.057	29.984	30.019	30.021	47.9	53.2	59.8	51.5	53.01
November,	29.870	29.876	.048	29.828	29.859	29.858	32.3	34.9	40.4	33.5	35.02
December,	30.163	30.106	.050	30.056	30.063	30.098	24.7	26.4	33.0	27.7	28.01
Ann. Mean,	29.935	29.967	.048	29.919	29.947	29.949	42.47	47.02	53.71	45.24	47.08

Barometer.	Inch.	External Thermometer.	°
Mean pressure for 1858, . . .	29.949	Mean of the year 1858, . . .	47.08
Maximum, Dec. 24th, 7 A. M.,	30.923	Maximum, July 8th, 2 P. M.,	91.00
Minimum, March 9th, 7 A. M.,	29.080	Minimum, Feb. 19th, 7 A. M.,	1.00
Range, ...	0.843	Range, ...	92.00

The indications of the Barometer are given corrected for capillary action, and reduced to the temperature of 32° Fahrenheit, but are not corrected for its height above the sea-level, which is 71 feet.

2. Rain, Winds, and Clouds, *Monthly Means of Observations.*

Months. 1858.	Force of Wind, 0—6.						Quantity of Clouds, 0–10.				Amount of Rain, in Inches.
	7 A. M.	9 A. M.	Diff.	2 P. M.	9 P. M.	Sum.	7 A. M.	9 A. M.	2 P. M.	9 P. M.	
January,	1.57	1.70	+.19	2.19	1.35	6.75	5.03	4.84	4.97	4.45	3.439
February,	1.53	2.00	.47	2.21	1.39	7.13	3.71	3.82	4.14	4.39	1.862
March,	1.22	1.61	.39	1.97	0.93	5.73	3.67	3.64	3.36	4.18	1.767
April,	1.33	1.93	.60	2.13	1.03	6.42	5.43	4.03	5.86	6.50	3.809
May,	1.32	1.68	+.36	2.00	1.13	6.13	6.06	7.00	5.87	4.26	3.714
June,	1.33	1.30	—.03	2.10	1.20	5.93	5.43	4.83	5.20	5.70	7.552
July,	1.19	1.61	+.42	1.87	1.12	5.79	6.48	6.00	6.67	4.80	4.360
August,	1.19	1.70	.51	1.96	0.83	5.68	5.12	5.26	5.80	4.93	5.567
September,	1.26	1.70	.44	1.93	0.96	5.85	2.86	2.00	3.43	2.86	5.111
October,	1.26	1.32	.06	2.03	0.93	5.54	5.00	5.06	4.58	4.93	2.869
November,	1.40	1.60	.20	2.20	1.16	6.36	6.13	6.03	6.46	5.36	2.375
December,	1.29	1.48	.19	1.90	1.13	5.80	5.51	5.90	5.87	5.54	3.040

Amount of rain during the year, 45.465 inches.

III. METEOROLOGICAL TABLE FOR PROVIDENCE, R. I.

Summary of Meteorological Observations made at Brown University. Lat. 41° 50′ 17″ N., Long. 71° 23′ 40″ W. from Greenwich. Barometer reduced to the Sea-level, and to 32° Fahr., and corrected for Capillarity. By Prof. A. Caswell.

1. Mean Barometric Pressure and External Thermometer.

Months.	Barometer. Means of three daily Observations.				External Thermometer. Means of three daily Observations, with Maximum and Minimum.					
	Sunrise or 6 A. M.*	2 P. M.	10 P. M.	Monthly Mean.	Sunrise or 6 A. M.	2 P. M.	10 P. M.	Monthly Mean.	Maxim.	Minim.
1853.	Inch.	Inch.	Inch.	Inch.	°	°	°	°	°	°
January,	30.09	30.03	30.08	30.067	29.4	38.3	31.7	31.1	67	6
February,	29.97	29.93	29.96	29.953	20.1	30.3	23.1	24.5	47	3
March,	29.83	29.81	29.87	29.837	27.5	40.3	30.8	32.9	60	2
April,	29.91	29.86	29.89	29.887	40.5	54.7	42.4	46.2	69	30
May,	29.99	29.97	30.01	29.990	49.6	60.7	49.8	53.3	75	41
June,	29.97	29.95	29.97	29.963	62.5	76.2	64.5	67.7	91	49
July,	29.98	29.96	29.99	29.977	65.3	77.5	66.7	69.8	93	57
August,	29.99	29.99	30.02	30.000	62.2	73.1	64.0	66.4	80	49
September,	30.05	30.02	30.07	30.047	56.6	70.6	59.3	62.2	85	39
October,	30.07	30.02	30.08	30.057	49.0	61.9	51.6	54.2	82	33
November,	29.90	29.86	29.90	29.887	34.3	41.7	35.7	37.2	68	21
December,	30.11	30.08	30.09	30.093	28.3	36.4	31.5	32.1	58	14
Ann. Mean,	29.990	29.957	29.992	29.980	43.9	55.1	45.9	48.13	93	2

2. Winds, Clouds, and Rain.

Months. 1858.	Number of Days in which the prevailing Winds came from some Point between				Quantity of Clouds, from 0—10.				No. of Days on which Rain or Snow fell.	Quantity of Rain and Snow in Inches of Water.
	N. and E.	E. and S.	S. and W.	W. and N.	Sunrise or 6 A. M.	2 P. M.	10 P. M.	Monthly Mean.		
January,	4	2	10	15	4.1	5.2	4.0	4.5	7	3.33
February,	5	0	6	17	3.5	4.2	4.3	4.0	8	2.80
March,	2	2	8	19	3.4	4.0	3.6	3.7	6	2.05
April,	5	1	9	15	4.7	5.3	5.1	5.0	10	3.63
May,	14	2	7	8	6.0	6.0	5.3	5.8	14	2.35
June,	11	3	13	3	5.2	4.5	4.6	4.8	8	5.55
July,	6	3	11	8	6.2	5.1	5.0	5.5	7	4.90
August,	12	1	11	5†	5.7	5.3	4.7	5.2	13	8.20
September,	6	2	11	8	2.8	3.2	2.3	2.4	5	3.05
October,	8	1	12	10	4.9	4.6	3.5	4.3	8	2.80
November,	8	0	4	18	5.8	5.8	4.2	5.3	11	2.40
December,	5	3	7	16	5.6	6.0	5.6	5.7	14	3.45
Monthly Mean,	7.2	1.7	9.6	11.9	4.9	5.0	4.4	4.7	9.2	3.71
Total for the Year,	86	20	115	142					111	44.51

Remarks. The greatest height of the barometer (reduced as above) was 30.74 inches, on the 23d of January. The least 29.12 inches, on the 9th of March. Showing the extreme range for the year to be 1.62 inches.

The maximum temperature was 93° on the 11th of July, which was also the hottest day of the season; the mean of three daily observations being 81°.3, wind southwest. On the evening of the same day there was a very heavy thunder-shower. The minimum temperature was 2° on the 4th of March. The coldest day was March 5th, the mean of three daily observations being 10°, with a cutting wind at northwest. Range for the year, 91°.

* Observations are made at 6 A. M. from April 1st to October 1st, and at sunrise from October to April.

† Two days not observed.

IV. METEOROLOGICAL TABLE FOR WORCESTER, MASS.

Lat. 42° 16′ 17″ N.; Long. 71° 48′ 13″ W.; elevation 536 feet. Hours of Observation, 7 A.M., 2 and 9 P.M.

1857-58.	December.	January.	February.	March.	April.	May.	June.	July.	August.	September.	Extremes.
Thermometer.	°	°	°	°	°	°	°	°	°	°	°
Mean at 7	30	23	18	27	40	42	65	67	62	56	3
Mean at 2	36	36	29	41	53	59	76	77	72	68	92
Mean at 9	28	30	21	30	44	50	65	67	63	57	
Barometer.	Inch.	Inch.	inch.	inch.	inch.	inch.	Inch.	Inch.	Inch.	Inch.	
Mean at 7	29.503	29.496	29.442	29.344	29.424	29.459	29.448	29.472	29.488	29.509	
Mean at 2	29.483	29.472	29.410	29.354	29.329	29.431	29.413	29.424	29.427	29.468	
Mean at 9	29.515	29.517	29.362	29.432	29.337	29.422	29.416	29.462	29.455	29.505	
Cloudiness.											
Mean at 7	6.5	6.0	5.1	6.0	5.2	6.4	4.5	5.0	5.2	2.7	
Mean at 2	6.4	6.0	5.5	5.5	6.2	6.6	3.7	4.0	5.7	4.2	
Mean at 9	5.4	3.5	3.5	4.2	5.2	5.5	4.0	4.0	4.7	2.9	Total.
Inches of rain,	5.33	2.13	1.10	2.29	3.37	4.13	5.16	4.18	4.00	5.70	37.4
" snow-water	0.78	0.93	0.	0.	0.77	0.	0.	0.	0.	0.	
" snow,	9.1	8.5	4.5	0.	5.00	0.	0.	0.	0.	0.	
No. of Days											
Clear,	1	0	0	0	2	0	0	0	1	3	7
Cloudy,	30	31	28	31	28	31	30	31	30	27	297
Rainy,	15	7	8	11	12	17	9	9	14	7	109
Days of											
N. & N. W. wind	2	1	1	4	0	0	0	0	3	5	16
W. & S. W. "	3	2	2	3	7	3	2	2	0	1	25
S. & S. E. "	0	0	0	0	0	1	0	0	2	1	4
E. & N. E. "	3	1	1	0	2	0	2	2	6	2	19

REMARKS. By clear days is meant entirely clear, i. e. no cloud whatever being visible. By rainy days, that more or less rain fell, without any reference to quantity.

V. AMOUNT OF RAIN AND SNOW REGISTERED AT THE STATE LUNATIC HOSPITAL, WORCESTER, MASS., FOR SEVENTEEN YEARS.

Year.	December.		January.		February.		March.		April.		May.
	Inches Rain.	Inches Snow.	Inches Rain.	Inches Snow.	Inches Rain.	Inches Snow.	Inches Rain.	Inches Snow.	Inches Rain.	Inches Snow.	Inches Rain.
1841-42	4.77	6.0	1.35	5.0	4.13	3.0	2.24	4.0	2.82		3.24
1842-43	5.30	26.0	5.05	2.0	4.45	30.0	5.23	26.0	3.13	10.0	1.73
1843-44	2.28	23.0	3.14	13.5	1.44	12.0	3.80	18.5	0.35		3.67
1844-45	2.05	8.0	4.17	12.0	2.61	20.0	3.29	10.0	1.61		3.23
1845-46	5.39	13.0	2.92	13.0	2.50	30.0	3.33		1.34		5.85
1846-47	2.67	9.0	4.66	5.0	4.08	17.0	3.89	8.0	1.67		1.63
1847-48	4.93	10.5	3.06	4.5	1.61	25.0	3.69	6.0	1.52	5.0	6.82
1848-49	3.93	25.0	0.98	2.0	1.30	14.5	6.30	3.0	1.95		3.56
1849-50	3.12	8.5	4.79	16.0	3.23	2.0	3.67	20.0	5.53	13.0	7.50
1850-51	4.19	23.5	2.07	2.5	4.01	1.5	1.40	18.0	6.76		4.73
1851-52	2.30	5.5	5.44	15.5	2.46	11.5	3.42	13.5	10.77	23.0	3.50
1852-53	4.78	4.0	3.02	10.0	8.09	11.0	3.60	8.0	4.92		4.45
1853-54	3.79	20.5	2.82	7.5	6.62	15.5	3.45		6.69		6.78
1854-55	3.43	15.5	8.11	9.0	4.48	8.0	0.23	4.0	5.39		1.64
1855-56	6.90	10.5	4.60	27.5	1.35	9.0	1.69	10.2	3.34		6.55
1856-57	4.08	3.0	4.48	20.0	2.24	6.5	2.80	11.75	8.87		4.56
1857-58	5.33	9.0	2.13	8.5	1.10	4.5	2.29		3.37		4.13
Sums,	69.45	220.5	62.81	181.5	55.70	221.0	54.52	160.95	71.03	51.0	74.20
Means,	4.08	12.9	3.69	1.06	3.27	13.0	3.20	9.46	4.17	3.0	4.36

V. Continued.

Year.	June. Inches Rain.	July. Inches Rain.	August. Inches Rain.	Sept. Inches Rain.	October. Inches Rain.	October. Inches Snow.	November. Inches Rain.	November. Inches Snow.	Total. Inches Rain.	Total. Inches Snow.
1841-42	4.93	1.96	7.12	3.60	0.83		3.36		40.25	18.0
1842-43	4.15	3.39	9.19	1.25	5.19		3.63		51.69	94.0
1843-44	1.92	3.50	3.39	3.68	7.34		3.06	5.0	37.57	72.0
1844-45	3.14	2.91	2.36	2.57	4.44		6.77	4.0	39.66	54.0
1845-46	2.37	3.81	2.44	0.90	2.19		4.08	5.0	37.12	61.0
1846-47	5.29	4.86	4.20	7.17	2.87		3.75		46.94	39.0
1847-48	1.31	3.13	3.19	2.36	5.75		1.94	8.0	39.53	59.0
1848-49	1.25	1.60	4.28	2.49	6.45		4.11		38.20	44.5
1849-50	3.35	3.75	6.05	7.92	3.37		2.14	0.5	54.42	59.0
1850-51	3.16	2.17	1.97	2.50	7.04	4	5.68	5.5	45.68	55.0
1851-52	3.53	3.42	11.38	3.36	3.89		5.88	4.0	59.00	73.0
1852-53	1.01	3.29	10.71	5.26	6.20		5.30		59.65	33.0
1853-54	3.05	5.68	0.35	5.53	5.03		9.82	2.5	59.51	46.0
1854-55	4.19	9.40	4.06	0.20	8.17		5.85	2.0	55.05	38.5
1855-56	1.44	2 68	13.14	3.39	2.65		2 03	2.5	49.76	69.7
1856-57	3.44	3.80	5.75	4.92	3.93		3.12		51.89	50.25
1857-58	5.16	4 18	4.00	5.70					37.39	22 0
Sums,	52.69	63.53	93.58	62.80	75.34	4	70.52	39.0	803.31	887.95
Means,	3.09	3.73	5.50	3.69	4.70	.25	4.40	2.29	47.25	52.23

The above Table, increasing in value as years are added, exhibits the mean quantity of Rain and Snow for each month, the yearly mean, and the amount falling in each month and year during the last seventeen years.

VI. METEOROLOGICAL TABLES FOR LAMBERTVILLE, N. J.

Lat. 40° 22′ 45″ N.; Long. 74° 55′ 30″ W. Barometer 96 feet above Mid-Tide. By L. H. Parsons.

1. Summary for the Year ending August 31, 1859.

Months.	Thermometer. Mean. 7 A. M.	Thermometer. Mean. 2 P. M.	Thermometer. Mean. 9 P. M.	Thermometer. Maximum.	Thermometer. Day of Mo.	Thermometer. Minimum.	Thermometer. Day of Mo.	Thermometer. Range.	Barometer. Mean. 7 A. M.	Barometer. Mean. 2 P. M.	Barometer. Mean. 9 P. M.	Barometer. Maximum.	Barometer. Day of Mo.	Barometer. Minimum.	Barometer. Day of Mo.	Barometer. Range.
1858.	°	°	°	°	.	°		°	inch.	inch.	inch.	inch.		inch.		in.
Sept.	55.34	76.41	59.30	89.5	9	34.5	28	55.0	30.073	30.075	30.069	30.40	19	29.40	16	1.00
October,	47.78	65.71	52.34	88.6	4	25.8	26	62 8	30.086	30.066	30.068	30.50	17	29.58	7	.92
Nov.	33.81	44.39	37.72	66.0	1	19.5	10	46.5	29.924	29.920	29.946	30.26	1	29.52	23	.74
Dec.	28.77	38.42	33.85	56.0	15	10.0	19	46.0	30.102	30.112	30.119	30.66	25	29.34	21	1.32
1859.																
January,	24.24	37.75	30.24	56.6	28	-7.0	10	63.6	30.103	30.123	30.153	30.62	24	29.49	7	1.13
February,	26.78	40.06	31.79	60 3	23	4.3	8	56.0	29.988	30.000	29.993	30.38	11	29.50	20	.88
March,	37.95	53.21	42.78	67 5	22	12.5	2	55.0	29 879	29.878	29.890	30.52	2	29.24	19	1.28
April,	42.11	55.52	45.38	76 0	30	28.0	6	48.0	29.875	29.830	29.863	30.57	9	29.00	23	1.57
May,	54.12	71.47	58.18	90.1	8	36.0	5	54.1	30.042	30.054	30.054	30.35	4	29.73	9	.62
June,	64.06	77.39	62.91	98.0	29	38.0	5	60 0	30 015	30.003	30.009	30.26	12	29.65	17	.67
July,	68.54	53.64	67.49	100½	13	44.0	5	56.5	30.014	30.004	30.012	30.34	5	29.72	22	.62
August,	66.09	32.29	65.14	96.5	4	41.5	29	55.0	29.992	29.986	29.998	30.10	9	29.82	25	.38
Year,	45.79	60.52	48.92	100½	13*	-7	10†	107½				30.66	25‡	29.00	23§	

* July. † January. ‡ December. § April.

2. Weather for Year ending August 31, 1859.

Months. 1858–59.	Clear.*	Cloudy.*	Rain or Snow.	Water, in Inches.	Months. 1859.	Clear.*	Cloudy.*	Rain or Snow.	Water, in Inches.
September,	3	2	6	1.335	April,	3	6	16	4.702
October,	6	5	8	1.990	May,	3	8	11	1.261
November,	0	7	9	3.592	June,	2	6	7	3.014
December,	3	11	13	4.130	July,	0	4	9	4.040
January, '59,	1	8	11	4.889	August,	1	1	9	3.010
February,	0	6	14	3.167					
March,	4	4	13	5.916	Year,				41.336

3. *Average Monthly Mean for 22 Years, from 1837 to 1858 inclusive.*

Month.	7 A. M.	2 P. M.	9 P. M.	Month.	7 A. M.	2 P. M.	9 P. M.	Month.	7 A. M.	2 P. M.	9 P. M.
Jan.	24°.69	36°.19	28°.92	May,	56°.32	69°.88	55°.93	Sept.	58°.21	73°.64	60°.03
Feb.	24.82	36.13	28.62	June,	65.46	78.82	64.69	Oct.	45.25	60.43	49.77
March,	32.10	45.66	36.83	July,	70.87	84.00	69.88	Nov.	36.02	48.96	40.12
April,	43.64	57.62	46.37	August,	67.19	80.56	67.82	Dec.	27.87	37.90	30.82

4. *Annual Mean and Extreme Temperature for 22 Years.*

Year.	7 A. M.	2 P. M.	9 P. M.	Max.	Day.	Min.	Day.	Range.
1837	47°.02	58°.28	45°.89	91°.0	August 8	6°.0	February 14	85°.0
1838	47.01	57.76	48.58	97.3	July 11	0.0	December 31	97.3
1839	50.00	60.03	48.95	95.0	July 19	1.0	January 1	94.0
1840	48.66	58.41	47.19	89.5	July 16	– 6.0	February 6	95.5
1841	45.41	55.52	46.88	92.5	June 8	0.7	January 4	91.8
1842	46.20	57.29	47.52	88.0	July 27	10.0	February 17	78.0
1843	48.48	56.40	47.05	94.5	July 2	4.5	December 14	90.0
1844	44.49	57.64	47.49	94.0	July 14	0.2	January 28	93.8
1845	45.50	58.25	47.86	98.5	July 16	3.0	February 9	95.5
1846	45.62	59.08	48.05	96.0	July 11	1.0	February 27	95.0
1847	46.25	59.67	49.64	93.8	July 18	4.0	January 13	89.8
1848	47.09	61.11	51.22	97.0	June 17	4.0	January 11	93.0
1849	46.02	59.39	49.87	96.8	June 27	– 6.2	January 11	103.0
1850	45.65	60.11	49.83	95.0	June 20	8.0	February 5	87.0
1851	45.08	59.92	49.97	95.0	Sept. 12	–16.5	December 27	111.5
1852	45.49	59.66	49.84	97.0	June 16	– 8.5	January 20	105.5
1853	47.32	61.73	49.28	98.5	June 22	6.0	January 16	92.5
1854	46.29	62.77	49.16	100.0	July 21	1.0	November 22	99.0
1855	46.26	59.89	47.56	100.0	June 29	– 5.0	December 7	105.0
1856	43.03	59.05	46.21	101.5	July 18	–10.0	January 9	111.5
1857	44.47	59.43	46.73	98.4	July 13	–20.0	January 24	118.4
1858	45.46	60.46	48.75	98.3	June 26	– 8.7	February 24	107.0
22 Yrs.	46.17	59.62	48.34	101.5		–20.0		121.5

5. *Quantity of Water from Rain and Snow, and Depth of Snow, for 21 Years.*

Year.	Water from Rain & Snow.	Depth of Snow. †	Rain or Snow.	Year.	Water from Rain & Snow.	Depth of Snow. †	Rain or Snow.	Year.	Water from Rain & Snow.	Depth of Snow. †	Rain or Snow.
	Inches.	Inch.	Days.		Inches.	Inch.	Days.		Inches.	Inch.	Days.
1838	37.997		86	1845	42.884	39	129	1852	45.210	14	116
1839	44.008	18	97	1846	45.199	29	134	1853	42.924	24	97
1840	41.612	66	110	1847	51.034	10	108	1854	43.135	30	99
1841	57.363	22	142	1848	34.138	38	106	1855	45.174	36	115
1842	41.856	29	139	1849	43.731	17	101	1856	32.319	37	93
1843	51.320	25	137	1850	53.254	11	118	1857	48.657	31	125
1844	40.319	28	131	1851	32.450	47	85	1858	40.415	32	108

* Perfectly clear or entirely cloudy during the whole day.
† During the season *ending* each year as indicated.

VII. METEOROLOGICAL TABLES FOR SAVANNAH, GA.

For the Year ending May, 1859. By Dr. John F. Posey.

1. Barometer.

Barometer cistern with constant level, No. 465, by J. Green. Scale, English inches, corrected for temperature reduced to the freezing point. 42 feet above half-tide in the river.

Months.	Highest.					Lowest.					Monthly Mean for each Hour.			Mean of all the daily Means.
	Day.	7 A. M.	2 P. M.	9 P. M.	Mean.	Day.	7 A. M.	2 P. M.	9 P. M.	Mean.	7 A. M.	2 P. M.	9 P. M.	
1858.		inch.	inch.	inch.	inch.		inch.	inch.	inch.	inch.	inch.	inch.	inch.	inch.
June,	7	30.21	30.17	30.20	30.193	14	29.55	29.78	29.83	29 822	30 068	30.029	30.044	30.045
July,	10	30.14	30.14	30.14	30.140	24	29 83	29.75	29.84	29.805	30.026	29.987	30.018	30 009
August,	25	30.12	30.09	30.13	30.115	28	29.89	29.81	29.87	29.857	30.023	29.996	30 024	30.013
Sept.	19	30.37	30.34	30.36	30.357	16	29.88	29.63	29.55	29 705	30.109	30.061	30.059	30 066
October,	16	30.39	30.34	30.38	30.383	22	29.94	29.76	29.89	29 864	30 101	30.058	30.085	30 081
Nov.	26	30.33	30.29	30.35	30.330	22	29.73	29.68	29.81	29.740	30.024	29.998	30.064	30.035
Dec.	25	30.48	30.50	30.52	30.501	21	29.81	29.67	29.98	29.822	30.179	30.123	30.159	30.154
1859.														
January,	23	30.50	30.51	30.59	30.535	15	29.86	29.83	30.07	29.922	30.262	30.211	30.261	30 246
Feb.	1	30.43	30.32	30.27	30.341	9	29.58	29.56	29.70	29.613	30.117	30.067	30.097	30.090
March,	2	30.27	30.29	30.28	30.281	29	29.59	29.64	29.60	29 578	30 000	29.950	29.996	29 982
April,	1	30.32	30.30	30.25	30.290	22	29.86	29.77	29.62	29 751	30.036	29.980	30 000	30.000
May,	25	30.26	30.21	30.24		10	29.72	29.69	29.76	29.726	30.044	30.011	30.026	30.027
An. M'n,											30.062	30.038	30.071	30.064

Barometer was highest, January 23d, 1859, ... 30.569 inches.
" " lowest, March 29th, 1859, ... 29.537 "

Difference, ... 1.052 "

2. Thermometer.

Made by J. Green, New York; housed as directed by the Smithsonian Institution.

Months.	Highest.					Lowest.					Monthly Mean for each Hour.			Mean of all the daily Means.	Rain-Gauge.	Rainy Days.	Relative Humidity.
	Day.	7 A. M.	2 P. M.	9 P. M.	Mean.	Day.	7 A. M.	2 P. M.	9 P. M.	Mean.	7 A. M.	2 P. M.	9 P. M.				
1858.		°	°	°	°		°	°	°	°	°	°	°	°	Inch.		
June,	1	76.0	93.3	82.6	83 97	14	67 6	82 6	75.0	75.07	75.8	86.8	78.1	80.07	2.901	6	.76
July,	4	81.6	96.9	78.9	85.77	7	70 3	72 4	70.7	71.13	77.2	87.7	79.6	81.49	5.774	15	.79
Aug.	3	79.5	95.6	85.5	86 87	30	69 3	83.9	76.1	76 43	76.5	86.5	78.9	80.50	3.324	11	.81
Sept.	3	75.5	89.8	80.5	81.93	29	55.8	71.8	65 0	64.20	68.4	77.5	72 0	72.65	14.198	12	.80
Oct.	7	71.1	87.8	78.3	79.07	15	53.8	68.0	61.5	61.10	64.9	75.8	69.4	70.03	1.543	8	.77
Nov.	2	68.7	79.9	69 0	72.53	25	34 2	52 0	46.3	44.17	47.5	59.0	52.4	52 62	3.371	10	.71
Dec.	8	64.0	75.4	68.9	69.43	10	36.0	52.8	44.1	34.30	53.9	63.0	57.5	58.15	5.948	11	
1859.																	.81
Jan.	21	64.0	73.5	63.3	66.93	24	26.1	46.1	43 5	38.23	45 7	56 2	50.9	50.91	3.134	6	.73
Feb.	25	62.2	80 5	71.3	71.33	1	37.0	52.9	47.8	45 90	49.3	62.3	55.2	55.72	2.764	5	.74
March	29	63.7	83.3	75.4	75.80	19	43.3	57.9	51.7	50.97	57 3	67.7	58.4	61.91	4.239	13	.73
April,	14	70.4	89.5	75 6	78.50	6	43 0	55.3	49.4	49 33	62.4	72.6	64.0	65.39	1.237	5	.68
May,	14	71.0	88.6	75.7	78.43	1	54.0	71.3	64 2	63.17	66 6	78.4	70.0	71.68	2.872	6	.74
Mean,											62.1	72.6	65.5	66.76	51.205	108	

Thermometer was highest, July 4th, 1858, ... 96°.9
" " lowest, January 24th, 1859, ... 26.1

Difference, ... 70.8

VIII. METEOROLOGICAL TABLES FOR MUSCATINE, Iowa.

For the Year 1858. *By* T. S. Parvin, *Smithsonian Observer.*

Lat. 41° 25′ *N., Long.* 92° 2′ *W. (proximate).*

Barometer 72.21 ft. above low water in (and 586.21 ft. above the mouth of) the Mississippi River.

Months.	Barometer, Height reduced to Freezing Point. 7 A. M.	2 P. M.	9 P. M.	Monthly Mean.	Thermometer, in the Open Air. 7 A. M.	2 P. M.	9 P. M.	Monthly Mean.	Maximum.	Minimum.	Force of Vapor. 7 A. M.	2 P. M.	9 P. M.	Relative Humidity. 7 A. M.	2 P. M.	9 P. M.
1858.	Inch.	Inch.	Inch.	Inch.	°	°	°	°	°	°	inch.	inch.	inch.			
January,	29.51	29.48	29.52	29.50	24.7	34.1	28.3	29.96	52	8	.380	.439	.429	67	66	63
Feb'ry,	.59	.58	.60	.58	10.5	22.1	15.1	15 98	46	-17	.306	.393	.368	61	66	63
March,	.64	.62	.63	.62	31.5	47.5	36 1	38.71	70	1	.430	.529	.517	71	73	74
April,	.47	.45	.37	.43	41.3	52.6	41.4	46.12	78	24	.289	.316	.323	83	84	80
May,	.45	.45	.50	.44	56.0	57.4	55.4	54.31	81	39	.417	.433	.503	80	67	86
June,	.47	.42	.38	.40	67.4	75.3	66.1	70.62	96	52	.698	.800	.724	89	85	86
July,	.49	.46	.44	.46	67.8	84.8	72 0	78.80	89	52	.745	.601	.809	87	82	89
August,	.52	.53	.49	.50	65.2	81.3	72 3	79.89	93	46	.681	.759	.781	86	81	87
Sept'ber,	.53	.52	.52	.51	55.7	72.9	62.0	66.93	87	42	.549	.573	.552	85	81	83
October,	.47	.45	.44	.45	46.9	56.6	50.7	51.99	85	30	.380	.381	.389	87	83	89
Nov'ber,	.51	.49	.50	.50	29.6	37.2	31.6	32.61	52	4	.293	.317	.342	75	70	72
Dec'ber,	29.52	29.68	29.59	29.60	20.1	31.2	22 2	25.53	43	-15	.345	.458	.434	67	63	64
Means,	29.51	29.50	29.49	29.50	43.0	54.7	46.1	49.29	73	22	.435	.516	.517	78	77	79

Clouds, Rains, Winds, etc.

Months. 1858.	Clouds, Amount and Course. Amount from 10 to 0. 7 A. M.	2 P. M.	9 P. M.	N.—N.E.	E.—S.E.	S.—S.W.	W.—N.W.	Weather (days). Clear.	Cloudy.	Variable.	Rain. Days.	Amount in inches.	Snow. Days.	Depth in inches.	Winds, Direction and Force. Force from 0 to 10. N.—N.E.	E.—S.E.	S.—S.W.	W.—N.W.	7 A. M.	2 P. M.	9 P. M.
January,	2.7	2.6	2.2			3	1	19	5	7	6	1.60			1	2	14	14	1.5	1.5	1.5
Feb'ry,	1.7	2.2	1.6				3	18	3	7		2.00	3	18.00	4	4	4	16	1.3	1.3	1.8
March,	2.6	3.3	3.3			3	3	15	6	10	6	2.20			2	11	7	11	1.3	1.8	1.5
April,	4.6	4.9	5.8	4	2	6	6	7	16	7	11	5.67	1	2.00	5	9	5	11	1.4	1.9	1.5
May,	4.9	4.9	5.6	2		4	5	6	19	6	21	8.40			6	9	6	10	1.4	1.6	1.7
June,	2.9	3.2	3.9			11		11	9	10	6	6.67			3	8	15	4	1.0	1.3	1.0
July,	6.0	6.8	5.6	4		13	5	6	19	6	16	7.30			6	11	9	5	.9	1.0	.6
August,	2.5	4.1	2.6		1	6	11	15	6	10	8	4.12			10	5	10	6	.9	1.0	.9
Sept'ber,	1.7	1.5	1.8	2		7	1	20	4	6	7	6.10			3	2	17	8	1.1	2.0	1.1
October,	6.3	5.6	6.3	3	1	5	1	9	14	18	13	4.95			2	9	11	9	1.4	1.9	1.3
Nov'ber,	8.0	7.3	6.4	2		3	2	4	19	7	11	4.00	8	5.40	11	2	3	14	1.2	1.4	1.1
Dec'ber,	3.6	4.1	4.3			6	2	14	10	7	5	1.70	3	12.00	2	1	18	10	1.3	1.7	1.1
An. M'n,	3.9	4.2	3.9	1	0	5	3	12	10	8	9	4.56	4	9.35	4	6	10	10	1.2	1.5	1.2

Lowest Temperature, February 10th, —17°. Highest, June 22d, 96°. Range, 113°. Mean, 49°.29. Average Mean for 19 years, 47°.12. Greatest Range of mean temperature, 6°.39. Lowest height of barometer, April 8th, 28.66 inches; thermometer attached, 45°. Greatest, January 7th, 30.17 inches; thermometer attached, 25°. Range, 1.51 inches. Mean height, 29.50 inches.

Frost, last in the spring, April 26th; first in the fall, September 12th. Disappearance of frost from the ground, April 1st. Depth of ground frozen, 1 foot. Thickness of ice in the river, 9 inches.

January, temperature mild; heavy snow first week; good stage of water and boats all the month. February, dry, with some severe cold weather; boats in the early part of the month; river then full of ice. April 13th, snow and hail storm; last half of month very wet; five inches rain. May, very wet; rivers high; farmers unable to plough. June, very wet;

high waters; low lands overflowed, and but little corn planted. July, continued rains and high waters. August, first half very hot, and last half very cool. September, first half wet, and last half dry; waters falling, with good stage in the Mississippi; corn ripened, with an average crop; wheat and oats failed. October, first half of month pleasant weather, last half very disagreeable, and with the whole of November, continued rains. December, weather mild; river open and boats running.

IX. METEOROLOGICAL TABLE FOR SACRAMENTO, CAL.

For the Year ending March 31st, 1859. Lat. 38° 34′ 41″ *N., Long.* 121° 27′ 44″ *W. Elevation above the Level of the Sea, at the Levee in front of the City,* 40 *feet. Height of the lower surface of the Mercury,* 41 *feet above the Sea at San Francisco. By Thomas M. Logan, M. D.*

1858 - 59.	April.	May.	June.	July.	August.	September.	October.	November.	December.	January.	February.	March.	Mean.
Barometer.	inch	inch.	inch.	inch.	inch.	inch.	inch.	inch	inch	inch.	inch	inch.	inch.
Maximum,	30.21	30.15	30.00	30.01	30.09	30.13	30.31	30.26	30.36	30.49	30.33	30 38	30.230
Minimum,	29.79	29.77	29.72	29.74	29.75	29.63	29.62	29.85	29.82	29.44	29.63	29.77	29.711
Mean,	29.99	29.96	29.86	29.88	29.90	29.91	29.99	30.07	30.11	30.21	30.03	30.16	30.005
Thermometer.	°	°	°	°	°	°	°	°	°	°	°	°	°
Maximum,	81.00	80.00	96.00	97.00	85.00	87.00	79.00	66.00	62.00	57.00	62 00	64.00	74 67
Minimum,	46.00	65.00	61.00	59.00	61.00	55.00	43.00	39.00	29.00	34.00	39.00	40.00	46 75
Mean,	59.50	65.19	69.43	70.81	70.57	68.90	59.51	54.23	44.47	44.57	50.49	51.47	59.15
Thermometrograph.													
Maximum,	85.00	81.00	92.00	98.00	90 00	92.00	80.00	69.00	53 00	58.00	63.00	66.00	77.25
Minimum,	42 00	46 00	52.00	53.00	55.00	50.00	38.00	34 00	23.00	30 00	34.00	36.00	41.06
Range,	43.00	35.00	40.00	45.00	35.00	42.00	42.00	35.00	30.00	28.00	29 00	30.00	36.17
Dew-Point.	p. ct	p. ct.	p. ct.	p. ct.	p. ct	p. ct.	p. ct.	p. ct.	p. ct.	p. ct	p. ct	p. ct.	p. ct.
Maximum,	87.00	82.00	92.00	76.00	79.00	74.00	88.00	94 00	92.00	93.00	94 00	92.00	86.08
Minimum,	38.00	30.00	22.00	19.00	33.00	22.00	26 00	29.00	19.00	32 00	60.00	19.00	29.08
Mean,	67.30	61.48	59.57	60.05	62.81	59.01	65.18	73.58	74.98	78.05	78.73	68.32	67.42
No. of Days													Total.
Clear,	15⅓	16	17⅓	24⅔	18⅓	19⅔	10⅓	13⅓	6⅓	7	3⅓	11	162⅔
Cloudy & foggy.	14⅔	15	12⅔	6⅓	12⅔	10⅓	20⅔	16⅔	24⅔	24	24⅔	20	202⅓
Rainy,	3	4	2	0	4	1	4	3	11	7	16	14	69
Inches of Rain,	1.214	0.203	0.096	0.000	sprinkle.	sprinkle.	3.010	0.147	4.339	0.964	3.906	1.637	15.518
Days of													
N. wind,	4⅓	2⅔	⅔	1	1	5	8⅓	11⅔	9⅓	11⅓	4⅓	8⅔	66⅓
N. W. "	7⅓	6⅔	4	1⅔	1⅓	3	7⅓	4	6⅔	2⅔	0	2⅔	45⅓
W. "	2⅓	1⅓	2	2⅔	3⅔	3	2⅓	⅓	0	0	2	4	23⅔
S W. "	5⅓	7⅔	7⅓	7	6⅓	4⅔	2⅓	1	2	1⅓	3⅔	4⅔	53⅓
S. "	3	6	10⅓	12	9⅔	5⅔	5	⅔	3⅓	2	8⅓	4	70
S. E. "	3⅔	4⅔	5	6⅔	6	7⅓	3⅔	5⅔	7⅓	6⅓	8	5	62⅓
E. "	1⅓	⅓	⅓	⅓	1⅔	⅓	⅔	4	1⅔	1⅓	⅔	1	14
N. E. "	2⅔	2⅔	⅓	⅓	1⅓	⅔	1⅓	2⅔	1⅔	6	1	1	22

REMARKS. The observations were made three times a day, conformably with the hours adopted by the Smithsonian Institution. The indications of the Barometer are given corrected for capillary action, and reduced to the temperature of 32° Fahrenheit, but are not corrected for its height above the sea-level. The rainy days are included under the head of cloudy and foggy days, and are also put separately to show the number of days on which rain fell during the month. The last rain of the season of 1857-58 occurred on the 18th of June. The first rain of 1858-59 occurred on the 21st of October, and is the heaviest on record for that period. From this date the winter or rainy season may be said to have set in, and proved the severest, both as to intensity and prolongation of cold, on record. The spring of 1859 was one month later than usual. White frost was seen as late as the 12th of April. The last frost of the season of 1857-58 was seen on the 28th of March. The Sacramento River, owing to the lateness of the melting of the snow on the mountains, did not reach its highest point until the 24th of May, 1859.

X. RAIN AT POWHATAN HILL, KING GEORGE CO., VA.

	1st quarter.	2d.	3d	4th.	Total.
1857.	0.86	8.32	12.105	8.725	30.01 inches.

		Inches.	Rain fell.			Inches.	Rain fell.
1857.	July,	6.085	11 days.	1857.	October,	2.015	5 days.
	August,	4.975	9 "		November,	1.28	5 "
	September,	1.045	6 "		December,	5.43	11 "
		12.105	26 "			8.725	21 "

	1st quarter.	2d.	3d.	4th.	Total.
1858.	2.835	8.94	8.315	9.91	30 inches.

		Inches.	Rain fell.			Inches.	Rain fell.
1858.	January,	0.635	5 days.	1858.	July,	1.635	7 days.
	February,	1.745	8 "		August,	3.225	9 "
	March,	0.455	5 "		September,	3.455	8 "
	April,	2.67	12 "		October,	1.80	8 "
	May,	5.145	15 "		November,	3.83	10 "
	June,	1.125	8 "		December,	4.28	14 "

	1st quarter.	2d.	Total.
1859.	7.735	12.965	In 6 months, 20.7 inches.

		Inches.	Rain fell.		Inches.	Rain fell.
1859.	January,	3.27	9 days.	April,	3.99	13 days.
	February,	1.77	9 "	May,	2.845	8 "
	March,	2.695	12 "	June,	6.13	12 "

Heaviest Rains from July to December, 1857.

Aug. 4th and 5th, 3.005; July 11th, 1.79; 1st, 1.685; Dec. 30th, 1.205; Oct. 16th, 1.085; Dec. 17th and 18th, 1.075; July 31st, 1.005. — Three rains over 1½ inches, 4, from 1 to 1½ inches, 6, from ½ to 1 inch, 32, under ½ inch.

Snow. — Dec. 25th, 2 inches.

Frost. — Sept. 30th, Oct. 1st, and 21st, killing frost; Nov. 19th, severe.

Ice. — Oct. 21st, a skim; Nov. 21st, 1 inch: Dec. 11th, a skim.

Heaviest Rains in 1858.

Sept. 15th and 16th, 1.505: Aug. 18th, 1.415: Nov. 3d, 1.12; May 18th, 1.085; Sept. 11th, 1.075; Dec. 29th, 30th, and 31st, 1.025; Dec. 7th and 8th, 1.02. — One rain over 1½ inches, 6 from 1 to 1½ inches, 12 from ½ to 1 inch, 75 under ½ inch.

Snow. — Feb. 13th, 5 inches; 20th, 2 inches; March 6th, ½ inch; 8th, 6 inches; April 26th, ground white.

Frost. — April 24th and 26th, frost; Oct. 9th, 26th, 27th, 28th, killing frost.

Ice. — Jan. 19th, a skim; 23d, ½ inch; 30th, a skim; Feb. 6th, ¼ inch; 11th, ¼ inch; 17th, 2¼ inches; 18th, 3 inches; 23d, 3 inches; Nov. 19th, ¼ inch; Dec. 1st, ¼ inch; 9th, ½ inch; 23d, a skim; 25th, ½ inch.

Heaviest Rains from January to July, 1859.

June 17th, 2.385; 16th, 2.345 (4.73 inches in 2 days); April 28th, 1.075; 22d and 23d, 1.045; Jan. 21st, 1.03. — Two rains over 2 inches, 3 from 1 to 1½ inches, 8 from ½ to 1 inch, 43 under ½ inch.

Snow. — Feb. 26th, 1 inch.

Frost. — April 1st, 2d, and 6th, killing; 7th and 9th, killing: 19th, May 2d, and June 5th.

Ice. — Jan. 2d, a skim; 11th, 3 inches; 24th 1½ inches; 26th, 2 inches nearly.

Flowering of Fruit Trees in 1858.

Apricot, March 22d. Peach, April 3d to 5th. Plum, April 5th to 8th. Cherry, April 5th to 8th. Pear, April 9th. Apple, April 13th to 17th.

Flowering of Fruit Trees in 1859.

Apricot, March 12th. Peach, March 18th to 23d. Plum, March 23d to 28th. Cherry, March 28th. Pear, April 4th. Apple, April 12th. — Fruit of Apricot, Plum, and some Peaches destroyed by frost of April 9th.

*** The Table of the "Flowering of Fruit Trees in 1859," for want of space here, is transferred to the "Corrections and Additions," at the end of the volume.

THE

AMERICAN ALMANAC,

FOR

1860.

PART II.

UNITED STATES.

I. PRESIDENTS OF THE UNITED STATES FROM THE ADOPTION OF THE CONSTITUTION.

			Term Began.	Term Ended.
1.	George Washington,	Virginia,	April 30, 1789,	March 3, 1797.
2.	John Adams,	Massachusetts,	March 4, 1797,	March 3, 1801.
3.	Thomas Jefferson,	Virginia,	March 4, 1801,	March 3, 1809.
4.	James Madison,	Virginia,	March 4, 1809,	March 3, 1817.
5.	James Monroe,	Virginia,	March 4, 1817,	March 3, 1825.
6.	John Quincy Adams,	Massachusetts,	March 4, 1825,	March 3, 1829.
7.	Andrew Jackson,	Tennessee,	March 4, 1829,	March 3, 1837.
8.	Martin Van Buren,	New York,	March 4, 1837,	March 3, 1841.
9.	William H. Harrison,*	Ohio,	March 4, 1841,	April 4, 1841.
10.	John Tyler,	Virginia,	April 4, 1841,	March 3, 1845.
11.	James Knox Polk,	Tennessee,	March 4, 1845,	March 3, 1849.
12.	Zachary Taylor,*	Louisiana,	March 4, 1849,	July 9, 1850.
13.	Millard Fillmore,	New York,	July 9, 1850,	March 3, 1853.
14.	Franklin Pierce,	New Hampshire,	March 4, 1853,	March 3, 1857.
15.	James Buchanan,	Pennsylvania,	March 4, 1857.	

II. EXECUTIVE GOVERNMENT.

The 18th Presidential term of four years, since the establishment of the government of the United States under the Constitution, began on the 4th of March, 1857; and it will expire on the 3d of March, 1861. An election in each State throughout the United States for Electors of President and Vice-President, for the 19th Presidential term of four years from the 4th of March, 1861, will be held on the Tuesday next after the first Monday of November, 1860 (November 6th).

		Salary.
JAMES BUCHANAN, of Pennsylvania,	*President,*	$25,000
John C. Breckinridge, of Kentucky,	*Vice-President,*	8,000

The Cabinet.

The following are the principal officers in the *executive department* of the government, who form the Cabinet, and who hold their offices at the will of the President.

Lewis Cass,	Michigan,	*Secretary of State,*	$8,000
Howell Cobb,	Georgia,	*Secretary of the Treasury,*	8,000
John B. Floyd,	Virginia,	*Secretary of War,*	8,000
Isaac Toucey,	Connecticut,	*Secretary of the Navy,*	8,000
Jacob Thompson,	Mississippi,	*Secretary of the Interior,*	8,000
Joseph Holt,	Kentucky,	*Postmaster-General,*	8,000
Jeremiah S. Black,	Pennsylvania,	*Attorney-General,*	8,000

* Died in office.

Department of State.

Lewis Cass, *Secretary*.

John Appleton, *Assistant Secretary*, salary, $ 3,000.

	Salary.		Salary.
William Hunter, *Chief Clerk*,	$ 2,200	Hugh C. McLaughlin, *Superintendent of Statistics*,	$ 2,000
Edward Stubbs, *Disburs. Agent*,	2,000		

Treasury Department.

Howell Cobb, *Secretary*.

Philip Clayton, *Assistant Secretary*, salary, $ 3,000.

Gilbert Rodman, *Chief Clerk of the Treasury Department*,	$ 2,200

Comptrollers.

William Medill, *1st Comp.*,	3,500
W. H. Jones, *Chief Clerk*,	2,000
James M. Cutts, *2d Comp.*,	3,000
Thos. J. Cathcart, *Chief Clerk*,	2,000

Auditors.

Thos. L. Smith, *1st Auditor*,	3,000
David W. Mahon, *Chief Clerk*,	2,000
Thos. J. D. Fuller, *2d Auditor*,	3,000
William Mechlen, *Chief Clerk*,	2,000
Robt. J. Atkinson, *3d Auditor*,	3,000
Samuel S. Rind, *Chief Clerk*,	2,000
A. J. O'Bannon, *4th Auditor*,	3,000
T. Hunter, *Chief Clerk*,	2,000
B. Fuller, *5th Auditor*,	3,000
Thos. M. Smith, *Chief Clerk*,	2,000
Thomas M. Tate, *Auditor of Treasury for P. O. Depart.*,	3,000
H. St. Geo. Offutt, *Chief Clerk*,	2,000

Commissioner of Customs.

Samuel Ingham,	3,000
Thomas Feran, *Chief Clerk*,	2,000

Geo. F. Emery,
Moses F. Odell,
Chas. V. Hagner,
J. W. Baughman, } *Appraisers at Large.*

Richard Roman, *Appraiser-General for the Pacific Coast*,	$ 6,000

Treasurer's Office.

Samuel Casey, *Treasurer*,	3,000
W. B. Randolph, *Chief Clerk*,	2,000

Assistant Treasurers.

Edward C. Pratt,	*Boston*,	2,500
John J. Cisco,	*New York*,	4,000
Jas. H. Walton,	*Philadelphia*,	2,500
B. C. Pressly,	*Charleston*,	2,500
Ant. J. Guirot,	*New Orleans*,	2,500
Isaac H. Sturgeon,	*St. Louis*,	2,500
Jacob R. Snyder,	*California*.	

Register's Office.

Finley Bigger, *Register*,	3,000
Charles T. Jones, *Chief Clerk*,	2,000

Solicitor's Office.

Junius Hillyer, *Solicitor*,	3,500
B. F. Pleasants, *Chief Clerk*,	2,000

Coast Survey.

Alex. D. Bache, *Superintendent*,	6,000

Office of Attorney-General.

Jeremiah S. Black,	*Attorney-General*.	
Alfred B. McCalmont,	*Assistant*,*	Salary, $ 3,000.

* For the act creating the Assistant Attorney-General, see "Titles and Abstracts of Public Laws," No. 33, *post*, p. 136.

Department of War.

John B. Floyd, *Secretary.*

Salary.

W. R. Drinkard, *Chief Clerk*, $2,200

Adjutant-General's Office.

Samuel Cooper, *Col., Adjutant-General.*

E. D. Townsend, *Major, Assist. Adj.-Gen.*

J. L Addison, *Principal Clerk*, 1,800

Quartermaster-General's Office.

Thos. S. Jesup, *Brev. Maj.-Gen., Quartermaster-General.*

E. S Sibley, *Major, Quartermaster.*

Wm. A. Gordon, *Principal Clerk*, 1,800

Paymaster-General's Office.

Benj. F. Larned, *Col., Paymaster-Gen.*

W. D. Beall, *Principal Clerk*, 1,800

Subsistence Office.

Joseph P. Taylor, *Col., Acting Com.-Gen. of Subsistence.*

A. E. Shiras, *Capt., Assistant.*

Richard Gott, *Principal Clerk*, 1,800

Salary.

Medical Bureau.

Thomas Lawson, *Brev. Brig.-Gen., Surg.-Gen.*

Robert C. Wood, *Surgeon Assistant to the Surgeon-General.*

R. Johnson, *Principal Clerk*, $1,800

Engineer Bureau.

Joseph G. Totten, *Brev. Brig.-Gen., Chief Engineer.*

H. G. Wright, *Capt., Assistant.*

F. N. Barbarin, *Principal Clerk*, 1,800

Topographical Bureau.

John J. Abert, *Col., Chief Top. Engineer.*

I. C. Woodruff, *Capt., Assistant.*

Geo. Thompson, *Principal Clerk*, 1,800

Ordnance Bureau.

Henry K. Craig, *Col., Chief of Ordnance.*

W. Maynadier, *Capt., Assist.*

Geo. Bender, *Principal Clerk*, 1,800

Navy Department.

Isaac Toucey, *Secretary.*

Charles W. Welsh, *Chief Clerk*,				2,200
Joseph Smith, *Chief of the Bureau of Docks and Navy-Yards*,				3,500
D. N. Ingraham,	*do.*	*do.*	*Ordnance and Hydrography*,	3,500
John Lenthall,	*do.*	*do.*	*Construct., Equip., & Repairs*,	3,500
Horatio Bridge,	*do.*	*do.*	*Provisions and Clothing*,	3,500
William Whelan,	*do.*	*do.*	*Med. and Surgery*,	3,500
Commander M. F. Maury, *Super. of Observatory at Washington*,				3,000
Samuel Archbold, *Engineer in Chief*,				3,000

Department of the Interior.

Jacob Thompson, *Secretary.*

Moses Kelly, *Chief Clerk*, $2,200

Peter Lammond, *Disbursing Clerk*, 2,000

General Land-Office.

Samuel A. Smith, *Commiss.*, 3,000

Jos. S. Wilson, *Chief Clerk, and Principal Clerk of Private Land Claims*, 2,000

W. V. H. Brown, *Principal Clerk of Public Lands*, 1,800

Asa F. Chapin, *Principal Clerk of Surveys*, 1,800

Julius N. Granger, *Recorder*, 2,000

J. B. Leonard, *Sec. to Pres. to sign Land Patents*, 1,500

	Salary.
Indian Office.	
A. B. Greenwood, *Commiss.*,	$3,000
Charles E. Mix, *Chief Clerk*,	2,000
Pension Office.	
Geo. C. Whiting, *Commissioner*,	3,000
John Robb, *Chief Clerk*,	2,000
Patent Office.	
Wm. D. Bishop, *Commiss.*,	3,000
S. T. Shugert, *Chief Clerk*,	2,000
R. R. Rhoades, *Examiner*,	2,500
Henry Baldwin, *do.*	2,500
Henry King, *do.*	2,500
James S. French, *do.*	2,500
Titian R. Peale, *do.*	2,500
R. D. Clarke, *do.*	2,500
A. B. Little, *do.*	2,500
De Witt C. Lawrence, *do.*	2,500
J. M. Henry, *do.*	2,500
William B. Taylor, *do.*	2,500
Edward Foreman, *do.*	2,500
H. P. K. Peck, *do.*	2,500
J. Van Santvoord, *Assist. Exam.*,	1,800
Thos. Antisell, *do.*	1,800
Edward Shaw, *do.*	1,800
A. M. Smith, *Assist. Exam.*,	$1,800
H. N. Taft, *do.*	1,800
A. T. Jenckes, *do.*	1,800
I. D. Toll, *do.*	1,800
Jos. H. Adams, Jr., *do.*	1,800
S. E. Coues, *do.*	1,800
Henry Wurtz, *do.*	1,800
Elias Yulee, *do.*	1,800
Alfred Herbert, *do.*	1,800
A. L. McIntire, *Draughtsman*,	1,600
D. J. Browne, *Agricult. Clerk*,	2,000
Samuel P. Bell, *Machinist*,	1,600
Wm. W. Turner, *Librarian*,	1,600
Public Buildings.	
John B. Blake, *Commissioner*,	2,000
Penitentiary.	
C. P. Sengstack, *Warden*,	1,800
Peter Force, *Inspector*,	250
Robert Ould, *do.*	250
George Parker, *do.*	250
United States Insane Asylum.	
C. H. Nichols, *Superintendent*,	2,500
W. P. Young, Jr., *Ass't Physician*,	700

Post-Office Department.

Joseph Holt, *Postmaster-General.*

Horatio King,	*1st Assistant Postmaster-Gen., Appointment Office,*	3,000
Wm. H. Dundas,	*2d do. do., Contract Office,*	3,000
A. N. Zevely,	*3d do. do., Finance Office,*	3,000
B. N. Clements,	*Chief Cl'k P. O. Dep't, and Chief of Inspection Office,*	2,200
Thomas M. Tate,	*Auditor of the Treasury for the Post-Office,*	3,000
H. St. George Offutt,	*Chief Clerk of the Auditor,*	2,000

Postmasters in the Chief Towns and Cities.*

(Corrected in the Post-Office Department, November 1, 1859.)

Place.	Postmaster.
Abingdon, Va.	Henry W. Baker.
Adrian, Mich.	C. B. Backus.
*Albany, N. Y.	C. Comstock.
*Alexandria, La.	E. R. Biossat.
Alexandria, Va.	T. W. Ashby.
Alton, Ill.	R. W. English.
Amherst, Mass.	Seth Nims.
Andover, Mass.	H. Clark.
Annapolis, Md.	Aug. Gassaway.
Ann Arbor, Mich.	H. D. Bennett.
Apalachicola, Fa.	B. F. Simmons.
Ashville, N. C.	W. L. Hilliard.
Astoria, Oregon,	T. P. Powers.
Athens, Ga.	Thos. Crawford.

* The places marked thus (*) are distributing offices, and those thus marked were *all* the distributing offices, November 1, 1859.

Place.	Postmaster.
Auburn, N. Y.	C. W. Pomeroy.
*Augusta, Ga.	J. M. Smythe.
Augusta, Me.	Wm. S. Badger.
Austin, Tex.	William Rust.
*Baltimore, Md.	Jacob G. Davies.
Bangor, Me.	L. Jones.
Batavia, N. Y.	Wm. Seaver.
Bath, Me.	Joseph C. Snow.
Baton Rouge, La.	Jos. McCormick.
Benicia, Cal.	T. T. Hooper.
Bennington, Vt.	Truman Heiling.
Binghampton, N.Y.	Virgil Whitney.
*Boston, Mass.	Nahum Capen.
Brattleboro', Vt.	Asher Spencer.
Bridgeport, Conn.	E. B. Goodsell.
Brooklyn, N. Y.	Wm. H. Peck.
Brunswick, Me.	Robert P. Dunlap.
*Buffalo, N. Y.	James G. Dickie.
Burlington, Iowa.	James Tizzard.
Burlington, N. J.	H. Hollenback.
Burlington, Vt.	D. A. Danforth.
*Cairo, Ill.	L. G. Faxon.
Calais, Me.	Edgar Whidden.
Cambridge, Mass.	Wm. Caldwell.
Cambridgeport, Ms.	Samuel James.
Camden, S. C.	Thos W. Pegues.
Canandaigua, N.Y.	G. M. Chapman.
Carlisle, Pa.	John B. Bratton.
Castine, Me.	Charles Rogers.
Catskill, N. Y.	J. Joesbury.
Chambersburg, Pa.	John Ligget.
*Charleston, S. C.	Alfred Huger.
Charlestown, Mass.	Chas. B. Rogers.
Charlestown, N.H.	J. H. Hubbard.
Charlottesville, Va.	W. M. Kellinger.
Chattanooga, Tenn.	H. T. Phillips.
*Chicago, Ill.	W. Price.
Chillicothe, Ohio,	John Hough.
*Cincinnati, Ohio,	John L. Vattier.
Clarksburg, Va.	B. S. Griffin.
*Cleveland, Ohio,	Benj. Harrington.
Columbia, S. C.	James B. Glass.
Columbia, Tenn.	E. F. Lee.
*Columbus, Ga.	Henry M. Jeter.
*Columbus, Ohio,	Thomas Miller.
Concord, N. H.	Jacob Carter.
Cooperstown, N.Y.	C. J. Stillman.
Corpus Christi, Tex.	Wm. J. Moore.
Cumberland, Md.	Sam. H. Taylor.
Cumb'd Gap, Tenn.	J. G. Newlee.
Darien, Ga.	Wm. T. Thorp.
Dayton, Ohio,	Edward A. King.
Dedham, Mass.	L. W. Tower.
*Detroit, Mich.	Henry N. Walker.
Donaldsonville, La.	A. Gingry.
Dover, N. H.	P. H. Burns.
Dover, Del.	Tim. C. Killen.
*Dubuque, Ia.	H. H. Heath.
Easton, Pa.	W. H. Hutten.
Eastport, Me.	W. Hathaway.
Elmira, N. Y.	Daniel Stephens.
Erie, Pa.	B. F. Sloan.
Evansville, Ind.	C. B. Rudd.
Exeter, N. H.	D. Melcher.
Fayetteville, N. C.	James G. Cook.
Fitchburg, Mass.	J. W. Mansur.
Florence, Ala.	John A. Smith.
Fort Gibson, Ark.	Thomas Lanigan.
Frankfort, Ky.	Benj. F. Johnson.
Frederick, Md.	C. B. McCaffray.
Fredericsburg, Va.	R. T. Thom.
Galena, Ill.	B. B. Howard.
*Galveston, Tex.	John B. Root.
Geneva, N. Y.	S. H. Parker.
Georgetown, D. C.	H. W. Tilley.
Georgetown, S. C.	Wm. McNulty.
Greenfield, Mass.	D. N. Carpenter.
Greensboro', Ala.	H. Kohnen.
Greensboro', N. C.	B. C. Graham.
Hagerstown, Md.	Saml. Ridenour.
Hallowell, Me.	T. W. Newman.
Hanover, N. H.	S. W. Cobb.
Harrisburg, Pa.	Geo. W. Porter.
Hartford, Conn.	W. J. Hamersley.
Hillsboro', N. C.	J. M. Palmer.
Hollidaysburg, Pa.	W. G. Murray.
Houston, Tex.	O. L. Cochran.
Hudson, N. Y.	Henry C. Miller.
Huntsville, Ala.	W. P. A. Murray.
Independence, Mo.	P. McClanahan.
*Indianapolis, Ind.	John M. Talbot.
Ithaca, N. Y.	O. B. Curran.

Place.	Postmaster.	Place.	Postmaster.
Jackson, Mich.	J. P. Shoemaker.	Nashua, N. H.	George Bowers.
Jackson, Miss.	C. R. Dickson.	*Nashville, Tenn.	S. R. Anderson.
Jacksonville, Ill.	Samuel Hunt.	Natchez, Miss.	Richard Elward.
Jefferson Bar., Mo.	E. Thompson.	Natchitoches, La.	Fairman F. Taber.
Jefferson City, Mo.	John M. Dixon.	New Albany, Ind.	F. M. Gwin.
Kalamazoo, Mich.	Wm. H. De Yoe.	Newark, N. J.	Charles T. Gray.
*Kanawha C.H., Va.	D. H. Snyder.	Newark, Ohio,	James E. Lewis.
Kaskaskia, Ill.	P. W. Unger.	New Bedford, Ms.	John Fraser.
Keene, N. H.	J. D. Colony.	Newbern, N. C.	J. C. Stevenson.
Kensington, Pa.	Peter Rambo.	N. Brunswick, N.J.	Henry Sanderson.
Key West, Fa.	J. C. Whalton.	Newburg, N. Y.	Jos. Casterline, Jr.
Knoxville, Tenn.	C. W. Charlton.	Newburyport, Ms.	Geo. W. Jackman.
Lafayette, Ind.	Thomas Wood.	Newcastle, Del.	J. Dunkin, Jr.
Lancaster, Pa.	H. M. Reigart.	New Haven, Ct.	L. A. Thomas.
Lansing, Mich.	J. M. Griswold.	New London, Ct.	Stanley G. Troth.
Lawrence, Mass.	Benj. F. Watson.	*New Orleans, La.	Saml. F. Marks.
Lecompton, Kan. T.	Jas. S. Rucker.	Newport, R. I.	James Atkinson.
Lexington, Ky.	Jesse Woodruff.	*New York, N. Y.	Isaac V. Fowler.
Litchfield, Conn.	G. H. Baldwin.	*Norfolk, Va.	A. M. Vaughan.
*Little Rock, Ark.	John E. Reardon.	Northampton, Ms.	H. H. Chilson.
Lockport, N. Y.	Asher Torrance.	Northumberland, Pa.	Jacob Ulp.
*Louisville, Ky.	F. S. J. Ronald.	Norwich, Conn.	John W. Stedman.
Lowell, Mass.	F. A. Hildreth.	Ogdensburg, N. Y.	Thomas Bacon.
Lynchburg, Va.	Robt. H. Glass.	Olympia, Wash. T.	Rufus Willard.
Lynn, Mass.	Leonard B. Usher.	Omaha City, Neb. T.	W. W. Wyman.
Macon, Ga.	E. L. Strohecker.	Oswego, N. Y.	Alfred B. Letty.
Madison, Ind.	Rolla Doolittle.	Owego, N. Y.	H. A. Beebe.
Madison, Wisc.	John N. Jones.	Oregon City, Or.	W. W. Buck.
Manchester, N. H.	Thos. P. Pierce.	Pass Christian, Mi.	Archibald Clark.
Marietta, Ohio,	A. W. McCormick.	Paterson, N. J.	William D. Quin.
Marysville, Cal.	W. C. Dougherty.	Pawtucket, R. I.	C. A. Leonard.
Maysville, Ky.	Benj. O. Picket.	Pensacola, Fa.	Dillon Jordon.
Meadville, Pa.	J. E. McFarland.	Peoria, Ill.	Geo. W. Raney.
*Memphis, Tenn.	Wm. H. Carroll.	Petersburg, Va.	Wm. E. Bass.
Middlebury, Vt.	Wm. P. Russell.	*Philadelphia, Pa.	Nath. B. Browne.
Middletown, Ct.	Sam. Babcock, Jr.	*Pittsburg, Pa.	Robt. Anderson.
Milledgeville, Ga.	E. S. Chandler.	Pittsfield, Mass.	Phineas Allen, Jr.
Milwaukee, Wisc.	Mitchell Steever.	Plattsburg, N. Y.	Chas. S. Mooers.
Mobile, Ala.	Loyd Bowers.	Plymouth, Mass.	C. A. S. Perkins.
Monterey, Cal.	Wm. Curtis.	Pontiac, Mich.	S. W. Denton.
*Montgomery, Ala.	Thomas Welch.	Port Gibson, Miss.	W. S. Morris.
Montpelier, Vt.	T. P. Redfield.	Portland, Me.	S. Jordan.
Muscatine, Iowa,	J. A. McCormick.	Portsmouth, N. H.	G. H. Rundlett.
Murfreesboro', Ten.	Wm. R. Butler.	P't Townsend, W.T.	F. W. Pettygrove.
Nantucket, Mass.	Charles P. Swain.	Pottsville, Pa.	Henry L. Acker.
*Napoleon, Ark.	Jas. T. Porter.	Poughkeepsie, N.Y.	G. P. Pelton.

Place.	Postmaster.	Place.	Postmaster.
Princeton, N. J.	Robert L. Clow.	St. Paul, Min.	W. H. Forbes.
Providence, R. I.	Albert S. Gallup.	Syracuse, N. Y.	H. J. Sedgwick.
Quincy, Ill.	W. H. Carlin.	Tallahassee, Fa.	Miles Nash.
*Raleigh, N. C.	George T. Cooke.	Taunton, Mass.	A. M. Ide, Jr.
Reading, Pa.	Philip K. Miller.	Terre Haute, Ind.	B. H. Cornwell.
*Richmond, Va.	Thos. B. Bigger.	Thomaston, Me.	A. Lermond.
Robbinston, Me.	J. W. Cox.	*Toledo, Ohio,	John E. Hunt.
Rochester, N. Y.	Nicholas E. Paine.	Trenton, N. J.	W. A. Benjamin.
Rome, N. Y.	D. E. Wager.	Troy, N. Y.	James R. Fonda.
Rutland, Vt.	J. Cain.	Tuscaloosa, Ala.	Wm. D. Marrast.
Saco, Me.	Charles Nutter.	Tuscumbia, Ala.	Samuel Finley.
Sacramento, Cal.	J. R. Hardenberg.	Uniontown, Pa.	A. Hadden.
Salem, Mass.	I. S. Perkins.	Utica, N. Y.	Joseph M. Lyon.
Salt Lake City, Ut.	Elias Smith.	Vicksburg, Miss.	Wm. B. Sloan.
San Diego, Cal.	J. W. Robinson.	Vincennes, Ind.	John Moore.
Sandusky, Ohio,	John M. Brown.	Ware, Mass.	Addison Sanford.
Sandwich, Mass.	Charles B. Hall.	*Washington, D.C.	William Jones.
*San Francisco, Cal.	Chas. L. Weller.	Watertown, N. Y.	W. H. Sigourney.
San José, Cal.	John W. Patrick.	Waterville, Me.	E. L. Getchell.
Santa Fé, N. Mex.	D. V. Whiting.	West Point, N. Y.	Mary Berard.
Saratoga Sp., N. Y.	Thos. G. Young.	*Wheeling, Va.	F. H. Feeney.
*Savannah, Ga.	Solomon Cohen.	Whitehall, N. Y.	H. W. Buel.
Schenectady, N. Y.	Luke Dodge.	Wilkesbarre, Pa.	E. R. Collings.
Sharon, N. Y.	H. Beekman.	Williamstown, Ms.	John M. Cole.
Shawneetown, Ill.	Sarah J. Seabolt.	Wilmington, Del.	Henry F. Askew.
Springfield, Ill.	Morris Lindsay.	Wilmington, N. C.	Daniel Dickson.
Springfield, Mass.	A. W. Chapin.	Winchester, Va.	Geo. B. Graves.
Steubenville, Ohio,	Thos. Brashears.	Windsor, Vt.	P. G. Skinner.
*St. Josephs, Mo.	Wm. A. Davis.	Worcester, Mass.	E. Bannister.
*St. Louis, Mo.	John Hogan.	Yorkville, S. C.	J. R. Alexander.
Stockton, Cal.	P. Edward Conner.	Zanesville, Ohio,	J. B. Roberts.

Collectors of Customs in the Principal Ports.

(Corrected in the Treasury Department, November 1, 1859.)

Port.	Collector.	Port.	Collector.
Alexandria, Va.	Edwd. S. Hough.	Benicia, Cal.	T. B. Storer.
Annapolis, Md.	J. T. Hammond.	Boston, Ms.	Arthur W. Austin.
Apalachicola, Fa.	Robert J. Floyd.	Bridgetown, N. J.	Wm. S. Bowen.
Astoria, Oregon.	John Adair.	Bristol, R. I.	G. H. Reynolds.
Baltimore, Md.	J. T. Mason.	Buffalo, N. Y.	Warren Bryant.
Bangor, Me.	D. F. Leavitt.	Burlington, Vt.	J. B. Bowdish.
Barnstable, Ms.	S. B. Phinney.	C. Vincent, N. Y.	Theop. Peugnet.
Bath, Me.	Joseph Berry.	Castine, Me.	John R. Redman.
Beaufort, N. C.	J. E. Gibble.	Charleston, S. C.	Wm. F. Colcock.
Beaufort, S. C.	B. R. Bythewood.	Chicago, Ill.	B. F. Strother.
Belfast, Me.	J. D. Dickerson.	Cleveland, Ohio,	Robert Parks.

Port.	Collector.	Port.	Collector.
Darien, Geo.	Woodford Maybry.	Oswego, N. Y.	O. Robinson.
Detroit, Mich.	M. Shoemaker.	Oxford, Md.	Tench Tilghman.
Dunkirk, N. Y.	O. F. Dickenson.	Pembina, Min. T.	J. McFetridge.
Eastport, Me.	Robert Burns.	Pensacola, Fa.	Joseph Sierra.
Eastville, Va.	John S. Parker.	Perth Amboy, N. J.	Amos Robins.
Edenton, N. C.	Edmund Wright.	Petersburg, Va.	Timothy Rives.
Edgartown, Ms.	C. Norton.	Philadelphia, Pa.	Joseph B. Baker.
Elizabeth City, N.C.	L. D. Starke.	Plattsburg, N. Y.	Henry B. Smith.
Ellsworth, Me.	Thomas D. Jones.	Plymouth, Ms.	W. Wadsworth.
Erie, Pa.	Murray Whallon.	Plymouth, N. C.	Joseph Ramsey.
Fairfield, Ct.	Wm. S. Pomeroy.	Point Isabel, Tex.	F. W. Latham.
Fall River, Ms.	P. W. Leland.	Portland, Me.	M. Macdonald.
Fernandina, Fa.	Felix Livingston.	Port Leon, Fa.	A. B. Noyes.
Franklin, La.	R. N. McMillan.	Port Orford, Oreg.	Benj. Brattain.
Galveston, Texas,	Hamilton Stuart.	Portsmouth, N. H.	Augustus Jenkins.
Gardiner, Oreg.	B. J. Burns.	Port Townsend, W.T.	M. H. Frost.
Georgetown, D. C.	H. C. Mathews.	Providence, R. I.	James A. Aborn.
Georgetown, S. C.	John N. Merriman.	Richmond, Va.	W. M. Harrison.
Gloucester, Ms.	G. Babson.	Rochester, N. Y.	P. M. Bromley.
Jacksonville, Fa.	Thos. Ledwith.	Sackett's H'r, N.Y.	Wm. Howland.
Kennebunk, Me.	John Cousens.	Saco, Me.	A. A. Hanscom.
Key West, Fa.	John P. Baldwin.	Sacramento, Cal.	Lewis Sanders, Jr.
Lamberton, N. J.	H. J. Ashmore.	Sag Harbor, N.Y.	J. M. Terbell.
Las Cruces, N. Mex.	S. J. Jones.	Salem & Beverly, Ms.	Wm. B. Pike.
La Salle, Texas,	D. M. Stapp.	San Diego, Cal.	Henry Hancock.
Lewiston, N. Y.	G. P. Eddy.	Sandusky, Ohio,	Geo. S. Patterson.
Machias, Me.	A. F. Parlin.	San Francisco, Cal.	B. F. Washington.
Marblehead, Ms.	Wm. Bartoll.	San Pedro, Cal.	P. H. Downey.
Michil'ck, Mich.	J. A. T. Wendell.	Savannah, Ga.	John Boston.
Middletown, Ct.	Patrick Fagan.	Shieldsboro', Miss.	Robert Eager.
Milwaukee, Wisc.	G. W. Clason.	Somerspoint, N. J.	Thos. D. Winner.
Mobile, Ala.	Thad. Sanford.	St. Augustine, Fa.	Paul Arnau.
Monterey, Cal.	James A. Watson.	St. Mary's, Ga.	J. A. Baratte.
Nantucket, Ms.	E. W. Allen.	Stockton, Cal.	Andrew Lester.
Natchez, Miss.	John Hunter.	Stonington, Ct.	Benj. F. States.
Newark, N. J.	Edwd. T. Hillyer.	Tappahannock, Va.	Geo. T. Wright.
New Bedford, Ms.	C. B. H. Fessenden	Toledo, Ohio,	E. D. Potter.
Newbern, N. C.	W. G. Singleton.	Tuckerton, N. J.	I. S. Jennings.
Newburyport, Ms.	James Blood.	Vicksburg, Miss.	Wm. D. Roy.
New Haven, Ct.	M. A. Osborn.	Vienna, Md.	Wm. S. Jackson.
New London, Ct.	J. P. C. Mather.	Waldoboro', Me.	J. H. Kennedy.
New Orleans, La.	F. H. Hatch.	Washington, N. C.	H. F. Hancock.
Newport, R. I.	Gilbert Chase.	Wilmington, Del.	Jesse Sharpe.
New York, N. Y.	Augustus Schell.	Wilmington, N.C.	Jas. T. Miller.
Norfolk, Va.	J. J. Simkins.	Wiscasset, Me.	T. Cunningham.
Ocracoke, N. C.	Oliver S. Dewey.	York, Me.	Luther Junkins.
Ogdensburg, N. Y.	Horace Moody.	Yorktown, Va.	Wm. F. Presson.

NAVAL OFFICERS *in Office, November*, 1859.

District.	Name.	District.	Name.
Baltimore, Md.	Levi K. Bowen.	Philadelphia, Pa.	C. McKibben.
Boston, Ms.	Charles G. Greene.	Portsmouth, N. H.	S. B. Lord.
Charleston, S. C.	John Laurens.	Providence, R.I.	Thos. J. Gardiner.
Newburyport, Ms.	Nicholas Brown.	Salem, Ms.	John Ryan.
New Orleans, La.	Joseph Genois.	San Francisco.	F. Tilford.
Newport, R. I.	William Rider.	Savannah, Ga.	S. P. Hamilton.
New York, N. Y.	A. Birdsall.	Wilmington, N.C.	Wm. N. Peden.
Norfolk, Va.	C. C. Robinson.		

REGISTERS, RECEIVERS, SURVEYORS, AND GEOLOGISTS CONNECTED WITH THE LAND-OFFICE.

Names of Registers and Receivers in Office, November 1, 1859.

State.	Place.	Register.	Receiver.
ALABAMA,	St. Stephens,	James Magoffin,	John Peebles.
"	Greenville,	John K. Henry,	B. Lloyd.
"	Huntsville,	James H. Ware,	John S. Nance.
"	Tuscaloosa,	Monroe Donoho,	James W. Warren.
"	Elba,	Joseph P. Baldwin,	Richard F. Cook.
"	Demopolis,	Lewis B. McCarty,	S. M. Torbert.
"	Montgomery,	Thos. O. Glascock,	E. M. Hastings.
"	Centre,	N. M. Warren,	L. M. Stiff.
ARKANSAS,	Batesville,	Wm. W. Lewis,	Wm. A. Bevins.
"	Little Rock,	Henry A. Powers,	Peter T. Crutchfield.
"	Washington,	William Moss,	Daniel Griffin.
"	Fayetteville,	L. B. Cunningham,	J. L. Dickson.
"	Helena,	Robert Maloney,	James C. Tappan.
"	Clarksville,	Oliver Bashan,	Moreau Rose.
"	Champagnole,	William J. Owen,	Wm. T. Sargent.
CALIFORNIA,	Los Angeles,	W. T. Harvey,	A. Olivera.
"	San Francisco,	Ira Munson,	P. Bequette.
"	Marysville,	E. O. F. Hastings,	J. Hopkins.
"	Humboldt,	W. McDaniel,	G. W. Hook.
"	Stockton,	A. C. Bradford,	W. B. Norman.
"	Visalia,	E. P. Hart,	Thomas Baker.
FLORIDA,	Tallahassee,	E. T. L. Blake,	A. L. Woodward.
"	St. Augustine,	James M. Gould,	F. P. Ferreira.
"	Newnansville,	L. G. Pyles,	George Helvenston.
"	Tampa,	Jesse Carter,	Madison Post.
ILLINOIS,	Springfield,	W. E. Keefer,	A. G. Herndon.
INDIANA,	Indianapolis,	George McOuat,	C. C. Campbell.
IOWA,	Fort Dodge,	J M. Stockdale,	T. Sargent.
"	Sioux City,	S. P. Yeomans,	Andrew Leech.
"	Fort Des Moines,	J. W. Griffith,	Isaac Cooper.
"	Council Bluffs,	L. S. Hills,	A. H. Palmer.
LOUISIANA,	New Orleans,	Lewis Palms,	Henry W. Palfrey.
"	Opelousas,	Robt. Benguerel,	John Posey.
"	Monroe,	J. McEnery,	Chris. H. Dobbs.
"	Greensburg,	Thomas Bennet,	J. B. McClendon.

State.	Place.	Register.	Receiver.
LOUISIANA,	Natchitoches,	John B. Cloutier,	Thos. C. Hunt.
MICHIGAN,	Detroit,	C. F. Heyerman,	J. Beeson.
"	East Saginaw,	M. B. Hess,	W. L. P. Little.
"	Ionia,	J. C. Blanchard,	H. J. Wilson.
"	Marquette,	Peter White,	E. Warner.
"	Traverse City,	Jacob Barns,	Oscar A. Stevens.
MISSISSIPPI,*	Washington,	J. G. G. Garrett,	Wm. N. Whitehurst.
"	Augusta,	Drury Bynum,	A. R. Carter.
"	Jackson,	Joseph Bell,	R. A. Clarke.
"	Grenada,	Saml. M. Hankins,	John J. Gage.
"	Columbus,	Francis G. Baldwin,	Robert D. Haden.
MISSOURI,	St. Louis,	Paris Pipkin,	J. S. Dougherty.
"	Booneville,	H. L. Brown,	E. E. Buckner.
"	Jackson,	Charles A. Davis,	J. J. Turnbaugh.
"	Warsaw,	M. L. Means,	Nathl. B. Holden.
"	Springfield,	W. H. Graves,	T. J. Bishop.
OHIO,	Chillicothe,	Jas. S. McGinnis,	Thomas McNally.
WISCONSIN,	Menasha,	D. R. Curran,	Samuel Ryan.
"	Hudson,	Orpheus Everts,	J. D. Reymert.
"	Stevens Point,	H. Brawley,	Albert G. Ellis.
"	La Crosse,	Charles S. Benton,	Theo. Rodolf.
"	Superior,	Wm. McAboy,	T. R. Spencer.
"	Eau Claire,	W. T. Galloway,	N. B. Boyden.
MINNESOTA.	Cambridge,	C. H. Wagner,	M. H. Abbott.
"	St. Cloud,	W. A. Caruthers,	S. L. Hays.
"	Chatfield,	John R. Bennett,	J. H. McKenney.
"	Forest City,	T. E. Massey,	J. D. Evans.
"	St. Peter,	S. Plumer,	B. F. Tillotson.
"	Henderson,	J. C. Dow,	Christ. Graham.
"	Portland,	J. S. Watrous,	John Whipple.
"	Ottertail City,	G. B. Clitheral,	William Sawyer.
OREGON.	Oregon City,	B. Jennings,	A. L. Lovejoy.
"	Winchester,	Lafayette Mosher,	William J. Martin.
KANSAS TER.	Lecompton,	Ely Moore,	William Brindle.
"	Kickapoo,	J. W. Whitfield,	D. Woodson.
"	Fort Scott,	J. Morin,	E. Ransom.
"	Junction City,	S. B. Garrett,	F. Patterson.
NEBR. TER.	Omaha City,	John A. Parker, jr.,	P. F. Wilson.
"	Brownsville,	G. H. Nixon,	C. B. Smith.
"	Nebraska City,	A. Hopkins,	E. A. Deslonde.
"	Dahkota City,	J. N. H. Patrick,	G. B. Graff.
WASH. TER.	Olympia,	W. B. Rankin,	Selucius Garfield.
NEW MEXICO.	Santa Fé,	W. A. Davidson,	W. A. Street.

Surveyors-General of the Public Lands, November 1st, 1859.

District.	Surveyor.	Residence.
Illinois and Missouri,	John Loughborough,	St. Louis, Mo.
Louisiana,	Wm. J. McCulloh,	Donaldsonville.
Wisconsin and Iowa,	Warner Lewis,	Dubuque, Iowa.
Florida,	F. L. Dancy,	St. Augustine.
California,	J. W. Mandeville,	San Francisco.
Oregon,	W. W. Chapman,	Salem, Oregon.

* R. W. Edmundson, Clerk of the Courts, Pontotoc, Mississippi, is Keeper of the Archives of the old Pontotoc Land District.

District.	Surveyor.	Residence.
New Mexico,	W. Pelham,	Santa Fé, N. M. Ter.
Washington Territory,	J. Tilton,	Olympia, W. Ter.
Kansas and Nebraska,	Ward B. Burnett,	Lecompton, K. Ter.
Utah Territory,	S. C. Stambaugh,	Salt Lake City.
Minnesota,	C. L. Emerson,	St. Paul, Min.

Recorder of Land Titles.

Adolphe Renard, St. Louis, Mo.

INDIAN DEPARTMENT.*

[Corrected in Office of Indian Affairs, November, 1859.]

Superintendencies.

Superintendency.	Superintendent.	Bond.	Salary.
Northern,	W. J. Cullen,	$100,000	$2,000
Central,	A. M. Robinson,	75,000	2,000
Southern,	Elias Rector,	75,000	2,000
Utah,	Jacob Forney.	50,000	2,000

Agencies

Designation of Agency.	Tribes in each Agency.	Name of Agent.	Bond.	Salary.
Central Superintend.				
Delaware,	Delawares,	Thomas B. Sykes,	$75,000	$1,500
Kansas,	Kansas,	M. C. Dickey,	10,000	1,500
Upper Arkansas,	Upper Arkansas,	W. W. Bent,	20,000	1,500
Kickapoo,	Kickapoos,	Wm. P. Badger,	20,000	1,500
Blackfeet,	Blackfeet and other neighboring tribes,	A. J. Vaughan,	20,000	1,500
Upper Platte,	Arapahoes, Cheyennes, &c.,	Thos. S. Twiss,	10,000	1,500
Pottawatomie,	Pottawatomies,	W. E. Murphy,	20,000	1,500
Sac and Fox,	Sacs and Foxes, Ottawas of Swan Creek, and Black River Chippewas,	Perry Fuller,	15,000	1,500
Upper Missouri,	Sioux, &c., &c.,	Bern'd Schoonover,	20,000	1,500
Osage River,	Weas, Piankeshaws, Kaskaskias, Peorias, and Miamies,	Seth Clover,	20,000	1,500
Shawnee,	Shawnees and Wyandotts,	B. J. Newsom,	75,000	1,500
Great Nemeha,	Iowas, and Sacs and Foxes of Missouri,	Danl. Vanderslice,	10,000	1,500
Omaha,	Omahas,	Wm. E. Moore,	20,000	1,500
Ottoe and Missouria,	Ottoes, Missourias, and Pawnees,	W. W. Dennison,	15,000	1,500
Southern Superintend.				
Yancton Sioux,	Yancton Sioux,	A. H. Redfield,	50,000	1,500
Choctaw & Chickasaw,	Choctaws and Chickasaws,	Douglas H. Cooper,	70,000	1,500
Creek,	Creeks,	Wm. H. Garrett,	20,000	1,500
Cherokee,	Cherokees,	George Butler,	20,000	1,500
Neosha,	Osages, Quapaws, Senecas, and Shawnees,	Andrew J. Dorn,	40,000	1,500
Seminole,	Seminoles,	S. M. Rutherford,	5,000	1,500
	Witchitas,	S. E. Blain.		
Northern Superintend.				
Winnebago,	Winnebagoes,	C. H. Mix,	20,000	1,500
Chippewa,	Chippewas of the Mississippi,	J. W. Lynde,	20,000	1,500
Saint Peters,	Sioux of Minnesota,	J. R. Brown,	50,000	1,500
Green Bay,	Menomonees, Oneidas, Stockbridges, and Munsees,	A. D. Bonesteel,	10,000	1,000
	Lake Superior Indians,	C. K. Drew,	20,000	1,500
Miscellaneous Agencies.				
Mackinac,	Ottawas and Chippewas, and Chippewas of Lake Superior,	A. M. Fitch,	40,000	1,500
New York,	Indians in New York,	B. H. Colegrove,	5,000	1,000

* The number of Indians within the territory of the United States in 1853 was estimated by the Commissioner of Indian Affairs at 400,764.

New Mexico.

James L. Collins, *Sup. of Ind. Affairs.* Salary $2,000. Bond $30,000.

Agent.	Salary.	Bond.	Agent.	Salary.	Bond.
Christopher Carson,	$1,550	$5,000	D. Archaleta,	$1,550	$5,000
Michael Steck,	1,550	5,000	Silas F. Kendrick,	1,500	10,000
S. M. Yost,	1,550	10,000	J. Walker,	1,500	10,000

Utah.

Jacob Forney,	*Superintend. of Ind. Affairs.*	Salary	$2,000	Bond	$50,000
Andrew Humphreys,	*Agent,*	"	1,550		20,000
Frederick Dodge,	"	"	1,000	"	5,000
W. H. Rogers,	"	"	1,000	"	5,000

California.

James Y. McDuffie,	*Super. of Ind. Affairs,*	Salary	$4,000	Bond	$200,000
J. R. Vineyard,	*Agent,*	"	3,000	"	20,000
D. E. Buel,	"	"	3,000	"	20,000
V. E. Geiger,	"	"	3,000	"	20,000

Henry L. Ford, M. B. Lewis, and H. Heintzleman, each *Sub-agents,* salary $1,500, bonds $20,000.

Washington and Oregon Territory.

E. R. Geary,	*Superintendent of Ind. Affairs,*	Salary	$2,500	Bond	$70,000
John F. Miller,	*Agent,*	"	1,500	"	5,000
Daniel Newcomb,	"	"	1,500	"	10,000
A. P. Dennison,	"	"	1,500	"	10,000
M. T. Simmons,	"	"	1,500	"	10,000
R. H. Lansdale,	"	"	1,500	"	20,000
Andrew J. Cain,	"	"	1,500	"	10,000

Joshua B. Sykes, G. H. Abbott, and John Owen, *Sub-agents,* with a salary each of $1,000, and each giving bonds in $2,000.

S. P. Ross and M. Leeper are Special Agents, for Indians in Texas. Their bonds are $5,000 each, and their salary is $1,500 per annum.

Army Pension-Agents *in Office, November,* 1859.

Place.	Name.	Place.	Name.
Albany, N. Y.	Isaac Vanderpoel.	Huntsville, Ala.	Wm. H. Moore.
Baltimore, Md.	John S. Gittings.	Indianapolis, Ind.	Wm. Henderson.
Boston, Mass.	Isaac O. Barnes.	Jackson, Miss.	D. N. Barrows.
Bradford, Vt.	B. F. Blodgett.	Jackson, Tenn.	Jos. B. Freeman.
Burlington, Vt.	Chas. F. Warner.	Jacksonville, Fa.	Arthur M. Reed.
Charleston, S. C.	John C. Cochran.	Jonesboro', Ten.	Wm. K. Blair.
Cincinnati, Ohio,	Joel C. Green.	Knoxville, Tenn.	Isaac Lewis.
Cleveland, Ohio,	E. Hessenmueller.	Little Rock, Ark.	P. T. Crutchfield.
Concord, N. H.	George Minot.	Louisville, Ky.	J. B. Kinkhead.
Detroit, Mich.	H. C. Kibbee.	Madison, Ind.	J. W. Chapman.
Fayetteville, N.C.	W. G. Broadfoot.	Milwaukee, Wis.	C. H. Larkin.
Fort Gibson, Ark.	Thos. Lanigan.	Mobile, Ala.	James A. Miller.
Hartford, Ct.	Seth Belden.	Morgantown, N.C.	R. C. Pierson.

Place.	Name.	Place.	Name.
Nashville, Tenn.	Joel M. Smith.	Richmond, Va.	M. D. Newman.
New Albany, Ind.	B. C. Kent,	San Francisco, Cal.	P. Bequette.
New Orleans, La.	S. W. Dalton.	Savannah, Ga.	Geo. A. Mercer.
New York, N. Y.	V. B. Livingston.	Springfield, Ill.	Harry Wilton.
Oregon City, Or.	A. L. Lovejoy.	St. Louis, Mo.	Thos. H. Clarke.
Ottumwa, Iowa,	P. C. Jeffries.	Tallahassee, Fla.	Francis H. Flagg.
Philadelphia, Pa.	Joseph E. Devitt.	Trenton, N. J.	Phil. Dickinson.
Pittsburg, Pa.	John Grayson.	Tuscaloosa, Ala.	Monroe Donoho.
Portland, Me.	George F. Emery.	Washington, D.C.	G. W. Riggs.
Portsmouth, N.H.	A. H. Hoyt.	Wheeling, Va.	S. Brady.
Providence, R. I.	A. M. Warner.		

NAVY PENSION-AGENTS *in Office, November*, 1859.

Place.	Name.	Place.	Name.
Baltimore, Md.	J. S. Gittings.	Philadelphia, Pa.	Joseph E. Devitt.
Boston, Mass.	Isaac O. Barnes.	Pittsburg, Pa.	John Grayson.
Charleston, S. C.	John C. Cochran.	Portland, Me.	George F. Emery.
Cincinnati, Ohio,	Joel C. Green.	Portsmouth, N.H.	A. H. Hoyt.
Detroit, Mich.	H. C. Kibbee.	Providence, R.I.	A. M. Warner.
Hartford, Ct.	Seth Belden.	San Francisco, Cal.	P. Bequette.
Louisville, Ky.	J. B. Kinkhead.	Savannah, Ga.	Geo. A. Mercer.
New Orleans, La.	S. W. Dalton.	St. Louis, Mo.	Thos. H. Clarke.
New York, N.Y.	V. B. Livingston.	Trenton, N. J.	Phil. Dickinson.
Norfolk, Va.	E. Pendleton.	Washington, D.C.	G. W. Riggs.
Pensacola, Fa.	A. E. Maxwell.		

SUPERVISING INSPECTORS OF STEAMBOATS, AND THEIR DISTRICTS, *November*, 1859.

Salary $1,500 each, and reasonable travelling expenses.

No. of Dist.	Inspector.	District.
1.	William Burnett, of Boston,	Maine to Connecticut, inclusive.
2.	Charles W. Copeland, of New York,	New York to Delaware Bay and tributaries, and the Hudson River as far north as Troy.
3.	John S. Brown, of Baltimore,	Delaware Bay to Cape Sable, Florida.
4.	O. A. Pitfield, of New Orleans,	Cape Sable to the Rio Grande; Mississippi River to Baton Rouge; California & Oregon.
5.	Charles Ross, of Cincinnati,	The Mississippi above Baton Rouge and its tributaries, excluding the Ohio, and including the Missouri River.
6.	John Shalcross, of Louisville,	The waters of the Ohio River to the Kentucky River.
7.	Benjamin Crawford, of Pittsburg,	Waters of the Ohio above the Kentucky River.
8.	Isaac Lewis, of Monroe (Mich.),	The waters north and west of Lake Erie, including the Illinois and Mississippi, above Missouri.
9.	Augustus Walker, of Buffalo,	The waters of Lake Erie, Ontario, and the St. Lawrence to Champlain.

LIGHTHOUSE BOARD.

Howell Cobb, *Secretary of the Treasury, President ex officio.*

Members.

*Wm. B. Shubrick, U. S. N.
A. H. Bowman, U. S. Eng. Corps.
A. A. Humphreys, U.S. Topog. Eng.
A. D. Bache, Supt. Coast Survey.
Joseph Henry, Sec'y Smithson. Inst.
Edward G. Tilton, U. S. N.

Secretaries.

Raphael Simmes, U. S. N.
W. B. Franklin, U. S. Top. Eng.

* Com. Kearney has been appointed temporarily, but Com. Shubrick has not been relieved.

III. ARMY LIST.‖

1. Winfield Scott,¶ *Major-General*, (commissioned June 25, 1841,) *General-in-Chief*. Head-quarters at New York.

*John E. Wool, *Brigadier-General*,	commissioned	June 25, 1841.
*David E. Twiggs, "	"	June 30, 1846.
William S. Harney, "	"	June 14, 1858.
Samuel Cooper, *Col. and Adj.-Gen.*,	"	July 15, 1852.
†Sylvester Churchill, *Col. and Inspector-Gen.*,	"	June 25, 1841.
Jos. K. F. Mansfield, *Col. and Inspector-Gen.*,	"	May 28, 1853.
*Thomas S. Jesup, *Brig.-Gen., and Quartermaster-General*,	"	May 8, 1818.
*George Gibson, *Col. and Commissary-Gen.*,	"	April 18, 1818.
†Thomas Lawson, *Col. and Surgeon-Gen.*,	"	Nov. 30, 1836.
Benj. F. Larned, *Col. and Paymaster-Gen.*,	"	July 20, 1854.
†Col. Joseph G. Totten, *Chief Engineer*,	"	Dec. 7, 1838.
Col. J. J. Abert, *Chief Topographical Engineer*,	"	July 7, 1838.
Col. Henry K. Craig, *Chief of Ordnance*,	"	July 10, 1851.
Brevet-Major John F. Lee, *Judge Advocate*,	"	Mar. 2, 1849.

2. Field Officers of the Corps of Engineers, Topographical Engineers, and Ordnance, and of Regiments.

Engineers.

†Col. Joseph G. Totten,
‡Lieut.-Col. Sylvanus Thayer,
" René E. De Russy,
Major Richard Delafield,**
" Henry Brewerton.
" Alexander H. Bowman.
" John G. Barnard,

Topographical Engineers.

Col. John J. Abert,
Lieut.-Col. James Kearney,
§Major Stephen H. Long,
" Hartman Bache,
§ " James D. Graham,
" Campbell Graham.

Ordnance Department.

Col. Henry K. Craig,
Lieut.-Col. James W. Ripley,
Major John Symington,
" William H. Bell,
" Alfred Mordecai,
‡ " Benjamin Huger.

First Dragoons.

Col. Thomas T. Fauntleroy,
Lieut.-Col. Benjamin L. Beall,
Major George A. H. Blake.
" Enoch Steen.

Second Dragoons.

Col. Philip St. G. Cooke,
Lieut.-Col. Marshall S. Howe,
‡Major Charles A. May,
" Lawrence P. Graham.

First Cavalry.

Col. Edwin V. Sumner,
Lieut.-Col. J. E. Johnston,
Major Wm. H. Emory,
" John Sedgwick.

Second Cavalry.

†Col. Albert S. Johnston,
‡Lieut.-Col. Robert E. Lee,
§Major Wm. J. Hardee,
" Geo. H. Thomas.

Mounted Riflemen.

Col. Wm. W. Loring,
Lieut.-Col. Geo. B. Crittenden,
Major John S. Simonson,
" Charles F. Ruff.

First Artillery.

Col. John Erving,
‡Lieut.-Col. John L. Gardner,
Major Robert Anderson,
" Erasmus D. Keyes.

Second Artillery.

Col. Matthew M. Payne,
‡Lieut.-Col. Justin Dimick,
‡Major Harvey Brown,
§ " Martin Burke.

Third Artillery.

Col. William Gates,
Lieut.-Col. Chas. S. Merchant,
§Major George Nauman,
" John B. Scott.

* Major-General by brevet.
† Brigadier-General by brevet.
‡ Colonel by brevet.
§ Lieutenant-Colonel by brevet.
‖ We are greatly indebted to the Adjutant-General for correcting this List to Nov. 1st, 1859.
¶ Lt.-Gen. by brevet, from March 29, 1847, by joint resolution of Feb. 15, 1855.
** Superintendent of the Military Academy at West Point, with local rank of Colonel.

Fourth Artillery.
Col. Francis S. Belton,
‡Lieut.-Col. John Munroe,
Major Giles Porter,
" William W. Morris.

First Infantry.
Col. Joseph Plympton,
Lieut.-Col. Gouverneur Morris,
Major Samuel P. Heintzelman,
" Sidney Burbank.

Second Infantry.
Col. Dixon S. Miles,
Lieut.-Col. J. J. Abercrombie,
Major Edgar S. Hawkins,
" Hannibal Day.

Third Infantry.
Col. Benjamin L. E. Bonneville,
Lieut.-Col. Electus Backus,
Major Nathaniel C. Macrae,
" Caleb C. Sibley.

Fourth Infantry.
Col. William Whistler,
Lieut.-Col. Thompson Morris,
Major Gabriel J. Rains,
§ " Robert C. Buchanan.

Fifth Infantry.
Col. Gustavus Loomis,
‡Lieut.-Col. Carlos A. Waite,
Major Thomas P. Gwynne,
" Seth Eastman.

Sixth Infantry.
†Col. Newman S. Clarke,
Lieut.-Col. George Andrews,
§Major William Hoffman,
" Albemarle Cady.

Seventh Infantry.
Col. Henry Wilson,
Lieut.-Col. Pitcairn Morrison,
§ " Joseph R. Smith,
" Isaac Lynde.

Eighth Infantry.
†Col. John Garland,
Lieut.-Col. Washington Seawell,
Major Thomas L. Alexander,
" Theophilus H. Holmes.

Ninth Infantry.
Col. George Wright,
Lieut.-Col. Silas Casey,
§Major Edward J. Steptoe,
" Robert S. Garnett.

Tenth Infantry.
Col. Edmund B. Alexander,
‡Lieut.-Col. Charles F. Smith,
§Major Wm. H. T. Walker,
§ " Edward R. S. Canby.

3. Military Commands.

Department of the East. — The country east of the Mississippi River; head-quarters at Troy, N. Y. Brev. Maj.-Gen. John E. Wool, Commander.

Department of the West. — The country west of the Mississippi River, and east of the Rocky Mountains, except that portion included within the limits of the Departments of Texas and New Mexico; head-quarters at St. Louis, Mo. Colonel Edwin V. Sumner, 1st Cavalry, Commander.

Department of Texas. — The State of Texas, and the territory north of it to the boundaries of New Mexico, Kansas, and Arkansas, and the Arkansas River, including Fort Smith. Fort Bliss, in Texas, is temporarily attached to the Department of New Mexico; head-quarters at San Antonio, Texas. Brevet Maj.-Gen. David E. Twiggs, Commander.

Department of New Mexico. — The Territory of New Mexico; head-quarters at Santa Fé, New Mexico. Colonel Thomas T. Fauntleroy, 1st Dragoons, Commander.

Department of Utah. — The Territory of Utah, except that portion of it lying west of the 117th degree of west longitude; head-quarters, Camp Floyd, U. T. Brevet Brig.-Gen. Albert S. Johnston, 2d Cavalry, Commander.

Department of Oregon. — The Territory of Washington and the State of Oregon, excepting the Rogue River and Umpqua districts in Oregon; head-quarters at Fort Vancouver, Washington Territory. Brig.-Gen. William S. Harney, Commander.

Department of California. — The country west of the Rocky Mountains except those portions of it included within the limits of the departments of Oregon, Utah, and New Mexico; head-quarters at San Francisco, California. Brevet Brig.-Gen. Newman S. Clarke, 6th Infantry, Commander.

The head-quarters of the army are in the city of New York. Brevet Lieut.-Gen. Winfield Scott, Commander.

4. Arsenals.

Arsenal.	State or Territory.	Post-Office.	Permanent Commander.	Regiment and Corps.
Kennebec,	Maine,	Augusta,	1st Lieut. J. W. Todd,	Ordnance.
Watertown,	Massachusetts,	Watertown,	Capt. R. A. Wainwright,	Ordnance.
Watervliet,	New York,	West Troy,	Maj. A. Mordecai,	Ordnance.
New York,	New York,	New York,	Bvt.Maj. W. A. Thornton,	Ordnance.
Alleghany,	Pennsylvania,	Pittsburg,	Maj. John Symington,	Ordnance.
Frankford,	"	Bridesburg,	Bvt. Maj. P. V. Hagner,	Ordnance.
Pikesville,	Maryland,	Pikesville,	Bvt. Col. B. Huger,	Ordnance.
Washington,	Dist. of Columbia,	Washington,	Bvt. Maj. G. D. Ramsay,	Ordnance.
Fort Monroe,	Virginia,	Old P. Comfort,	Capt. A. B. Dyer,	Ordnance.
North Carolina,	North Carolina,	Fayetteville,	Capt. J. A. J. Bradford,	Ordnance.
Charleston,	South Carolina,	Charleston,	Capt. Josiah Gorgas,	Ordnance.
Mount Vernon,	Alabama,	Mount Vernon,	Bvt. 2d Lt. G. C. Strong,	Ordnance.
Baton Rouge,	Louisiana,	Baton Rouge,	1st Lt. W. R. Boggs,	Ordnance.
Texas,	Texas,	San Antonio,	Capt. R. H. K. Whiteley,	Ordnance.
St. Louis,	Missouri,	St. Louis,	Maj. W. H. Bell,	Ordnance.
Benicia,	California,	Benicia,	Capt. F. D. Callender,	Ordnance.

There is a national armory at Springfield, Mass., James S. Whitney, Civil Superintendent, and one at Harper's Ferry, Va., Henry W. Clowe, Civil Superintendent. The Detroit Arsenal, at Dearbonville, Mich.; the Champlain Arsenal and Ordnance Depot at Vergennes, Vt.; the Rome, at Rome, N. Y.; the Augusta, at Augusta, Ga.; the Appalachicola, at Chattahoochee, Fla.; the Little Rock Arsenal, Ark.; and the Santa Fé, at Santa Fé, New Mexico, are under charge of military storekeepers. The Bellona Arsenal is not used at present. An Ordnance Sergeant is at the post in charge of the buildings and grounds.

5. Military Posts. — *October 5th*, 1859.

The places designated by asterisks (*) are upon the St. Louis and California overland mail route.

Post.	State or Territory.	Post-Office.	Permanent Commander.	Garrison.
Department of the	East.			
Fort Sullivan,	Maine,	Eastport,	Garrison	withdrawn.
Fort Preble,	"	Portland,	"	"
Fort Constitution,	N. Hampshire,	Portsmouth,	"	"
Fort Independence,	Massachusetts,	Boston,	Bvt.Maj.L.G.Arnold,2art.	2d artillery.
Fort Warren,	"	"		Not garrisoned.
Fort Adams,	Rhode Island,	Newport,	Bvt.Lt.-Col.Magruder,1ar.	1st artillery.
Fort Wolcott,	Rhode Island,	Newport,		Not garrisoned.
Fort Trumbull,	Connecticut,	New London,	Garrison	withdrawn.
West Point,	New York,	West Point,	Col. Rich'd Delafield, engs.	Engineers.
Fort Hamilton,	"	Fort Hamilton,	Col. Martin Burke,	2d artillery.
Fort Lafayette,	"	New York,		Not garrisoned.
Fort Columbus,	N. Y. Harbor,	"	Major T. H. Holmes, 8inf.	Recruits.
Fort Wood,	"	"		Not garrisoned.
Fort Niagara,	New York,	Youngstown,	Garrison	withdrawn.
Fort Ontario,	"	Oswego,	"	"
Madison Barracks,	"	Sackett's Harb.	"	"
Plattsburgh Barracks,	"	Plattsburgh,	Capt. H. A. Allen, 2art.	2d artillery.
Fort Mifflin,	Pennsylvania,	Philadelphia,	Garrison	withdrawn.
Carlisle Barracks,	"	Carlisle,	Maj. L. P. Graham, 2 drag.	Recruits.
Fort McHenry,	Maryland,	Baltimore,		Detachment.
Fort Washington,	"	F. Washington,	Garrison	withdrawn.
Fort Monroe,	Virginia,	Old P. Comfort,	Bvt. Col. H. Brown, 2 art.	1, 2, 3, & 4 art.
Fort Johnson, } Fort Caswell, }	North Carolina,	Smithville,	Garrison	withdrawn.
Fort Macon,	"	Beaufort,	"	"
Fort Moultrie,	South Carolina,	Charleston,	Col. J. L. Gardner, 1 art.	1st artillery.
Castle Pinckney, } Fort Sumter, }	"	"	Garrison	withdrawn.

Post.	State or Territory.	Post-office.	Permanent Commander.	Garrison.
Oglethorpe Bar'cks,	Georgia,	Savannah,	Garrison	withdrawn.
Key West Barracks,	Florida,	Key West,	Capt. J. M. Brannan, 1 art.	1st artillery.
Fort Pickens, Barrancas Barracks, Fort McRee,	Florida,	Pensacola,	Bvt. Lt.-Col. Winder, 1 art.	1st artillery.
Fort Marion,	"	St. Augustine,	Garrison	withdrawn.
Fort Morgan,	Alabama,	Mobile,	"	"
Baton Rouge Barracks,	Louisiana,	Baton Rouge,	Capt. J. B. Ricketts, 1st ar.	1st artillery.
Fort Pike,	"	Fort Pike,	Garrison	withdrawn.
Fort Macomb,	"	New Orleans,	"	"
Fort Jackson,	"	"	"	"
New Orleans Barracks,	"	"	"	"
Newport Barracks,	Kentucky,	Newport,	Major S. Burbank, 1 inf.	Recruits.
Fort Brady,	Michigan,	Sault S. Marie,	Garrison	withdrawn.
Fort Mackinac,	"	Mackinac,	Capt. H. C. Pratt, 2 art.	2d artillery.
Fort Gratiot,	"	Fort Gratiot,	Garrison	withdrawn.
DEPARTMENT OF THE WEST.				
Fort Ripley,	Minnesota,	Fort Ripley,	1st Lt. A. J. Perry, 2 art.	2d infantry.
Fort Ridgely,	"	Fort Ridgely,	Maj. W. W. Morris, 4 art.	2d.3d,& 4th art.
Fort Randall,	Nebraska,	*Via* Sioux City, Iowa.	Bvt. Col. Munroe,	2d & 4th art.
Fort Leavenworth,	Kansas,	F. Leavenworth	Bvt. Col. Dimick,	2d art., 2d inf.
Fort Riley,	"	Fort Riley,	Bvt. Lt.-Col. Brooks, 2 art.	1st cav., 2d inf.
Jefferson Barracks,	Missouri,	Jefferson B'ks,		Not garrisoned.
Fort Smith,	Arkansas,	Fort Smith,		" "
Fort Arbuckle,	Choctaw Na'n,	Fort Arbuckle,	Capt. W. E. Prince, 1 inf.	1st cav., 1st inf.
Fort Washita,	Chickasaw "	Fort Washita,	Capt. T. J. Wood, 1 cav.	1st cavalry.
Fort Kearny,	Nebraska,	Fort Kearny,	Bvt. Col. May, 2 drag.	2d drag., 2d inf.
Fort Laramie,	"	Fort Laramie,	Capt. C. S. Lovell, 2 inf.	2d drag., 2d inf.
Prairie Dog Creek,	"		Capt. N. Lyon, 2 inf.	2d infantry.
DEPARTMENT OF TEXAS.				
Fort Belknap,	Texas,	Fort Belknap,		Not garrisoned.
Fort Chadbourne,	"	*V.* F. Belknap,*	Capt. G. W. Wallace, 1 inf.	1st infantry.
Camp Colorado,	"	*V.* San Antonio,	Bvt. Maj. Van Dorn, 2 cav.	2d cavalry.
Fort Lancaster,	"	Fort Lancaster,	Capt. R. S. Granger, 1 inf.	1st infantry.
Fort Davis,	"	Fort Davis,	Lt.-Col. W. Seawell, 8 inf.	8th infantry.
Fort Quitman,	"	*Via* Fort Davis,	Bvt. Lt.-Col. Bomford,	8th infantry.
Camp Hudson,	"	*V.* San Antonio,	Bvt. Major L. Smith,	8th infantry.
Camp Verde,	"	"	Major S. P. Heintzelman,	1st infantry.
San Antonio Barracks,	"	San Antonio,	Capt. J. H. King, 1 inf.	1st infantry.
Fort Clark,	"	Fort Clark,	Bvt. Major W. H. French,	1st artillery.
Fort Inge,	"	*V.* San Antonio,	Capt. R. P. Maclay, 8 inf.	8th infantry.
Fort Mason,	"	"	2d Lieut. W. Owens,	2d cavalry.
Camp Stockton,	"	**V.* St. Louis, &c.	Capt. S. D. Carpenter,	1st infantry.
Fort Cobb,	"		Maj. W. H. Emory, 1 cav.	1st cav., 1st inf.
DEPARTMENT OF NEW MEXICO.				
Fort Garland,	New Mexico,	*Via* Santa Fé,	Capt. A. W. Bowman, 3 inf.	3d infantry.
Cantonment Burgwin,	"	"	Capt. T. Duncan, Mt. rifl.	Rifles, 3d inf.
Fort Union,	"	Fort Union,	Capt. J. G. Walker,	Mtd. rifles.
Fort Defiance,	"	*Via* Santa Fé,	Major J. S. Simonson,	3d infantry.
Fort Marcy,	"	Santa Fé,	1st Lt. M. Cogswell, 8 inf.	8th infantry.
Albuquerque,	"	Albuquerque,	Capt. J. Trevitt, 3 inf.	3d infantry.
Los Lunas,	"	*V.* Albuquerque,	1st Lt. Whistler, 3 inf.	3d infantry.
Fort Craig,	"	Fort Craig,	Bvt. Lt.-Col. A. Porter,	Mtd rifles.
Fort Stanton,*	"	*V.* Albuquerque,	*Major C. F. Ruff,	Mt. rifles, 8 inf.
Fort Fillmore,	"	Fort Fillmore,*	Bvt. Maj. Gordon, 3 inf.	3 inf. 1dr. rifles.
Fort Bliss,	Texas,	Fort Bliss,*	Capt. W. L. Elliott,	Mt. rifles, 8 inf.
Fort Buchanan,	New Mexico,	Ft. Buchanan,*	Bvt. Lt.-Col. J. V. D. Reeve,	1st drag., 8 inf.
DEPARTMENT OF UTAH.				
Fort Bridger,	Utah Ter.,	*V.* St. Joseph, Mo.	Bvt. Lt.-Col. Canby, 10 inf.	2 dr., 7 & 10 inf.
Camp Floyd,	"	Salt Lake City,	Lt.-Col. C. F. Smith,	2 dr., 4 art., 5, 7, & 10 inf.
DEPARTMENT OF OREGON.				
Harney Depot,	Washington T.	*V.* F. Walla-Walla,	Bvt Maj. P. Lugenbeel,	9th infantry.
Escort to N. W. Boundary Commission,	"	"	Capt. D. Woodruff, 9 inf.	9th infantry.
Fort Walla-Walla,	"	"	Col. George Wright, 9 inf.	1dr., 3art., 9inf.
Fort Vancouver,	"	Vancouver,	Lt.-Col. T. Morris, 4 inf.	3art., 4inf., 1dr.

Post.	State or Territory.	Post-Office.	Permanent Commander.	Garrison.
Fort Dalles,	Oregon,	Dalles of Col'bia	Capt. H. M. Black, 9 inf.	9th infantry.
Fort Yamhill,	"	Dayton,	Capt. D. A. Russell, 4 inf.	4th inf., 1st dr.
Fort Hoskins,	"	Portland,	Capt. C. C. Augur, 4 inf.	4th infantry.
San Juan Island,	Washington T.	V. Pt. Towns'd,	Lieut.-Col. S. Casey, 4 inf.	3 art., 4 & 9 inf., det. of engrs.
DEPARTMENT OF CALIFORNIA.				
Fort Umpqua,	Oregon,	Umpqua City,	Maj. J. B. Scott, 3 art.	3d artillery.
Fort Humboldt,	California,	Bucksport,	Maj. G. J. Rains, 4 inf.	4th infantry.
Fort Crook,	"	Am. Ranch,	Capt. J. Adams, 1 drags.	1st dragoons.
Benicia Barracks,	"	Benicia,	Bvt. Lieut.-Col. Hoffman,	6th infantry.
Fort Tejon,	"	V. LosAngeles,*	Lt.-Col. B. L. Beall, 1 dr.	1st dragoons.
Fort Yuma,	"	Fort Yuma,*		6th infantry.
Fort Gaston,	"	V. Ft. Humboldt	Capt. E. Underwood,	4th infantry.
New San Diego,	"	San Diego,	Capt. W. S. Ketchum,	6th infantry.
Fort Mojave,	New Mexico,*		Bvt. Maj. L. A. Armistead,	6th infantry.
Presidio San Francisco,	California,		Lt.-Col. C. S. Merchant,	3d artillery.

6. MILITIA FORCE OF THE UNITED STATES.

Abstract of the United States Militia, from the Army Register for 1859.

State or Territory.†	For what year.	General Officers.	General Staff Officers.	Field Officers, &c.	Company Officers.	Total Commissioned Officers.	Non-commissioned Officers, Musicians, Artificers, Privates.	Aggregate.
Alabama,	1851	32	142	775	1,883	2,832	73,830	76,662
Arkansas,	1854	10	39	128	955	1,132	34,922	36,054
California,	1857	18	126	11	175	330	207,400	207,730
Connecticut,	1858	3	9	82	199	293	51,312	51,605
Delaware,	1827	4	8	71	364	447	8,782	9,229
Florida,	1845	3	14	95	508	620	11,502	12,122
Georgia,	1850	39	91	624	4,296	5,050	73,649	78,699
Illinois,	1855							257,420
Indiana,	1832	31	110	566	2,154	2,861	51,052	53,913
Kentucky,	1852	43	145	1,165	3,517	4,870	84,109	88,979
Louisiana,	1858	16	129	542	2,101	2,788	88,496	91,284
Maine,	1856	13	52	36	203	304	73,248	73,552
Maryland,	1838	22	68	544	1,763	2,397	44,467	46,864
Massachusetts,	1858	10	47	125	421	603	152,850	153,453
Michigan,	1854	30	323	147	2,358	2,858	94,236	97,094
Minnesota,	1851	2	5			7	1,996	2,003
Mississippi,	1838	16	70	392	348	825	35,259	36,084
Missouri,	1853		17	4	67	88	117,959	118,047
N. Hampshire,	1854	11	202	119	895	1,227	32,311	33,538
New Jersey,	1852							81,984
New York,	1856	93	299	1,501	5,495	7,388	329,847	337,235
North Carolina,	1845	28	133	657	3,449	4,267	75,181	79,448
Ohio,	1845	91	217	462	1,281	2,051	174,404	176,455
Pennsylvania,	1855							147,973
Rhode Island,	1858	2	22	106	26	156	16,555	16,711
South Carolina,	1856	20	135	535	1,909	2,599	33,473	36,072
Tennessee,	1840	25	79	859	2,644	3,607	67,645	71,252
Texas,	1847	15	45	248	940	1,248	18,518	19,766
Vermont,	1843	12	51	224	801	1,088	22,827	23,915
Virginia,	1858							150,000
Wisconsin,	1855	15	8	215	904	1,142	50,179	51,321
D. of Columbia,	1852	3	10	28	185	226	7,975	8,201
Utah Ter.,	1853	2		48	235	285	2,536	2,821
Total,		608	2,596	10,309	40,076	53,589	2,036,520	2,727,466

† No returns from Iowa, and Oregon, and the Territories of New Mexico, Washington, Kansas, and Nebraska.

7. Table of Pay, Subsistence, Forage, etc. of Army Officers.

Rank and Classification of Officers.	Pay.	Subsistence. 30 cents for each Ration.		Forage. $8 p. mo. for each Horse.		Servants. Pay, &c. of a Private.		Total Monthly Pay.
	Per Month.	No. of Rations.	Monthly Commutation value.	No. of Horses.	Monthly Commutation value.	No. of Servants.	Monthly Commutation value.	
Lieutenant-General, ...	$270.00	40	$360		$50	4	$90.00	$770.00
Aids-de-camp, and military Secretary to Lieutenant-General, *each*, . . .	80.00	5	45	3	24	2	45.00	194.00
Major-General, ...	220.00	15	135	3	24	4	90.00	469.00
Senior Aide-de-camp to General-in-chief,	80.00	4	36	3	24	2	47.00	187.00
Aide-de-camp, besides pay of Lieutenant,	24.00			1	8			32.00
Brigadier-General, ...	124.00	12	108	3	24	3	67.50	323.50
Aide-de-camp, besides pay of Lieutenant,	20.00			1	8			19.00
Adjutant-General, — Colonel, ...	110.00	6	54	3	24	2	47.00	235.00
Assistant Adj.-General, — Lieut.-Colonel,	95.00	5	45	3	24	2	47.00	211.00
" " Major, .	80.00	4	36	3	24	2	47.00	187.00
" " Captain, .	70.00	4	36	1	8	1	23.50	137.50
Judge-Advocate, — Major, ...	80.00	4	36	3	24	2	47.00	187.00
Inspector-General, — Colonel, . . .	110.00	6	54	3	24	2	47.00	235.00
Quartermaster-General, — Brig.-General,	124.00	12	108	3	24	3	67.50	323.50
Assistant Quarterm.-Gen., — Colonel, .	110.00	6	54	3	24	2	47.00	235.00
Deputy Quarterm.-Gen., — Lieut.-Colonel,	95.00	5	45	3	24	2	47.00	211.00
Quartermaster, — Major, ...	80.00	4	36	3	24	2	47.00	187.00
Assistant Quartermaster, — Captain, .	70.00	4	36	1	8	1	23.50	137.50
Commissary-Gen. of Subsistence, — Col.,	110.00	6	54	3	24	2	47.00	236.00
Assist. Commissary-Gen., — Lieut.-Col.,	96.00	5	45	3	24	2	47.00	211.00
Commissary of Subsistence, — Major,	80.00	4	36	3	24	2	47.00	187.00
" " Captain, .	70.00	4	36	1	8	1	23.50	137.50
Assistant Comm'y, besides pay of Lieut.,	20.00							11.00
Paymaster-General, $2,740 per annum, .								228.33
Deputy Paymaster-General, ...	95.00	5	45	3	24	2	47.00	211.00
Paymaster, ...	80.00	4	36	3	24	2	47.00	187.00
Surgeon-General, $2,740 per annum, .								228.33
Surgeons of 10 years' service, . . .	80.00	8	72	3	24	2	47.00	223.00
Surgeons of less than 10 years' service,	80.00	4	36	3	24	2	47.00	187.00
Assistant Surgeons of 10 years' service, .	70.00	8	72	1	8	1	23.50	173.50
" of 5 years' service,	70.00	4	36	1	8	1	23.50	137.50
Assist. Surg. of less than 5 years' service,	53.33	4	36	1	8	1	23.50	120.83
Engineers, Topog. Engineers, and Ordnance Department.								
Colonel, ...	110.00	6	54	3	24	2	47.00	235.00
Lieutenant-Colonel, ...	95.00	5	45	3	24	2	47.00	211.00
Major, ...	80.00	4	36	3	24	2	47.00	187.00
Captain, ...	70.00	4	36	1	8	1	23.50	137.50
First Lieutenant, ...	53.33	4	36	1	8	1	23.50	120.83
Second Lieutenant (Brevet the same), .	53.33	4	36	1	8	1	23.50	120.83
Mounted Dragoons, Cavalry, Riflemen, and Light Artillery.								
Colonel, ...	110.00	6	54	3	24	2	47.00	235.00
Lieutenant-Colonel, ...	95.00	5	45	3	24	2	47.00	211.00
Major, ...	80.00	4	36	3	24	2	47.00	187.00
Captain, ...	70.00	4	36	2	16	1	23.50	145.50
First Lieutenant, ...	53.33	4	36	2	16	1	23.50	128.83
Second Lieutenant (Brevet the same), .	53.33	4	36	2	16	1	23.50	128.83
Adj. & Reg. Q'rm'r, besides pay of Lieut.,	10.00							10.00
Artillery and Infantry.								
Colonel, ...	95.00	6	54	3	24	2	45.00	218.00
Lieutenant-Colonel, ...	80.00	5	45	3	24	2	45.00	194.00
Major, ...	70.00	4	36	3	24	2	45.00	175.00
Captain, ...	60.00	4	36			1	22.50	118.50
First Lieutenant, ...	50.00	4	36			1	22.50	108.50
Second Lieutenant (Brevet the same), .	45.00	4	36			1	22.50	103.50
Adj. and Reg. Q'rm'r, besides pay of Lieut.,	10.00			1	8			18.00

Military Storekeepers attached to the Quartermaster's department, at armories and at arsenals of construction, the storekeeper at Watertown arsenal, and storekeepers of ordnance serving in Oregon, California, and New Mexico, $ 1,490 per annum, being $ 124.16 per month; at all other arsenals $ 1,040 per annum, being $ 86.66 per month.

On January 1, 1859, the whole number of commissioned officers in the regular army was 1.084; of non-commissioned officers, musicians, artificers, and privates, 11,859; total, 12,913.

IV. NAVY LIST.

1. Commanders of Squadrons. [Flag Officers.]

Wm. J. McCluney,	Home Squadron.	E. A. F. Lavallette,	Mediterranean.
Joshua R. Sands,	Coast of Brazil.	Cornelius K. Stribling,	East Indies.
J. B. Montgomery,	Pacific Ocean.	William Inman,	Coast of Africa.

2. Commanders of Navy Yards.

John Pope,	Portsmouth.	Charles H. Bell,	Norfolk.
William L. Hudson,	Boston.	James Mc. McIntosh,	Pensacola.
S. L. Breese,	New York.	R. B. Cunningham,	Mare Isl., Cal.
Charles Stewart,	Philadelphia.	G. N. Hollins,	Sackett's Harbor, N. Y.
Franklin Buchanan,	Washington.		

3. Naval Asylum.

William W. McKean, *Governor*, Philadelphia.

4. Naval Academy.

George S. Blake, *Superintendent*, Annapolis, Md.

5. Officers of the Navy.

Captains. (*Active List.*) — 80.

Wm. B. Shubrick.
Lawrence Kearny.
Joseph Smith.
Lawrence Rousseau.
George W. Storer.
Francis H. Gregory.
Charles S. McCauley.
E. A. F. Lavallette.
John H. Aulick.
Silas H. Stringham.
Isaac Mayo.
William Mervine.
Thomas Crabbe.
Thomas Paine.
James Armstrong.
Samuel L. Breese.
Hiram Paulding.
Uriah P. Levy.
French Forrest.
William Ramsay.
Thomas A. Conover.
John C. Long.
James Mc. McIntosh.
Josiah Tatnall.
William Inman.
William J. McCluney.
John B. Montgomery.
Cornelius K. Stribling.
Joshua R. Sands.
Charles H. Bell.
Joseph R Jarvis.
Wm. M. Armstrong.
G. J. Pendergrast.
William C. Nicholson.
Joseph B. Hull.
John S. Chauncey.
John Kelly.
William H. Gardner.
David G. Farragut.
Stephen B. Wilson.
T. Aloysius Dornin.
Rob. B. Cunningham.
James Glynn.
Victor M. Randolph.
Frederick Engle.
John Rudd.
Robert Ritchie.
Wm. W. McKean.
Franklin Buchanan.
Samuel Mercer.
Charles Lowndes.
L. M. Goldsborough.
George N. Hollins.
Duncan N. Ingraham.
John Marston.
Henry A. Adams.
William S. Walker.
George F. Pearson.
John S. Nicholas.
Samuel F. Du Pont.
William L. Hudson.
George A. Magruder.
John Pope.
Levin M. Powell.
Charles Wilkes.
Thomas O. Selfridge.
Henry Eagle.
Andrew K. Long.
G. J. Van Brunt.
William M. Glendy.
George S. Blake.
Samuel Barron.
Andrew A. Harwood.
Theodorus Bailey.
Hugh Y. Purviance.
Cadwalader Ringgold.
Wm. F. Lynch.
Henry W. Morris.
Isaac S. Sterett.
Francis B. Ellison.

Captains. (*Reserved List.*) — 20.

Charles Stewart.
George C. Read.
Jesse Wilkinson.
John D. Sloat.
Charles W. Skinner.
Philip F. Voorhees.
David Geisinger.
William D. Salter.
Thomas M. Newell.
John Percival.
William K. Latimer.
Charles Boarman.
William Jamesson.
Henry W. Ogden.
John H. Graham.
Hugh N. Page.
Stephen Champlin.
Lewis E. Simonds.
Harrison H. Cocke.
Horace B. Sawyer.

Commanders. (*Active List.*) — 114.

Edw. B. Boutwell.
Sidney Smith Lee.
Wm. C. Whittle.
T. Darrah Shaw.
Robert D. Thorburn.
Samuel Lockwood.
William S. Ogden.
Charles C. Turner.
James L. Lardner.
Robert G. Robb.
John Colhoun.
Thomas T. Craven.
Andrew H. Foote.
Wm. W. Hunter.
Edward G. Tilton.
James H. Ward.
Henry K. Hoff.
Murray Mason.
Charles H. Davis.
Ebenezer Farrand.
Henry H Bell.
William Smith.
Charles H. McBlair.
John W. Livingston.
William E. Hunt.
Archibald B. Fairfax.
Henry K Thatcher.
William D. Porter.
William McBlair.
John S. Missroon.
Richard L. Page.
Frederic Chatard.
Benjamin J. Totten.
Arthur Sinclair.
Robert B. Hitchcock.
C H A H Kennedy.
Thomas W. Brent.
Joseph Lanman.
John K. Mitchell.
Thomas Turner.
Charles H. Poor.
James F. Schenck.
Matthew F. Maury.
Timothy A. Hunt.

Sylvanus Wm. Godon.
James S. Palmer.
William Radford.
Samuel F. Hazard.
John M. Berrien.
George A. Prentiss.
John C. Carter.
Alfred Taylor.
Samuel Phillips Lee.
John P. Gillis.
Simon B. Bissell.
Samuel Swartwout.
John J. Glasson.
Raphael Semmes.
James P. McKinstry.
Oliver S. Glisson.
John A. Dahlgren.
Stephen C. Rowan.
Edward R. Thomson.
Guert Gansevoort.
Robert Handy.
Charles Green.
Edward L. Handy.
Melancton Smith.
Cicero Price.
J. R. Goldsborough.
Charles S. Boggs.
A. H. Kilty.
William Chandler.
Theodore P. Green.
John R. Tucker.
Richard W. Meade.
Thomas J. Page.
George Minor.
Percival Drayton.
Robert F. Pinkney.
Thomas R. Rootes.
Edward M. Yard.
Alexander Gibson.
William S Young.
Joseph F. Green.
John De Camp.
Charles W. Pickering.
Overton Carr.
William M. Walker.
John A. Winslow.
Benjamin M. Dove.
Henry Walke.
Thornton A. Jenkins.
John Rodgers.
John B. Marchand.
Wm. Rogers Taylor.
Henry J. Hartstene.
Benjamin F. Sands.
Henry French.
Henry S. Stellwagen.
James L. Henderson.
Daniel B. Ridgely.
William T. Muse.
Charles Steedman.
James Alden.
Augustus L. Case.
Roger Perry.
Alex. M. Pennock.
George F. Emmons.
Edward Middleton.
Thomas T. Hunter.
Gustavus H. Scott.
David McDougal.
Chas. F. McIntosh.

Commanders. (*Reserved List.*) — 16.

John J. Young.
Samuel W. Lecompte.
Charles T. Platt.
Ed. W. Carpender.
John L. Saunders.
Joseph Myers.
Henry Bruce.
Elisha Peck.
William Green.
Timothy G. Benham.
Oscar Bullus.
Charles H. Jackson.
Lloyd B. Newell.
Frederick A. Neville.
John Manning.
Amasa Paine.

6. Pay of the Navy, *per annum*.

Note. — One ration per day only is allowed to each officer when attached to vessels for sea service, since the passage of the law of the 3d of March, 1835, regulating the pay of the navy.

	Pay.
Captains, 100, the senior one in service,	$4,500
" " " on leave,	3,500
Captains of squadrons (flag officers),	4,000
Other captains on duty,	3,500
" on leave,	2,500
" on furlough,	1,250
Commanders, 130, in sea service,	2,500
" at navy yards, or on other duty,	2,100
" on leave, &c.,	1,800
" on furlough,	900
Lieutenants, 362, commanding,	1,800
" on other duty,	1,500
" waiting orders,	1,200
" on furlough,	600
Surgeons, 69, 1st 5 years in com.,	1,000
" in navy yards, &c.,	1,250
" in sea service,	1,333
" of the fleet,	1,500
" 2d 5 years, on leave,	1,200
" at navy yards, &c.,	1,500
" in sea service,	1,600
" of the fleet,	1,800
" 3d 5 years, on leave,	1,400
" at navy yards, &c.,	1,750
" in sea service,	1,866
" 3d 5 years, of the fleet,	2,100
" 4th 5 years, on leave,	1,600
" at navy yards, &c.,	2,000
" in sea service,	2,133
" of the fleet,	2,400
" 20 years and upwards, on leave,	1,800
" at navy yards, &c.	2,250
" in sea service,	2,400
" of the fleet,	2,700

	Pay.
Passed Assistant Surgeons, 39.	
Assistant Surgeons, 41, waiting orders,	$650
" after passing, &c.,	850
" at sea,	950
" " after passing,	1,200
" at navy yards,	950
" " after passing,	1,150
Pursers, 64, from $1,500 to	3,500
Chaplains, 23, in sea serv. or at navy-yds.	1,500
" on leave, &c.,	1,000
Professors of Mathematics, 11,	1,500
Masters in the line of promotion, 34.	
Passed Midshipmen, 2, on duty,	750
" " waiting orders,	600
Midshipmen, 49, in sea service,	400
Midshipmen, on other duty,	350
" on leave, &c.,	300
Acting Midshipmen, 194.	
Masters, of ship of the line at sea,	1,100
" on other duty,	1,000
" on leave, &c.,	750
Boatswains, 40; Gunners, 48; Carpenters, 46; Sailmakers, 41 — on leave, or waiting orders,	600
" shore duty,	700
" sea service,‡	900
Chief Engineers, 26, on duty, 1st 5 years,	1,500
" " " after 5 years,	2,000
" " on leave, 1st 5 years,	1,200
Chief Engineers on duty after 5 years,	1,400
1st Assistant Engineers, 36, on duty,	1,000
" " on leave,	850
2d Assistant Engineers, 21, on duty,	800
" " on leave,	600
3d Assistant Engineers, 95, on duty,	600
" " on leave,	400

‡ They have an addition of 2 per cent upon the foregoing rates for every year's sea service, and an addition upon sea pay of 10 per cent when serving in ships with 400 men, and 20 per cent when serving in ships with 900 men.

7. Vessels of War of the United States Navy. — *Nov.* 1, 1859.

(The officers marked thus (*) have the rank of *Commanders*; thus (†), *Lieutenants*; the rest are *Captains*.)

Name.	Guns.	Ton.	Where and when built.		Commanded by	Where stationed.
Ships of the Line.		10.				
Penns'vania,	120	3,241	Philadelphia,	1837	*Frederick Chatard,	Rec'g ship, Norfolk.
Columbus,	80	2,480	Washington,	1819	In ordinary,	Norfolk.
Ohio,	84	2,757	Brooklyn,	1820	*William Smith,	Rec'g ship, Boston.
N. Carolina,	84	2,633	Philadelphia,	1820	*James H. Ward,	" N. York.
Delaware,	84	2,633	Gosport,	1820	In ordinary,	Norfolk.
Vermont,	84	2,633	Charlestown,	1848	In ordinary,	Boston.
New Orleans,	84	2,805	Sackett's Harbor,	1815	On the stocks,	Sackett's Harbor.
Alabama,	84	2,633	Kittery,	1818	On the stocks,	Kittery, Me.
Virginia,	84	2,633	Charlestown,	1818	On the stocks,	Boston.
New York,	84	2,633	Gosport,	1818	On the stocks,	Norfolk.
Frigates.	10.					
Constitution,	50	1,607	Charlestown,	1797	In ordinary,	Kittery, Me.
United States,	50	1,607	Philadelphia,	1797	In ordinary,	Norfolk.
Potomac,	50	1,726	Washington,	1821	In ordinary,	New York.
Brandywine,	50	1,726	"	1825	In ordinary,	New York.
Columbia,	50	1,726	"	1836	In ordinary,	Norfolk.
Congress,	50	1,867	Kittery,	1841	L. M. Goldsborough,	Brazil Squadron.
Raritan,	50	1,726	Philadelphia,	1843	In ordinary,	Norfolk.
St. Lawrence,	50	1,726	Gosport,	1847	In ordinary,	Philadelphia.
Santee,	50	1,726	Kittery,	1855	In ordinary,	Kittery, Me.
Sabine,	50	1,726	Brooklyn,	1855	Henry A. Adams,	Home Squadron.
Sloops of War.		21.				
Cumberland,	24	1,726	Charlestown,	1842	In ordinary,	Kittery, Me.
Savannah,	24	1,726	Brooklyn,	1842	Joseph R. Jarvis,	Home Squadron.
Constellation,	22	1,452	Rebuilt, Gosport,	1854	John S. Nicholas,	African Squadron.
Macedonian,	22	1,341	Gosport,	1836	Uriah P. Levy,	Mediterranean.
Portsmouth,	22	1,022	Kittery,	1843	*John Colhoun,	Coast of Africa.
Plymouth,	22	989	Charlestown,	1843	*Thomas T. Craven,	Practice ship, N. Acad.
St. Mary's,	22	958	Washington,	1844	*William D. Porter,	Pacific Squadron.
Jamestown,	22	985	Gosport,	1844	*C H. A. H. Kennedy,	Home Squadron.
Germantown,	22	939	Philadelphia,	1846	*Richard L. Page,	East India Squadron.
Saratoga,	20	882	Kittery,	1842	*Thomas Turner,	Home Squadron.
John Adams,	20	700	Rebuilt, Gosport,	1831	*Murray Mason,	East India Squadron.
Vincennes,	20	700	Brooklyn,	1826	*Benjamin J. Totten,	Coast of Africa.
Falmouth,	20	703	Charlestown,	1827	In ordinary,	New York.
Vandalia,	20	783	Philadelphia,	1828	*Arthur Sinclair,	Pacific Ocean.
St. Louis,	20	700	Washington,	1828	*Charles H. Poor,	Home Squadron.
Cyane,	20	792	Charlestown,	1837	*Samuel Lockwood,	Pacific Squadron.
Levant,	20	792	Brooklyn,	1837	*William E. Hunt,	Pacific Squadron.
Decatur,	16	566	"	1839	In ordinary,	Navy Yard, Mare Isl'd.
Marion,	16	566	Charlestown,	1839	*Thomas W. Brent,	African Squadron.
Dale,	16	566	Philadelphia,	1839	In ordinary,	Portsmouth, N. H.
Preble,	16	566	Kittery,	1839	*T. A. Jenkins,	Home Squadron.
Brigs.	3.					
Bainbridge,	6	259	Charlestown,	1842	†Maxwell Woodhull,	Brazil Squadron.
Perry,	6	280	Gosport,	1843	†R. L. Tilghman,	Coast of Brazil.
Dolphin,	4	224	Brooklyn,	1836	*Charles Steedman,	Brazil Squadron.
Schooner.						
Fenimore Cooper,	3	95	Purchased,	1852	†J. M. Brooke.	Surveying in Pacific.
STEAMERS.						
Screw, 1st Class.		8.				
Niagara,	12	4,580	Brooklyn,	1855	In ordinary,	New York.
Roanoke,	40	3,400	Gosport,	1855	Wm. H. Gardner,	Home Squadron.
Colorado,	40	3,400	"	1855	In ordinary,	Boston.
Merrimack,	40	3,200	Charlestown,	1855	*Robt. B. Hitchcock,	Pacific Ocean.
Minnesota,	40	3,200	Washington,	1855	In ordinary,	Boston.
Wabash,	40	3,200	Philadelphia,	1855	Samuel Barron,	Mediterranean.
Franklin,	50	3,680	Kittery,	1854	In ordinary,	Kittery, Me.
Stevens' war steamer,	6	4,683	Commenced in	1842	Building,	Hoboken, N. J.
Screw, 2d Class.		6.				
San Jacinto,	13	1,446	Brooklyn,	1850	Wm. M. Armstrong,	African Squadron.
Lancaster,	18	2,360	Philadelphia,	1858	John B. Montgomery,	Pacific Squadron.
Pensacola,	16	2,158	Pensacola,	1858	In ordinary,	Pensacola.
Brooklyn,	14	2,070	New York,	1858	David G. Farragut,	Home Squadron.

Name. — Guns. — Ton.			Where and when built.		Commanded by	Where stationed.
Hartford,	14	1,990	Boston,	1858	Charles Lowndes,	East Indies.
Richmond,	14	1,929	Norfolk,	1858	In ordinary,	Norfolk.
Screw, 3d Class.	14.					
Massachusetts,	9	765	Transf'd from W. D.		In ordinary,	Mare Island.
John Hancock,	2	382	Charlestown,	1850	In ordinary,	Mare Island.
Mohican,	6	994	Kittery,	1858	*Sylvanus W. Godon,	Coast of Africa.
Narragansett,	3	809	Boston,	1858	*Timothy A Hunt,	Pacific Squadron.
Iroquois,	6	1,016	New York,	1858	*James S. Palmer,	Mediterranean Squad.
Wyoming,	6	997	Philad'phia,	1858	*John K. Mitchell,	Pacific Squadron.
Pawnee,	6	1,289	Philad'phia,	1858	Preparing for sea.	Philadelphia.
Dacotah,	6	996	Gosport,	1858	Preparing for sea.	Philadelphia.
Seminole,	3	801	Pensacola,	1858	Preparing for sea.	Pensacola,
Crusader,	8	549	Purchased,	1858	†Jno. N. Maffitt,	Home Squadron.
Mystic,	5	464	"	1858	†William E. LeRoy,	Coast of Africa.
Mohawk,	6	464	"	1858	†T. Aug. Craven,	Home Squadron.
Sumpter,	5	464	"	1858	†James F. Armstrong,	Coast of Africa.
Wyandott,	6	464	"	1858	†Fabius Stanly,	Home Squadron.
Screw Tenders.	2.					
Despatch,		558	Purchased,	1855	In ordinary,	Norfolk.
Anacostia,		217	"	1858	†T. S. Fillebrown,	Washing'n & Norfolk.
Side-wheel, 1st Class,	3.					
Mississippi,	10	1,692	Philadelphia,	1841	Wm. C. Nicholson,	East India Squadron.
Susquehanna,	15	2,450	"	1850	In ordinary,	New York.
Powhatan,	9	2,415	Gosport,	1850	George F. Pearson,	East India Squadron.
Side-wheel, 2d Class,	1.					
Saranac,	6	1,446	Kittery,	1848	Robert Ritchie,	Pacific Ocean.
Side-wheel, 3d Class,	3.					
Fulton,	5	698	Brooklyn,	1837	In ordinary,	Pensacola.
Michigan,	1	582	Erie, Penn.,	1844	*Joseph Lanman,	On the Lakes.
Saginaw,	3	453	San Francisco,	1859	*James F. Schenck,	East Indies.
Side-wheel Tenders.	2.					
Water-Witch,	1	378	Washington,	1845	†L. C. Sartori,	Home Squadron.
Pulaski,		395	Purchased,	1858	†Wm. H. Macomb,	Brazil Squadron.
Store Vessels,	3.					
Relief,	2	468	Philadelphia,	1836	*Benj. M. Dove,	Home Squadron.
Supply,	4	547	Purchased,	1846	*Henry Walke.	Coast of Africa.
Release,	1	327	"	1855	†G. W. Harrison,	Brazil Squadron.
Permanent Store and Receiving Ships.						
Independence,		2,257	Charlestown,	1814	*Simon B. Bissell,	Pacific, receiving ship.
Alleghany,		989	Pittsburg, Penn.,	1847	*W. W. Hunter,	Rec'g ship, Baltimore.
Princeton,		900	Rebuilt, Boston,	1851	*Henry K. Hoff,	Rec'g ship, Philadel'a.
Warren,		691	Charlestown,	1826	†Junius J. Boyle,	Panama.
Fredonia,		800	Purchased,	1846	†James M. Watson,	Pacific Squadron.

V. THE MARINE CORPS.*

THE Marine Corps has the organization of a brigade. The pay and allowances of the officers of the Marine Corps are similar to those of officers of the same grades in the infantry of the Army, except the Adjutant and Inspector, who has the same pay and allowances as the Paymaster of the Marines; namely, about $3,000 per annum. The Marine Corps is subject to the laws and regulations of the Navy, except when detached for service with the Army by the order of the President of the United States. The head-quarters of the Corps are at Washington.

John Harris, *Colonel-Commandant.*

General Staff.

† Henry B. Tyler, *Adj. & Inspector.*	James Edelin, *Lieutenant-Colonel.*
† Wm. W. Russell, *Paymaster.*	William Dulany, *Major.*
† Dan. J. Sutherland, *Quartermaster.*	Thomas S. English, *Major.*
‡ W. A. T. Maddox, *Assistant Quartermaster.*	Ward Marston, *Major.*
	Benjamin Macomber, *Major.*

* There are 14 Captains, 20 First Lieutenants, and 20 Second Lieutenants. The number of non-commissioned officers, musicians, and privates varies; it may average 1,100 men.
† With the rank of Major. ‡ With the rank of Captain.

VI. THE JUDICIARY.

Supreme Court.

	Residence.		Appointed.	Salary.
Roger B. Taney,	Baltimore, Md.,	*Chief Justice*,	1836,	$6,500
John McLean,	Cincinnati, Ohio,	*Associate Justice*,	1829,	6,000
James M. Wayne,	Savannah, Ga.,	"	1835,	6,000
John Catron,	Nashville, Tenn.,	"	1837,	6,000
Peter V. Daniel,	Richmond, Va.,	"	1841,	6,000
Samuel Nelson,	Cooperstown, N. Y.,	"	1845,	6,000
Robert C. Grier,	Pittsburg, Pa.,	"	1846,	6,000
John A. Campbell,	Mobile, Ala.,	"	1853,	6,000
Nathan Clifford,	Portland, Me.,	"	1858,	6,000
Jeremiah S. Black,	Washington, D. C.,	*Attorney-General*,	1857,	8,000
Benj. C. Howard,	Baltimore, Md.,	*Reporter*,	1843,	1,300
William T. Carroll,	Washington, D. C.,	*Clerk*,		Fees, &c.

The Supreme Court is held in the city of Washington, and has one session annually, commencing on the 1st Monday of December.

Circuit Courts.

The United States are divided into the following nine Judicial Circuits, in each of which a Circuit Court is held twice every year, for each State within the Circuit, by a Justice of the Supreme Court, assigned to the Circuit, and by the District Judge of the State or District in which the Court sits.

			Presiding Judge.
1st	Circuit,	Maine, Mass., N. Hampshire, and R. I.,	Mr. Justice Clifford.
2d	"	Connecticut, New York, and Vermont,	Mr. Justice Nelson.
3d	"	New Jersey and Pennsylvania,	Mr. Justice Grier.
4th	"	Delaware, Maryland, and Virginia,	Mr. Ch. Justice Taney.
5th	"	Alabama, Kentucky,* and Louisiana,	Mr. Justice Campbell.
6th	"	Georgia, N. Carolina, and S. Carolina,	Mr. Justice Wayne.
7th	"	Illinois, Indiana, Michigan, and Ohio,	Mr. Justice McLean.
8th	"	Kentucky, Missouri, and Tennessee,	Mr. Justice Catron.
9th	"	Arkansas, and Mississippi	Mr. Justice Daniel.

California Circuit, Matthew H. McAllister, of San Francisco.

The States of Florida, Iowa, Minnesota, Oregon, Texas, and Wisconsin, have not yet been attached to any Circuit, but the District Courts have the power of Circuit Courts, and the District Judges act as Circuit Judges. There is a local Circuit Court held in the District of Columbia, by three judges specially appointed for that purpose. The Chief Justice of that Court sits also as District Judge of that District.

Places and Times of Holding the Circuit Courts.†

Alabama, . . . *Mobile*, 2d Mon. in April and 4th Mon. in Dec.

Arkansas, . . . *Little Rock*, 2d Monday in April.

---

* The Judge of the 5th Circuit holds the Circuit Court for the District of Kentucky in the absence of the Judge of the 8th Circuit. Stat. 1849, Ch. 120.

† For the Terms in the States not attached to any Circuit, see Terms of the District Courts in those States. For the Terms in the District of Columbia and the Territories, see *post*, Part III.

CALIFORNIA, N. Dist., *San Francisco*, 1st Monday in January and July.
CALIFORNIA, S. Dist., *Los Angeles*, 1st Monday in March and September.
CONNECTICUT, . . *New Haven*, 4th Tuesday in April; — *Hartford*, 3d Tuesday in September.
DELAWARE, . . . *Wilmington*, 3d Tuesday in June and October.
GEORGIA, N. Dist., *Marietta*,* 2d Monday in March and September.
GEORGIA, S. Dist., . *Savannah*, 2d Monday in April; — *Milledgeville*. Thursday after 1st Monday in November.
ILLINOIS, N. Dist., *Chicago*, 1st Mon. in July and 3d Mon. in Dec.
ILLINOIS, S. Dist., *Springfield*, 1st Monday in January and June.
INDIANA, ... *Indianapolis*, 3d Monday in May and November.
KENTUCKY, . . . *Frankfort*, 3d Monday in May and October.
LOUISIANA, . . . *New Orleans*, 4th Mon. in April and 1st Mon. in Nov.
MAINE, ... *Portland*, 23d April and 23d September.
MARYLAND, . . . *Baltimore*, 1st Monday in April and November.
MASSACHUSETTS, . *Boston*, 15th May and 15th October.
MICHIGAN, . . . *Detroit*, 3d Monday in June and 2d Monday in Oct.
MISSISSIPPI, . . . *Jackson*, 1st Monday in May and November.
MISSOURI, . . . *St. Louis*, 1st Monday in April and (special) Oct.
NEW HAMPSHIRE, . *Portsmouth*, 8th May; — *Exeter*, 8th October.
NEW JERSEY, . . *Trenton*, 4th Tuesday in March and September.
N. YORK, S. Dist., . *New York*, 1st Monday in April and 3d Monday in October; and a special term for criminal cases and suits in equity on the last Monday in February.
N. YORK, N. Dist., *Albany*, 3d Tuesday in October and 3d Tuesday in May; — *Canandaigua*, Tuesday next after 3d Monday in June.
NORTH CAROLINA, . *Raleigh*, 1st Mon. in June and last Mon. in Nov.
OHIO, N. Dist., . . *Cleveland*, 2d Tuesday in July and November.
OHIO, S. Dist., . . *Cincinnati*, 3d Tuesday in April and October.
PENN., E. Dist., . *Philadelphia*, 1st Monday in April and October.
PENN., W. Dist., . *Pittsburg*, 2d Monday in May and November; — *Williamsport*, 3d Monday in June and September.
RHODE ISLAND, . *Newport*, 15th June; — *Providence*, 15th November.
SOUTH CAROLINA, . *Charleston*, 1st Monday in April; — *Columbia*, 4th Monday in November.
TENNESSEE, M. Dist., *Nashville*, 3d Monday in April and October.
TENNESSEE, E. Dist., *Knoxville*, 3d Mon. in May and 4th Mon. in Nov.
TENNESSEE, W. Dist., *Jackson*, 1st Monday in April and October.
VERMONT, ... *Windsor*, 4th Tuesday in July; — *Rutland*, 3d October.
VIRGINIA, E. Dist., *Richmond*, 1st Mon. in May and 4th Mon. in Nov.
VIRGINIA, W. Dist., *Lewisburg*, 1st Monday in August.

* This court is held by the District Judge, with special authority to exercise the powers and jurisdiction of a Judge of the Circuit Court.

* DISTRICT COURTS:—JUDGES, ATTORNEYS,

	District.		Judge.	Residence.	Attorney.	Residence.
1	Ala.	N. Dist.	W. G. Jones,	Mobile,	M. J. Turnley,	Talladega,
2		M. Dist.			†	
3		S. Dist.			A. J. Requier,	Mobile,
4	Ark.	E. Dist.	Daniel Ringo,	Little Rock	John M. Harrell,	Little Rock,
5		W. Dist.			Alfred M. Wilson,	Fayetteville,
6	Cal.	N. Dist.	Ogden Hoffman,	S. Francisco,	P. D. Torre,	San Francisco,
7		S. Dist.	Isaac S. K. Ogier,	Los Angeles,	J. R. Gitchell,	Los Angeles,
8	Connecticut,		Charles A. Ingersoll,	New Haven	Wm. D. Shipman,	Hartford,
9	Delaware,		Willard Hall,	Wilmington	Daniel M. Bates,	Wilmington,
10	Fa.	N. Dist.	McQueen McIntosh,	Jacksonville,	Chandler C. Yonge,	Mariana,
11		S. Dist.	William Marvin,	Key West,	J. L. Tatum,	Tampa,
12	Geo.	N. Dist.	John C. Nicoll,	Savannah,	Joseph Ganahl,	Savannah,
13		S. Dist.				
14	Ill.	N. Dist.	Thos. Drummond,	Chicago,	H. S. Fitch,	Chicago,
15		S. Dist.	Sam. H. Treat, Jr.,	Springfield,	Wm. K. Parish,	Springfield,
16	Indiana,		E. M. Huntington,	Cannelton,	D. W. Voorhees,	Terrehaute,
17	Iowa,		James M. Love,	Keokuk,	Joseph C. Knapp,	Keosauqua,
18	Kentucky,		Thomas B. Monroe,	Frankfort,	C. C. Rogers,	Lexington,
19	La.	E. Dist.	Theo. H. McCaleb,	N. Orleans,	Henry E. Miller,	New Orleans,
20		W. Dist.	Henry Boyce,	Alexandria,	J. H. New,	Baton Rogue,
21	Maine,		Ashur Ware,	Portland,	George F. Shepley,	Portland,
22	Maryland,		Wm. F. Giles,	Baltimore,	Wm. M. Addison,	Baltimore,
23	Massachusetts,		Peleg Sprague,	Boston,	Chas. L Woodbury,	Boston,
24	Michigan,		Ross Wilkins,	Detroit,	Joseph Miller, Jr.,	Kalamazoo,
25	Minnesota,		R. R. Nelson,	St. Paul,	E. M. Wilson,	Winona,
26	Miss.	N. Dist.	Samuel J. Gholson,	Aberdeen,	F. J. Lovejoy,	
27		S. Dist.			Vacant,	
28	Mo.	E. Dist.	Samuel Treat,	St. Louis,	Calvin F. Burnes,	St. Louis,
29		W. Dist.	Robert M. Wells,	Jeff'son City,	A. M. Lay,	Jefferson City,
30	N. Hampshire,		Matthew Harvey,	Concord,	A. S. Marshall,	Concord,
31	New Jersey,		Philemon Dickerson,	Paterson,	Garrett S. Cannon,	Bordentown,
32	N. Y.	N. Dist.	Nathan K. Hall,	Buffalo,	Jas. C. Spencer,	Ogdensburg,
33		S. Dist.	Samuel R. Betts,	New York,	Theod. Sedgwick,	New York,
34	North Carolina,		Asa Biggs,	Williamston,	Robert P. Dick,	Greensboro,
35	Ohio,	N. Dist.	H. V. Willson,	Cleveland,	G. W. Belden,	Canton,
36		S. Dist.	H. H. Leavitt,	Cincinnati,	Stanley Matthews,	Cincinnati,
37	Oregon,		M. P. Deady,	Winchester,	A. J. Thayer,	Portland,
38	Pa.	E. Dist.	John Cadwalader,	Philadelphia,	James C. Vandyke,	Philadelphia,
39		W. Dist.	W. McCandless,	Pittsburg,	R. Biddle Roberts,	Pittsburg,
40	Rhode Island,		John Pitman,	Providence,	George H. Browne,	Providence,
41	South Carolina,		A. G. Magrath,	Charleston,	James Conner,	Charleston,
42	Tenn.	W. Dist.	W. H. Humphreys,	Nashville,	Alex. W. Campbell,	Jackson,
43		M. Dist.			Thos. B. Childress,	Nashville,
44		E. Dist.			J. C. Ramsey,	Knoxville,
45	Tex.	E. Dist.	John C. Watrous,	Galveston,	George Mason,	Galveston,
46		W. Dist.	Thomas H. Duval,	Austin,	Jas. F. Warren,	Tyler,
47	Vermont,		David A. Smalley,	Burlington,	H. E. Stoughton,	Bellows Falls,
48	Va.	E. Dist.	Jas. D. Hallyburton,	Richmond,	John M. Gregory,	Richmond,
49		W. Dist.	J. W. Brockenbrough,	Lexington,	Fleming B. Miller,	Fincastle,
50	Wisconsin,		Andrew J. Miller,	Milwaukee,	D. A. J. Upham,	Milwaukee,

PLACES AND TIMES OF HOLDING THE DISTRICT COURTS.‡

ALABAMA, N. Dist., *Huntsville*, 2d Monday in May and November.

ALABAMA, Mid. Dist., *Montgomery*, 4th Monday in May and November.

ALABAMA, S. Dist., *Mobile*, 4th Monday in April and 2d Monday after 4th Monday in November.

ARKANSAS, E. Dist., *Little Rock*, 1st Monday in April and October.

---

* Corrected at the office of the Attorney-General, November, 1859. For the Judges, &c., of the Territories and District of Columbia, see the Territories, &c., respectively, *post*, Part III.

† The Attorney for the Northern District acts for this District.

‡ For the District of Columbia and the Territories, see *post*, Part III.

MARSHALS, AND CLERKS.

	Marshal.	Residence.	Pay.	Clerks.§	Residence.	Pay.
1	Benj. Patteson,	Huntsville,	$200†	B. F. Moore,	Tuscaloosa,	Fees.
2	‡			P. H. S. Gayle,	Montgomery,	"
3	Cade M. Godbold,	Mobile,	200†	R. B. Owens,	Mobile,	"
4	Jno. S. Halliburton,	Little Rock,	200†	William Field,	Little Rock,	"
5	Benj. J. Jacoway,	Van Buren,	200†	A. McLean,	Van Buren,	"
6	Perrin L. Solomon,	Sonora,	200†	H. Y. Gray,	San Francisco,	"
7	J. C. Pennie,	San José,	200†	C. Sims,	Los Angeles,	"
8	Curtiss Bacon,	Middletown,	200†	Alfred Blackman,	New Haven,	"
9	Wm. Morrow,	Wilmington,	200†	L. E. Wales,	Wilmington,	"
10	Elias E. Blackburn,	Monticello,	200†	B. Wright, Hugh A. Corley,	St. Augustine, Tallahassee,	" "
11	Fernando J. Moreno,	Key West,	200†	Jos. B. Browne,	Key West,	"
12 13	J. M. Spullock,	Savannah,	*	W. H. Hunt, Charles S. Henry,	Marietta, Savannah,	" "
14	Charles E. Pine,	Chicago,	200†	W. H. Bradley,	Chicago,	"
15	Wm. L. Dougherty,	Springfield,	200†	G. W. Lowry,	Springfield,	"
16	John L. Robinson,	Indianapolis,	200†	John H. Rea,	Indianapolis,	"
17	Laurel Summers,	Le Claire,	200†	T. S. Parvin,	Muscatine,	"
18	Thos. R. Dohoney,	Columbia,	200†	John A. Munroe,	Frankfort,	"
19	Joseph M. Kennedy,	New Orleans,	200†	N. R. Jennings,	New Orleans,	"
20	Samuel M. Hyams.	Natchitoches,	200†	A. Lastrappes,	Opelousas,	"
21	William K. Kimball,	Paris,	200†	Wm. P. Preble, Jr.	Portland,	"
22	John W. Watkins,	Baltimore,	*	Thomas Spicer,	Baltimore,	"
23	Watson Freeman,	Boston,	*	Seth E. Sprague,	Boston,	"
24	J. S. Bagg,	Detroit,	200†	Wm. D. Wilkins,	Detroit,	"
25	W. R. Gere,	Chatfield,	200†	G. W. Prescott,	St. Paul,	"
26	W. H. H. Tison,	Pontotoc,	200†	R. W. Edmundson,	Pontotoc,	"
27	Richard Griffith,	Jackson,	200†	W. H. Brown,	Jackson,	"
28	T. S. Bryant,	St. Louis,	200†	Thos. H. Reynolds,	St. Louis,	"
29	S. L. Jones,	Memphis,	200†	Jason Harrison,	Jefferson City,	"
30	S. W. Dearborn,	Exeter,	200†	Albert R. Hatch,	Portsmouth,	"
31	George H. Nelden,	Newton,	200†	Philemon Dickerson	Paterson,	"
32	S. B. Jewett,	Clarkson,	200†	Aurelian Conkling,	Buffalo,	"
33	Isaiah Rynders,	New York,	*	Geo. F. Betts,	New York,	"
34	Wesley Jones,	Raleigh,	200†	John M. Jones,	Albemarle,	"
35	Matthew Johnson,	Cleveland,	200†	F. W. Green,	Cleveland,	"
36	L. W. Sifford,	Cincinnati,	200†	J. M. McLean, Jr.,	Cincinnati,	"
37	Adolphus B. Hanna,	Portland,	200†			"
38	Jacob S. Yost,	Philadelphia,	*	Jno. M. Jones,	Philadelphia,	"
39	James G. Campbell,	Pittsburg,	200†	J. S. Bailey,	Pittsburg,	"
40	Francis C. Gardiner,	Providence,	200†	Henry Pitman,	Providence,	"
41	D. H. Hamilton,	Charleston,	200†	H. Y. Gray,	Charleston,	"
42	Hamden McClonahan,	Jackson,	200†	James L. Talbott,	Jackson,	"
43	Jesse B. Clements,	Nashville,	200†	Jacob McGavock,	Nashville,	"
44	Wm. M. Lowry,	Greenville,	200†	C. W. Crozier,	Knoxville,	"
45	Henry E. McCulloch,	Galveston,	200†	James Love,	Galveston,	"
46	William C. Young,	Sherman,	200†	Matthew Hopkins,	Austin,	"
47	Lewis L. Partridge,	Norwich,	200†	William H. Hoyt,	Burlington,	"
48	John F. Wiley,	Amelia C. H.	200†	John T. Francis,	Norfolk,	"
49	J. T. Martin,	Moundsville,	200†	J. W. Caldwell,	Clarksburg,	"
50	J. H. Lewis,	Milwaukee,	200†	John M. Miller,	Milwaukee,	"

ARKANSAS, W. Dist., *Van Buren*, 2d Monday in May and November.

CALIFORNIA, N. Dist., *San Francisco*, 1st Monday in June and December.

CALIFORNIA, S. Dist., *Monterey*, 1st Monday in June; — *Los Angeles*, 1st Monday in December.

CONNECTICUT, . . *New Haven*, 4th Tuesday in February and August; — *Hartford*, 4th Tuesday in May and November.

* Fees, &c.
† And fees.
‡ The Marshal for the Southern District acts for this District.
§ Besides the above list of clerks, John T. Francis is Clerk at Norfolk, Va.; B. F. Hays at Alexandria, La.; R. J. Wilson at Monroe, La.; W. H. Garretson at St. Joseph, La.;

DELAWARE, . . .	*Wilmington*, 2d Tuesday of January, April, June, and September.
FLORIDA, N. Dist., .	*Tallahassee*, 1st Monday in January; — *Apalachicola*, 1st Monday in February; — *Pensacola*, 1st Monday in March; — *St. Augustine*, 1st Monday in April.
FLORIDA, S. Dist., .	*Key West*, 1st Monday in May and November.
GEORGIA, N. Dist.,	*Marietta*, 2d Monday in March and September.
GEORGIA, S. Dist.,	*Savannah*, 2d Tuesday in February, May, August, and November.
ILLINOIS, N. Dist., .	*Chicago*, 1st Monday in July and 3d Monday in December.
ILLINOIS, S. Dist., .	*Springfield*, 1st Monday in January and June.
INDIANA, ...	*Indianapolis*, 3d Monday in May and November.
IOWA, N. Division,	*Dubuque*, 3d Tuesday in April and October.
IOWA, W. Division,	*Desmoines*, 2d Tuesday in November.
IOWA, S. Division,	*Keokuk*, 3d Tuesday in March and September.
KENTUCKY, . . .	*Frankfort*, 3d Monday in May and October.
LOUISIANA, E. Dist.,	*New Orleans*, 3d Monday in February, May, and November.
LOUISIANA, W. Dist.,	*Opelousas*, 1st Monday in August; — *Alexandria*, 1st Monday in September; — *Shreveport*, 1st Monday in October; — *Monroe*, 1st Monday in November; — *St. Joseph*, 1st Monday in December.
MAINE, ...	*Wiscasset*, 1st Tuesday in September; — *Portland*, 1st Tuesday in February and December; — *Bangor*, 4th Tuesday in June.
MARYLAND, . . .	*Baltimore*, 1st Tuesday in March, June, September, and December.
MASSACHUSETTS, .	*Boston*, 3d Tuesday in March, 4th Tuesday in June, 2d Tuesday in Sept., and 1st Tuesday in Dec.
MICHIGAN, . . .	*Detroit*, 3d Monday in June and 2d Monday in Oct.
MINNESOTA, . . .	*Preston*, 1st Monday in June; — *St. Paul*, 1st Monday in October.
MISSISSIPPI, N. Dist.,	*Pontotoc*, 1st Monday in June and December.
MISSISSIPPI, S. Dist.,	*Jackson*, 4th Monday in January and June.
MISSOURI, E. Dist.,	*St. Louis*, 3d Monday in February, May, and November.
MISSOURI, W. Dist.,	*Jefferson City*, 1st Monday in March and September.
NEW HAMPSHIRE, .	*Portsmouth*, 3d Tuesday in March and September; — *Exeter*, 3d Tuesday in June and December.
NEW JERSEY, . .	*Trenton*, 3d Tuesday in January, April, June, and September.
NEW YORK, N. Dist.,	*Albany*, 3d Tuesday in January; — *Utica*, 2d Tuesday in July; — *Rochester*, 3d Tuesday in May; — *Auburn*, 3d Tuesday in August; — *Buffalo*, 2d Tuesday in November; — one term annually in the county of St. Lawrence, Clinton, or Franklin, at such time and place as the Judge may direct.

Wm. Davenport, at Tyler, Texas; and F. J. Parker, at Brownsville, Texas. — The Clerks of the Circuit Courts, where they are not also Clerks of the District Courts, are as follows: Portland, Me., Geo. F. Emery; Boston, Mass., Henry W. Fuller; New York, N. Dist., A. A. Boyce, Utica; S. Dist., Kenneth G. White, New York; Pennsylvania, E. Dist., Ben. Patton, Philadelphia; W. Dist., Henry Sprowl, Pittsburg; Virginia, W. Dist., Thos. L. Moore; North Carolina, Henry R. Bryan, Raleigh; Louisiana, E. Dist., J. W. Gurley, New Orleans; Indiana, Horace Bassett, Indianapolis; Michigan, John Winder, Detroit; Missouri, B. F. Hickman, St. Louis.

New York, S. Dist., *New York*, 1st Tuesday in each month.

North Carolina, . *Edenton*, 3d Monday in April and October; — *Newbern*, 4th Monday in April and October; — *Wilmington*, 1st Monday after 4th Monday in April and October.

Ohio, N. Dist., . . *Cleveland*, 2d Tuesday in July and November.

Ohio, S. Dist., . . *Cincinnati*, 3d Tuesday in April and October.

Oregon, ... *Salem*, 2d Monday in April and September.

Pennsylvania, E. Dist., *Philadelphia*, 3d Monday in February, May, August, and November.

Pennsylvania, W. Dist., *Pittsburg*, 1st Monday in May and 3d Monday in October; — *Williamsport*, 3d Monday in June and 1st Monday in October.

Rhode Island, . . *Newport*, 2d Tues. in May and 3d Tues. in October; — *Providence*, 1st Tuesday in February and August.

South Carolina, E. Dist., *Charleston*, 1st Monday in January, May, July, and October.

South Carolina, W. Dist., *Greenville Court-House*,* 1st Monday in Aug.

Tennessee, E. Dist., *Knoxville*, 3d Mond. in May and 4th Mond. in Nov.

Tennessee, M. Dist., *Nashville*, 3d Monday in April and October.

Tennessee, W. Dist., *Jackson*, 1st Monday in April and October.

Texas, E. Dist., . *Galveston*, 1st Monday in May and December; — *Brownsville*, 1st Monday in March and October.

Texas, W. Dist., . *Austin*, 1st Monday in January and June; — *Tyler*, 4th Monday in April and 1st Monday in November.

Vermont, ... *Rutland*, 6th October; — *Windsor*, Monday next after 4th Tuesday in July.

Virginia, E. Dist., *Richmond*, 12th May and 12th November; — *Norfolk*, 30th May and 1st November.

Virginia, W. Dist., *Staunton*, 1st May and 1st October; — *Wythe Court-House*, 4th Monday in May and October; — *Charleston*, 19th April and 19th September; — *Clarksburg*, 24th March and 24th August; — *Wheeling*, 6th April and 6th September.

Wisconsin, . . . *Milwaukee*, 1st Monday in January; — *Madison*, 1st Monday in July.

COURT OF CLAIMS.†

Judges.			Appointed.	Salary.
Isaac Blackford,	of Indiana,	*Presiding Judge*,	1855,	$ 4,000
Geo. P. Scarburgh,	of Virginia,	*Judge*,	1855,	4,000
Edward G. Loring,	of Massachusetts,	"	1858,	4,000
Ransom H. Gillett,	of Dist. of Columbia,	*Solic. for U. States*,	1858,	3,500
Daniel Ratcliffe,	of Dist. of Columbia,	*Assist. Solicitor*,	1856,	3,500
J. D. McPherson,	of Dist. of Columbia,	*Deputy Solicitor*,	1856,	2,500
S. H. Huntington,	of Connecticut,	*Chief Clerk*,	1855,	3,000
Edgar M. Garnett,	of Florida,	*Assistant Clerk*,	1856,	2,000

* This Court has Circuit Court jurisdiction, except in appeals and writs of error.

† This Court holds its sessions at Washington, D. C.

VII. INTERCOURSE WITH FOREIGN NATIONS.

By the Act of Congress of Aug. 18, 1856, "To regulate the Diplomatic and Consular Systems of the United States," (see Public Laws, No. 56, Ch. CXXVII., American Almanac for 1857, pp. 147–152,) the Ministers and other Diplomatic Agents of the United States in foreign countries are paid by salaries, and the outfit is abolished.

1. Ministers and Diplomatic Agents of the United States in Foreign Countries.

[Corrected at the Department of State, November 1, 1859.]

Envoys Extraordinary and Ministers Plenipotentiary.

		Appointed.	Salary.	Foreign State.	Capital.
George M. Dallas,	Pa.	1856	$17,500	Great Britain,	London.
Francis W. Pickens,	S. C.	1858	12,000	Russia,	St. Petersburg.
Vacant.			17,500	France,	Paris.
William Preston,	Ky.	1858	12,000	Spain,	Madrid.
Joseph A. Wright,	Ind.	1857	12,000	Prussia,	Berlin.
Robert M. McLane,	Md.	1859	12,000	Mexico,	Mexico.
Richard K. Meade,	Va.	1857	12,000	Brazil,	Rio Janeiro.
John Bigler,	Cal.	1857	10,000	Chile,	Santiago.
John R. Clay,	Pa.	1847	10,000	Peru,	Lima.
John E. Ward,	Ga.	1858	12,000	China,	Canton.
Ministers Resident.					
James Williams,	Tenn.	1858	$7,500	Turkey,	Constantinople.
Theodore S. Fay,	Mass.	1853	7,500	Switzerland,	Berne.
Henry C. Murphy,	N. Y.	1857	7,500	Netherlands,	Hague.
John M. Daniel,	Va.	1853	7,500	Sardinia,	Turin.
James M. Buchanan,	Md.	1858	7,500	Denmark,	Copenhagen.
J. Glancy Jones,	Pa.	1858	9,000	Austria,	Vienna.
Elisha Y. Fair,	Ala.	1858	7,500	Belgium,	Brussels.
Joseph R. Chandler,	Pa.	1858	7,500	Naples,	Naples.
Benj. F. Angel,	N. Y.	1857	7,500	Sweden & Nor.	Stockholm.
George W. Morgan,	Ohio,	1858	7,500	Portugal,	Lisbon.
John P. Stockton,	N. J.	1858	7,500	Rome,	Rome.
John C. Smith,	Conn.	1858	7,500	Bolivia,	La Paz.
Chas. R. Buckalew,	Pa.	1858	7,500	Ecuador,	Quito.
John F. Cushman,	Ga.	1859	7,500	Argentine Conf.	Paraná.
George W. Jones,	Iowa.	1859	7,500	New Granada,	Bogotá.
Edward A. Turpin,	N. Y.	1858	7,500	Venezuela,	Caraccas.
Beverly L. Clarke,	Ky.	1858	7,500	Guatemala,	Guatemala.
Alexander Dimitry,	La.	1859	7,500	Nicaragua,	Nicaragua.
Townsend Harris,	N. Y.	1859	7,500	Japan,	Yedo.
Commissioner.					
James W. Borden,	Ind.	1858	$7,500	Sandwich Isl.	Honolulu.

*Secretaries of Legation.**

		Salary.			Salary.
Philip N. Dallas,	England,	$2,625	G. W. Ryckman,	Chile,	$1,500
John E. Bacon,	Russia,	1,800	Robert W. Woolley,	Spain,	1,800
W. Wallace Ward,†	China,	3,000	G. L. Brent,	Arg. Confed.,	1,500
W. R. Calhoun,	France,	2,625	Romaine Dillon,	Brazil,	1,800
E. G. W. Butler, Jr.,	Prussia,	1,800	Henry R. LaReintrie,	Mexico,	1,800
Geo. W. Lippitt,	Austria,	1,800	Z. B. Caverly,	Peru,	1,500

John P. Brown, *Sec'y of Legation and Dragoman*, Turkey, $3,000.

* Secretaries of Legation are authorized in each country where there is a Minister Plenipotentiary or Minister Resident. Appointments have been made only to the above-named places. Assistant Secretaries are authorized at London and Paris. The Assistant Secretary at London is Benjamin Moran, salary $1,500; at Paris, J. B. Wilbor, Jr., salary $1,500.

† S. Wells Williams is Interpreter in China, salary $5,000; Frederic Jenkins at Shanghai, salary $1,500; T. Hart Hyatt, Jr, at Amoy, salary $1,000. An Interpreter is authorized at Ningpo, salary $1,500.

2. List of Consuls-General, Consuls, and Commercial Agents of the United States in Foreign Countries, and the Places of their Residence.

[Corrected at the Department of State, November 5, 1859.]

☞ Those marked thus (*) are Commercial Agents. Consuls only at places marked thus (†) are at liberty to transact business.

		Salary.
	Africa.	
——,	Algiers,	fees.
*W. H. Browne,	†Monrovia,	$1,000
Daniel H. Mansfield,	†Zanzibar,	1,000
*——,	†Gaboon,	1,000
W. Walker,‡	Gaboon,	
W. D. Miller,	†St. Paulo de Loando,	1,000
*Daniel R. B. Upton,	†Bathurst,	fees.
John Seys, *Agent*,	†Liberia,	1,500
	Argentine Republic, or Buenos Ayres.	
Wm. H. Hudson,	Buenos Ayres,	2,000
Wm. H. Smiley,	†Rio Negro,	fees.
*Benjamin Upton,	Rosario.	fees.
	Austria.	
Edward C. Stiles,	Vienna,	1,500
Stephen S. Remak,	Trieste,	2,000
Ferdinand L. Sarmiento,	†Venice,	750
	Baden.	
——,	†Carlsruhe,	fees.
	Barbary States.	
Geo. V. Brown,	Tangiers, Morocco,	3,000
G. W. S. Nicholson,	Tunis, Tunis,	3,000
Marcus J. Gaines,	Tripoli, Tripoli,	3,000
*Juda Sol. Levy,	†Tetuan, Barbary,	fees.
——,	†Laraché & Arzila, Morocco,	fees.
	Bavaria.	
Andrew Ten Brook,	Munich,	1,000
Chas. Obermayer,	†Augsburg,	fees.
Philip Geisse,	†Nuremberg,	fees.
	Belgium.	
J. W. Quiggle,	Antwerp,	2,500
	Bolivia.	
Lewis Joel,	†Cobija,	500
	Borneo.	
——,	†Bruni,	fees.
	Brazil.	
Robert G. Scott, Jr.,	Rio Janeiro,	6,000
Walter W. Stapp,	Pernambuco,	2,000
Eben P. Bailey,	†Para,	1,000
Robt. S. Cathcart,	†St. Catherine's Isl.	fees.
George F. Upton,	†Rio Grande,	1,000
J. S. Gillmer,	†Bahia de San Salv.	1,000
Wm. H. McGrath,	†Maranham Isl.	1,000
W. T. Wright, Jr.,	†Santos,	fees.
	Brunswick.	
——,	†Brunswick,	fees.

		Salary.
	Chili.	
William Trevitt,	Valparaiso,	$3,000
Albert G. Blakey,	†Talcahuano,	1,000
——,	†Coquimbo,	fees.
	China.	
Oliver H. Perry,	Canton,	4,000
Thomas H. Hyatt,	Amoy,	3,000
Charles W. Bradley,	Ningpo,	3,000
S. L. Gouvernau, Jr.,	Fouchou,	3,500
W. L. G. Smith,	Shanghai,	4,000
G. Nye,‡	†Macao,§	fees.
James Keenan,	†Hong Kong,¶	3,500
	Costa Rica.	
Marquis L. Hine,	†San José,	fees.
	Denmark.	
J. P. M. Epping,	Elsineur,	1,500
——,	†Copenhagen,	fees.
L. A. Heckscher,‖	Copenhagen,	
Diedrich Kohlsat,	†Altona,	fees.
	West Indies.	
Robert P. Waring,	St. Thomas,	4,000
Robert A. Finlay,	†Santa Cruz,	750
	Ecuador.	
J. N. Casanova,	†Guayaquil,	750
	Egypt, *Pachalic of.*	
Edw. DeLeon, *Con.-Gen.*,	Alexandria,	3,500
	France.	
Henry W. Spencer,	Paris,	5,000
——,	Havre,	6,000
Gabriel G. Fleurot,	Bordeaux,	2,000
Thos. W. Rountree,	La Rochelle,	1,500
Joel W. White,	Lyons,	1,500
Alexander Derbes,	Marseilles,	2,500
——,	†Sedan,	fees.
Hypolite Roques,	†Nantes,	fees.
——,	†Bayonne,	fees.
Charles Audouy,	†Napoleon Vendee,	fees.
	West Indies.	
Charles W. Kimball,	†Pointe-à-Pitre, Guadaloupe,	fees.
Alex. Campbell,	†Martinique,	fees.
	America.	
Samuel E. Fabens,	†Cayenne, Fr. Guiana,	fees.
*George Hughes,	†St. Pierre, Miquelon,	fees.
	Africa.	
——,	†Algiers,	fees.

‡ Vice Com. Agent. § Portuguese Colony. ¶ English Colony. ‖ Vice-Consul.

FRANKFORT ON THE MAIN. *See* HANSEATIC OR FREE CITIES.

GREAT BRITAIN.

England.		Salary.
Robt. B. Campbell,	London,	$7,500
Beverly Tucker,	Liverpool,	7,500
Duncan Macauley,	Manchester,	2,000
William Thomson,	Southampton,	2,000
Albert Davy,	Leeds,	2,000
Samuel Ward,	†Bristol,	fees.
——,	†Falmouth,	fees.
Thos. W. Fox, Jr.,	†Plymouth,	fees.
——,	†Newcastle,	fees.

Scotland.

Joseph B. Holderby,	Dundee,	2,000
George Vail,	Glasgow,	3,000
James McDowell,	†Leith,	fees.

Ireland.

Theodore Frean,	Belfast,	2,000
Robert Dowling,	Cork,	2,000
Samuel W. Talbot,	†Dublin,	fees.
Alex. Henderson,	†Londonderry,	fees.
Thomas M. Persse,	†Galway,	fees.

In and near Europe and Africa.

Geo. H. Fairfield,	Port Louis, Mauritius,	2,500
Horatio J. Sprague,	†Gibraltar,	fees.
Wm. Winthrop,	†Island of Malta,	fees.
Gid. S. Holmes,	†Cape-Town, C.G.H.,	1,000
Geo. W. Kimball,	†Isl. of St. Helena,	fees.

North America.

Wyman B. S. Moor, *Con.-Gen. Br. N. A. Prov.*,	Montreal,	4,000
C. Dorwin, *Dep. Con.-Gen.*,	Montreal,	
Albert Pillsbury,	Halifax, N. S.,	2,000
Albert G. Catlin,	P. E. Island,	1,000
——,	†St. John, N. B.,	fees.
Benj. H. Norton,	Pictou, N. S.,	fees.
Wm. S. H. Newman,	†St. John, N. F.,	fees.
——,	†Gaspé Basin, C.E.,	fees.

West Indies.

Isaac J. Merritt,	Nassau, N. P.,	2,000
James B. Hayne,	Turk's Island,	2,000
Isaac Wendon,	Kingston, Jam.,	2,000
F. B. Wells,	†Bermuda,	fees.
*E. S. Delisle,	†St. Christopher's,	fees.
*R. S. Higinbotham,	†Antigua,	fees.
Noble Towner,	†Barbadoes,	fees.
R. S. Newbold,	†Isl. of Trinidad,	fees.

South America.

A. V. Colvin,	Demerara, B. G.,	2,000
*Wm. H. Smiley,	†Falkland Isles,	1,000

Australia.

James P. Maguire,	Melbourne,	4,000
Robert D. Merrill,	†Sydney, N.S.W.	fees.

Tasmania, or Van Diemen's Land.		Salary.
——,	†Hobart Town,	fees.

New Zealand.

——,	†Bay of Islands,	$1,000

East Indies.

Chas. Huffnagle, *Con.-Gen. of British India*,	Calcutta,	5,000
A. H. Rhodes, Jr., *Vice Con.-Gen.*	Calcutta,	
John P. O'Sullivan,	Singapore,	2,500
Luther H. Hatfield,	†Bombay,	fees.
*John Black,	†Isl. of Ceylon,	fees.

China.

James Keenan,	Hong Kong,	3,500

GREECE.

John D. Diomatari,	†Athens,	1,000

GUATEMALA.

James S. Peacock,	†Guatemala,	fees.

HANOVER.

——,	†Hanover,	fees.

HANSEATIC OR FREE CITIES.

Saml. Ricker, *Con.-Gen.*,	Frankfort,	3,000
John B. Miller,	Hamburg,	2,000
Isaac R. Diller,	Bremen,	2,000

HAWAIAN ISLANDS. *See* PACIFIC ISLANDS, *Independent.*

HAYTI AND ST. DOMINGO.

*Joseph N. Lewis,	Port au Prince,	2,000
*Jonathan Elliot,	St. Domingo,	1,500
*Richmond Loring,	†Aux Cayes,	500
*G. Eustis Hubbard,	†Cape Haytien,	1,000

HESSE-DARMSTADT.‡

Samuel Ricker,	†Frankfort,	fees.

HONDURAS.

A. Follin,	†Omoa & Truxillo,	1,000
——,	†Comayagua & Tegucigalpa,	fees.
*Gilbert S. Miner,	Amapula,	fees.

IONIAN REPUBLIC.

Amos S. York,	†Zante,	fees.

JAPAN.

——, *Con.-Gen.*,	Simoda,	5,000
*Elisha E. Rice,	†Hakodadi,	fees.

LIBERIA. *See* AFRICA.

MECKLENBURG SCHWERIN AND STRELITZ.

——,	†Schwerin,	fees.

MEXICAN REPUBLIC.

Isaac S. McMicken,	Acapulco,	2,000
R. B. J. Twyman,	Vera Cruz,	3,500
John Black,	†Mexico,	1,000
Richard Fitzpatrick,	†Matamoras,	1,000
Franklin Chase,	†Tampico,	1,000
——,	†Chihuahua,	fees.
Edward Conner,	†Mazatlan,	fees.
A. C. Allen,	†Minatitlan,	fees.

‡ Including Hesse-Cassel, Nassau, and Hesse-Homburg.

		Salary.
——,	†San Blas,	fees.
Joseph Walsh,	†Monterey,	fees.
E. P. Johnson,	†Tabasco,	$500
Rafael Preciat,	†Campeché,	fees.
——,	†Aguas Calientes,	fees.
Robert Rose,	†Guayamas,	fees.
Dav. R. Diffenderffer,	†Paso del Norte,	fees.
Charles R. Webster,	†Tehuantepec,	fees.
R. J. y Patrullo,	†Merida & Sisal,	fees.
——,	†Laguna,	fees.
Wm. Foster,	†Manzanillo,	fees.
*Thomas Sprague,	†La Paz,	fees.

MOLDAVIA.

H. T. Romertze,	†Galatza,	fees.

MUSCAT, *Dominion of the Sultan of.*

Daniel H. Mansfield,	†Isl. of Zanzibar,	1,000
——,	†Muscat,	fees.

THE NETHERLANDS, OR HOLLAND.

R. G. Barnwell,	Amsterdam,	1,000
Wm. S. Campbell,	Rotterdam,	2,000

Colonies.

Henry Sawyer,	†Paramaribo,	fees.
*Moses Jesurun,	†Curaçoa,	fees.
Henry Anthon, Jr.,	†Batavia, Java,	1,000
——,	Padang,	fees.
*Charles Rey,	†Isl. St. Martin's,	fees.

NEW GRANADA.

Charles J. Fox,	Aspinwall,	2,500
Amos B. Corwine,	Panamá,	3,500
Henry L. Jessup,	†Bogotá,	fees.
Albert Mathieu,	†Carthagena,	500
John Capela, Jr.,	†Turbo,	fees.
——,	†Santa Martha,	fees.
——,	†Sabanilla,	500
Nicolas Daniee,	†Rio Hacha,	fees.
*E. M. Uribe,	†Medellin,	fees.

NICARAGUA.

*Thomas S. Bell,	San Juan del Norte & Punta Arenas,	2,000
John Priest,	San Juan del Sur,	2,000

OLDENBURG.

——,	†Oldenburg,	fees.

PACIFIC ISLANDS, *Independent.*

Abner Pratt,	Honolulu, S. Isl.,	4,000
Anson G. Chandler,	Lahaina, "	3,000
Thomas Miller,	†Hilo, "	fees.
*J. B. Williams,	†Lanthala, Fej. Isl.,	1,000
*J. C. Dirickson,	†Apia, Navigators' & Friendly Isl.,	1,000
Vicesimus Turner,	†Tahiti, Soc. Isl.,	1,000

PARAGUAY.

Louis Bamberger,	†Asuncion,	fees.

PERU.

		Salary.
William Miles,	Callao,	3,500
John T. Lansing,	†Arica,	fees.
Fayette M. Ringgold,	†Paita,	500
Leonard G. Sanford,	†Tumbez,	$500

PORTUGAL.

John F. Porteous,	Oporto,	1,500
——,	†Lisbon,	fees.

Islands.

John H. March,	Funchal, Madeira,	1,500
Chas. W. Dabney,	†Fayal, Azores,	750
——,	†Macao,	fees.
Clarimundo Martins,	†Bissao,	fees.
——,	†Mozambique,	fees.
W. H. Morse,	†St. Jago, Cape de Verds,	750
*J. G. Willis,	†St. Paulo de Loando, W. Africa,	1,000

PRUSSIA.

Abel French,	Aix-la-Chapelle,	2,500
Rudolph F. Schillow,	†Stettin,	1,000

ROME, OR PONTIFICAL STATES.

Horatio de V. Glentworth,	†Rome,	fees.
——,	†Ancona,	fees.
——,	†Ravenna,	fees.
——,	†Carrara, Modena,	fees.

RUSSIA.

Francis S. Claxton,	Moscow,	2,000
John Ralli,	Odessa,	2,000
Charles A. Leas,	Revel,	2,000
Caleb Croswell,	St. Petersburg,	2,000
——,	†Riga,	fees.
Edmund Brandt,	†Archangel,	fees.
Reynold Frenckell,	†Helsingfors,	fees.
H. T. Romertze,	†Galatza, Moldavia,	fees.
*Perry McD. Collins,	†Amoor River,	1,000

SANDWICH ISLANDS. *See* PACIFIC ISLANDS, *Independent.*

SAN SALVADOR.

Joseph W. Livingston,	†La Union,	fees.

SARDINIA.

W. L. Patterson,	Genoa,	1,500
——,	†Nice,	fees.
Robert H. Leese,	†Spezzia,	1,000

SAXE-MEININGEN HILDBURGHAUSEN.

Louis Lindner,	†Sonneberg,	fees.

SAXONY.

P. A. Stockton,	Leipsic,	1,500
J. J. Springer,	†Dresden,	fees.

SIAM.

H. R. Pollard,	†Bangkok,	fees.

SPAIN.

T. T. Tunstall,	Cadiz,	1,500
J. Somers Smith,	Malaga,	1,500
Wm. L. Giro,	†Alicante,	fees.
——,	†Bilboa,	fees.
John Morand,	†Denia,	fees.
Ernest Volger,	†Barcelona,	fees.
Manuel Barcena,	†Vigo,	fees.

		Salary.
Peter Moraud,	†Valencia,	fees.
Spiridion Ladico,	†Port Mahon, Isl. Min.,	fees.
Louis Gallo,	†Santander,	fees.
John Cunningham,	†Seville,	fees.
	Cuba.	
Chas. J. Helm, *Con.-Gen.*,	Havana,	$6,000
T. Savage, *Dep. Con.-Gen.*,	Havana,	
Hugh Martin, Jr.,	Matanzas,	2,500
John R. Kooken,	Trinidad de Cuba,	2,500
Stephen Cochran,	Santiago de Cuba,	2,500
	Puerto Rico.	
James C. Gallaher,	Ponce,	1,500
Charles De Ronceray,	St. John's,	2,000
	Other Spanish Islands.	
Felipe Bodmann,	†Teneriffe, Canary,	fees.
Chas. Griswold,	†Manilla, Philipp.,	fees.
	SUMATRA.	
——,	†Padang,	fees.
	SWEDEN AND NORWAY.	
A.W. Prestadius, Jr.,	†Stockholm,	fees.
F. Cyrus,	†Gothenburg,	fees.
——,	†Bergen, Nor.,	fees.
——,	†Porsgrund, Nor.,	fees.
	SWITZERLAND.	
John Endlich,	Basel, or Bâle,	2,000
Wm. F. Giles, Jr.,	Geneva,	$1,500
Geo. H. Goundie,	†Zurich,	fees.
	TURKEY.	
——, *Con.-Gen.*,	Constantinople,	3,000
Jerem. A. Johnson,	Beyrout,	2,000
John W. Gorham,	Jerusalem,	1,500
E. S. Offley,	Smyrna,	2,000
W. L. Ellsworth,	†Cyprus,	1,000
Augustus Canfield,	†Candia,	1,000
Edward P. Peters,	†Trebizond,	fees.
	TUSCANY.	
J. A. Binda,	Leghorn,	1,500
*E. J. Mallett,	†Florence,	fees.
	TWO SICILIES.	
Alex. Hammett,	Naples,	1,500
Henry H. Barstow,	Palermo,	1,500
C. H. Morgan,	Messina,	1,500
	URUGUAY, OR CISPLATINE REPUBLIC.	
Richard H. Gayle,	†Monte Video,	1,000
	VENEZUELA.	
Andrew J. Smith,	Laguayra,	1,500
William Bliss,	†Puerto Cabello,	fees.
R. H. Swift,	†Maracaibo,	fees.
Henry Tay,	†Ciudad Bolivar,	fees.
	WURTEMBERG.	
Tapley W. Young,	†Stuttgard,	1,000

3. FOREIGN MINISTERS AND THEIR SECRETARIES,

Accredited to the Government of the United States.

Foreign State.	Envoy Ex. and Min. Plen.	Secretaries, &c.
Belgium,	M. Blondeel Van Cuelebrouk.	M. Alfred Berghmans, *Sec. Leg.* M. Valere de Brabandère, *Attaché.*
Brazil,	The Commander M. M. Lisboa.	M. Montezuma, *Sec. of Legation.*
Costa Rica,	Señor Luis Molina.	
France,	M. le Comte de Sartiges.	M. le Vte. Treilhard, *Ch. d'Affaires.* Chas. de Hell, *Sec. Leg.* M. Paul Hoemelle, *Attaché.* M. de Vaugrigneuse, *Chancelier.*
Gt. Britain,	Lord Lyons.	Hon. W. Douglas Irvine, *Sec. Leg.* Hon. Ed. Monson, *Priv. Sec.* M. Manley, *Clerk.*
Guatemala,	Señor Don J. A. de Yrisarri, *Min. Plen.*	
Mexico,	Señ. J. M. Mata.	
New Granada,	Señor Gen. P. A. Herran.	Don Rafael Pombo, *Sec. Leg.*
Nicaragua,	Señor Louis Molina, *Chargé ad. in.*	Don Jeronimo Perez, *Sec. Leg.*
Prussia,	Baron Fr. Von Gerolt.	Baron Guido de Grabow, *Sec. Leg.* Alexander Gau, *Sec. de Chancell.*
Portugal,	The Commander J. C. de Figaniere é Morsô.	
Russia,	Edward de Stoeckl,	Baron d'Osten Sacken, 1*st Sec. Leg.* M. Waldemar de Bodisco, 2*d Sec.*

Foreign State.	Envoy Ex. and Min. Plen.	Secretaries, &c.
San Salvador,	Señor Don J. A. de Yrisarri, *Min. Plen.*	
Spain,	Señor Don Gabriel Garcia y Tassara.	Don Carlos Villalba, *1st Sec. Leg.* Don F. Moreno, *Attaché.* Don F. Barreyro, *Priv. Sec.*

Ministers Resident.

Austria,	Chev. J. G. Hülsemann.
Bremen,	J. M. R. Schleiden.
Netherlands,	Theodore Marinus Roest van Limburg.
Peru,	Señor Don Cipriano C. Zegarra.
Sweden,	Baron Wetterstedt.

Chargés d'Affaires.

Denmark,	W. de Raasloff.
Sandwich Islands,	Schuyler Livingston.
Sardinia,	Chevalier Bertinatti.
Two Sicilies,	Chev. P. Mussone.

4. Foreign Consuls and Vice-Consuls in the United States.‡

Those marked thus (*) are *Consuls-General*; thus (†) *Vice-Consuls*; the rest are *Consuls*.

Anhalt-Dessau, Duchy of.	
New York,	Herman Gelpcke.
Argentine Republic.	
Baltimore,	Carlos M. Stewart.
Boston,	S. C. Bello, *act.*
Charleston,	Motte A. Pringle.
New York,	S. Livingston.
Philadelphia,	N. Frazier.
Austria.	
New York,	*Chas. F. Loosey.
Apalachicola,	†J. M. Wright.
Baltimore,	†J. D. Kremelberg.
Boston,	†F. A. Hirsch.
Charleston,	†B. S. Wilkins, *act.*
Galveston,	†Julius Kauffman.
Mobile,	†J. E. Dumont.
New Orleans,	Jacob H. Eimer.
N. York,	Henry Kohen, *Chancellor.*
Norfolk,	†E. T. Hardy.
Philadelphia,	†S. Morris Waln.
Richmond,	†E. W. de Voss.
San Francisco,	C. Fischer, *Cons. Agt.*
Savannah,	†Andrew Low.
St. Louis,	†E. C. Angelrodt.
Baden.	
New York,	*J. W. Schmidt.
Baltimore,	W. Dresel.
Cincinnati,	C. F. Adae.
Louisville,	John Smidt.
Milwaukee,	Emil. Spangenberg.
New Orleans,	Jacob H. Eimer.
New York,	†Leopold Schmidt.
Philadelphia,	C. F. Hagedorn.
St. Louis,	E. C. Angelrodt.
Bavaria.	
Philadelphia,	*C. Fred. Hagedorn.
Baltimore,	W. Dresel.
Cincinnati,	Chas. F. Adae.
Louisville,	John Smidt.
Milwaukee,	L. von Baumbach.
New Orleans,	J. H. Eimer.
New York,	G. Heinrich Siemon.
St. Louis, Mo.,	E. C. Angelrodt.
Belgium.	
New York,	*Henry W. T. Mali.
Apalachicola,	†William G. Porter.
Baltimore,	G. O. Gorter.
Boston,	Ives G. Bates.
Charleston,	C. E. Stewart.
Chicago,	J. F. Henrotin.
Cincinnati,	J. F. Meline.
Green Bay,	J. B. A. Massé.

‡ This list is corrected from the record of their *exequatur* in the Department of State, Washington, November, 1859, and by correspondence.

Key West, Oliver O'Hara.
Mobile, Hy. V. H. Voorhees.
New Orleans, Joseph Degnoott.
New Orleans, †A. P. Noblom.
Norfolk, Duncan Robertson.
Philadelphia, M. F. Mange.
Philadelphia, †G. E. Matile.
Richmond, E. O. Nölting.
San Francisco, Jules May.
Savannah, Wm. C. O'Driscoll.
St. Louis, Charles Hunt.

Brazil.

New York, *L. H. F. de Aguiar.
Baltimore, †C. Oliver O'Donnell.
Boston, Mass., N. H., & Maine, †Archibald Foster.
Charleston, †Eugenio Esdra.
New Orleans, Andres F. Walls.
New York, †L. F. de Figaniere.
Norfolk, †Myer Myers.
Pensacola, †W. Henry Judah.
Philadelphia, †Edw. S. Sayres.
Richmond, †Heman R. Baldwin.
Washington, Georg., & Alexandria, Va., †Adolph T. Kieckhoefer.

Bremen.

Baltimore, *Alb. Schumacher.
Boston, F. A. Hirsch.
Charleston, J. L. H. Thiermann.
Galveston, Julius Kauffman.
Indianola, Tex. H. A. H. Runge,
New Orleans, Fred. Rodewald.
New York, F. W. Keutgen.
Norfolk, Myer Myers, *Cons. Agt.*
Philadelphia, John T. Plate.
Richmond, E. W. de Voss.
San Francisco, C. A. C. Duisenberg.
Savannah, Heinrich Müller.
St. Louis, J. Wolff.

Brunswick and Luneburg.

Cincinnati, R. K. Topp.
Chicago, F. A. Hoffman.
Cleveland, A. Rettberg.
Louisville, H. Beckurts.
Milwaukee, Jacob Mahler.
Mobile, J. Sampson.
New Orleans, F. W. Freudenthal.
New York, *G. J. Bechtel.
Philadelphia, C. F. Hagedorn.
St. Louis, E. C. Angelrodt.
St. Paul, James Wenz.

Buenos Ayres.

Baltimore, C. M. Stewart.
Boston, ———.
New York, C. F. Zimmerman.
Philadelphia, †N. Frazier.

Chile.

Baltimore, R. B. Fitzgerald.
Boston, H. V. Ward.
New York, E. F. Fallon.
Philadelphia, F. V. Cleeman.
San Francisco, F. S. Alvarez.
Washington, Jas. H. Causten.

Costa Rica.

New York, *Royal Phelps.
Boston, Patrick Grant.
New Orleans, ———.
Philadelphia, S. Morris Waln.
San Francisco, Samuel H. Greene.

Denmark.

Alexandria, †James Dempsey.
Baltimore, †Hen. G. Jacobsen.
Boston, Mass., Me., N. H., & R. I., E. C. Hammer.
Charleston, †Wm. H. Ladson.
Chicago, †G. V. Hanson.
Cincinnati, †J. F. Meline.
Mobile, R. B. Searing.
New Orleans, Henry Frellsen.
N. Y., Conn., and part of N. J., N. York, H. Dollner.
Philadelphia, †Godfrey Weber.
San Francisco, G. O'Hara Taafe.
St. Louis, †J. E. Schuetze.
St. Paul, †C. W. Borup.
Wash'ton, D.C., G. P. Todson.
Wilmington, N. C., †P. K. Dickinson.

Ecuador.

Washington, *Aaron H. Palmer.‡

‡ Charged with the affairs of the Legation at Washington.

Baltimore, James J. Fisher.
Boston, Seth Bryant.
New Orleans, J. Gardette.
New York, Gregorio Dominguez.
Philadelphia, Edward J. Fisher.
San Francisco, Daniel Wolff.
Washington, James H. Causten.

France.

N. Y., *C.F.F. Marquis de Montholon.
Baltimore, †M. Arbeltier.
Boston, J. E. Souchard.
Charleston, M. St. Croix de Belligny.
Charleston, †M. Fauconnet.
Cincinnati, †J. F. Meline.
Galveston, ——.
Key West, W. Pinkney, *Cons. Agt.*
Louisville, J. J. Perrin, *Cons. Agt.*
Mobile, A. de la Forest.
Monterey, Cal, J. Lombard, *Cons. Agt.*
New Orleans, †H. Germain.
New Orleans, M. le Comte de Mejon
New York, †Louis Borg.
Newport, †Fauvel Gouraud.
Norfolk, †Pascal Schisano.
Philadelphia, F. C. A. L. de la Forest.
Portland, E. P. le Prohon, *Cons. Agt.*
Richmond, Alfred Paul.
San Francisco, Albert F. Gautier.
San Francisco, †E. Guys.
Savannah, ——.
St. Louis, F. J. Kunemann.

Frankfort on the Maine.

Chicago, F. A. Hoffman.
Cincinnati, C. F. Adae.
Milwaukee, A. C. Willmans.
New York, Fred. Weissmann.
Philadelphia, J. H. Harjes.
St. Louis, F. A. Reuss.

Great Britain.

Alexandria, †James P. Smith.
Baltimore, Hy. W. Ovenden.
Boston, Mass., Francis Lousada.
Buffalo, Denis Donahoe.
Charleston, †Benjamin Walker.
Charleston, N. C. and S. C., Robert Bunch.
Chicago, Ill, John E. Wilkins.
Cincinnati, ——.
Darien, Wm. Cooke, *Cons. Agt.*
Eastport, †G. D. Sherwood.
Galveston, Arthur T. Lynn.
Mobile, Flor. and Ala., Charles Tulin.
Nantucket, W. Barney, *Cons. Agt.*
N. Haven (N.Y.), †Fred. A. Bartlett.
New Orleans, William Mure.
New York, Edward M. Archibald.
New York, †Pierrepont Edwards.
Ogdensburg (N.Y.), †Chas. W. Bartlett.
Oswego (N.Y.), †C. H. H. Castle.
Pensacola, †H. T. Ingraham.
Philadelphia, C. E. K. Kortright.
Portland, Me. and N. H., James Grignon.
Portland, †George H. Starr.
Richmond, Va., George Moore.
San Francisco, Wm. Lane Booker.
Savannah, Ga., Edmund Molyneux.
Wilmington, †G. W. Davis.

Greece.

Boston, Henry G. Andrews.
New Orleans, Nicholas Benachi.
New York, D. Botassis.

Guatemala.

New York, *Bartolomeo Blanco.
Boston, Patrick Grant.
Key West, E. J. Gomez.
New Orleans, Joseph Mitchell.
Philadelphia, S. Morris Waln.
San Francisco, Samuel H. Greene.

Hamburg.

Baltimore, *Alb. Schumacher.
Baltimore, F. Rodewald.
Boston, F. A. Hirsch.
Charleston, Lewis Trapman.
Cincinnati, J. F. Meline.
Galveston, J. W. Jockusch.
Indianola, Tex, Henry Runge.
Mobile, H. A. Schroeder.
New Orleans, Charles Kock.
New York, G. E. Kunhardt.
Philadelphia, Charles Lorenz.

Richmond, Henry Ludlaw.
San Francisco, N. T. Stockfleth.
Savannah, J. N. Hudtwalker.

Hanover.

New York, *Adolph Gosling.
Baltimore, Edward Uhrlaub.
Boston, Francis A. Hirsch.
Charleston, G. C. Baurmeister.
Cincinnati, Carl F. Adae.
Cleveland, Ad. Rettberg.
Galveston, Julius Frederich.
Louisville, Theodore Schwartz.
Milwaukee, Ill., Ind., Mich., Min., & Wisc., A. C. Willmans.
New Orleans, Aug. Reichard.
New York, L. H. Meyer.
Philadelphia, C. C. Schöttler.
San Francisco, Otto H. Frank.
Savannuh, K. H. Muller.
St. Louis, Adolphus Meier.

Hawaiian Islands.

New York, *Sch. Livingston.
Baltimore, Md. & Del., †Granville S. Oldfield.
Boston, H. A. Pierce,
Olympia, Or., W. G. Dunlap.
Oregon City, G. F. Allen.
San Francisco, †Chas. E. Hitchcock.

Electorate of Hesse-Cassel and Grand Duchy of Fulda.

Philadelphia, for Eastern States, *C. F. Hagedorn.
St. Louis, for Western States, *E. C. Angelrodt.
Cincinnati, C. F. Adae.
Galveston, Th. Wagner.
New Orleans, R. Thiele.
New York, Fred. Kühne.
St. Louis, E. C. Angelrodt.

Grand Duchy of Hesse-Darmstadt.

Baltimore, W. Dresel.
Cincinnati, C. F. Adae.
Galveston. †J. W. Jockusch,
Louisville, John Smidt.
Milwaukee, for Wisc. & Min., Emil Spangenberg.
New Orleans, A. Reichard.
New York, F. W. Keutgen.
San Francisco, G. Ziel.

Honduras.

To reside in California, *Wm. V. Wells.

Lippe, Principality of.

New York, Frederick Kühne.

Lubec.

Baltimore, Hermann von Kapff.
Boston, H. C. Lauterbach.
Charleston, J. L. H. Thiermann.
Cincinnati, J. F. Meline.
Galveston, Died. H. Klaener.
New York, Fred. A. Schumacher.
New York, Geo. E. Kunhardt, *Act.*
New Orleans, Friedrich Kirchhoff.
Philadelphia, F. H. Harjes.
San Francisco, H. Ernst.

Mecklenburg-Schwerin.

Charleston, *Leon Herckenrath.
Boston, F. A. Hirsch,
Cincinnati, J. F. Meline.
Galveston, H. Schultz.
Milwaukee, Ind., Ill., Mich., Ia., Wis., Min., L. von Baumbach.
New Orleans, Wilhelm Prehn.
New York, H. Gelpcke.
Philadelphia, for Pennsyl., N.Y., & Del. F. H. Harjes.
San Francisco, J. de Fremery.
St. Louis, E. C. Angelrodt.

Mecklenburg-Strelitz.

New York, Frederick Kühne.

Mexico.

New Orleans, *Francisco Ribaud.
Baltimore, †J. A. Pizarro.
Boston, †S. Cancio Bello.
Brownsville, Tex., C. M. Trevino.
Charleston, †F. Montanez.
Franklin, N. Mex., †R. Ramires.
Galveston, Tex., † H. de Saint Cyr.
Mobile, †Charles L. Le Baron.
New Orleans, O. L. Dabelsteen.
New Mexico, †Guadalupe Miranda.

New York, J. M. Duran.
Philadelphia, †Felix Merino.
Pittsburg, †Juan Herbert.
San Francisco, J. Mugarieta.
Santa Fé, M. Armendair.
St. Louis, †P. J. Marallano.

Montevideo.

Baltimore, Frederic B. Graf.
New Orleans, Bartholomew Watts.

Nassau.

New York, *Wilh. A. Kobbe.
Cincinnati, C. F. Adae.
Galveston, F. H. Steil.
Milwaukee, Wilh. Finkler.
New Orleans, Fred. W. Freudenthal.
New Braunfels, Tex., F. Moureau.
San Francisco, A. von Witzleben.
St. Louis, E. C. Angelrodt.

Netherlands, or Holland.

New York, *R. C. Burlage.
Baltimore, Md. and D. C., Claas Vocke.
Boston, for Mass., Me., N.H., & R.I., F. A. Hirsch.
Charleston, †Carl Epping.
Charleston, N. C., S. C., and Ga., Dan'l Lesesne.
Cincinnati, Ohio, Ind., and Ky., J. F. Meline.
Galveston, Tex., Edward Kauffman.
Key West, †Oliver O'Hara.
Mobile, Ala. & Florida, J. J. Van Wanroy.
New Orleans, for La. & Mi., Amedée Conturié.
New York, †J. Z. Zimmerman, *Chanc.*
Norfolk, Myer Myers.
Philadelphia, Pa., G. K. Ziegler.
Philadelphia, †D. L. Kurtz.
Portage City, Wisc., for Mich., Wisc., & Minn., J. P. V. Dorselen.
St. Louis, Ill., Mo., & Iowa, F. R. Toe Water.
San Francisco, P. H. Gildemeester.
Savannah, †Carl Epping.

New Granada.

New York, *I. M. Gaitan.
Baltimore, Robert A. Fisher.
New Orleans, J. E. Beylle.
New York, †Anibal de Mosquera.
New York, Greg. Dominguez.
San Francisco, O. H. Burrows.

Nicaragua.

Baltimore, Oliver O'Donnell.
New Orleans, E. G. Gomez.
New York, *Armory Edwards.

Oldenburg.

New York, *J. W. Schmidt.
Baltimore, Henry Oelrichs.
Charleston, Charles T. Lowndes.
Cincinnati, Carl F. Adae.
Galveston, Julius Frederich.
Louisville, Theo. Schwartz.
Milwaukee, Wisc., Mich., Ia., & Min., E. Spangenberg.
New Orleans, R. Thiele.
New York, †G. Janssen.
Philadelphia, C. F. Hagedorn.
San Francisco, for Cal., H. Hansmann.
San Francisco, H. F. von Lengerke.
Savannah, Heinrich Muller.
St. Louis, E. C. Angelrodt.

Paraguay.

New York, R. Mullowny.

Parma.

San Francisco, J. M. Satrustegui.

Peru.

Baltimore, R. B. Fitzgerald.
Boston, Santiago C. Bello.
Charleston, A. A. Cay.
New Orleans, M. M. de Castillo.
New York, Felipe N. Casado.
Philadelphia, A. S. Christian.
San Francisco, N. Fejerina.
Wash'n, D.C., C. C. Zegarra, M. R.

Portugal.

New York, *Thos. R. dos Santos.

Alexandria, Va., & Dist. Colum'a, †Christ. Neale.
Baltimore, Md., †C. Oliver O'Donnell.
Boston, Mass., N.H., & R.I., †Archibald Foster.
Charleston, †Eugenio Esdra.
Mobile, †Charles L. Baron.
New Orleans, †Antonio J. de Silva.
New York, †L. E. Amsinck.
Norfolk,‡ †Rob. W. dos Santos.
Pensacola, Jule Pescay.
Philadelphia, Pa., Del., & N. Jersey, †Edw. Smith Sayres.
San Francisco, Jona. Searle.
Savannah, †José J. Martin.
St. Augustine, W. H. Allen.
Wilmington, J. A. Sintas.

Prussia.

New York, *J. W. Schmidt.
Baltimore, L. Brauns.
Boston, F. A. Hirsch.
Charleston, Wm. H. Trappman.
Cincinnati, C. Fr. Adae.
Galveston, J. W. Jockusch.
Louisville, J. Von Borries.
Milwaukee, E. Spangenberg.
New Orleans, A. Reichard.
New Bedford, †George Hussey.
New York, E. von der Heydt.
Philadelphia, T. Schottler.
San Francisco, H. Hansmann.
Savannah, F. N. Hudtwalcker.
St. Louis, E. C. Angelrodt.

Reuss, Prince of, Senior and Junior Line.

New York, *Hy. Schondorff.

Rome, or Pontifical States.

Baltimore, †B. T. Elder.
Boston, †Nicholas Reggio.
Charleston, †E. Mottet.
Cincinnati, ——.
New Orleans, C. J. Daron.
New York, *Louis B. Binsse.
Philadelphia, ——.

Russia.

New York, *J. de Nottbeck.
Baltimore, †Augustus Kohler.
Boston, †Robert B. Storer.
Charleston, Thomas H. Deas.
Galveston, †F. Wolff.
Mobile, †Joseph E. Murrell.
New Orleans, E. Johns.
Philadelphia, ——.
San Francisco, †Peter Kostromitinoff.
Savannah, †John R. Wilder.

Salvador.

New York, *R. Phelps.
San Francisco, R. W. Heath.

Sardinia.

New York, *G. Bertinatti.
Baltimore, †C. A. Williamson.
Boston, Mas., Me. N.H., & R.I., †Nicholas Reggio.
Charleston, †E. L. Trenholm.
Cincinnati, †J. F. Meline.
Mobile, †L. O. Townsley.
New Orleans, Joseph Lanata.
New Orleans, †Wm. Pinckney.
New York, G. Valerio.
Norfolk, †D. Robinson.
Philad., Penn., N. J., and Del., †Vittorio Sartori.
San Francisco, B. Davidson.
San Francisco, †F. Biesta.
St. Louis, †L.A.J. Baptiste Paris.

Saxe-Altenburg.

New York, C. E. L. Hinrichs.
New York, Frederick Kühne.
St. Louis, E. C. Angelrodt.

Saxe-Coburg and Gotha.

New York, *C. E. L. Hinrichs.
Chicago, Francis A. Hoffman.
Cincinnati, A. Eggers.
New York, Frederick Kühne.
Philadelphia, C. F. Hagedorn.

‡ And for all other ports in Virginia except Alexandria.

St. Louis, E. C. Angelrodt.

Saxe-Weimar.

Chicago, Francis A. Hoffman.
Cincinnati, F. Augustus Eggers.
New York, H. Gelpcke.
Philadelphia, C. F. Hagedorn.
St. Louis, E. C. Angelrodt.

Saxony.

New York, *J. W. Schmidt.
Baltimore, W. Dresel.
Cincinnati, C. F. Adae.
Galveston, J. Kauffman.
Louisville, John Smidt.
Milwaukee, F. A. Borchardt.
New Orleans, T. Hamman.
Philadelphia, J. T. Plate.
San Francisco, J. Kreyinhagen.
St. Louis, E. C. Angelrodt.

Schaumburg-Lippe.

New York, C. B. Richard.

Schwarzburg-Rudolstadt and Schwarzburg-Sondershausen.

New York, C. E. Borsdorf.

Spain.

New York, *Francis Stoughton.
Baltimore, †José Pizarro.
Boston, †L. L. de Arze y Noel.
Charleston, N.C. & S.C., V. Anto. Larrañaga.
Galveston, †José de Espinar.
Key West, Mariano Alvarez.
Mobile, J. G. Miranda.
New Orleans, Juan Callejon.
New Orleans, †A. Ferando.
New York, †Carlos Chacon.
Norfolk, †Duncan Robertson.
Pensacola, †Francisco Moreno.
Philadelphia, Geronimo Roca.
Portland, J. Avendaño.
Portsmouth, †Wm. B. Parker.
San Francisco, Camilo Martin.
Savannah, †Francisco Uncilla.
St. Louis, †Robt. H. Betts.
Wilmington, N.C., †Fred. B. Lord.

Sweden and Norway.

Washington, D.C., *N. W. Wetterstedt.
Alexandria, †James Dempsey.
Baltimore, †Frederic B. Graf.
Boston, Mass., Me., & N. H., †Bartol Schlesinger.
Charleston, †Jos. A. Winthrop.
Chicago, †P. Van Schneidaer.
Cincinnati, †James P. Meline.
Key West, †Asa F. Tift.
Madison, Wisc., †G. Bjornson.
Mobile, †R. Westfelt.
New Orleans, †Ambrose Lanfear.
New York, C. E. Habicht.
Norfolk, †D. Robertson.
Philadelphia, †E. S. Sayres.
San Francisco, G. C. Johnson.
Savannah, †Fran. H. Wilman.
St. Louis, †W. de Kantzow.

Switzerland.

Washington, for D.C., Del., Md., and Va., *John Hitz.
Charleston, N. C., S.C., Geo., & Flor., Henri Meyer.
Detroit, Mich., Wisc., Iowa, & Min., Ch. Dominé.
Highland, Ill., Mo. & Ill., C. Rilliet.
Louisville, Ind., Ohio, Ky., ——.
N. Orleans, Ala., Miss., La., Tenn., & Ark., A. Piaget.
New York, New England & N.Y. Louis P. De Luze.
New York, †A. Iselin.
Philadelphia, Pa., N. Jersey, A. Korady.
San Francisco, †A. de Stouz.
San Francisco, H. Hentsch.
Texas, Galveston, J. C. Kuhn.

Turkey.

Baltimore, G. Porter.
Boston, Joseph Iasigi.
New York, J. Hosford Smith.

Tuscany.

New York, G. B. Talliaferri.
New York, †W. H. Aspinwall.
New Orleans, Carlo G. Manzoni.

Two Sicilies.

New York, *C. A. di Licignano.
Baltimore, †A. C. Rhodes.
Boston, †N. Reggio.
Charleston, †J. H. Holmes.
Dist. Columbia, †N. E. Fowles.
Key West, †Wm. Pinkney.
New Haven, †Ira Clisbe.
New Orleans, †J. T. Barelli.
New York, †L. Contencin, *Cons. Agt.*
Norfolk, †L. Schisano.
Philadelphia, †Vito Viti.
Richmond, Daniel Groning.
San Francisco, †W. A. Darling.
Savannah, †G. C. Michels.

Uruguay.

New York, *G. F. Darby.
Baltimore, P. Murguiondo.
Boston & Salem, †C. Soule, Jr.
Galveston, Tex., †F. A. Stokes.
Mobile, †C. G. Mansony.
New Orleans, †A. F. Valls.
Philadelphia, John F. Cabot.
San Francisco, T. P. Hamilton.

Venezuela.

Washington, *Victor de la Cova.
Baltimore, J. F. Strohm.
Boston, Silas G. Whitney.
New Orleans, Geo. B. Dieter.
New York, Simon Comacho.
Norfolk, ———.
Philadelphia, W. G. Boulton.

Wurtemberg.

Baltimore, W. Dresel.
Cincinnati, Carl. Fred. Adae.
Louisville, John Smidt.
Milwaukee, L. von Baumbach.
New Orleans, Ch. Honold.
New York, Leopold Bierwirth.
Philadelphia, W. Dresel, *Act. Balt.*
San Francisco, Friedrich Frank.
St. Louis, E. C. Angelrodt.

VIII. TITLES AND ABSTRACTS OF THE PUBLIC LAWS,

Passed at the Second Session of the 35th Congress.

[The references by Chapters are to Little, Brown, & Co.'s authorized edition of the Laws of the United States. The omitted Chapters are private laws.]

General Appropriations for the Years ending June 30, 1859, and June 30, 1860.

	June 30, 1859.	June 30, 1860.
Deficiencies for year 1858,	$ 9,704,209.89	
Military Academy,	182,804.00	$ 179,588.00
Legislative, Executive, and Judicial Expenses,	6,057,878.61	6,976,833.77
Consular and Diplomatic Expenses,	912.120.00	1,047,745.00
Civil Expenses,	5,897,148 07	3,374,537.37
Expense of Collecting Revenue from Customs,	3.600,000.00	
Naval Service Appropriation,	14,508,354.23	10,527,163.55
Army Appropriation,	17,185,806.46	15,279,845.76
Post-Office Appropriation,	17,535,520 00	
Ocean Mail Steamers,	1,460,750.00	341,229.16
Indian Department and Treaty Stipulations with Indian Tribes,	2,298,061.85	2,418,468.52
Deficiency in Indian Appropriations for 1858,	339,595.00	
Deficiency for Paper, Printing, &c., for 33d and 34th Congresses,	341,189.58	
Invalid and other Pensions,	769,500.00	852,000.00
Military and Wagon Roads in Territories,	30,000.00	
Treaty with Denmark,	408,731.44	
Lighthouses, Light-Boats, Buoys, &c.,		331,507.70
Relief of Sundry Individuals,	76 156.27	88,504.76
Miscellaneous,	522,000.00	26,400.00
Total definite Appropriations for the years 1859 and 1860,	$ 81,829,825.40	$ 41,443,825.59

Some of the principal items of the appropriations for legislative, executive, and judicial expenses for the two years are as follows: —

Legislative. — Congress, pay of members and mileage,	$743,000.00	$1,557,861.72
" " " Officers and Clerks of both Houses,	165,992.00	157,639.60
" Contingent expenses of Senate, including engraving, reporting, stationery, newspapers, &c.	196,125.70	216,191.28
" Contingent expenses of House, including as above,	439,064.60	287,306.00
" Paper and printing of both Houses,	184,614.00	170,000.00
" Library of Congress. — Books and expenses,	17,600.00	17,000 00
Executive. — President of the United States,	31,450.00	31,450.00
Vice-President,	8,000.00	8,000.00
Department of State,	82,400 00	85,625.00
Treasury Department,	703,310.00	670,153.50
Department of the Interior (exclusive of Surveyor-Gen. & clerks),	537,970.00	518,870.00
Surveyors-General and their Clerks,	137,020 00	102,870.00
War Department,	123,570.00	126,720.00
Navy Department,	102,140.00	102,140 00
Post-Office Department,	200,800.00	172,800.00
Attorney-General's office,	24,600 00	18,967.00
Territorial Governments,	198,000 00	125,275.22
Mint and Branches, and Assay Office,	497,255 00	606,423.50
Independent Treasury,	48,800.00	46,300 00
Office of Superintendent of Public Printing,	14,614.00	13,615.92
Paper and Printing for Executive Departments,	65,000 00	68,500.00
Public Lands, Collection of Revenue from,	120,000.00	356,800.00
Executive Buildings,	55,763.00	54,463.00
Judicial. — Judges, Attorneys, and Marshals,	207,100.00	209,100.00
Law Expenses and Prosecutions for Crime,	1,053,300 00	835,000.00
Penitentiary,	22,530 25	22,530.00
Auxiliary Guard and Police,	19,400 00	44,930 52
Court of Claims,	36,300.00	36,300.00

No. 1. Ch. I. *An Act to continue the Office of Register of the Land Office at Vincennes, Indiana.* The office of Register is continued for three years; a Register is to be appointed to act as register and receiver, with a salary of $500 and fees, to reside at Vincennes, and give the usual bond. Dec. 21, 1858.

No. 2. Ch. V. *An Act to confirm the Land Claim of certain Pueblos and Towns in the Territory of New Mexico.* The claim of the United States alone is relinquished, and all adverse rights are saved. Dec. 22, 1858.

No. 3. Ch. VI. *An Act making Appropriations for the Support of the Military Academy for the Year ending June 30, 1860.* $179,588 are appropriated. Jan. 12, 1859.

No. 4. Ch. VIII. *An Act to repeal an Act entitled "An Act authorizing the Secretary of the Treasury to change the Names of Vessels, in certain Cases."* Approved March 5, 1856. Jan. 17, 1859.

No. 5. Ch. X. *An Act to authorize the President to make Advances of Money to Hiram Powers.* Partial payments may be made, from time to time, under the contract for certain statuary. Jan. 19, 1859.

No. 6. Ch. XI. *An Act authorizing the Issue of Registers to the Steamships America and Canada, and to change the Names of said Steamships.* The America is to be called the "Mississippi," and the Canada the "Coatzacoalcos," and both are to be deemed United States vessels. Jan. 19, 1859.

No. 7. Ch. XIII. *An Act to Provide for Holding the Courts of the United States in the State of Alabama.* In case of the disability of the Federal District Judge, the Federal Supreme Judge for the fifth circuit, upon notice, may hold general or special terms of the Federal District Court. This act to be in force until March 4, 1861. Jan. 25, 1859.

No. 8. Ch. XVII. *An Act for the Enforcement of Mechanics' Liens on Buildings, and so forth, in the District of Columbia.* Any person hereafter performing labor, or furnishing materials, engine, or machinery, to an amount exceeding $20, in constructing or repairing any building, under a contract with the owner, or agent of such owner, shall have a lien therefor on such building, and the lot of ground on which it stands, to certain limits, upon filing notice in the Circuit Court Clerk's office for the district, after commencing, and within three months after completing the building or repairs, setting forth specifically his claim, and his intention to hold a lien, and bringing his action in said Circuit Court to enforce such lien, within one year after completing the building or repairs, if the claim is then due; and, if not, within three months after it falls due. All having liens on the same building may join in the action; and if several such actions are brought, the Court may order them consolidated. The notice is to be recorded in the Clerk's Office. When suit is brought, due notice is to be given to those interested. If the premises have been sold, the purchaser may be made defendant. The proceedings in such action shall be the same generally as in other actions.

Liens by this act have priority over all other liens created subsequent to the notice. If upon sale on execution the proceeds are not sufficient to satisfy the liens, the Court shall order payment *pro rata;* and other property of defendant may be taken on the execution, and sold for the amount.

When any person has a lien, and his claim and costs are paid, or tendered to him, he shall, within six days, enter satisfaction in the said Clerk's office; and if he fails to do so, he shall pay $50 to those aggrieved, and all damages they may suffer. The lien may also be discharged by the defendant's giving security, approved by the Court, to pay any judgment and costs that may be recovered in the action.

Any person in possession of, and performing labor on, any article of personal property, at the request of the owner, or of the person in possession, may, in the absence of any special agreement, have a lien thereon for his reasonable charges for such labor, and may retain possession thereof until such charges are paid. If he parts with the possession, he loses his lien. The Act of 1833, ch. 80, and all inconsistent Acts, are repealed. Feb. 2, 1859.

No. 9. Ch. XVIII. *An Act to provide for the Lighting with Gas certain Streets across the Mall.* The streets are Four and a-Half, Seventh, and Twelfth Streets. The Act takes effect from its passage. $6,400 are appropriated. Feb. 2, 1859.

No. 10. Ch. XIX. *An Act to fix and regulate the Compensation of Receivers and Registers of the Land-Offices under the Provisions of the Act approved April* 20, 1818. Their pay is to be Commissions on moneys received, not to exceed, in the aggregate, $2,500 per annum each, and *pro rata* for any quarter or fraction of a quarter, to commence when they begin to discharge their duties. Feb. 2, 1859.

No. 11. Ch. XX. *An Act authorizing the Secretary of the Treasury to grant a Register for the Schooner "William A. Hamill."* Feb. 2, 1859.

No. 12. Ch. XXI. *An Act providing for the Payment of the Expenses of Investigating Committees of the House of Representatives.* $10,000 are appropriated, no part to be paid for constructive mileage for summoning witnesses. The mileage for serving precepts of either House shall not exceed ten cents for each mile necessarily and actually travelled. Feb. 5, 1859.

No. 13. Ch. XXII. *An Act providing for Keeping and Distributing all Public Documents.* The Secretary of the Interior is to receive, keep, and distribute the printed journals of the two Houses of Congress, and all public documents now or hereafter printed or purchased for Government use, except those printed for the particular use of Congress, or of either House, or of the Executive, or any department, and except "Wilkes's Exploring Expedition." Proper rooms in the Patent Office Building are to be set apart for this sole purpose, whither all such documents shall be removed, and where, and whence, they shall hereafter be delivered. A register thereof shall be kept, showing the quantity and kind received, and what, when, and to whom distributed; and a report of the same shall be made at the first session of each Congress. The Secretary of the Interior shall deliver the same only on the written order of the persons authorized to receive them, except when he is required by law to deliver them without such requisition. The books and documents shall be distributed hereafter, for the purposes now prescribed by law. Those for colleges, &c., shall be sent to such institutions in the several States, &c., as the Senators, Representatives, and Delegates, shall designate to the Secretary of the Interior, to be sent first to those districts to which there has been no distribution heretofore. When such books, &c., are received at the proper offices, libraries, &c., they shall not be removed therefrom.

All matters pertaining to Copyright are transferred to the Department of the Interior, and all books, &c., heretofore deposited for copyright, are to be sent thither, — the law requiring a copy of every publication to be sent to the Smithsonian Institution and the Congressional Library is repealed. The joint committee on said library may dispose of "duplicate, injured, or wasted books, or any other matter not deemed proper to it," as they may deem best. Of the Statutes at Large, in said library, ten copies shall be retained there for the Judges of the Supreme Court; and of the remainder, one-third shall be sent to the Senate, and two-thirds to the library of the House of Representatives. Feb. 5, 1859.

No. 14. Ch. XXIII. *An Act for the Punishment of the Crime of Forgery of or Counterfeiting Military Bounty-Land Warrants, Military Bounty-Land Certificates, Certificates of Location, Certificates of Purchase, and Receivers' Receipts.* Such forgery, and the knowingly uttering such forged papers, &c., is made a felony, and punishable by imprisonment at hard labor, not less than three, or over ten, years. The jurisdiction of State Courts is not limited hereby. Feb. 5, 1859.

No. 15. Ch. XXVI. *An Act granting the Right of Way over, and Depot Grounds on, the Military Reserve at Fort Gratiot, in the State of Michigan, for Railroad Purposes.* The grant is to any railroad company, or companies, constructing a railroad or railroads from Detroit, to or near Port Huron, and is made in case the President shall deem it not injurious to the public defence, — the price of the land used to be determined by the Secretary of War, and approved by the President. If the price is not paid in thirty days after the approval of the President, or if either road is not completed in three years, or if ever discontinued, the grant shall cease. All the buildings erected shall be of wood; and if the military authorities shall destroy them by fire or otherwise, there shall be no claim against the United States for damages. Feb. 8, 1859.

No. 16. Ch. XXVII. *An Act to provide for the Payment of the Claims of the State of Maine, for Expenses incurred by that State in organizing a Regiment of Volunteers for the Mexican War.* Feb. 9, 1859.

No. 17. Ch. XXVIII. *An Act to authorize the Attorney-General to represent the United States in the Proceeding in Equity, now pending in the Supreme Court, between the Commonwealth of Massachusetts and the State of Rhode Island and Providence Plantations.* He may also consent to a conventional line, if the parties agree thereon; and this line, when confirmed by a decree of the court, shall be taken to be the true boundary line for all purposes affecting the jurisdiction of the United States. Feb. 9, 1859.

No. 18. Ch. XXXIII. *An Act for the Admission of Oregon into the Union.* "Whereas the people of Oregon have framed, ratified, and adopted a constitution of State government which is Republican in form, and in conformity with the Constitution of the United States, and have applied for admission into the Union on an equal footing with the other States: Therefore ..... Oregon is received into the Union on an equal footing with the other States in all respects whatever, with the following boundaries, to wit: Beginning one marine league at sea due west from the point where the 42° N. latitude intersects the same; thence northerly, at the same distance from the line of the coast, lying west and opposite the State, including all islands within the jurisdiction of the United States, to a point due west and opposite the middle of the north ship channel of the Columbia river; thence easterly, to and up the middle channel of said river, and, where it is divided by islands, up the middle of the widest channel thereof, to a point near Fort Walla-Walla, where the 46° N. latitude crosses said river; thence east, on said parallel, to the middle of the main channel of the Shoshones or Snake River; thence up the middle of the main channel of said river, to the mouth of the Owyhee River; thence due south, to 42° N. latitude; thence west, along said parallel, to the place of beginning."

The State has concurrent jurisdiction over all waters forming a common boundary between it and other States, and all navigable waters are made common highways. Until the next census it is entitled to one Representative in Congress.

The following propositions are offered to the people of Oregon, if accepted, to bind both the United States and Oregon: — 1st. Sections 16 and 36 in every township of public lands, or their equivalent, in case said sections are otherwise disposed of, shall be granted for the use of schools. 2d. 72 sections shall be set apart for a State University, to be selected by the Governor of the State, and to be applied by the Legislature for this purpose, and no other. 3d. 10 entire sections, to be selected by the Governor, in legal subdivisions, shall be granted to the State for completing, or erecting, public buildings at the seat of government, under the direction of the Legislature. 4th. All salt springs in the State, not over twelve in number, and not otherwise disposed of, with six sections of contiguous land, to be selected by the Governor in one year, shall be granted to the State for its use, under the direction of the Legislature. 5th. Five per cent. of the net proceeds of the sales of public lands in the State, sold after its admission into the Union, shall be paid the State for public roads and internal improvements, under the direction of the Legislature. *All of the above propositions* are on the condition that the State shall never interfere with the primary disposal of the soil within the same by the United States, or with any regulations Congress may make to secure title in said soil to *bona fide* purchasers; and that non-resident proprietors shall not be taxed higher than residents. 6th. The State shall never tax the lands or property of the United States within the State. If any lands herein granted to the State have been heretofore confirmed to the territory for the purposes specified herein, the amount so confirmed shall be deducted herefrom. The residue of the Territory of Oregon is made part of the Territory of Washington. Feb. 14, 1859.

No. 19. Ch. XXXV. *An Act for the Relief of the Mobile and Ohio Railroad Company.* Certain transfers by Alabama and Mississippi are confirmed; and the time for completing the road is extended to September 20, 1865; but no condition of the original act is released either to the road or the States. Feb. 18, 1859.

No. 20. Ch. LVIII. *An Act to authorize Settlers upon 16th and 36th Sections, who settled before the Surveys of the Public Lands, to pre-empt their Settlements.* Feb. 26, 1859.

No. 21. Ch. LIX. *An Act to protect the Land Fund for School Purposes in Sarpy County, Nebraska Territory.* The Superintendent of Schools in said county may select for school purposes public lands in lieu of those pre-empted, &c. Feb. 26, 1859.

No. 22. Ch. LX. *An Act to incorporate the Washington National Monument Society.* "For the purpose of completing the erection, now in progress, of a great national monument to the memory of Washington, at the seat of the Federal Government," Winfield Scott and others are incorporated, under the name in the title, with the usual powers of such a corporation. All the rights, property, &c., of the Association called "The Washington National Monument Society," are vested in this corporation. Any member of said corporation may be removed by a four-fifths vote of the members. When any vacancy happens from any cause, the other members shall elect a successor in ten days after the vacancy happens, and if they do not fill it in thirty days, the Federal Attorney for the district shall proceed against them for a forfeiture of their charter, in the Circuit Court, and its judgment thereon shall be conclusive. For other purposes than the removal of members, five corporators shall constitute a quorum. The President of the United States shall be *ex officio* President of the Corporation, and the Governors of the several States, Vice-Presidents. All meetings shall be held and records kept in Washington. Corporators are individually liable for debts contracted since October 20, 1858. This corporation cannot issue notes as currency, and the charter may at any time be amended or repealed. It shall take effect from its passage. Feb. 26, 1859.

No. 23. Ch. LXIV. *An Act to amend an Act entitled "An Act authorizing Repayment for Land erroneously sold by the United States."* When any sale cannot be confirmed, the purchase-money may be repaid; if it has been invested in stocks, &c., held in trust, they may be sold, and the money repaid from the proceeds of such sale. Feb. 28, 1859.

No. 24. Ch. LXV. *An Act giving the Assent of Congress to a Law of the Missouri Legislature for the Application of the reserved two per cent. Land Fund of said State.* Feb. 28, 1859.

No. 25. Ch. LXVI. *An Act making Appropriations for the current and contingent Expenses of the Indian Department, and for fulfilling Treaty Stipulations with various Indian*

Tribes, for the Year ending June 30, 1860. $1,797,301.86 are appropriated. Reservations for Indian purposes in California may be increased, not to exceed in the aggregate 125,000 acres. No new Indian agents, &c., are authorised hereby. None of this appropriation to go for arms and ammunition, unless treaties require it. The tracts occupied by the Pimas and Maricopas in Arizona Territory are to be surveyed, and reservations, not over 100 square miles in extent, are to be set apart for them. Rules, &c., for the Indian service, are to be prepared and submitted to Congress. The law obliging the United States, in certain cases, to indemnify the whites for trespasses of the Indians is repealed. Feb. 28, 1859.

No. 26. Ch. LXVIII. *An Act to authorize the Enrolment, Registry, and License of certain Steamboats, or Vessels, owned by the Buffalo and Lake Huron Railroad Company.* March 1, 1859.

No. 27. Ch. LXXIV. *An Act supplemental to an Act for the Admission of the State of Minnesota into the Union.* A Term of the District Court is established at Preston in June, and at St. Paul in October, and the appointment of a Clerk authorized. For the terms, &c., of the District Court, see *ante*, p. 116. March 3, 1859.

No. 28. Ch. LXXV. *An Act making Appropriations for the Consular and Diplomatic Expenses of the Government for the Year ending June* 30, 1860. $1,047,745 are appropriated. No minister, &c., except to certain designated places, shall receive pay. The salary of the Consul-General for British North America shall be his entire compensation. All fees received by him, and by vice-consuls, and commercial agents in British North America, beyond their established compensation, must be accounted for with the federal treasury. The fee for certifying invoices, &c., of free goods under the reciprocity treaty, shall be fifty cents; and no such certificate shall be required unless the goods exceed $ 200 in value. March 3, 1859.

No. 29. Ch. LXXVI. *An Act making Appropriations for the Naval Service for the Year ending June* 30, 1860. $10,527,163.55 are appropriated. Not more than $1000 shall be expended in any navy yard, in the repair of any vessel, until after a report thereon, by a board of not less than three officers of the navy. The general order of the Secretary of the Navy, of January 30, 1859, as to the rank of engineer officers, is confirmed. Navy officers dropped by the retiring board, and since restored, shall, while dropped, receive furlough pay if restored to the "furlough" list, or leave pay if to the "leave pay" list. March 3, 1859.

No. 30. Ch. LXXVII. *An Act to carry into Effect the Convention between the United States and China, concluded November* 8, 1858, *at Shanghai.* When the Chinese revenue officers issue the debentures or duty receipts, provided for in the Convention, the chief diplomatic officer of the United States in China shall select some suitable depositary therefor, and determine his compensation. The President, with the advice of the Senate, shall appoint two Commissioners, at a salary of $ 3,000 each, to form a board in China, to hear and determine claims under the Convention, at such time and place as the chief diplomatic officer shall designate; they shall terminate their duties in one year from the time of their meeting; and they shall report to such diplomatic officer their several awards, which shall be sent to the depositary, and he shall distribute ratably the debentures or their proceeds. The records of the Commission, when its duties are completed, shall be deposited in the office of the Secretary of State. March 3, 1859.

No. 31. Ch. LXXVIII. *An Act to protect the Timber growing upon Lands of the United States, reserved for Military and other Purposes.* The unlawful cutting or wanton destruction of such timber is punishable by fine of not over $ 500, and by imprisonment of not over twelve months. March 3, 1859.

No. 32. Ch. LXXIX. *An Act making Appropriations for fulfilling Treaty Stipulations with the Yancton and Tonawanda Indians for the Year ending June* 30, 1860, *and for other Purposes.* $ 621,166.66 are appropriated for Indian purposes; and $ 341,229.16 for payments under existing contracts for carrying the ocean mails. March 3, 1859.

No. 33. Ch. LXXX. *An Act making Appropriations for the Legislative, Executive, and Judicial Expenses of Government for the Year ending June* 30, 1860. $ 6,976,835.77 are appropriated. No officer, &c., of the House of Representatives shall receive pay for discharging the duties of two offices at the same time. The creditors of the republic of Texas may file their claims up to January 1, 1861. The Attorney-General may appoint an assistant, at a salary of $ 3,000; two 3d class clerks, salary $ 1,600; one 2d class, at $1,400; and may employ temporary clerks, at an expense of not over $1,000 a year. All moneys hereafter drawn from the Treasury, on the requisition of the Attorney-General, shall be disbursed by an officer designated by the Secretary of the Treasury. Cents may be paid out at the mint, for Spanish and Mexican quarters, eighths, and sixteenths of a dollar, at their nominal value of 25, 12½, and 6¼ cents, for two years from February 21, 1859. When both Houses of Congress order any document to be printed, the printer of the House first ordering it shall do the whole, with the same price for composition as though it had been ordered but by one House. In no case shall more than 1550 copies of a document be printed, unless extra numbers are ordered. The office of printer to either House shall not be transferred, directly or indirectly; and any attempt to sell or transfer it shall vacate the office. The Patent Office Report, mechanical, must hereafter be so prepared as to make but one volume of 800 pages. March 3, 1859.

No. 34. Ch. LXXXI. *An Act making Appropriations for Lighthouses, Light-boats, Buoys, &c., and providing for the Erection and Establishment of the same, and for other Purposes.* $ 331,507.70 are appropriated. Hereafter, when light vessels require rebuilding, permanent structures shall be erected in their place, when advisable and practicable. The Secretary of the Treasury, at the recommendation of the Lighthouse Board, may discontinue lights that have become useless by mutations of commerce, and changes in channels, &c. Necessary preliminary surveys for the sites for lighthouses may be made on the seaboard by the Coast Survey, and on the Northwestern Lakes by the Topographical Engineers. If reports are adverse, they shall be submitted to Congress at its next session; if favorable, work may be commenced as soon as a valid title is obtained to the site. The authority to discontinue the light at Port Clinton, Portage Bay, Ohio, is repealed. March 3, 1859.

No. 35. Ch. LXXXII. *An Act making Appropriations for sundry Civil Expenses of the Government for the Year ending June* 30, 1860. $ 3,374,537.37 are appropriated. No part of the expenses of the Agricultural Congress to be paid. The Capitol Extension shall not be embellished with sculpture or paintings unless approved by the Art Commission, excepting works by Crawford and Rogers, and painting certain rooms already partly painted. Certain lots of land in Philadelphia shall be sold at auction, and proceeds applied to a building for a Court-House and Post-Office. The power to issue and reissue Treasury notes, by the Act of December 23, 1857, is extended to July 1, 1860. The Secretary of the Treasury, under the Act of 1858, ch. 165, may issue coupon or registered stock, as the purchaser may elect. The Post Office in Boston is not to be removed from its present location, until after the next session of Congress, if remonstrants indemnify the Government from additional expense growing out of any contracts for another site. Officers placed on the "furlough list," by the Naval Retiring Board, transferred to the leave list, shall have "leave pay" while on the "furlough list;" and in case of his death, after the transfer, his representatives may receive what was his due. The Superintendent of Public Printing, on default of contractor to supply paper, may advertise for proposals, or buy in open market the necessary paper, and the contractor shall pay the increase of cost, if any. Patents for lands, with restrictions for their benefit, may issue to Indians in Kansas under treaty stipulations. March 3, 1859.

No 36. Ch. LXXXIII. *An Act making Appropriations for the Support of the Army for the Year ending June* 30, 1860. $15,279,845.76 are appropriated. No permanent barracks shall be constructed without previous detailed estimates being submitted to Congress, and a special appropriation therefor. Mileage shall not be allowed an officer transferred or relieved at his own request. The claim of Massachusetts for disbursements during the war of 1812, as due by Mr. Poinsett's Report, of Dec. 23, 1837, is to be paid in cash or 5 per cent stock, redeemable in ten years, or sooner. The number of Commissioners of the Military Asylum is reduced to three, — the Commissary-General of Subsistence, the Surgeon-General, and the Adjutant-General, — any two of whom form a quorum. Invalid, &c., soldiers of the war of 1812, and subsequent wars, to have the benefits of the asylum. Pensioners, while in the asylum, to surrender their pensions for the benefit of the asylum. All persons in the asylum to be subject to the articles of war; 12½ cents only to be deducted from the monthly pay of soldiers, &c. The "Military Asylum" to be called hereafter the "Soldiers' Home." March 3, 1859.

No. 37. Ch. LXXXIV. *An Act to provide for the Care and Preservation of the Works constructed by the United States, for bringing the Potomac Water into the Cities of Washington and Georgetown, for the Supply of said Water for all Governmental Purposes, and for the Uses and Benefits of the Inhabitants of the said Cities.* The Potomac Water-Works are placed under the care of an officer of the Engineer Corps, U. S. A., who is to act under the direction of the Department of the Interior, and for compensation is to have his pay as such Engineer officer, and no more. The Corporations of the two cities may distribute the water by pipes, without expense to the United States, and may establish and collect water rates; but the rates shall never be a source of revenue to the cities. The Federal Government shall lay only such pipes as are necessary to give the Government the necessary supply of water. The two cities may establish a complete system of sewerage; they may borrow money for the purposes of this Act, Washington not over $150,000, and Georgetown not over $50,000, redeemable in ten years out of any revenue from water rents. The unauthorized opening of pipes is punishable by a fine of not less than $50, nor over $500, for each offence. The wilful, &c. breaking, &c. of any pipe, hydrant, &c. is punishable by imprisonment for not over two years. Wilfully, &c. making the water impure is punishable by a fine of not less than $500, or over $1,000; or by imprisonment of not less than one year, nor over three years, in the Penitentiary in the district. March 3, 1859.

* No. 38. Ch. LXXXV. *An Act to provide for extending the Laws and Judicial System of the United States to the State of Oregon, and for other Purposes.* Oregon is made a Judicial District. The salary of the judge is $2,500, and that of the Marshal and District Attorney the same as that of those officers in Iowa. In cases of appeals pending in the Federal Supreme Court from the Supreme Court of Oregon Territory, the mandates shall go either to the Federal or State Courts of Oregon, as the nature of the appeal may require. Iowa is divided into three districts, for the trial of issues of fact by the jury in the Federal District Court, as follows: —

Northern Division. — The counties of Clinton, Jones, Linn, Benton, Tama, Marshall, Grundy, Hardin, Webster, and all counties north of the same, and east of Calhoun, Pocahontas, Palo Alto, and Emmett.

Southern Division. — The counties of Scott, Cedar, Johnson, Iowa, Powasheik, Mahaska, Marion, Lucas, Clark, Decatur, and all counties south and east of the same.

Western Division. — The remaining counties in the State. For the times and places of holding the Federal Courts in Oregon and Iowa, see *ante*, pp. 116, 117. March 3, 1859.

No. 39. Ch. LXXXVI. *An Act for the Relief of Congressional Township number twenty-seven, North, of Range number six, East, in Wabash County, Indiana.* The Auditor of the County may enter certain lands in lieu of a deficit of school lands, and patents may issue therefor. March 3, 1859.

No. 40. Ch. LXXXVII. *An Act making an Appropriation for the Payment of the Expenses of Investigating Committees, and for other Purposes.* $10,000 are appropriated for the expenses of such Committees of the House during the present Congress. March 3, 1859.

No. 41. Ch. LXXXVIII. *An Act making Appropriations for the Payment of Invalid and other Pensions of the United States for the Year ending June 30, 1860.* $852,000 are appropriated. The application for payment of pensions to invalids must be supported, once in every two years, by the affidavit of two surgeons or physicians, whose credibility as such shall be certified by the magistrate before whom the affidavit is made. The affidavit shall describe the disability, state its continuance, and its rate at the present time. If the affidavit shall state a rate below that for which the pension was originally granted, payment shall be made for the rate in the affidavit. The affidavit is not necessary where the pension was granted for a total disability, as the loss of a limb. March 3, 1859.

IX. PUBLIC RESOLUTIONS.

[The omitted numbers are private resolutions.]

No. 1. *A Resolution for the Appointment of two Regents of the Smithsonian Institution, Alexander Dallas Bache and George E. Badger are appointed to fill vacancies in the class of "others than members of Congress."* Jan. 17, 1859.

No. 2. *Joint Resolution authorizing Townsend Harris, United States Consul-General at Japan, and H. C. J. Heusken, his Interpreter, respectively, to accept a Snuffbox from her Majesty, the Queen of England.* Jan. 25, 1859.

No. 4. *A Resolution authorizing the Secretary of the Treasury to convey a Portion of the Government Lot on which the United States Court-House stands in Rutland, Vermont, in Exchange for other Land adjoining said Lot.* Feb. 5, 1859.

No. 6. *A Resolution for the Payment of an unexpended Balance to the State of Georgia, on Account of Militia Services.* Feb. 9, 1859.

No. 7. *A Resolution for changing the Plan of the Custom-House at Galveston, in the State of Texas.* The cost, however, is not to exceed the amount already appropriated, and the consent in writing of the contractors thereto is to be first obtained. Feb. 9, 1859.

No. 8. *Joint Resolution giving the Consent of Congress to the Acceptance by Captain M. F. Maury and Professor A. D. Bache of Gold Medals from the Sardinian Government.* Feb. 14, 1859.

No. 9. *Joint Resolution in Relation to the Tobacco Trade of the United States with Foreign Nations.* There are restrictions on the Tobacco trade in certain foreign countries; these restrictions are unsatisfactory to certain of the tobacco-growing States of the United States; the Federal Government ought, therefore, to use its utmost power to have these restrictions modified, and, to that end, to open diplomatic negotiations with those countries; and it should encourage the introduction of American tobacco into China and Japan, as an article of use among the people of those nations. Feb. 14, 1859.

No. 10. *Joint Resolution to authorize the Secretary of the Treasury to sell a certain Plat of Land in the City of Petersburg, Virginia, belonging to the United States.* A minimum shall be fixed by the Secretary of the Treasury, below which the lots shall not be sold. Feb. 18, 1859.

No. 12. *A Resolution conferring the Rank of Senior Flag Officer on the Active Service List of the United States Navy on Captain Charles Stewart.* March 2, 1859.

No. 13. *A Resolution in Relation to the Second Section of the Act of Congress entitled "An Act to provide for the Location of certain confirmed private Land Claims in the State of Missouri, and for other Purposes."* March 3, 1859.

No. 14. *A Joint Resolution amendatory of an Act entitled "An Act to Regulate the Compensation of Members of Congress," approved August 16, 1856, so far as relates to such Members as shall die during their Terms of Service.* Any member dying after the commencement of the Congress to which he shall have been elected, his widow, or if he has no widow, his heirs, shall receive his pay from the commencement of such Congress to his death. In all cases compensation shall be paid for not less than three months; but constructive mileage shall never be allowed. This shall apply to the widows and heirs of those who were elected to the 35th Congress. The pay of the member elected to fill the vacancy shall begin when the pay of the deceased terminated. March 3, 1859.

X. REVENUE AND EXPENDITURE.

1. *Statement of Duties, Revenues, and Public Expenditures, during the Fiscal Years ending June 30, 1857, and June 30, 1858.*

[From Reports of the Secretary of the Treasury, Dec. 8, 1857, and Dec. 6, 1858.]

The receipts into the Treasury were as follows: —	Year ending June 30, 1857.	Year ending June 30, 1858.
From customs, viz.: —		
During the first quarter, ending Sept. 30,	$20,677,740.40	$18,573,729.37
During the second quarter, " Dec. 31,	14,243,414.90	6,237,723.69
During the third quarter, " Mar. 31,	19,055,328.55	7,127,900.69
During the fourth quarter, " June 30,	9,899,421.20	9,850,267.21
Total customs,	63,875,905.05	41,789,620.96
From sales of public lands,	3,829,486.64	3,513,715.87
From miscellaneous sources,	926,121.98	1,254,232.76
Total receipts, exclusive of loans, &c.,	68,631,513.67	46,557,569.59
Treasury-Notes, under act Dec. 23, 1857,		23,716,300.00
Balance in the Treasury, July 1, 1856 and '57,	19,901,325.45	17,710,114.27
Total means,	88,532,839.12	87,983,983.86
The expenditures, exclusive of trust funds, and treasury-notes funded, were as follows: —		
Civil List.		
Legislative, including books,	3,498,109.77	3,583,523.79
Executive,	1,990,363.51	1,856,017.53
Judiciary,	1,117,629.72	1,062,631.61
Governments in the Territories,	224,186.73	184,673.89
Surveyors and their clerks, &c.,	146,319.40	163,717.13
Officers of Mint, branches, and Assay Office,	112,242.19	88,283.33
Supervising and local Inspectors, &c.,	78,419.42	81,133.70
Assistant Treasurers and their clerks,	39,841.68	39,215.77
Total civil list,	7,207,112.42	7,059,196.75
Foreign Intercourse.		
Salaries of Ministers, Chargés d'Affaires, &c.,	311,153.19	255,534.12
Salaries of Secretaries of Legation,	28,568.73	20,795.40
Salaries of Consuls,	251,359.58	296,189.14
Dragoman to Turkey and contingencies,	2,625.00	3,000.00
Contingent expenses of all the missions abroad,	42,501.11	50,536.84
Contingent expenses of foreign intercourse,	35,000.00	40,002.21
Office-rent of Consuls who cannot trade,	10,209.44	8,263.00
Relief and protection of American seamen,	149,328.35	133,648.71
Interpreters to Consuls in China,		4,500.00
Secretary and Interpreter to Chinese Mission,	2,750.00	6,151.32
Commissioner to Sandwich Islands,	6,375.00	
Intercourse with Barbary powers,	2,069.65	8,684.82
Interpreters, guards, &c. at the Consulates in Turkish dominions,	1,733.94	1,042.05
French seamen at Toulon and their families,	1,000.00	
Acknowledgment to masters, &c. of foreign vessels rescuing American citizens,	3,004.48	3,000.00

	Year ending June 30, 1857.	Year ending June 30, 1858.
Blank-books, stationery, &c. for Consuls, .	$ 11,500.00	$ 53,079.62
Preservation of archives of Consulates, .	11,900.00	
Loss by exchange on drafts of Consuls, &c.	3,724,72	7,767.55
Other diplomatic and consular expenses,	12,509.98	
Expenses under Reciprocity Treaty, .	76,340.00	15,460.00
Restoration of ship Resolute, ...	40,000.00	
Suppression of Slave-trade, ...	3,783.33	4,375.00
Audubon's Birds, &c. for foreign governments,	16,000.00	
Treaty with Denmark, Art 3d, ...		393,011.00
Treaty with Denmark, Art. 6th, . . .		15,720,44
Commission on boundary of Wash. Territory,		71,000.00
Execution of Neutrality Act, ...		1,370.00
Miscellaneous, ...	1,316.61	161.20
Total foreign intercourse, . .	*1,024,753.11	†1,393,292.42
Miscellaneous.		
Surveys of public lands, ...	409,523.31	417,270.44
Surveys of public lands, &c. in California,	308,254.85	186,294.98
Collecting revenue from sales of public lands,	215,329.51	329,566.30
Support and maintenance of lighthouses, &c.,	1,067,097.17	1,162,857.51
Building lighthouses, for buoys, beacons, &c.,	966,398 20	758,663.29
Marine hospital establishment, . .	354,053 90	376,806.96
Building marine hospitals, and repairs, .	303,979.23	333,323.16
Public buildings, grounds, &c. in Washington,	109,625 00	132,910.00
Patent fund and drawings, ...	214,460.73	204,908.99
Mail service for government, ...	200,000.00	200,000.00
Mail service for Congress, &c., . . .	500,000.00	500,000.00
Deficiency in Post-Office revenue, . . .	2,916,883.00	3,969,173 00
Building, &c. custom-houses, warehouses, &c.	1,824,686.01	2,021,193.74
Building Post-Offices, Court Houses, &c.,		138,241.41
Expenses of collecting revenue from customs,	3,161,935.86	2,907,431.63
Survey of the coast of the United States, .	280,0'0.00	250,000.00
Survey of the western coast of United States,	130,000.00	96,500.00
Survey of Islands on the coast of California,	14,000 00	30,000.00
Survey of Florida reefs and keys, &c., .	52,000.00	59,500.00
Publishing observations by Coast Survey,	7,500.00	8,000.00
Other Expenses of Coast Survey, . .	5,500.00	33,000.00
Continuation, &c. Treasury buildings, .	377,000.00	541,050 46
Patent-Office building, and furnishing rooms,	138,964 28	219,000.00
Mint establishment, ...	661,130 66	613,487 21
Relief of sundry individuals, ...	1,110,753.23	112,112.36
Auxiliary guard in the city of Washington,	19,255.84	19,252 87
Expenses incident to loans and Treas.-notes,	3,737.90	11,019.58
Penitentiary in District of Columbia, . .	19,395.00	18,255.00
Support of insane paupers in Dist. Columbia,	20,500.00	20,500.00
Erecting asylum, &c. for insane in Dist. Col.,	37,200.00	55,500.00
Support of transient paupers, ...	3,000.00	3,000.00
Bridges, and draw-keepers, ...	54,397.33	50,945.97
Three per cent to Ohio, ...	263.30	
Three per cent to Illinois, ...	27,007.90	13,791.69
Three per cent to Missouri, ...		79,030.09

* Deducting a repayment of $ 5,317.96, gives $ 1,019,435.16 as the total of foreign intercourse.

† Deduct from this, repayment of $ 1,884.51, and there remains $ 1,391,407.91, as the true total of foreign intercourse.

	Year ending June 30, 1857.	Year ending June 30, 1858.
Two and three per cent to Alabama, .		$26,071.76
Two and three per cent to Mississippi, .	$161,036.58	19,943.26
Five per cent to Arkansas, ...		18,700.79
Five per cent to Michigan, ...	18,911.13	7,358.24
Five per cent to Florida, ...		5,535.18
Five per cent to Iowa, ...	185,785.32	34,219.34
Five per cent to Louisiana, ...		10,971.30
To Vermont, to preserve neutrality, . .	4,009.18	
Debentures, drawbacks, bounties, &c.,	508,699.34	487,755.35
Excess of deposits for duties repaid importers,	1,257,225.04	656,226.11
Debentures and other charges (customs),	10,671.54	8,283.14
Payment of horses, &c. lost in military service,	1,607.83	11,170.01
Refunding duties on foreign merchandise,	564,647.35	151,154.96
Refunding duties under warehouse system,	4,838.85	1,775.86
Refunding duties under Reciprocity Treaty with Great Britain, ...	2,913.30	466.90
Repayment for lands erroneously sold, .	72,405.78	60,762.19
Settling land claims and suits in California,	17,400.00	2,535.85
Account, &c. of the Exploring Expedition,	10,410.00	33,414.22
Smithsonian Institution, act Aug. 10, 1846,	30,910.14	30,910.14
Safe-keeping the public revenue, . .	35,600.78	35,211.09
Building vaults in 66 depositories, . .		5,796.18
Claims not otherwise provided for, . .	5,191.31	7,526.95
Building and equipping revenue-cutters,	15,563.16	182,614.12
Pay to each designated depositary (½ per cent),	6,330.23	4,818.14
Purchase of land and buildings, &c., . .	630,184.14	
Public buildings in Territories, . .	84,901.92	24,257.41
Books for Territorial Libraries, . . .	6,000.00	
Special examiners of drugs and medicines,	7,416.24	6,748.27
Boundary line, United States and Mexico,	29,407.81	19,097.54
Cherokees that remained in North Carolina,		4,000.00
Increase of pay to collectors, &c., . .	9,311.59	6,180.45
Oregon, defence against Cayuse Indians,	3,453.24	1,920.25
Tri-monthly mail, New Orleans & Vera Cruz,		69,750.00
Mail, Charleston and Havana, two months,		10,000.00
500 burial lots in Cong. bury. ground, .		5,000.00
Bringing Electoral vote to Washington, .	16,156.00	
Agricultural statistics, and distributing seeds,	85,000.00	60,000.00
Public gardener, gate-keepers, laborers, .	17,677.00	19,048.00
Sundry items, ...	21,692.64	35,407.90
Total miscellaneous, ...	*19,339,831.75	17,937,217.54
Under the direction of the Depart. of Interior.		
Indian department, ...	4,008,062.79	4,812,815.09
Pensions, military, ...	1,191,667.58	1,075,637.14
Pensions, naval, ...	135,195.89	143,246.17
Relief of sundry individuals, ...	23,348.46	20,224.98
Total under direction of Depart. of Interior,	5,358,274.72	6,051,923.38
Under the direction of the War Department.		
Army proper, &c., ...	12,380,684.56	17,455,976.85
Military Academy, ...	175,784.70	164,301.31
Fortifications, and other works of defence,	1,631,563.74	2,667,448.11
Armories, arsenals, and munitions of war, .	1,105,141.69	1,443,235.74

* Deducting $33,814.86 for repayments, gives $19,305,374.79 as total miscellaneous.

	Year ending June 30, 1857.	Year ending June 30, 1858.
Harbors, roads, rivers, &c.,	$614,124.70	$577,792.16
Arming and equipping the militia,	141,249.81	361,609 86
Payments to militia and volunteers,	391,764.99	50,234.34
Extension of the Capitol, and new dome,	930,000.00	1,000,000.00
General Post-Office building,	260,000.00	350,000.00
Washington Aqueduct,	175,000.00	945,036 99
Relief of individuals, and miscellaneous,	1,456,459.97	469,748.24
Total under direction of the War Dep't,	19,261,774.16	25,485,383.60
Under the direction of the Navy Department.		
Pay and subsistence, including medicines, &c.,	4,241,321.25	4,761,000.89
Increase, repairs, ordnance, and equipment,	2,886,102.95	3,394,646.29
Contingent expenses,	862,467.73	904,314.45
Navy yards and docks,	1,781,124.45	1,982,923 62
Navy hospitals, asylums, and magazines,	126,622.02	274,195.84
Naval Academy,	39,172.23	43,731.22
Relief of individuals, and miscellaneous,	385,951.73	301,300.46
Marine Corps and barracks,	503,670.93	587,242.25
Steam mail service,	1,059,866.67	885,322.20
Six steam-frigates,	840,556.73	368,932.41
Five steam-sloops of war,		472,390.96
Total under direction of the Navy Dep't,	12,726,856 69	13,976,000.59
Public Debt.		
Old public debt,	503.21	
Interest on the public debt and Treasury-notes,	1,678,265.23	1,567,055.67
Redemption bounty land stock,	400.00	225.00
Reimbursement Treasury-notes in specie,	100.00	200.00
Payment Texas creditors, Act September 9th, 1850,	629,353.24	38,788.42
Redemption of stock, loan of 1842,	516,539.58	614,270.82
Redemption of stock, loan of 1846,	714,013.26	26,400.00
Redemption of stock, loan of 1847,	1,000,000.00	1,759,950.00
Redemption of stock, loan of 1848,	898,150.00	1,435,900.00
Premium, commission, &c. on stock redeemed,	363,572.39	574,443.08
Redemption Texan indemnity stock,	143,000.00	28,000.00
Payment Treasury-notes, act Dec. 23, 1857,		3,639,300.00
" " act Feb. 24, 1815,		5.00
Total public debt paid,	5,943,896.91	9,684,537.99
Total expenditures,	70,822,724.85	81,585,667.76
Balances in the Treasury, July 1, 1857 and '58,	17,710,114.27	6,398,316.10

2. *Statement of Public Revenues and Public Expenditures during the Fiscal Year ending June 30, 1859, agreeably to warrants issued, exclusive of Trust Funds and Treasury-notes funded.*

RECEIPTS.

From Customs, quarter ending Sept. 30, 1858,	$13,444,520.28	
Dec. 31, 1858,	9,054,228.60	
Mar. 31, 1859,	12,786,252.19	
June 30, 1859,	14,280,823.31	
		$40,565,824.38
Lands, quarter ending Sept. 30, 1858,	421,171.84	
Dec. 31, 1858,	402,190.97	
Mar. 31, 1859,	490,947.78	
June 30, 1859,	442,376.71	
		1,756,687.30
Miscellaneous and incidental sources,		2,082,559.33
Treasury-notes, Act of Dec. 23, 1857,		9,667,400.00
Loan Act of June 14, 1858,		18,620,000.00
Total receipts,		$81,692,471.01
Balance in Treasury, July 1, 1858,		6,398,316.10
Total means,		$88,090,787.11

EXPENDITURES.

For civil list,	$5,963,705 66
" foreign intercourse,	1,036,860.02
" miscellaneous,	16,636,165.26
Under direction of the Department of the Interior (Indian and Pensions),	4,753,972.60
" " " War Department,	23,243,822.38
" " " Navy "	14,712,610.21
For public debt,	17,405,285.44
Total expenditures,	$83,751,511.57
Balance in Treasury, July 1, 1859,	$4,339,275.54

3. *Receipts and Expenditures of the United States for the quarter ending September 30, 1859, exclusive of Trust Funds.*

RECEIPTS.

From customs,	$15,947,670.62
" Sales of public lands,	470,244 62
" Loan under Act of June 14, 1858,	210,000.00
" Treasury-notes, under Act of Dec. 23, 1857,	3,611,300.00
" Miscellaneous and incidental sources,	379,650.61
Total receipts,	$20,618,865.85

Expenditures.

Civil, foreign intercourse, and miscellaneous, ...		$4,748,130.89
Interior (Pensions and Indian), ...		1,739,176.11
War		5,473,949.10
Navy		3,381,551.90
Interest on Public Debt, including Treasury-notes,	$248,825.22	
Redemption of bounty land stock, ...	200.00	
Payment to creditors of Texas, per Act of Sept. 9, 1850, ...	841.54	
Payment of Treasury-notes issued per Act of 23d Dec., 1857, ...	4,414,500.00	
		4,664,366.76
		$20,007,174.76

4. *Statement of the Debt of the United States on the 1st of July, 1858.**

Denomination of Debt.	Rate of Interest per Cent.	When redeemable.	Amount.
Principal and interest of the old funded and unfunded debt, Treasury-notes of 1812, and Yazoo scrip, ...		On present'ion	$114,118.54
Treasury-notes issued previous to Dec. 23, 1857, ...		On present'ion	107,011.64
Loan of April 15, 1842, .	6	Dec. 31, 1862	2,883,364.11
" July 22, 1846, . .	6	Nov. 12, 1856	7,600.00
" January 28, 1847, .	6	Jan. 1, 1868	9,412,700.00
" March 31, 1848, . .	6	July 1, 1868	8,908,341.80
Texan indemnity, . .	5	Jan. 1, 1865	3,461,000.00
Texas debt, act Feb. 28, 1855, .	. .	. .	261,841.57
Present amount as above, .	. .	. .	$25,155,977.66
Treasury-notes under act of Dec. 23, 1857, ...		$23,716,300	
Settled and entered as redeemed previous to July 1, 1858, .	$3,639,300		
Redeemed but not entered, .	322,200		
		3,961,500	
			19,754,800.00
Total debt, ...			$44,910,777.66

* For later official statements in regard to the public debt of the United States, if received, see the Additions and Corrections at the end of the volume. There was received from loans and Treasury-notes from July 1, 1858, to Sept. 30, 1859, $32,108,700. The payments on the same account and on account of the public debt during the same period were $21,819,785.44. This would make an increase of the public debt, Sept. 30, 1859, of $10,288,914.56.

5. *Statement of the Expenditures of the United States for 70 years, exclusive of Payments on account of the Public Debt and from Trust Funds, fractions excluded.*

Years.	Civil List, Foreign Intercourse, and Miscellaneous.	Military Establishment.†	Naval Establishment.	Aggregate of Expenditures.	
				In each Year.	In each Period of four Years.
1789 - 91	$1,083,401	$835,618	$570	$1,919,589	
1792	654,257	1,223,594	53	1,877,904	$3,797,493
1793	472,450	1,237,620		1,710,070	
1794	705,598	2,733,540	61,409	3,500,547	
1795	1,367,037	2,573,059	410,562	4,350,658	
1796	772,485	1,474,661	274,784	2,521,930	12,083,205
1797	1,246,904	1,194,055	382,632	2,823,591	
1798	1,111,038	2,130,837	1,381,348	4,623,223	
1799	1,039,392	2,582,693	2,858,082	6,480,167	
1800	1,337,613	2,625,041	3,448,716	7,411,370	21,338,351
1801	1,114,768	1,755,477	2,111,424	4,981,669	
1802	1,462,929	1,358,589	915,562	3,737,080	
1803	1,842,636	944,958	1,215,231	4,002,825	
1804	2,191,009	1,072,017	1,189,833	4,452,859	17,174,433
1805	3,768,588	991,136	1,597,500	6,357,224	
1806	2,891,037	1,540,431	1,649,641	6,081,109	
1807	1,697,897	1,564,611	1,722,064	4,984,572	
1808	1,423,286	3,196,985	1,884,068	6,504,339	23,927,244
1809	1,215,804	3,771,109	2,427,759	7,414,672	
1810	1,101,145	2,555,693	1,654,244	5,311,082	
1811	1,367,291	2,259,747	1,965,566	5,592,604	
1812	1,683,088	12,187,046	3,959,365	17,829,499	36,147,857
1813	1,729,435	19,906,362	6,446,600	28,082,397	
1814	2,208,029	20,608,366	7,311,291	30,127,686	
1815	2,898,871	15,394,700	8,660,000	26,953,571	
1816	2,989,742	16,475,412	3,908,278	23,373,432	108,537,086
1817	3,518,937	8,621,075	3,314,598	15,454,610	
1818	3,835,839	7,019,140	2,953,695	13,808,674	
1819	3,067,212	9,385,421	3,847,640	16,300,273	
1820	2,592,022	6,154,518	4,387,990	13,134,530	58,698,087
1821	2,223,122	5,181,114	3,319,243	10,723,479	
1822	1,967,996	5,635,187	2,224,459	9,827,642	
1823	2,022,094	5,258,295	2,503,766	9,784,155	
1824	7,155,308	5,270,255	2,904,582	15,330,145	45,665,421
1825	2,748,544	5,692,831	3,049,084	11,490,459	
1826	2,600,178	6,243,236	4,218,902	13,062,316	
1827	2,314,777	5,675,742	4,263,878	12,254,397	
1828	2,886,052	5,701,203	3,918,786	12,506,041	49.313,213
1829	3,092,214	6,250,530	3,308,745	12,651,489	
1830	3,228,416	6,752,689	3,239,429	13,220,534	
1831	3,064,346	6,943,239	3,856,183	13,863,768	
1832	4,574,841	7,982,877	3,956,370	16,514,088	56,249,879
1833	5,051,789	13,096,152	3,901,357	22,049,298	
1834	4,399,779	10,064,428	3,956,260	18,420,467	
1835	3,720,167	9,420,313	3,864,939	17,006,419	
1836	5,388,371	18,466,110	5,800,763	29,655,244	87,130.428
1837	5,524,253	19,417,274	6,852,060	31,793,587	
1838	5,666,703	19,936,312	5,975,771	31,578,785	
1839	4,994,562	14,268,981	6,225,003	25,488,647	
1840	5,581,878	11,621,438	6,124,456	23,327,772	112,188,691
1841	6,490,881	13,704,982	6,001,077	26,196,840	
1842	6,775,625	9,188,469	8,397,243	24,361,337	
6 mo. of 1843	2,867,289	4,158,384	3,672,718	10,698,301	
*1844	5,231,747	8,231,317	6,496,991	19,960,055	81.216,623
*1845	5,608,207	9,533,203	6,228,639	21,370,049	
*1846	6,783,000	13,579,428	6,450,862	26,813,290	
*1847	6,715,854	41,281,606	7,931,633	55,929,093	
*1848	5,585,070	27,820,163	9,406,737	42,811,970	146.924.402
*1849	14,017,640	17,290,936	9,869,818	57,631,667	
*1850	14,839,725	12,801,764	7,923,313	43,002,168	
*1851	17,872,967	11.811,793	8,967,798	48,005,879	
*1852	17,379,768	13,424,075	8,928,236	46,007,896	194,647.610
*1853	17,175,797	15,476,828	10,891,640	43,543,263	
*1854	25,907,372	14,342,684	10.768,192	51,018.249	
*1855	24,183.487	18,900,565	13,281,341	56,365,393	
*1856	25,274.331	20,821,024	14.077,047	60,172,402	211 099,507
*1857	27,531,922	24,619,049	12,728,857	64,878,828	
*1858	26.387,822	31.537.307	13.976.001	71.901,130	

* For the year ending June 30. † Including Dep't of the Interior for and since 1850.

6. *Statement of the Receipts into the National Treasury, from Customs, Internal Revenue, and Direct Taxes, and Sales of Public Lands, — fractions of a Dollar being excluded, — for 70 years, from 1789 to 1858 inclusive.*

Years.	Customs.	Internal and Direct Taxes.	Sales of Lands and Miscellaneous.	Aggregate of Receipts. In each Year.	Aggregate of Receipts. In each Period of four Years.
1789 - 91	$4,399,473			$4,399,473	
1792	3,443,071	$208,943		3,652,014	$8,051,487
1793	4,255,306	337,706		4,593,012	
1794	4,801,065	274,090		5,075,155	
1795	5,588,461	337,755		5,926,216	
1796	6,567,988	475,290	$4,836	7,048,114	22,642,497
1797	7,549,650	575,491	83,541	8,208,682	
1798	7,106,062	644,358	11,963	7,762,383	
1799	6,610,449	779,136		7,389,585	
1800	9,080,933	1,543,620	444	10,624,997	33,985,647
1801	10,750,779	1,582,377	167,726	12,500,882	
1802	12,438,236	828,464	188,628	13,455,328	
1803	10,479,418	287,059	165,676	10,932,153	
1804	11,098,465	101,139	487,527	11,687,231	48,575,694
1805	12,936,487	43,631	540,194	13,520,312	
1806	14,667,698	75,865	765,246	15,508,809	
1807	15,845,522	47,784	466,163	16,359,469	
1808	16,363,550	27,370	647,939	17,038,859	62,427,419
1809	7,296,021	11,562	442,252	7,749,835	
1810	8,583,309	19,879	696,549	9,299,737	
1811	13,313,223	9,962	1,040,238	14,363,423	
1812	8,958,778	5,762	710,428	9,674,968	41,087,963
1813	13,224,623	8,561	835,655	14,068,839	
1814	5,998,772	3,882,482	1,135,971	11,017,225	
1815	7,282,942	6,840,733	1,287,959	15,411,634	
1816	36,306,875	9,378,344	1,717,985	47,403,204	87,900,902
1817	26,283,348	4,512,288	1,991,226	32,786,862	
1818	17,176,385	1,219,613	2,606,565	21,002,563	
1819	20,283,609	313,244	3,274,423	23,871,276	
1820	15,005,612	137,847	1,635,872	16,779,331	91,440,032
1821	13,004,447	98,377	1,212,966	14,315,790	
1822	17,589,762	88,617	1,803,582	19,481,961	
1823	19,088,433	44,580	916,523	20,049,536	
1824	17,878,326	40,865	984,418	18,903,609	72,750,896
1825	20,098,714	28,102	1,216,090	21,342,906	
1826	23,341,332	28,228	1,393,785	24,763,345	
1827	19,712,283	22,513	1,495,945	21,230,641	
1828	23,205,524	19,671	1,018,309	24,243,504	91,580,396
1829	22,681,966	25,838	1,517,175	24,224,979	
1830	21,922,391	29,141	2,329,356	24,280,888	
1831	21,224,412	17,440	3,210,815	27,452,697	
1832	28,465,237	18,422	2,623,381	31,107,040	107,065,604
1833	29,032,509	3,153	3,967,682	33,003,344	
1834	16,214,957	4,216	4,857,601	21,076,774	
1835	19,391,311	14,723	4,757,601	34,163,635	
1836	23,409,940	1,099	4,877,180	48,288,219	136,531,972
1837	11,169,290		6,863,556	18,032,846	
1838	16,158,800		3,214,184	19,372,984	
1839	23,137,925		7,261,118	30,399,043	
1840	13,499,502		3,494,356	16,993,858	84,798,731
1841	14,487,217		1,470,295	15,957,512	
1842	18,187,909		1,456,058	19,643,967	
6 mo. of 1843	7,046,844		1,018,482	8,065,326	
*1844	26,183,571		2,320,948	28,504,519	72,171,324
*1845	27,528,113		2,241,021	29,769,134	
*1846	26,712,668		2,786,579	29,499,247	
*1847	23,747,864		2,598,926	26,346,790	
*1848	31,757,070		3,679,679	35,436,750	121,051,921
*1849	28,346,738		2,727,608	31,074,347	
*1850	39,668,686		3,707,112	43,375,798	
*1851	49,017,568		3,295,412	52,312,979	
*1852	47,339,326		2,389,060	49,728,386	176,491,510
*1853	58,931,865		2,405,709	61,337,574	
*1854	64,224,190		9,325,514	73,549,705	
*1855	53,025,794		11,978,136	65,003,930	
*1856	64,022,863		9,895,278	73,918,141	273,809,330
*1857	63,875,905		4,755,609	68,631,514	
*1858	41,789,621		4,767,949	46,557,570	

* For the year ending June 30.

7. *Statement of the Debt of the United States, the Total Value of Imports and Exports, and the Total Tonnage, each Year for 69 years, from 1790 to 1858, fractions excluded.*

Years.	Debt.	Imports.‡	Exports.‡	Tonnage.
1790-91	$ 75,463,476	$ 52,200,000	$ 39,217,197	502,146
1792	77,227,924	31,500,000	20,753,098	564,437
1793	80,352,634	31,100,000	26,109,572	491,780
1794	78,427,405	34,600,000	33,026,233	628,817
1795	80,747,587	69,756,268	47,989,472	747,964
1796	83,762,172	81,436,164	67,064,097	831,900
1797	82,064,479	75,379,406	56,850,206	876,913
1798	79,228,529	68,551,700	61,527,097	898,328
1799	78,408,670	79,068,148	78,665,522	946,408
1800	82,976,294	91,252,768	70,971,780	972,492
1801	83,038,051	111,363,511	94,115,925	1,033,219
1802	80,712,632	76,333,333	72,483,160	892,104
1803	77,054,686	64,666,666	55,800,033	949,147
1804	86,427,121	85,000,000	77,699,074	1,042,404
1805	82,312,150	120,600,000	95,566,021	1,140,369
1806	75,723,271	129,410,000	101,536,963	1,208,735
1807	69,218,399	138,500,000	108,343,150	1,268,548
1808	65,196,318	56,990,000	22,430,960	1,212,595
1809	57,023,192	59,400,000	52,203,233	1,350,281
1810	53,173,217	85,400,000	66,757,970	1,424,783
1811	48,005,588	53,400,000	61,316,833	1,232,502
1812	45,209,738	77,030,000	38,527,236	1,269,997
1813	55,962,828	22,005,000	27,855,997	1,666,628
1814	81,487,846	12,965,000	6,927,441	1,159,209
1815	99,833,660	113,041,274	52,557,753	1,368,127
1816	127,334,934	147,103,000	81,920,452	1,372,218
1817	123,491,965	99,250,000	87,671,569	1,399,912
1818	103,466,634	121,750,000	93,281,133	1,225,184
1819	95,529,648	87,125,000	70,142,521	1,260,751
1820	91,015,566	74,450,000	69,691,669	1,280,166
1821	89,987,428	62,585,724	64,974,382	1,298,958
1822	93,546,677	83,241,541	72,160,281	1,324,699
1823	90,875,877	77,579,267	74,699,030	1,336,566
1824	90,269,778	80,549,007	75,986,657	1,389,163
1825	83,788,433	96,340,075	99,535,388	1,423,112
1826	81,054,060	84,974,477	77,595,322	1,534,191
1827	73,987,357	79,484,068	82,324,827	1,620,608
1828	67,475,044	88,509,824	72,264,686	1,741,392
1829	58,421,414	74,492,527	72,358,671	1,260,798
1830	48,565,406	70,876,920	73,849,508	1,191,776
1831	39,123,192	103,191,124	81,310,583	1,267,847
1832	24,322,235	101,029,266	87,176,943	1,439,450
1833	7,001,699	108,118,311	90,140,443	1,606,151
1834	4,760,082	126,521,332	104,336,973	1,758,907
1835	37,733	149,895,742	121,693,577	1,824,940
1836	37,513	189,980,035	128,663,040	1,882,103
1837	1,878,224	140,989,217	117,419,376	1,896,686
1838	4,857,660	113,717,404	108,486,616	1,995,640
1839	11,983,738	162,092,132	121,028,416	2,096,380
1840	5,125,078	132,085,946	107,141,519	2,180,764
1841	6,737,398	127,946,177	121,851,803	2,130,744
1842	15,028,486	100,162,087	104,691,534	2,092,391
1843	26,898,953	64,753,799*	84,346,480*	2,158,603
1844	26,143,996	108,435,035†	111,200,046†	2,280,095
1845	16,801,647	117,254,564†	114,646,606†	2,417,002
1846	24,256,495	121,691,797†	113,488,516†	2,562,085
1847	45,659,659	146,545,638†	158,648,622†	2,839,046
1848	65,804,450	154,998,928†	154,032,131†	3,154,042
1849	64,704,693	147,857,439†	145,755,820†	3,334,015
1850	64,228,238	178,138,318†	151,898,720†	3,535,454
1851	62,560,395	216,224,932†	218,388,011†	3,772,439
1852	67,560,395	212,945,442†	209,658,366†	4,138,441
1853	56,336,157	267,978,647†	230,976,157†	4,407,010
1854	44,975,456	304,562,381†	278,241,064†	4,802,903
1855	39,969,731	261,468,520†	275,156,846†	5,212,001
1856	30,963,910	314,639,942†	326,964,908†	4,871,652
1857	25,165,155	360,890,141†	362,960,682†	4,940,843
1858	44,910,778	282,613,150†	324,644,421†	5,049,808

* Only nine months of 1843. † For the year ending June 30.

‡ Total imports for 69 years, $7,941,044,687; total Exports, $7,184,644,755.

XI. COMMERCE AND NAVIGATION.

1. Value of Different Articles Imported.

Value of Goods, Wares, and Merchandise imported into the United States in all Vessels, from July 1, 1857, *to June* 30, 1858.

[The letters n. o. p. mean not otherwise provided for.]

Species of Merchandise.	Value.
Free of Duty.	
Animals, living, of all kinds,	$ 81,331
Argols, or crude tartar,	66,786
Articles.	
From British provinces under reciprocity treaty,	14,572,255
All for use of United States,	13,178
Produce of U. S. brought back,	1,244,692
Specially for seminaries of learning, &c.,	64,341
Crude used in dyeing or tanning,	322,456
Bark, Peruvian,	813,184
Bells, old, and bell-metal,	473
Berries, nuts, &c., for dyeing or composing dyes,	12,823
Bismuth,	3,266
Bitter Apples,	1,575
Bolting Cloths,	107,612
Bone black,	619
Bone, burnt,	9,206
Brass.	
Old,	12,490
Pigs,	470
Bullion.	
Gold,	2,286,000
Silver,	408,879
Burr-stones, unmanufactured,	65,423
Cabinets of coins, medals, &c.,	14
Coffee,	18,341,081
Coins.	
Gold,	9,279,969
Silver,	7,209,649
Copper.	
For sheathing vessels,	111,698
In bars or pigs,	745,932
Old,	322,619
Ore,	1,131,362
Cotton, unmanufactured,	41,356
Dragon's blood,	223
Dyewoods, in sticks,	887,486
Effects.	
Personal and household,	40,296
Personal, of emigrants and others, including wearing apparel and tools of trade, &c.,	232,825
Household, of persons or families arriving in U. S.,	47,139
Personal and household, of citizens dying abroad,	1,671
Felt, adhesive, for sheathing vessels,	10,843
Flax, unmanufactured,	197,934
Glass, old, and fit only to be remanufactured,	364
Hair of the alpaca goat or other like animals,	500
Ivory, unmanufactured,	401,387
Linseed, not embracing flax-seed,	3,243,174
Madder, Root,	$ 78,144
Ground or prepared,	643,642
Manures.	
Guano,	525,376
Other substances expressly for manure,	56
Maps and Charts,	6,562
Models of inventions and improvements in the arts,	3,866
Oils and products of American fisheries.	
Oils, spermaceti, whale, and other fish,	199,258
Other products of fisheries,	137,654
Old junk and oakum,	62,331
Paintings and statuary,	504,634
Palm leaf, unmanufactured,	34,880
Plaster of Paris, unmanufact'd,	82,313
Platina, unmanufactured,	37,681
Rags, of every material, except wool,	971,126
Rattans and Reeds, unmanuf'd,	171,813
Seeds, trees, shrubs, bulbs, plants, &c.,	392,440
Sheathing metal, no part iron, ungalvanized,	183,394
Shingle bolts and stave bolts,	3,889
Silk, raw or reeled, from the cocoon,	1,300,065
Specimens of natural history, &c.,	2,092
Tea,	6,777,295
Tin, Bars,	228,426
Blocks,	470,023
Pigs,	594,258
Wool, sheep's, unmanufactured, not over 20 cents per lb.,	3,843,320
All other articles,	460,263
Total free of duty,	80,319,275
Paying Duties *ad Valorem*.	
Acids.	
Acetic, benzoic, boracic, &c.,	113,736
Acetous, chromic, nitric, &c.,	592
Alum,	3,514
Arrow Root,	19,573
Bark, Quilla,	600
Of all kinds, n. o. p.,	26,963
Beer, Ale, and Porter.	
In casks,	146,095
In bottles,	485,039
Black-lead pencils,	93,779
Boots and shoes, other than leather,	30,754
Borax, refined.	67,890
Brass, and Manufactures of.	
Pins, in packs or otherwise,	33,132
Sheet and rolled,	281
Wire,	2,136
Manufactures of, not specified,	166,935

Species of Merchandise.	Value.
Breadstuffs.	
Barley,	$ 10,368
Indian corn and cornmeal,	34,936
Oats,	95
Oatmeal,	3,305
Rye,	772
Ryemeal,	9
Wheat,	26,651
Wheat-flour,	19,818
Brimstone.	
Crude,	249,317
Rolled,	9,639
Bristles,	265,720
Brushes and brooms,	170,078
Butter,	5,757
Buttons.	
Metal,	12,788
All other, and button-moulds,	483,141
Camphor, Crude,	92,953
Refined,	4
Candles.	
Spermaceti,	923
Stearine,	34,466
Wax,	7,808
Cheese,	152,272
Chloride of lime, or bleaching powder,	387,101
Chronometers, and parts thereof,	9,090
Clocks and Watches.	
Clocks, and parts thereof,	54,038
Watches, and parts thereof,	2,118,838
Watch materials, and unfinished parts of watches,	44,130
Clothing.	
Articles of wear,	961,514
Ready made,	322,024
Coal,	772,925
Cochineal,	221,332
Cocoa,	213,644
Coffee, from places other than of its production,	28,759
Copper, and Manufactures of.	
Copper bottoms,	5,194
Nails and spikes,	68
Rods and bolts,	8
Wire,	243
Manufactures of, not specified,	104,032
Cordage.	
Tarred and cables,	73,627
Untarred,	96,632
Cotton, Manufactures of, plain.	
Cords, galloons, and gimps,	40,969
Hatters' plush, cotton and silk,	4,818
Hos'y and art. made on frames,	2,120,868
Piece goods,	741,077
Thread, twist, yarn,	1,080,671
Velvets,	298,134
Manufactures not specified,	966,017
Cottons, bleached, printed, painted, or dyed.	
Piece goods, wholly of cotton,	12,391,713
All other manufactures wholly of cotton,	390,863
Daguerreotype plates,	1,828
Dolls and toys of all kinds,	350,486
Engravings or plates,	133,059
Extracts & decoctions of logwood and other dye woods, n. o. p.,	4,038
Extract of madder,	40,567
Extract of indigo,	382

Species of Merchandise.	Value.
Feathers and flowers, artificial or ornamental,	$ 654,132
Fish, dried, smoked, or pickled	
Fish, dried or smoked,	111,709
Herrings,	905
Mackerel,	369
Salmon,	2,416
All other,	5,209
Fish in oil, sardines and all other,	274,137
Flax, and Manufactures of.	
Hosiery and articles made on frames,	5,316
Linens, bleached or unbleached,	5,598,571
Manufactures of, not specified,	953,436
Tow of flax (codilla),	29,691
Floor cloth, patent, painted, &c.,	1,336
Fruits, green, ripe, or dried.	
Currants,	342,869
Dates,	31,567
Figs,	308,472
Lemons,	301,492
Limes,	2,024
Oranges,	476,694
Plums,	158,580
Prunes,	133,524
Raisins,	1,411,471
Other green, ripe, or dried fruits,	236,086
Fruit preserved in sugar, brandy, &c.,	121,058
Furs.	
Dressed, on the skin,	199,714
Undressed, on the skin,	321,935
Hatters' furs, dressed or undressed, not on the skin,	876,156
Manufactures of fur,	64,412
Glass, and Manufactures of.	
Bottles,	29,841
Demijohns,	32,016
Crystals for watches,	35,141
Painted or colored glass,	33,103
Polished plate glass,	397,310
Porcelain,	3,276
Silvered glass,	198,109
Ware, cut,	101,496
" plain,	63,681
Window glass, broad, crown, and cylinder,	626,747
Manufactures of, not specified,	138,249
Glaziers' diamonds,	1,533
Glue,	14,637
Gold and Silver, Manufactures of.	
Epaulettes, galloons, laces, tassels, tresses, &c.,	35,294
Gems, set,	3,915
" not set,	339,241
Gold and silver leaf,	40,087
Jewelry, real, or imitations of,	385,945
Silver plated metal,	6,731
" " ware,	8,439
Manufactures of, not specified,	55,282
Grass-cloth,	32,144
Gums.	
Arabic, Barbary, copal, &c.,	389,402
All other, and resins in a crude state,	118,277
Gum, benzoin or Benjamin,	6,803
Gunny bags,	420,966

Species of Merchandise.	Value.
Gunny cloth,	$ 1,016,801
Gunpowder,	4,458
Gutta Percha.	
Manufactures of,	586
Unmanufactured,	41,648
Hair.	
Manufactures of,	67,725
Unmanufactured,	263,472
Angora, Thibet, and all other goats' hair, or mohair,	
Piece goods,	515,641
Unmanufactured,	1,371
Hats and Bonnets.	
Of straw or other vegetable substance,	1,182,837
Of hair, whalebone, or other material, not otherwise provided for,	14,352
Hemp, and Manufactures of.	
Burlaps,	78,221
Cotton bagging,	8,296
Sail-duck, Russia, Holland, and Ravens,	7,592
Ticklenburgs,	528
Manufactures of, not specified,	520,029
Unmanufactured,	331,307
Tow of (codilla),	40,931
Honey,	149,915
India-Rubber.	
Manufactures of,	89,245
Unmanufactured,	666,583
Indigo,	945,063
Ink and ink powders,	23,410
Iron and Steel, Manufactures of.	
Anchors, and parts thereof,	8,072
Anvils, and parts thereof,	45,275
Bar iron,	3,318,913
Cables, chain,	155,406
Cutlery,	1,489,054
Fire-arms not specified,	382,610
Hoop iron,	273,326
Muskets and rifles,	17,024
Nails, spikes, tacks, &c.,	100,481
Needles,	202,163
Old and scrap iron,	87,113
Pig iron,	739,949
Railroad iron,	2,987,576
Rod iron,	426,499
Saws, mill, cross-cut, and pit,	34,210
Sheet iron,	945,073
Side-arms,	4,747
Steel, cast, shear, and German,	1,147,773
All other,	725,338
Wire, cap or bonnet,	6,900
Other manufactures of iron not specified,	2,260,402
Manufactures of steel, all other,	970,133
Ivory, manufactures of,	15,094
" black,	45
Jute, sisal, grass, coir, &c.,	2,298,709
Laces, &c.	
Braids of cotton,	13,971
Embroideries of cotton, linen, silk, and wool,	2,845,029
Insertings of cotton,	88,007
Laces of cotton,	405,439
Laces of thread,	189,494
Trimmings of cotton,	112,263
Lard,	422
Lasting and mohair-cloth for buttons and shoes,	$ 65,090
Lead, and Manufactures of.	
Bar, pig, sheet, and old,	1,972,243
Pipes,	1,501
Shot,	8,132
Manufactures not specified,	855
Leather, and Manufactures of.	
Boots and shoes,	87,101
Gloves,	1,449,672
Japanned leather, or skins of all kinds,	226,142
Skins, tanned and dressed,	806,412
Skivers,	35,976
Tanned, bend, sole, and upper,	1,259,711
Manufactures not specified,	278,946
Liquorice.	
Paste,	477,995
Root,	18,217
Machinery to manufacture flax and linen,	1,643
Marble.	
Manufactures of,	16,491
Unmanufactured,	167,634
Mathematical instruments,	21,437
Matting, Chinese or other, of flags, jute, &c.,	216,441
Meats and Vegetables.	
Bacon,	1,725
Beef,	11,606
Ham,	7,329
Pork,	595
Potatoes,	97,160
Meats, game, poultry, and vegetables, prepared in cans or otherwise,	45,320
Molasses,	4,116,759
Musical instruments,	378,928
Nuts.	
Almonds,	213,145
Cocoa-nuts,	42,656
Nuts not otherwise provided for,	236,907
Oil and Bone of foreign Fishing.	
Spermaceti,	157
Whale and other fish,	18,470
Whalebone,	13,475
Oil.	
Castor,	143,458
Essential, expressed, or volatile,	231,736
Hempseed and Rapeseed,	14,531
Linseed,	164,757
Neat's-foot, and other animal,	4,127
Olive, in casks,	110,172
Olive, in bottles,	199,615
Palm and cocoa-nut,	405,681
Oil-cloth of all kinds,	21,549
Opium,	447,534
Paints, Painters' colors, &c.	
Litharge,	7,539
Ochre, dry,	12,534
Painters' colors,	27,368
Paris white,	5,162
Red lead,	50,652
Spanish brown, in oil,	392
Sugar of lead,	12,612
Water colors,	29,012
White lead,	58,774

Species of Merchandise.	Value.
Whiting,	$ 20,608
Paints not specified,	199,748
Paper, and Manufactures of.	
Blank books,	18,343
Boxes, paper,	15,842
Boxes, fancy	17,681
Cards, playing,	18,595
Hangings,	104,758
Papier-maché, articles and wares of,	22,954
Writing-paper,	256,322
Manufactures of, not specified,	123,169
Parchment,	4,340
Pens, metallic,	83,630
Pewter.	
Old,	2,543
Manufactures of, not specified,	2,062
Printed books, magazines, &c.	
In English,	456,450
In other languages,	175,508
Newspapers, illustrated,	18,445
Periodicals,	3,519
Periodicals in course of republication,	158
Quicksilver,	1,029
Raw hides and skins,	9,884,358
Saddlery.	
Common, tinned, or japanned,	56,669
Plated, brass, or polished steel,	138,490
Salt,	1,124,920
Saltpetre.	
Crude,	1,270,251
Refined, or partially refined,	383
Seines,	979
Silk, and Manufactures of.	
Caps, bonnets, and hats,	94,396
Floss silk,	16,067
Hosiery and articles made on frames,	417,168
Piece goods,	16,121,395
Piece goods of silk and worsted,	1,249,385
Raw,	242,130
Sewing-silk,	111,912
Twist,	11,992
Manufactures not specified,	3,207,043
Slates of all kinds,	85,775
Soap.	
Perfumed,	37,515
Other than perfumed,	52,786
Soda.	
Ash,	1,211,305
Carbonate,	373,599
Sal,	123,083
Spices.	
Cassia,	356,614
Cinnamon,	18,419
Cloves,	63,978
Ginger, dried, green, ripe, preserved, or pickled,	53,141
Mace,	29,923
Nutmegs,	378,257
Pepper, black,	631,723
" red,	5,493
Pimento,	203,143
Spirits, Foreign Distilled, &c.	
Brandy,	2,232,452
From grain,	1,158,517
From other materials,	324,905
Cordials,	104,269
Starch,	4,308

Species of Merchandise.	Value.
Sugars.	$
Brown,	23,317,435
Candy,	2,205
Loaf, and other refined,	1,001
Syrup of sugar-cane,	6,165
White, clayed, or powdered,	109,887
Sulphate of barytes,	39,958
Sulphate of quinine,	54,166
Tallow,	7,413
Tea, from places other than of its production,	484,520
Tin, and Manufactures of.	
Foil,	25,317
Plates and sheets,	3,842,968
Manufactures of, not specified,	27,675
Tobacco.	
Cigars,	4,123,208
Snuff,	5,153
Manufactured, other than cigars and snuff,	22,898
Unmanufactured,	1,255,831
Twine,	73,010
Umbrellas, parasols, and sunshades, of silk or other,	47,790
Verdigris,	21,142
Vitriol.	
Blue or Roman (sulphate of copper),	5,438
Green (sulphate of iron, copperas),	2,414
White (sulphate of zinc),	1,515
Oil of (sulphuric acid),	25
Wares, China, &c.	
Chemical, earthen, or pottery, over 10 gallons,	18,959
China, earthen, porcelain, and stone,	3,215,236
Britannia,	4,275
Gilt or plated,	95,991
Japanned,	29,863
Wines, in casks.	
Austria and other of Germany,	46,733
Burgundy,	10,864
Claret,	385,750
Fayal and other Azores,	10,409
Madeira,	72,429
Port,	226,781
Sherry and St. Lucar,	343,100
Sicily & other Mediterranean,	56,612
Teneriffe and other Canary,	3,377
Red wines not enumerated,	421,368
White wines not enumerated,	285,125
Wines, in bottles.	
Burgundy,	2,714
Champagne,	860,942
Claret,	227,246
Madeira,	1,600
Port,	7,901
Sherry,	10,059
All other,	273,378
Woad or pastel,	1,203
Wood, Manufactures of.	
Cabinet & household furniture,	51,958
Cedar,	1,922
Ebony,	1,029
Mahogany,	9,978
Rose,	12,165
Satin,	254
Willow,	112,725
Other manufactures of,	288,334

Species of Merchandise.	Value.
Wood, unmanufactured.	
Box,	$ 7,507
Cedar,	68,467
Ebony,	2,365
Grenadillo,	1,586
Lignumvitæ,	14,083
Mahogany,	217,731
Rose,	81,440
Satin,	835
All other cabinet woods,	260
Fire-wood,	4,091
Willow,	35,141
Other woods not specified,	966
Bark of the Cork-tree.	
Cork,	167,181
Manufactures of,	86
Unmanufactured,	13,922
Wool and Worsted, Manufactures of.	
Baizes, bindings, & bockings,	124,006
Blankets,	1,574,716
Carpeting, viz., Aubusson, Brussels, Saxony, treble, ingrained, Turkey, Venetian, and other ingrained not specified, Wilton,	1,542,606
Flannels,	137,687
Hosiery and articles made on frames,	1,837,561
Piece goods of wool, including wool and cotton,	7,626,830

Species of Merchandise.	Value.
Piece goods of worsted, including worsted and cotton,	$ 10,780,379
Shawls of wool, wool and cotton, silk, and silk and cotton,	2,002,653
Woollen and worsted yarn,	196,285
Manufactures of wool or worsted not specified,	663,372
Wool, unmanufactured, not otherwise provided for,	179,315
Zinc, Manufactures of.	
Nails,	1,166
Pigs,	28,701
Sheets,	209,736
Spelter,	212,823
Manufactures of zinc not specified,	4,865
Value of Merchandise not enumerated.	
At 4 per cent,	1,387,425
At 8 "	291,633
At 12 "	8,576
At 15 "	2,314,065
At 19 "	169,254
At 24 "	1,496,074
At 30 "	35,017
Value of Merchandise paying Duties ad valorem,	202,293,875
Free of Duty,	80,319,275
Total,	282,613,150

Year ending June 30, 1854.	$	*Year ending June* 30, 1856.	$
Merchandise at ad valorem,	268,975,060	Merchandise at ad valorem,	257,684,236
" free of duty,	32,519,034	" free of duty,	56,955,706
Total,	301,494,094	Total,	314,639,942
Add Imports at San Francisco,	3.068.287		
Total,	304,562,381		
Year ending June 30, 1855.	$	*Year ending June* 30, 1857.	$
Merchandise at ad valorem,	221,378,184	Merchandise at ad valorem,	294,160,835
" free of duty,	40,090,336	" free of duty,	66,729,306
Total,	261,468,520	Total,	360,890,141
Deduct for deficiency in invoices,	85,560		
Total,	261,382,960		

For the amount of the imports for the year ending June 30, 1859, see the Additions and Corrections at the end of the volume.

For the annual average price of flour in Boston, New York, Philadelphia, and Baltimore from 1800 to 1855 inclusive, in New Orleans from 1813 to 1855 inclusive, and in St. Louis from 1833 to 1835 inclusive; for the amount of specie, and for the bank-notes in circulation at different years between 1800 and 1855; and for the amount of coin and bullion imported and exported annually from 1821 to 1855 inclusive, see the American Almanac for 1857, page 173.

2. Exports of the Produce of the United States.

Summary Statement of the Value of the Exports of the Growth, Produce, and Manufacture of the United States, during the Four Years ending June 30, 1858.

The Sea.	Year ending June 30, 1855.	Year ending June 30, 1856.	Year ending June 30, 1857.	Year ending June 30, 1858.
Fisheries.				
Dried fish, or cod fisheries,	$ 379,892	$ 578,011	$ 570,348	$ 487,007
Pickled fish, or river fisheries (herring, shad, salmon, mackerel),	94,111	173,939	211,383	197,441
Whale and other fish oil,	485,506	526,338	363,665	597,107
Spermaceti oil,	45,411	977,005	1,216,888	1,097,505
Whalebone,	781,680	1,036,647	1,307,322	1,105,223
Spermaceti and sperm candles,	136,463	64,857	70,038	66,012
Total Fisheries,	3,516,894	3,356,797	3,739,644	3,550,295
The Forest.				
Skins and furs,	709,531	952,452	1,116,041	1,002,378
Ginseng,	19,796	175,706	58,331	193,736
Products of Wood.				
Staves, shingles, boards, plank, scantling, hewn timber,	4,916,308	4,252,749	6,956,206	6,291,996
Other lumber,	677,659	803,684	638,406	1,240,425
Oak bark and other dye,	99,168	121,030	322,754	392,825
All manufactures of wood,	3,683,420	2,501,583	3,158,424	2,234,678
Naval stores, tar, pitch, rosin, and turpentine,	2,049,456	1,457,553	1,753,182	1,564,869
Ashes, pot and pearl,	448,499	429,428	696,367	554,744
Total Products of the Forest,	12,603,837	10,694,184	14,699,711	13,475,671
Agriculture.				
Products of Animals.				
Beef, tallow, hides, and horned cattle,	4,399,616	3,047,154	2,620,341	5,021,348
Butter and cheese,	932,757	1,467,991	1,240,507	1,273,773
Pork (pickled), hams, bacon, lard, live hogs,	11,607,165	12,770,648	12,467,029	9,430,372
Horses and mules,	191,904	323,972	366,816	527,568
Sheep,	18,837	18,802	22,758	49,319
Wool,	27,802	27,455	19,007	211,861
Total Products of Animals,	17,178,080	17,655,922	16,736,458	16,514,241
Vegetable Food.				
Wheat,	1,829,246	15,115,661	22,240,857	9,061,504
Flour,	10,896,908	29,275,148	25,882,316	19,328,884
Indian corn,	6,961,571	7,622,565	5,184,666	3,259,039
Indian meal,	1,237,122	1,175,688	957,791	877,692
Rye meal,	236,246	214,563	115,828	56,235
Rye, oats, and other small grain and pulse,	238,976	2,718,620	680,108	642,764
Biscuit, or ship-bread,	657,783	497,741	563,266	472,372
Potatoes,	203,416	153,061	205,616	206,791
Apples,	107,643	143,884	135,280	74,363
Rice,	1,717,953	2,390,233	2,290,400	1,870,578
Onions,	64,496	83,742	77,048	75,626
Total Vegetable Food,	23,651,362	59,390,906	58,333,176	35,924,848
Tobacco,	14,712,468	12,221,843	20,260,772	17,009,767
Cotton,	88,143,844	128,382,351	131,575,859	131,386,661
Hemp,	121,320	28,598	46,907	47,875
All other Agricultural Products.				
Flaxseed,	6,016	18,043	525	
Hops,	1,310,720	146,966	84,852	41,704
Brown sugar,	286,408	404,145	190,012	375,062
Clover-seed,	13,570	41,875	330,166	332,250
Total, other Ag. Products,	1,616,714	611,029	605,555	749,016
Total Agricul. Products,	145,423,786	218,290,649	227,558,727	201,632,408
Manufactures.				
Soap and candles,	1,111,349	1,200,764	1,207,483	934,303
Leather, boots and shoes,	1,652,406	1,313,311	1,311,709	1,269,494
Household furniture,	803,960	982,042	579,448	932,499
Coaches, carriages, and cars,	290,525	370,259	476,394	777,921

	Year ending June 30, 1855.	Year ending June 30, 1856.	Year ending June 30, 1857.	Year ending June 30, 1858.
Hats,	$ 177,914	$ 226,682	$ 254,208	$ 126,525
Saddlery,	61,886	31,249	45,222	55,280
Wax,	69,905	74,005	91,983	85,926
Beer, ale, porter, and cider,	45,069	45,086	39,732	59,532
Snuff and tobacco, manufactured,	1,500,113	1,829,207	1,458,553	2,410,224
Linseed oil,	49,580	57,190	54,144	48,225
Spirits of turpentine,	1,137,152	839,048	741,346	1,069,282
Cables and cordage,	315,267	367,182	286,163	212,840
Iron.				
Pig, bar, and nails,	288,337	286,980	397,313	205,931
Castings,	306,439	288,316	289,967	464,415
All other manufactures of,	3,158,596	3,585,712	4,197,687	4,059,528
Spirits from molasses,	1,418,280	1,329,151	1,216,635	1,267,691
Spirits from grain,	384,144	300,945	1,248,234	476,722
Spirits from other materials,	101,836	95,484	120,011	249,432
Sugar, refined,	526,463	360,444	368,206	200,724
Chocolate,	2,771	1,476	1,932	2,304
Gunpowder,	356,051	644,974	398,244	365,173
Copper and brass, and manufactures of,	690,766	534,846	607,054	1,955,223
Medicinal drugs,	788,114	1,066,294	886,909	681,278
Cotton Piece Goods.				
Printed or colored,	2,613,655	1,966,845	1,785,685	2,069,194
White other than duck,	2,793,910	4,290,361	3,463,230	1,598,136
Duck,	113,366	325,903	252,109	183,889
All other manufactures of,	336,250	384,200	614,153	1,800,285
Total of Cotton Goods,	5,857,181	6,967,309	6,115,177	5,651,504
Flax and Hemp.				
Cloth and thread,	2,506	802	1,066	1,326
Bags & other manufactures of,	34,002	25,233	33,687	87,766
Wearing-apparel,	223,801	278,832	333,442	210,695
Combs and buttons,	32,049	32,653	39,799	46,349
Brooms and brushes of all kinds,	10,856	8,385	7,324	49,153
Billiard-tables and apparatus,	4,916	2,778	733	8,791
Umbrellas, parasols, sun-shades,	8,441	5,989	6,846	6,339
Morocco and other leather not sold per pound,	36,045	5,765	2,119	13,099
Fire-engines and apparatus,	14,829	29,088	21,524	7,220
Printing-presses and type,	36,405	67,517	52,747	106,498
Musical instruments,	106,857	133,517	127,748	99,275
Books and maps,	207,218	202,502	277,647	209,774
Paper and stationery,	185,637	203,013	224,767	229,991
Paints and varnish,	163,096	217,179	223,320	131,217
Vinegar,	17,281	26,034	30,788	24,336
Earthen and stone ware,	32,119	66,696	34,256	36,783
Glass, manufactures of,	204,679	216,439	179,900	214,608
Tin, "	14,279	13,610	5,622	24,186
Pewter & lead, manufactures of,	5,233	5,628	4,818	27,327
Marble and stone, "	168,546	162,376	111,403	138,590
Gold and silver, and gold-leaf, manufactures of,	9,051	6,116	15,477	26,386
Gold and silver coin and bullion,	53,957,418	44,148,279	60,078,352	42,407,246
Artificial flowers and jewelry,	22,043	26,386	28,070	28,901
Molasses,	189,830	154,630	108,003	115,893
Trunks and valises,	35,203	38,457	37,748	59,441
Bricks and lime,	57,393	64,297	68,002	103,821
Salt,	156,879	311,495	190,699	162,650
Coal,	637,006	677,420	616,861	558,014
Lead,	14,298	27,512	58,624	48,119
Ice,	190,793	191,744	219,816	200,525
Quicksilver,	806,119	831,724	665,480	129,184
India-rubber boots and shoes,	686,769	427,936	331,125	115,931
All other manufactures of,	722,338	665,602	312,387	197,448
Lard oil, and oil-cake,	822,534	1,298,202	1,279,479	1,496,819
Articles not enumerated.				
Manufactured,	3,274,843	3,559,613	3,292,722	2,601,789
Other articles (raw produce),	1,545,518	1,119,295	1,266,828	1,561,940
Total,	$ 246,708,553	$ 310,586,330	$ 338,985,065	$ 293,758,279

3. Imports from and Exports to Foreign Countries,

During the Year ending June 30, 1858.

	Countries.	Value of Imports.	Value of Exports.		
			Domestic Produce.	Foreign Produce.	Total.
1	Russia on the Baltic and North Seas,	$ 2,061,660	$ 4,263,554	$ 72,390	$ 4,335,944
2	Asiatic Russia,	19,611	25,519	26,521	52,040
3	Russian Possessions in North America,	54,007	47,608	2,226	49,834
4	Sweden and Norway,	625,210	496,121	6,881	503,002
5	Swedish West Indies,	33,882	82,533	106	82,639
6	Denmark,	9,028	36,179		36,179
7	Danish West Indies,	325,895	748,363	46,461	794,824
8	Hamburg,	3,712,292	2,279,330	1,257,373	3,536,703
9	Bremen,	10,452,194	8,617,457	1,058,461	9,675,918
10	Other German ports,	50	54,614		54,614
11	Holland,	2,328,142	3,033,454	338,053	3,371,507
12	Dutch West Indies,	434,655	347,748	13,099	360,847
13	Dutch Guiana,	225,314	264,290	7,741	272,031
14	Dutch East Indies,	817,998	270,361	237,762	508,123
15	Belgium,	3,777,996	2,192,868	1,626,093	3,818,961
16	England,	90,454,611	151,573,714	11,707,330	163,281,044
17	Scotland,	5,160,767	3,124,551	104,442	3,228,993
18	Ireland,	115,280	1,307,935	277,876	1,585,811
19	Gibraltar,	92,238	403,454	15,665	419,119
20	Malta,	51,214	57,845	2,339	60,184
21	Canada,	11,581,571	13,663,465	3,365,789	17,029,254
22	Other British N. American Possessions,	4,244,948	5,975,494	646,979	6,622,473
23	British West Indies,	1,907,738	5,452,202	105,496	5,557,698
24	British Honduras,	412,316	419,745	32,851	452,596
25	British Guiana,	329,687	881,521	2,980	884,501
26	British Possessions in Africa,	1,061,647	441,216	2,311	443,527
27	British Australia,	65,254	3,119,411	86,279	3,205,690
28	British East Indies,	12,140,783	1,198,455	80,250	1,278,705
29	France on the Atlantic,	32,900,796	30,013,271	1,162,621	31,175,892
30	France on the Mediterranean,	2,391,725	1,502,395	63,630	1,566,025
31	French North American Possessions,	91,072	147,938	29,602	177,540
32	French West Indies,	103,639	622,436	10,642	633,078
33	French Guiana,	49,411	82,565	743	83,308
34	French Possessions in Africa,		27,616	334	27,950
35	Spain on the Atlantic,	563,910	2,054,369	24,268	2,078,637
36	Spain on the Mediterranean,	2,458,667	6,555,799	77,209	6,633,008
37	Canary Islands,	2,529	79,795	981	80,776
38	Philippine Islands,	3,033,989	57,649	17,350	74,999
39	Cuba,	27,214,846	11,673,167	2,760,024	14,433,191
40	Porto Rico,	4,455,586	1,612,048	298,302	1,910,350
41	Portugal,	142,056	269,484	10,008	279,492
42	Madeira,	30,199	19,806	512	20,318
43	Cape de Verde Islands,	2,256	46,460	2,414	48,874
44	Azores,	48,209	130,595	6,288	136,883
45	Sardinia,	291,458	2,779,368	188,685	2,968,053
46	Tuscany,	1,396,631	582,396	8,590	590,986
47	Two Sicilies,	1,737,328	525,374	40,869	566,243
48	Austria,	396,195	910,769	206,048	1,116,817
49	Austrian Possessions in Italy,	5,817	1,058,699	8,543	1,067,242
50	Ionian Republic,	42,218	3,060		3,060
51	Turkey in Europe,	112,311	509,985	1,360	511,345
52	Turkey in Asia,	974,591	273,420	53,112	326,532
53	Egypt,	93,083	107,637	560	108,197
54	Other ports in Africa,	1,597,249	1,767,965	136,334	1,904,299
55	Hayti,	2,185,862	1,978,865	248,744	2,227,609
56	San Domingo,	199,370	112,427	6,001	118,428
57	Mexico,	5,477,465	2,785,852	529,973	3,315,825
58	Central Republic,	132,427	115,611	19,351	134,962
59	New Granada,	3,099,721	1,489,583	199,084	1,688,667
60	Venezuela,	3,601,847	1,194,294	73,632	1,267,926
61	Brazil,	16,932,396	4,735,834	218,872	4,954,706
62	Uruguay, or Cisplatine Republic.	621,888	552,067	26,061	578,128
63	Buenos Ayres, or Argentine Republic,	2,725,218	765,043	139,551	904,594
64	Chili,	2,655,263	1,680,187	292,354	1,972,541
65	Bolivia,	38,658	12,373		12,373
66	Peru,	1,000,541	603,827	82,082	685,909
67	Sandwich Islands,	315,345	606,104	113,229	719,333
68	China,	10,570,536	3,007,748	2,689,603	5,697,351
69	Other Islands in the Pacific,	32,456	45,201	10,177	55,378
70	Whale Fisheries,	86,623	261,390	4,645	266,035
	Total,	*282,613,150	293,758,279	30,886,142	324,644,421

* Included in this there are from "Russia on the Black Sea," $ 2,905; "other British Possessions in S. America," $ 1,498; "the Papal States," $ 2,259; "Greece," $ 139,907; "other Ports in Asia," $ 121,444; and "Uncertain Places," $ 25,692. In the Total Exports of Domestic Produce there are to Prussia, $ 5,100; to Ecuador, $ 13,700.

4. Tonnage of Vessels engaged in Foreign Trade,

During the Year ending June 30, 1858.

	Countries.	American Tonnage.		Foreign Tonnage.	
		Entered.	Cleared.	Entered.	Cleared.
1	Russia on the Baltic and North Seas,	12,911	21,698	2,235	1,587
2	Russia on the Black Sea,	525			
3	Asiatic Russia,	132	132		2,546
4	Russian Possessions in North America,	2,578	2,447	1,523	1,517
5	Prussia,				425
6	Sweden and Norway,	6,001	1,363	3,753	1,313
7	Swedish West Indies,	2,975	2,654		
8	Denmark,				1,121
9	Danish West Indies,	28,501	22,516	3,757	416
10	Hamburg,	6,242	1,052	56,896	50,374
11	Bremen,	25,058	26,611	112,164	86,413
12	Other German ports,			267	1,049
13	Holland,	20,935	18,330	12,293	25,016
14	Dutch West Indies,	6,807	10,031	1,692	1,004
15	Dutch Guiana,	5,019	5,779	796	806
16	Dutch East Indies,	7,322	9,387	1,032	1,509
17	Belgium,	39,201	27,974	6,740	4,431
18	England,	835,308	863,484	328,721	354,451
19	Scotland,	15,390	28,711	66,816	37,375
20	Ireland,	1,384	18,298	10,122	18,725
21	Gibraltar,	1,441	8,485	2,184	1,162
22	Malta,	424	2,782		
23	Canada,	1,344,717	1,364,580	922,920	1,012,358
24	Other British North American Possessions,	171,024	242,407	390,926	475,329
25	British West Indies,	101,332	117,974	39,429	32,762
26	British Honduras,	7,605	6,430	4,070	2,910
27	British Guiana,	6,753	12,763	4,853	3,538
28	Other British Possessions in South America,				
29	British Possessions in Africa,	8,227	13,564	880	2,971
30	British Australia,	5,402	60,381	3,319	10,878
31	British East Indies,	93,233	53,875	4,732	7,482
32	France on the Atlantic,	221,076	209,815	16,412	7,756
33	France on the Mediterranean,	19,055	17,972	2,477	3,489
34	French North American Possessions,	240	1,135	3,100	2,782
35	French West Indies,	8,100	27,225	2,335	1,440
36	French Guiana,	2,207	1,687		
37	French Possessions in Africa,		364	744	1,949
38	Spain on the Atlantic,	16,583	29,333	2,217	6,338
39	Spain on the Mediterranean,	21,247	20,531	24,935	62,387
40	Canary Islands,	1,542	1,459		2,401
41	Philippine Islands,	23,389	3,122	932	
42	Cuba,	568,521	549,389	61,354	11,857
43	Porto Rico,	63,313	40,034	9,065	2,214
44	Portugal,	3,777	6,680	1,671	1,676
45	Madeira,		870	475	
46	Cape de Verde Islands,	1,011	1,847	1,211	218
47	Azores,	3,603	5,319	1,862	2,267
48	Sardinia,	8,672	15,886	6,513	4,766
49	Tuscany,	15,013	1,931	3,063	218
50	Papal States,				
51	Two Sicilies,	41,534	4,325	15,297	3,763
52	Austria,	7,698	8,591	2,065	1,661
53	Austrian Possessions in Italy,		5,748		743
54	Ionian Republic,		300	138	
55	Greece,			890	
56	Turkey in Europe,	1,207	6,590		877
57	Turkey in Asia,	10,907	4,277	817	
58	Egypt,		2,828	2,317	
59	Other ports in Africa,	18,477	14,096	530	324
60	Hayti,	48,679	33,108	4,786	2,151
61	San Domingo,	2,781	3,441	670	1,187
62	Mexico,	56,645	68,578	7,439	14,213
63	Central Republic,	7,796	3,428	958	425
64	New Granada,	110,126	119,706	1,179	853
65	Venezuela,	25,150	16,284	3,164	641
66	Brazil,	89,675	86,242	19,511	3,975
67	Uruguay, or Cisplatine Republic,	3,781	13,864	924	690
68	Buenos Ayres, or Argentine Republic,	17,297	25,170	261	1,216
69	Chili,	16,760	28,657	5,297	7,845
70	Bolivia,		279	333	
71	Peru,	98,180	35,565	3,836	8,699
72	Ecuador,	326	984		

	Countries.	American Tonnage.		Foreign Tonnage.	
		Entered.	Cleared.	Entered.	Cleared.
73	Sandwich Islands,	11,109	15,302	708	578
74	China,	49,958	67,972	15,814	10,696
75	Other ports in Asia,	1,444		626	
76	Other Islands in the Pacific,	1,935	2,063	1,313	666
77	Whale Fisheries,	40,049	64,268		
78	Uncertain places,	272			
	Total,	4,395,642	4,490,033	2,209,403	2,312,759

5. *Table showing the Quantity and Average Value of Cotton, Rice, and Tobacco, and the Value of Breadstuffs, exported annually, from* 1821 *to* 1858, *inclusive.*

[From Report of the Secretary of the Treasury on the Finances, Dec. 6, 1858.]

Years.	Cotton.		Rice.		Tobacco.		Breadstuffs and Provisions.
	Pounds.	Average price per pound.	Tierces.	Average price per tierce.	Hogsheads.	Average price per hhd.	Value.
		cents.		$		$	$
1821	124,893,405	16.2	88,221	16.94	66,858	84.49	12,341,901
1822	144,675,095	16.6	87,089	17.84	83,169	74.82	13,886,856
1823	173,723,270	11.8	101,365	17.96	99,009	63.45	13,767,847
1824	142,369,663	15.4	113,229	16.63	77,883	62.34	15,059,484
1825	176,449,907	20.9	97,015	19.84	75,984	80.48	11,634,449
1826	204,535,415	12.2	111,063	17.26	64,098	83.42	11,303,496
1827	294,310,115	10.0	113,518	17.55	100,025	65.75	11,685,556
1828	210,590,463	10.7	175,019	14.97	96,278	54.73	11,461,144
1829	264,837,186	10.0	132,923	18.92	77,131	64.60	13,131,858
1830	298,459,102	9.9	130,697	15.20	83,810	66.66	12,075,430
1831	276,979,784	9.1	116,517	17.30	86,718	56.41	17,538,227
1832	322,215,122	9.8	120,327	17.89	106,806	56.17	12,424,703
1833	324,698,604	11.1	144,163	19.04	83,153	69.20	14,209,128
1834	384,717,907	12.8	121,886	17.41	87,979	74.96	11,524,024
1835	387,358,992	16.8	119,851	19.94	94,353	87.44	12,009,399
1836	423,631,307	16.8	212,983	11.97	109,042	92.24	10,614,130
1837	444,211,537	14.2	106,084	21.76	100,232	57.82	9,588,359
1838	595,952,297	10.3	71,048	21.23	100,593	73.48	9,636,650
1839	413,624,212	14.8	93,320	26.36	78,995	124.47	14,147,779
1840	743,941,061	8.5	101,660	19.10	119,484	82.72	19,067,535
1841	530,204,100	10.2	101,617	19.78	147,828	85.07	17,196,102
1842	584,717,017	8.1	114,617	16.64	158,710	60.11	16,902,876
1843*	792,297,106	6.2	106,766	15.23	94,454	49.24	11,204,123
1844†	663,633,455	8.1	134,715	16.20	163,042	51.50	17,970,135
1845†	872,905,996	5.9	118,621	18.21	147,168	50.75	16,743,421
1846†	547,558,055	7.8	124,007	20.68	147,998	57.28	27,701,121
1847†	527,219,958	10.3	144,427	24.97	135,762	53.34	68,701,921
1848†	814,274,431	7.6	100,403	23.23	130,665	57.78	37,472,751
1849†	1,026,602,269	6.4	128,861	19.94	101,521	57.17	38,155,507
1850†	635,381,604	11.3	127,069	20.71	145,729	68.28	26,051,373
1851†	927,237,089	12.1	105,590	20.56	95,945	96.09	21,948,651
1852†	1,093,230,639	8.0	119,733	20.63	137,097	73.17	25,857,027
1853†	1,111,570,370	9.8	67,707	24.48	159,853	70.81	32,985,322
1854†	987,833,106	9.5	105,121	25.05	126,107	79.42	65,941,323
1855†	1,008,424,601	8.74	‡52,520	25.51	‡150,213		38,895,348
1856†	1,351,431,701	9.49	‡58,668	20.01	‡116,962		77,187,301
1857†	‡1,048,282,475	12.55	‡64,332	19.08	‡156,848		74,667,852
1858†	1,118,624,012	11.70	‡64,015	17.46	‡127,670		50,683,285
Total,	21,993,602,428		4,207,767		4,235,172		923,373,394

* Nine months to June 30th. † Year ending June 30th.

‡ In 1855, there were, besides the quantities given above, 19,774 barrels of rice, and 12,913 bales and 13,366 cases of tobacco exported; in 1856, 81,038 barrels of rice, and 17,772 bales and 9,384 cases of tobacco; in 1857, 74,309 barrels of rice, and 14,432 bales and 5,631 cases of tobacco; and in 1858, 49,283 barrels of rice, and 12,640 bales and 4,841 cases of tobacco. The total value of cotton exported during the year ending June 30th, 1858 is given at $131,386,661, and for the whole 38 years, $2,221,592,613;—of rice for the year, $1,870,578; for the 38 years, $83,079,964;—of tobacco for the year, $17,009,767; for the 38 years, $318,200,482.

6. *Average Quarterly Prices of certain leading Articles of Domestic Produce at New York, for the Years ending June 30, 1857, and 1858; and the Average Price for the Years ending June 30, 1856, 1857, and 1858.*

[From the Report of the Secretary of the Treasury, Dec. 6, 1858, pp. 54, 59. In the Report can be found the *monthly* average prices for the whole three years.]

Articles.		Fiscal Year, 1856-1857.		Fiscal Year, 1857-1858.				Year ending June 30, 1856.	Year ending June 30, 1857.	Year ending June 30, 1858.
		Quarter ending Sept. 30.	Quarter ending March 31.	Quarter ending Sept. 30.	Quarter ending Dec. 31.	Quarter ending March 31.	Quarter ending June 30.			
Breadstuffs.		$	$	$	$	$	$	$	$	$
Wheat flour, sup.,	bbl.	6.00	6.18	6.07	4.60	4.23	4.03	7.47	6.23	4.73
Corn meal,	"	3.50	3.37	4.22	3.62	3.25	3.58	4.14	3.54	3.67
Wheat, white, western,	bush.	1.65	1.70	1.76	1.40	1.32	1.24	2.06	1.69	1.43
Wheat, red, w'ter,	"	1.56	1.53	1.67	1.18	1.16	1.08	1.83	1.56	1.24
Wheat, Spring,	"	1.36	1 38	1.28	.99	.92	.89	1.65	1.39	1.02
Rye,	"	.86	.92	1.00	.76	.70	.68	1.14	.92	.79
Oats,	"	.44	.48	.51	.41	.38	.42	.44	.49	.43
Corn,	"	.65	.72	.85	.76	.68	.73	.81	.73	.76
Cotton.										
mid. uplands,	lb.	.12	.13	.15	.12	.11	.12	.10	.13	.12
sheetings, heavy,	yd.	.08	.09	.09	.09	.08	.08	.08	.09	.08
Copper, Amer. ingot,	lb.	.25	.28	.24	.21	.21	.21	.27	.26	.22
Glass, window, 8×11 to 10×15,	box.	1.58	1.55	1.55	1.53	1.51	1.51	1.63	1.56	1.52
Hay,	cwt.	.56	.93	.69	.68	.68	.42	.90	.75	.59
Hemp, undressed,	ton.	201.66	198.33	177.50	113.33	100.00	121.66	174.46	201.41	128.12
Iron,										
pig,	"	25.50	26.50	25.58	23.75	21.25	20.50	26.96	26.69	22.77
common bar,	"	56.67	58.33	53.33	50.00	49.33	47.50	61.62	57.29	50.04
railroad bar,	"	55.83	60.00	54.17	46.33	44.67	46.00	59.25	57.92	47.79
Lead,	cwt.	6.50	6.59	7.17	5.58	5.87	6.42	6.82	6.66	6.26
Leather, hemlock sole,	lb.	.26	.32	.27	.22	.21	.23	.22	.28	.23
Molasses, N. Orleans,	gall.	.51	.77	.68	.38	.31	.36	.41	.66	.43
Nails,	lb.	.04	.04	.04	.03	.04	.03	.04	.04	.03
Naval Stores.										
Spirits Turp'tine,	gall.	.41	.51	.47	.41	.44	.47	.41	.46	.45
Rosin, common (310 lbs),	bbl.	1.60	1.68	1.88	1.39	1.39	1.49	1.64	1.69	1.54
Oils.										
Sperm, crude,	gall.	1.51	1.43	1.29	1.11	1.14	1.23	1.77	1.42	1.19
Whale, crude,	"	.79	.73	.71	.65	.55	.53	.77	.76	.61
Linseed,	"	.91	.84	.77	.59	.57	.64	.87	.87	.64
Provisions.										
Pork, mess,	bbl.	19.87	22.08	24.58	19.22	15.88	17.59	19.16	21.20	19.32
Beef, State mess,	"	8.95	12.17	14.75	10.92	10.00	11.00	11.08	11.13	11.67
Lard,	lb.	.13	.14	.15	.12	.09	.11	.11	.13	.12
Butter,	"	.17	.21	.19	.17	.17	.18	.20	.20	.18
Cheese,	"	.08	.11	.08	.07	.08	.07	.09	.10	.06
Rice,	cwt.	4.33	4 25	5.04	3.59	3.29	3.50	4.97	4.47	3.85
Seeds.										
clover,	lb.	.13	.13	.11	.10	.09	.07	.12	.12	.09
timothy,	bush.	3.50	3.42	3.73	2.58	2.23	2.12	3.31	3.48	2.67
Steel, spring,	lb.	.05	.05	.05	.05	.06	.05	.06	.05	.06
Sugar, New Orleans,	"	.08	.10	.10	.07	.06	.06	.07	.09	.07
Tallow,	"	.11	.12	.12	.10	.10	.10	.12	.12	.10
Tobacco, Kentucky,	"	.14	.13	.15	.11	.11	.12	.11	.14	.12
Wool.										
common fleece,	"	.33	.39	.37	.32	.26	.25	.30	.36	.30
medium fleece,	"	.43	.50	.48	.44	.38	.37	.43	.47	.42

7. Imports and Exports of each State, *During the Year ending June* 30, 1858.

States.*	Value of Exports.			Value of Imports.		
	American Produce.	Foreign Produce.	Total.	In Amer. Vessels.	In Foreign Vessels.	Total.
Alabama,	$21,019,266	$ 2,883	$21,022,149	$ 432,416	$ 174,526	$ 606,942
California,	12,035,393	3,003,854	15,039,247	4,471,361	4,518,369	8,989,733
Connecticut,	1,320,527	9,714	1,330,241	902,690	52,415	955,105
Delaware,	106,571		106,571	2,821		2,821
Florida,	1,877,552		1,877,552	151,859	13,091	164,950
Georgia,	9,597,559		9,597,559	332,740	78,910	411,650
Illinois,	1,713,077		1,713,077	75,527	147,403	222,930
Louisiana,	88,270,224	605,771	88,875,995	16,650,815	2,935,218	19,586,033
Maine,	2,445,142	416,917	2,862,059	1,488,590	369,802	1,858,392
Maryland,	9,878,386	564,230	10,442,616	7,561,407	1,368,750	8,930,157
Massachusetts,	16,630,571	5,831,806	22,462,377	29,826,274	12,486,146	42,312,420
Michigan,	5,168,031	20,676	5,188,707	623,126	49,808	672,934
New Hampshire,	1,699	101	1,800	7,866	10,095	17,961
New Jersey,	14,021		14,021	135	6,483	6,618
New York,	89,039,790	19,301,134	108,340,924	123,928,283	54,547,453	178,475,736
North Carolina,	541,216		541,216	169,348	4,924	174,272
Ohio,	339,561		339,561	105,805	93,488	199,293
Oregon [Territory],	9,935		9,935	4,067	35,510	39,577
Pennsylvania,	5,662,384	374,027	6,036,411	11,795,160	1,097,055	12,892,215
Rhode Island,	409,007	12,339	421,346	416,054	71,762	487,816
South Carolina,	16,924,056	380	16,924,436	1,644,380	427,139	2,071,519
Texas,	2,428,169	296	2,428,465	51,397	61,694	113,091
Vermont,	237,686	727,979	965,665	2,196,088		2,196,088
Virginia,	7,262,765	14,035	7,276,800	785,217	293,839	1,079,056
Wisconsin,	543,280		543,280	48,506	58,098	106,604
Washington Ter.,	265,701		265,701	4,935	7,782	12,717
District of Columbia	16,710		16,710	23,146	3,374	26,520
Total,	293,758,279	30,886,142	324,644,421	203,700,016	78,913,134	282,613,150

8. Vessels built, and the Tonnage thereof, in the United States, *During the Year ending June* 30, 1858.

States.*	Class of Vessels.					Total number of Vessels built.	Total Tonnage.	
	Ships and Barq's.	Brigs.	Schooners.	Sloops and canal-boats.	Steamers.		Tons.	95ths.
Alabama,			6	1	4	11	1,386	84
California,			6	5	6	17	2,109	47
Connecticut,	3	1	20	6	1	31	7,118	30
Delaware,	1	2	12	2	3	20	3,917	74
Florida,			2	1	2	5	548	93
Georgia,			1		3	4	614	62
Illinois,			1	6		7	586	42
Kentucky,					28	28	8,302	74
Louisiana,			7	1	7	15	1,488	13
Maine,	56	28	77	2	4	167	55,959	48
Maryland,	5	7	45	1	3	61	6,996	33
Massachusetts,	33	3	70	1	3	110	32,599	41
Michigan,		1	13	13	11	38	5,633	42
Mississippi,			6	1		7	245	85
Missouri,					9	9	5,603	83
New Hampshire,	5		1			6	5,075	77
New Jersey,			35	13	2	50	6,704	20
New York,	7	3	47	91	42	193	37,185	92
North Carolina,	1		20	1		22	1,351	28
Ohio,	4		22	8	32	66	19,521	34
Oregon [Territory],			1			1	14	68
Pennsylvania,	2		14	104	50	170	21,583	05
Rhode Island,	3	1	3			7	3,111	54
South Carolina,			3			3	193	83
Tennessee,					3	2	648	88
Texas,			5	1	1	7	323	87
Vermont,					1	1	231	07
Virginia,	2		10	2	11	25	2,605	35
Wisconsin,			4		1	5	951	32
District of Columbia,				137		137	9,672	28
Total,	122	46	431	400	226	1,225	242,286	69

* There are no returns for the omitted States and Territories.

9. Comparative View of the Tonnage of the United States, *From* 1815 *to* 1858, *inclusive, in Tons* (95*ths not counted*).

Years.	Registered Tonnage.	Enrolled & licensed Tonnage.	Reg. Tonn. in Whale Fishery.	Enrolled and Licensed Tonnage in			Tonnage in Steam Navigation
				Coasting Trade.	Cod Fishery.	Mackerel Fishery.	
1815	854,294	513,833		435,066	26,510		
1816	800,759	571,458		479,979	37,879		
1817	800,724	590,186	4,871	481,457	53,990		
1818	606,088	619,095	16,134	503,140	58,551		
1819	612,930	647,821	31,700	523,556	68,044		
1820	619,047	661,118	35,391	539,080	60,842		
1821	619,896	679,062	26,070	559,435	51,351		
1822	628,150	696,548	65,449	573,080	58,405		
1823	639,920	699,644	39,918	566,408	67,621		24,879
1824	669,972	729,190	33,165	589,223	68,419		21,609
1825	700,787	722,323	35,379	587,273	70,626		23,061
1826	737,978	796,212	41,757	666,420	63,761		34,058
1827	747,170	873,437	45,653	732,937	74,048		40,197
1828	812,619	928,772	54,621	758,922	74,947		39,418
1829	650,142	610,654	57,284	508,858	101,796		54,036
1830	576,675	615,311	38,911	516,978	61,554	35,973	64,471
1831	620,451	647,394	82,315	539,723	60,977	48,210	34,435
1832	686,989	752,460	72,868	649,627	54,027	47,421	90,813
1833	750,026	856,123	101,158	744,198	62,720	48,725	101,849
1834	857,438	901,468	108,060	783,618	54,403	61,082	122,815
1835	885,821	939,118	97,640	792,301	72,374	64,443	122,815
1836	897,774	984,321	144,680	873,023	62,307	64,425	145,566
1837	810,447	1,086,238	127,242	956,980	80,551	46,810	154,764
1838	822,591	1,173,047	119,629	1,041,105	70,064	56,649	193,413
1839	834,244	1,262,234	131,845	1,153,551	72,258	35,983	204,938
1840	899,764	1,280,999	136,926	1,176,694	76,035	28,269	201,339
1841	845,803	1,184,940	157,405	1,107,067	66,551	11,321	175,088
1842	975,358	1,117,031	151,612	1,045,753	54,804	16,096	229,661
1843	1,009,315	1,149,297	152,374	1,076,155	61,224	11,775	236,867
1844	1,068,764	1,211,330	168,293	1,109,614	85,224	16,170	273,179
1845	1,095,172	1,321,829	190,695	1,190,898	69,825	21,413	326,018
1846	1,130,286	1,431,798	189,980	1,289,870	72,516	36,463	347,893
1847	1,241,312	1,597,732	193,858	1,452,623	70,177	31,451	404,841
1848	1,360,886	1,793,155	192,179	1,620,988	82,651	43,558	427,891
1849	1,438,941	1,895,073	180,186	1,730,410	42,970	73,853	462,394
1850	1,585,711	1,949,743	146,016	1,755,796	85,646	58,111	525,946
1851	1,726,307	2,046,132	181,644	1,854,317	87,475	50,539	583,607
1852	1,899,448	2,238,992	193,797	2,008,021	102,659	72,546	643,240
1853	2,103,674	2,303,336	193,202	2,134,256	109,227	59,850	514,094
1854	2,333,819	2,469,083	181,901	2,273,900	102,194	35,041	676,607
1855	2,535,136	2,676,864	186,773	2,491,108	102,927	21,627	770,285
1856	2,491,402	2,380,249	189,213	2,211,935	95,816	29,886	673,077
1857	2,463,967	2,476,875	195,771	2,300,399	104,572	28,327	705,784
1858	2,499,741	2,550,066	198,593	2,361,595	110,896	29,593	729,390

The columns of "Registered," and "Enrolled and Licensed" Tonnage give together the total tonnage. The other columns indicate how parts of the total tonnage are specifically employed.

No separate returns of tonnage employed in the mackerel fishery were made by the collectors prior to the year 1830; and none given of steam navigation prior to 1823. For a table giving the total tonnage since 1790, see *ante*, page 147.

10. *Entries and Clearances of American and Foreign Vessels, with their Tonnage and Crews, during the Year ending June* 30, 1858.

		Tonnage.
American vessels entered during the year ending June 30, 1858, from foreign countries, ...	10,735	4,395,642
Foreign vessels entered from do., ...	11,024	2,209,403
Total of American and foreign vessels, . . .	21,759	6,605,045
American vessels cleared for foreign countries, .	11,124	4,490,033
Foreign vessels cleared for do., ...	10,155	2,312,759
Total of American and foreign vessels, . .	21,279	6,802,792

Crews of American vessels entered. Men, 141,897. Boys, 337. Total, 142,234.

Crews of foreign vessels entered. Men, 102,476. Boys, 1,080. Total, 103,556.

Crews of American vessels cleared. Men, 144,657. Boys, 405. Total, 145,062.

Crews of foreign vessels cleared. Men, 103,777. Boys, 1,047. Total, 103,824.

11. Number and Class of Vessels built, and the Tonnage thereof, in the United States, from 1815 to 1858, *inclusive*.

Years.	Class of Vessels.					Total number of Vessels built.	Total Tonnage.
	Ships.	Brigs.	Schooners.	Sloops and canal-boats.	Steamers.		Tons. 95ths.
1815	136	224	681	274		1,315	154,624 39
1816	76	122	781	424		1,403	131,668 04
1817	34	86	559	394		1,073	86,393 37
1818	53	85	428	332		898	82,421 20
1819	53	82	473	242		850	79,817 86
1820	21	60	301	152		521	47,784 01
1821	43	89	247	127		507	55,856 01
1822	64	131	260	168		623	75,346 93
1823	55	127	260	165	15	622	75,007 57
1824	56	156	377	166	26	781	90,939 00
1825	56	197	538	168	35	994	114,997 25
1826	71	187	482	227	45	1,012	126,438 35
1827	58	153	464	241	38	934	104,342 67
1828	73	108	474	196	33	881	98,375 58
1829	44	68	485	145	43	785	77,098 65
1830	25	56	403	116	37	637	58,094 21
1831	72	95	416	94	34	711	85,962 68
1832	132	143	568	122	100	1,065	144,539 16
1833	144	169	625	185	65	1,188	161,626 36
1834	98	94	497	180	68	937	118,330 37
1835*	25*	50*	301*	100*	30*	507*	46,238 52*
1836	93	65	444	164	124	890	113,627 49
1837	67	72	507	168	135	949	122,987 22
1838	66	79	501	153	90	898	113,135 44
1839	83	89	439	122	125	858	120,989 34
1840	97	109	378	224	64	872	118,309 23
1841	114	101	310	157	78	762	118,893 71
1842	116	91	273	404	137	1,021	129,083 64
1843*	58*	34*	138*	173*	79*	482*	43,617 77*
1844	73	47	204	279	163	766	103,589 29
1845	124	87	322	342	163	1,038	146,018 02
1846	100	164	576	355	225	1,420	188,203 93
1847	151	168	689	392	198	1,598	243,732 67
1848	254	174	701	547	175	1,851	318,075 54
1849	198	148	623	370	208	1,547	256,577 47
1850	247	117	547	290	159	1,360	272,218 54
1851	211	65	522	326	233	1,367	298,203 60
1852	255	79	584	267	259	1,444	351,493 41
1853	269	95	681	394	271	1,710	425,572 49
1854	334	112	661	386	281	1,774	535,616 01
1855	381	126	605	669	253	2,034	583,450 04
1856	306	103	594	479	221	1,703	469,393 73
1857	251	58	504	358	263	1,434	378,804 70
1858	122	46	431	400	226	1,225	242,286 69

The amount of registered tonnage sold to foreigners during the year ending June 30, 1858, is stated to be 25,925.73 tons; being 40 ships or barques, 13 brigs, 21 schooners, 1 sloop, and 5 steamers. Amount condemned as unseaworthy, 13,699.45 tons; being 28 ships or barques, 4 brigs, 3 schooners, 2 sloops, and 3 steamers. Amount lost at sea, 46,198.18 tons; being 65 ships or barques, 24 brigs, 9 schooners, and 5 sloops.

* For nine months.

12. Indirect Trade.

Statement of the Value of Imports, the Produce and Manufacture of the States forming the German Zoll Verein, Switzerland, England, and other countries, during the Year ending June 30, 1858.

Imported from	Via the Ports of			
	Belgium.	Bremen.	England.	France.
Baden,	$ 265,353	$ 66,776	$ 20,344	$ 89,676
Bavaria,	73,788	469,296	8,985	45,038
Frankfort,	69,710	132,644	36,760	197,298
Hesse (Cassel & Darmstadt),	63,380	192,410	24,101	74,365
Prussia,	866,549	1,220,468	993,138	824,205
Saxony,	8,549	2,195,572	240,022	158,142
Wurtemberg,	3,484	42,378	8,388	46,205
Countries not specified,	3,510	81,665	132,591	5,139
Total Zoll Verein,	1,359,323	4,401,209	1,464,329	1,440,068
Total Austria,	8,829	203,940	32,068	73,982
Total Belgium,			127,240	55,873
Total England,	31,386	31,627		73,855
Total France,	74,869	762,506	5,735,753	
Total Hamburg,		19,821	2,577	1,290
Total Switzerland,		373,754	1,279,641	2,951,149
Total other countries,		10,559	951,685	54,441
Total value,	1,474,407	5,803,416	9,593,293	4,650,658

Imported from	Via the Ports of				
	Hamburg.	Holland.	New Granada.	Other Countries.	Total.
Baden,	$ 40	$ 146,685			$ 588,874
Bavaria,	56,125	6,568	$ 9,348		669,148
Frankfort,	30,078	10,625			477,115
Hesse (Cassel & Darmstadt),	11,807	16,124			276,940
Prussia,	690,907	23,660	1,641	$ 394	4,621,052
Saxony,	595,085	14,325			3,211,695
Wurtemberg,	8,826	13,759	2,228		125,268
Countries not specified,	3,186	475			
Total Zoll Verein,	1,396,144	232,221	13,217	394	10,306,905
Total Austria,	71,523				390,342
Total Belgium,		3,140			186,253
Total England,	36,825	2,047	62,275	24,677	262,692
Total France,	21,961	1,449	156,861	27,394	6,780,793
Total Hamburg,			22,527	553	46,768
Total Switzerland,	33,650		6,979		4,645,173
Total other countries,	22,793	34,677	315,228	257,919	1,647,302
Total value,	1,582,896	273,534	577,087	310,937	24,266,228

Exports to, and Imports from, Canada and other British Possessions in North America, from July 1, 1851, to June 30, 1858.

[From the Report of the Secretary of the Treasury, Dec. 6, 1858, p. 343.]

Year ending June 30.	Exports.			Imports.	Increase of each successive year over 1852.	
	Foreign.	Domestic.	Total.		Exports.	Imports.
1852	$ 3,853,919	$ 6,655,097	$ 10,509,016	$ 6,110,299		
1853	5,736,555	7,404,087	13,140,642	7,550,718	$ 2,631,626	$ 1,440,419
1854	9,362,716	15,204,144	24,566,860	8,927,560	14,057,844	2,817,261
1855	11,999,378	15,806,642	27,806,020	15,136,734	17,297,004	9,026,435
1856	6,314,652	22,714,697	29,029,349	21,310,421	18,520,333	15,200,122
1857	4,326,369	19,936,113	24,262,482	22,124,296	13,753,466	16,013,997
1858	4,012,768	19,638,959	23,651,727	15,806,519	13,142,711	9,696,220
Total,	45,606,357	107,359,739	152,966,096	96,866,547	79,402,984	54,194,454

13. *Statement of Foreign Imports into, and of the Exports of Foreign Goods from, and the Expenses at each Custom-House in each Collection District for the Year ending June 30, 1858.*

Districts.	Value of Imports.			Expenses at each Custom House.	Value of Exports.	
	Free.	Paying Duties.	Total Imports.		Foreign Dutiable Goods.	Total Foreign Exports.
Passamaquoddy,	$ 389,275	$ 76,425	$ 465,700	$ 31,902	$ 52,387	$ 92,502
Frenchman's Bay,		1,323	1,323	4,704		
Penobscot,	2,181	4,920	7,101	4,669		
Waldoborough,	5,232	98	5,330	6,869		
Wiscasset,	680	3,101	3,781	6,656		
Bath,	12,907	4,166	17,073	6,970		
Portland & Falmouth,	98,754	1,192,449	1,291,203	31,449	313,554	324,415
Saco,	1,453		1,453	1,075		
Belfast,	2,075	4,978	7,053	5,686		
Bangor,	3,036	55,339	58,375	7,092		
Portsmouth,	7,531	10,430	17,961	11,720	46	101
Vermont,	2,152,554	43,534	2,196,088	17,069	722,660	727,979
Newburyport,	26,640	15,295	41,935	5,910		
Gloucester,	68,773	134,005	202,778	6,128	3,441	4,062
Salem and Beverly,	430,992	942,982	1,373,974	20,154	101,953	120,663
Marblehead,	29,526		29,526	2,218	449	509
Boston & Charlestown,	13,398,625	27,034,085	40,432,710	385,166	3,787,215	5,706,061
Plymouth, Mass.,	1,447		1,447	2,966		
Fall River,	24,409	5,804	30,213	2,604		
New Bedford,	78,883	93,717	172,600	7,271	521	521
Edgartown,	64	240	304	3,501		
Nantucket,	3,124	23,809	26,933	2,832		
Providence,	202,242	200,037	402,279	12,281	10,994	11,017
Bristol and Warren,	1,358	49,111	50,469	4,159	966	1,322
Newport,	3,265	31,803	35,068	5,376		
New London,	4,459	3,565	8,024	13,289	1,171	3,468
New Haven,	65,739	862,705	928,444	20,321	1,228	4,888
Fairfield,	9,563	1,306	10,869	1,780		158
Stonington,	758	7,010	7,768	1,667	825	1,200
Sackett's Harbor,	2,892	147	3,039	3,930		
Genesee,	271,335	712	272,047	6,748	4,032	14,552
Oswego,	1,863,279	7,495	1,870,774	14,137		197,163
Niagara,	893,578	23,391	916,969	11,824	21,515	273,551
Buffalo Creek,	1,366,923	13,701	1,380,624	14,737	8,787	80,600
Oswegatchie,	949,157	11,959	961,116	8,225		30,135
New York,	33,072,680	137,208,207	170,280,887	967,853	7,461,443	17,299,097
Champlain,	1,533,598	26,298	1,559,896	13,665	829,314	1,138,531
Cape Vincent,	1,224,733	5,651	1,230,384	6,684	267,302	267,505
Perth Amboy,	1,025		1,025	4,747		
Newark,	5,593		5,593	1,494		
Philadelphia,	2,852,258	10,038,111	12,890,369	214,508	313,996	374,027
Presque Isle,	1,805	41	1,846	2,280		
Delaware,	2,821		2,821	14,701		
Baltimore,	4,423,217	4,506,940	8,930,157	161,763	228,308	564,230
Georgetown, D. C.,	3,121	23,399	26,520	3,077		
Richmond,	513,479	152,427	665,906	7,204	2,195	13,035
Norfolk & Portsmouth,	34,084	140,913	174,997	43,953		1,000
Tappahannock,	2,723		2,723	1,606		
Petersburg,	16,434	105,731	122,165	5,937		
Alexandria,	52,544	60,721	113,265	5,661		
Camden,	14,936	4,785	19,721	606		
Edenton,		631	631	397		
Plymouth, N. C.,	2,527	866	3,393	590		
Washington,	30,766	3,622	34,388	404		
Newbern,	3,081	2,896	5,977	2,093		
Beaufort, N. C.,		37,163	37,163	1,110		
Wilmington,	127	72,872	72,999	6,230		
Charleston,	299,711	1,770,538	2,070,249	66,535	380	380
Georgetown, S. C.,		1,270	1,270	477		
Savannah,	46,976	363,616	410,592	34,026		
St. Mary's,		1,058	1,068	719		
Mobile,	257,691	349,251	606,942	34,863	2,883	2,883
Pensacola,		504	504	2,290		

Districts.	Value of Imports.			Expenses at each Custom-House.	Value of Exports.	
	Free.	Paying Duties.	Total Imports.		Foreign Dutiable Goods.	Total Foreign Exports.
Key West,	$7,066	$22,969	$30,055	$7,346		
St. John's,		87	87	3,233		
Apalachicola,		16,401	16,401	4,912		
Fernandina,		117,903	117,903	2,475		
New Orleans,	9,338,920	10,247,113	19,586,033	265,543	$378,065	$605,771
Texas,	350	71,031	71,381	20,530	296	296
Saluria,	4,668	37,042	41,710	8,232		
Miami,	5,999		5,999	3,990		
Sandusky,	12,443	32	12,475	13,349		
Cuyahoga,	161,713	19,106	180,819	6,587		
Detroit,	626,286	36,715	663,001	17,899	18,299	20,676
Michilimackinac,	9,827	106	9,933	4,322		
Chicago,	174,065	48,865	222,930	14,286		
Milwaukee,	1,551	105,053	106,604	6,226		
Puget's Sound,	1,231	11,486	12,717	22,827		
Oregon,	775	38,802	39,577	12,188		
San Francisco,	3,205,742	5,778,946	8,984,688	425,886	374,017	3,003,669
Sonoma,		5,045	5,045	3,919		
Monterey,					150	195
Total,	80,319,275	202,293,875	282,613,150		14,908,391	30,886,142

XII. THE MINT.

It is lawful for any person to bring to the Mint gold and silver bullion to be coined; and the bullion so brought is there assayed and coined, as speedily as may be after the receipt thereof, and, if of the standard of the United States, free of expense, except gold, which is subject to a coinage charge of one half of one per cent. But the Treasurer of the Mint is not obliged to receive, for the purpose of refining and coining, any deposit of less value than one hundred dollars, nor any bullion so base as to be unsuitable for minting. And there must be retained from every deposit of bullion below the standard such sum as shall be equivalent to the expense incurred in refining, toughening, and alloying the same; an accurate account of which expense, on every deposit, is kept, and of the sums retained on account of the same, which are accounted for by the Treasurer of the Mint with the Treasurer of the United States.

Officers of the Mint at Philadelphia.

	Salary.		Salary.
J. R. Snowden, *Director*,	$3,500	James C. Booth, *Melter and Refiner*,	$2,000
James H. Walton, *Treasurer*,	2,000	W. E. Dubois, *Assist. Assayer*,	1,500
George K. Childs, *Chief Coiner*,	2,000	John H. Taylor, *Assist. Melter and Refiner*,	1,500
Jacob R. Eckfeldt, *Assayer*,	2,000		
Jas. B. Longacre, *Engraver*,	2,000		

Officers of the Branch at New Orleans, La.

Wm. A. Elmore, *Superint.*,	$2,500	B. F. Taylor, *Coiner*,	$2,000
Howard Millspaugh, *Assayer*,	2,000	A. J. Guirot, *Treasurer*,	4,000
M. F. Bonzano, *Melter & Refiner*,	2,000		

Officers of the Branch at Dahlonega, Ga.

	Salary.		Salary.
J. M. Patton, *Sup. and Treas.*,	$2,000	John D. Field, Jr., *Coiner*,	$1,500
Isaac L. Todd, *Assayer*,	1,500		

Officers of the Branch at Charlotte, N. C.

G. W. Caldwell, *Sup. & Treas.*,	$2,000	John R. Bolton, *Coiner*,	$1,500
John H. Gibbons, *Assayer*,	1,500		

Officers of the Branch at San Francisco.

C. H. Hempstead, *Superint.*,	$4,500	R. W. Slocum, *Coiner*,	$3,000
J. R. Snyder, *Treasurer*,	4,500	Louis A. Garnett, *Melter and Refiner*,	3,500
Joseph H. Snyder, *Assayer*,	3,000		

Assay Office, New York.

S. F. Butterworth, *Superint.*,	$3,500	Clarence Morfit, *Assist. Melter and Refiner*,	$2,000
John Torry, *Assayer*,	3,000	Andrew Mason, *Assist. Assayer*,	2,000
Edward N. Kent, *Melt. & Ref.*,	3,000		

1. *Statement of the Deposits for Coinage at the Mint of the United States and its Branches, and the Assay Office, during the Year ending June 30, 1858.*

Gold.		Silver.	
Foreign Coin, ...	$1,636,909.23	Deposited, including purchases,	$8,883,482.31
Foreign Bullion, ...	290,135.01	United States Bullion, parted from gold, ...	300,849.36
United States Coin, old standard, .	5,219.27	United States Bullion (Lake Superior), ...	15,623.00
United States Bullion, .	49,549,570.43		
Do. parted from Silver, . .	12,477.35		
Total of Gold, . . .	$51,494,311.29	Total of Silver, .	$9.199,954.67

Total Gold and Silver Deposits, ...	$60,694,265.96
Less value of gold ($8,572,401.88) and silver ($2,300,362.21) redeposited at the different institutions, ...	10,872,764.09
Total, ...	$49,821,501.87

2. *Statement of the Coinage of the Mint and Branches, and of the Assay Office, during the Year ending June 30, 1858.*

Denominations.	Pieces.	Value.	Denominations.	Pieces.	Value.
Gold.			Silver.		
Double Eagles,	1,401,944	$28,038,880.00	Dollars,		
Eagles,	62,990	629,900.00	Half-Dollars,	8,860,000	$4,430,000.00
Half-Eagles,	154,555	772,775.00	Quarter-Dollars,	12,079,000	3,019,750.00
Three-Dollars,	22,059	66,177.00	Dimes,	2,260,000	226,000.00
Quarter-Eagles,	206,253	515,632.50	Half-Dimes,	6,540,000	327,000.00
Dollars,	230,361	230,361.00	Three-cent Pieces,	1,266,000	37,980.00
Fine Bars,	7,105	21,819,779.14	Fine Bars,	900	192,557.77
Unparted Bars,	488	816,295.65	Total silver,	31,005,900	8,233,287.77
Total Gold,	2,085,755	52,889,800.29			
Copper.			Total Coinage, including Fine and unparted Bars,	56,491,655	61,357,088.06
Cents,	23,400	234,000.00			
Half-Cents,					
Total Copper,	23,400	234,000.00			

From June 30, 1858, to June 30, 1859, there were coined at the Mint and branches 811,836 double eagles, 14,600 eagles, 80,342 half-eagles, 11,524 three-dollar pieces, 85,204 quarter-eagles, 259,065 gold dollars. The value of the gold coined in fine bars was $13,113,876.70; in unparted bars, none. The total gold coinage in value for this period was $30,409,953.70; the total silver coinage, including silver bars, was $6,833,631.47; the total cent coinage, $307,000. The whole number of pieces coined in this period was 53,550,522. Their value was $37,550,585.17. The deposits of gold at the Mint and branches during this period were $29,563,380.63: the deposits and purchases of silver amounted to $7,336,609.67. The entire deposit of domestic gold at the Mint and branches, to June 30, 1859, was $470,341,478.46, of which $451,310,840.26 were from California.

3. *Coinage of the Mint of the United States, from 1792, including the Coinage of the Branch Mints from the Commencement of their Operations in 1838, and of the Assay Office.*

Years.	Gold.	Silver.	Copper.	Whole Coinage.	
	Value.	Value.	Value.	No. of Pieces.	Value.
1793 – 95	$71,485.00	$370,683.80	$11,373.00	1,834,420	$453,541.80
1796	102,727.50	79,077.50	10,324.40	1,219,370	192,129.40
1797	103,422.50	12,591.45	9,510.34	1,095,165	125,524.29
1798	205,610.00	330,291.00	9,797.00	1,368,241	545,698.00
1799	213,285.00	423,515.00	9,106.68	1,365,681	645,906.68
1800	317,760.00	224,296.00	29,279.40	3,337,972	571,335.40
1801	422,570.00	74,758.00	13,628.37	1,571,390	510,956.37
1802	423,310.00	58,343.00	34,422.83	3,615,869	516,075.83
1803	258,377.50	87,118.00	25,203.03	2,780,830	370,698.53
1804	258,642.50	100,340.50	12,844.94	2,046,839	371,827.94
1805	170,367.50	149,388.50	13,483.48	2,260,361	333,239.48
1806	324,505.00	471,319.00	5,260.00	1,815,409	801,084.00
1807	437,495.00	597,448.75	9,652.21	2,731,345	1,044,595.96
1808	284,665.00	684,300.00	13,090.00	2,935,888	982,055.00
1809	169,375.00	707,376.00	8,001.53	2,861,834	884,752.53
1810	501,435.00	638,773.50	15,660.00	3,056,418	1,155,868.50
1811	497,905.00	608,340.00	2,495.95	1,649,570	1,108,740.95
1812	290,435.00	814,029.50	10,755.00	2,761,646	1,115,219.50
1813	477,140.00	620,951.50	4,180.00	1,755,331	1,102,275.50
1814	77,270.00	561,687.50	3,578.30	1,833,859	642,535.80
1815	3,175.00	17,308.00		69,867	20,483.00
1816		28,575.75	28,209.82	2,888,135	56,785.57
1817		607,783.50	39,484.00	5,163,967	647,267.50
1818	242,940.00	1,070,454.50	31,670.00	5,537,084	1,345,064.50
1819	258,615.00	1,140,000.00	26,710.00	5,074,723	1,425,325.00
1820	1,319,030.00	501,680.70	44,075.50	6,492,509	1,864,786.20
1821	189,325.00	825,762.45	3,890.00	3,139,249	1,018,977.45
1822	88,980.00	805,806.50	20,723.39	3,813,788	915,509.89
1823	72,425.00	895,550.00		2,166,485	967,975.00
1824	93,200.00	1,752,477.00	12,620.00	4,786,894	1,858,297.00
1825	156,385.00	1,564,583.00	14,926.00	5,178,760	1,735,894.00
1826	92,245.00	2,002,090.00	16,344.25	5,774,434	2,110,679.25
1827	131,565.00	2,869,200.00	23,557.32	9,097,845	3,024,342.32
1828	140,145.00	1,575,600.00	25,636.24	6,196,853	1,741,381.24
1829	295,717.50	1,994,578.00	16,580.00	7,674,501	2,306,875.50
1830	643,105.00	2,495,400.00	17,115.00	8,357,191	3,155,620.00
1831	714,270.00	3,175,600.00	33,603.60	11,792,284	3,923,473.60
1832	798,435.00	2,579,000.00	23,620.00	9,128,387	3,401,055.00
1833	978,550.00	2,759,000.00	28,160.00	10,307,790	3,765,710.00
1834	3,954,270.00	3,415,002.00	19,151.00	11,637,643	7,388,423.00
1835	2,186,175.00	3,443,003.00	39,489.00	15,996,342	5,668,667.00
1836	4,135,700.00	3,606,100.00	23,100.00	13,719,333	7,764,900.00
1837	1,148,305.00	2,096,010.00	55,583.00	13,010,721	3,299,898.00
1838	1,809,595.00	2,315,250.00	53,702.00	15,780,311	4,178,547.00
1839	1,375,760.00	2,098,636.00	31,286.61	11,811,594	3,505,682.61
1840	1,690,802.00	1,712,178.00	24,627.00	10,558,240	3,427,607.00
1841	1,102,197.50	1,115,875.00	15,973.67	8,811,968	2,233,946.17
1842	1,833,170.50	2,325,750.00	23,833.90	11,743,153	4,182,754.40
1843	8,302,797.50	3,722,250.00	24,283.20	4,640,582	11,967,830.70
1844	5,428,230.00	2,235,550.00	23,987.52	9,051,834	7,687,767.52
1845	3,756,447.50	1,873,200.00	38,948.04	1,806,196	5,668,595.54
1846	4,034,177.50	2,558,580.00	41,208.00	10,133,515	6,633,965.50
1847	20,221,385.00	2,374,450.00	61,836.69	15,392,344	22,657,671.69
1848	3,775,512.50	2,040,050.00	64,157.99	12,649,790	5,879,720.49
1849	9,007,761.50	2,114,950.00	41,984.32	12,666,659	11,164,695.82
1850	31,981,738.50	1,866,100.00	44,467.50	14,588,220	33,892,306.00
1851	62,614,492.50	774,397.00	99,635.43	28,701,958	63,488,524.93
1852	56,846,187.50	999,410.00	50,630.94	32,964,019	57,896,228.44
1853	55,213,906.94	9,077,571.00	67,059.78	76,484,062	64,358,537.78
1854	52,094,595.47	8,619,270.00	42,638.35	44,645,011	60,756,503.82
1855	52,795,457.20	3,501,245.00	16,030.79	16,997,807	56,312,732.99
1856	59,343,365.35	5,196,670.17	27,106.78	33,870,966	64,567,142.30
1857*	25,183,138.66	1,601,644.46	63,510.46	19,440,547	26,848,293.60
1858†	52,889,800.29	8,233,287.77	234,000.00	56,491,655	61,357,088.06
Total,	534,311,878.99	115,861,205.30	1,896,623.55	680,132,154	650,969,907.84

* For the six months ending June 30, 1857. † For the year ending June 30.

XIII. POST-OFFICE DEPARTMENT.

1. *Post-Office Statistics for the Year ending June* 30, 1858.

Number of mail routes, 8,296; number of contractors, 7,044; length of routes, 260,603 miles; amount of annual transportation in miles, 78,765,491; cost of same, $7,795,418; being by coach 19,555,734 miles, at a cost of $1,909,844, or nearly 9.8 cents a mile; by railroad, 25,763,452 miles, at $2,828,301, or nearly 11 cents a mile; by steamboat, 4,569,610 miles, at $1,233,916, or nearly 27.2 cents a mile; by inferior grades, 28,876,695 miles, at $1,823,357, or 6.3 cents a mile.*

During the year the inland mail transportation has increased 3,859,424 miles, or about 5.11 per cent, at an increase of $1,173,372 cost, or about 17.46 per cent, as follows: — *Increase* of railroad service, 1,495,508 miles, or 6.05 per cent, at a cost of $268,454, or 10.44 per cent; of steamboat service, 51,491 miles, or 1.10 per cent, at a cost of $241,918, or 24.38 per cent; of service by coaches, 464,804 miles, or 2.43 per cent, at a cost of $499,018, or 35.37 per cent; of inferior routes, 1,847,261 miles, or 6.83 per cent, at a cost of $163,892, or 9.87 per cent. The length of railroad routes in 1842 was 3,091 miles, and the cost of service, $432,568; and in 1852 the length of routes was 10,146 miles, at a cost of $1,275,520.

The number of post-offices, December 1, 1858, was 28,573. There were June 30, 1858, 27,977; of which 400 were of the class to which postmasters are appointed by the President, the yearly commissions exceeding $1,000. There were (June 30) 440 route agents whose pay was $334,750; 28 express route agents, pay $28,000; 23 local agents, pay $29,989; 1,464 mail messengers, pay $184,634.41.

The gross revenue for the contract year ending June 30, 1858, was $8,186,792.86; total expenditures, $12,722,470.01; making the excess of expenditure $4,535,677.17.† The details are as follows: —

Receipts.	
Letter postage in money,	$904,299.13
Registered letters,	28,146.16
Stamps and stamped letters,	5,700,314.03
Newspapers and pamphlets,	591,976.90
Fines,	85.00
Excess of emolum'ts of postmasters,	80,644.96
Letter-carriers,	174,038.10
Dead-letter money unclaimed,	3,410.66
Miscellaneous receipts,	3,878.92
Annual appropriations for mail service performed for government,	700,000.00
Gross revenue for the year,	8,186,792.86
Total expenditures for the year,	12,722.470.01
Excess of expenditures,	4,535.677.15
Add "bad debts," &c., $91.90, and deduct $925.35, gain from suspense account, it gives for	
Total deficiency for the year,	$4,534,843.70

Expenditures.	
Transportation of inland mails,	$7,821,556.83
Transportation of foreign mails,	424,497.34
Compensation to postmasters,	2,355,016.28
Ship, steamboat, and way letters,	16,613.38
Wrapping-paper,	50,229.67
Office furniture for post-offices,	2,927.70
Advertising,	128,034.92
Mail-bags,	38,454.19
Blanks,	106,277.76
Mail locks, keys, and stamps,	13,485.09
Mail depredations and special agents,	73,527.01
Clerks in post-offices,	918,272.73
Postage stamps & Stam'd envelopes,	93,019.10
Payments to letter-carriers,	174,038.10
Balance due on British mails,	282,406.17
Balance due on Bremen mails,	2,859.14
Balance due on French mails,	26,343.47
Balance due on Hamburg mails,	1,366.13
Miscellaneous payments,	193,566.00
Total expenditures,	$12,722,470.01

* There are, besides, eight routes of the aggregate length of 21,087 miles, connecting this with foreign countries. For this service and its pay, see *post*, p. 170.

† For the gross receipts and expenditures of the Department for the contract year ending June 30, 1859, see the Additions and Corrections, at the end of the volume.

During the year, 2,121 post-offices were established, and 730 were discontinued, — net increase, 1,391. 4,595 postmasters were appointed to fill vacancies by resignations; 1,998, by removals; 278, by deaths; 292, by change of names and sites; 2,121, by establishment of new offices; — in all, 8,284.

2. *Table of Mail Service for the Year ending June 30, 1858.**

States.	Length of Routes.	Annual Transportation.				Total Transportation.	Total Cost.
		Mode not specified.	In Coaches.	In Steamboat.	By Railroad.		
	Miles.	Miles.	Miles.	Miles.	Miles.	Miles.	$
Alabama,	8,893	7,158	1,187	34	514	2,587,546	324,880
Arkansas,	9,708	7,686	1,186	836		1,709,704	221,297
California,	4,734	2,179	1,301	1,254		944,710	276,897
Connecticut,	2,202	719	478	260	745	1,404,916	117,483
Delaware,	562	174	303		85	325,124	24,690
Florida,	4,545	1,670	784	1,971	120	664,644	153,732
Georgia,	10,371	5,947	1,273	1,979	1,172	3,012,656	281,103
Illinois,	12,915	8,239	1,992	101	2,583	5,292,950	385,743
Indiana,	9,273	6,728	1,048		1,497	2,968,512	254,961
Iowa,	8,969	6,395	2,183	140	251	2,076,127	140,021
Kentucky,	9,314	6,838	1,641	†614	221	2,479,992	184,822
Louisiana,	8,049	4,707	943	‡2,229	170	2,054,416	515,977
Maine,	4,847	2,425	1,945		477	1,917,812	122,348
Maryland,	2,950	1,751	451		§748	1,933,178	233,846
Massachusetts,	3,086	912	632	240	1,302	2,345,120	196,299
Michigan,	7,909	5,502	877	650	880	2,266,002	173,176
Minnesota,	7,313	4,033	2,600	680		1,106,213	85,746
Mississippi,	9,626	7,118	1,202	907	399	2,503,692	286,555
Missouri,	14,685	10,710	3,156	614	205	2,594,311	450,417
New Hampshire,	1,880	837	554	60	429	902,148	56,995
New Jersey,	2,404	606	1,331	12	455	1,342,168	96,949
New York,	13,078	5,055	4,961	168	2,894	7,969,843	518,060
North Carolina,	9,791	7,086	1,986	213	506	2,307,192	190,628
Ohio,	13,968	8,341	2,184	187	3,292	5,565,602	530,391
Oregon,	1,222	938	140	144		139,000	33,686
Pennsylvania,	13,969	7,594	4,702	55	1,618	5,493,353	374,713
Rhode Island,	403	178	88	28	109	270,660	19,859
South Carolina,	6,679	4,531	348	880	917	1,970,658	198,206
Tennessee,	9,338	7,393	1,153	249	538	2,391,882	179,651
Texas,	16,838	11,589	4,068	1,140	39	2,592,060	434,200
Vermont,	2,349	546	1,314		489	1,072,814	83,284
Virginia,	15,141	10,652	2,208	1,135	1,146	4,069,214	354,678
Wisconsin,	7,274	4,517	2,044	83	630	1,839,012	120,501
Kansas Ter.	2,321	2,000	321			349,544	36,748
Nebraska Ter.	2,032	1,390	642			194,528	24,635
New Mexico Ter.	440	70	370			25,040	24,536
Utah Ter.	1,242	1,102	140			59,968	33,107
Washington Ter.	285	105		180		24,180	24,308
Total,	260,603	165,429	53,700	17,043	24,431	78,765,491	7,795,418
Route and local agents and mail messengers,							577,373
Total,	260,603	165,429	53,700	17,043	24,431	78,765,491	8,372,791

* The entire service and pay are set down to the State under which the route is numbered, though extending into other States, instead of being divided among the States in which each portion of it lies.

† This includes steamboat service from Louisville to Cincinnati.

‡ This includes the route from New Orleans to Mobile; also from Cairo to New Orleans.

§ The Baltimore, Wilmington, and Philadelphia Railroad is under a Maryland number.

3. *Number of Post-Offices, Extent of Post-Routes, and Revenue and Expenditures of the Post-Office Department; with the Amount paid to Postmasters and for Transportation of the Mail, since* 1790.

Year.	No. of Post-Offices.	Extent of Post-Routes in Miles.	Revenue of the Department.	Expenditures of the Department.	Amount paid for Compen. of Postmast'rs.	Amount paid for Transport'n of the Mail.
1790	75	1,875	$37,935	$32,140	$5,195	$22,081
1795	453	13,207	160,620	117,893	30,272	75,359
1800	903	20,817	280,804	213,994	69,243	128,644
1805	1,558	31,076	421,373	377,367	111,552	239,635
1810	2,300	36,406	551,684	495,969	149,438	327,966
1815	3,000	43,748	1,043,065	748,121	241,901	487,779
1816	3,260	48,673	961,782	804,422	265,944	521,970
1817	3,459	52,089	1,002,973	916,515	303,916	589,189
1818	3,618	59,473	1,130,235	1,035,832	346,429	664,611
1819	4,000	67,586	1,204,737	1,117,861	375,828	717,881
1820	4,500	72,492	1,111,927	1,160,926	352,295	782,425
1821	4,650	78,808	1,059,087	1,184,283	337,599	815,681
1822	4,709	82,763	1,117,490	1,167,572	355,299	788,618
1823	4,043	84,860	1,130,11	156,995	360,462	767,464
1824	5,182	84,860	1,197,750	1,[illegible]88,019	383,804	768,939
1825	5,677	94,052	1,306,525	1,229,043	411,183	785,646
1826	6,150	94,052	1,447,703	1,366,712	447,727	885,100
1827	7,003	105,336	1,524,633	1,468,959	486,411	942,345
1828	7,530	105,336	1,659,915	1,689,945	548,049	1,086,313
1829	8,004	115,000	1,707,418	1,782,132	559,237	1,153,646
1830	8,450	115,176	1,850,583	1,932,708	595,234	1,274,009
1831	8,686	115,486	1,997,811	1,936,122	635,028	1,252,226
1832	9,205	104,466	2,258,570	2,266,171	715,481	1,482,507
1833	10,127	119,916	2,617,011	2,930,414	826,283	1,894,638
1834	10,693	119,916	2,823,749	2,910,605	897,317	1,925,544
1835	10,770	112,774	2,993,356	2,757,350	945,418	1,719,007
1836	11,091	118,264	3,408,323	2,841,766	812,803	1,638,052
1837	11,767	141,242	4,236,779	3,544,630	891,352	1,996,727
1838	12,519	134,818	4,238,733	4,430,662	933,948	3,131,308
1839	12,780	133,999	4,484,657	4,636,536	980,000	3,285,622
1840	13,468	155,739	4,543,522	4,718,236	1,028,925	3,296,876
1841	13,778	155,026	4,407,726	4,499,528	1,018,645	3,159,375
1842	13,733	149,732	4,546,849	5,674,752	1,147,256	3,087,796
1843	13,814	142,295	4,296,225	4,374,754	1,426,394	2,947,319
1844	14,103	144,687	4,237,288	4,296,513	1,358,316	2,938,551
1845	14,183	143,940	4,289,841	4,320,732	1,409,875	2,905,504
*1846	14,601	152,865	3,487,199	4,084,297	1,042,079	2,716,673
*1847	15,146	153,818	3,955,893	3,979,570	1,060,228	2,476,455
*1848	16,159	163,208	4,371,077	4,326,850		2,394,703
*1849	16,749	163,703	4,905,176	4,479,049	1,320,921	2,577,407
*1850	18,417	178,672	5,552,971	5,212,953	1,549,376	2,965,786
*1851	19,796	196,290	6,727,867	6,278,402	1,781,686	3,538,064
*1852	20,901	214,284	6,925,971	7,108,459	1,296,765	4,225,311
*1853	22,320	217,743	5,940,725	7,982,957	1,406,477	4,906,308
*1854	23,548	219,935	6,955,586	8,577,424	1,707,708	5,401,382
*1855	24,410	227,908	7,342,136	9,968,342	2,135,335	6,076,335
*1856	25,565	239,642	7,620,822	10,405,286	2,102,891	6,765,639
*1857	26,586	242,601	8,053,952	11,508,058	2,285,610	7,239,333
*1858	27,977	260,603	8,186,793	12,722,470	2,855,016	8,246,054

* The returns for 1846, 1847, 1848, 1849, 1850, and 1851 are for the six years under the law of March 3, 1845. Those for 1852, 1853, 1854, 1855, 1856, 1857, and 1858, are for the seven years under the new law.

4. Foreign Mail Service.

Foreign Mail Service of the United States in Operation September 30, 1858.*

Routes.	Distance in miles.	Number of trips.	Contractors.	Annual Pay.	Remarks.
1. New York, by Southampton, to Bremen Haven,	3,700	13 a year	Not under contract.	†	Mails carried under Act June 14, 1858.
2. Charleston, by Savannah and Key West, to Havana.	669	2a month	M. C. Mordecai.	60,000	Contracts with P. M. G., Acts Mar. 3, '47, & July 10, 1848.
3. New York to Aspinwall, Havana to Aspinwall, New York, by Havana, to New Orleans,	2,000 1,200 2,000	2 a mo.	M. O. Roberts, and B. R. McIlvain, & M. Taylor	290,000	Contract with Secretary of Navy, Acts Mar. 3, 1847, and Mar. 3, 1851.
4. Astoria, by Port Orford, San Francisco, Monterey, and San Diego, to Panama,	4,200	2a month	Pacific Mail Steam. Co., W. H. Davidge, *Pres.*	348,250	Contract with Sec. of Navy, & P. M. G. Acts Mar. 3, 1847 and 1851, and June 14, 1858.
5. New York to Liverpool,	3,100	20 a year	E. K. Collins, J. & S. Brown.	335,000	Cont. with Sec. of N. Act Mar. 3, 1847.‡
6. New York, by Cowes, to Havre,	3,270	13 a year	Not under contract.	†	Mails carried under Act June 14, 1858.
7. Aspinwall to Panama,	48	2a month or as often as required.	Panama Railroad Co.	100,000	Contract with Postmaster-General.
8. New Orleans to Vera Cruz,	900	2a month	Not under contract.		Mails carried under Act June 14, 1858.
	21,087				

The gross amount accruing to the United States for the fiscal year for postages on mails transported by the Bremen line was $92,523.18; the net revenue (i. e. deducting commissions paid postmasters and United States inland postages) was $78,491.22. By the Collins line the gross amount was $100,016.75; the net revenue, $56,707.79. By the "miscellaneous" (i. e. the substitutes for the Collins steamships) line, the gross amount was $37,599.77; the net revenue, $22,807.55. By the Havre line the gross revenue was $97,782.36; the net revenue, $63,366.92. The net revenue on the four lines was $221,373.48. The postages on the Charleston and Havana line were $9,125.42; by the New York and California lines, $295,202.50; by the New Orleans and Vera Cruz line, $4,359.37.§ The revenue by the Cunard line was as follows: — Total letter postage, $557,624.72; the United States' portion, five twenty-fourths, being United States inland postage, was $116,171.81; add newspaper postage, $19,124.94; total, $135,296.75. On these postages the United States pays for commissions $136,257.25, making a deficit of $960.50; and to this should be added for United States inland postage on British mails, $116,171.81, which makes the whole deficit to the Department $117,132.31.

The amount of postages for the year, on mails received and sent between the United States and British Provinces, under the existing postal arrangements, by which each party retains what it collects, was $156,479.80, and of this there was collected in the United States $85,607.44, and in the Provinces $70,872.36, giving a balance to the United States of $14,735.08. In 1854 there was a balance in favor of the Provinces of $1,793.99; in 1855, a balance in favor of the United States of $4,354.33; in 1856, of $5,226.81; and in 1857, of $7,964.12.

* The service is substantially the same, October 1, 1859, although the contractors and pay may be different.

† The pay is United States postage (sea and inland) on mails conveyed.

‡ The contractors withdrew their steamships, February, 1858. The mails have since been transported by temporary steamers for the postages, under the Act of June 14, 1858.

§ For receipts of these lines in former years, see the American Almanac for 1856, pages 183, 184; for 1857, page 180; for 1858, page 181; and for 1859, page 176.

The number of letters and newspapers exchanged between the United States and Great Britain, in British mails, during the year, was: —

Lines.	Letters.			Newspapers.		
	Received.	Sent.	Total.	Received.	Sent.	Total.
Cunard,	1,326,023	1,051,895	2,377,918	1,009,223	956,247	1,965,470
Collins,	175,851	190,362	366,213	119,363	199,748	319,111
Miscellaneous,	37,110	96,397	133,607	27,210	108,000	135,210
Bremen,	122,051	137,231	259,282	106,061	166,141	272,202
Havre,	103,980	127,724	231,704	93,394	139,937	233,331
Total,	1,765,015	1,603,609	3,368,624	1,356,251	1,570,073	2,925,324

The number of letters and newspapers exchanged between the United States and France during the year, was: —

Lines.	Letters.			Newspapers.		
	Received.	Sent.	Total.	Received.	Sent.	Total.
Cunard,	441,941	437,826	879,767	110,155	222,510	332,665
Collins,	54,527	63,019	117,546	11,869	32,958	44,827
Miscellaneous,	26,587	32,058	58,645	3,184	13,378	16,562
Havre,	50,288	61,086	111,374	7,464	24,548	32,002
Bremen,	51,452	45,917	97,369	11,460	22,753	34,233
Total,	624,795	639,906	1,264,701	144,142	316,147	460,289

The number exchanged between the United States and Bremen, in *Bremen* mails and all by the Bremen line, was: *Letters* received, 112,734; sent, 81,766; total, 194,500. *Newspapers* received, 9,038; sent, 14,113; total, 23,151.

The number of letters and newspapers exchanged between the United States and Prussia in closed mails was: —

Lines.	Letters.			Newspapers.		
	Received.	Sent.	Total.	Received.	Sent.	Total.
Cunard,	247,324	387,006	634,330	15,492	50,840	66,332
Collins,	49,872	86,604	136,476	4,837	9,478	14,315
Miscellaneous,	6,899	45,525	52,424	663	5,675	6,338
Bremen,	64,412	72,646	137,058	5,526	9,481	15,007
Havre,	51,257	42,150	93,407	4,814	6,275	11,089
Total,	419,764	633,931	1,053,695	31,332	81,749	113,081

The number of letters and newspapers conveyed in the home lines was as follows, viz.: —

Lines.	Letters.	Postage.	Newspapers.	Postage.
New York, Chagres, and California,	2,044,266	$255,706.67	3,949,583	$39,495.83
Charleston and Havana,	76,359	7,960.98	58,222	1,164.44
New Orleans and Vera Cruz,	33,532	4,359.37		
West India Islands,	306,411	40,948.36	136,341	2,726.82
Panama,	40,285	10,377.61	29,184	1,167.36
Total,	2,500,853	319,352.99	4,173,330	44,554.45

In 1855, (for the year ending June 30th,) there were carried in the *British* mails, as above, 3,842,228 letters, and 3,154,600 newspapers; in 1856, 3,909,128 letters, and 3,196,014 newspapers; in 1857, 3,879,076 letters, and 3,322,052 newspapers; in the *Bremen* mails, in 1855, 361,657 letters, and 16,396 newspapers; in 1856, 353,195 letters, and 23,165 newspapers; in 1857, 194,500 letters, and 23,151 newspapers; in the *Prussian* closed mails, in 1855, 978,442 letters, and 47,734 newspapers; in 1856,

974,499 letters, and 63,131 newspapers; in 1857, 1,085,327 letters, and 90,378 newspapers; and by the home lines, in 1855, 3,099,997 letters, and 3,973,264 newspapers; in 1856, 2,682,437 letters, and 3,643,626 newspapers; in 1857, 2,627,336 letters, and 4,394 newspapers.

5. Revenue and Expenditure.

Revenue and Expenditure of the Post-Office under the old Law (prior to 1845), under the Law of 1845, and under that of 1851.

	Letter Postage.	Newspapers and Pamphlets.	Total Annual Receipts.	Total Annual Expenditures.
Average of nine years under the old law,	$3,807,993	$528,979	$4,364,825	$4,499,595
Average of the six years of the law of 1845,	3,900,000	791,045	4,833,197	4,684,547
Average of seven years under the law of 1851,	5,570,109	643,606	7,274,857	9,753,265

"Letter postage" includes receipts from stamps sold and registered letters. A reference to the detailed statement of the receipts and expenditures, *ante*, p. 167, will show how the annual receipts, &c. are made up.

Under the act of 1845, the gross revenue from letter postage fell off in 1846, the first year of the reduction, $988,738.92, or 27 per cent; in the second year, 1847, it increased $363,950.49, or 13.6 per cent over 1846.

In the year ending June 30, 1852, the first year after the reduction by the act of 1851, the gross revenue from letter postage was reduced $1,185,993.73, or 22.33 per cent; in 1853 the increase from the same source over that of 1852 was $246,434, or 5.83 per cent of the whole income from this source in 1852; in 1854 the increase over this revenue in 1853 was $950,359, or 21.25 per cent thereof; in 1855 the increase over 1854 was $322,281, or 5.94 per cent; in 1856 the increase over 1855 was $244,345, or 4.25 per cent; in 1857 the increase over 1856 was $445,170, or 7.39 per cent; in 1858 the increase over 1857 was $165,909.70, or nearly 2.57 per cent.

The cost of the transportation of the mails has increased rapidly. In 1845 it was $2,905,504; in 1850, $2,965,786; in 1855, $6,076,335; in 1858, $8,246,054. See table, *ante*, page 169.

The details of the receipts and expenditures of the Department for the contract year ending June 30, 1857, are given *ante*, p. 167.

6. Compensation of Postmasters.

The commissions allowed postmasters are as follows, viz.:—

1. On the postage collected at their respective offices, not exceeding $100 in any one *quarter*,	60 per cent.
But if mails arrive regularly at any office between 9 P.M. and 5 A.M., then	70 "
2. On any sum between $100 and $400 in any *quarter*,	50 "
3. On any sum between $400 and $2,400 in any *quarter*,	40 "
4. On any sum over $2,400 in any *quarter*,	15 "
5. On the amount of letters and packets received for distribution at general distribution offices,	12½ "
6. On newspaper postages in all cases,	50 "
7. Box rents not exceeding $2,000 per annum.	

No postmaster can receive a larger compensation from commissions than $500 per quarter. The postmasters at New Orleans and Washington have special allowances for extra labor. To postmasters whose pay does not exceed $500 in any quarter, one cent is paid for the delivery of each free letter or document, except for the delivery of such as are for himself.

On postages on letters received at a frontier office to be sent to Canada, 3½ per cent is allowed; if received from Canada for distribution, 7 per cent is allowed. Those postmasters who are required to keep a register of the arrival and departure of the mails, are allowed ten cents for each monthly return made to the Postmaster-General. Two mills are allowed for delivery of each newspaper not chargeable with postage. Additional allowances may be made to the postmasters at distributing and separating offices, to defray actual and necessary expenses, when the commissions, allowances, and emoluments are insufficient.

The term *letter postage* includes all postages received, except those which arise from newspapers sent from the offices of publication to subscribers, and from pamphlets and magazines.

7. Rates of Postage within the United States.*

For every single letter in manuscript, or paper of any kind in which information is asked for, or communicated in writing, or by marks, or signs, sent in the mail not exceeding 3,000 miles, ... 3 cents.

Sent over 3,000 miles, ... 10 "

Upon all letters passing through or in the mail, except such as are to or from a foreign country, the postage must be prepaid, except upon letters and packages addressed to officers of the government on official business, and so marked on the envelope. This is not, however, to interfere with the franking privilege.

For a double letter double the above rates are charged; for a treble letter, treble the above rates, &c. Every letter or parcel not exceeding half an ounce (avoirdupois) in weight is a single letter, and every additional weight of half an ounce or of less than half an ounce is charged with an additional single postage. When advertised, one cent additional is charged on each letter. For a letter delivered by a carrier, there is an additional charge of not exceeding one or two cents.

For drop letters, prepayment optional, (not to be mailed,) each 1 "

For all letters or packages (*ship letters*) conveyed by any vessel not employed in conveying the mail, ... 2 "

To this charge of 2 cents is added 4 cents, when the letters are not transmitted through the mail, but are delivered at the post-office where deposited; and the ordinary rates of United States postage are added when the letter is transmitted through the mails.

---

* Established by the act of March 3, 1855.

Each newspaper, periodical, unsealed circular, or other article of printed matter, not exceeding three ounces in weight, to any part of the United States, ... 1 cent.

For every additional ounce or fraction of an ounce, . . . 1 "

If the postage on any newspaper or periodical is paid quarterly or yearly in advance, at the office where the same is either mailed or delivered, then half the above rates are charged. Newspapers and periodicals not weighing over one and a half ounces, circulated in the State where published, are likewise charged but half of the above rates.

Small newspapers and periodicals, published monthly or oftener, and pamphlets not containing more than sixteen octavo pages each, when sent in single packages, weighing at least eight ounces, to one address, and prepaid by affixing postage stamps thereto, are charged only half a cent for each ounce or fraction of an ounce, notwithstanding the postage calculated on each separate article of such package would exceed that amount. The postage on all transient matter must be prepaid.

Books, bound or unbound, not weighing over four pounds, are deemed mailable matter, and pay,

For all distances under 3,000 miles, per ounce, . . . 1 cent.

For all distances over 3,000 miles, ... 2 "

Fifty per cent will be added in all cases when not prepaid. All printed matter chargeable by weight will be weighed when dry. The publishers of newspapers and periodicals may send to each other from their respective offices of publication, free of postage, one copy of each publication; and may also send to each actual subscriber, enclosed in their publications, bills and receipts for the same, free of postage. The publishers of weekly newspapers may send to each actual subscriber, within the county where their papers are printed and published, one copy thereof free of postage.

No printed matter shall be sent at the above rates, unless either without any wrapper, or with one open at the ends or sides, so that the character of the matter may be seen without removing the wrapper; or if any written or printed communication is put on the same after its publication, or upon the cover or wrapper, except the name and address of the person to whom the same is sent; or if anything else is enclosed in such printed paper. If these conditions are not complied with, letter postage shall be charged.

When any printed matter, received during any quarter, has been in the post-office for the whole of the succeeding quarter, the postmaster shall sell it, and credit the amount of the sales as directed by the Post-Office Department.

The establishment of private expresses for the conveyance of any letters, packets, or packages of letters, or other matter transmissible in the United States mail (newspapers, pamphlets, magazines, and periodicals excepted), from one city, town, or other place, to any other city, town, or place in the United States, between which the United States mail is regularly transported, is prohibited, but letters, &c. may be carried by carriers in *stamped* envelopes. Contractors may carry newspapers out of the mails, for sale or distribution among subscribers. A penalty of $5,000 is imposed on any person taking letters *through* or over any part of the United States for the purpose of being sent out of the United States without the payment of postage.

Letters addressed to different persons cannot be enclosed in the same envelope or package, under a penalty of ten dollars, unless addressed to foreign countries.

8. Privilege of Franking.

1. The President, ex-Presidents, the Vice-President, ex-Vice-Presidents, Mrs. Harrison, and Mrs. Polk, have the franking privilege, as regulated by former laws.

2. Members of Congress and Delegates from Territories, *from thirty days before the commencement* of each Congress until the first Monday in December after the expiration of their term of office*, the Secretary of the Senate, and the Clerk of the House of Representatives, during their *official terms*, may *send* and *receive free letters or packages* not exceeding two ounces in weight, and public documents not exceeding three pounds in weight.

3. The Governor of any State may send free the laws, records, and documents of the Legislature to the Governors of other States.

4. The Secretaries of the Departments, and Assistant Secretaries; the Attorney-General, Postmaster-General and Assistant Postmasters-General; Comptrollers, Auditors, Register, and Solicitor of the Treasury; Treasurer; Commissioners of the different Offices and Bureaus; Chiefs of Bureaus in the War and Navy Departments, General-in-Chief, and Adjutant-General; and the Superintendent of the Coast Survey and his Assistant, may *send and receive free* all letters and packages upon official business, but *not* their private letters or papers.

5. The Chief Clerks in the Departments may send free public official letters and documents.

6. Deputy postmasters may *send free* all such letters and packages as relate exclusively to the business of their respective offices; and those whose compensation did not exceed $200 for the year ending the 30th of June, 1846, may also send free, through the mails, letters written by themselves, and receive free all written communications on their own private business, not weighing over one half-ounce, but not transient newspapers, handbills, or circulars.

7. Exchange newspapers, magazines, &c. between editors pass free.

8. All publications entered for copyright, and which, under the act of August 10, 1846, are to be deposited in the library of Congress and in the Smithsonian Institution, pass free.†

For other free matter, see *Rates of Postage*.

Public Documents are those printed by the order of either house of Congress, and publications or books procured or purchased by Congress, or either house, for the use of the members.

* The commencement of each Congress for this purpose dates from the 4th of March (i. e. the day next) succeeding the termination of the preceding Congress.

† See "Titles and Abstracts of Public Laws," No. 13, *ante*, pp. 132, 133.

9. *Rates of Postage to various Foreign Countries and Cities.*†

[The asterisk (*) indicates that in cases where it is prefixed prepayment is optional unless the letter be registered; in all other cases prepayment is required.]

COUNTRIES.	Letters. Not exceeding ¼ oz.	Letters. Not exceeding ½ oz.	Printed Matter. Newspapers.	Printed Matter. Pamphlets per oz.
	Cents.	Cents.	Cents.	Cents.
Acapulco, over 2,500 miles		20	2	1
" under 2,500 miles		10	2	1
Aden, British mail, via Southampton		33	4	
" " via Marseilles	39	45	8	
" French mail	30	60		
Africa (West Coast), British mail		33	4	
Alexandretta, Prussian closed mail		40	6	
" French mail	*30	*60	2	1
" open mail, via Engl'd, by Am. packet		21	2	
" " " by Br. packet		5	2	
Alexandria, Prussian closed mail		*38	6	
" by Bremen or Hamburg mail		*30		
" French mail	*30	*60	2	1
" open mail, via Engl'd, by Am. packet		21	2	
" " " by British packet		5	2	
" via Marseilles, by American packet		21	2	
" " " by British packet		5	2	
Algeria, French mail	*15	*30	2	1
Altona, Prussian closed mail		*33	6	
" by Bremen or Hamburg mail		*22	3	1
" French mail	*27	*54		1
Anegada. See *West Indies.*				
Angostura. See *Venezuela.*				
Antigua. See *West Indies.*				
Arabia, British mail, via Southampton		33	4	
" " via Marseilles	39	45	8	
Argentine Republic. See *Buenos Ayres.*				
Ascension, via England		33	4	
Aspinwall, for distances not exceeding 2,500 miles		10	2	1
" " exceeding 2,500 miles		20	2	1
Assumption. See *Paraguay.*				
Australia, British mail, via Southampton		33	4	
" " via Marseilles	39	45	8	
" by private ship, from N. York or Boston		5	2	1
" by French mail	30	60		1
" by Bremen or Hamburg mail, via Marseilles and Suez	50	102		
" by Bremen or Hamburg mail, via Trieste		55		
" by mail to San Francisco, thence by private ship		10		
Austria and its States, Prussian closed mail		*30	6	
" " by Bremen or Hamburg mail		*15	3	1
" " French mail	*21	*42		
Aux Cayes		34	6	
Azores Islands, via England	29	37	4	
" " private ship		5	2	1
Baden, Prussian closed mail		*30	6	
" by Bremen or Hamburg mail		*22	3	1
" French mail	*21	*42	2	1
Bahamas and other British West India Islands. See *West Indies*				
Batavia, British mail, via Southampton		33	4	
" " via Marseilles	39	45	8	
" French mail	30	60		
Bavaria, Prussian closed mail		*30	6	
" by Bremen or Hamburg mail		*15	3	1
" French mail	*21	*42		
Belgium, French mail	*21	*42	2	1
" open mail, via London, by Amer. packet		21	2	

† Five cents the single letter, of a half-ounce or under, must be added to the rates named in this table by "British mail," "via England," or "via London," respectively, if the letter is from California, Oregon, or Washington Territory.

COUNTRIES.	Letters.		Printed Matter	
	Not exceeding ½ oz.	Not exceeding ½ oz.	Newspapers.	Pamphlets per oz.
	Cents.	Cents.	Cents.	Cents.
Belgium, open mail, via London, by British packet		5	2	
Belgrade, " " by Amer. packet		21	2	
" " " by British packet		5	2	
" " " by French mail..	*21	*42		
Beyrout, Prussian closed mail		*40	6	
" French mail	*30	*60	2	1
Bogota. See *New Granada.*				
Bolivia		34	6	4
Bombay. See *East Indies.*				
Borneo, British mail, via Southampton............		33	6	
" " via Marseilles	39	45	10	
" French mail	30	60		
Bourbon, British mail, via Southampton		33	6	
" " via Marseilles..............	39	45	10	
" French mail............................	*30	*60		
Bourghas, Prussian closed mail		40	6	
" French mail............................	*30	*60		
Brazils, via England		45	4	
Bremen, Prussian closed mail		*30	6	
" Bremen mail............................		*10	2	1
" Hamburg mail...........................		*15	3	1
" French mail............................	*21	*42	2	1
British N. A. Provinces, when not exceeding 3,000m.		*10	1	
" " when exceeding 3,000 miles		*15		
Brunswick, Prussian closed mail..................		*30	6	
" by Bremen or Hamburg mail		*15	3	1
" French mail............................	*21	*42	2	
Buenaventura		18	6	4
Buenos Ayres, via England		33	4	
Buene Ayre. West India Islands.....................		34	6	
Burmah,† via Marseilles, by Amer. packet.........		21	8	
" " by British packet........		5	8	
Caiffa, Prussian closed mail		40	6	
Calcutta,† via Marseilles, by Amer. packet.........		21	8	
" " by British packet........		5	8	
" Prussian closed mail.....................		38	6	
" French mail............................	30	60		
Canada. See *British North American Provinces.*				
Canary Islands, via England	33	45	6	
Candia, Prussian closed mail		*40	6	
" open mail, via London, by Amer. packet..		21	4	
" " " by British packet..		5	4	
Canea, Prussian closed mail.........................		*40	6	
" French mail	*30	*60		
" via Marseilles or Southampton, by Am. pkt.		21	2	
" " " by Br. pkt.		5	2	
Canton. See *China* (1st and 2d lines)..............				
Cape of Good Hope, via England, by Amer. packet.		21	2	
Cape de Verde Islands, via England	29	37	4	
Cardenas, West India Islands, not over 2,500 miles.		10	2	
" " " over 2,500 miles....		20	2	
Carthagena..		18	6	
Cayenne, French Guiana		34	6	
Central America, Pacific slope, via Panama.........		20	2	1
Cephalonia, Cerigo, Cesme. See *Turkey*...........				
Ceylon, via Marseilles, by Amer. packet		21	8	
" " by British packet...........		5	8	
" via Southampton, by Amer. packet........		21	4	
" " by British packet		5	4	
" French mail	30	60		
Chagres (New Granada), not exceeding 2,500 miles		10	2	1
" " exceeding 2,500 miles....		20	2	1
Chile		34	6	4
China (except Hong Kong), via Southampton		33	4	

† Via Southampton, the letter postage is the same as via Marseilles, the newspaper postage is 6 cents.

COUNTRIES.	Letters.		Printed Matter.	
	Not exceeding ½ oz.	Not exceeding ½ oz.	Newspapers.	Pamphlets per oz.
	Cents.	Cents.	Cents.	Cents.
China, (except Hong Kong), via Marseilles.........	39	45	8	
" " Bremen & Hamburg, via Trieste		55		
" " " via Suez..	40	72		
" " French mail...................	30	60		
" by m'l to San Francisco, thence by private ship		10	2	1
Chincha Islands..................................		34	6	
Constantinople, Prussian closed mail..............		*40	6	
" French mail..........................	*30	*60	2	1
" by Bremen and Hamburg mail		*32		
" via Mars. or South'pton, by Am. pkt.		21	2	
" " " by Br. pkt.		5	2	
Corfu. See *Ionian Islands.*				
Corsica, by American packet.......................		21	2	
" by British packet..........................		5	2	
Cuba, when distance does not exceed 2,500 miles...		10	2	1
" " does exceed 2,500 miles......		20	2	1
Curacoa, W. India Islands, via England...........		33	4	
Cuxhaven, Prussian closed mail....................		*30	6	
" by Bremen or Hamburg mail		*15	3	1
" French mail............................	*21	*42	2	1
Dardanelles, Prussian closed mail.................		*40	6	
" French mail.........	*30	*60	2	1
Demerara. See *Guiana, British.*				
Denmark, Prussian closed mail		*35	6	
" by Bremen or Hamburg mail............		*29	3	1
" French mail	*27	*54		1
Dominica, same as West Indies, British				
East Indies, via Mars. or Southampton, by Am. pkt.		21	8	
" " " by Br. pkt.		5	8	
" Prussian closed mail, via Trieste......		70	13	
" (English Possessions,) Prussian closed mail, via Trieste...................		38	10	
" by Bremen or Hamburg mail, via Marseilles and Suez	40	72		
East Indies, by Bremen or Hamburg mail, via Trieste		64		
" French mail............................	30	60		
Ecuador		34	6	4
Egypt (except Alexandria), Br. m'l, via Southampton		33	4	
" " " via Marseilles..	39	45	8	
" " Prussian closed mail....		38	6	
" " Bremen or Hamburg m'l		*30		
" " French mail	30	60	2	1
Falkland Islands, via England.....................		33	4	
Fayal. See *Azores Islands.*				
Florence, Prussian closed mail....................		*35	6	
" French mail............................	*27	*54	2	1
" Bremen or Hamburg....................		*28	3	1
Fowchow. See *China*, 1st and 2d lines.				
France	*15	*30	2	1
Frankfort, French mail	*21	*42	2	1
" Prussian closed mail		*30	6	
" Bremen or Hamburg mail		*15	3	1
Galatz, Prussian closed mail......................		*40		
" French mail..............................	*30	*60	2	1
" via Marseilles or Southampton, by Am. pkt.		21	2	
" " " by Brit. pkt.		5	2	
Gallicia, Prussian closed mail.....................		*30	6	
" Bremen or Hamburg....................		*15	3	1
French mail......................................	*21	*42	2	
Gallipoli, Prussian closed mail....................		*40	6	
" French mail..............................	*30	*60	2	1
Gambia, via England		33	4	
Genoa, Prussian closed mail........................		*38	6	
" French mail................................	*21	*42		1
Genoa, Bremen or Hamburg........................		*30	3	1
German States, Prussian closed mail...............		*30	6	
" French mail....................	*21	*42	2	1

COUNTRIES.	Letters.		Printed Matter.	
	Not exceeding ¼ oz.	Not exceeding ½ oz.	Newspapers.	Pamphlets per oz.
	Cents.	Cents.	Cents.	Cents.
German States, by Bremen or Hamburg mail, (except Baden and Luxemburg)....		*15	3	1
Gibraltar, French mail	21	42		
" open mail, via England, by Amer. packet		21	2	
" " " by British packet		5	2	
Gonaives		34	6	4
Great Britain and Ireland (California, Oregon, or Washington Territory excepted)		*24	2	†
Greece, Prussian closed mail........................		*42	6	
" French mail..................................	*30	*60		1
" by Bremen or Hamburg mail..............		*35	3	1
" via England, by American packet.........		21	2	
" " by British packet		5	2	
Guadaloupe, via England		33	4	
Guatemala, Old and New......................		34	6	4
Guiana, British, not over 2,500 miles...............		10	2	
" " over 2,500 miles		20	2	
" Dutch, same as British				
" French		34	6	
Hamburg, by Hamburg mail direct from New York		*10	2	1
" Bremen mail		*15	3	1
" Prussian closed mail.....................		*30	6	
" French mail.............................	*21	*42		
Hanover, Prussian closed mail.....................		*30	6	
" Bremen or Hamburg mail		*15	3	1
" French mail..............................	*21	*42		
Havana. See *Cuba.*				
Hayti, via England..................................		33	4	4
Heligoland, Island of, via England..................		33	4	
Hindostan. See *East Indies.*				
Holquin, Spanish W. Indies. Same as *Guiana Brit.*				
Holland, French mail	*21	*42	2	1
" via England, by American packet		21	2	
" " by British packet		5	2	
Holstein, Prussian closed mail........................		*35	6	
" by Bremen or Hamburg mail...............		*25	3	1
" French mail..............................	*27	*54	2	1
Honduras		34	6	4
Hong Kong, via England, by American packet		21	2	
" " by British packet.........		5	2	
" French mail............................	30	60		
" by Bremen or Hamburg mail...........		30		
" Prussian closed mail		38	10	
Ibraila, French mail.................................	*30	*60	2	1
" Prussian closed mail........................		*40	6	
Indian Archipelago, French mail....................	30	60		
" via Marseilles	39	45	8	
Indies. See *East Indies, West Indies.*				
Ineboli, Prussian closed mail.........................		40	6	
" French mail	*30	*60	2	1
Ionian Islands, Prussian closed mail		*38	6	
" French mail	*30	*60	2	
" by American packet..................		21	2	
" by British packets..................		5		
" via Marseilles.......................	39		6	
" via Southampton....................		33	4	
Isle of Pines, Spanish West Indies. Same as *Guiana, British.*				
Italy. See *Sardinian States; Lombardy; Modena; Parma; Tuscany; Papal States;* and *Two Sicilies.*				
Ithica, Prussian closed mail		*38	6	
" French mail	*30	*60		
Janina, by French mail..............................	*30	*60		
Java, British mail, via Southampton................		33	4	

† 2 cents each if not over 2 ounces, and 4 cents an ounce or fraction of an ounce over 2 ounces, to be collected in all cases in the United States.

COUNTRIES.	Letters. Not exceeding ¼ oz.	Letters. Not exceeding ½ oz.	Printed Matter. Newspapers.	Printed Matter. Pamphlets per oz.
	Cents.	Cents.	Cents.	Cents.
Java, British mail, via Marseilles	39	45	8	
" " via French mail	30	60		
Jaffa, Prussian closed mail		40		
" French mail	*30	*60		
" via England, by American packet		21	2	
" " by British packet		5	2	
Jamaica. See *West Indies.*				
Japan, via Southampton		33	4	
" via Marseilles	39	45	8	
Jeremie		34	6	1
Jerusalem, via England, by American packet		21	2	
" " by British packet		5	2	
Karikal, French mail	*30	*60		
Kerassunde, French mail	*30	*60	2	1
Labuan, British mail, via Southampton		33	6	
" " via Marseilles	39	45	10	
" French mail	30	60		
Larnica, by French mail	*30	*60		
Lauenburg, Prussian closed mail		*33	6	
" by Bremen or Hamburg mail		*25	3	1
" French mail	*27	*54	2	1
Latakia, Prussian closed mail		40	6	
" French mail	*30	*60	2	
Liberia, British mail		33	4	4
Lombardy, Prussian closed mail		33	6	
" by Bremen or Hamburg mail		*15	3	1
" French mail	*21	*42	2	1
Lubec, Prussian closed mail		*30	6	
" by Bremen or Hamburg mail		*15	3	1
" French mail	*21	*42	2	1
Luxemburg Grand Duchy, Prussian closed mail		*30	6	
" " French mail	*21	*42		
" " by Bremen or Hamb'g m'l		*22	3	1
Madeira, Island of, via England and Lisbon	29	37	4	
Madras, via Marseilles and Southamp'n, by Am. pkt.		21	8	
" " " by Br. pkt.		5	8	
" French mail	30	60		
" Prussian closed mail		38	10	
Mahé, French mail	*30	*60		
Majorca and Minorca, via England		33		
Malta, Isl. of, via Mars. & Southampton, by Am. pkt.		21	2	
" " " " by Br. pkt.		5	2	
" " French mail	*30	*60		
Manila. See *Philippine Islands.*				
Martinique, via England		33	4	
Matanzas. Same as *Guiana, British.*				
Mauritius, British mail, via Southampton and India		33	4	
" " via Marseilles and India	39	45	8	
" French mail	30	60		
Mexico, for distances under 2,500 miles		10	2	1
" " over 2,500 miles		20	2	1
Mecklenburg (Strelitz, &c.). See *German States.*				
Messina, Prussian closed mail		40	6	
" by Bremen or Hamburg mail		22		
" French mail	*30	*60	2	
Miquelon, British steamer to Halifax		5	2	
" land mail to Halifax		10	1	
Mitylene (Metelin), Prussian closed mail		40		
" French mail	*30	*60	2	1
Modena, Prussian closed mail		*33	6	
" French mail	*27	*54	2	1
" by Bremen or Hamburg mail		*25	3	1
Moldavia, Prussian closed mail		30	6	
" by Bremen or Hamburg mail		*32		
" French mail	*30	*60		
Moluccas, British mail, via Southampton and India		33	6	
" " via Marseilles and India	39	45	10	

COUNTRIES.	Letters.		Printed Matter.	
	Not exceeding ¼ oz.	Not exceeding ½ oz.	Newspapers.	Pamphlets per oz.
	Cents.	Cents.	Cents.	Cents.
Moluccas, French mail	30	60		
Montenegro, by French mail	21	42		
Montevideo, via England		33	4	
Mosquitia		34	6	
Naples, Kingdom of, Prussian closed mail		30	6	
" " French mail	*30	*60	2	1
" " by Bremen or Hamburg mail		22		
Netherlands, The, French mail	*21	*42	2	1
" " via England, by American packet		21	2	
" " " by British packet		5	2	
Nevis. See *West Indies, British.*				
New Brunswick. } See *British N. A. Provinces.*				
Newfoundland. }				
New Granada (except Aspinwall, and Panama)		18	6	4
New Providence. See *West Indies, British.*				
New South Wales. See *Australia.*				
New Zealand, via Southampton and Suez		33	4	
" via Marseilles	39	45	8	
" French mail	30	60		
Nicaragua		34	6	4
Norway, Prussian closed mail		*46	6	
" by Bremen or Hamburg mail		*38	3	1
" French mail	*33	*66		
Nova Scotia. See *British North American Provinces.*				
Oldenburg, Prussian closed mail		*30	6	
" by Bremen or Hamburg mail		*13	3	1
" French mail	*21	*42		1
Padang, via Marseilles	39	45	10	
" via Southampton		33	6	
Palermo. See *Sicilies, The Two.*				
Panama, when distance does not exceed 2,500 miles		10	2	1
" " does exceed 2,500 miles		20	2	1
Paraguay, via England		33	4	
Paramaribo. See *Guiana, Dutch.*				
Parma, Prussian closed mail		*33	6	
" French mail	*27	*54	2	1
" by Bremen or Hamburg mail		*25	3	1
Penang. See *East Indies.*				
Peru		22	6	4
Philippine Islands, British mail, via Southampton		33	6	
" " via Marseilles	39	45	10	
" French mail	30	60		
Placentia, Prussian closed mail		30	6	
" by Bremen or Hamburg mail		*25		
" French mail	27	54		
Poland, Prussian closed mail		*37	6	
" by Bremen or Hamburg mail		*29	3	1
" French mail	*30	*60		
Pondicherry, French mail	*30	*60		
Port au Prince, Porto Bello, Porto Rico		34	6	4
Portugal, via England	29	37	4	
" by Bremen or Hamburg mail	30	42		
" French mail	21	42		
Prevesa, Prussian closed mail		40	6	
Prince Edward's Island. See *B. N. A. Provinces.*				
Prussia, Prussian closed mail		*30	6	
" by Bremen or Hamburg mail		*15	3	1
" French mail	*21	*42		1
Puerto Principe. See *Guiana, British.*				
Rhodes, Prussian closed mail		*40	6	
" French mail	*30	*60	2	1
Rio de Janeiro		45	4	
Roman or Papal States, Prussian closed mail		*35	6	
" " French mail	*27	*54	2	1
" " by Bremen or Hamburg m'l		*28		
Russia, Prussian closed mail		*37	6	
" by Bremen or Hamburg mail		*29		

COUNTRIES.	Letters. Not exceeding ½ oz.	Letters. Not exceeding ½ oz.	Printed Matter. Newspapers.	Printed Matter. Pamphlets per oz.
	Cents.	Cents.	Cents.	Cents.
Russia, French mail	*30	*60	2	1
Salonica, Prussian closed mail		*40	6	
" French mail	*30	*60	2	1
Samsoun, Prussian closed mail		*40		
" French mail	*30	*60	2	1
Sandwich Islands, via San Francisco		10	2	1
San Juan, San Salvador, San Martha		34	6	4
Sardinian States, Prussian closed mail		*38	6	
" French mail	*21	*42		1
" by Bremen or Hamburg mail		*30	3	1
Saxe-Altenburg, Prussian closed mail		*30	6	
" by Bremen or Hamburg mail		*15	3	1
" French mail	*21	*42		1
Saxe Coburg-Gotha, Meiningen, and Weimar, Pr. m.		*30	6	
" " " by Bremen or Hamburg mail		*22	3	1
" Meiningen, and Weimar, Fr. m.	*21	*42		1
Saxony, Kingdom of, Prussian closed mail		*30	6	
" " by Bremen or Hamburg mail		*15	3	1
" " French mail	*21	*42		1
Schleswig, by Bremen or Hamburg mail		*25	3	1
" French mail	*27	*54		1
" Prussian closed mail		*35	6	
Scio, by French mail	*30	*60		
Scutari (Asia), Prussian closed mail		30	6	
" " French mail	30	60	2	
" " open mail, via London, by Am. pkt.		21	2	
" " " " by Br. pkt.		5	2	
Servia (except Belgrade), Prussian closed mail		30	6	
" French mail, via Austria	21	42	2	1
Shanghai. See *China*, 1st and 2d lines.				
Siam		33	4	
Sicilies, The Two, Prussian mail		30	6	
" " French mail	*30	*60	2	
" " open mail, via London, Am. pkt.		21	2	
" " open mail, via London, Br. pkt.		5	2	
" " by Bremen or Hamburg mail		22		
Singapore. See *East Indies.*				
Sinope, via England, by Amer. packet		21	2	
" " by British packet		5	2	
" French mail	*30	*60	2	1
" Prussian closed mail		40		
Sisal		34	6	
Smyrna, Prussian closed mail		40	6	
" French mail	*30	*60	2	1
Sophia, by French mail	*30	*60		
Spain, via London, by American packet		21	2	
" " by British packet		5	2	
" via French mail	21	42	2	
" via Bremen or Hamburg mail	30	42		
St. Helena, via England		33	4	
St. Thomas, via Havana		34	6	
Sulina, French mail	*30	*60	2	1
Sumatra, British mail, via Southampton		33	6	
" " via Marseilles	39	45	10	
" French mail	30	60		
Surinam		34	6	
Sweden, Prussian closed mail		*42	6	
" by Bremen or Hamburg mail		*33	3	1
" by French mail	*33	*66		1
Switzerland, Prussian closed mail		*35	6	
" French mail	*21	*42	2	1
" by Bremen or Hamburg mail		*27	3	1
Syria, open mail, via London, by American packet		21	2	
" " " by British packet		5	2	
" British mail, via Marseilles, by French pkt.	33	45	4	
" French mail	30	60	2	1

COUNTRIES.	Letters.		Printed Matter.	
	Not exceeding ¼ oz.	Not exceeding ½ oz.	Newspapers.	Pamphlets per oz.
	Cents.	Cents.	Cents.	Cents.
Tangiers, French mail	*30	*60		
Tasmania. See *Van Diemen's Land.*				
Tchesme, Prussian closed mail		*40	6	
" open mail, via London, by Amer. packet		21	4	
" " " by British packet		5	4	
Tenedos, " " by Amer. packet		21		
" " " by British packet		5		
" Prussian closed mail		40	6	
" French mail	*30	*60		
Trebisond, open mail, via London, by Am. packet		21	2	
" " " by Br. packet		5	2	
" Prussian closed mail		*40	6	
" French mail	*30	*60	2	1
Tripoli in Syria, French mail	*30	*60	2	
Tultcha, French mail	*30	*60	2	1
" Prussian closed mail		*40	6	
Tunis, French mail	*30	*60	2	1
" British mail, via Marseilles, by French pkt.	33	45	4	
Turkey in Europe and Turkish Islands in the Mediterranean, except as herein mentioned: —				
Prussian closed mail		30	6	
By Bremen or Hamburg mail		*32		
Turkey, open mail, via London, by American packet		21	2	
" " by British packet		5	2	1
Turk's Island, under 2,500 miles		10	2	1
" over 2,500 miles		20	2	1
Tuscany, Prussian closed mail		*35	6	
" French mail	*27	*54	2	1
" by Bremen or Hamburg mail		*28	3	1
Valona, Prussian closed mail		40		
" French mail	*30	*60		
Vancouver's Island, via California		10	1	
Van Diemen's Land, British mail, via Southampton		33	4	
" " " via Marseilles	39	45	8	
" " French mail	30	60		
Varna, Prussian closed mail		*40	6	
" French mail	*30	*60	2	1
" open mail, via London, by American packet		21	2	
" " " by British packet		5	2	
Venetian States, Prussian closed mail		*30	6	
" French mail	27	54	2	1
" by Bremen or Hamburg mail		*15	3	1
Venezuela		34	6	4
Victoria (Port Philip), via Southampton		33	4	
" " via Marseilles	39	45	8	
Volo, Prussian closed mail		40	6	
" French mail	*30	*60	2	1
Wallachia, Prussian closed mail		*30	6	
" by Bremen or Hamburg mail		30	3	1
West Indies, British, via Havana, not over 2,500 m.		10	2	1
" " " over 2,500 miles		20	2	1
" " via Halifax		10	2	
West Indies, not British (except Cuba)		34	6	4
Wurtemberg, Prussian closed mail		*30	6	
" French mail	*21	*42	2	
" by Bremen or Hamburg mail		*15	3	1
Yancoi and Yanaon, French mail	*30	*60	2	
Yucatan		34	6	
Zanzibar, via England		65	4	
Zante, Prussian closed mail		*38	6	
" French mail	30	60	2	

Routes of Transmission, &c.

To prevent mistakes at the exchange offices, the particular routes by which letters are to be forwarded from the United States to Europe should be distinctly written on the covers. Letters for transmission in the open mail to England should bear the direction, "open mail via England;" if for transmission in the French mail, they should be directed "via France in French mail;" if for transmission by closed mail to Prussia, they should be directed "via Prussian closed mail;" and if for transmission by the New York and Bremen line to Bremen, or by the New York and Hamburg line to Hamburg, they should be directed "via Bremen," or "via Hamburg." Letters addressed to Germany and other European countries via France, where the single rate per quarter ounce is 21 cents, should be plainly marked to be sent via France; otherwise they may be missent in the open mail to Liverpool by U. S. Packet, the 21 cent rate per half-ounce being also chargeable on letters thus forwarded.

On a letter or packet of any weight the *whole* postage or *none at all* should be prepaid, where the prepayment is optional. If anything less than the whole is prepaid, *it is entirely lost to the sender.*

On British sea and American inland postage, the single letter is ½ ounce and under; on foreign postage, the single letter is less than ¼ ounce. Letters weighing ¼ ounce and under ½ ounce are charged two rates; ½ ounce and under ¾, three rates, &c.; an additional rate being charged for each quarter of an ounce. Where a letter pays both British, &c. postage and foreign postage, if it weighs more than ¼ ounce and less than ½ ounce, it pays a single rate of British, &c. postage, and two rates for the foreign postage; the *foreign* postage only being doubled for each ¼ ounce.

Upon *periodicals and pamphlets* sent to Great Britain, the rates of postage have been given (*ante*, p. 179, note). An additional British postage of the same rate, when not exceeding 2 ounces, must be paid in England; but the third ounce raises the British charge to 6*d*. (12 cents), with 2*d*. (4 cents) additional for each additional ounce. No pamphlet can be sent weighing over 8 ounces, and no periodical over 16 ounces, without being subject to letter postage. Pamphlets and periodicals are not entitled to conveyance through England, except addressed to France, Algeria, or cities of Turkey, Syria, or Egypt in which France has post-offices.

Newspapers, periodical works, books stitched or bound, pamphlets, catalogues, papers of music, prospectuses, circulars, and all other kinds of printed matter addressed to France, Algeria, or cities of Turkey, Syria, and Egypt in which France has post-offices, (viz. Alexandria, Alexandretta, Beyrout, Constantinople, Dardanelles, Galatz, Gallipoli, Ibraila, Ineboli, Jaffa, Kerassund, Latakia, Messina in Asiatic Turkey, Mitylene, Rhodes, Salonica, Samsoun, Sinope, Smyrna, Sulina, Trebisond, Tripoli in Syria, Tultcha, Varna, and Volo,) can be despatched to France *direct*, or by way of England, on prepayment of the United States postage, viz. newspapers, 2 cents each; periodical works, catalogues, or pamphlets, one cent an ounce or fraction of an ounce; and all other kinds of printed matter the same as domestic rates; to be in all cases collected in the United States, whether sent or received. France in like manner collects its own postage on all kinds of printed matter, whether sent or received. This mail is sent by every steamer.

The United States exchange offices for French mails are New York, Boston, and Philadelphia.

Newspapers and periodicals published in the United States, and sent to regular subscribers in the British North American Provinces, or published in those Provinces and sent to regular subscribers in the United States, are chargeable with the regular prepaid quarterly rates of United States postage to and from the line; which postage must be collected at the office of mailing in the United States on matter sent, and at the office of delivery in the United States on matter received. In like manner, such matter, if transient, is chargeable with the regular domestic transient printed matter rates to and from the line, to be collected at the office of mailing or delivery in the United States, as the case may be. Editors, however, may exchange free of expense.

Letters received from Canada, to which are affixed United States postage-stamps of sufficient value to prepay the full postage chargeable thereon, should be delivered without charge by the United States offices.

Newspapers and periodicals to the Sandwich Islands, China, and New South Wales, must be prepaid the regular domestic rates to San Francisco. The rate payable on letters at the point of destination in the Sandwich Islands is 5 cents, and on newspapers 2 cents each. In China and New South Wales the ship postage, it is understood, is comparatively trifling.

Newspapers and periodicals to foreign countries, and particularly to the Continent of Europe, must be sent in narrow bands, open at the sides or end; otherwise they are chargeable there with letter postage.

Overland mails are made up in London, and despatched as follows: — For Aden, Alexandria, Arabia, Burmah, Calcutta, East Indies, Egypt, Hindostan, Madras, Malta, and Penang, on the 3d, 10th, 18th, and 26th, of each month, via Marseilles; and on the 4th, 12th, 20th, and 27th, via Southampton. For Bombay, on the 3d and 18th of each month, via Marseilles, and on the 12th and 27th, via Southampton. For Batavia, Borneo, Bourbon, Canton, China, Java, Labuan, Manila, Moluccas, Padang, Singapore, and Sumatra, on the 10th and 26th of each month, via Marseilles; and on the 4th and 20th, via Southampton. For Australia, Mauritius, New Zealand, and Tasmania, on the 18th of each month, via Marseilles; and on the 12th, via Southampton. For Brazil, Buenos Ayres, and Montevideo, on the 9th of each month. When any of these dates fall on Sunday, the Marseilles mails are despatched the following evening, and the Southampton mails, the previous morning.

10. Registration of Letters.

The act of March 3, 1855, authorized the Postmaster-General to establish a uniform plan for the registration of valuable letters posted for transmission in the mails, for their greater security, upon the application of parties posting the same. A registration fee, to be prepaid, is charged upon each letter or packet, in addition to the regular postage. The registration is not compulsory, nor does it render the United States or the Department responsible for the safe carriage of such letters or packets.

Valuable letters, addressed to Germany or any part of the German Austrian Postal Union, by the Bremen line via New York, or by the Prussian closed mail via New York and Boston, as also letters addressed to Great Britain and Canada, will be *registered* on the application of the person posting the same, in the same manner and on the same terms as those deliverable in the United States, *provided* that the full postage chargeable thereon to destination, together with *a registration fee of five cents on each letter*, is prepaid at the mailing office. Such letters should be mailed and forwarded to the respective United States exchange offices, in the same manner as domestic registered letters are mailed to those offices.

11. *Amounts actually credited for the Transportation of the Mails, and other Expenses, by States and Territories, and the Amount of Postages collected in the same, in the Year ending June 30, 1858, fractions of a dollar omitted.*

States and Territories.	Letter Postage.	News-paper Postage.	Registered Letters.	Stamps Sold.	Total Receipts.	Transportation.	Compensation allowed Post-masters.	Total Expenses.
	$	$	$	$	$	$	$	$
Alabama,	5,706	12,218	1,046	92,122	111,092	188,260	44,172	248,750
Arkansas,	1,988	5,314	127	28,298	35,727	222,368	20,010	244,569
California,	67,241	14,690	547	184,269	256,746	176,914	59,185	283,421
Connecticut,	10,395	16,553	286	172,091	199,324	113,806	78,032	209,452
Delaware,	1,178	2,079	84	18,482	21,822	22,488	8,783	32,703
Florida,	1,316	2,356	190	20,821	24,683	144,603	12,231	166,888
Georgia,	6,466	15,558	1,230	138,362	161,617	267,984	57,716	348,801
Illinois,	50,672	37,602	1,663	350,929	440,866	377,628	164,008	627,629
Indiana,	14,155	24,358	983	153,053	192,548	254,234	93,127	361,235
Iowa,	15,543	17,829	620	122,801	156,792	123,860	68,523	213,261
Kentucky,	8,553	13,968	792	116,735	140,049	192,156	62,305	260,031
Louisiana,	23,706	14,480	798	141,058	180,042	504,025	27,517	565,191
Maine,	13,678	13,697	678	125,300	153,163	120,693	72,073	209,676
Maryland,	24,054	10,774	902	140,289	176,019	234,551	34,353	298,671
Massachusetts,	77,827	28,981	1,176	460,649	565,633	187,243	151,069	435,237
Michigan,	18,875	16,126	992	129,889	165,882	184,175	71,784	274,897
Mississippi,	3,772	11,985	559	72,142	88,458	284,669	43,033	332,506
Missouri,	28,155	17,237	697	144,091	190,180	362,531	66,410	448,510
New Hampshire,	4,757	10,376	309	89,973	105,415	55,671	53,266	113,276
New Jersey,	15,947	10,555	260	94,510	121,272	94,178	53,549	154,456
New York,	285,207	90,244	2,875	1,080,385	1,458,711	625,950	316,267	1,164,111
North Carolina,	2,759	10,429	763	67,454	81,405	187,463	39,612	230,582
Ohio,	42,312	43,671	2,332	414,704	503,019	524,787	181,906	750,776
Pennsylvania,	76,168	52,892	3,053	485,644	617,757	359,878	184,039	642,104
Rhode Island,	4,401	3,674	120	52,860	61,054	19,299	15,360	45,494
South Carolina,	11,240	7,572	803	81,530	101,145	243,688	28,927	284,600
Tennessee,	4,391	12,286	920	101,216	118,814	165,201	45,447	228,153
Texas,	7,167	11,955	374	65,963	85,449	428,365	38,522	472,300
Vermont,	4,272	12,071	267	83,769	100,379	80,175	53,782	135,045
Virginia,	10,949	25,021	1,369	205,612	242,951	347,709	95,930	473,848
Wisconsin,	27,244	16,839	744	140,402	185,228	116,718	76,179	206,954
Kansas Territory,	2,228	1,727	47	17,981	21,984	26,322	11,311	37,857
Minnesota Territ.	8,335	5,003	225	38,219	51,781	87,757	23,015	115,005
Nebraska Territ.	1,258	978	22	6,821	9,079	21,859	4,876	26,787
New Mexico Ter.	139	106	4	1,511	1,760	30,680	760	31,446
Oregon Territory,	2,805	1,791	19	8,961	13,576	35,370	6,115	41,602
Utah Territory,	569	128	35	603	1,300	31,568	702	32,275
Washington Ter.	664	164	5	1,594	2,426	23	1,407	1,450
Dist. Columbia,	6,031	2,218	365	42,287	50,902		2,959	39,596

For all post-offices where the compensation of the postmaster exceeds $1,000 per annum, the postmaster is appointed by the President with the advice and consent of the Senate, and is removable by the President only; for all other offices, the Postmaster-General has the sole power of appointment and removal.

A surplus of commissions accrued at the following post-offices, after deducting the maximum compensation of the postmasters, and the necessary incidental expenses of the offices, viz. : —

Albany, N. Y.	$3,463.24	Independence, Mo.	$158.45	Raleigh, N. C.	$121 68
Augusta, Ga.	703.14	Jersey City, N. J.	274.99	Richmond, Va.	438.08
Baltimore, Md.	1,134 29	Kensington, Pa.	25.76	Rochester, N. Y.	860 09
Boston, Mass.	22,125.97	Louisville, Ky.	1,984.19	Rockford, Ill.	192.83
Brooklyn, N. Y.	235.87	Lancaster, Pa.	64 66	San Francisco, Cal.	3,727.38
Buffalo, N. Y.	3,141.42	Lockport, N. Y.	102.00	Savannah, Ga.	40.93
Cleveland, Ohio,	2,476.89	Memphis, Tenn.	1,614.43	Springfield, Mass.	505.36
Columbus, Ohio,	1.86	Milwaukee, Wis.	229 81	St. Louis, Mo.	9,532.29
Chicago, Ill.	12,596.17	Madison, Wis.	833.24	Syracuse, N. Y.	290.65
Charleston, S. C.	368.52	New Bedford, Mass.	238.82	Toledo, Ohio,	1,861.49
Cincinnati, Ohio,	695.94	Newark, N. J.	319.73	Troy, N. Y.	1,377.07
Detroit, Mich.	1,968.98	Nashville, Tenn.	694.25	Utica, N. Y.	161.00
Dayton, Ohio,	193.67	New York, N. Y.	71,130.27	Washington, D. C.	2,892.98
Davenport, Iowa,	160 69	New Haven, Conn.	82.16	Worcester, Mass.	430.50
Dubuque, Iowa,	2,567.71	Norfolk, Va.	208.82	Williamsburg, N. Y.	57.87
Erie, Pa.	1,907.56	New Orleans, La.	10,647.01	Wilmington, Del.	906.28
Galveston, Texas,	387.27	Oswego, N. Y.	81 75		
Hartford, Conn.	935.97	Portland, Me.	695.89	Total,	$174,262.93
Harrisburg, Pa.	579.69	Philadelphia, Pa.	2,841.84		
Indianapolis, Ind.	946.14	Pittsburg, Penn.	2,278.39		

12. *Letters, Circulars, Newspapers, and Pamphlets, delivered by Carriers, during the Year ending June* 30, 1858.

Places.	Number of Letters.	Number of Circulars.	Newspapers & Pamphlets.	Amount for Carriage.
Baltimore, Md. . .	886,403	34,126	166,690	$18,902.78
Boston, Mass. .	37,984	*1,304,718	87,786	13,799.68
Harrisburg, Penn. .	22,257		2,896	883.25
Lowell, Mass. . .	96,273		7,683	1,963.90
Manchester, N. H. .	57,284		4,430	1,167.63
New Orleans, La. .	117,289	8,708	11,304	2,469.36
New York, N. Y. .	3,913,649	550,809	532,093	87,041.53
Philadelphia, Pa. .	2,040,225	39,114	359,822	43,069.75
Providence, R. I. .	†132,174		21,349	2,750.22
Roxbury, Mass. .	†20,717		4,880	438.73
Syracuse, N. Y. .	35,902			716,04
Total, . . .	7,390,057	1,937,477	1,198,937	$173,222.97

The amount of postage accounted for on foreign dead letters returned to and sent from the United States, for the year ending June 30th, 1858, was as follows: —

Great Britain to United States,	$1,639 45	United States to Great Britain,	$11,546.25
Prussia to United States,	760.84	United States to Prussia,	1,645.42
Bremen to United States,	None.	United States to Bremen,	560.12
France to United States,	None.	United States to France,	None.
Hamburg to United States,	10.15	United States to Hamburg,	4.10

13. *Overland Mail Route.* — In September, 1858, service commenced on the overland mail route to California. The mail leaves St. Louis and Memphis, the eastern termini, and San Francisco, the western terminus, twice a week. The time for the trip across (2795 miles from St. Louis to San Francisco) is 25 days. The contract pay is $600,000 per annum for six years.

* In this, many letters are included, being of same rate as circulars.

† From October 1, 1857.

XIV. CONGRESS.*

The Congress of the United States consists of a Senate and House of Representatives, and must assemble at least once every year, on the first Monday of December, unless it is otherwise provided by law.

The Senate is composed of two members from each State; and, of course, the regular number is now 66. They are chosen by the Legislatures of the several States, for the term of six years, one third being elected biennially.

The Vice-President of the United States is the President of the Senate, in which body he has only a casting vote, which is given in case of an equal division of the votes of the Senators. In his absence, a President *pro tempore* is chosen from among the Senators by the Senate.

The House of Representatives is composed of members from the several States, elected by the people, in separate districts composed of contiguous territory, for the term of two years. The Representatives are apportioned among the different States according to population, as follows. After each decennial enumeration, the aggregate representative population of the United States is ascertained by the Secretary of the Interior, by adding to the whole number of free persons in all the States, including those bound to service for a term of years, and excluding Indians not taxed, three fifths of all other persons. This aggregate is divided by 233, and the quotient, rejecting fractions, if any, is the ratio of apportionment among the several States. The representative population of each State is then ascertained in the same manner, and is divided by the above-named ratio, and this quotient gives the apportionment of Representatives to each State. The loss by fractions is compensated for by assigning one additional member to as many States having the largest fractions as may be necessary to make the whole number of Representatives 233. If after the apportionment new States are admitted, Representatives are assigned to such States upon the above basis, in addition to the limited number of 233; but such excess continues only until the next apportionment under the succeeding census. The present number of Representatives is 237, an additional representative being temporarily assigned to California, two being allowed to Minnesota, and one to Oregon. There are, besides, five Delegates, one each from Utah, New Mexico, Washington, Kansas, and Nebraska, who have a right to speak, but not to vote. For table of apportionment, &c. among the several States, see *post*, p. 214.

The compensation of members is, mileage (being $8 for every twenty

* The American Almanac for 1844, p. 149, contains a complete list of the Senators and Representatives in Congress from the several States, from the commencement of the government under the Constitution to the end of the 27th Congress, March 23, 1843, with the beginning and termination of their respective periods of office. The American Almanac for 1854, p. 213, brings down the list from the commencement of the 28th Congress to the end of the 32d Congress, March 3, 1853.

miles of travel in the usual road, in going to and returning from the seat of government), and $6,000 for each Congress, payable as follows: on the first day of each regular session, the mileage and the pay then due from the beginning of the term, at the rate of $250 a month, and, during the session, compensation at the same rate; on the first day of each subsequent session, mileage, and pay at the same rate that has accrued since the adjournment, and during said session at the same rate. Members dying before the commencement of the first session receive no pay or mileage; dying afterwards, their representatives receive what was then due them.* Deductions from the monthly pay of each member are made for each day's absence, unless the cause of absence be his sickness or that of some member of his family. The pay of the Speaker, and of the President of the Senate *pro tempore*, is $12,000 for each Congress.

Thirty-sixth Congress. 1st Session. The Senate.

[The figures denote the expiration of the terms of the Senators.]

Hon. John C. Breckinridge, *President, ex officio.*

Asbury Dickins, *Secretary.* William Hickey, *Chief Clerk.*

Alabama.			*Indiana.*		
Benj. Fitzpatrick,	Wetumpka,	1861	Graham N. Fitch,	Logansport,	1861
Clem. C. Clay, Jr.,	Huntsville,	1865	Jesse D. Bright,	Jeffersonville,	1863
Arkansas.			*Iowa.*		
Robt. W. Johnson,	Pine Bluffs,	1861	James Harlan,	Mt. Pleasant,	1861
Wm. K. Sebastian,	Helena,	1865	James W. Grimes,	Burlington,	1865
California.			*Kentucky.*		
Wm. M. Gwin,	San Francisco,	1861	John J. Crittenden,	Frankfort,	1861
Vacancy,†		1863	Laz. W. Powell,	Henderson Co.,	1865
Connecticut.			*Louisiana.*		
Lafayette S. Foster,	Norwich,	1861	John Slidell,	New Orleans,	1861
James Dixon,	Hartford,	1863	J. P. Benjamin,	New Orleans,	1865
Delaware.			*Maine.*		
James A. Bayard,	Wilmington,	1863	Hannibal Hamlin,	Hampden,	1863
Willard Saulsbury,	Georgetown,	1865	Wm. Pitt Fessenden,	Portland,	1865
Florida.			*Maryland.*		
David L. Yulee,	Homossassa,	1861	James A. Pearce,	Chestertown,	1861
Steph. R. Mallory,	Key West,	1863	Anthony Kennedy,	Baltimore,	1863
Georgia.			*Massachusetts.*		
Alfred Iverson,	Columbus,	1861	Charles Sumner,	Boston,	1863
Robert Toombs,	Washington,	1865	Henry Wilson,	Natick,	1865
Illinois.			*Michigan.*		
Lyman Trumbull,	Alton,	1861	Zachariah Chandler,	Detroit,	1863
Stephen A. Douglas,	Chicago,	1865	Kinsley S. Bingham,	Kensington,	1865

* See "Public Resolutions," No. 14, *ante*, p. 138.

† Occasioned by the death of Hon. David C. Broderick.

Minnesota.

Henry M. Rice, St. Paul, 1863
Vacancy, 1865

Mississippi.

Jefferson Davis, Hurricane, 1863
Albert G. Brown, Newtown, 1865

Missouri.

James S. Greene, Canton, 1861
Trusten Polk, St. Louis, 1863

New Hampshire.

Daniel Clark, Manchester, 1861
John P. Hale, Dover, 1865

New Jersey.

John R. Thomson, Princeton, 1863
John C. Ten Eyck, Mt. Holly, 1865

New York.

Wm. H. Seward, Auburn, 1861
Preston King, Ogdensburg, 1863

North Carolina.

Thos. L. Clingman, Ashville, 1861
Thomas Bragg, Northampton, 1865

Ohio.

George E. Pugh, Cincinnati, 1861
Benj. F. Wade, Jefferson, 1863

Oregon.

Joseph Lane, 1861
Vacancy, 1865

Pennsylvania.

William Bigler, Clearfield, 1861
Simon Cameron, Harrisburg, 1863

Rhode Island.

James F. Simmons, Providence, 1863
Henry B. Anthony, Providence, 1865

South Carolina.

Jas. H. Hammond, Beech Isl'd, 1861
James Chesnut, Kershaw, 1865

Tennessee.

Andrew Johnson, Greenville, 1863
A. O. P. Nicholson, Columbia, 1865

Texas.

Vacancy, 1863
John Hemphill, Austin, 1865

Vermont.

Jacob Collamer, Woodstock, 1861
Solomon Foot, Rutland, 1863

Virginia.

James M. Mason, Winchester, 1863
R.M.T.Hunter, Lloyds, EssexCo. 1865

Wisconsin.

Charles Durkee, Kenosha, 1861
James R. Doolittle, Racine, 1863

House of Representatives of the Thirty-sixth Congress, *which will expire on the 3d of March*, 1861.

[The First Session of the 36th Congress commences on the 5th of December, 1859. The numbers prefixed to the names of the members show the District in each State from which they are chosen. The number after the name of the State indicates the number of Representatives to which, under the present apportionment, the State is entitled.]

Alabama. — 7.

3. Clopton, David, Tuskegee.
6. Cobb, W. R. W., Bellefonte.
7. Curry, J. L. M., Talladega.
5. Houston, Geo. S., Athens.
4. Moore, Sydenham, Greensboro'.
2. Pugh, James L., Eufaula.
1. Stallworth, Jas. A., Evergreen.

Arkansas. — 2.

1. Hindman, T. C.
2. Rust, Albert, El Dorado.

California. — 2.

2. Burch, John C., Trinity.
1. Scott, Chas. L., Sonora.

Connecticut. — 4.

3. Burnham, Alfred A., Windham.
4. Ferry, Orris S., Norwalk.
1. Loomis, Dwight, Rockville.
2. Woodruff, John, New Haven.

Delaware. — 1.

Whiteley, Wm. G., Newcastle.

Florida. — 1.

Hawkins, Geo. S., Pensacola.

Georgia. — 8.

2. Crawford, Martin J., Columbus.
4. Gartrell, Lucius J., Atlanta.

3. Hardeman, Thos. Jr., Macon.
7. Hill, Joshua, Madison.
6. Jackson, James, Athens.
8. Jones, John J., Waynesboro'.
1. Love, Peter E. Thomasville.
5. Underwood, J.W.H., Rome.

Illinois. — 9.

2. Farnsworth, J. F., Chicago.
8. Fouke, Philip B., Belleville.
4. Kellogg, William, Canton.
9. Logan, John A., Benton.
3. Lovejoy, Owen, Princeton.
6. McClernand, J.A.,* Springfield.
5. Morris, Isaac N., Quincy.
7. Robinson, James C., Marshall.
1. Washburne, E. B., Galena.

Indiana. — 11.

10. Case, Charles, Fort Wayne.
9. Colfax, Schuyler, South Bend.
7. Davis, John G., Rockville.
3. Dunn, Wm. M., Madison.
2. English, Wm. H., Lexington.
4. Holman, Wm. S., Lawrenceburg.
5. Kilgore, David, Yorktown.
1. Niblack, Wm. E., Vincennes.
11. Pettit, John U., Wabash.
6. Porter, Albert G., Indianapolis.
8. Wilson, James, Crawfordsville.

Iowa. — 2.

1. Curtis, Samuel R., Keokuk.
2. Vandever, W., Dubuque.

Kentucky. — 10.

6. Adams, Green.
4. Anderson, Wm. C.
3. Bristow, Francis M.
5. Brown, J. Young.
1. Burnett, Henry C., Cadiz.
7. Mallory, Robert.
9. Moore, Laban T.
2. Peyton, Samuel O., Hartford.
8. Simms, Wm. E.
10. Stevenson, John W., Covington.

Louisiana. — 4.

1. Bouligny, J. E., New Orleans.
3. Davidson, T. G., Baton Rouge.
4. Landrum, John M., Shreveport.
2. Taylor, Miles, Donaldsonville.

Maine. — 6.

6. Foster, Stephen C., Pembroke.
3. French, Ezra B., Damariscotta.
4. Morse, Freeman H., Oxford.
2. Perry, John J., Bath.
1. Somes, Daniel E., Biddeford.
5. Washburne, Israel, Jr., Orono,

Maryland. — 6.

4. Davis, H. Winter, Baltimore.
3. Harris, J. Morrison, Baltimore.
6. Hughes, Geo. W., West River.
5. Kunkel, Jacob M., Frederic City.
1. Stewart, James A., Cambridge.
2. Webster, Edward H., Bel Air.

Massachusetts. — 11.

3. Adams, Charles F., Quincy.
6. Alley, John B., Lynn.
2. Buffinton, James, Fall River.
5. Burlingame, Anson, Cambridge.
11. Dawes, Henry L., N. Adams.
10. Delano, Charles, Northampton.
1. Eliot, Thomas D., New Bedford.
7. Gooch, Daniel W., Melrose.
4. Rice, Alexander H., Boston.
9. Thayer, Eli, Worcester.
8. Train, Charles R., Framingham.

Michigan. — 4.

1. Cooper, George B., Jackson.
3. Kellogg, F. W., Grand Rapids.
4. Leach, Dewitt C., Lansing.
2. Waldron, Henry, Hillsdale.

Minnesota. — 2.

1. Aldrich, Cyrus, Hennepin.
2. Window, William, Winona.

Mississippi. — 5.

3. Barksdale, Wm., Columbus.

* Elected in November, 1859, to fill the vacancy caused by the death of Thomas L. Harris, the member elect.

2. Davis, Reuben, Aberdeen.
1. Lamar, Lucius Q. C., Abbeville.
5. McRae, John J., Clark Co.
4. Singleton, Otho R., Canton.

Missouri. — 7.

2. Anderson, Thos. L., Palmyra.
1. *Barrett, James R., St. Louis.
3. Clark, John B., Fayette.
4. Craige, James, St. Joseph.
7. Noell, John W., Perryville.
6. Phelps, John S., Springfield.
5. Woodson, S. H., Independence.

New Hampshire. — 3.

3. Edwards, T. M., Keene.
1. Marston, Gilman, Exeter.
2. Tappan, Mason W., Bradford.

New Jersey. — 5.

3. Adrain, G. B., N. Brunswick.
1. Nixon, John T., Bridgeton.
5. Pennington, Wm., Newark.
4. Riggs, Jetur R., Patterson.
2. Stratton, J. L. N., Mount Holly.

New York. — 33.

4. †Barr, Thomas J., New York.
12. Beale, Charles L., Kinderhook.
7. †Briggs, George, New York.
31. Burroughs, Silas M., Medina.
25. Butterfield, Martin, Palmyra.
1. Carter, Luther C., Flushing.
8. †Clark, Horace F., New York.
18. Cochrane, C. B., Schenectady.
6. †Cochrane, John, New York.
20. Conkling, Roscoe, Utica.
21. Duell, R. Holland, Courtlandville.
29. Ely, Alfred, Rochester.
33. Fenton, Reuben E., Frewsburg.
30. Frank, Augustus, Warsaw.
19. Graham, James H., Delhi.
9. Haskin, John B., Fordham.
23. Hoard, Charles B., Watertown.
2. Humphrey, James, Brooklyn.
28. Irvine, William, Corning.
11. Kenyon, Wm. S., Kingston.
22. Lee, M. Lindley, Fulton.
5. †Maclay, Wm. B., New York.
15. McKean, James B., Saratoga.
13. Olin, Abram B., Troy.
16. Palmer, Geo. W., Plattsburg.
26. Pottle, Emory B., Naples.
14. Reynolds, John H., Albany.
24. Sedgwick, Charles B., Syracuse.
3. †Sickles, Daniel E., New York.
32. Spaulding, E. G., Buffalo.
17. Spinner, Francis E., Mohawk.
10. Van Wyck, C. H., Bloomingburg.
27. Wells, Alfred, Ithaca.

North Carolina. — 8.

4. Branch, L. O'B., Raleigh.
7. Craige, Burton, Salisbury.
5. Gilmer, John A., Greensboro'.
6. Leach, J. M., Lexington.
2. Ruffin, Thomas, Goldsboro'.
1. Smith, W. N. H., Murfreesboro'.
8. Vance, Z. B., Ashville.
3. Winslow, Warren, Fayetteville.

Ohio. — 21.

4. Allen, William, Lima.
5. Ashley, James M., Toledo.
21. Bingham, John A., Cadiz.
14. Blake, Harrison G., Medina.
9. Carey, John, Wyandotte.
7. Corwin, Thomas, Lebanon.
12. Cox, Samuel S., Columbus.
18. Egerton, Sidney, Akron.
2. Gurley, John A., Cincinnati.
15. Helmick, Wm., N. Philadelphia.
6. Howard, William, Batavia.
20. Hutchins, John, Warren.
11. Martin, Chas. D., Lancaster.
1. Pendleton, Geo. H., Cincinnati.
13. Sherman, John, Mansfield.

---

* Contested by F. P. Blair.

† The election returns for these districts were made out for "Member of Congress," and not for "Representative in Congress," and the State canvassers have withheld certificates from these six gentlemen. The 5th district is partly in Kings County, and partly in New York. The returns from Kings County were correctly made, and they gave Philip Hamilton a majority of the votes for "Representative in Congress," but Mr. Maclay's majority in New York for "Member of Congress" was greater than Mr. Hamilton's in Kings County for "Representative in Congress."

8. Stanton, Benjamin, Bellefontaine.
17. Theaker, Thom. C., Bridgeport.
16. Tomkins, C. B., McConnelsville.
10. Trimble, Carey A., Chillicothe.
3. Vallandingham, C. L., Dayton.
19. Wade, Edward, Cleveland.

Oregon. — 1.

*Stout, Lansing.

Pennsylvania. — 25.

25. Babbitt, Elijah, Erie.
18. Blair, Samuel S., Holidaysburg.
11. Campbell, James H., Pottsville.
19. Covode, John, Lockport Station.
13. Dimmick, Wm. H., Honesdale.
1. Florence, Thos. B., Philadelphia.
14. Grow, Galusha A., Glenwood.
15. Hale, James T., Bellefonte.
24. Hall, Chapin, Warren.
6. Hickman, John, West Chester.
16. Junkin, Benj. F., Bloomfield.
10. Kellinger, John W., Lebanon.
7. Longnecker, H. C. Doylestown.
22. McKnight, Robert, Pittsburg.
17. McPherson, Edward, Gettysburg.
4. Millward, Wm., Philadelphia.
20. Montgomery, Wm., Washington.
21. Morehead, James K., Pittsburg.
2. Morris, Ed. Joy, Philadelphia.
8. Schwartz, John, Reading.
12. Scranton, Geo. W., Scranton.
9. Stevens, Thaddeus, Lancaster.
23. Stewart, William, Mercer.
3. Verree, John P., Philadelphia.
5. Wood, John, Philadelphia.

Rhode Island. — 2.

2. Brayton, Wm. D., Warwick.
1. Robinson, C., Woonsocket Falls.

South Carolina. — 6.

5. Ashmore, John D., Anderson.
4. Bonham, M. L., Edgefield.
6. Boyce, Wm. W., Monticello.
3. Keitt, L. M., Orangeburg C. H.
1. McQueen, J., Marlborough C.H.
2. Miles, Wm. P., Charleston.

Tennessee. — 10.

10. Avery, Wm. T., Memphis.
3. Brabson, Reese B., Chatanooga.
9. Etheridge, Emerson, Dresden.
5. Hatton, Robert, Lebanon.
2. Maynard, Horace, Knoxville.
1. Nelson, Thos. A. R., Jonesboro'.
8. Quarles, James M., Clarksville.
4. Stokes, W. B., Smithville.
6. Thomas, James H., Columbia.
7. Wright, John V., Purdy.

Texas. — 2.

2. Hamilton, A. H.
1. Reagan, James H., Palestine.

Vermont. — 3.

2. Morrill, Justin S., Strafford.
3. Royce, Homer E., Berkshire.
1. Walton, E. P., Montpelier.

Virginia. — 13.

5. Bocock, T. S., Appomatox C. H.
8. Boteler, Alex. R., Charlestown.
10. Clemens, Sherard, Wheeling.
3. Dejarnette, D. C., Bowling Green.
12. Edmondson, H. A., Salem.
1. Garnett, M. R. H., Lloyds, Essex.
9. Harris, John T., Harrisburg.
11. Jenkins, A. G., Green Bottom.
6. Leake, S. F., Charlottesville.
13. Martin, Elbert S., Lee C. H.
2. Millson, John S., Norfolk.
4. †Pryor, Roger A., Petersburg.
7. Smith, William, Warrenton.

Wisconsin. — 3.

3. Larrabee, C. H., Ozaukee.
1. Potter, John F. East Troy.
2. Washburne, C. C., Mineral Point.

Kansas Territory. — 1.

Parrott, Marcus J., Leavenworth City.

Nebraska Territory. — 1.

Estabrook, Experience, Omaha City.

New Mexico Territory. — 1.

Otero, Miguel A., Albuquerque.

Utah Territory. — 1.

Hooper, Wm. H., Salt Lake City.

Washington Territory. — 1.

Stevens, Isaac J., Olympia.

---

* Contested by David Logan.

† Elected in October, 1859, to fill the vacancy caused by the death of William O. Goode, the member elect.

ALPHABETICAL LIST OF THE HOUSE OF REPRESENTATIVES.

Adams, C. F., Mass.
Adams, Green, Ky.
Adrain, G. B., N. J.
Aldrich, Cyrus, Minn.
Allen, William, O.
Alley, J. B., Mass.
Anderson, T. L., Mo.
Anderson, W. C., Ky.
Ashley, J. M., O.
Ashmore, J. D., S. C.
Avery, W. T., Tenn.
Babbitt, Elijah, Pa.
Barksdale, Wm., Miss.
Barr, T. J., N. Y.
Barrett, J. R., Mo.
Beale, C. L., N. Y.
Bingham, John A., O.
Blair, S. S., Pa.
Blake, H. G., O.
Bocock, Thos. S., Va.
Bonham, M. L., S. C.
Boteler, A. R., Va.
Bouligny, J. E., La.
Boyce, W. W., S. C.
Brabson, R. B., Tenn.
Branch, L. O'B., N. C.
Brayton, Wm. D., R. I.
Briggs, George, N. Y.
Bristow, F. M., Ky.
Brown, J. Y., Ky.
Buffinton, Jas., Mass.
Burch, John C., Cal.
Burlingame, A., Mass.
Burnett, H. C., Ky.
Burnham, A. O., Conn.
Burroughs, S. M., N. Y.
Butterfield, M., N. Y.
Campbell, J. H., Pa.
Carey, John, O.
Carter, L. C., N. Y.
Case, Charles, Ind.
Clark, Horace F., N. Y.
Clarke, J. B., Mo.
Clemens, Sherrard, Va.
Clopton, David, Ala.
Cobb, W. R. W., Ala.
Cochrane, C. B., N. Y.
Cochrane, John, N. Y.
Colfax, Schuyler, Ind.
Conkling, R., N. Y.
Cooper, G. B., Mich.
Corwin, Thomas, O.
Covode, John, Pa.
Cox, Samuel S., O.
Craige, Burton, N. C.
Craig, J., Mo.
Crawford, M. J., Ga.
Curry, J. L. M., Ala.
Curtis, S. R., Iowa.
Davidson, Thos. G., La.
Davis, John G., Ind.
Davis, H. Winter, Md.
Davis, Reuben, Miss.
Dawes, Henry L., Mass.
Dejarnette, D. C., Va.
Delano, C., Mass.
Dimmick, W. H., Pa.
Duell, R. H., N. Y.
Dunn, W. M., Ind.
Edmondson, H. A., Va.
Edwards, T. M., N. H.
Egerton, S., O.
Eliot, T. D., Mass.
Ely, Alfred, N. Y.
English, Wm. H., Ind.
Estabrook, E., Neb. T.
Etheridge, E., Tenn.
Farnsworth, J. F., Ill.
Fenton, R. E., N. Y.
Ferry, O. L., Conn.
Florence, Thos. B., Pa.
Foster, S. C., Me.
Fouke, P. B., Ill.
Frank, Augustus, N. Y.
French, E. B., Me.
Garnett, M. R. H., Va.
Gartrell, L. J., Ga.
Gilmer, John A., N. C.
Gooch, Danl. W., Mass.
Graham, J. H., N. Y.
Grow, Galusha A., Pa.
Gurley, J. A., O.
Hale, J. T., Pa.
Hall, Chapin, Pa.
Hamilton, A. H., Tex.
Hardeman, T. Jr., Ga.
Harris, J. Morrison, Md.
Harris, J. T., Va.
Haskin, John B., N. Y.
Hatton, Robert, Tenn.
Hawkins, G. L., Fla.
Helmick, W., O.
Hickman, John, Pa.
Hill, Joshua, Ga.
Hindman, T. C., Ark.
Hoard, C. B., N. Y.
Holman, W. S., Ind.
Hooper, Wm. H., U.T.
Houston, Geo. S., Ala.
Howard, W., O.
Hughes, Geo. W., Md.
Humphrey, J., N. Y.
Hutchins, J., O.
Irvine, W., N. Y.
Jackson, James, Ga.
Jenkins, A. G., Va.
Jones, John J., Ga.
Junkin, B. F., Pa.
Keitt, L. M., S. C.
Kellinger, J. W., Pa.
Kellogg, F. W., Mich.
Kellogg, William, Ill.
Kenyon, W. S., N. Y.
Kilgore, D., Ind.
Kunkel, J. M., Md.
Lamar, L. Q. C., Miss.
Landrum, John M., La.
Larrabee, C. H., Wis.
Leach, D. C., Mich.
Leach, J. M., N. C.
Leake, Shelton F., Va.
Lee, M. L., N. Y.
Logan, J. A., Ill.
Longnecker, H. C., Pa.
Loomis, Dwight, Conn.
Love, Peter E., Ga.
Lovejoy, Owen, Ill.
Maclay, W. B., N. Y.
Mallory, Robert, Ky.
Marston, G., N. H.
Martin, C. D., O.
Martin, E. S., Va.
Maynard, Horace, Tenn.
McClernand, J. A., Ill.
McKean, J. B., N. Y
McKnight, Robert, Pa.
McPherson, Edw'd, Pa.
McQueen, John, S. C.
McRae, John J., Miss.
Miles, W. P., S. C.
Millson, John S., Va.
Millward, Wm., Pa.
Montgomery, Wm., Pa.
Moore, L. T., Ky.
Moore, Sydenham, Ala.
Morehead, J. K., Pa.
Morrill, Justin S., Vt.
Morris, E. Joy, Pa.
Morris, Isaac N., Ill.
Morse, F. H., Me.
Nelson, T. A. R., Tenn.
Niblack, W. E., Ind.
Nixon, J. T., N. J.
Noell, J. W., Mo.
Olin, A. B., N. Y.
Otero, M. A., N. M. T.
Palmer, G. W., N. Y.
Parrott, M. J., Kan. T.
Pendleton, G. H., O.
Pennington, Wm., N. J.
Perry, J. J., Me.

Pettit, J. U., Ind.
Peyton, Samuel O., Ky.
Phelps, John S., Mo.
Porter, A. G., Ind.
Potter, J. F., Wisc.
Pottle, E. B., N. Y.
Pryor, R. A., Va.
Pugh, J. L., Ala.
Quarles, J. M., Tenn.
Reagan, J. H., Tex.
Reynolds, J. H., N. Y.
Rice, A. H., Mass.
Riggs, J. R., N. J.
Robinson, C., R. I.
Robinson, J. C., Ill.
Royce, H. E., Vt.
Ruffin, Thomas, N. C.
Rust, Albert, Ark.
Schwartz, John, Pa.
Scott, Chas. L., Cal.
Scranton, G. W., Pa.
Sedgwick, C. B., N. Y.
Sherman, John, O.
Sickles, Dan'l E., N. Y.
Simms, W. E., Ky.
Singleton, O. R., Miss.
Somes, D. E., Me.
Smith, William, Va.
Smith, W. N. H., N. C.
Spaulding, E. G., N. Y.
Spinner, F. E., N. Y.
Stallworth, Jas. A., Ala.
Stanton, Benjamin, O.
Stevens, Isaac J., W. T.
Stevens, Thaddeus, Pa.
Stevenson, J. W., Ky.
Stewart, James A., Md.
Stewart, William, Pa.
Stokes, W. B., Tenn.
Stout, Lansing, Or.
Stratton, J. L. N., N. J.
Tappan, Mason W., N. H.
Taylor, Miles, La.
Thayer, Eli, Mass.
Theaker, T. C., O.
Thomas, J. H., Tenn.
Tomkins, C. B., O.
Train, C. R., Mass.
Trimble, C. A., O.
Underwood, J. W. H., Ga.
Vallandingham, C. L., O.
Vance, Z. B., N. C.
Vandever, W., Iowa.
Van Wyck, C. H., N. Y.
Verree, J. P., Pa.
Wade, Edward, O.
Waldron, Henry, Mich.
Walton, E. P., Vt.
Washburne, C. C., Wisc.
Washburne, E. B., Ill.
Washburne, Isr., jr., Me.
Webster, Edw. H., Md.
Wells, Alfred, N. Y.
Whiteley, W. G., Del.
Wilson, James, Ind.
Windom, Wm., Minn.
Winslow, Warren, N. C.
Wood, John, Pa.
Woodruff, John, Conn.
Woodson, S. H., Mo.
Wright, J. V., Tenn.

XV. THE LEVIATHAN OR GREAT EASTERN.

Experience had shown that an ordinary sea steamer of 1,800 tons burden, making the quickest passages to and from England and Australia, with a full cargo and complement of passengers, lost by the voyage from £1,000 to £10,000. A great portion of the expense was caused by the necessity of supplying coal-depots at different points where the steamer could touch during her voyage. These deviations from the shortest route also protracted the passage so much that clipper ships taking a direct course made as quick passages as steamers, and at such less expense that they superseded steamers. A problem then to be solved was this: supposing that a steamer could be built to move eighteen miles an hour, what ought to be the size of a steamer which could carry out and back fuel for a voyage from England to Australia, 25,000 miles? To work a steamer profitably it had been found that the tonnage must be nearly a ton to a mile. Mr. Brunel, therefore, conceived the idea of constructing a steamer of from 20,000 to 25,000 tons burden, capable of carrying coals for full steaming on the longest voyage, — to be built on the tubular plan, with the screw, the paddle, and the sail, for propelling power. The Eastern Steam Navigation Company was formed with a capital of £1,200,000, in shares of £20 each, with power to increase the capital to £2,000,000. The place where she was to be built, on the bank of the Thames at Millwall, consisting of a layer of mud thirty feet thick, on a bed of gravel, was prepared by driving upwards of 1,400 piles, in lines parallel to the river, as the vessel was to be launched sideways, — and the first plate of the vessel was laid May 1, 1854.

The ship consists of two skins, — an inner and outer skin, — two feet ten inches apart, with longitudinal webs at intervals of six feet, running the whole length of the vessel; and these are subdivided by transverse plates into water-tight spaces of about six feet square, so that should the outer skin be damaged the water could only get in between the webs and inner skin. The ship is divided by transverse bulkheads into twelve water-tight compartments below the lower deck, and nine above the lower deck: so that if both the outer and inner skin were fractured, the water could only enter into one of these compartments,—two of which could be filled without danger to the safety of the vessel. Besides these transverse bulkheads there are two which extend from the bottom of the ship to the upper deck, and run longitudinally for a length of 350 feet. There are also two tubular iron platforms extending from the gunwale to the longitudinal bulkheads, running fore and aft, 36 feet apart, and connected together about every 60 feet by iron platforms seven feet wide. The greatest care has been taken to make the bow strong enough to resist any impediment, and to enable the vessel to resist the constant vibration of the screw.

The vessel has no keel, the bottom being flat. A keel plate was first laid along a level platform prepared for it about five feet from the ground; then the centre-web, which somewhat resembles the keel of an ordinary ship, only that it is put *inside* instead of *outside*, was fitted to it;—then came other plates laid flat on the top of the centre web. The iron plates of which the skins of the vessel are composed are three quarters of an inch thick, except the keel-plate, which is one inch thick. Their average size is about 10 feet by 2 feet 9 inches, and their weight 825 pounds. For the sternpost and keel some enormous plates were required. Two were 27 feet long, 3 feet 3 inches wide, 1¼ inches thick, and weighed two tons each; others were 25 feet long, 4 feet wide, and 1¼ inch thick, and weighed 2½ tons each. About 30,000 plates, of an average weight of 600 pounds each, were used in the construction of the hull. Each plate, before being placed in its proper position, was a separate study to the engineer. For each a model in wood was made, and by steam shears the plates were cut according to the pattern; the proper curve was given to it, and the holes for the rivets were punched by machinery. They were riveted together by rivets, fastened at a white heat, some ⅞-inch, and some ¾-inch in diameter, about 2½ inches apart where the plates were to be made water-tight, and from 4 to 6 inches apart in other places. The total number of rivets was not far from 2,000,000. About 8,000 tons of iron were used in her hull.

The propelling power, as heretofore stated, is to be the screw, the paddle, and sails. The summary of statistics of the vessel given below states the number and dimensions of the engines, boilers, propeller, and paddle-wheels. Provision is made for drawing in, to the distance of 10 feet, the floats of the paddle-wheels, when the vessel is deeply laden. The wheels are connected to the engines by friction straps, so that they can be disconnected at any time, if it should be necessary to use the screw by itself. The building of the paddle-engines was commenced about the same time as the ship. They were originally put together in the erecting shop, and were then taken down and re-erected in the ship. The time occupied in doing all this was about sixteen months. The after length of the propeller shaft is 47 feet, and weighs 35 tons; the other lengths are each about 25 feet long, and weigh 16 tons. The coal-bunkers are on either side above and between the boilers, and can contain about 12,000 tons of coal. The estimated consumption of coal is about 180 tons for 24 hours. The vessel is provided with six masts; the after one being of wood, and the rest of iron. Reckoning from the bow, the 1st, 5th, and 6th are 2 feet 9 inches in diameter; the others are 3 feet 6 inches. The 2d, 3d, and 4th are crossed with yards, and carry square-sails; and all carry fore-and-aft sails. She can spread about 6,500 square yards of canvas. The standing rigging is 7½-inch wire rope, except for the after mast, where it is of hemp rope. She has no bowsprit and no figure-head. For her compasses a framework is erected against her after mast some fifty feet high. There are five capstans, three forward and two aft, fitted so that they can be worked either by hand or steam. Her bower chains are 2¾ inches in diameter; each link weighs 72 pounds, and each cable is 120 fathoms in length.

The vessel carries twenty large boats, fitted with masts and sails. In addition she carries two small screw steamers, which hang astern abaft the paddle-boxes, each of which is 100 feet long, 16 feet beam, 120 tons burden, and 40 horse power. These will be raised and lowered by the auxiliary steam-engines. Both of the little screws will be kept in readiness for sea, and be used for embarking and landing the passengers. The crew will number about 400 men all told; about one third being sailors, one third being cooks, stewards, and servants, and one third belonging to the engineering department.

The cabins and saloons are placed in the centre of the vessel, and at each end of the cabins there is a large hold for the cargo, 60 feet long, and the whole depth and breadth of the vessel, and capable of containing about 1,000 tons of cargo. It will be easy, as is said, to stow 6,000 tons of cargo in the holds and other unappropriated places. The vessel has 20 ports on the lower deck, each five feet square, to receive railway wagons; and 60 ports on each side, 2 feet 9 inches square, for ventilation. The lower ports are 16 feet above the water when the ship is loaded. The bulwarks are 9 feet 6 inches high forward, and slope down to above 5 feet high midships and aft. The wrought-iron deck is covered with teak planking placed about 6 inches distant from the iron. The estimated weight of the whole vessel when voyaging with every article and every person on board will be not less than 25,000 tons.

For the purpose of launching the vessel, two ways were constructed, with pile foundations, one at the fore part of the vessel, and one at the after part, each 300 feet long, and 120 feet wide, with about 120 feet of space between them. The cradles, two in number, were of the same width as the ways. Their bottom was composed of iron plates, 7 inches wide and 1 inch thick, placed at intervals of one foot apart, with their edges carefully rounded off, so as to offer the least resistance to the railway metals of the ways down which they had to pass.

The first attempt to launch the vessel was made November 3, 1857, and the vessel moved six feet down in her ways. Several other unsuccessful attempts were made on different days, but at length, January 31, 1858, she was afloat. The cost of building and launching the vessel is stated in round numbers at £730,000, exceeding the original estimate by £230,000. In November, 1858, the Eastern Steam Navigation Company, finding it impossible to go on, was dissolved, and a new corporation called The Great Ship Company was formed with a capital of £330,000. Of this capital, it is said that £160,000 was to be paid to shareholders of the former corporation, that the fitting and finishing for sea would not exceed £120,000, and that £40,000 would be left for working expenses.

Summary of Statistics of the Great Eastern.

Length of upper deck, 691 feet; length between perpendiculars, 680 feet; breadth across paddle-boxes, 118 feet; breadth of hull, 83 feet; depth from deck to keel, 58 feet; number of decks, 4; number of masts, 6; diameter of masts, 2 feet 9 inches to 3 feet 6 inches; quantity of canvas under full sail, 6,500 square yards; number of anchors, 10; number of boats, 20; tonnage, old measurement, 22,500 tons; stowage for cargo, 6,000 tons; capacity of coal-bunkers, 12,000 tons; draught of water, unladen, 15 feet 6 inches; draught of water, laden, 30 feet; number of water-tight compartments, 12.

Paddle-Wheels. — Diameter of paddle-wheels, 56 feet; weight of ditto, 185 tons; length of floats, 13 feet; width of ditto, 3 feet; number of ditto to each wheel, 30; length of paddle-shafts, 38 feet; weight of ditto, 30 tons; length of intermediate cranked shaft, 21½ feet; weight of ditto, 31 tons.

Paddle-Engines. — Nominal horse-power, 1,000; number of cylinders, 4; diameter of ditto, 6 feet 2 inches; weight of ditto, including piston and rod, 38 tons; length of stroke, 14 feet; strokes per minute, 14.

Paddle-Engine Boilers. — Number of boilers, 4; furnaces to each, 10; length of boilers, 17 feet 6 inches; width of ditto, 17 feet 9 inches; height of ditto, 13 feet 9 inches; weight of each, 50 tons; weight of water, 40 tons; area of heating surface, 4,800 square feet; number of tubes, 400; thickness of plates, $\frac{3}{8}$ and $\frac{7}{16}$ inches.

Screw Propeller. — Diameter of screw, 24 feet; pitch of ditto, 37 feet; number of fans, 4; weight of screw, 36 tons; length of propeller shaft, 160 feet.

Screw Engines. — Nominal horse-power, 1,600; number of cylinders, 4; diameter of each cylinder, 84 inches; length of stroke, 4 feet; number of revolutions per minute, 50.

Screw Boilers. — Number of boilers, 6; funnels to each ditto, 12; length of ditto, 18 feet 6 inches; width of ditto, 17 feet 6 inches; height of ditto, 14 feet; weight of ditto, 57 tons; weight of water, 45 tons; area of heating surface, 5,000 square feet; number of tubes, 420; thickness of plates, $\frac{7}{16}$ and ½ inches.

Number of auxiliary engines, 4; number of donkey engines, 10.

Total horse-power about *twelve thousand.*

Passenger Accommodation. — Number of passengers, 1st class, 800; number of ditto, 2d class, 2,000; number of ditto, 3d class, 1,200; aggregate length of saloons and berths, 350 feet; number of saloons, 10; length of principal saloon, 100 feet; width of ditto, 36 feet; height of ditto, 13 feet; length of berths, 14 feet; width of ditto, 7 to 8 feet; height of ditto, 7 feet 4 inches.

XVI. VOTES FOR PRESIDENTS AND VICE-PRESIDENTS FROM 1789 TO 1857.

For Explanations of this table, and remarks upon it, see page 200.
The years given are the dates of the declaration of the votes in Convention, being the year subsequent to that of the popular vote. In 1789 the vote was declared April 6th; in the other years on the second Wednesday of February.

		1. Alabama.	2. Arkansas.	3. California.	4. Conn.	5. Delaware.	6. Florida.	7. Georgia.	8. Illinois.	9. Indiana.	10. Iowa.	11. Kentucky.	12. Louisiana.	13. Maine.	14. Maryland.	15. Mass.	16. Michigan.	17. Mississippi.	18. Missouri.	19. New Hamp.	20. New Jersey.	21. New York.	22. N. Carolina.	23. Ohio.	24. Penn.	25. R. Island.	26. S. Carolina.	27. Tennessee.	28. Texas.	29. Vermont.	30. Virginia.	31. Wisconsin.	32. Total.
1789.	George Washington, Va.				7	3		5							6	10				5	6				10		7				10		69
	John Adams, Mass.				5											10				5	1				8						5		34
	Scattering (see *Remarks*).				2	3		5							6						5				2		7				5		35
1793.	George Washington, Va.				9	3		4				4			8	16				6	7	12	12		15	4	8			4	21		132
	John Adams, Mass.				9	3									8	16				6	7				14	4	6			4			77
	George Clinton, N. Y.							4				sc.										12	12		1		sc.				21		50
1797.	John Adams, Mass.				9	3									7	16				6	7	12	1		1	4				4	1		71
	Thomas Jefferson, Va.							4				4			4								11		14		8	3			20		68
	Thomas Pinckney, S. C.				4	3									4	13					7	12	1		2		8			4	1		59
	Aaron Burr, N. Y.											4			3								6		13			3			1		30
	Scattering, (sc.)				5			4							2	3				6			5			4					19		48
1801.	Thomas Jefferson, Va.							4				4			5							12	8		8		8	3			21		73
	John Adams, Mass.				9	3									5	16				6	7		4		7	4				4			65
	Aaron Burr, N. Y.							4				4			5							12	8		8	sc.	8	3			21		73
	Chas. C. Pinckney, S. C.				9	3									5	16				6	7		4		7	3				4			64
1805. Pres.	Thomas Jefferson, Va.							6				8			9	19				7	8	19	14	3	20	4	10	5		6	24		162
	Chas. C. Pinckney, S. C.				9	3									2																		14
V. Pres.	George Clinton, N. Y.							6				8			9	19				7	8	19	14	3	20	4	10	5		6	24		162
	Rufus King, N. Y.				9	3									2																		14
1809. Pres.	James Madison, Va.							6				7			9						8	13	11	3	20		10	5		6	24		122
	Chas. C. Pinckney, S. C.				9	3									2	19				7		sc.	3			4							47
V. Pres.	George Clinton, N. Y.							6				7			9	19					8	13	11	sc.	20		10	5			24		113
	Rufus King, N. Y.				9	3									2					7		sc.	3			4				sc.			47
1813. Pres.	James Madison, Va.							8				12	3		6								15	7	25		11	8		8	25		128
	DeWitt Clinton, N. Y.				9	4									5	22				8	8	29				4							89
V. Pres.	Elbridge Gerry, Mass.							8				12	3		6	2				1			15	7	25		11	8		8	25		131
	Jared Ingersoll, Pa.				9	4									5	20				7	8	29				4							86
1817. Pres.	James Monroe, Va.							8		3		12	3		8					8	8	29	15	8	25	4	11	8		8	25		183
	Rufus King, N. Y.				9	3										22																	34
V. Pres.	Danl. D. Tompkins, N.Y.				sc.	sc.		8		3		12	3		8	sc.				8	8	29	15	8	25	4	11	8		8	25		183
1821. Pres.	James Monroe, Va.	3			9	4		8	3	3		12	3	9	11	15		3		7 sc	8	29	15	8	25	4	11	8		8	25		231
V. Pres.	Danl. D. Tompkins, N. Y.	3			9	sc.		8	3	3		12	3	9	10 sc	7 sc		3		7 sc	8	29	15	8	25	4	11	8		8	25		218

		1.	2.	3.	4.	5.	6.	7.	8.	9.	10.	11.	12.	13.	14.	15.	16.	17.	18.	19.	20.	21.	22.	23.	24.	25.	26.	27.	28.	29.	30.	31.	32.
1825.	Andrew Jackson, Tenn.	5							2	5			3		7			3			8	1	15		28		11	11					99
Pres.	John Q. Adams, Mass.				8	1			1				2	9	3	15				8		26				4				7			84
	Wm. H. Crawford, Ga.					2		9							1							5									24		41
	Henry Clay, Ky.											14							3			4		16									37
V. Pres.	John C. Calhoun, S. C.	5				1			3	5		7	5	9	10	15		3		7	8	29	15		28	3	11	11		7			182
	Nathan Sanford, N. Y.				sc.	sc.		sc.				7			sc.				sc.	sc.		7		16							sc.		30
Vote in the House of Representatives.	Adams,	3			6							8	2	7	5	12			1	6	1	18	1	10	1	2				5	1		13
	Jackson,								1	3		4	1		3			1			5	2	2	2	25		9	9			1		7
	Crawford.					1		7							1	1						14	10	2							12		4
1829.	Andrew Jackson, Tenn.	5						9	3	5		14	5	1	5			3	3			20	15	16	28		11	11			24		178
Pres.	John Q. Adams, Mass.				8	3								8	6	15				8	8	16				4				7			83
	John C. Calhoun, S. C.	5						2	3	5		14	5	1	5			3	3			20	15	16	28		11	11			24		171
V. Pres.	Richard Rush, Pa.				8	3								8	6	15				8	8	16				4				7			83
	William Smith, S. C.							7																									7
1833.	Andrew Jackson, Tenn.	7						11	5	9			5	10	3			4	4	7	8	42	15	21	30		sc.	15			23		219
Pres.	Henry Clay, Ky.				8	3						15			5	14										4				sc.			49
V. Pres.	Martin Van Buren, N. Y.	7						11	5	9			5	10	3			4	4	7	8	42	15	21				15			23		189
	John Sergeant, Pa.				8	3						15			5	14									sc.	4	sc.			sc.			49
1837.	Martin Van Buren, N. Y.	7	3		8			sc.	5				5	10			3	4	4	7		42	15		30	4	sc.	sc.			23		170
Pres.	Wm. H. Harrison, Ohio.					3				9		15			10	sc.					8			21						7			73
V. Pres.	R. M. Johnson, Ky.	7	3		8				5				5	10			3	4	4	7		42	15		30	4							147
	Francis Granger, N. Y.					3		sc.		9		15			sc.	14					8			21			sc.	sc.		7	sc.		77
1841.	Wm. H. Harrison, Ohio.				8	3		11		9		15	5	10	10	14	3	4			8	42	15	21	30	4		15		7			234
Pres.	Martin Van Buren, N. Y.	7	3						5										4	7							11				23		60
V. Pres.	John Tyler, Va.				8	3		11		9		15	5	10	10	14	3	4			8	42	15	21	30	4		15		7			234
	R. M. Johnson, Ky.	7	3						5										4	7							sc.				22		48
1845.	James K. Polk, Tenn.	9	3					10	9	12			6	9			5	6	7	6		36			26		9				17		170
Pres.	Henry Clay, Ky.				6	3						12			8	12					7		11	23		4		13		6			105
V. Pres.	George M. Dallas, Pa.	9	3					10	9	12			6	9			5	6	7	6		36			26		9				17		170
	T. Frelinghuysen, N. Y.				6	3						12			8	12					7		11	23		4		13		6			105
1849.	Zachary Taylor, La.				6	3	3	10				12	6		8	12					7	36	11		26	4		13		6			163
Pres.	Lewis Cass, Mich.	9	3						9	12	4			9			5	6	7	6				23			9		4		17	4	127
V. Pres.	Millard Fillmore, N. Y.				6	3	3	10				12	6		8	12					7	36	11		26	4		13		6			163
	Wm. O. Butler, Ky.	9	3						9	12	4			9			5	6	7	6				23			9		4		17	4	127
1853.	Franklin Pierce, N. H.	9	4	4	6	3	3	10	11	13	4		6	8	8		6	7	7	5	7	35	10	23	27	4	8		4		15	5	254
Pres.	Winfield Scott, N. Y.											12				13												12		5			42
V. Pres.	William R. King, Ala.	9	4	4	6	3	3	10	11	13	4		6	8	8		6	7	7	5	7	35	10	23	27	4	8		4		15	5	254
	Wm. A. Graham, N. C.											12				13												12		5			42
1857.	James Buchanan, Pa.	9	4	4		3	3	10	11	13		12	6					7	9		7		10		27		8	12	4		13		174
Pres.	John C. Fremont, Cal.				6						4			8		13	6			5		35		23		4				5		5	114
	Millard Fillmore, N. Y.														8																		8
	J. C. Breckinridge, Ky.	9	4	4		3	3	10	11	13		12	6					7	9		7		10		27		8	12	4		13		174
V. Pres.	William M. Dayton, N. J.				6						4			8		13	6			5		35		23		4				5		5	114
	A. J. Donelson, Tenn.														8																		8

RECAPITULATION AND REMARKS.

1st Term, 1789. Electors 73, and 69 votes for G. Washington. J. Adams had 34; John Jay (N. J. 5, Del. 3, Va. 1) 9; R. H. Harrison (Md. 6) 6; J. Rutledge (S. C. 6) 6; J. Hancock (Pa. 2, Va. 1, S. C 1) 4; G. Clinton (Va. 3) 3; S. Huntington (Ct. 2) 2; John Milton (Ga. 2) 2; J. Armstrong (Ga. 1) 1; Ed. Telfair (Ga. 1) 1; B. Lincoln (Ga. 1) 1:—total 69. Rhode Island, New York, and North Carolina did not assent to the Constitution in season to vote for President in 1789. These votes would have made 91 electoral votes. Two votes of Maryland and two of Virginia were not given.

2d, 1793. Electors 135. 132 votes for G. Washington, and 3 (Md. 2, Vt. 1) vacancies. J. Adams received 77 votes; G. Clinton 50; T. Jefferson (Ky. 4) 4; A. Burr (S. C. 1) 1:—total, 132.

3d, 1797. Electors 138. J. Adams received 71 votes; T. Jefferson 68; T. Pinckney 59; A. Burr 30; S. Adams (Va. 15) 15; Ol. Ellsworth (N. H. 6, Mass. 1, R. I. 4) 11; G. Clinton (Va. 3, Ga. 4) 7; John Jay (Ct. 5) 5; James Iredell (N. C. 3) 3; G. Washington (Va. 1, N. C. 1) 2; J. Henry (Md. 2) 2; S. Johnson (Mass. 2) 2; Charles C. Pinckney (N. C. 1) 1.

4th, 1801. Electors 138. T. Jefferson received 73 votes; A. Burr 73; J. Adams 65; Ch. C. Pinckney 64; John Jay (R. I. 1) 1. The election was carried to the House of Representatives, and Mr. Jefferson was, on the 36th ballot, chosen President by the votes of Vt., N. Y., N. J., Pa., Md., Va., N. C., Ga., Tenn., and Ky.; and Mr. Burr, Vice President. Two States (Del. and S. C.) threw a blank vote. After this, the Constitution was altered, so as to require the President and Vice-President to be separately voted for.

5th, 1805. For a full view of the votes, see Table.

6th, 1809. For *President;* J. Madison 122 votes; C. C. Pinckney 47; G. Clinton (N. Y. 6) 6; 1 vacancy (Ky.):—total 176. For *Vice-President;* G. Clinton 113 votes; Rufus King 47; J. Langdon (Vt. 6, Ohio 3) 9; J. Madison (N. Y. 3) 3; J. Monroe (N. Y. 3) 3; 1 vacancy (Ky.):—total 176.

7th, 1813. See Table. One vacancy in Ohio.

8th, 1817. For *President;* J. Monroe 183 votes; Rufus King 34; 4 vacancies (Del. 1, Md. 3) 4:—total 221. For *Vice-President;* Daniel D. Tompkins 183 votes; John E. Howard (Mass. 22) 22; James Ross (Ct. 5) 5; J. Marshall (Ct. 5) 5; R. G. Harper (Del. 3) 3; 4 vacancies (Del. 1, Md. 3):—total 221.

9th, 1821. For *President;* J. Monroe 231; J. Q. Adams (N. H. 1) 1:—total 232. For *Vice President;* D. D. Tompkins 218; R. Stockton (Mass. 8) 8; D. Rodney (Del. 4) 4; R. Rush (N. H. 1) 1; R. G. Harper (Md. 1) 1:—total 232.

10th, 1825. For *President;* A. Jackson 99 votes; J. Q. Adams 84; Wm. H. Crawford 41; Henry Clay 37:—total 261. Mr. Adams was elected by the House of Representatives by a vote of thirteen States. See Table. For *Vice-President;* J. C. Calhoun 182; N. Sanford 30; N. Macon (Va. 24) 24; A. Jackson (N. H. 1, Ct. 8, Md. 1, Mo. 3) 13; M. Van Buren (Ga. 9) 9; Henry Clay (Del. 2) 2; 1 vacancy (R. I.):—total 261.

11th, 1829. See Table.

12th, 1833. For *President;* A. Jackson 219 votes; Henry Clay 49; J. Floyd (S. C. 11) 11; W. Wirt (Vt. 7) 7; 2 vacancies (Md.):—total 288. For *Vice-President;* M. Van Buren 189; John Sergeant 49; Wm. Wilkins (Pa. 30) 30; Henry Lee (S. C. 11) 11; Amos Ellmaker (Vt. 7) 7:—total 286.

13th, 1837. For *President;* M. Van Buren 170; Wm. H. Harrison 73; Hugh L. White (Ga. 11, Tenn. 15) 26; Daniel Webster (Mass. 14) 14; W. P. Mangum (S. C. 11) 11:—total 294. For *Vice-President;* R. M. Johnson 147; Francis Granger 77; John Tyler (Md. 10, S. C. 11, Ga. 11, Tenn. 15) 47; Wm. Smith (Va. 23) 23:—total 294. Mr. Johnson was chosen Vice-President by the Senate.

14th, 1841. For *President;* W. H. Harrison 234; M. Van Buren 60:—total 294. For *Vice-President;* John Tyler 234; R. M. Johnson 48; L. W. Tazewell (S. C. 11) 11; J. K. Polk (Va. 1) 1:—total 294.

15th, 1845.
16th, 1849.
17th, 1853.
18th, 1857. } For a full view of votes see Table.

2. *Popular Vote at each Presidental Election since and including* 1824.

States.	1824.*				1828.		1832.	
	Adams.	Jackson.	Crawford.	Clay.	Jackson.	Adams.	Jackson.	Clay.
Alabama,	2,416	9,443	1,680	67	17,138	1,938	no op. to	Jackson.
Connecticut,	7,587		1,978		4,448	13 829	11,269	17,755
Delaware,	By Legislature.				4,349	4,769	4,110	4,276
Georgia,	By Legislature.				18,709	None.	20,750	None.
Illinois,	1,542	1,901	219	1,047	6,763	1,581	14,147	5,429
Indiana,	3,095	7,343		5,315	22,287	17,052	31,552	15,472
Kentucky,		6,453		16,782	39 084	31,172	36,247	43,396
Louisiana,	By Legislature.				4 605	4,097	4,049	2,528
Maine,	6,870	2,330			13,927	20,773	33,291	27,204
Maryland,	14,632	14,523	3,646	695	24,578	25,759	19,156	19,160
Massachusetts,	30,687		6,616		6,019	29,836	14,545	33,003
Mississippi,	1,694	3,234	119		6,763	1,581	5,919	None.
Missouri,	311	987		1,401	8,232	3,422	5,192	majority
New Hampshire,	4,107	643			20,692	24,076	25 486	19,010
New Jersey,	9,110	10,985	1,196		21,950	23,758	23,856	23 393
New York,	By Legislature.				140,763	135,413	168,497	154 896
North Carolina,		20,415	15,621		37,857	13,918	24,862	4,563
Ohio,	12,280	18,457		19,255	67,597	63 396	81,246	76,539
Pennsylvania,	5,440	36,100	4,206	1,609	101,652	50,848	90,983	66 716
Rhode Island,	2,145		200		821	2,754	2,126	2,810
South Carolina,	By Legislature.							
Tennessee,	216	20,197	312		44,090	2,240	28,740	1.436
Vermont,	By Legislature.				8,205	24,784	7,870	11,152
Virginia,	3,189	2,861	8,489	416	26,752	12,101	33,609	11,451
Total,	105,321	152,899	47,265	47,087	650,028 512,158	512,158	687,502 550,189	550,189
Majority,					137,870		137,313	

States.	1836.		1840.			1844.		
	Van Buren.	Others.	Harrison.	Van Buren.	Birney.	Polk.	Clay.	Birney.
Alabama,	19,068	15,637	28,471	33,991		36,223	24 850	
Arkansas,	2,400	1,238	4,363	6,049		9,546	5,504	
Connecticut,	19,234	18,466	31,601	25,296	174	29,841	32,842	1,943
Delaware,	4,155	4.738	5,967	4,884		5,969	6,257	
Georgia,	22,126	24,930	40,264	31,933		44,155	42,106	
Illinois,	18,097	14,983	45,537	47,476	149	58,515	45,612	3,579
Indiana,	32,480	41,281	65,308	51,695		70,181	67,867	2,106
Kentucky,	33,435	36,955	58,489	32,616		51,980	61,262	
Louisiana,	3,653	3,383	11,297	7,617		13,477	12,818	
Maine,	22,300	15,239	46,612	46,201	194	45,719	34,378	4,836
Maryland,	22,167	25 852	33,528	28,752		33,676	35,984	
Massachusetts,	33,501	41,093	72,874	51 948	1,621	52,985	66,872	10,830
Michigan,	7,360	4,000	22,907	21,098	321	27,703	24,223	3,632
Mississippi,	9,979	9,688	19,518	16,995		25,188	19,193	
Missouri,	10,995	8,337	22,972	29,760		41,369	31 251	
New Hampshire,	18,722	6,228	26,434	32,670	126	27,150	17,866	4,161
New Jersey,	26,347	26 892	33 262	31,034	69	37,495	38,318	131
New York,	166,815	138,543	225,812	212,519	2,798	237,588	232,473	15,812
North Carolina,	26,910	23,626	46,676	34,218		39,287	43,232	
Ohio,	96.948	105,405	148,157	124,782	903	149,061	155,113	8,050
Pennsylvania,	91,475	87,111	144,019	143,676	343	167,535	161,203	3,126
Rhode Island,	2,964	2.710	5,278	3,301	42	4,848	7,323	107
South Carolina,	By Legislature.							
Tennessee,	26,120	35,962	60,391	48 289		59,915	60,039	
Vermont,	14 037	20,991	32,445	18,009	319	18,041	26,770	3,957
Virginia,	30,261	23,368	42,501	43,893		49,417	43,677	
Total,	762,149 736,736	736,736	1,274,783 1,128,702	1,128,702	7,609	1,335,884 1,297,033	1,297,033	62,270
Majority,	25,413		146,081			38,801		

* The vote for 1824 is taken from the New York Herald of September 24, 1856.

States.	1848.			1852.			1856.		
	Taylor.	Cass.	Van Buren.	Pierce.	Scott.	Hale.	Buchanan.	Fremont.	Fillmore.
Alabama	30,482	31,363		26,881	15,038		46,817		28,557
Arkansas	7,588	9,300		12,173	7,401		21,908		10,816
Cal.				39,665	34,971	100	42,460	16,721	28,327
Conn.	30,314	27,046	5,005	33,249	30,359	3,160	34,995	42,715	2,615
Del.	6,440	5,910	80	6,318	6,293	62	8,103	306	6,175
Florida,	4,539	3,238		4,318	2,875		6,368		4,843
Georgia,	47,693	44,736		34,705	16,660		56,617		42,372
Illinois,	53,215	56,629	15,804	80,597	64,934	9,966	104,279	96,280	37,451
Indiana,	69,907	74,745	8,100	95,299	80,901	6,934	118 672	94,816	23,386
Iowa,	10,557	12,051	1,126	8,624	7,444	777	36,241	44,127	9,444
Ky.	67,141	49,720		53,806	57,068	265	72,917	369	65 822
La.	18,273	15,380		18,647	17,255		22,169		20,709
Maine,	35,273	40,195	12,157	41,609	32,543	8,030	38,035	65,514	3,233
Md.	37,702	34,528	125	40,022	35,077	54	39,115	281	47,462
Mass.	61,072	35,284	38,133	46.880	56,063	29,993	39,240	108,190	19,626
Mich.	23,940	30,687	10,389	41,842	33,860	7,237	52,139	71,762	1,560
Miss.	25,921	26,555		26,876	17,548		35,665		24,490
Mo.	32 671	40,077		36,642	28,944		58,164		48,524
N. H.	14,781	27,763	7,560	29,997	16,147	6,695	32,567	38,158	414
N. J.	40,009	36,880	849	44,305	38,556	350	46,943	28,351	24,115
N. Y.	218,551	114,592	120,519	262,083	234,882	25,329	195,878	274,705	124,604
N. C.	43,519	34,869	85	39,744	39,058	59	48,246		36,886
Ohio,	138,356	154,783	35,494	169,220	152,526	31,682	170,874	187,497	28,125
Pa.	186,113	172,661	11,262	198,568	179,122	8,524	230,154	147,350	82,178
R. I.	6,689	3,600	703	8,735	7,626	644	6,680	11,467	1,675
S. C.	By	Legislat	ure.						
Tenn.	64,705	58,419		57,018	58,898		73,638		66,178
Tex.	3,777	8,801		13,552	4,995		28,575		15,244
Vt.	23,122	10,948	13,857	13,044	22,173	8,621	10,577	39,561	511
Va.	45,124	46,586	9	72,413	57,132		89,975	291	60,039
Wisc.	13,747	15,001	10,418	33,658	22,240	8,814	52,867	66,092	579
Total,	1,362,031 1,222,455	1,222,455	291,678	1,590,490 1,378,589	1,378,589	157,296	1,850,960	1,334,553	885,960
Majority,	139,576			211,901					

3. *Number of Electoral Votes to which each State has been entitled at each Presidential Election since* 1789.

States.	1. 1789.	2. 1792.	3. 1796.	4. 1800.	5. 1804.	6. 1808.	7. 1812.	8. 1816.	9. 1820.	10. 1824.	11. 1828.	12. 1832.	13. 1836.	14. 1840.	15. 1844.	16. 1848.	17. 1852.	18. 1856.	19. 1860.
Alabama,									3	5	5	7	7	7	9	9	9	9	9
Arkansas,													3	3	3	3	4	4	4
California,																	4	4	4
Connecticut,	7	9	9	9	9	9	9	9	9	8	8	8	8	8	6	6	6	6	6
Delaware,	3	3	3	3	3	3	4	4	4	3	3	3	3	3	3	3	3	3	3
Florida,																3	3	3	3
Georgia,	5	4	4	4	6	6	8	8	8	9	9	11	11	11	10	10	10	10	10
Illinois,									3	3	3	5	5	5	9	9	11	11	11
Indiana,								3	3	5	5	9	9	9	12	12	13	13	13
Iowa,																4	4	4	4
Kentucky,		4	4	4	8	8	12	12	12	14	14	15	15	15	12	12	12	12	12
Louisiana,							3	3	3	5	5	5	5	5	6	6	6	6	6
Maine,									9	9	9	10	10	10	9	9	8	8	8
Maryland,	8	10	10	10	11	11	11	11	11	11	11	10	10	10	8	8	8	8	8
Massachusetts,	10	16	16	16	19	19	22	22	15	15	15	14	14	14	12	12	13	13	13
Michigan,													3	3	5	5	6	6	6
Minnesota,																			4
Mississippi,									3	3	3	4	4	4	6	6	7	7	7
Missouri,									3	3	3	4	4	4	7	7	9	9	9
New Hampshire,	5	6	6	6	7	7	8	8	8	8	8	7	7	7	6	6	5	5	5
New Jersey,	6	7	7	7	8	8	8	8	8	8	8	8	8	8	7	7	7	7	7
New York,	8	12	12	12	19	19	29	29	29	36	36	42	42	42	36	36	35	35	35
North Carolina,	7	12	12	12	14	14	15	15	15	15	15	15	15	15	11	11	10	10	10

States.	1. 1789.	2. 1792.	3. 1796.	4. 1800.	5. 1804.	6. 1808.	7. 1812.	8. 1816.	9. 1820.	10. 1824.	11. 1828.	12. 1832.	13. 1836.	14. 1840.	15. 1844.	16. 1848.	17. 1852.	18. 1856.	19. 1860.
Ohio,					3	3	8	8	8	16	16	21	21	21	23	23	23	23	23
Oregon,																			3
Pennsylvania,	10	15	15	15	20	20	25	25	25	28	28	30	30	30	26	26	27	27	27
Rhode Island,	3	4	4	4	4	4	4	4	4	4	4	4	4	4	4	4	4	4	4
South Carolina,	7	8	8	8	10	10	11	11	11	11	11	11	11	11	9	9	8	8	8
Tennessee,			3	3	5	5	8	8	8	11	11	15	15	15	13	13	12	12	12
Texas,																4	4	4	4
Vermont,		4	4	4	6	6	8	8	8	7	7	7	7	7	6	6	5	5	5
Virginia,	12	21	21	21	24	24	25	25	25	24	24	23	23	23	17	17	15	15	15
Wisconsin,																4	5	5	5
No. of States,	*13	15	16	16	17	17	18	19	23	24	24	24	26	26	26	30	31	31	33
Whole No.	91	135	138	138	176	176	218	221	232	261	261	288	294	294	275	290	296	296	303

4. *Apportionment of Federal Representatives, and Ratio of Representation by the Constitution and at each Census.*

States.	Date of Admission into the Union.	No. of Rep. to which entitled till next Apportionment.	Representatives to which each State is entitled by Constitution, 1789.	1st Census, from March 3, 1793.	2d Census, from March 3, 1803.	3d Census, from March 3, 1813.	4th Census, from March 3, 1823.	5th Census, from March 3, 1833.	6th Census, from March 3, 1843.	7th Census, from March 3, 1853.
Ratio of	*Representation,*		30,000	33,000	33,000	35,000	40,000	47,700	70,680	93,423
Alabama,	Dec. 14, 1819	1					3	5	7	7
Arkansas,	June 15, 1836	1							1	2
California,	Sept. 9, 1850	2								2
Connecticut,			5	7	7	7	6	6	4	4
Delaware,			1	1	1	2	1	1	1	1
Florida,	Mar. 3, 1845	1								1
Georgia,			3	2	4	6	7	9	8	8
Illinois,	Dec. 3, 1818	1					1	3	7	9
Indiana,	Dec. 11, 1816						3	7	10	11
Iowa,	Dec. 28, 1846	1								2
Kentucky,	June 1, 1792	2		2	6	10	12	13	10	10
Louisiana,	April 8, 1812	1					3	3	4	4
Maine,	Mar. 15, 1820	7					7	8	7	6
Maryland,			6	8	9	9	9	8	6	6
Mass.			8	14	17	20	13	12	10	11
Michigan,	Jan. 26, 1837	1							3	4
Minnesota,	May 11, 1858	2								2
Mississippi,	Dec. 10, 1817	1					1	2	4	5
Missouri,	Aug. 10, 1821	1					1	2	5	7
New Hamp.			3	4	5	6	6	5	4	3
New Jersey,			4	5	6	6	6	6	5	5
New York,			6	10	17	27	34	40	34	33
N. Carolina,			5	10	12	13	13	13	9	8
Ohio,	Nov. 29, 1802	1				6	14	19	21	21
Oregon,	Feb. 14, 1859	1								1
Pennsyl.			8	13	18	23	26	28	24	25
R. Island,			1	2	2	2	2	2	2	2
S. Carolina,			5	6	8	9	9	9	7	6
Tennessee,	June 1, 1796	1			3	6	9	13	11	10
Texas,	Dec. 29, 1845	2								2
Vermont,	Mar. 4, 1791	2		2	4	6	5	5	4	3
Virginia,			10	19	22	23	22	21	15	13
Wisconsin,	May 29, 1848	3 from 4th March 1849.								3
Whole No.			65	105	141	181	213	240	223	234

* New York, Rhode Island, and North Carolina had not then ratified the Constitution; so that properly there were but 10 States, and 73 Electoral Votes.

XVII. SOME OF THE COLLEGES AND PROFESSIONAL

	Name.	Place.		President.	Founded.
1	Bowdoin,	Brunswick,	Me.	Leonard Woods, D. D.	1792
2	Waterville,*	Waterville,	"	James T. Champlin,	1820
3	Dartmouth,	Hanover,	N. H.	Nathan Lord, D. D.	1769
4	University of Vermont,	Burlington,	Vt.	Rev. Calvin Pease, D. D.	1791
5	Middlebury,	Middlebury,	"	Benjamin Labaree, D. D.	1800
6	Norwich University,†	Norwich,	"	Rev. Edward Bourns, LL. D.	1834
7	Harvard University,	Cambridge,	Mass.	James Walker, D.D., LL. D.*	1636
8	Williams,	Williamstown,	"	Rev. Mark Hopkins, D. D.	1793
9	Amherst,	Amherst,	"	Rev. Wm. A. Stearns, D. D.	1821
10	Holy Cross,§	Worcester,	"	Peter J. Blenkinsop,	1843
11	Tufts College,	Medford,	"	Rev. Hosea Ballou, 2d, D. D.	1854
12	Brown University,*	Providence,	R. I.	Rev. Barnas Sears, D. D.	1764
13	Yale,	New Haven,	Conn.	T. D. Woolsey, D.D., LL. D.	1700
14	Trinity,†	Hartford,	"	Rev. Daniel R. Goodwin, D. D.	1823
15	Wesleyan University, ‡	Middletown,	"	Rev. Joseph Cummings, D. D.	1831
16	Columbia,†	New York,	N. Y.	Charles King, LL. D.	1754
17	Union,	Schenectady,	"	Eliphalet Nott, D. D., LL.D.	1795
18	Hamilton,	Clinton,	"	Rev. Samuel W. Fisher, D.D.	1812
19	Madison University,*	Hamilton,	"	Stephen W. Taylor, LL. D.	1846
20	Hobart Free College,†	Geneva,	"	Rev. A. Jackson, D. D.	1824
21	University of City of N. Y.	New York,	"	Isaac Ferris, LL.D., *Chanc'r*,	1831
22	University of Rochester,*	Rochester,	"	M. B. Anderson, LL.D.	1850
23	St. John's,§	Fordham,	"	Rev. Remigius Tellier, S J.	1840
24	College of New Jersey,	Princeton,	N. J.	John Maclean, D. D., LL.D.	1746
25	Rutgers,	New Brunswick,	"	Theo. Frelinghuysen, LL. D.	1770
26	Burlington,†	Burlington,	"		1846
27	University of Pennsylvania,	Philadelphia,	Penn.	Henry Vethake, LL.D., *Prov.*	1749
28	Dickinson,‡	Carlisle,	"	Charles Collins, D. D.	1783
29	Jefferson,	Canonsburg,	"	Joseph Alden, D. D., LL. D.	1802
30	Washington,	Washington,	"	John W. Scott, D. D.	1806
31	Allegheny,‡	Meadville,	"	John Barker, D. D.	1817
32	Pennsylvania,	Gettysburg,	"	H. L. Baugher, D. D.	1832
33	Lafayette,	Easton,	"	D. V. McLean, D. D.	1832
34	Franklin and Marshall,	Lancaster,	"	Rev. E. G. Gerhart, A. M.	1836
35	University at Lewisburg,*	Lewisburg,	"	Rev. Justin R. Loomis, P. D.	1847
36	Polytechnic,	Philadelphia,	"	A. L. Kennedy, M.D., *P.Fac.*	1853
37	Delaware,	Newark,	Del.	E. J. Newlin,	1833
38	St. Mary's,§	Wilmington,	"	Rev. P. Reilly,	1847
39	St. John's,	Annapolis.	Md.	C. K. Nelson,	1784
40	St. Charles's,§	Ellicott's Mills,	"	Rev. O. L. Jenkins, A. M.	1848
41	Mount St. Mary's,§	Emmetsburg,	"	John McCaffrey, A. M.	1830
42	St. James's,†	Washington Co.	"	Rev. John B. Kerfoot, D. D.	1842
43	Washington,	Chestertown,	"	E.F.Chambers, *Pres.of Trus.*	1783
44	Georgetown,§	Georgetown,	D. C.	Rev. John Early,	1792
45	Columbian,*	Washington,	"	Rev. J. G. Binney, D. D.	1821
46	William and Mary,†	Williamsburg,	Va.	Benjamin S. Ewell,	1692
47	Hampden-Sidney,	Prince Ed. Co.	"	Rev. J. M. P. Atkinson, D. D.	1789
48	Washington,	Lexington,	"	George Junkin, D. D.	1781
49	University of Virginia,	Charlottesville,	"	S. Maupin, M. D., *Ch. of Fac.*	1819
50	Randolph-Macon,‡	Boydon,	"	William A. Smith, D. D.	1832
51	Emory and Henry,‡	Washington Co.	"	Rev. Ephraim E. Wiley,	1838
52	Rector,*	Taylor Co.,	"	Charles Wheeler, A. M.	1839
53	Bethany College,	Bethany,	"	Alexander Campbell, A. M.	1841
54	Richmond,*	Richmond,	"	Rev. Robert Ryland, A. M.	1840
55	Virginia Military Institute,	Lexington,	"	Col. F.H. Smith, A.M., *Sup't*,	1839
56	University of N. Carolina,	Chapel Hill,	N. C.	Hon. David L. Swain, LL. D.	1789
57	Davidson,	Mecklenburg Co.	"	Rev. Drury Lacy, D. D.	1840
58	Wake Forest,*	Forestville,	"	John B. White, A. M.	1838
59	Charleston,	Charleston,	S. C.	N. R. Middleton,	1785
60	South Carolina,	Columbia,	"	A. B. Longstreet, D. D.	1801
61	Franklin,	Athens,	Ga.	Alonzo Church, D. D.	1785
62	Oglethorpe,	Milledgeville,	"	Samuel K. Talmage, D. D.	1836
63	Emory,‡	Oxford,	"	James R. Thomas, D. D.	1837
64	Mercer University,*	Penfield,	"	N. M. Crawford, D. D.	1838
65	Wesleyan Female,	Macon,	"	Rev. O. L. Smith, D. D.	1839
66	University of Alabama,	Tuscaloosa,	Ala.	Landon C. Garland, LL. D.	1831
67	Florence Wesleyan,‡	Florence,	"	R. H. Rivers, D. D.	1830
68	Spring Hill,§	Spring Hill,	"	Rev. F. Gautrelet, S. J.	1830
69	Howard,*	Marion,	"	Henry Talbird, D. D.	1848
70	Madison,‡	Sharon,	Miss.	T. C. Thornton, D. D.	
71	University of Mississippi,	Oxford,	"	Rev. F. A. P. Barnard, LL. D.	1848
72	Mississippi College,*	Clinton,	"	J. N. Urner, A. M.	1831
73	Semple Broaddus,*	Centre Hill,	"	Rev. William C. Crane, A. M.	1856
74	University of Louisiana,	New Orleans,	La.	C. W. Sears,	1849

* Dr. Walker has resigned.

	Instr'ors.	No. of Alumni.	No. Ministers.	Students.	Volumes in Libraries.	Commencement.
1	11	1,284	243	209	27,045	First Wednesday in August.
2	6	380	116	66	10,000	Second Wednesday in August.
3	16	3,068	779	304	33,699	Last Thursday in July.
4	7	659	141	104	13,000	First Wednesday in August.
5	6	981	425	85	9,000	Second Wednesday in August.
6	4	8		80	1,650	Second Thursday in August.
7	24	6,876	1,561	409	123,400	Third Wednesday in July.
8	9	1,602	563	224	18,355	First Wednesday in August.
9	14	1,288	637	235	24,700	Second Thursday in August.
10	8	100		75	6,600	Near the middle of July.
11	5	12	4	52	6,500	Second Wednesday in July.
12	10	1,970	520	169	34,000	First Wednesday in September.
13	21	6,810	1,721	502	67,000	Last Thursday in July.
14	9	494	180	56	13,500	Thursday before 4th July.
15	8	603	206	148	13,000	Fourth Wednesday in June.
16	12	1,400		173	14,000	Last week in June.
17	15	3,578	1,200	326	15,500	Thurs. after fourth Wednes. in July.
18	9	1,232	369	134	12,500	Third Thursday in July.
19	9	391	280	145	7,457	Third Wednesday in August.
20	7	260	50	80	13,100	Last Wednesday in June.
21	16	510	150	138	4,300	Wednesday preceding 4th of July.
22	8	114	35	165	5,200	Second Wednesday in July.
23	14	172		48	14,972	July 15th.
24	17	3,656	730	300	21,400	Wedn. before last Wednesday in June.
25	8	619	241	116	12,000	First Wednesday in July.
26	29			118	1,200	September 29th.
27	12	1,269		129	5,100	July 3d.
28	8	816	211	139	21,138	Second Thursday in July.
29	10	1,575	758	215	10,000	First Wednesday in August.
30	6	730	260	103	3,900	Third Wednesday in September.
31	6	299	74	104	9,600	Last Wednesday in June.
32	7	253	155	87	9,000	Third Thursday in September.
33	6	200	55	100	4,500	Last Wednesday in July.
34	6	249	105	90	10,000	Last Wednesday in July.
35	4	67	26	54	4,000	Last Wednesday in July.
36	6	7		34		Last Friday in June.
37	6	106	29	50	10,000	First Wednesday in July.
38	7	4	10		5,300	Last Thursday in June.
39	6	384	12	115	8,000	First Wednesday in August.
40	8	146	10	104	450	Middle of July.
41	24	137		126	4,000	Last Wednesday in June.
42	14	67	9	52	9,500	Second Wednesday in July.
43	5			70	1,200	August 20th.
44	17	308	14	215	26,000	Middle of July.
45	8	308	175	66	7,600	Last Wednesday in June.
46	6	3,000		64	9,000	July 4th.
47	5	361	83	128	7,000	Second Thursday in June.
48	8	893	117	75	6.200	Beginning of July.
49	14	148		417	30,000	June 20th, unless it be Sunday.
50	6	255	60	130	8,000	Fourth Thursday in June.
51	5	103	11	54	8,470	Second Wednesday in June.
52	3			50	2,500	Last Wednesday in September.
53	6	80	3	141	3,500	July 4th.
54	6	43	19	87	2,125	July 1st.
55	13	288	8	150	4,000	July 4th.
56	15	1.511	90	450	21,000	First Thursday in June.
57	6	206	45	113	5,800	Thursday after 2d Monday in July.
58	5	42	14	76	5,000	Second Thursday in June.
59	6	124		40	6,500	Last Tuesday in March.
60	8	3,000	3	202	24,000	First Monday in December.
61	10	800	90	113	18,250	First Wednesday in August.
62	4	231	50	97	4,500	Wednesday after 3d Monday in July.
63	6	282	45	126	1,700	Wednesday after 3d Monday in July.
64	8	152	26	89	7,500	Last Wednesday in July.
65	10	347		173	1,600	Wednesday after 2d Monday in July.
66	9	313	24	120	12,000	Thursday after 2d Monday in July.
67	5	140	7	112	2,000	First Wednesday in July.
68	20	225		30	7,000	The 15th of October.
69	6	53	16	83	3,000	Last Thursday in June.
70	4					
71	10	222	9	140	5,000	Wednesday after 1st Monday in July.
72	6	25	12	42	1,650	July 31st.
73	4			75		Last Wednesday in June.
74	7					July.

	Name.	Place.	President.	Founded.
75	Centenary,‡	Jackson, La.	Rev. John C. Miller, A. M.	1845
76	Washington,	Washington Co., "	E. T. Bard, A. M.	1795
77	University of Nashville,	Nashville, Tenn	J. B. Lindsley, D. D.	1806
78	Franklin,	Near Nashville, "	Tolbert Fanning, A. M.	1844
79	East Tennessee,	Knoxville, "	Rev. William D. Carnes,	1806
80	Cumberland University,	Lebanon, "	Rev. Thos. C. Anderson, D.D.	1844
81	Jackson,	Columbia, "	B. F. Mitchell, A. M.	1833
82	Union,*	Murfreesboro', "	Joseph H. Eaton, LL. D.	1848
83	Greenville,	Greenville, "	Wm. B. Rankin,	1796
84	Transylvania,	Lexington, Ky.	M. C. Johnson, LL. D.,	1798
85	St. Joseph's,§	Bardstown, "	Thomas O'Neil, S. J.	1819
86	Centre,	Danville, "	John C. Young, D. D.	1823
87	Georgetown,*	Georgetown, "	Rev. D. R. Campbell, LL. D.	1829
88	Kentucky Military Institute,	Franklin Springs, "	Col. E. W. Morgan, *Sup.*	1846
89	Paducah,	Paducah, "	M. H. Fisk,	1852
90	Ohio University,	Athens, Ohio,	Solomon Howard, D. D.	1804
91	Miami University,	Oxford, "	Rev. J. W. Hall, D. D.	1824
92	Franklin,	New Athens, "	Rev. A. D. Clark,	1824
93	Western Reserve,	Hudson, "	Henry L. Hitchcock, D. D.	1826
94	Kenyon,†	Gambier, "	Lorin Andrews, LL. D.	1826
95	Denison,*	Granville, "	Jeremiah Hall, D. D.	1832
96	Marietta,	Marietta, "	Israel W. Andrews, D. D.	1835
97	Oberlin College,	Oberlin, "	Rev. Charles G. Finney,	1834
98	Ohio Wesleyan University,‡	Delaware, "	Edward Thomson, D.D., LL.D.	1854
99	Wittenberg,	Springfield, "	Samuel Sprechen, D. D.	1845
100	Urbana University,	Urbana, "	Milo G. Williams, *Dean*,	1850
101	Antioch,	Yellow Springs, "	Rev. Thomas Hill,	1853
102	Indiana State University,	Bloomington, Ind.	Wm. M. Daily, D. D., LL. D.	1830
103	Hanover College,	South Hanover, "	Rev. S. H. Thomson, *Act.*	1832
104	Wabash,	Crawfordsville, "	Rev. Charles White, D. D.	1833
105	Indiana Asbury University,‡	Greencastle, "	Rev. Cyrus Nutt, A. M., *Act.*	1837
106	Illinois,	Jacksonville, Ill.	J. M. Sturtevant, D. D.	1830
107	Shurtleff,*	Upper Alton, "	Rev. N. N. Wood, D. D.	1835
108	McKendree,‡	Lebanon, "	Rev. N. E. Cobleigh, A. M.	1835
109	Knox,	Galesburg, "	Jonathan Blanchard,	1837
110	St. Louis University,§	St. Louis, Mo.	Rev. F. Coosemans, S. J.	1832
111	St. Vincent's,	Cape Girardeau, "	Rev. R. Henesy,	1843
112	Masonic,	Lexington, "	W. T. Davis,	1844
113	University of State of Mo	Columbia, "	William W. Hudson, A. M.	1839
114	St. Charles,‡	St. Charles, "	John W. Robinson,	1837
115	University of Michigan,	Ann Arbor, Mich.	Henry P. Tappan, D D., LL.D.	1837
116	Wisconsin University,	Madison, Wisc.	Henry Barnard, *Chancellor*,	1851
117	Beloit,	Beloit, Rock Co., "	Rev. Aaron L. Chapin, D. D.	1847
118	Lawrence University,‡	Appleton, "	Russell Z. Mason, *pro tem.*	1849
119	Milwaukee Female,	Milwaukee, "	I. A. Lapham,	1852
120	Iowa State University,	Iowa City, Iowa,	Amos Dean, LL.D.	1855
121	Iowa Wesleyan University,‡	Mt. Pleasant, "	Lucien W. Berry, D. D.	1856
122	Santa Clara,§	Near San José, Cal.	Rev. Felix Cicaterri, S. J.	1855
123	Carroll,	Waukesha, Wisc.	John A. Savage, D. D.	1850
124	Racine,†	Racine, "	Roswell Park, D. D.	1852

The Colleges marked thus (*) are under the direction of the *Baptists;* thus (†), *Episcopalians;* thus (‡), *Methodists;* thus (§), *Catholics.* With respect to the Colleges which are *unmarked*, the prevailing religious influence of those that are in the New England States is *Congregationalism;* of most of the others, *Presbyterianism.*

By Instructors, in the above table, is meant those connected with the undergraduates; and by *students*, except the Roman Catholic institutions and a few of the Colleges in the Southern and Western States, is meant *undergraduates*, or members of the four collegiate classes; not including such as are pursuing a professional education, or such as are members of a preparatory department. Some of the Colleges above enumerated are not in full operation, and scarcely deserve a place in the table. The column of *Libraries* includes the number of volumes in the *College Libraries* and in the *Students' Libraries.*

The above table shows the condition of the Colleges near January, 1859. Returns have not been received from several of the Colleges to so late a date. Any one noticing errors or imperfections in the list is requested to send the necessary corrections to the editor.

	Instr'ors.	No. of Alumni.	No. of Ministers.	Students.	Volumes in Libraries.	Commencement.
75	9	169	9	98	5,200	Last Thursday in July.
76	3	116	38	22	1,800	Third Thursday in July.
77	8	445		104	9,668	Last Thursday in June.
78	6	51	2	106	3,500	July 4th.
79		169	15		8,000	First Wednesday in July.
80	11	95	37	165	4,000	Last Thursday in June.
81	5	86	11	84	4,400	St. John's Day (June 24th).
82	6	84	28	150	4,500	First Wednesday in July.
83	2			20	3,500	First Thursday in July.
84	8	610		25	14,000	Last Thursday in June.
85	16	185			7,100	Near 4th July.
86	5	452	114	180	5,600	Third Thursday in September.
87	8		105	157	7,500	Last Thursday in June.
88	9	132		154	3,000	Third Wednesday in June.
89	6			18	650	Last Thursday in June.
90	6	200	70	78	7,000	Second Wednesday before 4th July.
91	8	614	195	127	7,500	First Thursday in July.
92	4	230	130	85	2,000	Last Wednesday in September.
93	7	206	58	27	8,451	Second Thursday in July.
94	10	232	65	127	12,635	Last Thursday in June.
95	5	62	36	47	4,950	Last Thursday in June.
96	6	205	70	56	15,500	Thursday before 4th of July.
97	8	277	135	110	4,000	Fourth Wednesday in August.
98	8	139	28	147	10,361	Second Thursday in June.
99	6	33	12	46	6,000	Last Thursday in June.
100	8			21	3,500	June 19th.
101	12	22	2	98	4,200	Wednesday before 4th July.
102	6	212	30	115	2,200	Third Thursday in July.
103	8	223	126	73	5,400	First Thursday in August.
104	7	119	45	49	6,400	Second Wednesday in July.
105	6	170	46	266	12,000	Last Wednesday in June.
106	7	130	43	70	3,660	Last Thursday but one in June.
107	6	17	7	40	1,900	Fourth Thursday in June.
108	6	107	20	62	5,500	Third Thursday in June.
109	7	32	5	56	3,300	Fourth Thursday in June.
110	18	160	110	134	22,000	Near 4th of July.
111	10	85	7	3	5,500	Last Thursday in July.
112	3	19		28	1,200	Last Thursday in June.
113	10	139	10	102	3,500	July 4th.
114	6	25	3	50	1,000	Third Thursday in June.
115	14	248	2	267	10,000	Last Wednesday in June.
116	7	6		30	1,900	Fourth Wednesday in July.
117	9	32	4	52	4,000	Second Wednesday in July.
118	8	16	4	90	4,000	Last Wednesday in June.
119	4	20		36	700	Third Wednesday in July.
120	4				200	First Wednesday in July.
121	9	50				First Week in July.
122	16			153		Near the middle of July.
123	5	13		20	1,650	Third Wednesday in July.
124	5	36	2	24	1,700	Third Thursday in July.

Annual College Expenses.

Name.	Instruction.	Room-rent and other Coll. Exp.	Total College Charges.	Board.	Wood, Lights, and Washing.
Bowdoin,	$24.00	$22.00	$46.00	39 weeks, $58.50	$35.00
Dartmouth,	27.00	13.24	40.24	38 " 57.00	9.00
Harvard,	75.00	20.00	95.00	40 " 110-160	
Williams,	30.00	9.00	39.00	39 " 65.00	
Amherst,	30.00	15.00	45.00	40 " 60.00	17.00
Brown,	40.00	23.00	63.00	39 " 60.00	
Yale,	45.00	30.00	75.00	40 " 110-150	24-40
Wesleyan,	36.00	11.25	47.25	39 " 58.50	20.00
Hamilton,	26.00	14.00	40.00	38 or 39 w. 58.00	
New Jersey,	50.00	28.14	78.14	40 weeks, 60.00	28.00
Dickinson,	33.00	14.00	47.00	43 " 75.25	22.75
University of Virginia,	75.00	23.00	98.00	44 " 110.00	20.00
North Carolina Univ.,	50.00	10.00	60.00	40 " 140.00	29-40
Transylvania,	40.00	12.00	52.00	40 " 100.00	25.00
Western Reserve,	30.00	11.00	41.00	42 " 80.00	12.00
University of Miss.,	80.00*			per month, 10.00	
Kenyon College,	30.00	15.00	45.00	38 w. 38-100	20-27

* This includes fuel.

2. Theological Schools.

Name.	Place.	Denomination.	Commenced Operation.	No. Profess'rs.	Stud'ts near 1858-59.	Number educated.	Volumes in Library.
Bangor Theological Seminary,	Bangor, Me.	Congregation.,	1816	4	40	330	10,300
Meth. Gen. Bib. Institute,	Concord, N. H.	Methodist,	1847	3	40		2,000
Gilmanton Theol. Seminary,	Gilmanton, "	Congregation.,	1835	3	23	69	4,300
N. Hampton Theol. Seminary,	New Hampton, "	Baptist,	1825	2	36		2,000
Theological Seminary,	Andover, Mass.	Congregation.,	1807	5	110	1,006	21,259
Divinity School, Harv. Univ.,	Cambridge, "	Cong. Unit.,	1816	2	17	295	8,700
Theological Institution,	Newton, "	Baptist,	1825	4	33	201	5,500
Theol. Dep. Yale College,	New Haven, Conn.	Congregation.,	1822	5	21	670	
Theol. Inst. of Connecticut,	East Windsor, "	"	1834	3	17	151	5,000
Theol. Inst. Episc. Church,	New York, N. Y.	Prot. Episcop.,	1817	5	58	430	11,963
Union Theological Seminary,	" "	Presbyterian,	1836	5	106	211	18,000
Theol. Sem. of Auburn,	Auburn, "	"	1821	4	30	580	6,000
Hamilton Theol. Seminary,	Hamilton, "	Baptist,	1820	3	24	252	7,500
Rochester Theol. Seminary,	Rochester, "	"	1850	3	36	50	5,500
Hartwick Seminary,	Hartwick, "	Lutheran,	1816	2	5	52	1,250
Theol. Sem. Ass. Ref. Church,	Newburg, "	Ass. Ref. Ch.,	1836	1	11	143	3,200
Th. Sem. Dutch Ref. Church,	N. Brunswick, N. J	Dutch Ref.,	1784	3	50	179	7,000
Theol. Sem. Presbyt. Church,	Princeton, "	Presbyterian,	1812	5	153	1,626	11,000
Wittemburg Theol. Seminary,	Gettysburg, Pa.	Evang. Luth.,	1825	3	25	250	10,000
German Reformed,	Mercersburg, "	Germ. Ref. Ch.	1825	2	18	121	6,000
Western Theol. Seminary,	Alleghany T., "	Presbyterian,	1828	2	48	252	6,000
Theological School,	Canonsburg, "	Asso. Church,	1792	2	33	147	2,000
Theological Seminary,	Pittsburg, "	Asso. Ref.,	1828	3	35	85	1,500
Western Theological School,	Meadville, "	Cong. Unit.,	1844	4	17	60	8,000
Georgetown College,	Georgetown, D. C.	Rom. Catholic,	1816	2	18		
Theol. Dep. Lewisburg Univ.	Lewisburg, "	Baptist,	1856	1	10	12	
St. Mary's Seminary,	Baltimore, Md.	Rom. Catholic,	1791	6	27		10,000
Episc. Theol. School of Va.,	Fairfax Co., Va.	Prot. Episcop.,	1822	4	47	336	7,500
Union Theological Seminary,	Prince Ed. Co., "	Presbyterian,	1824	3	20	175	4,000
Virginia Baptist Seminary,	Richmond, "	Baptist,	1832	3	67		1,000
Theological Seminary,	Columbia, S. C.	Presbyterian,	1828	4	42	249	17,260
Theological Seminary,	Lexington, "	Lutheran,	1835	2	10	20	1,800
Furman Theological Seminary,	Fairfield Dist., "	Baptist,	1826	2	30	30	1,000
Theol. Sem. of Mercer Univ.,	Penfield, Ga.	"	1844	2	10	6	2,200
Howard Theol. Institution,	Marion, Ala.	"	1848	1	6		1,000
Western Bap. Theol. Institut.,	Georgetown, Ky.	"	1845	2	16	180	500
Danville Theol. Seminary,	Danville, "	Presbyterian.	1853	4	47	115	
Southwest Theol. Seminary,	Maryville, Tenn.	"	1821	2	24	90	6,000
Theol. School, Cumb. Univ.	Lebanon, "	Cumb. Presbyt.	1855	2	33		
Theol. Dep. St. Louis Univ.	St. Louis, Mo.	Rom. Catholic,	1829	4	14	86	4,000
Lane Seminary,	Cincinnati, Ohio,	Presbyterian,	1829	3	36	257	10,500
Theol. Dep. Kenyon College,	Gambier, "	Prot. Episcop.,	1827	3	22	85	6,000
Theol. Dep. West. Res. College,	Hudson, "	Presbyterian,	1830	3	14		79
Granville Theol. Department,	Granville, "	Baptist,	1832	2	8		500
Oberlin Theol. Department,	Oberlin, "	Congregation.,	1835	3	24	157	500
Theol. Sem. Ass. Ref. Church,	Oxford, "	Asso. Ref.,	1839	1	12	31	1,500
Wittenberg,	Springfield, "	W. Lutheran,	1845	1	6	49	
Bibl. Dep't Ohio Wesl. Univ.,	Delaware, "	Methodist,	1849	1	11		
New Albany Theol. Seminary,	Hanover, Ind.	Presbyterian,	1832	3	15	156	4,000
Alton Theological Seminary,	Upper Alton, Ill.	Baptist,	1835				
Nashotah Theol. Seminary,	Nashotah, Wisc.	Prot. Episcop.,	1841	8	49	46	3,000

3. Law Schools.

Name.	Place.	Founded.	Professors.	Students 1858-59.	Graduates.	Vols. in Library.
Dane Law School, H. Univ.	Cambridge, Mass.,	1817	3	146	966	14,500
Law School, Yale College,	New Haven, Conn.,	1820	2	33	114	2,200
University of Albany,	Albany, N. Y.,	1851	3	121	37	State Lib.
Law School, Col. College,	New York, N. Y.,	1859	3	30		2,000
University of Pennsylvania.	Philadelphia, Pa.,	1850	3	60	80	
William and Mary College,	Williamsburg, Va.,	1782	1			
Law School, Univ. of Va.,	Charlottesville, Va.,	1825	2	109	247	2,000
North Carolina University,	Chapel Hill, N. C.,	1845	2	23		
University of Louisiana,	New Orleans, La.		3			
Transylvania University,	Lexington, Ky.,		3			
University of Louisville,	Louisville, Ky.,		3			
Kentucky Military Inst.,	Franklin Springs,	1858	1	20		
Cumberland University,	Lebanon, Tenn.,	1847	3	188	79	500
Law School, Cincinn. Coll.,	Cincinnati, Ohio,	1833	3	85	512	3,000
Indiana State University,	Bloomington, Ind.,	1840	1	18	78	
Indiana Asbury University,	Greencastle, Ind.,	1853	1	10	40	
Maynard L. S. Hamil'n Col.	Clinton, N. Y.,	1853	1	9	36	500
N. Y. State & National L. S.	Poughkeepsie, N.Y.	1845	4	119		3,000
University of Mississippi,	Oxford, Miss.,	1854	1	28	25	1,000

4. Medical Schools.

Name.	Place.	Founded.	Prof.	Stu.	Graduates.	Lectures commence.
Maine Medical School,	Brunswick, Me.	1820	7	50	774	February.
N. H. Medical School,	Hanover, N.H.	1797	6	50	948	Thurs. after Com't.
Castleton Medical College,	Castleton, Vt.	1818	7	104	555	4th Thurs. in Aug.
Med. Dep Univ. Vt.,	Burlington, Vt.	1821	6	49	163	Last of February.
Vermont Medical College,	Woodstock, Vt.	1835	8	91	350	1st Th. in March.
Medical School, Harv. Univ.,	Boston, Mass.	1782	6	104	1,125	1st Wed. in Nov.
Berkshire Medical School,	Pittsfield, "	1823	5	103	473	1st Th. in Sept.
Medical Inst. Yale College,	N. Haven, Ct.	1813	6	34	695	September.
Coll. Phys. & Surg., N. Y.,	N. York, N.Y.	1807	6	219	852	1st Mon. in Nov.
Med. Inst. Geneva Coll.,	Geneva, "	1835	9	16	545	1st Wednes. in Oct.
Med. Faculty, Univ. N. Y.,	N. York, "	1831	9	300	1,715	3d Mon. in Oct.
Albany Medical College,	Albany, "	1839	8	114	58	1st Tues. in Oct.
Med. Dep. Univ. Penn.,	Philadel., Pa.	1765	9	463	7,100	Early in October.
Jefferson Medical College,	" "	1824	7	514	2,036	1st Mon. in Nov.
Med. Dep. Penn. College.	" "	1839	7	140	35	11th October.
Philadelphia Coll. of Med.,	" "		7	75	250	
Med. School, Univ. Md.,	Baltimore, Md.	1807	6	100	909	October 31st.
Washington Med. College,	" "	1827	6	25		1st Mon. in Nov.
Nat. Med. Col., Columb. Col.,	Wash'ton, D.C.	1821	8	17	86	4th Mon. in Oct.
Med. Dep Georgetown Coll.	" "	1851	6	32	10	4th Mon. in Oct.
Med. School, Univ. Va.,	Charlottesville,	1827	5	99	35	1st October.
Med. Dep. Hamp.-Sid. Coll.,	Richmond, Va.	1838	7	90	40	October 13.
Winchester Med. College,	Winchester, "		5			1st Mon. in Oct.
Med. Coll. State of S. C.,	Charleston, S.C.	1833	8	158		2d Mon. in Nov.
Med. College of Georgia,	Augusta, Ga.	1830	7	115	124	2d Mon. in Nov.
Med. Dep. Univ. Louisiana,	N. Orleans, La.	1835	8	222		3d Mon. in Nov.
Med. Dep. Univ. Nashville,	Nashville, Ten.	1850	8	436	669	1st Mon. in Oct.
Med. Dep. E. Tenn. Univ.,	Knoxville, "	1856	8			October.
Med. Dep. Transylv. Univ.,	Lexington, Ky.	1818			1,351	
Med. Dep. Univ. Louisville,	Louisville, "	1837			53	
Med. Dep West. Reserve Col.	Cleveland, Oh.	1844	6	160	631	1st Wed. in Nov.
Medical College of Ohio,	Cincinnati, "	1819	8	130	331	1st Mon. in Nov.
West. Coll Homœpath. Med.	Cleveland, "	1850	8	62	17	1st Mon. in Nov.
Starling Medical College,	Columbus, "	1847	8	124	53	1st Mon. in Nov.
Rush Medical College,	Chicago, Ill.	1842	6	70	16	1st Mon. in Nov.
University of Michigan,	Ann Arbor,	1850	7	143	305	October 1st.
Med. Dep. of St. Louis Univ.,	St. Louis, Mo.	1836	9	125		1st Mon. in Nov.
Med. Dep. of Missouri Univ.,	Columbia, "	1846	7	103	13	1st Mon. in Nov.
Med. Dep. State Univ.,	Keokuk, Iowa,	1849	6	80	64	1st Mon. in Nov.
Med. Dep. State Univ..	Madison, Wisc.	1856	6			

XVIII. SMITHSONIAN INSTITUTION. — November, 1859.

Members, *ex Officio.*

James Buchanan, *Pres. U. States,*
Lewis Cass, *Sec. of State,*
Howell Cobb, *Sec. of Treas.,*
John B. Floyd, *Sec. of War,*
Isaac Toucey, *Sec. of Navy,*
Joseph Holt, *P. M. General,*
Jeremiah S. Black, *Att'y-General,*
Roger B. Taney, *Chief Justice U. S.*
William D. Bishop, *Com. of Patents,*
J. G. Berret, *Mayor of Wash.*

Board of Regents.

J. C. Breckinridge, Vice-President U. States,
Roger B. Taney, Chief Justice United States,
J. G. Berret, Mayor of Washington,
James A. Pearce, U. S. Senator,
James M. Mason, " "
Stephen A. Douglas, " "
Wm. H. English, U. S. Representative,
Lucius J. Gartrell, U. S. Representative,
Benj. Stanton, " "
Gideon Hawley, N. Y., } Citizens,
George E. Badger, N. C., } Citizens,
Cornelius C. Felton, Mass., } Citizens,
A. Dallas Bache, } Members of Nat. Inst.
Joseph G. Totten, } Members of Nat. Inst.

Officers.

The President of the United States, *ex Officio Presiding Officer.*
The Vice-President of the United States, *ex Officio Second Presiding Officer.*
Roger B. Taney, *Chancellor.*
Joseph Henry, LL. D., *Secretary.*
Spencer F. Baird, *Assistant Secretary.*
W. W. Seaton, *Treasurer.*
Wm. J. Rhees, *Chief Clerk.*

Executive Committee.

A. Dallas Bache, Joseph G. Totten, James A. Pearce.

Surviving Honorary Members.

Benjamin Silliman, A. B. Longstreet, Jacob Thompson.

XIX. RELIGIOUS DENOMINATIONS IN THE UNITED STATES,

According to the Census of 1850.

Denominations.	No. of Churches.	Aggregate Accommodations.	Av'age Accommodat.	Total Value of Church Property.	Average Value of Property.
Baptist, . . .	8,791	3,130,878	356	$ 10,931,382	$1,244
Christian, . .	812	296,050	365	845,810	1,041
Congregational, .	1,674	795,177	475	7,973,962	4,763
Dutch Reformed,	324	181,986	561	4,096,730	12,644
Episcopal, . .	1,422	625,213	440	11,261,970	7,919
Free, . . .	361	108,605	300	252,255	698
Friends, . . .	714	282,823	396	1,709,867	2,395
*German Reformed,	327	156,932	479	965,880	2,953
Jewish, . . .	31	16,575	534	371,600	11,967
*Lutheran, . .	1,203	531,100	441	2,867,886	2,383
Mennonite, . .	110	29,900	272	94,245	856
Methodist, . .	12,467	4,209,333	337	14,636,671	1,174
Moravian, . .	331	112,185	338	443,347	1,339
Presbyterian, .	4,584	2,040,316	445	14,369,889	3,135
Roman Catholic, .	1,112	620,950	558	8,973,838	8,069
Swedenborgian, .	15	5,070	338	108,100	7,206
Tunker, . . .	52	35,075	674	46,025	885
Union, . . .	619	213,552	345	690,065	1,114
Unitarian, . .	243	137,367	565	3,268,122	13,449
Universalist, .	494	205,462	415	1,767,015	3,576
Minor Sects, . .	325	115,347	354	741,980	2,283
Total, . .	36,011	13,849,896	384	$ 86,416,639	$ 2,400

XX. *Table exhibiting the Seats of Government, the Times of the Election of State Officers, and the Meeting of the Legislatures, of the several States.*

State.	Seat of Government.	Time of Holding Elections.	Time of the Meeting of the Legislatures.
Alabama,	Montgomery,	1st Monday in August,	2d Monday in Nov., *bienn.*
Arkansas,	Little Rock,	1st Monday in August,	1st Monday in Nov., *bienn.*
California,	Sacramento,	Tu. after 1st Mon. in Sept.,	1st Monday in January.
Connecticut,	Hartford,	1st Monday in April,	1st Wednesday in May.
Delaware,	Dover,	2d Tuesday in November,	1st Tues. in Jan., *biennially.*
Florida,	Tallahassee,	1st Monday in October,	4th Monday in Nov., *bienn.*
Georgia,	Milledgeville,	1st Mon. in Octob., *bienn.*,	1st Monday in Nov., *ann.*
Illinois,	Springfield,	Tu. after 1st Mon. in Nov.,	2d Monday in Jan., *bienn.*
Indiana,	Indianapolis,	2d Tuesday in October,	Thurs. af. 1st Mon. in Jan., *bi.*
Iowa,	Des Moines,	2d Tuesday in October,	2d Monday in Jan., *bienn.*
Kentucky,	Frankfort,	1st Monday in August,	1st Monday in December.
Louisiana,	Baton Rouge,	1st Monday in November,	3d Monday in January.
Maine,	Augusta,	2d Monday in September,	1st Wednesday in January.
Maryland,	Annapolis,	1st Wednesday in Nov.,	1st Wednesday in Jan., *bien.*
Massachusetts,	Boston,	Tu. after 1st Mon. in Nov.,	1st Wednesday in January.
Michigan,	Lansing,	Tu. after 1st Mon. in Nov.	1st Wed. in Jan., *bienn.*
Minnesota,	St Paul.	2d Tuesday in October,	1st Monday in December.
Mississippi,	Jackson,	1st Monday in October,	1st Monday in Nov., *bienn.*
Missouri,	Jefferson City,	1st Monday in August,	Last Mon. in Dec., *bienn.*
N. Hampshire,	Concord,	2d Tuesday in March,	1st Wednesday in June.
New Jersey,	Trenton,	Tu. after 1st Mon. in Nov.,	2d Tuesday in January.
New York,	Albany,	Tu. after 1st Mon. in Nov.,	1st Tuesday in January.
N. Carolina,	Raleigh,	1st Thursday in August,	3d Monday in Nov., *bienn.*
Ohio,	Columbus,	2d Tuesday in October,	1st Monday in Jan., *bienn.*
Oregon,	Salem,	1st Monday in June,	2d Monday in Sept., *bienn.*
Pennsylvania,	Harrisburg,	2d Tuesday in October,	1st Tuesday in January.
Rhode Island,	{ Newport, Providence, }	1st Wednesday in April,	{ Last Tuesday in May. By adjourn. from Newport.
S. Carolina,	Columbia,	2d Monday in October,	4th Monday in November.
Tennessee,	Nashville,	1st Thursday in August,	1st Monday in Oct., *bienn.*
Texas,	Austin,	1st Monday in August,	December, *bienn.*
Vermont,	Montpelier,	1st Tuesday in September,	2d Thursday in October.
Virginia,	Richmond,	4th Thursday in May,	1st Monday in Dec., *bienn.*
Wisconsin,	Madison,	Tu. after 1st Mon. in Nov.,	2d Wednesday in January.

* The German Reformed and Lutheran denominations use the same building in many places.

XXI. GOVERNORS OF THE SEVERAL STATES AND TERRITORIES,

With their Salaries, Terms of Office, and the Expiration of their respective Terms; the Number of Senators and Representatives in the State Legislatures, with their respective Terms.

State.	Governor.	Salary.	Governor, Term years.	Term expires.	Senators.	Term years.	Representatives.	Term years.
Alabama,	Andrew B. Moore,	$4,000	2	Dec. 1861	33	4	100	2
Arkansas,	Elias N. Conway,	2,000*	4	Nov. 1860	25	4	75	2
California,	Milton S. Latham,	8,000	2	Jan. 1862	16	2	36	1
Connecticut,	Wm. A. Buckinghaln,	1,100	1	May 1860	21	1	232	1
Delaware,	William Burton,	1,333⅓	4	Jan. 1863	9	4	21	1
Florida,	Madison S. Perry,	1,500	4	Oct. 1861	19	4	40	1
Georgia,	Joseph E. Brown,	3,000	2	Nov. 1861	52	2	150	2
Illinois,	William H. Bissell,	1,500	4	Jan. 1861	25	4	75	2
Indiana,	Ashbel P. Willard,	1,500*	4	Jan. 1861	50	4	100	1
Iowa,	S. J. Kirkwood,	2,000	2	Jan. 1862	30	4	59	2
Kentucky,	Beriah Magoffin,	2,500	4	Sept. 1863	38	4	100	2
Louisiana,	Thomas O. Moore,	4,000	4	Jan. 1864	32	4	88	2
Maine,	Lot M. Morrill,	1,500	1	Jan. 1861	31	1	151	1
Maryland,	Thomas H. Hicks,	3,600*	4	Jan. 1862	22	4	74	2
Massachusetts,	Nathl. P. Banks,	3,500	1	Jan. 1861	40	1	240	1
Michigan,	Moses Wisner,	1,000	2	Jan. 1861	32	2	81	2
Minnesota,	Alexander Ramsay,	2,500	2	Jan. 1862	37	2	80	1
Mississippi,	John J. Pettus,	4,000	2	Nov. 1861	32	4	92	2
Missouri,	Robt. M. Stewart,	3,000*	4	Nov. 1860	18	4	49	2
N. Hampshire,	Ichabod Goodwin,	1,000	1	June 1860	12	1	332	1
New Jersey,	Charles S. Olden,	1,800†	3	Jan. 1863	21	3	60	1
New York,	Edwin D. Morgan,	4,000	2	Jan. 1861	32	2	128	1
N. Carolina,	John W. Ellis,	3,000*	2	Jan. 1861	50	2	120	2
Ohio,	William Dennison, Jr.,	1,800	2	Jan. 1862	35	2	100	2
Oregon,	John Whitaker,	1,500	4	1862	16	4	34	2
Pennsylvania,	William F. Packer,	4,000	3	Jan. 1861	33	3	100	1
Rhode Island,	Thomas G. Turner,	1,000	1	May 1860	32	1	72	1
S. Carolina,	William H. Gist,	3,800*	2	Dec. 1860	46	4	124	2
Tennessee,	Isham G. Harris,	3,000	2	Oct. 1861	25	2	75	2
Texas,	Samuel Houston,	3,000	2	Dec. 1861	21	4	66	2
Vermont,	Hiland Hall,	1,000	1	Oct. 1860	30	1	230	1
Virginia,	John Letcher,	5,000	4	Jan. 1864	50	4	152	2
Wisconsin,	Alex. W. Randall,	1,250	2	Jan. 1862	30	2	97	1
Kansas Ter.,	Samuel Medary,	2,500	4	1862	13	2	26	1
Nebraska Ter.	Samuel W. Black,	2,500	4	1863	13	2	26	1
N. Mexico T.,	Abraham Rencher,	3,000	4	1861	13	2	26	1
Utah Ter.,	Alfred Cummings,	2,500	4	1861	13	2	26	1
Washington T.	Richard D. Gholson,	3,000	4	1863	9	3	18	1

In all the States, except South Carolina, the Governor is voted for by the people; and if no one has a majority of all the votes, in the States in which such a majority is required, the Legislature elects to the office of Governor one of the candidates voted for by the people. See also the Individual States, and the Additions and Corrections at the end of the volume.

* With the use of a furnished house. † And fees.

XXII. COMPARATIVE VIEW OF

States.	Absolute Debt.	Contingent Debt.	Total Debt.	Annual Interest on Absolute Debt.
	$	$	$	$
Alabama,	5,098,000		5,098,000	257,000
Arkansas,	2,981,133		2,981,133	178,868
California,	3,900,000	143,485	4,043,485	273,000
Connecticut,	None.		None.	
Delaware,	None.		None.	
Florida,	158,000		158,000	11,060
Georgia,	2,604,750	750,000	3,354,750	162,590
Illinois,	11,138,454		11,138,454	668,000
Indiana,	7,357,074		7,357,074	316,726
Iowa,	128,010		128,010	10,000
Kentucky,	5,574,244		5,574,244	335,000
Louisiana,	4,379,091	6,322,551	10,701,642	300,000
Maine,	699,000	335,277	1,034,277	41,940
Maryland,	10,754,204	4,100,000	14,854,204	600,000
Massachusetts,	1,314,000	4,999,456	6,313,456	70,000
Michigan,	2,337,630		2,337,630	140,258
Minnesota,	250,000		250,000	20,000
Mississippi,	2,271,707	5,000,000	7,271,707	136,000
Missouri,	602,000	18,436,000	19,038,000	35,805
New Hampshire,	None.		None.	
New Jersey,	95,000		95,000	5,700
New York,	31,671,944	770,000	32,441,944	1,900,000
North Carolina,	7,181,923		7,181,923	430,000
Ohio,	17,131,219		17,131,219	1,006,986
Oregon,				
Pennsylvania,	39,268,111		39,268,111	1,958,218
Rhode Island,		396,311	386,311	
South Carolina,	3,192,743	3,000,000	6,192,743	209,388
Tennessee,	3,844,607	12,799,000	16,643,607	248,571
Texas,	None.		None.	
Vermont,	None.		None.	
Virginia,	29,106,659	3,898,500	33,005,159	1,705,000
Wisconsin,	100,000		100,000	7,000
Total, near Jan. 1, 1859,	193,139,503	60,940,580	254,080,083	11,072,110
Total, " " 1858,	194,528,345	57,121,638	251,649,983	11,063,667
Total, " " 1857,	187,292,039	57,919,220	245,211,259	10,628,871
Total, " " 1856,	182,030,283	56,872,259	238,902,542	10,006,812
Total, " " 1855,	192,026,298	44,767,851	236,794,149	9,866,995
Total, " " 1854,	191,671,391	30,133,112	221,804,503	9,949,841
Total, " " 1853,	184,303,865	31,863,921	216,167,786	9,291,334
Total, " " 1852,	169,076,638	33,481,124	202,557,762	8,696,888
Total, " " 1851,	170,535,238	31,006,386	201,541,624	8,455,351
Total, " " 1850,	169,549,334	38,756,218	209,305,552	8,577,646
Total, " " 1849,	170,749,453	40,502,979	211,252,432	8,684,035
Total, " " 1848,	169,776,030	35,932,008	205,708,038	8,521,671
Total, " " 1847,	165,129,900	51,781,654	216,911,554	9,072,939
Total, " " 1846,	179,635,022	44,388,805	224,023,827	9,930,052

These tables are believed to be accurate, being compiled almost exclusively from official reports made by the Treasurers and Auditors to the Legislatures of the several States, most of them near the 1st of January, 1859. The account of the State debts, in particular, is full, and may be depended upon; that of the several kinds of property owned by the States of course is more defective, — for the State archives seldom afford complete materials for accurate accounts of this sort, and the property is sometimes estimated at a nominal valuation, which is much above its market value. The editor

THE FINANCES OF THE STATES.

States.	Amount of School Fund.	Other Productive Property.	Other Property not now Productive	Ordinary annual Expenditure exclusive of Debts & Schools
	$	$	$	$
Alabama, . .	1,425,933	132,000		100,000
Arkansas, .				75,000
California, . .	739,487			600,000
Connecticut, .	2,044,672	406,000		130,000
Delaware, . .	440,506	109,250		25,000
Florida, . .				45,000
Georgia, . .	440,900	4,461,532	250,000	140,000
Illinois, . .	4,109,476			230,000
Indiana, . .	4,912,012			80,000
Iowa, . .	1,000,000	58,571		25,000
Kentucky, . .	1,455,332			250,000
Louisiana, . .	1,036,500	207,000		500,000
Maine, . . .	149,085			150,000
Maryland, . .	181,167	13,647,276	14,060,000	170,000
Massachusetts, .	1,522,898	8,961,229	3,080,678	800,000
Michigan, . .	1,384,288			125,000
Minnesota, . .				
Mississippi, .			2,000,000	130,000
Missouri, . .	595,668			110,000
New Hampshire,	None.	None.		80,000
New Jersey, .	437,754	275,528	764,671	130,000
New York, .	6,775,889	38,800,000		750,000
North Carolina, .	2,181,850	4,600,000		85,000
Ohio, . .	2,500,000	18,000,000		200,000
Oregon, . .				
Pennsylvania, .		12,933,997		435,000
Rhode Island, .	299,436	400,532		60,000
South Carolina, .		5,654,622		115,000
Tennessee, . .	584,060	3,292,717		165,000
Texas, . .	2,192,000	1,400,000		100,000
Vermont, . .	None.	None.		100,000
Virginia, . .	1,677,652	4,885,856	25,313,514	600,000
Wisconsin, . .	2,358,791			285,000
Total, near Jan. 1, 1859,	40,445,356	118,226,110	45,408,863	6,810,000
Total, " " 1858,	37,752,481	128,590,351	48,083,770	6,466,000
Total, " " 1857,	37,700,334	137,498,801	44,203,461	6,461,000
Total, " " 1856,	34,385,476	135,169,816	43,648,393	6,356,000
Total, " " 1855,	29,179,871	134,878,928	44,802,609	6,217,000
Total, " " 1854,	26,509,820	145,015,799	30,903,978	5,832,000
Total, " " 1853,	25,669,096	141,934,707	29,955,182	5,832,000
Total, " " 1852,	25,170,730	134,982,644	30,598,069	5,812,000
Total, " " 1851,	20,456,605	134,936,578	29,855,912	5,812,000
Total, " " 1850,	21,542,683	125,369,722	27,584,443	5,673,121
Total, " " 1849,	21,420,275	118,508,448	28,236,755	5,258,652
Total, " " 1848,	20,338,246	111,638,746	31,498,469	5,062,310
Total, " " 1847,	17,631,553	108,643,384	30,660,945	5,435,285
Total, " " 1846,	16,608,719	110,396,552	23,232,715	5,455,186

of the American Almanac respectfully invites his correspondents in the several States to communicate such errors as they may detect in these tables. The object here is to give only a summary of the facts, so as to afford the means of comparing the States with each other. Their financial condition is shown at much greater length under the head of "Individual States," and in some cases later statements are given. Official returns published in this work for 1843 (page 135) show that the total of the debts of the States in 1842 was $198,818,736.

XXIII. SEVENTH CENSUS OF THE UNITED STATES.

POPULATION OF THE UNITED STATES ACCORDING TO THE SEVENTH CENSUS, AND REPRESENTATIVES IN CONGRESS.*

States.	White Population.	Free Color'd Population.	Total Free.	Slaves.	Federal Representative Population.	No. of Representatives.	Gain or loss fm. last Cens.	Fractions over.
Alabama,	426,486	2,293	428,779	342,892	634,514	7		†73,976
Arkansas,	162,189	608	162,797	47,100	191,057	2	+1	4,211
California,	91,632	965	92,597		92,597	‡2		
Connecticut,	363,099	7,693	370,792		370,792	4		†90,523
Delaware,	71,169	18,073	89,242	2,290	90,616	1		
Florida,	47,211	924	48,135	39,309	71,720	1		
Georgia,	521,572	2,931	524,503	381,682	753,512	8		6,128
Illinois,	846,035	5,435	851,470		851,470	9	+2	10,663
Indiana,	977,628	10,788	988,416		988,416	11	+1	†54,186
Iowa,	191,879	335	192,214		192,214	2		5,368
Kentucky,	761,417	10,007	771,424	210,981	898,012	10		†57,205
Louisiana,	255,491	17,462	272,953	244,809	419,836	4		46,146
Maine,	581,813	1,356	583,169		583,169	6	−1	22,631
Maryland,	417,943	74,723	492,666	90,368	546,886	6		†79,771
Massachusetts,	985,450	9,064	994,514		994,514	11	+1	†60,284
Michigan,	395,097	2,557	397,654		397,654	4	+1	†23,962
Mississippi,	295,718	930	296,648	309,878	482,574	5	+1	15,495
Missouri,	592,004	2,618	594,622	87,422	647,075	7	+2	†86,537
New Hampshire,	317,456	520	317,976		317,976	3	−1	37,707
New Jersey,	465,513	23,820	489,333	222	489,466	5		22,351
New York,	3,048,325	49,069	3,097,394		3,097,394	33	−1	14,435
North Carolina,	553,028	27,463	580,491	288,548	753,619	8	−1	6,235
Ohio,	1,955,108	25,319	1,980,427		1,980,427	21		18,544
Pennsylvania,	2,258,463	53,323	2,311,786		2,311,786	25	+1	†69,634
Rhode Island,	143,875	3,670	147,545		147,545	2		†54,122
South Carolina,	274,567	8,956	283,523	384,984	514,513	6	−1	†47,398
Tennessee,	756,753	6,401	763,154	239,460	906,830	10	−1	†66,023
Texas,	154,034	397	154,431	58,161	189,327	2		2,481
Vermont,	313,402	718	314,120		314,120	3	−1	33,851
Virginia,	894,800	54,333	949,133	472,528	1,232,649	13	−2	18,150
Wisconsin,	304,756	635	305,391		305,391	3		25,122
Total,	19,423,915	423,384	19,847,301	3,200,634	21,767,673	234		
Minnesota,	6,038	39	6,077					
New Mexico,	61,530	17	61,547					
Oregon,	13,088	206	13,294					
Utah,	11,330	24	11,354	26				
Dist. of Columbia,	38,027	9,973	48,000	3,687				
Total,	19,553,928	433,643	19,987,573	3,204,347				
Total by last pub. Census Tables.	19,553,068	434,495	19,987,563	3,204,313				

RECAPITULATION.

	Total Population in 1840.	Slaves in 1840.	Total Population in 1850.§	Total Free Population in 1860.	Slaves in 1850.	RepresentativePop in 1850.	Rep in 1850	Gain or loss.
Free States,	9,654,865	1,102	13,434,922	13,434,798	222	13,436,931	144	+1
Slave States,	7,290,719	2,481,632	9,612,969	6,412,503	3,200,412	8,330,742	90	−1
Dist. & Ter.	117,769	4,721	143,985	140,272	3,713			
Total,	17,063,353	2,487,355	23,191,876	19,987,573	3,204,347	21,767,673	234	

* The aggregate representative population (21,767,673), divided by 233, — the number of Representatives established by law, — gives 93,423 as the ratio of apportionment among the several States. But this gives only 219 members, leaving 11 to be assigned to the States having the largest residuary fractions, after allowing one each to Delaware, Florida and California.

† In the column of fractions, those marked with a † entitle the State to an additional Representative, who is included in the number given the State in the column of Representatives.

‡ By the act of July 30, 1852, an additional Representative is assigned to California, making the whole number of Representatives 234. The ratio of representation remains unchanged. The last published census tables differ slightly from the above, but as the apportionment of representation is made by the above table, it is continued.

§ This column is from the last published census returns. See page 215.

XXIV. POPULATION OF THE UNITED STATES.*

States.	1790.	1800.	1810.	1820.	1830.	1840.	1850.†
Alabama,	. .	. .	20,845	127,901	309,527	590,756	771,623
Arkansas,	. .	. .	. .	14,273	30,388	97,574	209,897
California,	. .	. .	. .	. .	. .	. .	92,597
Connecticut,	238,141	251,002	262,042	275,202	297,665	309,978	370,792
Delaware,	59,098	64,273	72,674	72,749	76,748	78,085	91,532
Florida,	. .	. .	. .	. .	34,730	54,477	87,445
Georgia,	82,548	162,101	252,433	340,987	516,823	691,392	906,185
Illinois,	. .	. .	12,282	55,211	157,455	476,183	851,470
Indiana,	. .	4,875	24,520	147,178	343,031	685,866	988,416
Iowa,	. .	. .	. .	. .	. .	43,112	192,214
Kentucky,	73,077	220,955	406,511	564,317	687,917	779,828	982,405
Louisiana,	. .	. .	76,556	153,407	215,739	352,411	517,762
Maine,	96,540	151,719	228,705	298,335	399,955	501,793	583,169
Maryland,	319,728	341,548	380,546	407,350	447,040	470,019	583,034
Massachusetts,	378,717	423,245	472,040	523,287	610,408	737,699	994,514
Michigan,	. .	. .	4,762	8,896	31,639	212,267	397,654
Minnesota,	. .	. .	. .	. .	. .	. .	6,077
Mississippi,	. .	8,850	40,352	75,448	136,621	375,651	606,526
Missouri,	. .	. .	20,845	66,586	140,445	383,702	682,044
New Hampshire,	141,899	183,762	214,360	244,161	269,328	284,574	317,976
New Jersey,	184,139	211,949	249,555	277,575	320,823	373,306	489,555
New York,	340,120	586,756	959,949	1,372,812	1,918,608	2,428,921	3,097,394
North Carolina,	393,751	478,103	555,500	638,829	737,987	753,419	869,039
Ohio,	. .	45,365	230,760	581,434	937,903	1,519,467	1,980,329
Oregon,	. .	. .	. .	. .	. .	. .	13,294
Pennsylvania,	434,373	602,365	810,091	1,049,458	1,348,233	1,724,033	2,311,786
Rhode Island,	69,110	69,122	77,031	83,059	97,199	108,830	147,545
South Carolina,	249,073	345,591	415,715	502,741	581,185	594,398	668,507
Tennessee,	35,791	105,602	261,727	422,813	681,904	829,210	1,002,717
Texas,	. .	. .	. .	. .	. .	. .	212,592
Vermont,	85,416	154,465	217,713	235,764	280,652	291,948	314,120
Virginia,	748,308	880,200	974,642	1,065,379	1,211,405	1,239,797	1,421,661
Wisconsin,	. .	. .	. .	. .	. .	30,945	305,391
Dist. of Columbia,	. .	14,093	24,023	33,039	39,834	43,712	51,687
Total,	3,929,872	5,305,952	7,239,814	9,638,131	12,866,920	17,063,353	23,191,876

XXV. SLAVES IN THE UNITED STATES.

States.	1790.	1800.	1810.	1820.	1830.	1840.	1850.†
Alabama,	. .	. .	. .	41,879	117,549	253,532	342,844
Arkansas,	. .	. .	. .	1,617	4,576	19,935	47,100
California,	. .	. .	. .	. .	. .	. .	. .
Connecticut,	2,759	951	310	97	25	17	. .
Delaware,	8,887	6,153	4,177	4,509	3,292	2,605	2,290
Florida,	. .	. .	. .	. .	15,501	25,717	39,310
Georgia,	29,264	59,404	105,218	149,656	217,531	280,944	381,682
Illinois,	. .	. .	168	117	747	331	. .
Indiana,	. .	135	237	190	. .	3	. .
Iowa,	. .	. .	. .	. .	. .	16	. .
Kentucky,	11,830	40,343	80,561	126,732	165,213	182,258	210,981
Louisiana,	. .	. .	34,660	69,064	109,588	168,452	244,809
Maine,	. .	. .	. .	. .	. .	. .	. .
Maryland,	103,036	105,635	111,502	107,398	102,294	89,737	90,368
Massachusetts,	. .	. .	. .	. .	. .	. .	. .
Michigan,	. .	. .	24	. .	32	. .	. .
Minnesota,	. .	. .	. .	. .	. .	. .	. .
Mississippi,	. .	3,489	17,088	32,814	65,659	195,211	309,878
Missouri,	. .	. .	3,011	10,222	25,081	58,240	87,422
New Hampshire,	158	8	. .	. .	. .	1	. .
New Jersey,	11,423	12,422	10,851	7,557	2,254	674	236
New York,	21,324	20,343	15,017	10,088	75	4	. .
North Carolina,	100,572	133,296	168,824	205,017	235,601	245,817	288,548
Ohio,	. .	. .	. .	. .	. .	3	. .
Oregon,	. .	. .	. .	. .	. .	. .	. .
Pennsylvania,	3,737	1,706	795	211	403	64	. .
Rhode Island,	952	381	108	48	17	5	. .
South Carolina,	107,094	146,151	196,365	258,475	315,401	327,038	384,984
Tennessee,	3,417	13,584	44,535	80,107	141,603	183,059	239,459
Texas,	. .	. .	. .	. .	. .	. .	58,161
Vermont,	17	. .	. .	. .	. .	. .	. .
Virginia,	293,427	345,796	392,518	425,153	469,757	448,987	472,528
Wisconsin,	. .	. .	. .	. .	. .	11	. .
Dist. of Columbia,	. .	3,244	5,395	6,377	6,119	4,694	3,687
Total,	697,897	893,041	1,191,364	1,538,064	2,009,031	2,487,355	3,204,313

* For any later returns of the population of the States and Territories, see the several States and Territories.

† No slaves are returned in the Territories of New Mexico and Oregon; in Utah 26 are returned; for their population, see p. 214, and the Territories themselves.

‡ Apprentices by the State act to abolish slavery, of April 18, 1846.

XXVI. POPULATION OF SOME OF THE PRINCIPAL CITIES,*

According to the several Censuses of the United States.

Cities.		1790.	1800.	1810.	1820.	1830.	1840.	1845.†	1850.
Albany,	N. Y.,	3,498	5,349	9,356	12,630	24,238	33,721	41,139	50,763
Baltimore,	Md.,	13,503	26,614	46,555	62,738	80,625	102,313		169,054
Bangor,	Me.,			850	1,221	2,867	8,627		14,432
Boston,	Mass.,	18,038	24,027	32,250	43,298	61,392	93,383	114,366	136,881
Brooklyn,	N. Y.,		3,298	4,402	7,175	12,042	36,233	59,566	96,838
Buffalo,	"			1,508	2,095	8,653	18,213	29,773	42,261
Charleston,	S. C.,	16,359	18,712	24,711	24,480	30,289	29,261		42,985
Chicago,	Ill.,						4,479		29,963
Cincinnati,	Ohio,		750	2,540	9,644	24,831	46,338		115,436
Cleveland,	"			547	606	1,076	6,071		17,034
Columbus,	"					2,435	6,048		17,882
Detroit,	Mich.,				1,422	2,222	9,102		21,019
Hartford,	Ct.,			3,955	4,726	7,074	12,793		13,555
Louisville,	Ky.,			1,357	4,012	10,352	21,210		43,194
Lowell,	Mass.,					6,474	20,796	28,841	33,383
Manchester,	N. H.,			615	761	877	3,235		13,932
Milwaukee,	Wis.,						1,700		20,061
Mobile,	Ala.,					3,194	12,672		20,515
Nashville,	Tenn.,					5,566	6,929		10,478
Newark,	N. J.,				6,507	10,953	17,290	34,140	38,894
New Haven,	Ct.,			5,772	7,147	10,180	14,890		20,345
New Orleans,	La.,			17,242	27,176	46,310	102,193		116,375
New York,	N. Y.,	33,131	60,489	96,373	123,706	203,007	312,710	371,102	515,547
Paterson,	N. J.,						7,596		11,334
Philadelphia,‡	Pa.,	42,520	70,287	96,664	108,116	167,188	258,037		408,762
Pittsburg,	"		1,565	4,768	7,248	12,542	21,115		46,601
Portland,	Me.,		3,677	7,169	8,581	12,601	15,218		20,815
Providence,	R. I.,		7,614	10,071	11,767	16,832	23,171		41,513
Richmond,	Va.,		5,537	9,735	12,046	16,060	20,153		27,570
Rochester,	N. Y.,				1,502	9,269	20,191	25,265	36,403
Salem,	Mass.,	7,921	9,457	12,613	12,721	13,886	15,082		20,264
San Francisco,	Cal.,								15,000
Savannah,	Ga.,				7,523	9,748	11,214		15,312
Springfield,	Mass.,			2,767	3,914	6,784	10,985		11,766
St. Louis,	Mo.,				4,598	5,852	16,469	63,491	77,860
Syracuse,	N. Y.,						6,502		22,271
Troy,	"			3,885	5,264	11,401	19,334	21,709	28,785
Utica,	"				2,972	8,323	12,782		17,565
Washington,	D. C.,		3,210	8,208	13,247	18,827	23,364		40,001
Williamsburg,	N. Y.,					1,620	5,680		30,780
Worcester,	Mass.,						7,497		17,049

XXVII. PUBLIC LANDS.

THE public lands that have belonged, and now belong, to the General Government are situated, — 1st. Within the limits of the United States, as defined by the treaty of 1783, and are embraced by the States of Ohio, Indiana, Illinois, Michigan, Wisconsin, and that part of Minnesota east of the Mississippi River, all of which have been formed out of the Northwestern Territory, as conveyed with certain reservations to the United States by New York in 1781, by Virginia in 1784, by Massachusetts in 1785, and by Connecticut in 1786; also the lands within the boundaries of the States of Mississippi and Alabama north of 31° north latitude, as conveyed to the United States by Georgia in 1802. 2d. Within the Territories of Orleans

* If there are later enumerations, see the several States.

† By the State census of this year.

‡ Including the County.

and Louisiana, as acquired from France by the treaty of 1803, including the portion of the States of Alabama and Mississippi south of 31°; the whole of Louisiana, Arkansas, Missouri, Iowa, and that portion of Minnesota west of the Mississippi River; the Indian Territory; Oregon; Kansas, and Nebraska Territories. 3d. Within the State of Florida, as obtained from Spain by the treaty of 1819. 4th. In New Mexico and California, as acquired from Mexico by the treaty of 1848. 5th. The "Gadsden Purchase" of 23,161,000 acres south of the Gila River, from Mexico, in 1854.

This public domain covered a surface, exclusive of water, of 1,450,000,000 acres. Of this there have been prepared for market, exclusive of school lands, 401,604,988 acres; of which 57,442,870 acres are subject to public sale, and 80,000,000 acres to entry at private sale. Of the whole domain there have been disposed of, to Sept. 30, 1857, 363,862,464 acres, which left then undisposed of, 1,086,137,536 acres. Exclusive of the lands in Oregon, California, New Mexico, Utah, Kansas, and Nebraska Territories, the entire area of the public domain is stated, after a careful examination, to have been 471,892,439 acres. The average cost per acre to the government of acquiring title, &c. to these lands is 14.41 cents; of survey, 2.07 cents; of selling and managing, 5.32 cents; in all 21.80 cents; while it receives $1.25 per acre, or a net profit on each acre sold of $1.032.

During the five quarters ending Sept. 30, 1858, there were sold, for cash, 4,804,919.46 acres, for which $2,534,192.20 were received, there were located with military warrants, 6,977,110 acres, and there were reported under swamp-land grants, 1,401,565.08 acres, making an aggregate of 13,183,594.54. The area of *unoffered* land surveyed and ready for market Sept. 30, 1858, including all previous operations, was 61,951,049 acres, and of this amount, 15,209,376 acres were surveyed during the five quarters ending Sept. 30, 1858. The following table gives the sales, &c., for the year ending June 30, 1858, in detail, in the several States:—

States.	Gross Amount of Lands sold during Fiscal Year.		Amount received in		Amount of Incidental Expenses.	Amount paid into the Treasury.
	Acres.	Purchase-money.	Cash.	Military Land Scrip.		
Alabama,	210,963.02	$46,690.98	$46,490.98		$14,312 43	$ 36,250.38
Arkansas,	836,101.35	512,100.27	512,033.17	$67.10	34,134.01	513,520.17
California,	6,130.00	7,662.52	7,662.52		17,843.38	
Florida,	37,704.37	18,262.01	18,262.01		5,487.92	18,927.90
Illinois,	27,939.06	43,097.27	43,097.27		2,826.45	51,616.62
Indiana,	8,301.11	3,480.23	3,480.23		3,272.12	6,658.26
Iowa,	61,383.13	83,764.88	77,155.15	6,609.93	28,121.11	237,285.85
Kansas T.,	93,464.46	116,832.60	116,832.60		9,573.68	1,209,489.37
Louisiana,	235,968.71	142,001.38	142,001.38		23,460.58	146,417.69
Michigan,	47,223.10	32,255.96	32,180.96	75.00	11,009.78	34,379.55
Minnesota,	68,165.83	85,339.03	85,339.03		15,298.51	134,118.76
Mississippi,	129,589.06	67,936 86	67,936.86		9,848.08	75,507.81
Missouri,	1,891,209.69	781,125.82	736,453.97	44,671.85	49,239.15	837,719.53
Nebraska T.,	58,309.61	72,887.32	72,887.32		8,435 32	80,755.29
Ohio,	1,310.29	1,687.69	1,687 69		1,106.19	2,169.03
Oregon,	10,584.99	13,233.82	13,233.82		11,146.66	16,079.35
Wash. Ter.,	2,420.90	3,026.15	3,026.05		4,394.56	3,657.46
Wisconsin,	78,139.78	85,583.03	44,283.03	300 00	11,886 92	109,133.55
Total,	3,804,908.46	2,116,768.02	2,065,044.14	51,723.88	261,405.85	3,513,715.57

The following table shows the sales of public lands and the cash proceeds thereof from the year 1833 to 1857, inclusive. The sales, however, as the above table indicates, do not show the amount of public lands disposed of during the year. Full details of the condition of the public lands, and of the various grants and donations thereof for purposes of education and of internal improvement, are given in the American Almanac for 1850, pp. 180 et seq.

Quantity of Public Land sold, and the Amount paid for it, in each Year, from 1833 to 1858, inclusive.

Years.	Acres.	Dollars.	Years.	Acres.	Dollars.
1833	3,856,227.56	4,972,284.84	1847	2,521,305.59	3,296,404.08
1834	4,658,218.71	6,099,981.04	1848	1,887,553.04	2,621,615.26
1835	12,564,478.85	15,999,804.11	1849	1,329,902.77	1,756,890.42
1836	20,074,870.92	25,167,833.06	1850*	769,364.48	998,841.26
1837	5,601,103.12	7,007,523.04	1851†	1,846,847.49	2,390,947.45
1838	3,414,907.42	4,305,564.64	1852†	1,553,071.00	1,975,658.54
1839	4,976,382.87	6,464,556.79	1853†	1,083,495.21	1,804,653 24
1840	2,236,889.74	2,789,637.53	1854†	7,035,735.07	9,000,211.81
1841	1,164,796.11	1,463,364.06	1855†	15,729,524.88	11,248,301 36
1842	1,129,217.58	1,417,972.06	1856†	9,227,878.98	8,750,440.34
1843	1,605,264.06	2,016,044.30	1857†	4,142,744.47	3,445,199.51
1844	1,754,763.13	2,207,678.04	1858†	3,804,908.46	2,116,768.02
1845	1,843,527.05	2,470,303.17	Total,	118,076,709.31	134,773,115.24
1846	2,263,730.81	2,904,637.27			

The following table shows the number of land-warrants issued under the acts of 1847, 1850, 1852, and 1855; the number located, and the number outstanding September 30, 1858.

Acts.	Number issued.	Acres therein.	Number located.	Acres.	Number Outstand'g.	Acres.
Act of 1847,	87,874	13,154,560	80,448	12,139,200	7,426	1,015,360
" 1850,	189,004	13,156,480	166,036	11,812,160	22,968	1,344,320
" 1852,	11,982	693,840	9,698	552,560	2,284	141,280
" 1855,	227,903	28,727,010	160,450	19,734,110	67,458	8,992,900
Total, . .	516,763	55,731,890	416,632	44,238,030	100,136	11,493,860

The following table exhibits the quantity of swamp and overflowed lands selected as enuring to the several States under the acts of March 2, 1849, and Sept. 28, 1850; the quantity approved under said acts; and the quantity patented under the act of Sept. 20, 1850, to Sept. 30, 1858: —

States.	Quantity selected.	Quantity approved.	Total Patented.	States.	Quantity selected.	Quantity approved.	Total Patented.
Alabama,	2,596	2,696		Michigan,	7,273,725	5,465,232	4,985,538
Arkansas,	8,562,753	6,255,435	4,418,430	Mississippi	2,836,676	2,918,379	2,549,618
Florida,	11,790,637	10,701,495	10,618,549	Missouri,	4,248,204	3,615,967	2,586,480
Illinois,	3,243,891	1,371,620	801,592	Ohio,	54,438	25,641	25,641
Indiana,	1,334,733	1,250,938	1,256,350	Wisconsin,	2,827,199	1,650,712	1,674,588
Iowa,	1,752,296	63,632		Total,	55,129,492	40,923,182	28,716,833
Louisiana,	11,202,344	7,601,535					

* From January 1 to June 30. † For year ending June 30.

The following table shows the names and lengths of such of the railroads in the several States to which Congress has granted lands, as were in process of adjustment at the General Land-Office, Sept. 30, 1858, and the quantities of land enuring to the same: —

States.	Name of Road.	Length of Road, Miles.	Length in the State.	[illegible] Acres.	Grant to the State.
Alabama,	Alabama and Florida,	114.00	468.00	[illegible]	1,148,500
	Alabama and Tennessee,	125.50		[illegible]	
	Mobile and Girard,	228.50		[illegible]	
Florida,	Florida,	151.50	517.25	*[illegible]	1,374,465
	Florida and Alabama,	15.00		[illegible]	
	Florida, Alabama, and Gulf Central,	60.00		27,778	
	Pensacola and Georgia,	290.75		*301,000	
Iowa,	Burlington and Missouri,	276.50	1,263.00	252,655	2,176,321
	Dubuque and Pacific,	330.50		1,137,143	
	Iowa Central Air Line,	338.00		[illegible]	
	Mississippi and Missouri,	318.00		400,000	
Louisiana,	New Orleans, Opelousas, and Great Western,	263.00	429.00	684,000	1,047,670
	Vicksburg, Shreveport, and Texas,	166.00		363,670	
Michigan,	Chicago, St. Paul, and Fond du Lac (Michigan part),	159.00	712.25	575,000	1,910,000
	Detroit and Milwaukee,	107.00		35,000	
	Flint and Pierre Marquette,	173.50		625,000	
	Grand Rapids and Indiana,	183.00		600,000	
	Point Huron and Milwaukee,	89.75		15,000	
Minnesota,	Minneapolis and Cedar Valley (branch),	112.00	458.00	*150,000	1,400,000
	Minnesota and Pacific (main),	230.00		*350,000	
	Minnesota and Pacific (branch),	116.00		*400,000	
Mississippi,	Southern,	110.00	110.00	207,731	207,731
Wisconsin,	Chicago, St. Paul, and Fond du Lac (Wisconsin part),	167.00	662.00	*600,000	*2,225,000
	La Crosse and Milwaukee,	252.00		*725,000	
	St. Croix and Lake Superior,	243.00		*900,000	
Total,		4,649.50	4,649.50	11,789,687	11,789,687

XXVIII. BANKS IN THE UNITED STATES.†

The following abstract of the condition of the State Banks throughout the Union is taken from a letter of the Secretary of the Treasury to the Speaker of the House of Representatives, dated February 28, 1859, which is printed as House Ex. Document No. 112. The information was obtained in compliance with a resolution of the House adopted as long since as July 10, 1832.

The following statement embraces, with a few trifling exceptions, all the chartered banks in the Union that were in operation on the 1st of January, 1859. To complete the statement, it has been found necessary to give the "stocks," "other investments," and "other liabilities," of the banks of Rhode Island as they stood on the 25th of May, 1858, the returns from that State for January, 1859, not embracing those items; and also to give the banks of Mississippi as they were in January, 1858.

The "specie funds" appear to consist (a few small amounts of coin and mint certificates excepted) almost exclusively of notes of other banks, checks on other banks, and other obligations payable on demand.

* Estimated.

† For later returns of the Banks, if any, see the Individual States.

Comparative View of the Condition of the Banks in the different States, from their Returns received nearest to January 1, 1859.

States.	Date.	No. banks and br's.	Capital.	Loans and Discounts.	Stocks.	Real Estate.	Other Investments.	Due by other Banks.
Alabama,	Jan. '59	6	$3,663,490	$9,058,379	$160,219	$160,410		$2,192,019
Connecticut,	Apr. '58	76	20,917,169	25,799,430	938,755	1,085,173	$877,000	2,584,819
Delaware,	Jan. '59	12	1,638,185	3,009,285	22,610	81,499		308,222
Georgia,	Jan. '59	28	12,479,111	17,929,066	1,605,127	4,791,022	678,274	4,073,665
Illinois,	Oct. '58	48	4,000,334	1,296,616	6,486,652	87,769	1,837	2,627,694
Indiana,	Jan. '59	37	3,617,629	6,468,308	1,252,981	195,711	111,089	1,177,489
Kentucky,	Dec. '58	37	12,216,725	24,404,942	793,641	608,503	144,075	6,535,215
Louisiana,	Dec. '58	12	24,215,689	29,424,278	5,564,590	2,395,500	873,471	9,268,254
Maine,	Jan. '59	68	7,408,945	11,815,127		145,665		1,478,896
Maryland,	Jan. '59	32	12,560,635	21,854,934	892,965	484,625	67,574	1,017,641
Mass.,	Oct. '58	174	61,819,825	101,602,947		1,584,864		9,187,245
Michigan,	Dec. '58	3	745,304	1,153,547	259,776	124,357	14,440	137,059
Minnesota,	Jan. '59	2	50,000	5,185	50,000		1,250	30,806
Mississippi,	Jan. '58	2	1,110,600	393,216	1,007	780,767	30,209	219,086
Missouri,	Jan. '59	22	5,796,781	9,830,426	417,335	169,459		597,679
N. Hamp.,	Dec. '58	52	5,011,000	8,250,754		66,086		889,330
New Jersey,	Jan. '59	46	7,369,122	12,449,460	785,623	421,793	391,194	2,223,935
New York,	Dec. '58	300	110,258,480	200,577,198	25,268,884	8,264,425	397,330	15,169,559
N. Carolina,	Jan. '59	28	6,525,200	12,247,300	128,951	216,347	45,696	1,291,343
Ohio,	Nov. '58	53	6,707,151	11,171,343	2,069,769	586,670	711,157	2,613,615
Pennsylv.,	Nov. '58	87	24,565,805	46,825,266	2,934,443	1,423,253	453,521	4,418,436
R. Island,		90	20,321,069	25,131,150	161,309	636,403	93,365	1,491,522
S. Carolina,	Dec. '58	20	14,888,451	24,444,044	3,321,969	677,641	2,964,540	2,204,450
Tennessee,	Jan. '59	39	8,361,357	13,262,766	1,577,578	486,622	8,258	2,575,465
Vermont,	Aug. '58	41	4,082,416	6,392,992	106,500	222,564	73,954	701,545
Virginia,	Jan. '59	63	14,685,370	22,419,512	3,569,437	954,629	413,675	2,567,182
Wisconsin,	Jan. '59	98	7,995,000	9,262,457	5,114,415	304,142		892,776
Nebraska T.	Nov. '58	2	66,000	97,037		1,155	1,341	3,127
Total,		1478	403,086,842	657,577,015	63,503,456	26,757,264	8,353,250	78,464,073

Comparative View continued.

States.	Notes of other Banks.	Specie Funds.	Specie.	Circulation.	Deposits.	Due to other Banks.	Other Liabilities.
Alabama,	$872,746		$3,371,956	$6,651,117	$3,830,607	$1,006,832	$2,131
Connecticut,	273,381	$262,595	915,844	5,380,247	4,140,068	684,997	893,156
Delaware,	61,446	114,812	217,342	960,846	832,657	86,180	
Georgia,	720,692	402,451	3,751,988	11,687,682	5,317,923	1,727,995	652,254
Illinois,	271,626	9,272	269,585	5,707,048	640,058	15,621	525,344
Indiana,	505,695	36,623	1,869,000	5,379,933	1,723,840	176,366	68,215
Kentucky,	1,017,580	199	4,984,141	14,345,696	5,144,879	4,338,364	
Louisiana,			16,218,027	9,094,009	21,822,538	2,198,982	1,781,056
Maine,	273,303		663,754	3,886,539	2,382,910	89,271	90,082
Maryland,	69,963	1,521,663	3,120,011	3,977,971	9,028,664	1,725,807	477,667
Massachusetts,	4,933,427		11,112,715	20,839,438	30,538,153	7,654,234	1,537,853
Michigan,	54,963	22,579	42,018	331,978	556,693	35,165	126,011
Minnesota,	4,223	512	15,272	48,643	13,131		
Mississippi,	975	47,254	591	169,400	49,781	31,792	60
Missouri,	1,007,575	349,658	3,921,879	6,069,120	3,123,622	579,530	
N. Hampshire,	170,994		294,423	3,115,643	1,069,990		
New Jersey,	578,006		952,231	4,054,770	4,239,235	770,935	
New York,	2,044,765	18,436,967	28,335,984	28,507,990	110,465,798	35,134,049	2,824,615
N. Carolina,	317,362	51,612	1,248,525	6,202,626	1,502,312	184,356	7,766
Ohio,	1,162,433	180,741	1,845,441	8,040,304	4,389,851	488,878	206,235
Pennsylvania,	834,124	3,349,824	11,345,636	11,980,480	26,064,668	4,569,625	429,167
Rhode Island,	802,660		608,833	3,318,681	3,130,475	936,081	296,869
S. Carolina,	600,290		2,601,414	9,170,333	3,897,840	3,746,604	3,214,920
Tennessee,	581,723	1,287,077	2,863,018	6,472,822	4,659,909	1,073,269	441,165
Vermont,	41,780	232,625	178,656	3,024,141	615,874	5,441	1,443
Virginia,	814,080	496,663	3,077,687	10,340,342	7,401,701	982,351	58,780
Wisconsin,	862,283	83,893	706,009	4,695,170	3,022,384		1,573,894
Nebraska T.	1,399	26	6,629	23,346	23,748	4,418	
Total,	18,859,261	28,856,076	104,538,409	193,476,218	259,618,059	68,244,443	15,048,487

XXIX. RAILROADS IN THE UNITED STATES.

The following table gives the names of the principal railroads in the United States, and their condition near January, 1859. The roads of less importance are put together under the item "Other roads;" and against that line, in the column headed State, is given the aggregate length of railroads in the State. The length of each road includes the branches, but not the double track. When a road is in two or more States, it is put in the list in the State in which the greater portion of it lies.

State.	Name of Road.	Length in operation.	Capital Stock paid in.	Debt, Funded and Floating.	Cost of Construction and Equipment.	Receipts in 1858.	Expenses in 1858.
		Miles	$	$	$	$	$
Alabama	Montgomery & W. Point,	116	1,414,924	992,884	2,411,722	391,000	275,500
	Mobile & Ohio. *See* Mississippi.						
	Ala. & Tenn. Rivers, .	95	1,031,958	700,000	1,678,211	113,152	92,445
	Ala. and Miss., Seluca to U. Town, . . .	30			600,000		
	Ala. and Fla., Montgomery to Greenville, .	43			1,000,000		
395	Other roads, . . .	111					
Ark.	Memphis and Little Rock,	39			1,000,000		
Califor.	Sacramento Valley, .	22			1,500,000		
Conn.	New Haven and Hartford,	72	2,330,000	964,000	3,320,667	628,245	363,400
	New York & New Haven,	62	2,980,839	2,194,051	5,324,527	836,612	607,503
	New London, Willimantic, and Palmer, . . .	66	510,000	1,052,000	1,573,769	101,484	73,973
	Housatonic, . . .	74	2,000,000	355,175	2,438,847	271,273	227,571
	Hartford, Prov., & Fishkill,	122	2,042,540	2,182,625	4,202,519	298,595	163,925
	Naugatuck, . . .	57	1,031,800	334,095	1,578,301	199,536	133,266
	New Haven, New London, and Stonington, . .	62	738,538	846,452	1,434,040	76,758	67,818
591	Other roads, . . .	79					
Del.	Delaware, ...	71	301,198	856,000	1,200,000	95,413	
93	Other roads, . . .	22			834,350		
Florida,	Florida (Fernan. to Gainsville), ...	62					
119	Other roads, . . .	57					
Georgia,	Georgia (W. W. & Ath. br.)	232	4,156,000	477,000	4,200,000	1,036,572	210,400
	Augusta and Savannah,	53					
	Central (Savan. to Macon),	191	3,725,916	191,767	3,750,000	1,122,646	582,310
	Southwestern & Muscogee (Am. Br.), . . .	175	1,400,000	440,978	2,270,000	547,876	210,107
	Macon & West (to Atlanta),	103	1,438,700	96,000	1,647,000	293,247	160,620
	Western and Atlantic, .	138			5,901,499		
	Atlanta and Lagrange,	87	1,000,000	199,000	1,172,000	317,700	125,810
1,160	Other roads, . . .	181					
Illinois,	Ohio and Miss. (W. Div.)	148	1,780,295	3,292,403	4,870,586		
	Terre Haute, Alt. & St. Lo.	193	3,011,150	5,925,927	8,726,764	823,767	247,757
	St Louis Alton & Chicago,	256					
	Chic. Burling'n, & Quincy,	310	4,632,000	2,990,000	8,042,430	1,044,573	672,958
	Chicago and Milwaukee,	85					
	Chicago and Rock Island,	182	5,248,000	1,734,318	6,628,272	1,886,196	850,039
	Peoria Branch, . .	47					
	Chicago, St. Paul, & Fond du Lac (now Chicago & Northwestern), . .	194	2,300,000	1,325,000	3,625,000		
	Galena & Chicago Union,	250	6,023,800	3,899,015	9,395,455	2,315,786	1,123,744
	Ill. Central & Branches,	706	6,556,435	20,315,692	23,437,669	2,293,965	1,727,993
	Great Western (Danville to Naples), . . .	167					
	Peoria and Oquawkua,	180	1,560,859	2,200,000	5,400,000		
2,851	Other roads, . . .	136					
Indiana,	See Ohio, Mich. & Illinois						
	Northern Indiana, air line,	Included	in Mich.	S. and N.	Indiana		

State.	Name of Road.	Length in operation.	Capital Stock paid in.	Debt, Funded and Floating.	Cost of Construction and Equipment.	Receipts in 1858.	Expenses in 1858.
		Miles.	$	$	$	$	$
Indiana,	Evansville & Crawfordsv.,	109	986,061	1,270,872	2,158,713	249,868	125,728
	Indiana Central, . .	68	612,350	1,261,179	1,909,911	368,189	153,504
	Indianapolis & Cincinnati,	110	1,686,809	1,564,584	3,029,989	491,743	246,121
	Jeffersonville, . . .	108	1,014,252	694,000	1,839,576	222,737	128,419
	Lafayette & Indianapolis,	64					
	Madison and Indianapolis,	87	1,647,700	1,336,816	2,984,516	260,214	141,586
	New Albany and Salem,	288	2,535,121	5,281,848	7,029,494	645,827	274,425
	Peru and Indianapolis,	74		858,314	2,000,000	150,000	60,000
	Terre Haute & Richmond,	73	1,361,450	250,125	1,585,809	481,272	275,193
	Ohio and Miss. (E. Div.)	192			10,000,000		
1,284	Other roads, . .	111					
Iowa,	Burlington and Mo. River,	75					
	Miss. & Missouri & Br.	105					
	Dubuque and Pacific, .	60					
	Keokuk, Fort Des Moines, and Minnesota, . .	38					
319	Chic., Iowa, & Nebraska,	81					
Kent'ky,	Kentucky Central, .	111	1,384,850	3,065,917	4,091,604	426,408	205,502
	Louisville and Lexington,	95	1,128,291	825,960	2,247,821	338,842	182,684
	Louisville and Nashville,	111					
340	Other roads, ...	23					
La.	N. Orleans, Jackson, and Gt. Northern, . .	206	4,428,266	3,035,715	7,461,236	593,093	935,323
	N. O., Opelousas & Great Western.	80	2,800,000	750,000	3,877,525	284,178	156,728
	West Feliciana, . . .	27					
	Mexican Gulf, . . .	28	174,458				
	Vicksburg, Shreveport, & Texas, ...	21					
400	Other roads, . . .	38					
Maine,	Androscoggin & Kennebec,	55	912,176	1,835,308	2,218,316	159,513	76,145
	Atlantic and St. Lawrence,	149	2,494,900	3,481,000	7,077,379	524,538	441,591
	Kennebec and Portland,	72	1,107,526	1,763,738	2,871,264	213,255	
	Portland, Saco, & Portsm'th	51	1,500,000		1,359,973	253,717	132,806
543	Other roads, . .	216					
Md.	Baltimore and Ohio, .	386	13,118,902	10,986,804	24,802,645	3,856,486	2,531,199
	Washington Branch, . .	31	1,650,000	25,000	1,650,000	369,229	234,246
	Northern Central, . .	138	2,260,000	5,461,319	7,238,540	731,688	448,404
639	Other roads, . . .	84					
Mass.	Boston and Lowell, .	28	1,830,000	451,025	2,422,598	407,399	217,621
	Boston and Maine, .	83	4,076,974		4,219,326	754,787	431,887
	Boston & N. York Central,	75	223,176	073,210		16,606	14,959
	Boston and Providence, .	56	3,160,000	195,220	3,524,981	537,764	278,590
	Boston and Worcester,	63	4,500,000	560,774	4,689,098	923,223	545,815
	Cape Cod, . . .	47	681,689	259,016	1,031,625	106,846	57,352
	Connecticut River, .	52	1,591,100	251,000	1,801,943	238,390	117,512
	Eastern, ...	60	2,853,400	2,277,717	4,590,741	616,783	332,267
	Fitchburg, ...	68	3,540,000	100,000	3,540,000	572,967	294,112
	New Bedford and Taunton,	21	500,000	12,600	544,965	137,914	108,107
	Norwich and Worcester,	66	2,122,300	775,280	2,613,694	283,556	183,189
	Old Colony & Fall River,	87	3,015,100	173,600	3,362,945	551,399	283,765
	Providence & Worcester,	43	1,510,200	300,000	1,789,476	270,402	160,067
	Taunton Branch, .	11	250,000	3,000	313,156	134,184	112,282
	Vermont & Massachusetts,	77	2,214,225	1,010,175	3,288,165	225,079	120,042
	Western, ...	155	5,150,000	6,276,320	10,881,281	1,700,293	890,930
	Worcester and Nashua, .	46	1,141,000	200,766	1,328,897	185,127	112,513
	Horse Railroads, . .	38	1,643,850	298,784	602,825	548,603	438,363
1,457	Other roads, . . .	381					
Mich.	Detroit and Milwaukee,	186	838,000	1,128,964	1,966,969		
	Michigan Central & Jol. Br.	329	6,057,840	8,366,640	12,846,000	1,072,732	817,045
	Mich. South. & North. Ind.,	500	8,876,400	10,459,680	19,336,084	2,309,487	1,765,176
1,073	Other roads, . .	58					
Miss.	Mississippi & Tennessee,	79	757,540	611,812	1,151,152	161,001	61,171
	Mississippi Central (N. & S. Div.), ...	194	1,575,175	1,729,500	3,508,000	953,527	744,236

State.	Name of Road.	Length in operation.	Capital Stock paid in.	Debt, Funded and Floating.	Cost of Construction and Equipment.	Receipts in 1858.	Expenses in 1858.
		Miles.	$	$	$	$	$
Miss.	Mobile and Ohio (S. Div.), open to Okalona, Miss.,	275	6,784,800	2,066,460	10,701,400	555,000	275,000
	Southern Mississippi,	82	1,000,000	1,400,000	2,400,000	264,205	128,386
657	Other roads, ...	27					
Missouri	North. Missouri, St. Louis to St. Joseph, . .	304	2,612,100	3,600,000	4,346,229	160,564	
	Hannibal and St. Joseph,	70	1,664,773	6,868,000	8,533,229		
	Pacific and S. W. Br., .	86	3,330,650	8,203,000	12,288,490	676,310	374,806
546	St. Louis & Iron Mount'n,	86	1,847,358	547,419	5,042,660		
N. H.	Boston, Concord, & Montr'l,	93	1,808,898	1,100,062	2,848,977	222,283	145,711
	Concord, ...	35	1,500,000	8,242	1,412,576	275,793	146,742
	Cheshire, ...	54	2,085,925	829,296	1,108,859	297,332	188,814
	Manchester & Lawrence,	27	840,000	240,000	1,000,000	183,862	87,828
	Northern, ...	82	3,068,400	225,299	3,068,400	353,100	176,110
507	Other roads, ...	216					
N. Jer.	Camden and Amboy, . .	94	1,500,000	8,794,100	6,576,796	1,640,327	874,167
	Camden and Atlantic, .	61	656,635	1,445,885	1,787,970	133,222	75,257
	Belvidere Delaware, .	63	1,100,000	2,036,000	3,173,285	224,303	131,220
	Central, ...	64	2,000,000	3,593,000	5,620,745	870,950	350,280
	Morris and Essex, .	53	1,157,805	340,000	1,610,294	231,222	136,703
	New Jersey, ...	31	3,749,000	789,000	3,617,510	903,458	554,090
467	Other roads, . . .	101					
N. York,	Buffalo, Corning, & N. Y.,	100	1,487,874	1,601,183	2,819,096	172,476	106,143
	Buffalo and N. York City,	92	798,439	2,587,849	3,401,868	288,392	256,496
	Buffalo and State Line,	69	1,300,000	1,040,000	2,494,364	679,750	323,987
	Canandaigua and Elmira,	69	434,111	922,393	1,275,796	174,089	104,583
	Canandaigua & Niag. Falls,	99	1,315,000	2,279,854	3,495,832		
	Cayuga and Susquehanna,	35	687,000	506,689	1,187,562	135,433	86,784
	Hudson River, . . .	144	3,758,466	9,250,352	12,737,898	1,902,828	1,213,945
	L. Island (B. & J. R. R., 11m.)	95	3,000,000	647,193	2,555,966	325,813	269,627
	New York Central, .	556	24,182,400	14,402,535	30,732,518	6,528,413	3,487,293
	New York and Erie, .	465	11,000,000	28,081,468	34,469,324	5,742,607	4,288,575
	New York and Harlem, .	133	5,717,100	4,822,498	8,758,203	1,040,393	715,502
	Northern (Ogdensburg),	122	1,633,022	4,406,874	5,470,714	520,153	364,399
	Oswego and Syracuse, .	36	306,130	213,025	752,036	149,373	70,619
	Rensl. & Sar., & Sar. & Sch.	46	910,000	244,000	1,380,000	241,149	168,549
	Saratoga and Whitehall,	48	500,000	395,600		71,909	50,820
	Syracuse and Southern,	80	768,369	1,578,804	2,272,777	159,484	137,981
	Watertown and Rome, .	97	1,500,000	700,979	2,200,500	440,290	278,253
	Brooklyn City roads, .	20	844,344				
	New York City roads, .	30	3,757,660				
2,580	Other roads, . .	244					
N. C.	North Carolina, . .	223	4,000,000		4,235,000	337,003	161,790
	Raleigh and Gaston, .	97	973,300	126,200	1,256,146	302,402	156,465
	Wilmington and Weldon,	162	1,350,000	900,000	2,846,806	446,600	221,141
	Wilmington & Manchester,	171	1,123,888	1,216,000	2,380,000		
763	Other roads, . .	110					
Ohio,	See Pa., Md., Va., & Ind.						
	Central Ohio, ...	139	1,627,907	6,226,650	6,496,822	670,092	405,396
	Cincinnati and Chicago,	108	4,196,679	1,006,126	2,080,433		
	Cin., Hamilton, & Dayton,	60	2,156,000	1,528,000	3,130,350	489,437	239,771
	Cin., Wil., & Zanesville,	131	2,421,176	3,782,040	5,696,210	223,506	193,218
	Clevel'd, Columbus, & Cin.,	141	4,746,000	90,400	4,751,845	1,113,639	538,480
	Cleveland and Erie, .	95					
	Cleveland and Pittsburg,	202	2,780,744	3,043,992	5,537,466	581,677	272,359
	Cleveland and Toledo, .	200	3,350,000	4,225,560	7,192,874	796,155	383,699
	Clevel'd, Zanesville, & Cin.,	87			1,725,000		
	Columbus & Indianapolis,	102			2,000,000		
	Columbus and Xenia, .	55	1,490,450	149,000	1,582,475	403,212	221,524
	Dayton and Michigan,	72	1,076,602	393,011	1,185,826		
	Dayton and Western, .	40	310,000	700,481	1,035,173	125,940	59,687
	Little Miami, . . .	65	2,961,282	1,266,000	3,925,157	775,442	485,319
	Marietta and Cincinnati,	196					

State.	Name of Road.	Length in operation.	Capital Stock paid in.	Debt, Funded and Floating.	Cost of Construction and Equipment.	Receipts in 1858.	Expenses in 1858.
		Miles.	$	$	$	$	$
Ohio,	Mad River and Lake Erie,	174	2,697,090	3,368,000	6,065,090		
	Sand.. Mansf'd, & Newark,	126	1,350,000	2,206,357	3,562,357	328,966	164,479
	Scioto & Hocking Valley,	56	403,975	509,050	888,858		
	Pitts., Ft. Wayne & Chic.	465	6,247,040	9,822,550	14,279,704	1,546,359	968,572
	Pittsb'g, Columb & Cinn.	124					
	Indianap, Pitts. & Clevel.	206	2,708,460	2,249,400	4,843,253		
	Toledo, Wabash, & West.	242	2,965,100	7,577,500	10,542,600		
3,337	Other roads, ...	252					
Penn.	Phil., Germ, & Norrist'n,	38	899,350	376,800	1,274,150	206,981	93,538
	Phil., Wilmington, & Balt.	98	5,600,000	2,673,450	8,568,369	1,143,853	764,977
	Philadelphia and Reading,	93	11,375,541	9,423,506	19,263,720	3,065,522	1,461,746
	Penn. (Phil to Pittsburg),	353	13,206,625	15,690,524	27,266,962	4,855,670	3,000,743
	Northern Pennsylvania,	65	3,051,865	2,820,165	5,106,342	248,784	112,157
	Del., Lackawanna, & West.,	135	3,292,772	6,194,551	8,013,761	815,768	774,629
	Cat., Williamsport & Erie,	63	1,700,000	1,940,000	3,640,000	219,253	166,803
	Williamsport and Elmira,	78	1,600,000	1,990,000	3,464,454	274,564	117,096
	Cumberland Valley, . .	52	1,013,900	213,509	1,226,675	156,463	79,371
	Pittsburg & Steubenville,	42	1,221,277	280,000	914,695		142,626
	Pittsburg & Connellsville,	60	1,748,062	1,613,403	2,265,606	45,587	41,269
	Sunbury and Erie, . .	40	3,676,030	875,293	3,238,293	105,860	65,360
	Coal roads, ...	300	6,000,000				
2,317	Other roads, ...	900					
R. Island,	N. York, Prov., & Boston,	50	1,608,000	306,500	2,158,000	208,439	112,000
65	Prov., Warren, & Bristol.	15	284,717	152,007	439,138		
S. C.	S Carolina, Cam & Col. brs.	242	4,179,200	3,318,525	7,558,037	1,449,803	709,268
	Charlotte & South Carolina,	109	1,201,000	380,000	1,719,046	240,722	119,167
	Greenville and Columbia,	165	1,295,000	970,000	1,907,278	1,449,800	709,265
	Northeastern, . .	102	886,650	1,819,990	1,907,278	99,404	61,132
733	Other roads, . .	115					
Tenn.	See Va., S. C., Ga., Ala., and Miss., ...						
	East Tenn. & Virginia,	130	626,075	1,728,664	3,208,138	61,314	22,252
	East Tenn. & Georgia,	110	1,192,974	1,739,669	2,703,428	227,363	122,371
	Nashville & Chattanooga,	159	2,263,905	1,632,798	3,896,703	641,552	422,292
	Tennessee and Alabama,	29	309,754	626,889	679,906	53,775	24,370
	Memphis and Charleston,	287	2,228,177	3,495,288	5,572,470	642,022	307,518
	Memphis and Ohio,	82	725,000	97,242	1,489,420		
830	McMinnville & Man'ster,	34	140,097	414,671	565,459		
Texas,	Buffalo Bayou, Braz & Col.	32	429,300	401,155	581,865	35,969	17,648
	Houston & Texas Central,	60	265,000		1,000,000	117,542	
	Galves., Hous. & Hender.,	25					
129	Other roads, . . .	22					
Vermont	Connecticut & Passump. R.,	90	1,200,000	800,000	2,631,146	192,122	110,121
	Rutland and Burlington,	119	2,233,376	6,392,141	4,691,217	354,288	272,726
	Rutland and Washington,	62	950,000		1,171,883	172,825	136,702
	Western Vermont, . .	54	332,000	331,600	1,084,000		
	Vermont Central, .	118	5,000,000	5,276,300	8,402,054	702,271	556,595
	Vermont and Canada, .	48					
	Vermont Valley, .	24	516,163		1,212,274	45,785	38,520
523	Other roads, ...	13					
Virginia,	Central (to Jackson's Riv.)	195	3,122,968	1,833,170	5,384,260	585,832	290,056
	Manassa's Gap, . .	75					
	Orange and Alexandria,	102	1,457,000	1,006,484	2,028,066	275,791	136,969
	Rich., Fred'b'g, & Potom.,*	75	1,000,000	730,506	1,708,169	232,172	111,960
	Richmond & Petersburg,	22	834,900	231,000	1,206,121	157,542	76,056
	Petersb'g(& Gast Br. 18m.)	82	769,000	158,502	1,009,115	263,784	140,128
	Richmond and Danville,	141	1,977,399	326,407	3,487,685	461,918	206,382
	Seaboard and Roanoke. .	80			1,365,834		
	Pet'bg & Lynchb'g (Saide),	133	1,457,000	1,006,484	2,028,068	275,791	136,969
	Virginia and Tennessee,	204	3,503,200	3,261,955	6,765,156	672,976	377,200
1,230	Other roads, . . .	121					
Wisc.	La Crosse and Milwaukee.	200	10,872,000	8,316,743	15,974,670	882,918	510,127

* From Washington to Acquia Creek by steamboat is 55 miles, which makes steamboat and railroad route 130 miles.

State.	Name of Road.	Length in operation.	Capital Stock paid in.	Debt, Funded and Floating.	Cost of Construction and Equipment.	Receipts in 1858.	Expenses in 1858.
		Miles.	$	$	$	$	$
Wisc.	Watertown Division,	64					
	Milwaukee & Mississippi,	235	3,440,673	4,610,583	8,161,255	882,818	510,127
	Milwaukee and Horicon,	42	1,101,200		919,757	60,066	
	Racine and Mississippi,	101	1,566,405	498,479	2,681,056	192,459	73,992
	Mineral Point,	32					
702	Kenosha, Rockf. & R. Isl.	28					
	Total in United States,	28,752					
	Panama (Aspinwall to Pa.)	49	3,743,000		6,564,832	1,305,819	845,183

The American Railroad Journal of January 1, 1859, gives the length of the railroads in operation in the United States, January 1, 1859, at 27,857 miles; cost $961,047,364. The Secretary of the Treasury (Report on the Finances, December 8, 1857, pp. 44, 45) states the capital paid in of the railroads in the United States to be $491,435,661; the debt, $417,243,664; annual interest on the debt, $25,093,203: the net income, $48,406,488; the available income, $24,290,826.

The American Railroad Journal for May 15, 1858, gives a table of the *Canals* in the United States, compiled by Richard S. Fisher, Esq. Their aggregate length is said to be 5,131.53 miles.

Railroads in Canada.

Name of Road.	Length. Miles.	Name of Road.	Length. Miles.
Buffalo & Lake Huron (Buff. to Goderich),	161	Great West. (Niagara Falls to Detroit),	229
Champ & St. Law. (Rous. Pt. to Montr.),	44	Guelph Branch,	28
Cobourg and Peterboro,	28	Toronto Branch (Hamilton to Toronto),	38
Erie & Ontario (Niag. Falls to Chippewa),	17	Mont. & N.Y. (Mont. to Mooer's Junc.),	42
Grand Trunk. For Portland Dist. see Maine.		Plattsb'g & Mont. (Mooer's J. to Platts.),	20
Montreal District,	143	Ont., Sim. & Huron (Tor. to Collingwood),	95
Quebec Dist. (Richmond to Quebec),	96	Ottawa & Prescott (Pres. to Bytown),	54
Montreal and Toronto Districts,	333	Other roads,	37
Tor. & Sarnia District (Tor. & Lond.)	120		
St. Thomas Branch,	49	Total,	1,534

Surveyed Routes for a Railroad from the Mississippi or its Tributaries to the Pacific Ocean. — From the Report of the Secretary of War.

Description of Route.	Distance in straight line.	Distance by proposed route.	Sum of ascent and descent.	Estimated Cost.	Through arable lands.
	Miles.	Miles.	Feet.	$	Miles.
1. Route near 47th and 49th parallels, from St. Paul to Vancouver,	1,455	1,864	18,100	130,781,000	374
a. Extension thence to Seattle,	45	161	1,000	10,090,000	161
2. Near the 41st and 42d parallels, *via* South Pass from Council Bluffs to Benicia,	1,410	2,032	29,120	116,095,000	632
3. Near the 38th and 39th parallels, from Westport to San Francisco, by the Coo-che-to-pa and Tah-ee-chay-pah Passes,	1,740	2,080	49,986	So great that road is impracticable.	620
b. Same, from Westport to San Francisco by the Coo-che-to-pah and Madelin Passes,	1,740	2,290	56,514	do.	670
4. Near the 35th parallel, from Fort Smith to San Pedro,	1,360	1,892	48,812	169,210,265	416
c. Near the 35th parallel, from Fort Smith to San Francisco,		2,174	50,670	169,210,265	644
5. Near the 32d parallel, from Fulton to San Pedro,	1,400	1,618	32,784	68,970,000	408
d. Fulton to San Francisco,	1,620	2,039	42,008	93,120,000	759

Route	Through sterile Land.	Miles of Route elevated. Less than 1,000 feet.	Between 1 & 2,000 feet.	Between 2 & 3,000 feet.	Between 3 & 4,000 feet.	Between 4 & 5,000 feet.	Between 5 & 6,000 feet.	Between 6 & 7,000 feet.	Between 7 & 8,000 feet.	Between 8 & 9,000 feet.	Between 9 & 10,000 feet.	Length of level Route of equal Working Expenses.	Summit of highest Pass.
	Miles.											Miles.	Feet.
1	1,490	470	530	720	130	97	23					2,207	6,044*
a		161										180	
2	1,400	180	170	210	160	580	285	270	107	20		2,583	8,373
3	1,460	340	276	165	343	466	170	60	155	80	20	3,125	10,032†
b	1,620	275	398	190	143	725	284	110	155	80	20	3,360	10,032†
4	1,476	303	347	263	185	160	305	235	95			2,816	7,472
c	1,530											3,137	
5	1,210	485	300	100	170	503	60					2,239	5,717
d	1,230	706	410	160	205	504	60					2,834	5,717

XXX. LINES OF LAND AND SUBMARINE TELEGRAPH.

The length in miles of the lines of land telegraph in operation in the different parts of the world, January 1, 1858, is stated in round numbers as follows: —

	Miles.		Miles.
America (United States),	35,000	India,	5,000
America (British Provinces),	5,000	Italy,	2,500
America (other parts and Islands),	5,000	Prussia,	4,000
Australia,	1,200	Russia,	5,000
Austria and Germany,	10,000	Switzerland,	1,500
Bavaria and Saxony,	1,700	Rest of Europe,	1,400
Belgium,	550	Other parts of the World,	500
England,	10,000		
France,	8,000	Total,	96,350

The estimated cost of the lines in the United States is $4,000,000; in the British Provinces, $500,000; in England, $7,500,000. The number of messages passing over all the lines in the United States in a year is estimated at near 4,000,000.

Lines of Submarine Telegraph.

	Miles.	Wires.	Date.
Dover and Calais	25	4	1851
Dover and Ostend	75	6	1852
Holyhead and Howth	65	1	1852
England and Holland	115	3	1853
Port Patrick and Donaghadee	13	6	1853
Port Patrick and Donaghadee, second cable,	13	6	1853
Across the Soland, Isle of Wight (England)	3	4	1855
Across the Frith of Forth (Scotland)	4	4	1855
Denmark, across the Great Belt	15	3	1854
Denmark, across the Little Belt	5	3	1854
Denmark, across the Sound	12	3	1855
Petersburg to Cronstadt	10	1	1856
Italy and Corsica	65	6	1854
Corsica and Sardinia	10	6	1854
Messina to Reggio	5	1	1856
Across the Danube, at Shumla	1	1	1855
Six cables across the mouths of the Danube, at the Isle of Serpents, each one mile long and having one conductor	6	6	1857
Varna and Balaklava (across the Black Sea)	340	1	1855
Balaklava and Eupatoria	60	1	1855
Across the Bosphorus, at Kandili	1	1	1856
Across the Hoogly River	2.50		
Across the Gulf of St. Lawrence	74	1	1856
Across the Straits of Northumberland, Prince Edward Island	10.50	1.	1856
Across the Gut of Canso, Nova Scotia	3	3	1856
Across the St. Lawrence, at Quebec		1	1855
Across the Mississippi at Paducah	1	1	1851
Across the Atlantic, from Trinity Bay to Valentia Bay	1,950	7	1858
Small river crossings	20		
Total length of submarine cables	2,904		

The cost of the Atlantic Telegraph Cable, as originally made, was as follows: 2,500 miles at $485 a mile; 10 miles deep-sea cable at $1,450 a mile; 25 miles shore ends at $1,250 a mile. Total cost, $1,258,250.

* Tunnel at elevation of 5,219 feet. † Tunnel at elevation of 9,540 feet.

INDIVIDUAL STATES.*

I. ALABAMA.

Capital, Montgomery. *Area*, 50,722 sq. m. *Population*, 1855, 841,704.

Government for the Year 1860.

			Salary.
Andrew B. Moore, of Marion,	*Governor* (term of office expires on the 1st Monday in December, 1861),		$4,000
James H. Weaver,	of Coosa Co.,	*Secretary of State*,	Fees and 1,200
Wm. J. Greene,	of Macon Co.,	*Compt. of Pub. Accounts*,	" 2,000
William Graham,	of Autauga Co.,	*State Treasurer*,	1,800
Thos. C. McIvor,	of Wilcox Co.,	*Adj. and Insp.-General*,	not over 200
P. H. Brittan,	of Montgomery,	*Quartermaster-General*,	150
Gabriel B. Du Val,	of Montgomery,	*Supt. of Education*,	2,000
John Whiting,	of Montgomery,	*Comm'r & Trustee to settle Affairs of State Bank and Branches*,	2,500
Watkins Phelan,	of Montgomery,	*Private Secretary to Governor, and Keeper of State-House*,	650
John D. Rather,	of Morgan Co.,	*President of Senate.*	
Joseph H. Phelan,	of Coosa Co.,	*Secretary of the Senate.*	
A. B. Meek,	of Mobile,	*Speaker of the House.*	
Albert S. Elmore,	of Montgomery,	*Clerk of the House.*	

The Senate consists of 33 members, elected for four years, one half going out every two years. The House of Representatives consists of 100 members, elected for two years. The Legislature meets *biennially* in the city of Montgomery, on the second Monday of November. The seventh biennial session commenced in November, 1859. The pay of the members of both houses is $4 a day each. The Legislature in 1857 raised the salary of the Governor from $2,500 to $4,000.

Judiciary.

		Supreme Court.	Term ends.	Salary.
A. J. Walker,	of Montgomery,	*Chief Justice*,	Jan. 1862,	$3,000
George W. Stone,	of Montgomery,	*Associate Justice*,	" "	3,000
†Richard W. Walker,	of Florence,	"	" 1864,	3,000
Marion A. Baldwin,	of Montgomery,	*Attorney-General*,		Fees and 425
J. W. Shepherd,	of Montgomery,	*Reporter*,		1,200
John D. Phelan,	of Montgomery,	*Clerk*,		Fees.

The judges of the Supreme Court, and the chancellors, are elected by a joint vote of the two houses of the General Assembly, for six years. The

* For the table exhibiting the Seats of Government, the times of the election of State Officers, and the meeting of the Legislatures, of the several States, see *ante*, p. 210; and for their population at the several censuses, see pp. 214, 215.

† R. W. Walker is Judge by executive appointment. The Legislature, at the session in 1859, elects a Judge.

Supreme Court has appellate jurisdiction only, and holds its sessions at the seat of government on the first Monday of January and June of each year, for hearing and determining points of law taken by appeal from the Chancery, Circuit, and Probate Courts. The volumes of reported decisions are fifty-two in number.

	Court of Chancery.		Term ends.	Salary.
Milton J. Saffold,	of Montgomery,	*Chancellor Southern Div.*,	1865,	$2,000
James B. Clark,	of Eutaw,	" *Middle* "	1860,	2,000
John Foster,	of Jacksonville,	" *Northern* "	1862,	2,000

The State is divided into three chancery divisions and thirty-nine districts, in each of which one session of the court is held annually, and in some of the larger districts two sessions are held.

Circuit Courts.

Circuit.	Judges.	Residence.	Salary.	Solicitors.	Salary.
1st.	Porter King,	Marion,	$2,000	Y. L. Royston,	$350 & fees.
2d.	Nathan Cook,	Haynesville,	"	R. Gaillard,	250 & fees.
3d.	William S. Mudd,	Elyton,	"	L. V. B. Martin,	"
4th.	John E. Moore,	Florence,	"	John S. Kennedy,	"
5th.	S. D. Hale,	Huntsville,	"	Nicholas Davis, Jr.,	"
6th.	Charles W. Rapier,	Mobile,	"	Robert Armistead,	"
7th.	A. A. Coleman,	Livingston,	"	A. E. Van Hoose,	"
8th.	John Gill Shorter,	Eufaula,	"	Marion A. Baldwin,	"
9th.	Robert Dougherty,	Tuskegee,	"	J. J. Woodward,	"

The judges of the Circuit Courts are elected by the people of the circuit for the term of six years, and are required to alternate with each other in holding the circuits. These courts have original jurisdiction in all criminal causes, and in all civil causes above $50. When less than $50, their jurisdiction is appellate only from the decisions of justices of the peace. Two sessions (spring and fall) are held each year in every county. The Solicitors, besides fees, receive a salary of $250, except in the First Circuit, where the salary is $350. The Attorney-General acts as Solicitor for the Eighth Circuit.

In Mobile County the criminal jurisdiction has been transferred to a special

	City Court for Mobile.		Term ends.	Salary.
Alexander McKinstry,	of Mobile,	*Judge*,	1862,	$2,000

This court holds three terms each year, on the first Monday of February and of June, and on the second Monday of October, and has concurrent jurisdiction with the Circuit Courts except in real actions.

Finances

For the Year ending September 30, 1859.

Balance in the Treasury, September 30, 1858,	$371,335.74	
Receipts for the year ending September 30, 1859,	945,900.16	
Total available means for the year,		$1,317,235.90
Disbursements for year ending September 30, 1859,		$685,556.90
Balance in the Treasury, September 30, 1859,		$631,679.00

This balance includes $46,079.00 of notes of the old State Bank and branches, which have been burned.

Chief Sources of Income.		*Principal Items of Expenditure.*	
Taxes,	$717,000.00	Executive,	$13,250.00
Banks, &c. for bonus and interest,	12,845.20	Judiciary,	39,332.89
Sales of 16th Section Lands,	72,577.00	Educational expenses,	293,376.00
Interest on such sales,	13,662.24	University of Alabama,	15,000.00
Foreign agencies, &c.,	1,923.00	Insane Hospital,	68,315.00
Bank attorneys,	30,000.00	Penitentiary and prisoners,	25,774.00
Mobile and Ohio R. R. Co.,	24,230.00	Railroads,	57,500.00
Two and Three per Cent Fund, &c.,	23,451.56	Trustee, State Bank & branches,	160,000.00
		Notes of old State Bank, &c. destroyed,	46,079.00

State Debt. — The foreign debt, Oct. 1, 1859, was $3,423,000.00 on which the annual interest is nearly $172,065.55. The domestic debt, Sept. 30, 1859, was $1,675,000.00, — being Common School Fund, $1,425,000.00; University Fund, $250,000.00. Annual interest nearly $85,000. The State has as security for its loans to roads, mortgages of the roads, first mortgage bonds, and in some cases individual notes. The State also owns Virginia and North Carolina stocks to the amount of $662,000.

To September 30, 1855, the State had lent to railroads and plank-roads $467,109.23.

Banks. — For the condition of the banks in this State in January, 1859, see *ante*, p. 220.

Common Schools. — A system of public instruction was established by the act of Feb. 15, 1854, and a Superintendent of Education was appointed. The money raised for the support of schools, and the income of the educational funds, are apportioned among the several townships, according to the number of children therein between 6 and 21 years of age. The amount apportioned for the year 1858 was $271,378.97. The number of children between 6 and 21 was 178,095; average per child, $1.30. The returns that were received showed in the summer of 1858 the existence of 2,597 schools. This does not include Mobile County, which has a separate and independent school system.

There is an Insane Hospital at Tuscaloosa. The amount advanced by the State to this institution up to Sept. 30, 1859, was $271,523.16. The State has made appropriations for an institution for the deaf and dumb, at Talladega, which is now in successful operation. There is an asylum for the blind at Mobile. The number of convicts in the State Penitentiary, October 1, 1858, was 217; of these 78 were committed for offences against the person; for offences against property, 121; for miscellaneous offences, 18.

State Census. — The census for the year 1855, taken under a special act, classifies the population as follows: — White males under 21 years, 140,077; over 21 years, 97,385; white females under 21 years, 135,422; over 21 years, 91,572; total whites, 464,456; insane persons, 464; slaves, 374,782; free persons of color, 2,466; total inhabitants, 841,704. There were 17 colleges, 160 academies, 1,074 common schools, 40,280 children at school, and 93,443 white children between 8 and 15 years of age.

II. ARKANSAS.

Capital, Little Rock. *Area*, 52,198 sq. m. *Population*, 1858, 331,213.

Government for the Year 1860.

	Salary.
ELIAS N. CONWAY, of Little Rock, *Governor* (term of office expires November, 1860),	$1,800*
Alexander Boileau, of Little Rock, *Sec. of State & School Commissioner*,	Perquisites and 1,000

* And $200 for rent of house. After the expiration of the term of the present Governor the salary will be $2,500.

			Salary.
William R. Miller,	of Little Rock,	*Aud. of Pub. Acc'ts,*	Fees and $ 1,200
John Quindley,	"	*Treasurer,*	Fees and 800
David Dale Owen,	of New Harmony, Ind.,	*State Geologist,*	2,500
J.W. McConaughey,	of Little Rock,	*Land Att'y & State Col.,*	5 per cent on col.
Thomas Fletcher,	of Arkansas Co.,	*President of the Senate.*	
Benj. T. Duval,	of Sebastian Co.,	*Speaker of the House.*	

State Land Agents. — B. F. Owen, Little Rock; J. C. O. Smith, Helena; W. W. Alexander, Batesville; L. C. Howell, Clarksville; J. M. Killgore, Washington; V. L. Kelley, Champagnolle. John D. Kimbell is *Swamp-Land Secretary.*

The Secretary of State, Auditor, and Treasurer are elected by a joint vote of both houses of the General Assembly. The term of office of the present members ends in November, 1860. The Legislature meets biennially at Little Rock. A session will commence in November, 1860. Number of Senators, 25; of Representatives, 75. Their compensation is $4 a day during the session, and $3 for every 20 miles' travel in going to and returning from the seat of government.

Judiciary.

Supreme Court.

			Term ends.	Salary.
Elbert H. English,	of Little Rock,	*Chief Justice,*	Nov. 1860,	$2,500
Henry M. Rector,	"	*Associate Justice,*	Nov. 1866,	2,500
Freeman W. Compton,	of Princeton,	"	Nov. 1864,	2,500
S. H. Hempstead,	of Little Rock,	*Solicitor-General,*	Nov. 1860,	1,500
J. L. Hallowell,	"	*Attorney-General,*		700
Luke E. Barber,	"	*Clerk and Reporter,*		Fees as Clerk, [and $ 400 as Reporter.

The Supreme Court has appellate jurisdiction only, except in particular cases pointed out by the constitution. It regularly holds annually two terms at Little Rock, in January and July, but by the act of 1858 it is required to hold four terms a year until the arrears of business are disposed of. The judges are elected by the General Assembly, by a joint vote of both houses, for eight years.

The Circuit Court has original jurisdiction over all criminal cases not expressly provided for otherwise by law; and exclusive original jurisdiction of all crimes amounting to felony at common law; and original jurisdiction of all civil cases which are not cognizable before justices of the peace; and in all matters of contract, where the sum in controversy is over $100. It holds annually two terms in each circuit. The judges and prosecuting attorneys are elected by the people, the former for four, and the latter for two years.

Chancellor of Pulaski County. — H. F. Fairchild, Term ends Nov. 1862. Salary, $1,800.

	Judge.	Term ends.	Salary.	Prosecut. Attorney.	Term ends.	Salary.
1st Circuit,	Mark W. Alexander,	1862,	$1,500	S. W. Childers,	1860,	Fees & $300
2d "	J. C. Murray,	1862,	1,500	S. M. Arnett,	1860,	" 300
3d "	William C. Bevens,	1862,	1,500	W. K. Patterson,	1860,	" 300
4th "	John M. Wilson,	1862,	1,500	Lafayette Gregg,	1860,	" 300

	Judge.	Term ends.	Salary.	Prosecut. Attorney.	Term ends.	Salary.
5th Circuit,	John J. Clendenin,	1862,	$ 1,500	J. L. Hallowell,	1860,	$ 700
6th "	Len. B. Green,	1862,	1,500	E. W. Gantt,	1860,	Fees & 300

Finances

For the Two Years ending 30th September, 1858.

Balance of specie in the treasury, October 1, 1856,	$ 177,226.62
Receipts in specie from all sources during the two years,	449,277.31
Total,	626,503.93
Total expenditures in specie for the two years,	368,420.16
Balance of specie in treasury, October 1, 1858,	$ 258,083.77

Of this balance, $ 235,194.39 were applicable to State expenditures, the rest being due certain funds. The receipts are chiefly from taxes. The principal items of expenditure were substantially as follows: Legislature, $ 35,000; Executive and contingencies, $ 35,000; Judiciary, $ 35,000; Prosecuting Attorneys, $ 6,700; Penitentiary, $ 37,000; Printing and distributing laws and law reports, $ 14,000; Digest of statute laws, $ 10,600; Seminary Fund and Schools, $ 30,000; Internal Improvement Fund, $ 110,000.

State Debt. — Outstanding bonds issued to the Real Estate Bank, principal,

October 1, 1858,		$ 946,000.00
Interest accrued and unpaid, October 1, 1858,		845,830.00
Total debt on account of Real Estate Bank, October 1, 1858,		$ 1,791,830.00
Outstanding bonds issued to Bank of the State of Arkansas, to October 1, 1858,	$ 616,000.00	
Interest accrued and unpaid to same date,	631,142.50	
Total debt on account of Bank of State, October 1, 1858,		1,247,142.50
Total debt on account of both banks, October 1, 1858,		$ 3,038,972.50

There has been since paid, up to October 1, 1859, for debt of both banks, principal, $ 26,000, interest, $ 31,839, — total, $ 57,839, — which deducted from the above gives $ 2,981,133 as the debt of the State October 1, 1859.

October 1, 1856, there was in the treasury $ 16,492.01 of Arkansas Bank paper. This has been burned. Amount received since and in the treasury October 1, 1858, $ 680.

By its charter, the Real Estate Bank is bound to pay the interest and redeem the principal of the bonds issued to its use, and the State took for security a mortgage from the 180 stockholders of 141,980 acres of land, valued at the time, by commissioners under oath, at $ 2,603,932.32, which mortgage it now holds. It is thought that from the increased value of the lands the State will be secured from loss, unless it waive the lien; and this would leave to the State the debt due for bonds issued on account of the Bank of the State.

$ 38,000 of the bonds are due in January, 1867, and $ 916,000 in January, 1868.

Taxable Property in 1858. — Number of acres of land 7,989,676; value with improvements, $ 39,069,146. Value of city, &c. lots and improvements, $ 3,316,558. Slaves between 5 and 60 years of age, 51,891; value, $ 34,794,169. 248 saw-mills; value, $ 256,306. 91 tan-yards; value, $ 27,856. 66 distilleries; value, $ 7,611. Value of household furniture, taxed, $ 102,589; of pleasure-carriages, $ 229,159; of horses over 2 years old, $ 3,720,802; of mules over 2 years, $ 1,701,766; of jacks and jennies, $ 120,719; of neat cattle over 2 years, $ 2,349,127; of stock in trade of *all* trades, &c., $ 1,507,018; of loans over debts, $ 885,898; of steamboats, ferries, &c., $ 35,290; gold watches and jewelry, $ 191,859. Capital in manufactories, $ 33,545. Total value of taxable property, $ 88,049,415. Amount of State tax, $ 154,798.79. Number of polls, 38,181.

State Census of 1858. — Returns were received from all the counties. From these it appears that there are in the State 132,790 white males, 114,341 white females; 387 free male negroes, and 361 free female negroes; 83,334 slaves. Total, 331,213. 331,628 acres of land were cultivated in cotton, and 979,366 in grain. There were raised 182,217 bales of cotton, 17,181,867 bushels of corn, 1,143,656 of wheat, 2,050,753 of oats.

Common Schools. — The Secretary of State is *ex officio* Commissioner of Common Schools. His last report that we have seen is dated November 13, 1854. The returns to him from the School Commissioners were exceedingly imperfect; only 40 schools were reported in the whole State. There is a great indifference to the subject of common school education throughout the State. The law provides for a large school fund. The seminary and saline funds are distributed to the counties to aid in the support of common schools. The seminary fund has distributed $ 79,321, and the saline fund $ 7,708, up to January 1, 1858. The accruing annual interest on money arising from the sales of the 16th section of land in any township is made a perpetual fund for the support of schools. The annual State and county taxes assessed upon 16th sections sold, proceeds of escheated estates, fines for certain offences and crimes, are by law to be paid into the treasury of the proper county for the support of schools. There is no official report of the amounts arising from those sources.

State Prison. — Number of convicts Oct. 1, 1856, 90; received since from State courts, 48; from U. S. courts, 15; runaway slaves, 4; in all, 67; making the whole number 157. There have been discharged of State prisoners, — by pardon, 19; expiration of sentence, 11; death, 5; escape, 4; otherwise 6; of U. S. prisoners — by expiration of sentence, 22; by death, 1. In all, 68, leaving in confinement Oct. 1, 1858, 89. Of these 28 were committed for murder or manslaughter, or for assault with intent to kill; 13 for horse stealing; 9 for negro stealing; 20 for petit larceny; 4 for burglary; 1 for arson; 1 for rape; 4 for forgery; 3 for passing counterfeit money. 10 were under 20 years of age, 43 between 20 and 30, 22 between 30 and 40; 84 were white males, 1 was an Indian, 2 free men of color, 2 runaway slaves; 75 were natives, 12 foreigners. The services of the prisoners and the prison itself are leased to contractors.

Geological Survey. — The Legislature in 1857 provided for a geological survey of the State. Dr. Owen was appointed State Geologist. During the years 1857 and 1858, assisted by William Elderhorst, Chemical Assistant, and Edward T. Cox, Assistant Geologist, he made a reconnoissance of the northern counties of the State, the results of which appear in his first report, already published.

III. CALIFORNIA.

Capital, Sacramento. *Area,* 160,000 sq. m. *Estimated population,* 1856, 507,067.

Government for the Year 1860.

			Term expires.	Salary.
Milton S. Latham,	of Sacramento,	*Governor,*	Jan. 1862,	$8,000
John G. Downey,	of Los Angelos,	*Lieut.-Gov. & Pres. of Senate,*		$12 a [day during session of Legislature.
Ferris Forman,*	of Sacramento,	*Sec'y of State,*	Jan. 1860,	3,500
Samuel H. Brooks,	of San Joaquim,	*Comptroller,*	Jan. 1862,	3,500
Thomas Findley,	of Nevada,	*Treasurer,*	"	3,500
Thos. H. Williams,	of El Dorado Co.,	*Attorney-General,*	"	2,000
Horace A. Higley,	of Nevada Co.,	*Surveyor-General,*	"	2,000
Andr. J. Moulder,	of San Francisco,	*Sup't of Pub. Instruc.,*	"	3,500
Wm. C. Kibbe,	of Calaveras Co.,	*Adj. and Q. M. Gen.,*		2,000
Charles T. Botts,	of Sacramento,	*State Printer,*	Jan. 1862,	Fees.

The Governor and Lieutenant-Governor are elected by the people, by a plurality vote, for two years. The Secretary of State is appointed by the Governor. The Comptroller, Treasurer, Attorney-General and Surveyor-General, and State Printer, are elected by the people for two years. The sessions of the Legislature are annual. The pay of the members is $ 10 per day for the first 90 days, and afterwards $ 5 a day and mileage, — $ 4 for every 20 miles of travel to the Capitol.

* It is said that Dr. Johnson Price is to be Secretary of State in place of Mr. Forman.

Supreme Court.

The Supreme Court consists of a chief justice and two associate justices. It has appellate jurisdiction where the matter in dispute exceeds $ 200, and where the legality of certain acts is questioned, and in certain criminal cases. The justices are elected by the people for six years, and are so classified that one goes out of office every two years. The senior judge in office is the chief justice. The clerk is elected for two years.

			Term expires.	Salary.
Stephen J. Field,	of Marysville,	*Chief Justice*,	Jan., 1862,	$ 6,000
Joseph G. Baldwin,	of San Francisco,	*Assoc. Justice*,	Jan., 1864,	6,000
W. W. Cope,	of Amador,	"	Jan., 1866,	6,000
Harvey Lee,	of Eldorado,	*Reporter*,	May, 1860,	4,000
Charles S. Fairfax,	of Marysville,	*Clerk*,	Jan. 1, 1862,	Fees.

District Courts.

Judges' Terms expire in 1865.

Dist.	Judge.	Residence.	Salary.	Dist.	Judge.	Residence.	Salary.
1.	Benjamin Hays,	San Diego,	$ 3,000	9.	W. P. Daingerfield,	Shasta,	6,000
2.	Joaquin Carillo,	Santa Barbara,	3,000	10.	S. M. Bliss,	Marysville,	6,000
3.	Sam Bell McKee,	San José,	4,000	11.	B. F. Myers,	Auburn,	6,000
4.	Caleb Burbank,	San Francisco,	7,500	12.	S. H. Brodie,	San Francisco,	7,000
5.	Charles M. Creaner,	Stockton,	6,000	13.	Nicholas Cleary,	Mariposa,	4,000
6.	J. H. McKune,	Sacramento,	6,000	14.	Niles Searles,	Downieville,	5,000
7.	E. W. McKinstry,	Sonoma,	5,000	15.	Warren T. Sexton,	Oroville,	4,000
8.	W. R. Turner,		6,000				

The District Courts have jurisdiction in law and equity, where the amount in dispute, exclusive of interest, exceeds $ 200. The judges are chosen by the people for six years. A county judge is elected in each county for four years, to act as judge of probate, to hold the County Court, and with two justices of the peace to hold Courts of Sessions for criminal business. Clerks of courts, district attorneys, sheriffs, coroners, &c. are elected by the people.

FINANCES.

State Debt. — The State debt January 1, 1859, was as follows: —

Bonds issued under act 28th April, 1857, ...	$ 3,900,000.00
Outstanding bonds and Comptroller's warrants not provided for, . .	143,485.63
Making an aggregate of	$ 4,043,485.63

The annual interest on the funded debt, as ratified by the people, is $ 273,900. A large part of the item $ 143,485 63 consists of old bonds which were presented for funding after the amount authorized by the act of April 28, 1857 ($ 3,900,000) had been funded. There are besides bonds to the amount of $ 245,374, issued by the State on account of Indian hostilities. They are made a claim on the Federal Government. They show on their face that they are not to be a charge on the State Treasury.

The total receipts for the year ending June 30, 1858, were	$ 1,215,128.61
The total expenditures for the same period were	992,553.35
Excess of receipts, ...	$ 222,575.26
The receipts from July 1, 1858 to December 15, 1858, inclusive, were .	493,332.28
Add amount in the Treasury July 1, 1858, ...	271,109.34
Total expended during the same period, ...	$ 764,441.62
	242,271.46
Balance on hand, December 15, 1858, ...	$ 522,170.26

For the year ending June 30, 1858, some of the principal items of receipts and expenditures were as follows: —

Receipts.		*Expenditures.*	
Property tax,	$ 710,211.63	Executive,	$ 106,428.55
Poll tax,	81,872.43	Judicial,	139,075.35
Stamp tax,	90,755.32	Legislative,	252,381.44
Foreign miners' licenses,	129,967.91	State Prison,	169,564.80
Merchants' licenses,	51,744.99	Printing,	83,054.58
Liquor licenses,	60,500.93	Insane Asylum,	90,106.31
Billiard and bowling licenses,	10,977.88	Hospital purposes,	10,224.46
Peddlers' licenses,	12,452.44	School purposes,	67,750.67
Other licenses,	11,905.96	State Agricultural Society,	10,000.00
Swamp and overflowed lands,	16,959.62	Military expenses,	1,089.48
Passenger brokers,	12,723.14	Translating laws,	1,397.60
Commutation tax,	9,172.00		

The valuation of the taxable property of the State, real and personal, was $ 123,955,877. The personal property constituted more than one third of the valuation. The whole number of acres of land reported was 5,037,557. Value, $ 27,917,641; value of improvements thereon, $ 15,888,534; value of city and town lots, $ 4,947,953; value of improvements thereon, $ 7,306,223. Value of personal property, $ 48,919,728. The State tax on the whole valuation, at 60 cents on each $ 100, amounted to 743,729. For 1856 the total valuation of taxable property was $ 113,458,000; for 1857, $ 131,806,269.

The total shipments of gold from San Francisco, from April 11, 1849, to Dec. 31, 1856, inclusive, were $ 322,393,856.

Abstract of Taxable Property for 1857. — Acres of land enclosed, 597,610; cultivated, 508,267. Acres of wheat, 126,038; bushels, 2,172,818; — of barley, 196,934; bushels, 4,449,581; — of oats, 36,894; bushels, 1,097,399; — of rye, 963; bushels, 31,967; — of corn, 12,141; bushels, 410,293; — of buckwheat, 1,065; bushels, 30,445; — of potatoes, 18,847; bushels, 1,522,397; — of hay, 66,836; tons, 84,837; — of tobacco, 14; pounds, 1,800. Pounds of butter, 1,942,861; of cheese, 1,067,418; of wool, 843,577; tons of grapes, 51,467; gallons of wine made, 288,400; value of fruit raised, $ 145,976. Number of American horses, 19,682; Spanish horses, tame, 26,104; wild, 51,019; number of stock cattle, 334,670; of beef cattle, 39,466; of sheep, 257,150; of cattle slaughtered, 69,661, value $ 1,924,675; of hogs slaughtered, 43,269, value $ 458,560; of sheep slaughtered, 43,977, value $ 226,568. Number of steam grist-mills, 42; water do., 52; bushels of grain ground per annum, 2,871,617. Steam saw-mills, 111; water do., 194; feet of lumber sawed, 308,531,500. Quartz mills, 132; value, $ 558,800; tons of quartz crushed, 206,547. Number of mining-ditches, 550; miles in length, 2,901; value $ 1,516,500. Turnpike roads, 22; length, 225 miles; cost, $ 91,500; income, $ 14,400; repairs, $ 1,950. Ferries, 109; cost, $ 79,200. Toll-bridges, 99; value, $ 286,500.

Common Schools. — The 500,000 acres of land granted by Congress to the State for purposes of internal improvement are by the constitution devoted to public schools. Of these lands, 448,934 acres had been sold January 1, 1859, for the sum of $ 739,487.50, the interest on which, at 7 per cent per annum, is credited semiannually to the School Fund. It was expected that the remaining 51,066 acres would be soon sold at the rate established by law, and the School Fund would then amount to $ 803,320 from this source. The 16th and 36th sections of land in each township, granted by Congress for the support of public schools, will amount, by estimation, to 5,500,000 acres. 72 sections of land, amounting to 46,080 acres, were granted to the State for the use of a seminary of learning. 8,579 acres have been sold for $ 10,724. The whole, when sold, will make the Seminary Fund $ 57,600. One fourth of the money from poll-taxes and escheated estates goes to the School Fund, and the constitution provides that the percentage on the sale of lands in the State allowed by Congress shall be inviolably appropriated to the use of common schools. Counties may levy special taxes for school purposes. To entitle any district to the benefit of an appropriation from the State School Fund, the school therein must have been kept at least three months in the year. There is a Board of Education, consisting of the Governor, the Superintendent of Public Instruction, and the Surveyor-General. The returns for the year ending October 31, 1858, are as follows: — Number of districts, 411; number of children between 4 and 18 years of age, 40,530 (boys 21,344, girls, 19,186); number under 4 years of age, 23,558; children of all ages born in California, 33,546; number of pupils attending schools, 19,822; daily average attendance, 11,183; number of teachers, 517 (male 333, female 184); number of schools, 432 (being 3 high, 17 grammar, 11 intermediate, 79 mixed, and 322 primary). State school money drawn for salaries, $ 55,383; amount paid teachers, $ 147,371; total drafts on account of salaries, $ 203,276; expended in erecting, rent, and repair of school-houses, $ 88,200; for school libraries and apparatus, $ 3,043; total expenditure for school purposes, $ 339,915; county tax received for school purposes, $ 162,890. Number of school-houses, 227 (of brick 14, of wood 213); number of private schools, 55; pupils in private schools, 2,422; number of schools kept open three months, 93; over three and less than six months, 166; over six and less than nine, 102; over nine months, 60.

State Prison. — At San Quentin, Marin County, 12 miles north of San Francisco. March 26, 1856, the prison, property, labor of prisoners, &c. was let to James M. Estell for five years, the State to pay him the sum of $ 10,000 a month for the whole period. The lease was unfortunate for the State and for the prisoners. It is claimed on the part of the State that the lease is void, and the State has resumed possession of the prison. Whole number of convicts received from Jan. 1, 1851, to Jan. 1, 1859, 1,649; 560 were discharged by expiration of sentence, 127 by pardon, 300 escaped, 35 died or were killed. There were in prison Jan. 1, 1859, 582; under 20 years of age, 54; between 20 and 30, 401; between 30 and 40, 98. 248 were natives of the United States, 78 of Mexico, 27 were from Ireland, 24 from England, 8 from France, 25 from Germany, 27 from China, and 15 from Chile. Of the whole number, 582, 46 were sentenced for murder, 28 for manslaughter, 38 for assault with intent to kill, 2 for mayhem, 32 for burglary, 33 for robbery, 10 for rape, 14 for assault with intent to commit rape, 5 for arson, 3 for perjury, and 312 for grand larceny.

Insane Asylum, Stockton. — Established in 1853. Number of patients, January 1, 1858, 188, — 156 males and 32 females; admitted to November 30, 1858, 244, — 201 males, 44 females; whole number, 432. Discharged during the same period, 159. Remaining November 30, 1858, 273. Of the 159 discharged, 32 — 30 males and 2 females — died, and 15 males eloped. Of the 244 admitted, the type of insanity of 122 was dementia; of 62 was mania; of 16, melancholia. Receipts, $ 46,338.88; expenditures, $ 46,149.67; balance in treasury December 1, 1858, $ 188.71.

Registration. — The Legislature, by the act of April 26, 1858, provided for the registration of marriages, births, divorces, and deaths in California. Edwin R. Campbell was appointed State Registrar, and Dec. 20, 1858, he made his report, covering a period of eight months. The returns are imperfect. They show 595 marriages, 3 divorces, 144 births, and 771 deaths. Of the deaths, 63 were from consumption, which was most fatal amongst the Chinese.

IV. CONNECTICUT.

Capitals, Hartford and New Haven. *Area*, 4,750 sq. m. *Population*, 1850, 370,792.

Government for the Year ending on the 1st Wednesday in May, 1860.

			Term ends.	Salary.
Wm. A. Buckingham,	of Norwich,	*Governor*,	May, 1860,	$ 1,100
Julius Catlin,	of Hartford,	*Lieut.-Governor*,	"	300
John Boyd,	of Winsted,	*Sec. of State*,	"	1,000
Lucius J. Hendee,	of Hebron,	*Treasurer*,	"	1,000
Wm. H. Buel,	of Clinton,	*Comptroller*,	"	1,000

			Salary.
Albert Sedgwick,	of Litchfield,	*Comm'r of the School Fund,*	$1,250 [and expenses.
David N. Camp,	of New Britain,	*Superintendent of Common Schools.*	
Charles J. Hoadly,	of Hartford,	*State Libr. & Registr.*	$2.50 a day.
Thaddeus Welles,	of Glastenbury,	*Pres. pro tem. of the Senate.*	
Calvin H. Carter,	of Waterbury,	*Clerk of the Senate.*	
Oliver H. Perry,	of Fairfield,	*Speaker of the House.*	
William W. Stone,	of New Haven,	*Clerks of House of Reps.*	
Daniel E. Holcomb,	of Granby,		

Judiciary.

Supreme Court of Errors and Superior Court.

			Salary.
William L. Storrs,*	of Hartford,	*Chief Justice,*	$2,000
Joel Hinman,*	of New Haven,	*Associate Justice,*	2,000
Wm. W. Ellsworth,*	of Hartford,	"	2,000
David C. Sanford,*	of New Milford,	"	2,000
John D. Park,	of Norwich,	"	2,000
Thomas B. Butler,	of Norwalk,	"	2,000
Origen S. Seymour,	of Litchfield,	"	2,000
Loren P. Waldo,	of Tolland,	"	2,000
Charles J. McCurdy,	of Lyme,	"	2,000
John Hooker,	of Hartford,	*Reporter,*	1,200

The Legislature at its May session, 1855, established two distinct courts, the "Supreme Court of Errors," and the "Superior Court," and abolished the County Courts. The Supreme Court of Errors is now to consist of the present judges of that Court, four in number, and the Superior Court is to consist of five judges. Each of the present four judges of the Supreme Court of Errors (Storrs, Hinman, Ellsworth, and Sanford) is a judge of the Superior Court also, and five judges of the Superior Court (Butler, Seymour, Waldo, Park, and McCurdy) have been recently appointed. Three judges constitute a quorum of the Supreme Court of Errors for the transaction of business, and two terms of the court are held annually in each county. The terms of the Superior Court are held by one judge, except for the trial of capital offences, and as often as four times a year in each county. Any judge may hold special terms of this court, but cannot at such term proceed to the trial or determination of any cause unless the parties consent thereto. A legal verdict may be found by any number of jurors, not less than nine, in any civil cause in which the parties so agree in writing before the verdict is rendered. The judges of this court appoint a State's Attorney in each county, and may remove him for cause. The judges of both courts are appointed by the concurrent vote of the Senate and House, and in all cases must be chosen by ballot, and those appointed in 1855 and since hold office for eight years; those previously ap-

* These judges form the Supreme Court.

pointed hold until seventy years of age. In the trial of capital cases, the court is held by a judge of the Supreme Court of Errors, who presides, and by a judge of the Superior Court. The same act establishes some new rules of practice in civil cases.

The Clerks of the Superior Court, who are *ex officio* Clerks of the Supreme Court of Errors in the several counties, are as follows: —

Counties.	Clerks.	Residence.	Counties.	Clerks.	Residence.
Hartford,	Chaun. Howard,	Hartford.	Windham,	Uriel Fuller,	Brooklyn.
New Haven,	Alfred H. Terry,	New Haven.	Litchfield,	F. D. Beman,	Litchfield.
New London,	Wm. L. Brewer,	Norwich.	Middlesex,	W. W. McFarland,	Middletown.
Fairfield,	E. S. Abernethy,	Bridgeport.	Tolland,	Joseph Bishop,	Tolland.

Finances

For the Year ending March 31, 1859.

Items of Expenditure, Civil List.	
Debenture and contingent expenses of General Assembly of 1858,	$34,450.81
Salaries of Executive and Judiciary,	24,180.00
Contingent expenses of government,	49,183.23
Judicial expenses, excl. of salaries,	93,822.22
Expense State paupers (contract),	1,800.00
Superintending common schools,	3,439.88
Salary of directors of State Prison,	300.00
Quartermaster-General's Departm.,	3,845.51
Public buildings and institutions,	24,081.33
Loans and interest,	$92,302.35
Balance to new account,	12,506.04
	$339,911.37

Sources of Income, Civil List.	
Taxes & dividends on bank stock,	$232,054.18
From avails of courts,	971.03
From forfeited bonds, &c.,	5,428.07
Military commutation tax,	10,604.29
Bonus from Banks,	21,637.80
Loans $65,000, and Mis. $377.06,	65,377.06
Balance of last year's account,	3,838.94
	$339,911.37

Total receipts for the year, including Civil List as above, School Fund $414,633.64, and other funds and former balance,	$800,397.29
Total payments, Civil List as above, Schools $407,613.96, Normal School $4,246.58, Reform School $3,500.00, Deaf and Dumb and Insane Poor Fund, $12,652.55,	762,382.93
Balance in the Treasury, April 1, 1859,	$38,014.36

The permanent fund of the State, April 1, 1859, consisting of bank stock not transferable, or subscriptions to the stock of certain banks which may be withdrawn on giving six months' notice, amounted to $406,000. The indebtedness of the State, consisting of a temporary loan, is $65,000. The amount of the Grand List of the taxable property of the State, October 1, 1858, was $7,199,423.69.

Banks. — There are 73 banks in the State, and their condition, April 1, 1859, was as follows: — Capital, $21,539,856; circulation, $7,555,369; total liabilities, $37,494,621; specie, $993,125; loans and discounts, $29,639,854; total resources, $37,494,621. The deposits were $5,288,169; and the loans to persons out of the State, $5,237,845. The deposits in the 35 savings banks, at the same date, were $14,052,182, of which is loaned on real estate, $8,788,567; on personal security, $934,020; invested in railroad bonds and stocks, $1,181,959; the whole number of depositors, 66,709; total assets, $14,467,270. There were, April 1, 1859, 39 "savings banks and building associations" organized under the act of 1850 that made reports. April 1, 1858, there were 42, which had 6,156 shareholders; stock paid in, $2,391,302; deposits, $2,390,643; making their total liabilities $4,781,945, of which $2,644,208 is loaned on personal security, and the residue on real estate, or invested in stocks and bonds. The Bank Commissioners say (April 1, 1859) "their depositors are perfectly secure." They are all winding up their business, under the law passed in 1858.

Common School Statistics. — Number of towns for year ending September 30, 1858, 159, and all but one made returns; of school districts, 1,614; number of common schools, 1,721; children in the State between 4 and 16 years of age, 103,103; average in each district, 64; number of scholars over 16 years, 3,845; attendance on winter schools, boys

39,414, girls 36,278; in summer, boys 29,726, girls 31,102; number of female teachers in winter, 935; in summer, 1,968; of male teachers in winter, 991; in summer, 172. Average wages of teachers per month, including board, males $30.84, females $16.66. The capital of School Fund, September 30, 1858, was $2,044,672; revenue divided for the year, $134,033; divided to each scholar $1.30. Capital of Town Deposit Fund, $763,662; revenue used for schools, $45,819; 1 per cent tax for schools, $71,656; number of districts assessing a property tax for schools, 245; property tax for schools, about $74,493; revenue of local funds for schools, $22,815; number of districts assessing rate-bills, 776; amount assessed by rate-bills, about $45,499. School-houses erected within the year, 74; estimated cost, $60,534. School-houses in very good condition, 782; in very bad condition, 245. Schools of two grades, 118; of three or more grades, 54. Schools furnished with outline maps, 690; with library, 467; with Holbrook's apparatus, 493. Lecturers were employed to visit the districts, and to lecture upon topics calculated to improve parents, teachers, and scholars. 8 Teachers' Institutes were held during the year; 769 members were in attendance.

Mode of Managing Schools. — Towns elect a board of school visitors of 3, 6, or 9 members, for three years, whose terms of office are so arranged that the term of one ends each year. If any town has a permanent school fund, it chooses annually a school-fund treasurer, who gives bond and takes charge of the fund. Districts are dissolved when there are therein less than 12 persons between the ages of 4 and 16; and no district is divided, if each part thereof, after the division, has less than 40 persons between 4 and 16 years of age. The income of the school fund is divided among towns in proportion to the number of children between 4 and 16 years of age in each town on the first Monday of January in each year. No district can have any portion of the public money, unless there has been a school therein kept by a qualified teacher at least six months in the year, and visited twice each season by the visitors of the towns; and unless the district committee certify that the public money received the previous year has been faithfully applied to the payment of teachers, and for no other purpose; nor shall towns receive any portion of it unless they report seasonably each year to the Superintendent of Schools. Towns must raise by taxation a sum of not less than one cent on the dollar of the Grand List, for the support of schools. School visitors take the general superintendence of the schools, and receive for the time actually employed therein $1.25 a day. Any school district raising $10 for a school library shall receive a like sum from the State; and the further sum of $5 annually, if $5 are annually raised by it for such purposes.

State Normal School. — This institution is at New Britain, and has David N. Camp, the Superintendent of Schools, for its Principal. It was opened for scholars May 15, 1850, and from that time to May, 1859, 1,628 pupils were connected with it. 121 have received the diploma of the school. During the last year, 266 pupils have been in attendance; their average age was 19. The number is limited to 220 at any one term, selections to be one from each school society. Tuition free. In Hartford, Middletown, and New London there are high schools, and in Norwich there is a free academy.

State Reform School, West Meriden. — Edward W. Hatch, Superintendent. This institution was opened for the reception of pupils March 1, 1854. From that time to April 1, 1859, 304 boys were received. In the school April 1, 1858, 150; 16 were received during the year, and 47 discharged, escaped, or died, leaving in the school, April 1, 1859, 119. Of the 304 committed, 179 were for theft, 14 for burglary, 41 for vagrancy, and 36 for stubbornness. 149 were committed during minority, 37 for two years, 23 for three years, 10 for five years, 7 for six years, 2 for ten years. 44 were born abroad, 260 were natives of the United States. Of those born in America, 49 were of Irish parentage, 2 of German, and 9 of English. 36 are colored. The average age of the boys when committed was nearly 13 years. The Legislature, in 1857, provided that no child should be sent there under ten years, nor for a period less than nine months. The grade-system is adopted. Records are kept, and the standing of each boy is determined by his daily conduct. The school is divided into four grades, and each grade into four classes. The discipline is maintained by promotion or degrading, by withholding food, by confinement, and, if necessity requires it, by corporal punishment. The time is allotted, school, 4½ hours; work at some mechanical employment or on the farm, 6 hours; meals and play, 3½ hours; the rest in sleep. There has already been gathered a library of 1,300 volumes. The buildings, when completed, are intended to accommodate from 300 to 350 pupils. The farm has 161½ acres of land. The ordinary expenses of the year were $15,567. The expense of each pupil is charged to the town sending him.

Births, Marriages, and Deaths. — During the year ending December 31, 1858, there were 11,299 births, — 5,872 males, and 5,360 females, and 67 sex not stated. Marriages, 3,737, of which 966 were between parties of foreign birth, and 243 between natives and foreigners. The parties to 3,210 marriages resided in the State; in 368, the husband was a non-resident; in 127, both were non-residents; in 127, the residence is not stated. Deaths 6,618, — males 3,234, females 3,255, sex not stated 129. 1,063 died of consumption, 346 of pneumonia, 150 of dropsy, 58 of scrofula, 13 of cholera, 237 of cholera infantum, 129 of croup, 158 of dysentery, 76 of erysipelas, 286 of typhus fever, and 326 of scarlatina. Returns were received from every town, though imperfect in some instances.

Retreat for the Insane, Hartford. — John S. Butler, M. D., Physician and Superintendent. The whole number of patients, April 1, 1858, was 208, of whom 102 were males and 106 females; 141 (63 males and 78 females) were admitted in the course of the year; making 349 in all, 165 of whom were males, and 184 females. 134 were discharged during the year, leaving in the Retreat, April 1, 1859, 215, — 105 of whom were males, and 110 females. Of the 134 patients discharged, 61 were recovered, 34 improved, 29 not improved, and 10 died. The whole number admitted, from the opening of the institution, in 1824, to April 1, 1859, is 3,407. 3,192 have been discharged; of whom 1,643 have recovered, and 347 have died. The terms of admission are, for patients belonging to the State, with the usual accommodations, $3 per week; for those belonging to other States, $4 per week. Extra accommodations and attendance are furnished at a corresponding additional charge. No patient is admitted for a shorter term than three months, and payment for that term only must be made in advance, to a Manager. Subsequent expenses are payable quarterly to the Steward. For admission, apply to either of the Managers, or to the Superintendent. The Managers are Gideon Welles, William T. Lee, and Russell G. Talcott, of Hartford. The expenses of the institution for the year were $44,568; receipts for support of patients $45,657.

American Asylum for the Deaf and Dumb, Hartford. — Rev. William W. Turner, A. M., Principal. During the year ending May 15, 1859, there were 234 different pupils, 135 males and 119 females. Of these 27 were supported by friends, 43 by Maine, 16 by New Hampshire, 27 by Vermont, 86 by Massachusetts, 12 by Rhode Island, 42 by Connecticut, and 1 by himself. For full statistics of the institution for 40 years, see the American Almanac for 1858, pp. 258, 259. The cost for each pupil, for board, washing, fuel, tuition, and the incidental expenses of the school-room, is $100 per annum. In sickness, the necessary extra charges are made. Payment must be made six months in advance, and a satisfactory bond for punctual payment will be required. Applicants for admission must be between 8 and 25 years of age, of good natural intellect, capable of forming and joining letters with a pen legibly and correctly, of good morals, and free from any contagious disease. Applications for the benefit of the legislative appropriations in Maine, New Hampshire, and Massachusetts should be made to the Secretaries of those States respectively, stating the name and age of the proposed beneficiary, and the circumstances of his parent or guardian. In the State of Rhode Island they should be made to the commissioners of the funds for the education of the deaf and dumb; and in Vermont and Connecticut, to the Governor. In all cases, a certificate from two or more of the selectmen, magistrates, or other respectable inhabitants of the township or place to which the applicant belongs, should accompany the application. The time of admission is the close of the summer vacation, or the third Wednesday of September. The expenses of the institution are about $40,000 a year.

State Prison, Wethersfield. — Daniel Webster, Warden. Number of convicts, March 31,

1858, 212; received during the year, 71; discharged, 80; leaving in confinement, March 31, 1859, 203. 62 were discharged by expiration of sentence, 10 were pardoned, and 8 died. Of those remaining in prison, 189 are males (167 white and 22 colored), 11 are females (7 white and 4 colored), and 3 are Indian half-breeds, sex not stated. Of the 203 prisoners, 11 were committed for murder, 5 for manslaughter, 2 for arson, 6 for other burnings, 7 for attempt to kill, 96 for burglary and theft, 7 for horse-stealing, 2 for adultery, 4 for rape, 5 for passing counterfeit money, 8 for forgery, 2 for perjury. 161 are natives of the United States, 42 are foreigners. The males are employed in making cabinet-work, cutlery, and shoes; and the females in washing, cooking, making and mending clothing, and binding boots. There is a library belonging to the prison of about 1,000 volumes, which are circulated among the prisoners every week. Instruction in the rudiments of learning is also given them. There is a Sunday school connected with the prison. The receipts for the year were $18,279.47; the expenditures, $16,407.98; excess of receipts, $1,871.49.

Idiocy. — The Commissioners on Idiocy, appointed in 1855, from the returns then obtained estimated there were from 1,100 to 1,200 idiots in the State. For the details of these returns, see the American Almanac for 1857, p. 258.

Hospitals for the Sick. — The city of New Haven has had a hospital for some years. The Hartford hospital was dedicated May 18, 1859. The plan of the structure is a centre building and four wings, each wing sufficient to accommodate 50 patients. It is provided with the most modern conveniences, and is thoroughly heated and ventilated. The heating is done by Brown's hot-water furnace. The lot of land contains eight and four-fifths acres, purchased at a cost of $16,754. The building has cost $31,407. The State contributed $10,000; the rest has been subscribed by individuals.

V. DELAWARE.

Capital, Dover. *Area*, 2,120 sq. m. *Population*, 1850, 91,532.

Government for the Year 1860.

			Term ends.	Salary.
William Burton,	of Milford,	*Governor*,	3d Tu. Jan. 1863,	$1,333⅓
Edward Ridgely,	of Dover,	*Secretary of State*,	"	Fees & 400
William J. Clark,	of Dover,	*State Treasurer*,	" 1861,	500
Aaron B. Marvel,	of Georgetown,	*Auditor*,	"	500
George P. Fisher,	of Dover,	*Attorney-Gen.*,	Mch. 1860,	Fees & 350
Manlove R. Carlisle,	of So. Milford,	*Speaker of the Senate.*		
John Stradley,	of Wilmington,	*Clerk of the Senate.*		
John W. V. Jackson,	of Camden,	*Speaker of the House of Rep.*		
John B. Pennington,	of Dover,	*Clerk of the House of Rep.*		

The term of office of the Secretary of State, who is appointed by the Governor, is four years. The State Treasurer and Auditor are elected by the Legislature for two years. The Attorney-General is appointed by the Governor, and holds office for five years. The pay of members of the Legislature is $3 a day and mileage. The pay of the Speaker of each House is $4 a day and mileage, and of the Clerk of each branch $3 a day and fees. The sessions are *biennial*. The last session commenced in January, 1859.

Judiciary.

Court of Chancery.

			Appointed.	Salary.
Samuel M. Harrington,	of Dover,	*Chancellor*,	1857,	$1,100

Superior Court.

			Appointed.	Salary.
Edward W. Gilpin,	of Wilmington,	*Chief Justice,*	1857,	$ 1,200
John J. Milligan,	of Wilmington,	*Associate Justice,*	1839,	1,000
Edward Wootten,	of Georgetown,	"	1847,	1,000
John W. Houston,	of Milford,	"	1856,	1,200
John W. Houston,	of Dover,	*State Reporter,*	1856,	
Turpin J. Moore,	of Sussex Co.,	*Prothonotary of Sup. Court,*		Fees.
Richard N. Merriken,	of Dover,	"	"	Fees.
John A. Alderdice,	of Newcastle,	"	"	Fees.

Orphans' Court.

The Orphans' Court consists of the Chancellor and a Judge of the Superior Court. The Clerks of the Court are, John D. Bird, of Newcastle Co.; James F. Allen, of Kent Co.; Isaac J. Jenkins, of Sussex Co.; and each is paid by fees.

Probate Court.

			Salary.
Peter B. Vandever,	of Newcastle,	*Register of Wills,*	Fees.
Daniel C. Godwin,	of Dover,	" "	Fees.
John Sorden,	of Georgetown,	" "	Fees.

The Chancellor and Judges are appointed by the Governor, and hold office during good behavior.

FINANCES.

The expenditures of the State in 1858, were $41,927.66; the receipts, including loans and balance of previous year, $60,725.18, and were from corporation taxes, dividends, and interest on loans, licenses, &c. The balance in the Treasurer's hands was $18,797.52. The State has as permanent resources, invested capital $109,250, and school fund $440,505.83, in all, $549,755.83.

For the number and condition of the banks in this State, in January, 1859, see the table, *ante*, page 220.

Common Schools.—The system provides a free school within reach of every family. The districts are laid off, numbered, and incorporated. 233 of them are organized. Each district entitles itself to a portion of the fund by establishing a school, and contributing towards its support not less than $25. But any district may lay a tax on itself of $300; or (by a special vote) may increase it to any sum deemed necessary for school purposes. Towns or populous districts may unite their resources and form schools of higher grades; the only condition is that they shall be *free*. The number of free schools in operation in the State in 1856 was 233; number of scholars (in a white population of 71,169), 11,468; average length of schools, 7.6 months; receipts from school fund, $27,482.69; and contributions, $53,067.02. Expended for support of free schools, tuition, $47,822.15; contingencies, $30,430.99.

VI. FLORIDA.

Capital, Tallahassee. *Area*, 59,268 sq. m. *Population*, 1855, 110,823.

Government for the Year 1861.

			Term expires.	Salary.
MADISON STARKE PERRY,	of Alachua Co.,	*Governor,*	Oct. 1861,	$1,500*

[and $500 annually for expenses of residence.

* The salary of the Governor has been raised to $2,500 and house-rent, to take effect on the expiration of the term of office of the present incumbent.

			Term expires.	Salary.
F. L. Villepigue,	of Leon Co.,	*Sec. of State*,	July, 1861, F. &	$600
T. W. Brevard,	of Tallahassee,	*Comptroller*,	Jan. 1861,	1,100
C. H. Austin,	of Tallahassee,	*Treasurer*,	"	800
———,		*Register of Public Lands, and*		
		Sup't of Schools, $1,200 and travelling expenses.		
John Finlayson,	of Jefferson Co.,	*President of the Senate*,		$3 a day.
John B. Galbraith,	of Leon Co.,	*Speaker of the House*,		3 a day.
Jos. E. Bowden,	of Hillsborough Co.,	*Secretary of the Senate*,		5 a day.
Robert B. Hilton,	of Leon Co.,	*Clerk of the House*,		5 a day.

The members of the General Assembly are chosen on the first Monday of October, *biennially*. The Assembly meets *biennially* on the fourth Monday in November. The last Assembly met in November, 1858. The Governor is elected by the people, by a plurality vote for four years. The Secretary of State, Comptroller, and Treasurer, are chosen for two years; the Register of Public Lands and Superintendent of Public Schools, for four years.

Judiciary.

Supreme Court.

			Term expires.	Salary.
Charles H. Dupont,	of Quincy,	*Chief Justice*,	1866,	$2,500
William A. Forward,	of Palatka,	*Associate Justice*,	1866,	2,500
David S. Walker,	of Tallahassee,	"	1866,	2,500
Mat. Papy,	"	*Clerk*,		Fees.

The Supreme Court holds four sessions annually; one in Tallahassee, on the first Monday in January; one in Jacksonville, on the third Monday in February; one in Tampa, on the first Monday in March; and one in Marianna, on the third Monday in March. When any one or two of the judges of the Supreme Court are disqualified from sitting in any cause, the vacancy is filled by a corresponding number of the Circuit Judges, who, in such case, constitute a part of the Supreme Court. The judges of the Supreme Court and of the Circuit Court are elected by the people for the term of six years.

Circuit Courts.

					Term expires.	Salary.
Benj. A. Putnam,	of St. Augustine,	*Judge*,	Eastern	Circuit,	1866,	$2,500
J. Wayles Baker,	of Tallahassee,	"	Middle	"	"	2,500
J. J. Finley,	of Marianna,	"	Western	"	"	2,500
Thomas F. King,	of Key West,	"	Southern	"	"	2,500
James M. Baker,	of Lake City,	"	Suwannee	"	"	2,500
M. D. Papy,	of Tallahassee,	*Attorney-General and Rep.*,				500
		[and $250 additional as Reporter.				
William D. Barnes,	of Marianna,	*Solicitor*,	Western	Circuit,	1861,	$800
Samuel B. Stephens,	of Quincy,	"	Middle	"	"	800
James B. Dawkins,	of Pilatka,	"	Eastern	"	"	800
Henry L. Mitchell,	of Tampa,	"	Southern	"	"	800
—— McLinn,		"	Suwannee	"	"	800

The State is divided into five circuits, Eastern, Middle, Western, Southern, and Suwannee; and the judges of the Circuit Court, in the order in which they are named above, preside in their respective circuits.

Finances. — The receipts into the Treasury, mostly from taxes and sales of lands, during the year ending Oct. 31, 1858, exclusive of the school and seminary funds, were $ 91,924.11, and the expenditures were $ 63,772.33. The principal items of expenditure were, — *Judiciary*, $ 20,305.13; *Executive*, $ 5,400.00; criminal prosecutions, $ 11,648.16; jurors and witnesses, $ 16,962.35; Indian hostilities, $ 7,780.72. The expenses of the Legislature, including printing, are about $ 25,000 for the biennial session. The receipts and disbursements for the two years ending Oct. 31, 1858, on all accounts were.

	Receipts.	Disbursements.	Balance.
Account of State,	$ 125,438.70	$ 90,484.04	$ 34,954 66
" School Fund,	44,907.46	18,255.68	26,651.88
" Seminary Fund,	13,211.67	7,560.44	5,651 23
			$ 183,557.83

The Governor in his message in November, 1858, says: "The present debt of the State (exclusive of the amount due for the suppression of Indian hostilities of 1855–56) may be summed up as follows, to wit: bonds outstanding of the State of Florida, $ 143,000; interest of State scrip, $ 15,000; balance due on account of Indian hostilities of 1856, estimated at $ 225,000. Of this sum, $ 143,000 is bearing interest at the rate of 7 per cent per annum, and only about $ 64,000 is the ultimate debt of the State, the balance being a *bonâ fide* debt due by the General Government."

Common Schools. — July 1, 1858, there were 20,885 children between the ages of 5 and 18 years; $ 6,542.60 were apportioned during the year. There are two State seminaries, one at Ocala, and one at Tallahassee.

State Census, 1855. — The returns include the whole State except Duval County. White males, 32,093; females, 28,395; total white, 60,493; increase per cent for five years, 31. There were 804 free colored persons, and 49,526 slaves, 24,597 males, and 24,929 females. Total population, 110,823. The census returned 2,265,503 acres of land; value per acre, $ 6.14; total value, $ 13,910,981. Value of slaves, $ 27,250,551; average, $ 550. Total value of all property, real and personal, $ 49,461,466.

VII. GEORGIA.

Capital, Milledgeville. *Area*, 58,000 sq. m. *Population*, 1859, 1,014,418.

Government for the Year 1860.

			Term ends.	Salary.
Joseph E. Brown,	of Canton,	*Governor*,	Nov. 1861,	$ 3,500
E. P. Watkins,	of Henry Co.,	*Secretary of State*,	"	1,600
John B. Trippe,	of Putnam Co.,	*Treasurer*,	"	1,600
Peterson Thweat,	of Muscogee Co.,	*Comptroller-Gen.*,	"	1,600
A. J. Boggess,	of Carrollton,	*Surveyor-General*,	"	1,600
William Turk,	of Baldwin Co.,	*Keeper of the Penitentiary.*		
Jesse H. Campbell,	of Floyd Co.,	*Commissioner of Deaf and Dumb.*		
Le Grand Guerry,	of Randolph Co.,	*President of the Senate*,		$ 8 a day.
Frederic West,	of Lee Co.,	*Secretary of the Senate*,		500
Isaiah T. Irvin,	of Wilkes Co.,	*Speaker of House of Rep.*,		$ 8 a day.
J. L. Diamond,	of Dekalb Co,	*Clerk of House of Rep.*,		500
Broughton & Nesbit,	of Milledgeville Co.,	*State Printers.*		

The Governor is elected by the people for two years. The Secretary of State, Treasurer, Comptroller, and Surveyor are chosen by the Legislature for two years. The pay of members of the Legislature is $5 a day. The members of both branches of the Legislature are elected biennially. The sessions of the Legislature are annual, and commence on the 1st Monday in November. The present number of Senators is 135, one for each county; of Representatives, 175.

Judiciary.

Supreme Court.

			Term ends.	Salary.
Richard F. Lyon,	of Albany,	*Judge,*	1865,	$3,500
Linton Stephens,	of Sparta,	"	1861,	3,500
Joseph H. Lumpkin,	of Athens,	"	1863,	3,500
Robert E. Martin,	of Milledgeville,	*Clerk.*		
Benjamin Y. Martin,	of Columbus,	*Reporter.*		

The judges of the Supreme Court are elected for six years (one every two years) by the General Assembly, and are removable upon address of two thirds of each house. All causes shall be determined at the first term; and in case the plaintiff is not ready for trial, unless he be prevented "by some providential cause," the judgment of the court below shall be affirmed. Judges of the Superior Court are elected for four years, by the people of the circuit over which they preside, with jurisdiction exclusive in criminal cases, and in land cases, and concurrent in all other civil cases. The Solicitors are chosen by the people. Justices of the inferior courts are elected by the people, for four years. Justices of the peace are elected by the people in districts. Each county elects an "ordinary," who holds office for four years, and has the ordinary jurisdiction of a judge of probate, and is paid by fees.

The State is divided into sixteen circuits, with a judge and solicitor for each. The salaries of the judges are $2,500 each. The Attorney-General is the solicitor for the Middle Circuit. An election for judges and solicitors, in most of the circuits, was held in January, 1859.

Superior Court.

Circuit.	Judge.	Residence.	Solicitor.	Residence.
Northern,	Thos. W. Thomas,	Sparta.	John C. Birch,	Elberton.
Eastern,	Wm. B. Fleming,	Savannah.	Y. J. Anderson,	Savannah.
Southern,	A. H. Hansell,	Thomasville.	Sam. B. Spencer,	Thomasville.
Western,	Nathan L. Hutchins,	Lawrenceville.	S. P. Thurmond,	Jefferson.
Middle,	W. W. Holt,	Augusta.	A. M. Rogers,	Augusta.
Ocmulgee,	R. V. Hardeman,	Clinton.	W. A. Lofton,	Monticello.
Flint,	Elbridge G. Cabaness,	Forsyth.	A. D. Hammond,	Forsyth.
Chattahoochee,	E. H. Worrell,	Talbotton.	Thaddeus Oliver,	Buena Vista.
Cherokee,	L. W. Crook,	Dalton,	J. A. W. Johnson,	Dalton.
Coweta,	O. A. Bull,	La Grange,	Thomas L. Cooper,	Atlanta.
Southwestern,	A. A. Allen,	Bainbridge.	William E. Smith,	Albany.
Macon,	H. G. Lamar,	Macon.	T. W. Monfort,	Oglethorpe.
Blue Ridge,	George D. Rice,	Marietta.	William Phillips,	Marietta.
Brunswick,	A. E. Cochran,	Brunswick.	William H. Dasher,	Brunswick.
Pataula,	W. C. Perkins,	Cuthbert.	F. D. Baily,	Cuthbert.
Tallapoosa,	Dennis F. Hammond,	Newnan.	Herbert Fielder,	Dallas.

			Salary.
A. M. Rogers,	of Augusta,	*Attorney-General,*	$250 & perquisites.
John M. Millen,	of Chatham Co.,	*Judge of Court of Oyer and Terminer,* Savannah,	$1,000
Wm. T. Gould,	of Richmond Co.,	*Judge of Court of Oyer and Terminer,* Augusta,	1,000

Finances.

The public debt of the State consists chiefly of bonds issued for the construction of the Western and Atlantic Railway. It amounted, 20th October, 1859, to $2,604,750.00, on which the annual interest is $162,590. Of this debt, $7,000 are due in 1860; $12,000 in 1861; $172,000 in 1862. The rest is redeemable from 1863 to 1879. The sum of $267,500 due in 1863 and 1868, can be by the terms of the loan, now redeemed. $702,500 is at 7 per cent interest; $1,830,250 at 6 per cent; and $72,000 at 5 per cent. The State also owes the Atlantic and Gulf Railroad Company, $250,000, and is pledged conditionally for a further subscription of $500,000. This would make the aggregate State indebtedness, $3,354,750.00. The semiannual dividends of interest, as well as the principal of the sterling bonds, are payable in London. The interest on the rest of the debt, nearly four fifths, is payable in New York or Georgia, as the holders may prefer.

The receipts into the treasury for the year ending Oct. 20, 1859, were,	$1,032,879.27
Add balance in the treasury Oct. 20, 1858,	455,918.65
Total means for the year,	$1,488,797.92
Total disbursements during the year,	874,465.92
Balance in the treasury Oct. 20, 1859,	$614,332.00

This balance is made up of Bank Stock (Education Fund), $290,900; Stock in Milledgeville and Gordon Railroad, $20,000; worthless, $14,654. Cash, $288.768.

Chief Sources of Income.			
General Tax of 1858,	$379,614.84	Poor School Fund,	$29,569.00
Net earnings W. & A. Railroad,	420,000.00	Public debt due,	50,565.00
Tax on Bank Stock,	33,417.52	Public debt not due,	99,250.00
" Railroads,	8,026.56	Interest on public debt,	138,677.48
" Lotteries,	5,323.09	Atlantic and Gulf railroad,	150,000.00
Dividends on Bank Stock,	25,005.00	Lunatic Asylum,	40,877.83
Bonds sold for At. & Gulf Railroad,	151,108.33	Deaf and Dumb Asylum,	9,000.00
Principal Items of Expenditure.		Academy for the Blind,	35,000.00
Civil Establishment,	$64,348.85	Penitentiary,	17,500.00
Printing,	19,070.02	Georgia Military Institute,	2,000.00
		State Census, 1859,	22,835.87

The productive property owned by the State, consists of the Western and Atlantic railroad which cost the State according to the report of the Comptroller, $4,441,532.15. It paid into the treasury as *net* earnings during the last year, $420,000. The State also owns, as above stated, $20,000 stock in the Milledgeville and Gordon railroad, which pays 6 per cent, and Bank Stock pledged to be used for purposes of education $290,000, paying an average dividend of 10 per cent. The State also owns $250,000 stock in the Atlantic and Gulf railroad, — already paid for. This road is not completed and the stock is not now productive. The State has heretofore invested in canal stocks, $148,500, — from which it realized $10,000 by the sale of a portion of them. The remainder are worthless. There are also the assets of the Central Bank to the nominal amount of about $200,000, but most of them are worthless.

The Comptroller's report shows the number of polls returned for the year 1859 to be 98,945; free persons of color, 1,213. Slaves, 443,364; value, $271,820,405; average value, $612.68. Acres of land, 33,750,233; value, $149,547,880; average per acre, $4.43. Value of city and town property, $32,129,814; amount of money and solvent debts, $96,124,701; merchandise, $13,531,687; capital in manufactures, $4,428,132; shipping and tonnage,

$631,731; household and kitchen furniture, $2,125,045; aggregate value of all property returned, $609,589,876. The very full and valuable report of the Comptroller, dated Oct. 20, 1859, gives the cost to the State (i. e. the appropriations without reckoning interest upon them), of the several public buildings, and of educational, benevolent, and charitable institutions. The cost of the railroads, of the penitentiary, the lunatic, and deaf and dumb asylums, and the academy for the blind are given under those various heads. The cost of the State-house is given at $200,000; of the executive mansion, $80,000. There has been appropriated to the Georgia military institute since 1852, $47,650; to medical colleges since 1833, $74,800; to the university of Georgia, Franklin college, since 1805, $242,500. Private donations to the college amount to $62,000. The cost to the college of its real estate is $156,500. It also has assets to the amount of $150,000, the interest of which is used to support the institution, making the value of the real estate and assets $306,500. From the same report, it appears that the State contributed to the capital stock of the Central Bank as available, $3,089,257.09, and issued bonds to pay its liabilities to the amount of $698,500, making in all $3,787,757.09. The bank paid back to the State $3,535,106.37; difference, $252,650.72.

Common Schools. — The old school fund is as stated before, $290,900. The annual income of this fund, $29,090, is distributed among the several counties and paid to teachers of schools and academies ratably. The Legislature at its last session appropriated $100,000 to be distributed in the same manner as, and in addition to, the income of the school fund. This amount is to be increased at the present session of the Legislature to $150,000, and will afterwards be increased annually until it reaches $500,000. Provision is also made for a school fund as follows. As each bond of the present State debt is paid a new one is to be issued; and these several bonds will constitute the fund, the income from which will be ratably distributed to pay teachers. November 1, 1859, $150,000 of these bonds had been issued, and are held by the Secretary of State as trustee of the Educational Fund of Georgia. The bonds run for 20 years, and pay six per cent interest. November 1, 1859, school returns had been received for 1859 from 102 counties. Number of children between 8 and 18, 107,825; whole number in the State by the State Census, 117,670; number taught, 67,155; total number taught, 79,922; males, 45,090; females, 34,832. Number taught the elementary branches, males, 29,238; females, 22,681; the higher branches, males, 8,032; females, 7,613. Cost of tuition, elementary branches, $15.50 per annum; higher branches, $26. Number of school-houses, 1,775, of schools, 1,777. Of the 102 counties, 99 have appointed boards to examine teachers.

The Georgia Military Institute at Marietta is under the patronage of the State. There are in the State, besides the State University with 105 students, eight colleges for males, and eleven for females under the control of particular religious sects. The male colleges are, Methodist, 4; students, 358. Baptist, 3; students, 297. Presbyterian, 1; students, 97. The female colleges are, Methodist, 4; students, 524. Baptist, 4; students, 322; Presbyterian, 3; students, 325; total female students in these colleges, 1,171. There are other colleges and high schools, not sectarian for males, 16, pupils, 773; for females, 16, pupils, 1,222. Number of academies, 57. Governor Brown in his message (Nov. 1859), recommends the appointment of a superintendent of education for the State.

State Penitentiary. — This building is at Milledgeville. It was commenced in 1811, and from that time to and including 1858, there had been appropriated for its erection, maintenance, repairs, and enlargement, $511,152. The convicts are now employed in repairing and reconstructing it.

Lunatic Asylum. — This institution is at Midway, near Milledgeville. The first appropriation made for it, was one of $20,000, in 1837. Since then to and including 1858, $348,200 had been appropriated for erecting, enlarging, and repairing the buildings, and $238,257 for the support of indigent and pauper patients, and for the pay of the officers, attendants, &c.

Deaf and Dumb Asylum. — This institution is near Cave Spring, Floyd County. The first appropriation for the support and education of the indigent deaf and dumb was made in 1834, when $3,000 were appropriated. In 1835, the sum was raised to $5,200. They were then educated in Hartford, Connecticut. In 1838, an annual appropriation of $ 4,500 was made for their education at Hartford. In 1845, the act was changed so as to authorize them to be educated in Georgia. In 1847, Commissioners were appointed to purchase land on which to build an asylum. The cost of the land and buildings is $ 20,231.44. Total appropriations for the Institution, $ 136,500.

Georgia Academy for the Blind. — This institution is at Macon. It was at first established by the citizens of Bibb County, and was incorporated in 1852, when the Legislature appropriated $ 10,000 to aid the funds and defray the expenses for the years 1852 and 1853. The State appropriations up to and including 1858, for all the purposes of the institution amounted to $ 91,500.

Banks. — For the condition of the Banks in Georgia in January, 1859, see *ante*, p. 220.

State Census. — The census returns for 1859 show the following: — White population, 571,534; slaves, 439,592; free persons of color, 3,292; total, 1,014,418; white males between 6 and 16, 81,719; males under 6, 62,109; males over 16, 131,592; females between 6 and 15, 73,480; under 6, 59,895; over 15, 138,323; deaf and dumb, 299; lunatics, 400; idiots, 442; representative population, 778,054; number of families, 99,695.

VIII. ILLINOIS.

Capital, Springfield. *Area*, 55,409 sq. m. *Population*, 1855, 1,306,576.

Government for the Year 1860.

			Term ends.	Salary.
WILLIAM H. BISSELL,	of Belleville,	*Governor, and ex officio Fund Commissioner,*	2d Monday in Jan. 1861,	$1,500
John Wood,	of Quincy,	*Lt.-Gov. & Pres. of Senate,*	"	$3 a day [during session, and 10 cents a mile travel.
Ozias M. Hatch,	of Griggsville,	*Sec. of State,*	Jan. 1861,	$800*
Jesse K. Dubois,	of Lawrenceville,	*Auditor,*	"	1,000*
William Butler,	of Springfield,	*Treasurer,*	"	800*
Newton Bateman,	of Jacksonville,	*State Sup. Pub. Instruc.*	"	1,500
A. H. Worthen,	of Springfield,	*State Geologist.*		
Moses K. Anderson,	of Pleasant Plains,	*Adjutant-General.*		
Wm. R. Morrison,	of Monroe Co.,	*Speaker of the House,*		$ 3 a day.
David E. Head,	of Hancock Co.,	*Clerk of the House,*		5 a day.
Finney D. Preston,	of Richland Co.,	*Clerk of the Senate,*		5 "

The Governor, Lieutenant-Governor, Secretary of State, and Auditor are elected by the people for four years; the Treasurer and Superintendent of Public Instruction for two years. Senators, twenty-five in number, are chosen for four years, one half every two years; and Representatives, seventy-five in number, every two years, for two years. The pay of the members of the Legislature is $ 2 a day for the first forty days, and $ 1 a day afterwards. The sessions of the Legislature are biennial. A session commences in January, 1861.

JUDICIARY.

Supreme Court.

				Term ends.	Salary.
1st Div.,	Sidney Breese,	of St. Clair Co.,	*Judge,*	June, 1861,	$1,200
"	Noah Johnson,	of Jefferson Co.,	*Clerk,*	"	Fees.

* Exclusive of clerk hire. The Secretary of State has fees also.

				Term expires.	Salary.
2d Div.,	P. H. Walker,	of Rushville,	*Judge,*	June, 1867,	$1,200
"	Wm. A. Turney,	of Springfield,	*Clerk,*	" 1861,	Fees.
3d Div.,	J. Deane Caton,	of Ottawa,	*Chief Justice,*	" 1864,	1,200
"	Lorenzo Leland,	of Ottawa,	*Clerk,*	" 1861,	Fees.
	Ebenezer Peck,	of Chicago,	*Reporter.*		

This court holds one session in each Division of the State each year. The terms are, — 1st Division, at Mt. Vernon, Jefferson Co., on the Tuesday after second Monday in November; 2d Division, at Springfield, on the Tuesday after first Monday in January; 3d Division, at Ottawa, La Salle Co., on the Tuesday after third Monday in April.

*Circuit Courts.**

Circ.	Judge.	Residence.	Salary.	Circ.	Judge.	Residence.	Salary.
1	D. M. Woodson,	Greene Co.,	$1,000	13	Isaac G. Wilson,	Kane Co.,	$1,000
2	H K.S. Omelveny.	Marion "	"	14	B. R. Sheldon,	Jo Daviess "	"
3	Wm. K. Parish,	Franklin "	"	15	Jos. Sibley,	Hancock "	"
4	Justin Harlan,	Clarke "	"	16	Elihu N. Powell,	Peoria "	"
5	P. H. Walker,	Schuyler "	"	17	Chas. Emerson,	Macon "	"
6	J. W. Drury,	Rock Isl. "	"	18	Edw. Y. Rice,	Montgomery "	"
7	Geo. Manierre,	Cook "	"	19	Wesley Sloan,	Pope "	"
8	David Davis,	McLean "	"	20	Chas. R Starr,	Kaukakee "	"
9	M. E. Hollister,	La Salle "	"	21	James Harriott,	Tazewell "	"
10	J. S. Thompson,	Mercer "	"	22	John V. Eustace,	Lee "	"
11	Jesse O. Norton,	Will "	"	23	Martin Ballou,	Putnam "	"
12	Edwin Beecher,	Wayne "	"	24	Wm. H. Snyder,	St. Clair, "	"

Superior Court of Chicago.

			Term ends.	Salary.
John M. Wilson,	of Chicago,	*Chief Justice,*	1861,	$ 1,000 and fees.
Grant Goodrich,	of "	*Associate* "	1863,	" "
Van H. Higgins,	of "	" "	1865,	" "

Clerks. — Walter Kimball, term ends 1861; U. R. Harley, term ends 1863; Caspar Büttz, term ends 1865.

The Superior Court of Chicago has concurrent jurisdiction in the county and city respectively with the Circuit Court and Common Pleas in all civil cases, and in all criminal cases except murder and treason. The Recorders' Court (Robert S. Wilson, Judge, and J. K. C. Forrest, Clerk), has jurisdiction in criminal cases, and in civil cases to the amount of $100. Each county has a County Court, with jurisdiction to the same amount as justices of the peace, but their business is chiefly probate matters.

Finances.

The indebtedness of the State January, 1859, was as follows:

81 old State bonds, bank and int. improvement stock, . .	$81,000.00	
Internal improvement scrip, ...	52,000.00	
		$ 133,000.00
Liquidation bonds, ...		271,849.00
Certificates new internal improvement stock, ...		2,583,368.15
Interest bonds, 1847, drawing interest from July, 1857, . . .		1,838,433.03
		$4,826,650.18

* The term of office of the several Judges ends in June, 1861. Their salary is $1,000 each.

Amount brought forward,		$4,826,650.18
Registered canal debt,	$2,713,113.19	
Unregistered canal debt,	1,468,505.61	
		4,181,618.80
		$9,008,268.98
Deduct State Debt Fund in Treasury Dec. 1, 1858, to be applied to payment of principal,		766,629.48
		$8,241,639.50
Certificates interest stock, to draw interest from Jan. 1, 1860,	$2,653,814.43	
Estimated arrears of interest, not yet funded, about	243,000.00	
		2,896,814.43
Total principal, interest stock, and arrears of interest,		$11,138,453.93
Upon which the annual interest at 6 per cent is		668,307.24

During the years 1857 and 1858 the principal of the public debt has been reduced $1,050,324.13; and the arrears of interest have been reduced $116,552.61; total payments during these years on account of the public debt, $1,166,876.74. The punctual collection of the tax of two mills on the dollar valuation provided by the constitution, for the purchase of the State bonds, has raised the value of those bonds above par.

The receipts into the Treasury for revenue purposes from Dec. 1, 1856 to Nov. 30, 1858,

were	$753,011.99
Add balance in the Treasury Dec. 1, 1856,	162,039.82
	$915,051.81
The expenditures for the same period were	761,977.68
Balance in the Treasury Dec. 1, 1858,	$153,074.13

Of the receipts, $750,530.24 were from taxes. Some of the principal items of expenditure for the two years were as follows:

Executive,	$29,169.28	Institution for Blind,	$28,000.00
General Assembly,	38,200.09	Geological Survey,	10,351.51
Judiciary,	82,576.19	County Agricultural Societies,	16,800.00
Prosecuting Attorneys,	26,740.62	Militia of Illinois,	132.37
Penitentiary and conveyance of convicts,	36,368.90	Public printing,	27,249.28
		Public building,	31,336.22
New Penitentiary,	81,281.00	Reports of Supreme Court,	5,150.00
Insane Hospital,	138,666.66	Bank Commissioners,	5,793.30
Institution for Deaf and Dumb,	74,979.95	Fugitives from justice,	610.07

The amount of taxable property in the State in the year 1857 was as follows: Personal property, $111,813,908; town lots, $44,398,666; lands, $201,693,234; railroad property, $7,529,703. Total value of real and personal property, $407,477,367. The aggregate value for 1856 was $349,951,272; for 1855, $334,396,425.

Common Schools. — In the year 1858, the whole number of public schools was 10,238; whole number of scholars in attendance, 457,113; being males, 243,859; females, 213,254; number of white persons in the State under 21, 809,879; number between 5 and 21, 470,540; number of colored persons under 21, 2,801; number between 5 and 21, 1,714; number of male teachers, 7,503; of female teachers, 5,878; average monthly wages of male teachers, $29.66, the highest being $200 and the lowest $10; average do. of female teachers, $19.48, the highest being $60 and the lowest being $5; number of school districts, 8,154; average number of months schools have been taught, 6.83; number of new school-houses erected during the last two years, 2,401; number of Teachers' Institutes held during the year, 38; amount paid to lecturers and instructors of Teachers' Institutes, $910; number of school district libraries purchased, 850. The amounts expended for schools during the year 1858 was as follows: Two mill tax apportioned, $743,000.00; interest apportioned, $50,871.25; amount raised by tax to extend schools after public money was exhausted, $563,460; expended for school furniture, $31,810; for building, repairing, and renting school-houses, $819,859; for school-house lots, $38,627; for school district libraries, $45,900. Total amount expended for school purposes, $2,705,052. The number of private schools reported was 530, with 18,571 scholars. There were reported also in the State 21 colleges and 58 academies and seminaries.

The corner-stone of the building for the *Normal University* was laid at Bloomington in September, 1857. The completion of the building has been delayed by the financial embarrassments of that year. A lot of land of 160 acres has been secured, and the buildings when completed will accommodate 300 normal scholars and 200 model school scholars. Temporary accommodations were obtained, and the school was opened therein in September, 1857. From that time to December, 1858, 127 scholars have been in attendance. Their average age at the time of entering the school was 20.16 years.

School Fund. — The school fund in December, 1858, was thus made up:

School Fund proper, being 3 per cent net proceeds sales of public lands in the State, one sixth part excepted,	$ 555,143.17
Surplus revenue,	335,592.32
College Fund, being one sixth of 3 per cent fund,	111,012.54
Seminary Fund, proceeds of sales of Seminary lands,	50,838.72
Township Funds, $3,335,680; County Funds, $218,653,	3,554,333.00
Total School Funds of the State,	$ 4,606,919.75

Illinois Institution for the Education of the Deaf and Dumb. — Jacksonville; Philip G. Gillet, Principal. The buildings in this Institution are now used for pupils. They are thoroughly heated by steam, and ventilated, and lighted by gas. During the two years 1857 and 1858 195 pupils were in attendance, 150 being in attendance at the date of the report. The annual expenses of the Institution are $150 to each pupil, and they are borne by the State. Pupils not under ten nor over thirty are admitted without charge if from Illinois, they paying only for clothing and travelling expenses. From other States they are charged $100, required in all cases in advance. The annual session commences first Wednesday in September and continues forty weeks, and pupils, except in extraordinary cases, will not be received unless they come at or about that time.

Illinois Institution for the Education of the Blind. — Jacksonville; Joshua Rhoads, M. D., Principal. The number of pupils belonging to the Institution at the date of its fifth biennial report (January, 1859) was 68. The Institution is open to all from Illinois, and the terms for scholars from other States are like those in the Institution for the Deaf and Dumb. The annual term commences the first Wednesday of October in each year.

Illinois State Hospital for the Insane. — Jacksonville; Andrew McFarland, M. D., Superintendent. The Hospital was opened for the admission of patients in November, 1851. Number of patients admitted to December 1, 1858, 1,017; recovered, 430; improved, 132; discharged as incurable, 134; died, 93; remaining, 229. The institution, when additions in progress are completed, will receive 500 patients. The buildings are heated by steam in the most approved manner, lighted with gas, and provided with complete apparatus for forced ventilation. The farm consists of 160 acres of land, laid out for farming, gardening, recreation, &c. Supported entirely by the State. Annual expense, $36,000.

State Penitentiaries. — T. S. Rutherford, Superintendent; Samuel K. Casey, Warden. January 1, 1859, there were 661 convicts. At *Alton*, 467 males and 3 females; at *Joliet*, 186 males and 5 females. In Nov. 1859, there were 710 convicts in the two prisons. The new prison at Joliet, was so far completed, that May 22, 1858, 53 convicts were removed from Alton to Joliet. It is expected that the buildings at Joliet will be completed in the spring of 1860, when all the convicts will be removed thither, and the prison at Alton be abandoned.

State Census. — The population in 1855 was 1,306,576, being a gain of 455,106 since 1850.

IX. INDIANA.*

Capital, Indianapolis. *Area*, 33,809 sq. m. *Population*, 1850, 988,416.

Government for the Year 1860.			Term expires.	Salary.
ASHBEL P. WILLARD,	of White Co.,	*Governor*,	Jan. 1861,	$3,000 [and furnished house.
Abr. A. Hammond,	of Vigo Co.,	*Lieut.-Governor and President of the Senate*,	Jan. 1861,	$3 a day [during session of Legislature.
Cyrus L. Dunham,	of Jackson Co.,	*Sec. of State*,		$2,000
N. F. Cunningham,	of Terre Haute,	*Treas. of State*,	Jan. 1861,	3,000
John W. Dodd,	of Grant Co.,	*Aud. Pub. Accts.*,	Feb. 1861,	2,500
Samuel L. Rugg,	of Fort Wayne,	*Sup. of Pub. Instr.*,	"	1,300
Samuel Beck,	of Indianapolis,	*Quartermaster-General*,		25
Wm. A. Morrison,	of Indianapolis,	*Adjutant-General*,		25
John C. Walker,	of La Porte,	*State Printer*,		Profits.
David W. Miller,	of Jeffersonville,	*Warden of State Prison*,		1,500
James R. Bryant,	of Indianapolis,	*State Librarian*,		800
Samuel Osbourne,	of Carroll Co.,	*Private Secretary to Governor*,		500
Jonathan W. Gordon,	of Indianapolis,	*Speaker of the House*,		$3 a day during session.
Richard F. Ryan,	of Indianapolis,	*Clerk of the House*,		4 a day during session.
James H. Vawter,	of Jennings Co.,	*Secretary of Senate*,		4 a day during session.

JUDICIARY.

Dist.	*Supreme Court.*			Term ends.	Salary.
1.	James L. Worden,	of Logansport,	*Judge*,	January, 1865,	$2,000
2.	Andrew Davidson,	of Greensburg,	"	" "	2,000
3.	Samuel E. Perkins,	of Indianapolis,	"	" "	2,000
4.	James M. Hanna,	of Vigo Co.,	"	" "	2,000
	Joseph E. McDonald,	of Montgomery Co.,	*Att.-Gen.*,	Dec. 1860,	1,000
	William B. Beach,	of Boone Co.,	*Clerk*,	"	Fees.
	Gordon Tanner,	of Marion Co.,	*Reporter*,	Jan. 1861.	
	Henry H. Nelson,	of Indianapolis,	*Sheriff*.		

Circuit Courts. †

Circ.	President Judge.		Prosecuting Attorney.	
1st.	J. W. Chapman,	of Jefferson Co.	Geo W. Richardson,	of ——.
2d.	George A. Bicknell,	of New Albany.	Robert M. Wier,	of New Albany.
3d.	M. F. Burke,	of ——.	Richard A. Clements, Jr.,	of Washington.
4th.	Reuben D. Logan,	of Rushville.	Henry C. Hanna,	of ——.
5th.	Fabius M. Finch,	of Franklin.	W. P. Fishback,	of Indianapolis.
6th.	Sol. Claypool,	of Vigo Co.	Isaac N. Pierce,	of ——.
7th.	Joseph S. Buckle,	of Muncietown.	David Moss,	of Noblesville.
8th.	John M. Cowan,	of Frankfort.	Robt. W. Harrison,	of ——.
9th.	Andrew L. Osborn,	of La Porte.	W. B. Biddle,	of ——.
10th.	Edw'd W. Wilson,	of Bluffton.	John Colerick,	of Fort Wayne.
11th.	John M. Wallace,	of Marion.	Richard P. De Hart,	of ——.
12th.	Charles H. Test,	of Lafayette.	John L. Miller,	of ——.
13th.	Jehu T. Elliott,	of New Castle.	Thos. M. Brown,	of Winchester.

The salary of each of these Judges is $1,500. Their term of office is six years. For the counties composing several of the circuits, see the American Almanac for 1856, pp. 321, 322.

* The Governor, Secretary, Treasurer, and Auditor are required to reside at Indianapolis during their term of office.

† Two new circuits, the 14th and 15th, have been recently created.

Court of Common Pleas.

For the Court of Common Pleas, the State is divided by counties into 44 districts, each of which elects a Judge to serve for four years, and until his successor is elected and qualified. The salaries of the Judges are $800 per annum. The American Almanac for 1859, page 320, contains a list of the present Districts, and of the Judges then in office. They are the same now, except that Alex. Anderson is Judge in the Floyd District, and Stanford J. Stoughton in the Noble and Whitley District.

By the act of March 1, 1859, the State is divided by counties into 21 districts, in each of which, in October, 1860, and every fourth year thereafter, a Judge of the Common Pleas is to be elected. The salaries of the Judges are to be $1,000, and three terms of the Court are to be held each year, beginning on the first Monday in January, and on the first Monday of every fourth month thereafter, unless the Circuit Court be in session, and then on the Monday succeeding the term of the Circuit Court.

FINANCES.

Balance in the treasury, November 1, 1857,	$660,653.48
Total receipts into the treasury for year ending October 31, 1858,	844,416.84
Total revenue from all sources,	$1,495,070.32
Total warrants on treasury for same period,	1,363,728.04
Balance in treasury, October 1, 1858,	$131,342.28

The Auditor's Report shows that the lands assessed for taxes of 1857 amounted to 21,510,601 acres; in 1858, to 21,918,659 acres. In 1857, these lands, without improvements, for the purposes of taxation, were valued at $101,844,254; improvements at $41,253,765; town lots and buildings at $33,796,862; railroad stock, $16,743,583; other corporation stock at $1,903,604; other personal property, $122,688,698. Total of taxable property in 1857, $317,932,958; in 1858, $318,204,964. Polls assessed for 1857, 185,193; in 1858, 199,621. Some of the items of taxation for the year 1857 were as follows: county tax, $1,073,782; road tax, $225,454; school tax, $371,593; township tax, $187,610; sinking fund tax, $56,939; total taxes, $2,459,336.

State Debt. — The provisions of the Constitution in relation to the State debt are as follows: — "The revenues of the public works and surplus taxes, after paying the ordinary State expenses and interest on the State debt, shall be applied to reduce the principal of the debt. No new debt shall be contracted, unless to meet casual deficits in the revenue, to pay the interest on the State debt, or to repel invasion, &c. The Assembly shall never assume any debts, nor shall any county lend its credit to, or borrow money to buy stock in, any incorporated company."

State debt November 1, 1857: — Amount of 5 per cent State Stock, $5,312,000; amount of 2½ per cent State Stock, $2,045,074. Total State debt, November 1, 1857, $7,357,074. November 1, 1858, the amount of 5 per cent State Stock was $5,312,500; of 2½ per cent, $2,045,511; total, $7,358,011. A statement of the entire debt of the State at this date gives, including the above, a debt to the School Fund of $1,100,342.67, and $783,175 of the old debt not surrendered and interest (being $413,000 of debt and $370,175 of interest), a total of $9,241,528.67.

The amount of *Canal Stock*, which depends on the Wabash and Erie Canal alone for its redemption, as to both principal and interest, issued and outstanding, Nov. 1, 1858, was as follows: — 5 per cent preferred canal stock, $4,079,500; 5 per cent preferred special canal stock, $1,216,737.50; 5 per cent deferred canal stock, $1,233,000; 5 per cent deferred special canal stock, $470,282.50. Total canal stock, $6,999,520. The American Almanac for 1857, pp. 323, 324, gives an extended account of the origin of the present debt, and of its history in its present form.

Sinking Fund. — This fund is chargeable with the payment of the principal and interest of the State Bonds issued for banking purposes. November 1, 1858, it amounted to $2,781,694.36.

Asylum for the Deaf and Dumb, Indianapolis, 1856. — All the deaf and dumb of the State between the ages of 10 and 21 are entitled to an education, without charge for board or tuition. The session is annual, and lasts ten months, from the 15th of September to the 15th of July. The course of instruction is for five years. For pupils from other States the charge is $100 for the session, for board and tuition. The average number of pupils is near 150.

Institute for the Blind, Indianapolis. — The boarding and tuition of pupils who are children of residents in the State are free. Generally applicants over 21 and under 8 years of age are not admitted. The average number of pupils is near 50. It is estimated that not one eighth part of the blind persons in the State avail themselves of the instruction of the school, although efforts are made to induce them to come. The session is for ten months, — from the first Monday in October to the last Wednesday in July.

Hospital for the Insane, Indianapolis. — This institution was opened (part of its buildings only being completed) in November, 1848. Since the opening of the Hospital, to October, 1856, there have been admitted 1,080; discharged, 845; of whom there had recovered, 594; improved, 93; unimproved, 58; died, 100. 308 were farmers, 46 laborers, 20 carpenters, 7 students, 12 teachers, and 10 tailors. Of the females, 461 were occupied in housework, 28 were school-girls, 13 tailoresses, and 14 teachers. The alleged probable cause of insanity in 86 cases was religious excitement and anxieties; in 35, spiritual rappings; in 31, intemperance; in 23, tobacco. The annual expenses of the institution average about $125 a patient. The average number of patients is near 150.

State Prison, Jeffersonville. — The labor of the prisoners was formerly let out to the highest bidder. But at the session of the Legislature in 1855, the mode of management was changed. Three directors, elected by the Legislature for four years (one each year), have the direction of its affairs, and appoint the Warden and other officers. The State assumes the entire care and control of the prisoners, and the change has been found most beneficial. Average number of prisoners, near 275.

Common Schools. — There is a State Board of Education, consisting of the Governor, Secretary of State, State Treasurer and Auditor, the Attorney-General, and the Superintendent of Public Instruction, who meet annually for conference, discussion, and the determination of questions arising under the school law. The Superintendent is elected by the people for two years, and has the general oversight of the schools, and must spend at least one day a year in each county. There is in each township a trustee, who has the general custody and management of the school property and lands, and a limited power to lay taxes for building school-houses. He also each year enumerates the children in his township between the ages of 5 and 21. The inhabitants of each school-district elect for a year a school director, who takes care of the school-house, provides fuel, employs the teachers, and reports to the trustee. The schools in each township are to be taught an equal length of time, without regard to the diversity in the number of pupils therein. There is to be assessed each year the sum of ten cents on each $100 worth of taxable property, and 50 cents on each poll, (except upon the property and polls of negroes and mulattoes, who have none of the benefits of this act,) for the use of common schools. The township library tax was limited to one year, and has not been extended. The *school fund* is made up of all funds heretofore appropriated to common schools, the surplus revenue, saline, bank-tax, and seminary funds; all fines, forfeitures, and escheats; all grants of land not otherwise specially devoted, the net proceeds of the swamp lands, unclaimed fees, and of all taxes specially laid therefor. The income of the fund is apportioned to the several counties of the State according to the enumeration of scholars therein. The special and common school funds for 1856 were $2,785,358.87. The amount apportioned from them during the year was $339,881.25. The Superintendent of Public Instruction, January 1, 1857, makes a statement of the educational funds of the State as follows: — Productive, $2,822,814.65; unproductive, $2,107,051.59. Total, $4,929,866.24.

Statistics of the Schools for the Year 1858. — The number of children reported in the State between the ages of 5 and 21 is 451,002, — 235,926 males and 215,076 females. Number of districts reported 6,575; number of common schools, 6,335; teachers, male 4,700, female 1,144; wages per month in 1856, males $23.76, females $16.84; average length of schools in 1856, 3.03 months. School-houses built in 1858, 660, at a cost of

$279,806; tax assessed for building school-houses, $308,436; books in school libraries in 1856, 188,499; number added during the year, 144,880.

Banks. — Of the Free Banks organized under the general banking law, a large number have suspended payment and are winding up. Their outstanding circulation, near November 1, 1858, was $1,233,880, to redeem which the securities were, at their then value in New York, $1,448,170. For the condition of the State Bank and 20 Branches, and of 16 Free Banks, in January, 1859, see *ante*, p. 220. In the first week of November, 1858, there were 18 specie-paying Free Banks in the State. Their circulation was $1,097,950, and their securities on deposit were $1,508,661.

Domestic and Farm Animals, Agricultural Products, &c. — The returns of the township assessors, June 1, 1857, show that there were 284,405 horses, mules, and asses, value $14,874,883; 727,057 cattle, value $7,179,828; 693,338 sheep, value $713,171; 2,159,627 swine, value $6,307,148; bushels of wheat, 9,350,975, value $8,828,485; of corn, 39,833,366, value $11,122,160; of rye, 183,063, value $103,876; of oats, 4,621,800, value $1,246,869; of potatoes, 1,195,485, value $635,360; of barley, 59,795, value $65,044; of grass seed, 113,848, value $211,336; barrels of pork, 342,937, value $2,266,439; pounds of bacon, 18,045,137, value $1,100,475; of lard, 4,337,272, value $388,640; value of slaughtered animals other than hogs, $740,889; value of poultry, $550,514; of orchard products, $404,998; of market-garden products, $196,382; of home-made manufactures, $2,474,262. Tons of hay, 342,118, value $1,699,432; of hemp, 413, value $3,035. Pounds of hops, 164,185, value $7,155; of tobacco, 486,734, value $36,047; of wool, 1,455,113, value $424,438; of maple-sugar, 960,823, value $110,989. Gallons of wine, 22,203, value $7,649.

X. IOWA.

Capital, Des Moines. *Area*, 50,914 sq. m. *Population*, 1859, 633,549.

Government for the Year 1860.

			Term ends.	Salary.
S. J. Kirkwood,	of Johnson Co.,	*Governor,*	Jan. 1862,	$2,000
N. J. Rusch,	of Scott Co.,	*Lt.-Governor & ex officio President of Senate,*	$6 a day during session of Legislature.	
Elijah Sells,	of Muscatine Co.,	*Secretary of State,*	Jan. 1861,	1,500
J. W. Cattell,	of Cedar Co.,	*Aud. of Pub. Accounts,*	"	1,500
J. W. Jones,	of Hardin Co.,	*Treasurer,*	"	1,500
Thos. H. Benton,	of Pottawatamie Co.,	*Sec. B. of Educ.,*	Jan. 1860,	1,500
A. E. Miller,	of Cerro Gordo,	*Reg. State Land-Office,*	Jan. 1861,	1,500
W. C. Drake,	of Wayne Co.,	*Com. Des Moines Impr't,*	"	1,000
J. P. Coulter,	of Linn Co.,	*Librarian,*	Jan. 1860,	400
P. T. Inskeep,	of Iowa Co.,	*Ward. of Penitentiary,*	"	1,000

The Governor, Lieutenant-Governor, Secretary of State, Auditor, and Treasurer, are elected by the people for two years, and hold office until their successors are qualified. The sessions of the Legislature are *biennial.* A session meets in January, 1860. Representatives, not over 100 in number, are elected for two years, and Senators, not over 50 in number, are elected for four years, one half every two years.

Judiciary.

The judicial power is vested in a Supreme Court, District Court, and such other courts inferior to the Supreme Court as the Assembly may establish. The Supreme Court, with appellate jurisdiction only in chancery cases, consists of three judges, elected by the people for six years, and until their successors are qualified, one every two years; and the one having the shortest time to serve is Chief Justice. They are, during their term, ineligible to any other State office. Judges of the District Court are elected in single districts for four years, and until their successors are qualified, and are during their term ineligible to any State office except that of Supreme Judge. Their pay shall not be increased or diminished during their term, and no reorganization of the districts or diminution of the number of judges shall remove a judge from office. A District Attorney is elected in each judicial district for four years, and until his successor is qualified.

Supreme Court.

			Term ends.	Salary.
Ralph P. Lowe,	of Lee Co.,	*Chief Justice*,	Jan. 1866,	$2,000
L. D. Stockton,	of Des Moines Co.,	*Associate Justice*,	" 1862,	2,000
Caleb Baldwin,	of Pottawattamie Co.,	"	" "	2,000
S. A. Rice,	of Mahaska Co.,	*Att'y-Gen.*,	Jan. 1861,	Fees & 1,000
Lewis Kinsey,	of Louisa Co.,	*Clerk*,		Fees.
W. Penn Clarke,	of Johnson Co.,	*Reporter.*		

District Courts.

Dist.	Judge.	Residence.	Salary.	District Attorney.	Residence.	Salary.
1.	F. A. Springer,	Louisa,	$1,200	J. F. Tracy,	Des Moines,	$800 & fees.
2.	J. S. Townsend,	Monroe,	1,200	Amos Harris,	Appanoose,	"
3.	E. H. Sears,	Fremont,	1,200	R. B. Parrott,	Clarke,	"
4.	A. W. Hubbard,	Woodbury,	1,200	O. C. Howe,	Dickinson,	"
5.	J. H. Gray,	Polk,	1,200	P. Cad. Bryan,	Warren,	"
6.	W. M. Stone,	Marion,	1,200	G. D. Woodin,	Keokuk,	"
7.	J. F. Dillon,	Scott,	1,200	H. O. Connor,	Muscatine,	"
8.	W. E. Miller,	Johnson,	1,200	I. L. Allen,	Tama,	"
9.	T. S. Wilson,	Dubuque,	1,200	W. T. Barker,	Dubuque,	"
10.	E. H. Williams,	Clayton,	1,200	M. McClatherty,	Fayette,	"
11.	John Porter,	Cerro Gordo,	1,200	W. P. Hepburn,	Marshall,	"

Board of Education.

One from each Judicial District. Salary $3.00 per day. Session limited to 20 days.

Dist.	Name.	Residence.	Dist.	Name.	Residence.
1.	Chas. Mason,	Des Moines Co.	7.	T. H. Canfield,	Jackson.
2.	T. B. Perry,	Monroe.	8.	F. M. Connelly,	Iowa.
3.	G. P. Kimball,	Page.	9.	O. H. P. Rozell,	Buchanan.
4.	D. E. Brainard,	Harrison.	10.	A. B. F. Hildreth,	Floyd.
5.	Daniel Mills,	Greene.	11.	I. J. Mitchell,	Boone.
6.	S. F. Cooper,	Poweshiek.			

Finances.

The funded debt of the State, November 1, 1857, was $122,295.75. There was at the same date $155,003.56 due on outstanding auditors' warrants, and $16,544.67 for interest on the above loans would become due January 1, 1858. The revenue is derived from taxes upon real and personal property.

The receipts into the State treasury for the year ending Oct. 31, 1857, including balance of previous year, were $255,327.75. The disbursements during the same period were $241,145.05; leaving $14,182.70 as the balance in the treasury, November 1, 1857.

The annual expenses of the State are, for executive, $12,147; judiciary, $19,226; printing, $27,588; deaf and dumb, $7,000; blind, $7,222; State debt and interest, $57,500; constitutional convention, $27,010; insane asylum, $100,338; agricultural societies, $4,967; geological survey, $9,965; stationery, $11,941; penitentiary, $26,726. The expenses of Legislature — the sessions are biennial — are near $32,000. The assessed State tax for 1854 was near $90,000; for 1855, $133,619; for 1856, $196,243; for 1857, $420,089. In 1854 the total valuation was, $72,327,204; in 1855, $106,895,390; in 1856, $164,394,413; in 1857, $240,044,534.

The Constitution provides that "the credit of the State shall not be given in any manner for any purpose. To meet casual deficits in the revenue, the State may borrow not exceeding $250,000 at any one time; and the State may contract debt to repel invasion or suppress insurrection. No corporation shall be created by special laws, and stockholders in banking corporations shall be individually liable. Bill-holders shall have a preference over other creditors; the suspension of specie payments shall not be sanctioned or permitted. Two thirds of each branch of the General Assembly may repeal all laws granting charters to corporations."

Common Schools. — The Constitution provides for a Board of Education, of which the Governor shall be a member, and the Lieutenant-Governor *ex officio* President, to consist of one member elected from each judicial district for four years; the members to be so classified that one half shall be chosen every two years. The members must be 25 years of age, and one year a resident of the State, and have the same pay as members of the Assembly. The Board choose a Secretary, and make all needful rules and regulations in regard to common schools and educational institutions. Common schools must be kept in each district at least 3 months in each year. The Assembly may abolish the Board of Education after 1863. The school funds and lands shall be managed by the General Assembly. All lands granted by the United States for schools, the 500,000 acres granted by Congress to new States, escheats, the percentage on sales of land in the State, money paid for exemption from military duty, and fines for breach of penal laws, shall be devoted to the support of common schools. The money shall be divided as the Assembly may direct, in proportion to the number of youths between 5 and 21 years of age. The School Fund, October 1, 1857, amounted to $2,030,544, nominally. This is subject to deductions for defalcations by the School Fund Commissioners in some of the counties. The unsold school lands contain 619,940 acres. The average price of land sold in Iowa for the year was $3.36 per acre. At this average price the school lands unsold would be worth $2,082,998. For the year ending October 31, 1857, there were reported 3,265 organized school districts; 2,708 district schools; 195,285 children in the State between 5 and 21 years of age; 79,572 pupils in schools; 1,572 male, and 1,424 female teachers employed; amount paid teachers, $126,358 from the teachers' fund, and $71,785 from voluntary subscription; cost of district school-houses, $571.06. Number of school-houses, brick, 168; stone, 47; frame, 936; log, 535. Amount raised in districts by tax for school-houses, $146,704; contingent expenses, $19,206. In March, 1857, there was apportioned among the schools, from the interest of the School Fund, $111,840.

Asylum for the Blind, Iowa City. — Samuel Bacon, Principal. This institution was opened for the reception of pupils, April 4, 1853. From the opening to January, 1858, 32 pupils had been admitted.

Asylum for the Deaf and Dumb, Iowa City. — H. C. Ijams, Principal. There were, in 1857, 50 pupils, 26 males 24 females, supported by the State in the Asylum. Total expenses for the year $9,804.

There is an Asylum for the Insane at Mount Pleasant in course of erection.

State Penitentiary. — Number in confinement, Oct. 1, 1856, 32; received during the year, 22; recaptured, 1; total for the year, 55. Discharges, 8; by expiration of sentence, 5; by pardon, 2; escaped, 1. In prison, Sept. 30, 1857, 47, — 46 males and 1 female. 18 were foreigners. 15 were convicted of offences against the person, and 32 of offences against property.

State Census for 1859. — The total population is 633,549, males 332,806, females 300,743. Number of legal voters, 136,457. Bushels of wheat in 1858, 3,293,253; of Indian corn, 23,368,634; of oats, 1,703,760. Acres of improved land, 3,109,436, of unimproved land, 7,335,657. Value of hogs sold in 1858, $2,111,425; of cattle, $2,950,187; of manufactures, $4,444,200. The population in 1856 was 509,414; in 1850, 192,214.

XI. KENTUCKY.

Capital, Frankfort. *Area*, 37,680 sq. m. *Population*, 1850, 982,406.

Government for the Year 1860.

			Salary.
BERIAH MAGOFFIN,	of Harrodsburg,	*Governor* (term of office expires September, 1863),	$2,500
Thos. B. Monroe,	of Lexington,	*Secretary of State*,	1,000
Grant Green,	of Henderson,	*Auditor of Public Accounts*,	2,000
James R. Watson,	of Frankfort,	*Assistant Auditor*,	900
Thos. J. Frazier,	of Jackson,	*Register of Land-Office*,	1,250
James H. Garrard,	of Frankfort,	*Treasurer*,	1,700
Scott Brown,	of Franklin Co.,	*Adjutant-General*,	250
M. D. West,	of Frankfort,	*Quartermaster-General*,	200
A. W. Vallandingham,	of Frankfort,	*State Librarian*,	400
Robert Richardson,	of Covington,	*Sup't of Public Instruction*,	1,000
James P. Bates,	of Barren Co.,	*Pres. Board of Inter. Impr't*,	1,500
John B. Major,	of Frankfort,	*Public Printer*.	
—— Porter,	of Woodford,	*President of the Senate*.	
David Meriwether,	of ——,	*Speaker of the House*.	

The Governor, Lieutenant-Governor, Auditor, Attorney-General, Register of Land-Office, and Superintendent of Public Instruction, are elected by the people for the term of four years. The Governor is ineligible for the four years succeeding the expiration of his term. If a vacancy in the office of Governor occur during the first two years of the term, the people fill it; if during the last two years, the Lieutenant-Governor, and after him the Speaker of the Senate, acts as Governor. The Treasurer is elected by the people every two years. The Secretary of State is appointed by the Governor, by and with the advice and consent of the Senate, during his term. Senators, 38 in number, are elected from single districts for four years, one half every two years. Representatives, 100 in number, are elected from single districts for two years. Sessions of the Assembly are biennial. They cannot continue longer than 60 days without a two-thirds vote of all the members elect to each branch. The members are paid $4 a day, and 15 cents a mile for travel.

JUDICIARY.

Court of Appeals.

			Salary.
James Simpson,	of Winchester,	*Chief Justice*,	$2,000
Henry J. Stites,	of Hopkinsville,	*Judge*,	2,000
Alvin Duvall,	of Georgetown,	"	2,000
Henry C. Wood,	of Louisville,		2,000
A. J. James,	of Frankfort,	*Attorney-General*,	$500 and fees.
R. R. Revill,	of Owenton,	*Clerk*,	Fees.
M. B. Chinn,	of Frankfort,	*Sergeant*,	$2 a day and fees.
James P. Metcalfe,	"	*Reporter*.	

Louisville Chancery Court.

			Salary.
Caleb W. Logan,	of Louisville,	*Chancellor,*	$1,800
Wm. R. Hervey,	"	*Clerk,*	Fees.
W. C. D. Whipps,	"	*Marshal,*	Fees.

Chancellors and Criminal Judges.

First Judicial District,	Joseph Bigger,	of Paducah,	$1,800
Second Judicial District,	Charles Green,	of Franklin,	1,500

Circuit Courts.

Judge.	Residence.	Attorney.	Residence.
1. R. K. Williams,	Mayfield.	A. P. Thompson,	Paducah.
2. Thomas C. Dabney,	Cadiz.	J. E. Arnold,	Madisonville.
3. James Stuart,	Brandenburg.	Cicero Maxwell,	Hartford.
4. A. W. Graham,	Bowling Green.	Wm. B. Jones,	Franklin.
5. G. W. Kavanaugh,	Lebanon.	Andy Barnett,	Greensburg.
6. Thos. E. Bramlette,	Columbia.	E. L. Van Winkle,	Somerset.
7. Peter B. Muir,	Louisville.	E. S. Craig,	Louisville.
8. E. F. Nuttall,	Henry County,	P. U. Major,	Frankfort.
9. Sam. Moore,	Covington.	W. E. Arthur,	Covington.
10. E. F. Phister,	Maysville.	R. H. Stanton,	Maysville.
11. W. H. Burns,	Mt. Sterling.	James N. Nesbitt,	Owingsville.
12. Granville Pearl,	London.	John Dishman,	Barboursville.
13. Wm. C. Goodloe,	Richmond.	W. S. Downey,	Winchester.

The salary of each circuit judge is $1,800; attorneys, $500, besides fees. All judges, justices of the peace, and officers of the court, are elected by the people; the judges of the Court of Appeals, from districts, for eight years, one every two years, and the one having the shortest time to serve being chief justice; judges of the Circuit Court, for six years; and justices of the peace, for four years. The officers of the several courts are elected for the same term as is the presiding judge of their court.

Finances.

Sinking Fund. — Certain resources are provided by law for the payment of the interest and principal of the public debt of the State. It is under the management of the Governor, who is chairman *ex officio*, and the Presidents of the Bank of Kentucky, Northern Bank of Kentucky, and Farmers' Bank of Kentucky. The Auditor is secretary *ex officio*. The receipts of the fund during the year ending October 10, 1859, including balance of 1858 ($41,163.68), were $572,877.29; the expenditures for the same year were $405,985.92; excess of receipts, $208,055.25. Add to this $550,228.03 lent by the commissioners at 6 per cent subject to call; and there is to the credit of the sinking fund, October 10, 1859, $758,283 28.

Ordinary Revenue. — Receipts into the treasury for the year ending October 10, 1859, $983,623.27; balance in 1858, $36,726.58; total means for 1859, $1,020,350.85; expenditures for the same time, $883,887.38; excess of receipts (including balance of previous year), $136,463.47. Value of taxable property in 1859, $493,409,363; increase since 1858, $28,480,550. The rate of taxation is 20 cents for every $100 worth of property; 10 cents of which are appropriated for ordinary expenses, 5 cents for the sinking fund, and 5 cents for the school fund. — *Items of Taxation*, 1858. 21,508,383 acres of land, valued at $219,081,552; town lots, 44,412, valued at $51,879,266; slaves, 207,559, valued at $95,588,479; horses, 351,400, value, $22,138,041; mules, 70,980, value, $5,068,557; jennies, 4,415, value, $523,506; cattle, 741,279, value, $6,180,157; stores, 4,510, value,

$11,844,220; surplus cash, bonds, &c., value, $53,809,903. — *Specific Taxation*, at 30 cents on $100. Value of carriages and barouches, omnibuses, gigs, buggies, stage-coaches, and other vehicles for passengers, $1,891,385; value of pianos, $618,804; value of gold, silver, and other metallic watches and clocks, $1,190,192; value of gold and silver plate, $527,233. Total white males over 21 years of age, who pay a poll-tax for county purposes, 177,372; studs, jacks, and bulls, 2,937, taxed $17,144; average value of land per acre, $10.11.

State Debt. — The entire debt of the State, October 10, 1858, was $5,574,244.03, composed of these items: — To individuals, $3,592,412; Southern Bank of Kentucky for stock, $600,000 (the State owns the stock, and the bank pays interest on the bonds); Board of Education, $1,381,832.03. To pay which the sinking fund receives annually a tax from the banks and dividends on stocks in the same; premiums on State bonds; dividends on stocks in turnpike roads; dividends from slack-water improvements; 5 cents on each $100 worth of property listed for taxation; taxes on brokers and insurance companies; and excess of revenue at the end of each year over $10,000. The interest on the State debt is punctually paid. The State debt, October 10, 1859, was $5,479,244 03, on which the annual interest is $275,421.94. The State owns stock in internal improvement companies of the nominal value of $4,830,475; in banks and railroads, $2,162,820; and the sinking fund, $758,283. Total, $7,751,578.

Common Schools. — The school fund amounted in 1857 to $1,455,332.03; consisting of State bonds and bank stocks, besides an annual tax of 5 cents on each $100 of property listed in the State, amounting to about $204,000. 103 counties made reports to the Superintendent for the year 1857. Number of children reported, 254,111; average number at school, 88,931. Money distributed during the year 1857, $304,933 20. Number of children in the State between the ages of 6 and 18 years, 240,799. Number of children in 1858, 267,712; average attendance at school, 97,001.

Board of Internal Improvement. — James P. Bates, of Glasgow, President, salary $1,500. Grant Green (Auditor), and ——, of —— County, members. The Auditor is Secretary *ex officio*.

State Institutions for the Relief of the Unfortunate. — Eastern Lunatic Asylum at Lexington. Number of inmates, 276. — Deaf and Dumb Asylum, at Danville. Number of pupils, 81. — School for the Blind, at Louisville. Pupils, 38. — Penitentiary. Number of prisoners, 234. — Western Lunatic Asylum at Hopkinsville. Number of inmates, 113.

Banking Institutions. — Bank of Kentucky; V. McKnight, President; S. H. Bullen, Cashier. Northern Bank of Kentucky; M. C. Johnson, President; A. F. Hawkins, Cashier. Farmer's Bank of Kentucky; Philip Swigert, President; J. B. Temple, Cashier. Bank of Louisville; J. F. Boles, President; C. Tilden, Cashier. Southern Bank of Kentucky; G. W. Norton, President; M. B. Morton, Cashier. Commercial Bank of Kentucky; L. M. Flournoy, President; J. L. Dallam, Cashier. Bank of Ashland; H. Means, President; E. W. Martin, Cashier. People's Bank of Kentucky; B. C. Grider, President; A. G. Hobson, Cashier. All of the above banks have branches at various points in the State, except the last-named one, whose place of business is at Bowling Green.

XII. LOUISIANA.

Capital, Baton Rouge. *Area*, 41,346 sq. m. *Population*, 1859, 646,971.

Government for the Year 1860.

			Term ends.	Salary.
Thos. O. Moore,	of Rapides,	*Governor*,	Jan. 1864,	$4,000
H. M. Hyams,	of N. Orleans,	*Lieut.-Gov. & Pres. of Senate*,	"	$8 a day [during the session of the Legislature.
Pliny D. Hardy,	of Opelousas,	*Secretary of State*,	Jan. 1864,	2,500
Thomas J. Semmes,	of New Orleans,	*Attorney-General*,	"	3,500

			Term ends.	Salary.
B. L. Defreese,	of Jackson Parish,	*Treasurer,*	Jan. 1862,	$ 2,500
E. W. Robertson,	of Iberville,	*Auditor of Accounts,*	"	4,000
Henry Avery,	of Baton Rouge,	*Supt. Pub. Education,*	"	2,000
Louis Bringier,	of New Orleans,	*Surveyor-General,*	Jan. 1860,	600
B. Haralson,	of St. Francisville,	*Register of Land-Office,*	"	Fees & 250
Louis Hebert,	of Bayou Goula,	*State Engineer,*	"	3,500
Maurice Grivot,	of New Orleans,	*Adjt. and Inspect.-Gen.,*	"	500
Henry Droz,	of New Orleans,	*State Librarian,*		1,200

August Duplantier, Lafayette Caldwell, G. W. Butler, and E. B. Towne constitute the Board of Swamp Land Commissioners; salary, $ 1,500 each. Term ends Jan. 1860.

The Governor, Lieutenant-Governor, Secretary of State, and Attorney-General are elected by the people, by a plurality vote, for four years. The Governor is ineligible for the four years next succeeding his term of office. The Treasurer, Auditor, and Superintendent of Education are chosen in the same way, but for two years. The Surveyor-General, Register of Land-Office, and Adjutant-General are appointed by the Governor, subject to confirmation by the Senate. Senators, 32 in number, are elected for four years; one half every two years. Representatives, not less than 70 nor more than 100 in number, (now 98,) are chosen for two years. The Legislature meets annually, on the 3d Monday in January. The pay of senators and representatives is $ 4 a day. The sessions are not to last more than 60 days: acts passed after 60 days are invalid.

Board of Public Works. — By the act of March 17, 1859, the State is divided into four Internal Improvement, Leveeing, Draining, and Reclaiming Districts, corresponding to the former Swamp Land Districts. Each district elects a Commissioner of the Board of Public Works, to hold office for four years from the first Monday in January, 1860, at a salary of $ 2,000 each. These four Commissioners constitute the Board of Public Works. Those first elected will designate by lot two of their number to hold office for only two years, and afterwards two will be elected every two years, to hold office for four years. The Board are to elect a Secretary, at a salary of not over $ 2,000; a Chief Engineer, at a salary of not over $ 3,000; and four assistants, at a salary of not over $ 2,000 each. The following Commissioners were elected November 7, 1859, 1st District, F. M. Kent; 2d District, Braxton Bragg; 3d District, G. W. Montgomery; 4th District, L. G. De Russy. Upon the organization of the Board of Public Works, the term of office of the State Engineer and Swamp Land Commissioners expire and their offices are abolished.

Judiciary.

The Chief Justice of the Supreme Court is elected by the people of the whole State, and for ten years: the four associates are chosen for the same period, but in districts. Their compensation is established by the constitution. The Court is in session in New Orleans from the first Monday in

November to the end of June. It has appellate jurisdiction when more than $ 300 is in dispute, when the legality of any tax or of any fine imposed by a municipal corporation is in question, and in criminal cases, on questions of law alone, when death, hard labor, or a fine of $ 300 is imposed. The Attorney-General and the District Attorneys are elected by the people for four years; the former by the State at large, the latter in their respective districts. The inferior judges, clerks of court, justices of the peace, sheriffs, and coroners are chosen by the people.

Supreme Court.

			Term ends.	Salary.
Edward H. Merrick,	of Clinton,	*Chief Justice*,	April, 1863,	$ 6,000
Thomas T. Land,	of Shreveport,	*Associate Justice*,	1861,	5,500
A. M. Buchanan,	of New Orleans,	"	1865,	5,500
James Cole,	of Thibodeaux,	"	1867,	5,500
Alfred Voorhies,	of St. Martinsville,	"	1869,	5,500
Thos J. Semmes,	of New Orleans,	*Attorney-Gen.*,	Jan. 1864,	3,500
A. N. Ogden,	"	*Reporter*,		2,500
Eugene La Sere,	"	*Clerk in New Orleans*,		Fees.

District Courts of New Orleans.

Dist.	Judge.	Clerk.	Dist.	Judge.	Clerk.
1.	Theo. G. Hunt.	N. Trepagnier.	4.	John W. Price.	J. O. Chalon.
2.	P. H. Morgan.	P. S. Wiltz.	5.	H. B. Eggleston.	C. F. White.
3.	Louis Duvignaud.	Ed. Toledano.	6.	R. K. Howell.	Isaac N. Phillips.

C. M. Bradford, *District Attorney*, Salary, $ 2,000. E. T. Parker, *Sheriff*, Fees.

The Courts of New Orleans constitute the first district. The salary of the judges is $ 3,500; their term ends in 1861. The clerks are paid by fees.

Other District Courts.

The term of office of the Judges will expire in April, 1861; that of the Attorneys in November, 1863.

District	Judge.	Residence.	Salary.	Attorney.	Residence.	Salary.
2	James Foulhouse,	St. Bernard,	$ 2,500	P. A. Ducros,	New Orleans,	$ 800
3	Victor Burthe,	Jefferson,	2,500	Robert Preston,	Carrollton,	800
4	Albert Duffel,	Donaldsonville,	2,500	Gervais Larsche,	St. James,	800
5	I. J. Roman,	Thibodeaux,	2,500	N H. Rightor,	Napoleonville,	800
6	R. G. Beale,	Baton Rouge,	2,500	T. Duncan Stuart,	Baton Rouge,	800
7	John McVea,	Clinton,	2,500	W. S. Vaughn,	Clinton,	800
8	J. E. Wilson,	Greensburg,	2,500	E. Ellis,	Covington,	800
9	A D.M. Haralson,	Point Coupee,	2,500	John Yoist,	Point Coupee,	800
10	Edgar D. Farrar,	St. Joseph,	2,500	James Nolan,	Madison,	800
11	Oran Mayo,	Caldwell,	2,500	W. H. Hough,	Caldwell,	800
12	R. W. Richardson,	Ouachita,	2,500	Francis P. Stubbs,	Ouachita,	800
13	E North Cullom,	Marksville,	2,500	C N. Hines,		800
14	Edward Simon,	Franklin,	2,500	Adolphus Olivier,	Franklin,	800
15	B. A. Martel,	Opelousas,	2,500	P. D. Hardy,	Opelousas,	800
16	Chich'r Chaplin,	Natchitoches,	2,500	C. Chaplin, Jr.,	Natchitoches,	800
17	W. B. Eagan,	Bienville,	2,500	J. D. Watkins,	Minden,	800
18	D. Criswell,	De Soto,	2,500	Hinton Smith,	De Soto,	800

Finances.

Total receipts into the Treasury for the year ending Dec. 31, 1858,	$ 1,819,741.69	
Balance, January 1, 1858,	1,058,058.76	
Total revenue for the year,		$ 2,877,800,45
Disbursements for the same period,		1,872,053.43
Balance in the Treasury, January 1, 1859,		$ 1,005,747.02

Chief Sources of Income.

State Taxes,	$ 622,357.48
Licenses of trades and professions,	202,312.82
Duty on auction sales,	22,428.42
Vacant estates,	3,967.22
Current School Fund,	417,602.53
Free School Fund,	73,253.06
Free School Accumulating Fund,	38,730.00
Seminary Fund,	4,210.00
Internal Improvement Funds,	127,319.70
Levee and Drainage Fund,	254,351.50
Road and Levee Fund,	4,094.50
Redemption State Debt Fund,	11,940.00

Principal Items of Expenditure.

Executive and Judiciary,	$ 157,934.27
Legislature, compensation and contingent expenses,	84,971.31
To owners of slaves convicted of crime,	$ 10,333,33
Free public schools,	351,414.66
Charitable institutions,	92,400.00
Seminary of learning,	30,000.00
Building Deaf, Dumb, and Blind Asylums,	45,725.10
Printing and advertising,	38,090.23
Interest on bonds,	173,390.00
Internal Improvement Fund,	46,051.21
Road and Levee Fund,	25,841.88
Levee and Drainage Fund,	268,801.75
Louisiana State Bank, loans, &c.	272,000.00
Criminal prosecutions,	100,134.64
Lessees of Penitentiary,	36,122.51
Decisions of Supreme Court,	5,350.75
State census,	10,683.93

State Debt. — The State debt, properly so called, amounted, Dec. 31, 1858, to $ 4,379,090.95

Add the State's indebtedness for the property banks,	$ 6,124,311.10	
Second Municipality of New Orleans,	198,240.00	
		6,322,551.10
Total State debt,		$ 10,701,641.75

This is the Auditor's statement, and in the debt proper are included United States surplus revenue, $ 479,919.14, of the Free School Fund, $ 529,000, and of the Seminary Fund, $ 136,000. Of this debt proper, $ 512,090.65 are stated to be due on demand, and $ 3,858,000 between 1867 and 1896. There have been issued of State bonds, included above, to the New Orleans and Nashville Railroad Co., $ 483,000; to the Mexican Gulf Railroad, $ 100,000; to the New Orleans, Opelousas, and Great Western, $ 621,000; to the New Orleans, Jackson, and Great Northern, $ 884,000; to the Vicksburg, Shreveport, and Texas, $ 174,000; to the Baton Rouge, G. T., and Op., $ 56,000.

The State has, in addition to the bonds that make up the Free School and Seminary Funds, bonds belonging to the redemption of the State Debt Fund, amounting in value to $ 207,000.

The assessed value of the taxable property of the State in 1857 was $ 378,911,905, upon which was assessed $ 1,398,349.61; 215,305 acres of land were cultivated in cane, 750,266 in cotton, 627,044 in corn, and 4,905 in rice. From these were produced 58,249 hogsheads of sugar, 95,421 barrels of molasses, 407,018 bales of cotton, 12,094,069 bushels of corn, and 21,147 barrels of rice.

Education. — The Constitution provides that "free public schools shall be established throughout the State; the proceeds of lands granted for the purpose, and of lands escheated to the State, shall be held as a permanent fund, on which six per cent interest shall be paid by the State for the support of these schools." The yearly sum of $ 250,000 is appropriated for the support of the free schools of the State, and is derived from the levy of a tax of one mill on the dollar, and from the imposition of a poll-tax of $ 1 on each white male inhabitant of the State. The Free School Fund, January 1, 1859, amounted to $ 899,500. There is, besides, the Seminary Fund, which at the same date was $ 137,000. Total of both funds, $ 1,036,500. The number of school districts in the State, January 1, 1856, was 638; number of public schools reported, 749; number of white children in the State between 6 and 10, 73,322. The report gives the number attending public schools as 17,949;

number not attending, 18,472. The amount apportioned to the several parishes for the year was $ 312,235.42. The number of educable youth in 1857 was 76,518, of which number only about one third are reported by the parish treasurers as having attended school during the year. The amount of public money apportioned among the different parishes in the State for the year ending March 31, 1859, was $ 303,324.34.

Banks. — For the condition of the banks in Louisiana in Dec. 1858, see *ante*, p. 220. The following table shows the condition of the New Orleans banks, in the particulars stated, at the given dates: —

	Loans.	Exchange.	Specie.	Circulation.	Deposits.
1858. Dec. 4,	19,089,952	9,759,156	14,951,536	7,825,629	22,425,067
1859. Jan. 1,	20,687,467		15,948,189	9,581,814	24,972,662
Feb. 5,	21,809,608	9,747,755	16,362,053	11,913,009	24,763,231
March 5,	22,915,914	9,203,800	16,806,889	12,698,604	25,283,033
April 2,	22,465,751	9,059,383	16,579,137	13,054,916	24,918,994
May 7,	19,444,970	9,270,514	15,539,236	12,712,026	23,426,987
June 4,	18,350,752	6,614,289	14,587,827	11,994,591	20,796,378
July 16,	16,750,441	4,044,114	13,666,522	10,743,394	17,972,879
Aug. 6,	17,526,593	2,787,371	13,504,546	10,091,039	17,350,740
Sept. 3,	19,827,317	2,455,097	13,154,963	9,805,674	17,394,654
Oct. 1,	22,797,077	2,175,440	12,767,783	9,293,719	17,785,359
Nov. 5,	24,650,794	4,578,644	12,309,920	9,876,084	19,563,935

Louisiana Penitentiary, Baton Rouge.—Prisoners in confinement December 31, 1857, 337; received to Dec. 31, 1858, 188; in all, 425. Discharged by expiration of sentence, 88; by pardon, 3; by death, 6; by escape, 2; in all, 99. Leaving in prison, Dec. 31, 1858, 326,—223 whites, 2 of whom were females, 58 colored men, and 15 colored females; and of these 96 were slaves. Of the 326 in prison there were committed for murder 78; manslaughter, 44; stabbing, 11; shooting, 7; poisoning, 4; attempt to kill, 10; attempt to poison, 4; rape, 4; attempt to commit rape, 6; assaulting white persons, 21; arson, 20; robbery, 20; larceny, 39; burglary, 14; horse stealing, 12; negro stealing, 7; aiding slaves to escape, 2. The prisoners are engaged in manufacturing cotton and bricks.

Deaf and Dumb and Blind Asylum. — This institution is at Baton Rouge, and embraces both a "mute department" and a "blind department." There were 46 pupils (29 males and 17 females) in the institution during the year 1856. All the deaf and dumb of the State, between 10 and 30 years of age, and all the blind between the ages of 8 and 25, are entitled to an education, free of charge for board or tuition, in this institution.

Insane Asylum, Jackson. — December 31, 1855, there were 133 patients in the asylum, 74 males and 59 females; admitted during the year, 59, 37 males and 22 females; whole number, 192. Discharged during the year, recovered, 28, 18 males and 10 females; removed, 3; eloped, 3; died, 56, 40 males and 16 females; in all 90, leaving in the Asylum, Dec. 31, 1856, 102, 49 males and 53 females. The whole number of patients since the opening of the institution is 587, of whom 132 were discharged recovered, 38 removed, 33 eloped, and 282 died.

Charity Hospital at New Orleans. — During the year 1858, 11,337 patients (9,135 males, 2,202 females) were admitted into the Hospital, 8,923 (7,071 males, 1,852 females) were discharged as cured, and 2,290 (1,927 males, 363 females) died. Remaining under treatment January 1, 1859, 644. Of the deaths, 134 were from diarrhœa, 69 from dysentery, 1,382 from yellow fever, 53 from typhoid, 50 from delirium tremens. Of the patients admitted, 9,568 were natives of foreign countries, 1,751 of the United States, and 18 unknown. The cost of the maintenance of the Hospital for the year, for all purposes, was $ 70,845.67. Its receipts, including former balance, were $ 73,039.47. The capitation tax on passengers for the use of the Hospital amounted to $ 19,640.25, and the tax on balls and concerts to $ 3,525.

State Census. — In 1859, there were 225,007 whites; 18,164 free colored persons, and 303,800 slaves; in all 546,971.

XIII. MAINE.

Capital, Augusta. *Area*, 35,000 sq. m. Population, 1850, 583,169.

Government for the Year ending the 1st Wednesday in January, 1860.

			Term ends.	Salary.
Lot M. Morrill,*	of Augusta,	*Governor*,	Jan. 1860,	$1,500
Noah Smith, Jr.,	of Calais,	*Secretary of State*,	"	900 & fees.
Lewis D. Moore,	of Augusta,	*Dep. Sec. of State*,	"	1,000
Benjamin D. Peck,	of Portland,	*Treasurer*,	"	1,600
Davis Tillson,	of Rockland,	*Adjutant-General*,	"	500
Noah Barker,	of Exeter,	*Land Agent*,	"	1,000
Thomas W. Hix,	of Rockland,	*Ward. of St. Prison*,	"	700
Henry M. Harlow,	of Augusta,	*Sup't of Insane Hospital*,		1,000
Seth Scammon,	of Saco,	*Sup't of State Reform School*,		1,500
Mark H. Dunnell,	of Norway,	*Sup't of Common Schools*,		1,200 [and travelling expenses.
Gilman Turner,	of Augusta,	*Sup't of Pub. Buildings*,		$1.25 per day.
Robert Goodenow,	of Farmington,	*Bank Commissioners*.		
William S. Cochran,	of Waldoboro',	*Bank Commissioners*.		
Charles W. Goddard,	of Auburn,†	*Pres. of Senate pro tem.*,		$4 per day.
Joseph B Hall,	of Presque Isle,†	*Secretary of the Senate*.		
William T. Johnson,	of Augusta,†	*Speaker of the House*,		4 " "
George W. Wilcox,	of Dixmont,†	*Clerk of the House*.		

Councillors. — Dennis L. Millikin, of Waterville; Aaron J. Wing, of Bangor; William Merriam, of Camden; George Thorndike, of South Thomaston; Rufus Horton, of Portland; Washington Long, of Fort Fairfield; Almon Lord, of Parsonsfield.

Judiciary.

Supreme Judicial Court.

			Term ends.	Salary.
John S. Tenney,	of Norridgewock,	*Chief Justice*,		$1,800
Daniel Goodenow,	of Alfred,	*Associate Justice*,		1,800
Richard D. Rice,	of Augusta,	"		1,800
John Appleton,	of Bangor,	"		1,800
Joshua W. Hathaway,	of Bangor,	"		1,800
Jonas Cutting,	of Bangor,	"		1,800
Seth May,	of Winthrop,	"		1,800
Woodbury Davis,	of Portland,	"		1,800
Nathan D. Appleton,	of Alfred,	*Attorney-General*,	Jan. 1860,	1,000
Wales Hubbard,	of Wiscasset,	*Reporter of Decisions*,		1,000

The State is divided into three Judicial Districts, denominated the *Western*, *Middle*, and *Eastern* Districts; and for the purpose of hearing and determining questions of law and equity, the terms are held for these districts, instead of being held, as heretofore, in the several counties. These terms are held annually in Portland for the Western, in Augusta for the

* Governor Morrill has been re-elected for the year ending January, 1861.

† Officers of session of 1859.

Middle, and in Bangor for the Eastern District. The other cases are tried, as heretofore, in the several counties where they are commenced.

Municipal and Police Courts.

Samuel Titcomb, of Augusta; Spencer A. Pratt, of Bangor; Jacob Smith, of Bath; Joseph Williamson, Jr., of Belfast; Henry Orr, of Brunswick; Luther Brackett, of Calais; William Palmer, of Gardiner; Samuel K. Gilman, of Hallowell; L. D. M'Lane, of Portland; John M. Meserve, of Rockland; William Berry, of Biddeford; and John Smith of Lewiston, are Judges at those places respectively. Some are paid by salaries, others by fees.

Probate Courts.

Counties.	Judges.	Residences.	Salary.	Registers.	Residences.	Salary.
Androscoggin	Edward T. Little,	Auburn,	$200	William P. Frye,	Lewiston,	$300
Aroostook,	Bradford Cummings	Maple Grove,	200	Chas. M. Herrin,	Houlton,	200
Cumberland,	Wm G. Barrows,	Brunswick,	700	Aaron B. Holden,	Portland,	950
Franklin,	Philip M. Stubbs,	Strong,	150	Benj. Sampson,	Farmington,	250
Hancock,	Parker Tuck,	Bucksport,	375	Alvin A. Bartlett,	Ellsworth,	400
Kennebec,	Henry K. Baker,	Hallowell,	450	Joseph Burton,	Augusta,	700
Lincoln,	Beder Fales,	Thomaston,	500	Erastus Foote,	Wiscasset,	650
Oxford,	Thomas H. Brown,	Paris,	275	David Knapp,	Rumford,	400
Penobscot,	John S. Godfrey,	Bangor,	350	Joseph Bartlett,	Bangor,	800
Piscataquis,	Jesse Stevens,	Sebec,	135	Samuel Whitney,	Sangerville,	125
Sagadahoc,	Charles R. Porter,	Bath,	200	Elijah Upton,	Bath,	300
Somerset,	David White,	Skowhegan,	250	Albert H. Ware,	Anson,	300
Waldo,	Hiram Bass,	Camden,	200	Bohan P. Field,	Belfast,	425
Washington,	Jotham Lippincott,	Columbia,	400	Wm. B. Smith,	Machias,	450
York,	Edward E. Bourne,	Kennebunk,	400	Francis Bacon,	Buxton,	620

Clerks of the Judicial Courts.

Counties.	Shire towns.	Clerks.	Counties.	Shire towns.	Clerks.
Androscoggin	Auburn,	Josiah D. Pulcifer.	Penobscot,	Bangor,	A. S. French.
Aroostook,	Houlton,	B. L. Staples.	Piscataquis,	Dover,	E. Flint.
Cumberland,	Portland,	Obadiah G. Cook.	Sagadahoc,	Bath,	A. C. Hewey.
Franklin,	Farmington,	Alanson B. Farwell.	Somerset,	Harmony,	Jas. W. Merrill.
Hancock,	Ellsworth,	Parker W. Perry.	Waldo,	Belfast,	S. L. Millikin.
Kennebec,	Augusta,	Wm. M. Stratton.	Washington,	Machias,	C. W. Porter.
Lincoln,	Wiscasset,	Edwin Rose,	York,	Alfred,	Caleb B. Lord.
Oxford,	Paris,	Sidney Perham,			

FINANCES.

Amount of receipts for the year ending December 31, 1858,	$373,984.70
Balance on hand, January 1, 1858,	48,423.30
Total means,	422,408.00
Amount of expenditures from January 1, 1858, to December 31, 1858,	346,039.48
Balance, December 31, 1858,	$76,368.52

Principal Items of Expenditure.

Pay of the Legislature,	$37,744.50	School funds,	$37,598 14
Pay-roll of the Council,	3,548.00	Military purposes,	3,681.00
Cont'g't fund of Governor & Council,	4,172.10	To Indians and Indian fund,	6,739.00
Salaries of State officers,	31,230.97	Militia pensions,	1,944.00
Clerks in public offices,	7,002.00	Maine Reports,	1,500.00
Rolls of accounts,	12,997.97	Agricultural Societies, &c.,	7,602.55
Printing, binding, and stationery,	12,000 00	Public debt paid,	30,500.00
Costs in criminal prosecutions,	34,376.59	Interest on public debt,	39,440.00
State Prison,	16,375 00	Teachers' Conventions,	2,000.00
Insane Hospital and insane paupers,	17,585.83	Publishing Revised Statutes,	3,299.99
Deaf, dumb, and blind,	3,614.16	Bank Commissioners,	1,200.00
Reform School,	17,125.00		

Chief Sources of Income.

State and County taxes, . . .	$ 203,277.00	Permanent School Fund, . . .	$ 5,068.58
Land Agent and lands, . . .	46,083.37	State loan and premium, .	31,252.50
Duties on commissions, . .	1,650.00	Northeastern boundary, . .	10,126.98
Bank tax, ...	74,642.03		

Public Debt. — The public funded debt of the State, January 1, 1859, was $ 699,000. There are besides funds to the amount of $ 335,277.32, held in trust by the State, and for which the State must provide the payment of interest. There are other liabilities to the amount of $ 130,094 45. A recent amendment of the Constitution limits the State indebtedness at any one time, to be afterwards created, to $ 300,000. The amount over this sum is the balance of the *old* debt. The resources of the State at the same date consisted of, — cash, $ 76,368.52; due on State taxes, $ 199,410.23; bank tax, $ 73,000.00; land office, $ 25,000.00; in all, $ 379,278.75. The State also owns about 2,000,000 acres of public lands.

School Fund. — The permanent school fund is $ 149,085.48, with a prospective increase from the sales of 487,567 acres of reserved lands, 20 per cent of all moneys hereafter accruing from the sales of all unsold public lands, and nearly $ 30,000 due on notes given for school lands. The amount apportioned for the year ending April 1, 1858, was $ 82,698.77. The bank tax for the support of schools is one per cent on their capital. The apportionment is made ratably among towns making returns. Towns are obliged by law to raise annually an amount of school money equal to 60 cents for each inhabitant.

School Statistics for the Year ending April 1, 1858. — Of the 394 towns and 90 plantations in the State, returns were received from 389 towns and 69 plantations. There were 4,127 school districts, and 394 parts of districts; number of children in the State between 4 and 21, 240,739; scholars in summer schools, 132,182; average number, 100,726; scholars in winter schools, 154,860; average,122,430; ratio of attendance throughout the year to the whole number of scholars, 49 per cent; male teachers, 2,828; female teachers, 4,506; average wages, exclusive of board, males per month $ 21.86, females per week $ 2.13. Average length of all the schools for the year, 19.9 weeks. Amount raised for schools by taxes, $ 402,761.11, being $ 54,712 01 more than the law requires. Amount received from State school funds, $ 82,698 27; from local funds, $ 14,286.76; expended for private schools, $ 26,561.56; school-houses built during the year, 134; cost, $ 66,739. Aggregate expended for school purposes, $ 623,699 69. Good school-houses, 1,926; poor do. 2,007; estimated value of all the school-houses, $ 1,105,967. Amount of school money raised per scholar, $ 1.59; received from the State, $ 0.348. 15 Teachers' Conventions were held in the several counties during the year, and were attended by 2,084 (911 males and 1,173 females) teachers.

Banks. — The banks are required to report semiannually, in January and June, to the Secretary of State. They also report their condition monthly, except in January and June, and their returns are published monthly in the State paper (now the Kennebec Journal). Their condition, Saturday, June 4, 1859, was as follows: Capital stock, $ 7,258,945.00; circulation, $ 3,945,656.00; deposits, $ 2,425,457.35; due other banks, $ 153,314.13; specie, $ 613,669 43; loans, $ 12,421,875.43; due from other banks, $ 869,047.92. For their condition near January, 1859, see *ante*, p. 220. At the end of the year 1858, there were eleven savings institutions in the State, which had $ 896,876.68 deposits. Their total resources are stated at $ 968,178.90. The returns of some of the institutions do not give the number of depositors.

Insane Hospital, Augusta. — Henry M. Harlow, Superintendent and Physician, Theodore C. Allan, Treasurer and Steward. Nov. 30th, 1857, there were in the Hospital 208 patients, 118 males and 90 females; received during the year, 126, 72 males and 54 females, in all 334. 126 (73 males and 53 females) have been discharged; of whom 59 (37 males and 22 females) were recovered, 25 (16 males and 9 females) improved, 18 (10 males and 8 females) unimproved, and 24 (10 males and 14 females) died; remaining 208 (117 males and 91 females). Of those admitted, 36 men and 32 women were married; 34 men and 15 women were unmarried; 2 were widowers, and 7 were widows. Their ages were between 20 and 80.

Supposed causes of insanity of those admitted during the year, ill health, 28; intemperance, 8; puerperal, 4; domestic trouble, 11; religious excitement, 11; business and loss of property, 2; masturbation, 5; spiritualism, 3; other causes, 24; not assigned, 30. Of those remaining, 56 are foreigners and non-residents, and receive their entire support from the State. Receipts for the year, $30,315.44. Expenditures, $31,577.63. Since opening the Hospital in 1840 there have been 1,978 patients admitted, and 1,770 discharged. Of the latter 813 have recovered; 347 were improved; 360 unimproved; and 250 died. The price of board is now $2.50 a week, and a bond must be given in the sum of $200 for the payment of all dues to the institution. The institution will accommodate 250 patients. The number of insane persons in the State is estimated at between 1,300 and 1,400.

State Prison, Thomaston. Number of convicts, December 31, 1857, 113; received up to December 31, 1858, 69; discharged during the same period, by expiration of sentence 22, by pardon 29, by death 2, and by escape 1, in all 54; leaving 128 in prison. 73 were committed for larceny, 2 for manslaughter, 8 for murder, 5 for arson, 6 for malicious burning, 2 for rape, 2 for assault with intent to ravish, 9 for burglary, 8 for shop-breaking, 2 for robbery, 2 for adultery. 5 convicts are colored and 2 are white females. The labor of a portion of the convicts is let by contract to be employed in the wheelwright business, and that of another portion for shoemaking. Most of those not so employed make baskets. The cost of "food" for each convict was 16.6 cents per day. The cost of clothing was $8.94 per year for each convict. Since July 2, 1824, 1,305 prisoners have been received. Of these there have been discharged, by expiration of sentence 883, pardon 246, death 33, escape 11, removal to Insane Hospital 4, writ of error 1. There is a library of 250 volumes for the use of the convicts.

State Reform School. This school is at Cape Elizabeth, and is under the superintendence of Seth Scammon. The first boy was received November 14, 1853; from that day to Nov. 30, 1858, 489 inmates were received, and 293 were discharged. 262 were committed for larceny, 3 for breaking and entering with felonious intent, 15 for shop-breaking, 68 as common runaways, 17 for truancy, 16 for assault, 13 for malicious mischief, 54 for vagrancy, 3 as common drunkards, and 1 as a common night-walker. 420 were reported born in the United States, and of these 64 were of foreign parentage; 69 were born abroad. The maximum age for admission is 18 years. The Trustees and Superintendent recommend that it should be reduced to 16. The Superintendent renews the suggestion, "that short terms of commitment are not for the good of the boy or the prosperity of the institution." The shortest sentence was one year. Each boy is employed six hours of each day at some mechanical, agricultural, or domestic labor. The farm connected with the school contains 160 acres. The cost of supporting each boy during the year is estimated to have been 10.75 cents a day.

Indigent and Idiotic Children. — The Legislature at its last session appropriated $1,500 for the support of this class of unfortunates, at any New England institution established for the training of such children.

XIV. MARYLAND.

Capital, Annapolis. *Area*, 11,000 sq. m. *Population*, 1850, 583,034.

Government for the Year 1860.

THOMAS H. HICKS, of Dorchester Co., *Governor* (term expires the 2d Wednesday in Jan., 1862), Use of a furnished house, and — Salary. $3,600

			Term ends.	
James R. Partridge,	of Baltimore,	*Sec. of State,*	Jan. 1862,	1,000
Dennis Claude,	of Annapolis,	*Treasurer,*	Jan. 1860,	2,500
Wm. H. Purnell,	of Worcester Co.,	*Compt. of Treas.,*	" 1862,	2,500
W. L. W. Seabrook,	of Frederick,	*Commissioner of Land-Office,*	1864,	Fees & 250

			Term ends.	Salary.
Lewellyn Boyle,	of Annapolis,	*State Librarian*,	April, 1861,	$ 1,0..0
Nathaniel Duke,	of Calvert Co.	*Commissioners of Public Works, & Sup't Buildings and Grounds*,		200
Lemuel Roberts,	of Q. Anne's Co.,			200
Henry R. Reynolds,	of Baltimore,			200
Frederic Schley,	of Frederick,			200
Nicholas Brewer,	of Ino,	*Adjutant-General*,		$ 500
Lemuel Jones,	of Howard Co.,	*Keep. Chanc'y Rec.*,	March 11, 1860,	1,000
Philip T. Tyson,	of Baltimore,	*State Agricult. Chem.*,	"	2,000
Otho Scott,	of Harford Co.,	*Commissioners to Revise and Codify the Laws.*		
Hiram McCullough,	of Cecil Co.,			

The Governor is elected by the people for four years; a Secretary of State is appointed by the Governor, by and with advice of the Senate, for the Governor's term, and removable by him; the Comptroller is elected by the people for two years, and the Commissioner of the Land-Office for six years. The Treasurer and the State Librarian are chosen by the Legislature, by joint ballot, for two years; the Commissioners of Public Works, &c., are elected by the people for four years; the Adjutant-General is appointed by the Governor for six years. The State Reporter is appointed by the Judges of the Court of Appeals for four years. He receives a salary of $ 500, and is entitled to the copyright of the Reports, and the State purchases 200 copies of each volume, at $ 5 each. Keeper of Chancery Records is elected by joint ballot of every Legislature for two years. The Commissioners to revise and codify the laws are appointed by concurrent vote of two houses of Legislature. The State Agricultural Chemist is appointed by the Governor every two years. Senators, 22 in number, are elected for four years, one half every two years; Representatives, 74 in number, are elected for two years. The pay of Senators and Representatives is $ 4 a day during the session, and 10 cents for every mile of travel, the presiding officer of each house to receive $ 5 *per diem*. The sessions of the Legislature are *biennial*. The next session will commence the first Wednesday (4th) in January, 1860.

Judiciary.

Court of Appeals.

	Elected.		Term expires.	Salary.
John C. LeGrand, of Baltimore,	1851,	*Chief Justice*,	1861,	$ 2,500
Wm. H. Tuck, of Upper Marlboro,	1851,	*Associate Justice*,	1861,	2,500
John B. Eccleston, of Chestertown,	1851,	"	1861,	2,500
James L. Bartol, of Baltimore,	1857,	"	1867,	2,500
William A. Spencer, of Annapolis,		*Clerk*,	1862,	Fees.
Oliver Miller, of Annapolis,		*Reporter*,		Copyright and $ 500

The judicial power of the State is vested in a Court of Appeals, and in Circuit Courts. The Court of Appeals has appellate jurisdiction only. Its judges, four in number, are elected from districts, by the voters therein, for ten years, unless they shall before reach the age of 70. They must be above

30 years of age, citizens of the State at least five years, residents of the judicial districts from which they are elected, and have been admitted to practise in the State. The Court of Appeals appoints its own clerk, to hold office for six years, and may reappoint him at the end of that time. When any judge of any court is interested in a case, or connected with any of the parties by affinity or consanguinity within the proscribed degrees, the Governor may commission the requisite number of persons, learned in the law, for the trial and determination of the case. The Governor, with the advice and consent of the Senate, designates one of the four judges as chief justice. The office of Attorney-General is abolished by the new Constitution.

Judges of the Circuit Courts.

Circuit.			Elected.	Term expires.	Salary.
1.	Peter W. Crain,	of Port Tobacco,	1851	1861	$2,000
2.	Nicholas Brewer,	of Annapolis,	1851	1861	2,000
3.	Madison Nelson,	of Frederic City,	1851	1861	2,000
4.	Thomas Perry,	of Cumberland,	1851	1861	2,000
6.	John H. Price,	of Harford Co.,	1855	1865	2,000
7.	Rich. B. Carmichael,	of Queen Anne's Co.,	1859	1869	2,000
8.	Thomas A. Spence,	of Worcester Co.,	1855	1865	2,000

The fifth Circuit comprises the city of Baltimore. The judges of that Circuit, all of whom reside in Baltimore, are: —

		Elected.	Term expires.	Salary.
Robert N. Martin,*	*Judge of Superior Court,*	1855	1861	$2,500
William Geo. Krebs,	*Judge of Circuit Court,*	1853	1863	2,500
Wm. L. Marshall,	*Judge of Court of Com. Pleas,*	1851	1861	2,500
Henry Stump,	*Judge of Criminal Court,*	1851	1861	2,000
Milton Whitney, of Baltimore,	*State Attorney,*	1859	1864	Fees to 3,000

The State is divided into eight judicial circuits, each of which elects a judge of the Circuit Court, to hold office for ten years. The qualifications of the judges are the same as those of the Court of Appeals, except that they must be citizens of the United States, and residents for two years in their judicial district. There is in the city of Baltimore a Court of Common Pleas, with jurisdiction in civil cases between $ 100 and $ 500, and exclusive jurisdiction in appeals from justices of the peace in that city; and a Superior Court, with jurisdiction in cases over $ 500. Each of these courts consists of one judge, elected by the people for ten years. There is also a Criminal Court, consisting of one judge, elected for ten years. Clerks of the Circuit Courts in each county, and of the Baltimore courts, are chosen for six years, and are re-eligible.

Each county, and Baltimore city, elect three persons as Judges of the Orphans' Court, to hold office for four years; a Register of Wills, for six years; Justices of the Peace, a Sheriff, and Constables, for two years. Attorneys for the Commonwealth are chosen in each county by the people, for four years.

* Appointed by the Governor, *vice* Z. Collins Lee, deceased, to hold office until the general election in November, 1861.

FINANCES.

The receipts into Treasury for fiscal year ending Sept. 30, 1859 (exclusive of balance in Treasury, Sept. 30, 1858), $ 1,200,552.77. The disbursements for the year, including the amounts for redemption of State debt, were $ 1,129,269.69. The balance in the Treasury, Sept. 30, 1859, was $ 513,291.16.

The whole nominal State debt, Sept. 30, 1859, was		$ 14,821,473
The Sinking Fund, representing, in fact, extinguished debt, the investment being solely in Maryland State stock, amounts to	$ 4,582,975	
This is included in the amount of the nominal State debt, given above.		
Also included in the nominal State debt above are the Tobacco loans, the interest of which is paid out of the proceeds of inspections, and loans on account of railroad companies, the interest of which is paid by those companies, or out of the State's receipts from those companies, representing in all a principal of, say . . .	4,100,000	
Other productive capital of the State, consisting of bank stocks, railroad stocks and bonds, paying dividends or interest, sums due from collectors, &c., considering the revenue derived from them, may now be estimated at, say	5,400,000	14,082,975

The Sinking Fund is treated as part of the State debt, and the interest on it is paid out of the proceeds of taxation, and applied to purchasing State stocks and bonds, to increase further the capital of that fund. All surpluses in the Treasury are applicable to the increase of the Sinking Fund. The increase of the Sinking Fund in the last year was $ 369,701.

The State direct tax is now 10 cents in every $ 100. The unproductive property of the State amounts to something more than $ 14,000,000, and consists of stocks, bonds, arrears of interest, uncollected taxes, &c., the greater part of which is considered desperate. The assessed value of real and personal property (1858), was $ 255,447,588. The School Fund, Sept. 30, 1859, was $ 327,263.

The provisions of the new Constitution in regard to the State's incurring new debts are as follows: — "No debt shall be contracted exceeding $ 100,000, nor unless the act creating it shall provide for a tax sufficient to pay the interest as it falls due, and the principal in fifteen years. Such taxes shall not be repealed or applied to any other purpose. The credit of the State shall never be given or lent, nor shall the State be in any way concerned in internal improvements. The moneys levied to pay the public debt shall never be diverted until the debt is paid, or until the sinking fund equals the outstanding debt."

Detail of Receipts and Expenditures for the Year ending 30th September, 1858.

Chief Sources of Income.		Judiciary, ...	$ 36,408.93
Auction duties, ...	$ 14,121.73	Legislature, ...	69,386.32
Bank dividends, ...	37,766.36	Public printing, ...	3,705.00
B. and O. Railroad Co. $\frac{1}{5}$ receipts from passengers on Washington Branch Road, ...	34,396.02	Sinking Fund, so much transferred,	19,312.49
		Surplus revenue, " "	34,069.36
		Pensions, ...	2,246.33
Do. interest on dividend and sterling bonds, ...	31,152.50	Colleges, academies, and schools,	21,750.00
		Penitentiary, ...	28,000.00
Taxes, direct and specific, all kinds,	360,327.85	House of Refuge, ...	10,000.00
Live stock scales, in Baltimore,	7,516.70	Hospital for the Insane, . . .	12,500.00
Lotteries, ...	51,000.00	Militia, ...	1,261.66
State tobacco inspections, Baltimore,	27,435.87	State Colonization Society, .	5,000.00
Licenses of all kinds, ...	273,035.06	Indigent deaf and dumb, . . .	2,363.82
Road stock, for dividends, .	50,235.00	State tobacco inspections, . .	21,558.43
Susquehannah and T. W. Canal Companies, ...	17,325.00	Contingent fund for library, .	998.05
		Library, increase of, ...	126.00
Principal Items of Expenditure.		Mayor and City Council of Baltimore,	15,612.79
Interest on public debt, . .	$ 665,405.12	Redemption State Stock, . . .	8,700.00
Civil officers, ...	19,106.11	Special appropriations, . . .	62,357.26

Banks. — For the condition of the banks in Maryland, in January, 1859, see the table, *ante*, p. 220.

State Penitentiary. — November 30, 1856, there were in confinement, 407 prisoners; received during the year, 138; in all, 545. Discharged during the year by expiration of sentence, 102; by pardon, 16; by death, 12; in all, 130; leaving in prison November 30, 1857, 415. The average number during the year was 413. Of those received during the year, 78 were white males and 47 colored males; 1 white and 12 colored females. Of the 415 in prison, 390 were first-comers, 18 second-comers, 3 third-comers, 3 fourth-comers, and 1 for the eighth time. 193 were sentenced for stealing; 34 for murder in 2d degree; 13 for manslaughter; 36 for assault with intent to kill; 19 for burglary; 14 for horse-stealing; and 19 for arson. 322 were Americans, and 93 foreigners, of whom 52 were natives of Germany, 31 of Ireland, and 7 of England. Among the 322 Americans are included 180 colored persons. During the year the north wing of the building, where manufacturing was carried on, was set on fire by two of the convicts and burned, but is now rebuilt. The expenses of supporting the institution are about $50,000 annually. The convicts earn something, being employed in spinning, weaving, and other manufacturing business. The prison buildings appear to be entirely insufficient and unfit for the purposes of a proper prison. The passable single cells number only 256, and yet there are 415 convicts.

XV. MASSACHUSETTS.

Capital, Boston. *Area*, 7,800 sq. m. *Population*, 1855, 1,132,369.

Government for the Year ending the 1*st Wednesday in January*, 1861.

			Term ends.	Salary.
NATHANIEL P. BANKS,	of Waltham,	*Governor*,	Jan. 1861,	$3,500
Eliphalet Trask,	of Springfield,	*Lieutenant-Governor*,	"	*600
Oliver Warner,	of Northampton,	*Secretary*,	"	2,000
Moses Tenney,	of Georgetown,	*Treas. & Receiver-Gen.*,	"	2,000
Charles White,	of Worcester,	*Auditor*,	"	2,000
Stephen H. Phillips,	of Salem,	*Attorney-General*,	"	2,500
			[and $1,000 for clerk hire.	
George S. Boutwell,	of Groton,	*Sec. of Board of Education and State Librarian*,		1,900
Charles L. Flint,	of Boston,	*Sec. Board of Agriculture*,		2,000
Ebenezer W. Stone,	of Roxbury,	*Adj.-Gen. & Quartermaster*,		1,800
Edward Hamilton,	of Roxbury,	*Supt. Alien Passengers*,		2,000
John Morrisey,	of Plymouth,	*Sergeant at Arms.*		
Charles W. Lovett,	of Boston,	*1st Clerk, Sec. of State's Office*,		1,500
Daniel H. Rogers,	of Kingston,	*1st Clerk, Treasurer's Office*,		1,500
Charles A. Phelps,†	of Boston,	*Pres't of the Senate*,		$600 per ses.
Charles Hale,†	of Boston,	*Speaker of House of Rep.*	"	"
Stephen N. Gifford†,	of Duxbury,	*Clerk of Senate*,		$2,000
William Stowe,†	of Springfield,	*Clerk of House*,		"

EXECUTIVE COUNCIL.

The State is divided into eight Districts, in each of which one Councillor is elected annually. The pay of the Councillors is $300 for the regular annual session of their board, and $3 a day for any subsequent session, and $2 for every 10 miles of travel.

---

* This is for the regular annual Session of the Executive Council. For attendance at any subsequent session he has $6 a day. He also receives $2 for every ten miles of travel.

† Officers at the session of 1858.

Councillors for the Year 1859.

Dist.	Name.	Residence.	Dist.	Name.	Residence.
1.	Jacob Sleeper,	Boston.	5.	Lyman Dimmock,	Westfield.
2.	John J. Baker,	Beverly.	6.	Aaron C Mayhew,	Milford.
3.	James M. Shute,	Somerville.	7.	Jos. McK. Churchill,	Milton.
4.	Hugh W. Greene,	Northfield.	8.	C. F. Swift,	Yarmouth.

The Senatorial Districts are 40 in number, and each District elects a single Senator. For the Districts, see the American Almanac for 1858, pp. 240, 241. The number of Representatives is 240, elected either from single districts, or from districts that elect two or three Representatives. The apportionment of Representatives among the Counties is as follows: —

County.	No.	County.	No.	County.	No.
Barnstable,	9	Franklin,	8	Norfolk,*	20
Berkshire,	11	Hampden,	12	Plymouth,*	16
Bristol,	20	Hampshire,	8	Suffolk,	28
Dukes,	1	Middlesex,	39	Worcester,	34
Essex,	32	Nantucket,	2	Total,	240

The pay of Senators and Representatives is $ 300 for the regular annual session to which the member is elected, and $ 1 for every five miles of travel, each way; payable, the mileage on the first day of such session, and the residue on the first of each month afterwards, at the rate of $ 2 a day, until the $ 300 are paid. If there is any balance due at the end of such session, it is then paid. $ 3 is deducted for each day's absence, unless the absence is excused by the house of which he is a member. The President of the Senate and the Speaker of the House have each $ 600 for the session. An extra (adjourned) session of the Legislature was held in the fall of 1859, to act upon the revision of the statutes.

Judiciary.

The Legislature of 1859 established a new court for hearing and determining questions of law, called "The Supreme Judicial Court for the Commonwealth." The judges are the same as the judges of the Supreme Judicial Court, and they appoint a clerk for five years. George C. Wilde, of Boston, now acts as clerk. This court holds a term in Berkshire, Hampshire (for Hampshire and Franklin), Hampden and Worcester, and in Suffolk for Suffolk and all the remaining counties. The same Legislature abolished the Court of Common Pleas and the Superior Court for the County of Suffolk, and the Municipal Court, and established in their stead the "Superior Court," consisting of a Chief Justice and nine Justices. All judges in the State are appointed by the Governor, with the advice and consent of the Council, and hold office during good behavior. The Supreme Judicial Court has exclusive cognizance of all capital crimes and exclusive chancery jurisdiction, so far as chancery powers are given by statute, and concurrent original jurisdiction of all civil cases where the amount in dispute exceeds $ 4,000 in Suffolk and $ 1,000 in other counties. It holds each year two *nisi prius* terms in Suffolk, on the first Tuesdays of April and October, and one *nisi prius* term in each of the other counties, except Dukes, which is attached to Barnstable. The Superior Court is held for the trial of civil cases above $ 20, and has criminal jurisdiction in all except capital cases. Frequent terms are held in every county. The district attorneys are elected in the several districts for three

* Cohasset is, in this apportionment, included in Plymouth County.

years. The assistant attorney in Suffolk is appointed by the Governor. Justices of the peace have jurisdiction in civil cases under $ 100, with the right of either party in cases over $ 20 to call in a jury of six, when all the parties to the suit file a written waiver of all right of appeal from the judgment of the justice on the verdict of the jury; and a right, in all other cases, of appeal to the Superior Court. In criminal cases justices of the peace have a limited jurisdiction to receive complaints and issue warrants, but only certain designated justices can try criminal cases. It is provided by statute that the number of such "designated" justices in the State shall not exceed 167 at any one time. In those places where the justices of the Police Court on stated days hold a "Justices' Court," justices of the peace cannot generally try causes. In Boston, a "Justices' Court" is held every Saturday. The jurisdiction of these courts is like that of justices of the peace, except in Suffolk County, where the jurisdiction extends to $ 300.

Supreme Judicial Court.

			Appointed.	Salary.
Lemuel Shaw,	of Boston,	*Chief Justice*,	1830,	$ 4,500
Charles A. Dewey,	of Northampton,	*Justice*,	1837,	4,000
Theron Metcalf,	of Boston,	"	1848,	4,000
Geo. Tyler Bigelow,	of Boston,	"	1850,	4,000
Pliny Merrick,	of Worcester,	"	1853,	4,000
Eben. Rockwood Hoar,	of Concord,	"	1859,	4,000
Horace Gray, Jr.,	of Boston,	*Reporter*, $ 300 and proceeds of Rep'ts.		

Superior Court.

			Appointed.	Salary.
Charles Allen,	of Worcester,	*Chief Justice*,	1859,	$ 3,700
Julius Rockwell,	of Pittsfield,	*Justice*,	1859,	3,500
Otis P. Lord,	of Salem,	"	1859,	3,500
Marcus Morton, jr.,	of Andover,	"	1859,	3,500
Ezra Wilkinson,	of Dedham,	"	1859,	3,500
Henry Vose,	of Springfield,	"	1859,	3,500
Seth Ames,	of Cambridge,	"	1859,	3,500
Thomas Russell,	of Boston,	"	1859,	3,500
John Phelps Putnam,	of Boston,	"	1859,	3,500
Lincoln F. Brigham,	of New Bedford,	"	1859,	3,500

Police Court of Boston.

John G. Rogers, Sebeus C. Maine, and Geo. D. Wells, *Justices*, salary, $ 2,200 each. Thomas Power, *Clerk*, salary, $ 1,800.

Courts of Probate and Insolvency.

The Legislature in 1858 united the Court of Probate and the Court of Insolvency. The judges of this court are appointed like other judges, and exercise the jurisdiction of the former judges of probate and of insolvency. For probate purposes, frequent courts are held at different places by the judge in the various counties; and they are so held for insolvency matters. A Register of Probate and Insolvency is elected by the voters of each county for a term of five years. There is an assistant Register in the counties of Suffolk (salary $1,500), Middlesex, Worcester, (each $1,000,) Essex ($800), and Norfolk ($600), for three years, subject to be sooner removed by the Judge.

Counties.	Judges.	Residence.	Salary.	Registers.	Residence.	Salary
Barnstable,	Joseph M. Day,	Barnstable,	$700	Jona. Higgins,	Orleans,	$700
Berkshire,	Jas. T. Robinson,	Adams,	800	A. J. Waterman,	Lenox,	800
Bristol,	E. H. Bennett,	Taunton.	1,100	John Daggett,	Attleborough,	1,300
Dukes,	T. G. Mayhew,	Edgartown,	250	Hebron Vincent,	Edgartown,	350
Essex,	Geo F. Choate,	Salem,	1,500	Abn. C. Goodell,	Lynn,	1,500
Franklin,	Charles Mattoon,	Greenfield,	600	C. J. J. Ingersoll,	Greenfield,	700
Hampden,	John Wells,	Chicopee,	800	W. S. Shurtleff,	Springfield,	800
Hampshire.	Sam'l F. Lyman.	Northampt.	650	Luke Lyman,	Northampton,	750
Middlesex,	W. A. Richardson,	Lowell,	2,000	Joseph H. Tyler,	E. Cambridge,	1,500
Nantucket,	Edw. M. Gardner,	Nantucket,	300	Wm. Barney,	Nantucket,	300
Norfolk,	George White.	Quincy.	1,400	Jona. H. Cobb,	Dedham,	1,000
Plymouth,	Wm. H. Wood,	Middleboro',	1,000	Dan E. Damon,	South Scituate,	1,000
Suffolk,	Isaac Ames,	Boston,	3,000	Wm. C. Brown,	Chelsea,	3,000
Worcester,	Henry Chapin,	Worcester.	1,800	John J. Piper,	Fitchburg,	1,500

District Attorneys in the Several Districts.

District.	Attorney.	Residence.	Salary.	District.	Attorney.	Residence.	Salary.
North.,	Isaac S. Morse,	Lowell,	$1,200	West.,	Edw. B. Gillett,	Westfield,	$1,200
South.,	Geo Marston,	Barnstable,	1,200	N.West.,	Dan. W. Alvord,	Greenfield,	1,000
East.,	A. A. Abbott,	Danvers,	1,200	Suffolk,	Geo. W. Cooley,	Boston,	3,000
S. East.,	B. W. Harris,	E.Bridgewater,	1,200	"	A. O. Brewster, *Ast.*,	Boston,	1,800
Middle,	P. E. Aldrich,	Worcester,	1,200				

The terms of the Attorneys expire January, 1863.

Sheriffs and Clerks of the Court in the Several Counties.

Counties.	Sheriffs.	Residence.	Clerks.	Residence.
Barnstable,	Charles C. Bearse,	Barnstable.	Frederick W. Crocker,	Barnstable.
Berkshire,	Graham A. Root,	Sheffield.	Henry W. Taft,	Lenox.
Bristol,	George H. Babbitt,	Taunton.	John S. Brayton,	Fall River.
Dukes,	Isaiah D. Pease,	Edgartown.	Richard L. Pease,	Edgartown.
Essex,	James Cary,	Lawrence.	Asahel Huntington,	Salem.
Franklin,	Samuel H. Reed,	Greenfield.	George Grennell,	Greenfield.
Hampden,	Frederick Bush,	Westfield.	George B. Morris,	Springfield.
Hampshire,	Henry A. Longley,	Belchertown.	Samuel Wells,	Northampton.
Middlesex,	Charles Kimball,	Winchester.	Benjamin F. Ham,	Natick.
Nantucket,	Uriah Gardner,	Nantucket.	George Cobb,	Nantucket.
Norfolk,	John W. Thomas,	Dedham.	Ezra W. Sampson,	Dedham.
Plymouth,	James Bates,	E. Bridgewater.	Wm. H. Whitman,	Plymouth.
Suffolk,	John M. Clark,	Boston.	George C. Wilde,	Boston.
Worcester,	J. S. C. Knowlton,	Worcester.	Joseph Mason,	Worcester.

Sheriffs are elected for three years, and Clerks for five years. They are paid by fees. The Clerks are the clerks both of the Supreme Court and Common Pleas. Their term expires in January, 1862; that of the Sheriffs and District Attorneys in January, 1863.

FINANCES.

Received into the Treasury during the year ending December 31st, 1858, on account of ordinary revenue, including State Tax, ...	$1,311,423.78
Received on all other accounts (including $405,000.00 temporary loans, borrowed in anticipation of the revenue), ...	1,123,714.74
Total receipts, ...	$2,435,138.52
Add cash on hand, January 1st, 1858, ...	110,196.17
Total means, ...	$2,545,334.69
The entire payments during the year on account of ordinary expenditures were	$1,247,131.31
On all other accounts, including $611,500 temporary loans repaid, . . .	1,101,356.10
Total payments, ...	$2,348,487.41
Excess of means for 1858, being cash on hand, January 1st, 1859,	$196,847.28

Of this $13,788.09 is borrowed on account of ordinary revenue, in anticipation of revenue, &c., and $183,059.19 on account of the school and other funds, railroad scrip, and the Back Bay Lands.

Principal Items of Expenditure.

Councillors,	$7,644.00
Legislature,	95,173.94
Executive and Judiciary,	116,810.58
District Attorneys' salaries,	10,043.51
Adj'nt and Q. M. General's Dep't,	4,169.42
Expenses of the Militia,	69,619.50
Repairs, fuel, &c. for State-House,	9,058.64
Stationery,	4,374.18
State Library,	2,685.00
Agent for discharged convicts,	1,000.00
Coroners' inquests,	1,120.74
Arrest of fugitives from justice,	833.73
Asylum for the Blind,	12,000.00
" " Deaf and Dumb,	7,844.10
Eye and Ear Infirmary,	2,500.00
Lunatic Hospital at Worcester,	3,250.00
Lunatic Hospital at Taunton,	3,225.00
Northampton Lunatic Hospital,	59,600.00
School for Idiots,	7,500.00
Pensioners,	770.00
Expenses State Reform School,	44,000.00
Industrial School for Girls,	9,000.00
Bank and Insurance Commissioners,	10,463.98
Alien and Pauper Commissioners,	7,969.29
State printing,	19,318.78
Newspapers,	3,051.79
Term Reports,	962.50
State Prison expenses,	15,000.00
State Prison indebtedness,	21,169.04
County Treasurers, § crim. costs,	$286,075.16
State paupers,	67,507.74
Expenses State Almshouses,	162,267.10
Indemnity to officers,	231.73
Interest on temporary loans,	22,174.64
Temporary loans repaid,	611,500.00
Interest on scrip,	70,290.00
Index and Journals,	12,516.36
New Plymouth Records,	8,919.64
State Board of Agriculture,	3,079.47
Agricultural Societies, bounty,	11,814.40
Courts of Insolvency,	20,645.18
Alien Passengers,	11,026.64
School and other funds,	272,135.05
State scrip,	200,391.67
Back Bay lands,	17,329.38

Chief Sources of Income.

Bank tax,	$606,100.05
Insurance tax,	2,561.81
Alien passengers,	14,795.37
Alien estates,	313.13
Interest on deposits,	1,828.06
Western Railroad dividends,	56,448.00
Temporary loans,	405,000.00
School and other Funds,	482,612.04
Scrip lent to railroads,	204,166.67
Back Bay lands,	31,936.03
State tax,	578,233.53

The funded debt of Massachusetts, on its own account, was, 1st January, 1859,	$1,314,000.00
Temporary loans, and sums due and unpaid,	135,419.43
Liability of the Commonwealth for scrip loaned to the various railroads,	4,999,455.56
Total absolute and contingent debt,	$6,448,874.99
The value of the productive property of the Commonwealth, January 1st, 1859, consisting of notes, mortgages, stocks and scrip, the Western Railroad Sinking Fund, School Fund, Indian Funds, &c.,	$5,494,671.40
Real estate, &c. unproductive,	3,060,677.71
Mortgages on the various railroads,	4,999,455.56
Total property of the Commonwealth,	$13,554,804.67
Total liabilities,	6,448,874.99
Excess of resources over liabilities,	$7,115,929.68

For a Table of Receipts and Expenditures in detail, from 1834 to 1853 inclusive, see American Almanac for 1855, page 232.

Institutions for Savings on the last Saturday in October, 1858. — In the 86 institutions that made returns, there were 182,655 depositors, and $33,914,971.71 deposits; $12,514,706.61 were loaned on mortgages; $3,363,989.83 to counties or towns; $7,751,265.74 on personal security; $6,611,431.94 were invested in bank stock; $104,363.75 in railroad stock; $207,190.35 in real estate; and $1,089,977.14 in public funds. The average dividend for the year was 5.06 per cent. The average annual per cent of dividends of the last five years is 6.74 per cent. The whole expense of managing these 86 Savings Banks was $105,328.83. The above includes the returns of 20 Five-Cent Savings Banks.

Banks. — The banks in Boston are required to report weekly their condition to the Secretary of State in the particulars in the headings of the columns in the tables given below, and these reports are published weekly. The banks out of Boston report, and their reports are published, monthly. Below, the condition of the banks near the first of each month is given, from December, 1858, the time of the reports published in the American Almanac for 1859 (page 240), to November, 1859.

Banks in Boston.

Date.	Capital.	Loans and Discounts	Specie in Bank.	Due from other Banks.	Due to other Banks.	Deposits.	Circulation.
1858 - 59.	$	$	$	$	$	$	$
* December 6,	33,230,600	57,678,912	9,564,716	7,126,044	8,613,337	22,881,34[illegible]	7,149,786
January 3,	33,303 300	60,069,424	8,548,934	7,083,737	10,789,135	22,357,838	6,543,134
February 7,	33,321,700	59,120,142	6,814,589	7,057,113	9,606,146	20,845,520	6,514,576
March 7,	33,921,700	58,892,981	6.386,580	6,673,623	8,477,968	19,935,649	6,578,472
April 4,	33,921,700	58,031,003	6,401,822	7,524,888	7,665,274	20,899,191	6,385,853
May 2,	33.921,700	58,178,264	6,910,187	7,346,135	7,850,530	21,990.246	6,658,260
June 6,	35,021,700	57,430,695	6,738,384	7,852,924	7,000,735	20,718,977	7,009,818
July 4,	35,115,733	59,037,935	5.493,396	7,283,020	7,076,162	20,017,147	6,935,903
August 1,	35,122,400	57,972,321	4,667,352	6,331,385	6,511,893	18,033,821	6,387,763
September 5,	35,125,433	58,567,981	5,115,478	6,153,490	6,921,705	18,159,586	6,495,9[illegible]0
October 3,	35,125,700	58,735,636	5,195,497	7,237,990	7,000,547	19,165,983	6,694,638
November							

Banks out of Boston.

Date.	Capital.	Loans and Discounts.	Specie in Bank.	Due from other Banks.	Due to other Banks.	Deposits.	Circulation.
1858 - 59.	$	$	$	$	$	$	$
December 4,	28,747,325	45.817,604	1,872,033	5,661,956	317,056	8,382,493	14,043,416
January 1,	28,748,100	46.031,432	1,841,543	5,404,933	345,043	8,266,863	13,804,461
February 5,	28,748,100	47.083,641	1,[illegible]9.124	6,165,985	423,491	8,563,260	14,089,445
March 5,	28,748,100	47.404,595	1,797,256	4.298,947	404,370	7,981,666	13,872,411
April 2,	28,695,600	47,621,484	1,767,798	4,412,118	377,293	7,939,964	14,311,278
" 30,	28,687,500	48,017,137	1,784,364	5.429.964	366,919	8,618,238	15 563,372
June 4,	28,687,500	47,907,915	1,784,921	5.129.611	418,716	8,661,843	14,958,755
July 2,	28,687,500	48.265.796	1,798.932	4,661,879	431,805	8,261,758	15,038,017
August, 1,	28.687,500	48.779,666	1,801,235	4.397,034	432,932	8,246,103	15,093,669
September 3,	28,687,500	48.707,583	1,797.201	4.092,729	494.414	8,028,084	14,569,375
October 1,	28,687,500	49,014,141	1,748,027	4,340,946	464,057	8,290,883	14,911,276

Joint-Stock Companies. There were, in January, 1859, 156 joint-stock companies organized, with a capital of $9,778,600, of which $6,908,863.70 was paid in.

Insurance Abstract for 1858. — Number of stock offices in the State, 34, 18 of which were in Boston. Capital actually paid in, $6,353.100. Amount of risk, Nov. 1, 1858, $203 713,779, being $132,854,841 fire risks, and $70,858,938 marine risks. The losses paid by them for the year ending Oct. 31, 1858, were, on fire risks, $422,953; on marine risks, $2,153,327; in all, $2,576,280. Number of mutual marine and mutual fire and marine companies, 14, of which 5 were in Boston. Amount at risk, Nov. 1, 1858, $59,632,147; being on marine risks, $49,640,173; on fire risks, $9,991,974. Losses paid during the same time, $2,201,509, being $14,138 on fire risks, and $2,187,371 on marine risks. Number of mutual fire offices, 69, 10 of which are in Boston. Amount of risk, Nov. 1, 1858, $204,733,847. Losses paid during the same time, $208,237. Amount at risk in the 5 home life insurance companies, Nov. 1, 1858, $17,408,714; amount insured by foreign agencies, over $7,000,000. The amount insured by 40 foreign agencies on fire and marine risks was $33,698,751. The amount of premiums received by foreign agents for the year was $776,035; $294,951 on fire and marine risks, and $481,084 on life risks. Amount of State tax received from such companies, $ 2,527. The Insurance Commissioners have made a very full report, and have printed full and carefully prepared abstracts of the returns of the various companies.

Schools for 1858. — Number of towns in the State, 332; number that made returns, 331. The towns raise by taxation for the support of schools, for wages, board, and fuel, $ 1,341,252. Aggregate raised and appropriated, except for erecting and repairing school-houses, $ 1,474,489. Number of children in the State from 5 to 15 years old, 223,304. Number that attend school under 5 years, 12,870; over 15 years, 16,894. Number of public schools in the State, 4,421. Number of teachers in summer, males 383, females 4,510; number in winter, males 1,598, females 3,482; different teachers during the year, males 1,C91, females 5,493. Number of scholars in summer schools, 199,792. Number in winter schools, 218,198. Average attendance in summer, 154,642; in winter, 175,526. Ratio of attendance to whole number of children between 5 and 15, .74. Average length of the schools, 7 months and 13 days. Average wages per month, inclusive of board, paid to male teachers, $ 49.87; do. to female teachers, $ 19.63. Amount of School Fund, December 31st, 1858, $ 1,522,898.00. From the interest of this fund about $ 48,000 are distributed annually among the towns for the support of schools; but to entitle a town to receive a portion thereof, it must raise by tax, for school purposes, at least $ 1.50 for each child in the town between 5 and 15. The amount raised by taxes (including income of surplus revenue) was $ 6.04 for each child between 5 and 15. There were 70 incorporated academies reported in the State, with an average of 4,338 pupils, and an aggregate of $ 84,401 paid for tuition; also, 672 unincorporated academies, private schools, &c., with an estimated average attendance of 18,044 scholars, and an estimated aggregate of $ 374,120 paid for tuition. Amount expended in 1856 to promote popular education, including Normal Schools, Teachers' Institutes, and the cost of repairing and erecting school edifices, but excluding cost of school-books and collegiate and professional instruction, and in charitable institutions, $ 2,846,309.76. There are local funds for the support of academies, &c. to the amount of about $ 650,000, yielding an income of about $ 35,000. There are four Normal Schools supported by the State, at an annual cost of about $ 13,500, — one at Westfield and one at Bridgewater for both sexes, and one at Framingham and at Salem for girls. There were in these schools, in 1858, 531 pupils, 108 males and 423 females. Since the opening of the first State Normal School, July 3, 1839, at Lexington, Mass. (the school now at Framingham), there have been to December, 1858, 4,065 pupils in attendance (3,171 females and 894 males), and of these 2,055 graduated. 113 pupils at the Normal Schools received State aid this year. Ten Teachers' Institutes were held during the year, attended by an average number of 153 teachers, at an expense of $ 350 for each Institute. Of the 1,533 persons enrolled as members, 609 were employed as teachers. Teachers' Associations have been formed in most of the counties of the State. The State allows $ 50 to each Association that holds each year two semiannual meetings of not less than two days each.

The Board of Education consists of the Governor and Lieutenant-Governor, and eight members, one being appointed each year by the Governor and Council for eight years. There is a Secretary of the Board, who has an assistant, and who is the executive officer of the Board. Provision is made by law for the education and training of young men to be principal teachers in the high schools in the Commonwealth, by establishing 48 State scholarships in the colleges of the State, and paying $ 100 annually to each. These scholarships are now filled, and their establishment has given a quickening impulse to the schools throughout the State. The report of the Secretary (22d report of the Board) gives the history of the School Fund of Massachusetts, and also a large correspondence with the town committees, tending to show the value of the Normal Schools as a means of educating teachers.

Perkins Institution and Massachusetts Asylum for the Blind. — The number of blind persons connected with the institution January 1, 1858, was 114; received up to Sept. 30, 1858, 15; discharged, 15; leaving, Sept. 30, 1858, 114. Of these 89 are resident at the household, and 25 are connected with the work department. 90 are beneficiaries from the other New England States; the rest are beneficiaries of Massachusetts. Young blind persons of good moral character can be admitted to the school on paying $200 per annum, which covers all expenses except for clothing. Indigent blind persons, of suitable age and character, belonging to Massachusetts, can be admitted gratuitously upon application to the Governor for a warrant. An obligation is required from some responsible person that the pupil shall be removed without expense to the institution, whenever it may be desirable to discharge him. Indigent blind persons residing in other New England States should apply to the Secretary of State in their own State. The usual period of tuition is from five to seven years. The State makes an annual grant to this institution of $ 12,000.

State Lunatic Hospital, Worcester. — Merrick Bemis, M. D., Superintendent. The Hospital was opened for patients January 18, 1833. Number of patients, December 1st, 1857, 372, — 177 males, 195 females; admitted during the year, 307, — 142 males, 165 females; under treatment during the year, 679, — 319 males, 360 females; discharged, 376, — 180 males, 196 females; remaining in the Hospital, September 30th, 1858, 301, — 141 males, 160 females. Of those admitted during the year, 151 (79 males, 72 females) were committed by the courts, and 22 (10 males, 12 females) by overseers of the poor. 136 foreigners (i. e. persons having no legal residence or settlement in the State), of whom 53 were males and 83 females, were admitted. 86 foreigners (33 males, 53 females) remained in the Hospital at the end of the year. Of the 376 patients discharged, 127 were recovered, 174 improved, 41 not improved, and 34 died. Supposed cause of insanity of some of those admitted since the opening of the Hospital: — Ill health, 651; intemperance, 472; domestic affliction, 383; epilepsy, 115; puerperal, 141; jealousy, 40; masturbation, 260; hard labor, 79; religious excitement, 289; Millerism 10; spiritualism, 25; fear of poverty, 39. Since the opening of the Hospital, 639 — 329 males, 310 females — have died. The principal diseases have been: — Marasmus, 92; consumption, 82; exhaustion, 70; epilepsy, 62; palsy, 29; apoplexy, 23; old age, 23; suicide, 21. The occupations of some of those admitted were as follows: — Housekeepers, 994; farmers, 450; laborers, 322; seamstresses, 312; shoemakers, 195; housemaids, 134; operatives in mill, 173; merchants, 111; sailors, 97; blacksmiths, 34; teachers, 50; clergymen, 18. Their ages were — under 15, 43, between 15 and 20, 382; between 20 and 30, 1,572; between 30 and 40, 1,451; between 40 and 50, 1,189; between 50 and 60, 869; between 60 and 70, 323; between 70 and 80, 101; over 80, 21. 2,782 were unmarried, 2,420 were married, 135 were widowers, and 343 widows. 3,247 were insane less than one year before their admission, 613 more than one year and less than two years; 48 had been insane for more than thirty years. The Hospital is full with 276 patients, but by crowding can accommodate 306. There is a small farm connected with the Hospital, which gives the patients opportunities for recreation and labor. Steam is used for warming the building, and ventilation is forced by mechanical power. The plan adopted has been in operation two years, and has accomplished its work in the most thorough and successful manner at a reasonable expense. The Hospital has been comfortably warmed in cold weather, been made cool in warm weather, and ventilated at all times. The receipts for the year were $ 60,302.42; expenditures $ 59,798.58.

State Lunatic Hospital, Taunton. — George C. S. Choate, M. D , Superintendent. This Hospital was opened for patients, and the first patient was admitted, April 7, 1854. The grounds contain nearly 134 acres, and the buildings are intended to accommodate 250 patients. Number of patients, September 30, 1857, 327 (177 males and 150 females); admitted during the year, 223 (120 males and 103 females); under treatment during the year, 550 (297 males, 253 females); discharged, 208 (115 males and 93 females); died, 40 (25 males and 15 females); eloped, 1 male. Remaining, September 30, 1858, 301 (156 males and 145 females). Of the 618 discharged during the four years, 334 (179 males and 155 females) were recovered, 85 (40 males and 45 females) were improved, and 199 (94 males and 105 females) were unimproved. Of the 1,112 patients admitted, the character of the insanity of 508 (257 males and 251 females) was *mania*; of 137 (62 males and 75 females) was *melancholia*; of 137 (73 males and 64 females) was *monomania*; of 330 (172 males and 158 females) was *dementia*. Of the 1,112, 554 were supported by the State, 263 by towns, and 295 by friends.

Restraint by mechanical apparatus is rarely resorted to, and the aim is to dispense, as far as possible, with physical force. Receipts for support of patients, $ 65,392; payments for supplies, fuel, labor, &c., $ 61,708.

State Lunatic Hospital, Northampton. — William H. Prince, M. D., Superintendent. The first patient was admitted to this Hospital August 16, 1858. The grounds contain 175 acres, and the buildings are constructed to accommodate 250 patients, and are arranged for twelve classes of each sex. There is a centre building four stories high, and, with its extension in the rear, 190 feet deep; and a range of wings on each side, three stories high, giving a front line of 512 feet. The stories are all twelve feet high. It is heated and ventilated by means of steam. Up to Sept. 30, 1858, there had been admitted 228 patients, (99 males and 129 females), and 8 (6 males and 2 females) had been discharged.

Besides the State hospitals at Worcester, Taunton, and Northampton, and the arrangements for the care of the insane at the almshouses, jails, &c., there are municipal and private establishments, as the city hospital at South Boston, the McLean Asylum at Somerville, and the institution at Pepperell.

State Prison. — Gideon Haynes, Warden. The number of prisoners, October 1st, 1857, was 440; 198 were received during the year ending 30th September, 1858, and 155 were discharged. Number of prisoners, 30th September, 1858, 483. Of those discharged, 126 were from expiration, and 26 from remission of sentence, 2 died, and 1 escaped. Of those in prison, 337 were committed for offences against property, and 146 for offences against the person, including larceny from the person, robbery, and perjury. 168 are natives of Massachusetts, 134 of other States, 180 are foreigners, and 1 is of unknown parentage. There are 58 second-comers, 16 third-comers, 1 fourth-comer, 2 fifth-comers, and 1 is a seventh-comer. Average daily number of convicts for the year, 469. Of those in prison, 49 are between 16 and 20 years of age; 146 from 20 to 25; 108 from 25 to 30; 108 from 30 to 40; 45 from 40 to 50; 19 from 50 to 60; 7 from 60 to 70; 1 from 70 to 80. 106 were sentenced for 2 years or less; 100 for 3, or more than 2; 112 for 5, or more than 3; 106 for 10, or more than 5; 17 for 15, or more than 10; 8 for 20, or more than 15; 1 for 30; and 34 for life. 359 convicts are employed, for contractors, in some mechanical employment, and the rest (or such as are not infirm or sick, or in close confinement) are engaged on work for prison account. $ 100 are appropriated each year to purchase books for the prison library, which now numbers 1,000 volumes. The ordinary expenses were $ 96,956, and the receipts $ 73,167; deficit of receipts, $ 23,789. Provision is made by statute that a record shall be kept of the conduct of each convict, and for every month that the convict observes the rules of the prison and is not subjected to punishment there shall be a deduction from the term of his sentence as follows: if the sentence is for less than three years, one day for each month of good conduct; if it is for three years or more and less than ten years, two days for each month; if for ten years or more, then five days for each month of such good conduct. The Warden submits the record and the scale of deduction once in three months to the Governor and Council.

State Reform School, Westborough. — William E. Starr, Superintendent. Boys in the school, Oct. 1st, 1857, 613; received since, 313; discharged during the year, 369; remaining, September 30th, 1858, 557. Of the 2,409 committed to the school since it was opened, 4 were six years of age, 18 were 7, 61 were 8, 127 were 9, 213 were 10, 261 were 11, 317 were 12, 364 were 13, 405 were 14, 487 were 15, 101 were 16, 39 were 17 and over, and the ages of 12 were unknown. 823 were committed for larceny, 1,023 for stubbornness, 107 as idle and disorderly, 143 for vagrancy, 34 for shopbreaking and stealing, 13 for assault, 22 as runaways, 26 for shopbreaking, with intent to steal, 12 as common drunkards, 57 for malicious mischief, 10 for burglary, 4 for robbery, 4 for forgery, and 4 for arson. 1,696 were committed during minority, 4 for 10 years, 1 for 9 years, 9 for 8 years, 5 for 7 years, 34 for 6 years, 76 for 5 years, and the remainder for shorter periods. 1,902 were born in the United States, and 507 in foreign countries. Of those born in this country, 1,304 are of American parentage, 489 of Irish, 64 of English, 16 of French, 16 of Scotch, 9 of German, and 1 each of Danish, Spanish, Swedish, and African. All the boys are employed during a portion of the day at some mechanical, agricultural, or domestic labor. They do the washing, ironing, and cooking, and make and mend their own clothes. Each day, 4 hours are devoted to school, 6 to labor, 8½ to sleep, and 5½ to recreation and miscellaneous duties. 180 acres of land were originally purchased, and since that time an adjoining farm has been added. The school can accommodate 600 inmates. The expenses of the institution for the year were $47,578 63. The principal building was destroyed by fire, set by one of the pupils, in August, 1859. The Legislature have since provided for rebuilding at Westborough on the family plan. They have also established a State Nautical School.

State Industrial School for Girls, Lancaster. — Bradford K. Peirce, *Superintendent.* This School, heretofore known as the "State Reform School for Girls," was inaugurated August 27, 1856. There are three buildings, each fitted to accommodate a separate family of 30 pupils, or 90 pupils in all. The object of the School is "for the instruction, employment, and reformation of exposed, helpless, evil-disposed, and vicious girls." Such girls, over 7 and under 16 years of age, upon complaint before the Judge of Probate, or a Commissioner appointed for the purpose, and notice to the parent or guardian, may be sent thither; and, in all cases, they are to be committed until they are 18 years of age, unless sooner discharged by the trustees, or bound out as apprentices. Up to Sept. 30, 1858, the date of the third report, 121 children were admitted, 85 of whom were American, 24 Irish, 6 English, 2 each Scotch and German, and 1 each Italian and French. Of 85 one or both parents are dead, or have separated. 17 have been indentured, and 2 escaped. The Trustees speak encouragingly of the influence of the school upon the inmates, and "that most of these girls will be saved from probable or inevitable ruin, and become useful members of society." The proceeds of the needlework and knitting by the girls during the year were $ 368.44.

School for Idiotic and Feeble-minded Youth, South Boston. — This school has been in operation since 1848, under the gratuitous and effective general superintendence of Dr. Samuel G. Howe. The resident Superintendent is Alexander McDonald. January 1, 1858, there were in the school 41 State pupils, and 20 private pupils. During 10 months there were admitted 20 (14 State beneficiaries and 6 private pupils); 18 pupils were discharged; leaving Sept. 30, 1858, 63, of whom 46 were supported entirely by the State, 4 partially by the State, and 13 by friends or other States. "Of those in the school (Dec. 1856), 8 do not make known their wants; 3 do not feed themselves; 12 do not, and 11 can partially, dress themselves; 7 are speechless; 2 can pronounce a few words; 31 form sentences; 18 know the names of several colors; 12 know their letters; 11 read words of two or three letters; 11 read understandingly; 21 count ten; 9 perform examples in mental arithmetic, and 5 in written; 8 have a general knowledge of geography; 10 can knit; 6 can do plain sewing; 7 sing well, and keep good time." The only treatment is kindness. Great attention is paid to cleanliness, and regularity of habits. There has been since 1848 a private establishment for the instruction of this class at Barre, in Worcester Co.

Pauperism in the Year 1858. — There were three State Almshouses opened for the reception of State paupers in 1854; one at Bridgewater, one at Monson, and one at Tewksbury. At *Bridgewater*, Oct. 1, 1857, there were 598 inmates; admitted since, including 76 born in the house, 1,611; and 1,367 were discharged and indentured, 30 deserted, 287 died; leaving, Sept. 30, 1858, 525 (131 men, 160 women, 134 boys under 15 years of age, and 100 girls). Average cost per week of each inmate, $ 1.02. A school is kept for each sex. Admissions to the hospital during the year, 1,568.

At *Monson*, Oct. 1, 1857, there were 638 inmates; admitted since, 2,300, including 22 born in the institution; discharged, deserted, and indentured, 2,271; died, 102; in all, 2,373; leaving Sept. 30, 1858, 565 (55 men, 74 women, 279 boys under 15 years of age, and 157 girls). The expenditures for the nine months were $ 30,525.27. The schools have 366 scholars. Number of admissions to the hospital, 1,032.

At *Tewksbury*, the average number of inmates during the ten months ending Sept. 30, 1858, was over 900. Average cost of support about 90 cents each per week. The number remaining Sept. 30, 1858, was 822. The school connected with this house averaged during the year 200 children daily as pupils. Admissions to the hospital during the year, 1,843. During the year, there were 97 births and 227 deaths.

There is a *State Hospital* at *Rainsford Island*, Boston Harbor, in which there were 1,160 pauper inmates during the year ending Sept. 30, 1858. 1,047 paupers have been sent out of the State during the nine months ending Sept. 30, 1857. 10,301 alien passengers, who gave bonds, or paid their commutation, amounting to $20,301, arrived in Boston by sea.

In addition to the above expenditures by the State for *State Paupers*, the individual towns in their corporate capacity support the town paupers, and relieve the poor. The statistics for the 11 mos. ending Sept. 30, 1858, are as follows: Persons relieved or supported as paupers, 37,206; number of almshouses, 212; acres of land appurtenant to almshouses, 21,296; value of almshouse establishments, $1,271,023; persons relieved in almshouses, 11,845; average cost per week, $1.57; paupers in almshouses unable to work, 2,282; estimated value of pauper labor in almshouses, $21,319; paupers made so by intemperance in themselves or others, 18,335. Number aided and supported out of almshouses, 23,071; average weekly cost, $1.10. Insane relieved and supported, 870; idiots, 306. Paupers by reason of insanity or idiocy, 1,090. Foreign paupers that have come into the State during the year, 290. Expense of supporting and relieving paupers, $550,620. 1,407 indigent children under 14 years of age (738 boys and 547 girls, sex of the rest not stated) were supported at the public charge in 1858.

Jails and Houses of Correction for the year ending Sept. 30, 1858. — Whole number committed, including 138 debtors, 14,599. There were 12,050 males; 2,549 females; 2,163 minors; 566 colored; 6,534 not able to read or write; 11 insane when committed; 3,050 natives of Massachusetts; 2,047 natives of other States; 9,502 foreigners; number of persons committed as witnesses, 657; number that had been addicted to intemperance, 8,155. Of the persons committed to jail for crime, 586 were discharged by order of court, 3,850 on expiration of sentence, 846 on payment of fine and costs, 3,630 as poor convicts unable to pay fine and costs, 96 by acquittal, 267 by pardon or discharge by overseers; remaining in confinement, Sept. 30, 1858, 1,969. Average cost of board of each prisoner per week, $1.52. Estimated value of labor in the Jails and Houses of Correction, $57,485. Expenses of both, $222,722.

Criminal Statistics for the Year 1858.

Offences.	Prosecutions.	Convictions.	Acquittals.	Nol. Pros'd.	Laid on file.	Still Pending.	No Bill.	Not Arrested.	Default on Recognizance.	Costs.
Against the person, feloniously,	119	60	10	8	6	20	11	3	1	$5,385.67
" " not feloniously,	635	211	61	80	79	100	30	4	20	13,016 14
Against property, ...	1191	579	84	79	141	140	125	17	26	28,631.45
Against the currency, and crim. frauds, ...	206	61	15	21	39	32	31	4	3	5,467.17
Against public justice, . . .	77	20	7	8	7	15	16	4		2,111.46
Against the public peace, . .	38	2	1	6	6	11	7	1	4	614.02
Against the public health, . .	1						1			25.26
Against chastity, morality, and decency, ...	556	212	38	58	108	71	50	7	12	10,583.72
Against public policy, ...	1732	383	174	176	437	325	150	48	39	36 288 53
Other offences, ...	164	14	5	17	40	73	8	5	2	2,332.18
Not stated, ...	363	1			2	122	232	6		2,087.10
Total, ...	5082	1573	395	453	865	909	631	99	107	$106,572.70

Before Justices of the Peace and Police Courts, there were in 1857, 8,705 complaints. In 5,325 cases there were convictions; 1,907 were discharged, and 1,322 were held to a higher court. *Offences.* — Assault, 2,116; drunkenness, 2,541; violation of the liquor law, 1,413; larceny, 884; total costs, $64,749; fines received, $6,208.

Births, Marriages, and Deaths, for the Year ending December 31, 1857. — *Sixteenth Registration Report.* — The number of births during that period was 35,320; 18,023 males and 17,121 females, the sex of 176 not given. Of these births, 15,235 were of foreign parentage, 16,261 of American, 1,975 mixed American and foreign, and the parentage of 1,851 was not stated. The number of marriages was 11,739; in 6,286 the parties were Americans, in 4,082 they were foreigners, and in 971 one party was an American and the other a foreigner. The number of deaths was 21,280, — 10,703 males and 10,485 females. Their average age was 27.44. During the 16 years and 8 months ending December 31, 1857, some of the causes of death were as follows: 54,166 (or 22.15 per cent) died of consumption; 15,864 (or 6.49 per cent) of dysentery; 15,229 (or 6.23 per cent) of typhus; 14,366 (or 5.87 per cent) of infantile diseases; 13,797 (or 5.64 per cent) of old age; 10,809 (or 4.42 per cent) of pneumonia; 10,800 (or 4.42 per cent) of scarlatina; 5,831 (or 2.38 per cent) of dropsy; 5,744 (or 2.35 per cent) of croup; 6,004 (or 2.46 per cent) were stillborn; 5,677 (or 2.32 per cent) of cholera infantum; 5,224 (or 2.14 per cent) of hydrocephalus; 5,469 (or 2.24 per cent) of disease of the heart; 4,516 (or 1.85 per cent) by accident; 4 396 (or 1.80 per cent) of convulsions; 3,453 (or 1.41 per cent) of paralysis; 1,990 (or .81 per cent) of apoplexy; 1,730 of epilepsy; 334 of delirium tremens; 434 of insanity; 2,378 of disease of the brain; 1,463 of pleurisy; 461 of bronchitis; 242 of asthma; 196 of hernia; 3,083 of disease of stomach; 1,424 of disease of liver; 301 of diabetes; 308 of calculus; 562 of disease of kidney; 615 of diseases of skin; 957 by suicide; 1,467 of small-pox; 2,387 of measles; 2,867 of whooping-cough; 2,063 of erysipelas; 2,709 of cholera; 596 of rheumatism; 806 of intemperance; 2,525 of cancer; 1,930 of canker; 152 of tetanus; 40 of gout; 72 of syphilis; 16 of hydrophobia; 2,220 of child-birth. This registration report is exceedingly valuable, and highly creditable to Dr. Josiah Curtis and the others engaged in its preparation. The report contains the Massachusetts Life, Population, and Annuity Table, with other tabular deductions and comments connected therewith, computed and prepared by E. B. Elliott of Boston.

The population of the State by counties, and that of the cities and principal towns, and the industrial statistics of the State, for 1855 and 1845, were given in the American Almanac for 1857, pp. 249, 250. Since then an additional volume has been published, giving the nativity, social statistics, and occupation of the people, as existing June 1, 1855, illustrated and developed in many carefully prepared tables, full abstracts of which are given in the American Almanac for 1858, p. 251.

The number of legal voters in the State, June 1, 1857, was 211,681.

XVI. MICHIGAN.

Capital, Lansing. *Area*, 56,243 sq. m. *Population*, 1854, 511,672.

Government for the Year 1860.

			Term expires.	Salary.
Moses Wisner,	of Pontiac,	*Governor*,	Jan. 1861,	$ 1,000
Edmund B. Fairfield,	of Hillsdale,	*Lieut.-Governor*,	"	$ 3 a day [during session of Legislature.
Nelson G. Isbell,	of Howell,	*Sec. of State*,	Dec. 31, 1860,	Fees & 800
Daniel L. Case,	of Lansing,	*Auditor-Gen.*,	"	1,000
John McKinney,	of Lansing,	*State Treasurer*,	"	1,000
Jacob M. Howard,	of Detroit,	*Attorney-General*,	"	800
John M. Gregory,	of Ann Arbor,	*Sup't of Pub. Instr.*	"	1,000
James W. Sanborn,	of Port Huron,	*Com. of Land-Office*,	"	800
F. W. Curtenius,	of Kalamazoo,	*Adj.-Gen. and Q. M.-Gen.*,		450
William L. Seaton,	of Jackson,	*Agent of State Prison*,		1,000
J. Eugene Tenney,	of Marshall,	*State Librarian*,		500

The Governor, Lieutenant-Governor, Secretary of State, Auditor-General, Treasurer, Superintendent of Public Instruction, Commissioner of the Land-Office, and the Attorney-General are each elected by the people, by a plurality vote, for two years. Senators, 32 in number, and representatives, 81 in number, are elected every two years by a similar vote for two years. The sessions of the Legislature are biennial, and the members receive pay for only forty days. The last session commenced in January, 1859.

Judiciary.

Supreme Court.

			Term ends.	Salary.
George Martin,	of Grand Rapids,	*Chief Justice*,	Dec. 30, 1867,	$2,500
Randolph Manning,	of Pontiac,	*Associate Justice*,	" 1861,	2,500
James V. Campbell,	of Detroit,	"	" 1863,	2,500
Isaac P. Christiancy,	of Monroe,	"	" 1865,	2,500
Thomas M. Cooley,	of Adrian,	*Reporter*,		500

Circuit Court. — Salary of Judges, $1,500 each.

Dist.	Judge.	Residence.	Term ends.	Dist.	Judge.	Residence.	Term ends.
1.	Edw. H. C. Wilson,	Hillsdale,	Dec. 30, 1863	6.	Sanford M. Green,	Pontiac,	Dec. 30, 1863
2.	Nathaniel Bacon,	Niles,	"	7.	Josiah Turner,	Howell,	"
3.	B. F. H. Witherell,	Detroit,	"	8.	Louis S. Lovell,	Grand Rapids,	"
4.	Edwin Lawrence,	Ann Arbor,	"	9.	Flavius J. Littlejohn,	Allegan,	Dec. 30, 1864
5.	Benj. F. Graves,	Battle Creek,	"	10.	W. F. Woodworth,	Midland City,	"

Daniel Goodwin, of Detroit, *District Judge*, Upper Peninsula, Salary $1,000.

The judges of the Supreme Court are elected by the people for eight years. After the first election in 1857, they were classified so that their several terms expired in two, four, six, and eight years. Judge Martin took the short term of two years and was re-elected in 1859, for the full term of eight years. Three judges constitute a quorum. Four terms of the Supreme Court are held annually, — two at Lansing on the Tuesday after the first Monday of January and July, and two at Detroit on the Tuesday after the first Monday of April and October, — and there may be special or adjourned terms at either of these places. The court shall be in session each term long enough to hear all the cases ready for argument, and all cases shall be determined either at the term they are argued, or early in the succeeding term. The clerk of the county in which the court is held is clerk of the Supreme Court. Judges of the Circuit Court are elected for six years by the people of their respective districts. Prosecuting officers are elected by the people of each county, to hold office for two years. By the Act of February 12, 1859, grand juries are not to attend any court, unless the judge thereof shall so direct in writing filed with the clerk of the court. Criminal proceedings are to be conducted by informations in the lieu of indictments, — the informations to be verified by the oath of the prosecuting officer, complainant or some other person, — and the same rules to govern in the setting forth of offences, as in indictment. The prosecuting attorney must subscribe his name thereto, and must indorse thereon the names of the witnesses known to him at the time of the filing of the information in court. The proceedings in holding to bail, &c. are the same as in indictments. No information can be found against any person for any offence, unless such person shall have had, or waived, a preliminary examination therefor.

Finances.

Balance in the Treasury, November 30, 1857,	$158,642.70
Receipts for the year ending November 30, 1858,	865,720.35
Total available means for the year,	$1,024,363.05
Expenditures for the year ending November 30, 1858,	848,015.85
Balance in the Treasury, November 30, 1858,	$176,347.20

State Debt.—The State debt, funded and fundable, November 30, 1858, was as follows:—

Penitentiary Bonds, principally due January 1, 1859, paid at maturity,	$20,000.00
" " " " 1860,	40,000.00
Full paid, $5,000,000 loan bonds, principal due January 1, 1863,	177,000.00
Adjusted, $5,000,000 " " " "	1,726,685.00
Part paid, $5,000,000 loan or unadjusted bonds, when funded will amount to	104,142.60
Outstanding Internal Improvement warrants,	3,752.07
New Bonds issued July, 1858, and due 1878,	266,000.00
Total,	$2,337,629.67
The annual interest on this sum, at 6 per cent, is	140,257.78

The State is also indebted to the several Trust Funds. These are derived from the sales of lands granted by the general government and appropriated by the Constitution of the State for educational purposes. In some instances, resort has been had to the principal of these funds to meet the appropriations of the Legislature. The Legislature of 1859 authorized the assessment and collection of a State tax of one mill on a dollar, on the aggregate of the real and personal property in the State, as equalized for 1856, for each of the years 1859 and 1860.

The receipts for the year ending Nov. 30, 1858, on account of the primary school funds were $83,232; university funds, $21,622; normal school funds, $3,402; swamp-land funds, $67,512; internal improvement funds, $5,297; general fund, $666,656. Some of the items of the receipts of the general fund were, proceeds of sales of lands for taxes, $76,132; delinquent taxes, $60,605; specific tax on railroads, $149,940; on plank roads, manufacturing and mining companies, $8,725; on banks, $7,597. Some of the items of the expenditures of the general fund were, salaries of public officers, $14,137; expenses of the judiciary, $25,840; extra session of legislature, $9,913; State Agricultural School and Society, $5,159; expenses and repairs of State prison, $34,000; house of correction for juvenile offenders, $15,000. The amount of lands sold during the year was 103,854 acres; amount of receipts for lands sold, $187,415.

Banks. — For the condition of the banks in Michigan, near Jan. 1, 1859, see *ante*, p. 220.

Common Schools for the Year ending Sept. 25, 1858. — Number of organized school districts in the State, 3,946; being 3,071 whole districts, and 875 fractional districts; number of children resident therein between 4 and 18 years of age, 225,592; average length of schools, 6 months; number of children attending school, 173,594, or near 77 per cent. of the whole number; number of qualified teachers, 7,231, 2,326 males and 4,905 females; paid for teachers' wages, $442,227.37; whole amount raised by tax upon the school districts for the support of schools, $316,580.71; of which $119,175.51 was raised to build, and $21,315.50 to repair school-houses. The amount raised by rate bill was $118,099.89. The amount of the mill tax raised in each county was $116,362.04. The number of volumes in the township libraries reported was 168,977. The Act of Feb. 15, 1859, provided that at the annual town-meeting in April, 1859, the voters in each town should decide by ballot for each town, for the continuance of the township library, or for the establishment of district libraries in lieu thereof.

The Act of Feb. 14, 1859, permits any districts containing more than 200 children between the ages of 4 and 18 years, by a two-thirds vote of the voters attending the annual meeting, to decide to elect a district board of six trustees, two for 1 year, two for 2 years, and 2 for three years, and afterwards two each year for three years, which trustees shall have the care and management of said district schools, with the power to classify and grade them, to establish a high school, to employ teachers, &c. Two contiguous districts, if their number of children united is not less than 200, may unite by a similar vote, and elect trustees in the same manner and with like powers.

The State Normal School at Ypsilanti was opened in October, 1852. During the year ending July, 1856, 253 students were in attendance, 103 males and 150 females. There is a Model School connected with the Normal School, which had, in 1856, 237 pupils. In December, 1859, the Normal School had 316 scholars, and the Model School, 63.

Agricultural College. — The Legislature of 1855 authorized the establishment of an Agricultural College. A farm of about 700 acres has been purchased, near the village of Lansing, and suitable buildings for professors and students, and for the uses of the farm, have been erected.

Asylum for the Education of the Deaf and Dumb and the Blind. — This institution was first opened in February, 1854, at Flint, in rooms rented for that purpose. The corner-stone of the main building was laid July 15, 1857. The building when completed will accommodate 350 pupils. The grounds contain 33.45 acres. 128 pupils have been received since its opening in 1854, 87 deaf and dumb, and 41 blind. The largest number in attendance at any one time has been 90. 111 pupils, 74 deaf and dumb and 37 blind, have been in attendance during the year ending Dec. 1, 1858. The Asylum is free to all the deaf and dumb and the blind in Michigan between the ages of 10 and 30, who have a good natural intellect, a good moral character, and no contagions. Board and tuition free, clothing and travelling expenses to be paid by the pupils, or parents or guardians. The vacation is from July 15, to 1st Wednesday in October, — and pupils should be admitted at the close of the vacation.

Asylum for the Insane. — This institution is at Kalamazoo. The grounds contain 167.76 acres. The buildings at the date of the last report, December, 1858, had not been completed. The centre building was laid in ashes February 11, 1858.

Crime. — By the report of the Attorney-General it appears that during the year 1858, there were 25 prosecutions for murder, in which there were 7 convictions, and 8 acquittals. Burglary, 56 prosecutions, 30 convictions, 2 acquittals. Larceny, 183 prosecutions, 126 convictions, 11 acquittals. Petit larceny, 77 prosecutions, 57 convictions, 4 acquittals. The remaining cases are pending, or the parties are not arrested, &c.

State Prison, Jackson. — Number of convicts in prison, 30th November, 1857, 411; of whom 268 were white and 24 colored males, and 1 half-breed Indian, and 9 white and 2 colored females; received during the year, 195; whole number, 606. Discharged during the year, 133, — by expiration of sentence 80, by pardon 40, 10 died, 2 escaped, and 1 was discharged by order of court. In prison, November 30, 1858, 473, of whom 10 are United States convicts. 460 are males, 424 white, 35 colored, 1 half-breed Indian; 13 are females, 12 white and 1 colored. Average number during the year, 443.6; average age of the prisoners, 27.2 years. The services of 296 convicts were let out on contract at an average of 42.4 cents for all the convicts so let out. Of those received during the year, 34 were sentenced for offences against the person, and 161 for offences against property. 143 were natives of the United States, and 52 were of foreign birth. The average length of sentence of those received during the year was 4.1 years; that of all the convicts in prison is 4.9 years. Since the opening of the prison in 1839, 1,521 prisoners have been received, and of these 108 were negroes, 30 mulattoes, 2 Indians, 2 half-breeds, and 35 females. The death penalty for murder in this State was abolished in 1846, and solitary confinement at hard labor in the State Prison for life substituted, March 2d, 1847. Since then, to Nov. 30, 1858, 28 persons have been convicted of murder, and sentenced to solitary confinement at hard labor for life. A separate building is erected for these convicts. The receipts of the prison for the year were $56,138.52, the expenditures, $56,227.01.

A House of Correction for Juvenile Offenders was opened at Lansing, Sept. 2, 1856. The name was changed by the Legislature of 1859 to that of the Reform School. The number of dormitories in the institution is 76. Since its opening there have been received 78 inmates. The number in the house, Nov. 18, 1857, was 39; number received during the year, 24; whole number, 63; left, 5; remaining Nov 18, 1858, 58. The average age of those received during the year was nearly 14.5 years. 9 were of American parentage. 20 were committed for larceny. A portion of the boys are employed by contractors in making chairs. The inmates are kept employed in some work or in attending school.

Geological Survey. — The Legislature in 1859 passed an act authorizing the completion of the Geological Survey of the State, the appointment of a geologist, &c.

Census of May, 1854. — Number reported under 5 years of age, males, 42,203; females, 38,714; over 5 and less than 10, males, 39,343; females, 36,032. Number of males over 10 and under 20, 61,736; over 21 and under 45, 92,764; over 45 and under 75, 30,096; over 75 and under 90, 1,251; over 90 and under 100, 71; 100 and over, 8. Number of females over 10 and under 18, 47,425; over 18 and under 40, 83,786; over 40 and under 75, 32,494; 75 and over, 1,598. Married males, 66.931; females, 86,315; unmarried males, 66,544; females, 54.188. Total population, 511,672. Number of blind reported, 178; of deaf and dumb, 206; of insane or idiotic, 428. Number of colored persons, 3,336. Number of marriages the preceding year, 3,876; of deaths, 4,754. Number of acres of land taxable, nearly 7,917,322; not taxable, 80,215; improved, 2,111,660; of wheat harvested the preceding year, 473,571; bushels raised, 7,027,932; acres of corn, 327,356; bushels harvested, 7,630,658; bushels of all other grains, 2,294,420; bushels of potatoes, 2,917,434; tons of hay, 496,041; pounds of wool, 2,680,747; pounds of pork, 11,258,841; of butter, 7,924,896; of cheese, 779,530; of sugar, 1,611,462. Number of horses one year old and over, 91,564; neat cattle do. other than oxen and cows, 141,253; of working oxen, 67,033; of milch cows, 139,260; of sheep, 964,333; swine, over six months old, 239,832. Barrels of flour made the preceding year, 998,503; number of flour-mills, 254,—25 steam, 220 water power, and power of 9 not stated; persons employed, 604; capital invested in flouring mills, $1,828,006; products of do. for past year, $3,567,978. Number of saw-mills, 922, —271 steam, 618 water power, and power of 33 not stated; persons employed, 4,579; capital invested, $2,442,577; products, $3,273,836. Barrels of peppermint oil manufactured during the preceding year, 10,782; gallons of wine, 1,215; barrels of cider, 2,829; barrels of fish caught, 47,203. Capital invested in manufactures, $2,832,965; persons employed, 5,769; products, $3,604,712. Persons employed in mining, 2,312; capital invested, $4,747,950; valuation of minerals produced, $902,961.

XVII. MINNESOTA.

Capital, St. Paul. *Area*, about 86.000 sq. m. *Population*, May, 1858, 150,042.

For the boundaries of the State and the act authorizing its admission into the Union, see the American Almanac for 1858, pp. 139, 140. For the act admitting the State into the Union, see the American Almanac for 1859, p. 143. The constitution was done in convention August 29, 1857, and adopted by the people October 13, 1857, by a vote of 36,506 for, to 703 against it. Some of its provisions are as follows: — *Voters.* — Every male person aged twenty-one, of either of the following classes, to wit: white citizens of the United States; white persons of foreign birth who have duly declared their intention to become citizens; persons of mixed white and Indian blood who have adopted the customs and habits of civilization; and persons of Indian blood, residing in the State, who have adopted the language, customs, and habits of civilization, when pronounced capable by any district court in the State, may vote if they have resided in the United States one year, in the State four months, and in the election district ten days next preceding the election. Persons convicted of treason or felony, unless restored to their civil rights, those under guardianship, or *non compos*, or insane, cannot vote. All elections, except for such town officers as the law otherwise directs, are by ballot. On election day no person can be arrested on civil process. *Legislative.* — The Legislature consists of a Senate and House of Representatives. The number of Senators and Representatives to be prescribed by law, — the representation in the Senate not to exceed one member for every 5,000 inhabitants, and in the House one member to every 2,000. Senators and Representatives — to be qualified voters and residents one year in the State and six months next before the election in their districts — are elected in single districts. Representatives for one year and Senators for two years, one half each year, except at the election next succeeding a new apportionment, when there is an entire new election of all the Senators. During any session, neither house shall adjourn for more than three days. The pay of members for the first session is $3 a day, afterwards as regulated by law. Members are privileged from arrest, except for treason, felony, or breach of the peace, and shall not be questioned in another place for words uttered in debate. No Senator or Representative shall hold any State office created, or whose emoluments were increased, while he was a member of the Legislature, until one year after the expiration of his term. No law shall be passed unless voted for by a majority of all the members elected to each branch, and the vote be entered on the journal of each house. Any presiding officer refusing to sign any bill which had previously passed both houses shall be incapable afterwards of holding any office of honor or profit in the State. Two or more members of either house may protest, and have their reasons entered on the journal. No law shall embrace but one subject, and that shall be expressed in its title. Every bill shall be read on three different days in each separate house, unless two thirds decide otherwise, and no bill can be passed unless previously twice read at length. The Legislature shall not grant divorces nor authorize any lottery or the sale of lottery tickets. In all elections by the Legislature the vote shall be *viva voce*, and the votes entered on the journal. No money shall be appropriated except by bill. The Legislature shall cause an enumeration of the inhabitants of the State to be made in 1865 and every tenth year afterward. A new apportionment of Senators and Representatives shall be made at the first session after the enumeration and at the first session after each federal census. Each house may punish during its session, by imprisonment of not over twenty-four hours, any person, not a member, guilty of contemptuous behavior in their presence. It may expel a member by a two-thirds vote. Any act passed during the last three days of the session shall, if signed by the Governor and filed in the office of the Secretary of State within three days after the adjournment of the Legislature, become a law.

Executive. — The Governor and Lieutenant-Governor, chosen by a plurality vote, hold office for two years, and until their successors are elected and qualified. They must each be twenty-five years old, and citizens and residents of the State for one year next before their election. The Governor may veto a bill, but two thirds of each house may by a yea and nay vote, and the names entered on the journal, pass it over his veto. Any bill retained by him three days, when the Legislature is in session, becomes a law. The Lieutenant-Governor is *ex officio* President of the Senate. In case of any vacancy in the office of Governor, he shall be Governor. Before the close of each session the Senate shall elect a President *pro tempore*, who shall be Lieutenant-Governor in case a vacancy occurs in that office. A Secretary of State, Auditor, Treasurer, and Attorney-General are elected by the people, — the Auditor for three years, the others for two years and until their successors are qualified.

The Judiciary. — The judicial power is vested in a Supreme Court, District Courts, Courts of Probate, Justices of the Peace, and such other courts inferior to the Supreme Court as the Legislature may, by a two-thirds vote, establish. The Supreme Court, with original jurisdiction in such remedial cases as are prescribed by law, and appellate jurisdiction in all cases, both in law and equity, consists of a Chief Justice and two Associate Justices, elected by the people at large, to hold office for seven years, and until their successors are qualified. The Legislature, by a two-thirds vote, may increase the number of Associate Justices to four. There shall be no trial by jury in this Court. The Court shall appoint a Reporter of its decisions. A Clerk is chosen for three years, and until his successor is qualified. There shall be six Judges of the District Courts, elected one in a district for seven years, and until their successors are chosen. A Clerk for the

District Court is elected in each county for four years. The District Courts have original jurisdiction in all cases in law and equity where over $ 100 is in controversy, and in criminal cases where the punishment may be imprisonment for over three months or a fine of over $ 100. The compensation of a Supreme or District Judge shall not be diminished during his continuance in office. There shall be a Probate Court in each organized county, the Judge to be elected by the voters of the county for two years. Justices of the Peace are elected in each county for two years. Their jurisdiction in civil cases does not exceed $ 100, and in criminal cases they cannot imprison over three months nor fine over $ 100. A Court Commissioner may be elected in each county. The number and boundaries of districts may be changed, but no such change shall vacate the office of any judge. The Justices of the Supreme and District Courts shall hold no other office, federal or State, nor be eligible during their term to any other than a judicial office.

Debts. — The credit of the State shall never be given or lent in aid of any individual, association, or corporation. To defray extraordinary expenditures, the State may contract public debts not exceeding in the aggregate $ 250,000. Every law establishing such debt must pass by a two-thirds vote of the members of each branch, taken by yeas and nays, and it must levy a tax annually sufficient to pay the annual interest and the principal in ten years; and these taxes cannot be repealed, postponed, or diminished until the principal and interest of the debt are paid. The State shall never contract any debts for works of internal improvement, or be a party in carrying on such works, except in cases where grants of land or other property shall have been made to the State especially dedicated by the grant to specific purposes; and in such cases the State shall devote thereto the avails of such grants, and may pledge or appropriate the revenues derived from such works in aid of their completion. All debts shall be contracted by loan on State bonds, — not to be sold by the State under par, — in sums of not less than $500, bearing interest, and payable in ten years. The estimated annual expenses of the State shall be defrayed by an annual tax.

The Legislature, by a two-thirds vote, may pass a general banking law, with certain specified restrictions. No corporation shall be formed under special acts except for municipal purposes, and each stockholder shall be individually liable to the amount of his stock.

Education. — The proceeds of lands granted by the United States for school purposes shall remain a perpetual school fund, and the principal of all funds arising from sales for educational purposes shall forever be preserved undiminished, and the income shall be distributed according to the number of scholars in each township between the ages of five and twenty-one years.

Miscellaneous. — The personal property of each person to the amount of $ 200 shall be exempt from taxation. No person shall be made incompetent as a witness in consequence of his opinion upon the subject of religion. No new county shall be made of less than 400 square miles, nor shall any county be reduced below that size. Any city of 20,000 inhabitants may be made a county, if a majority of the electors therein desire. No lease of agricultural lands longer than twenty-one years shall be valid. There shall be no slavery in the State, nor property qualification for voters or for holding office. Imprisonment for debt, except in cases of fraud, is abolished.

Amendments. — Amendments to the constitution must be passed by a majority of both branches of the Legislature, be published with the laws of that session, be submitted to the people, and be ratified by a majority of the votes cast. If two thirds of the members elected to each branch of the Legislature shall vote to call a convention to revise the constitution, the question shall be submitted to the people at the next election for members of the Legislature. If a majority of the votes are in favor of such a convention, the Legislature at its next session shall call a convention, to be composed of as many members, and to be chosen in the same manner as the House of Representatives, and to meet within three months after their election.

An amendment to the State Constitution was adopted by the people April 15, 1858, in regard to the State debt. It provides that the State credit shall not be lent, &c except to aid the construction of the four railroads to which Congress has granted aid. To these roads special bonds may be issued, bearing 7 per cent interest payable semiannually in New York, to an amount of not over $ 1,250,000 each, or not exceeding $ 5,000,000 in the whole. The bonds shall be called "Minnesota State Railroad Bonds," and shall be of not over $ 1,000, and be redeemable after 10 and before 25 years from their date. Upon satisfactory evidence verified by affidavit that 10 miles of a road are graded and ready for the superstructure, the Governor issues $ 100,000 of the bonds to the road, and $ 100,000 in addition for every additional 10 miles of grading, — and when the cars are running on any ten miles of road $ 100,000 additional of bonds are to be given, and so another like sum for each additional ten miles the cars run, until the whole amount is issued. Two fifths of the bonds issued to the Southern Minnesota Railroad must be expended in the construction and equipment of a line from La Crescent to the junction with the Transit road. The Minneapolis and Cedar Valley Railroad Company, shall commence their road at Faribault and Minneapolis, and construct it equally from both places. Within 30 days after the Governor has proclaimed that the State has voted to lend its credit to railroads, any railroad purposing to avail itself of the loan shall notify the Governor, shall commence its construction in 60 days, and shall within two years get at least 50 miles ready for the superstructure. Each road shall complete not less than 50 miles on or before the expiration of the year 1861, 100 before 1864, and four fifths by the year 1866, and failing to do this shall forfeit all its rights under the grant. Each company shall provide for the punctual payment of the interest and principal of the bonds, and shall pledge as security the net profits of the road, and shall convey to the State portions of its lands, and give first mortgage bonds to the State to an amount equal to the bonds received from the State.

Government for the Year 1860.

			Term ends.	Salary.
ALEXANDER RAMSEY,	of St. Paul,	*Governor,*	Jan. 1862,	$ 2,500
Ignatius Donnelly,	of Dakota,	*Lieut.-Governor,*	"	$ 6 a day [during session of Legislature.
J. H. Baker,	of Blue Earth,	*Sec'y of State,*	Jan. 1862,	1,500
Charles Scheffer,	of Washington,	*Treasurer,*	"	1,000
W. F. Dunbar,	of Caledonia,	*Auditor,*	Jan. 1861,	1,000
G. E. Cole,	of Rice,	*Att'y-General,*	" 1862,	1,000
W. F. Wheeler,	of St. Paul,	*State Librarian,*		800

The number of Senators is 37; of Representatives 80. The election for State officers and members of the Legislature is on the 2d Tuesday of October. The time of meeting of the Legislature is on the 1st Monday of December. The sessions of the Legislature are annual.

JUDICIARY.

Supreme Court.

			Term ends.	Salary.
Lafayette Emmet,	of St. Paul,	*Chief Justice,*	Jan. 1865,	$ 2,000
Isaac Atwater,	of Minneapolis,	*Associate Justice,*	"	2,000
Chas. E. Flandrau,	of Traverse de Sioux,	"	"	2,000
J. J. Noah,	of St. Paul,	*Clerk,*	Jan. 1861,	1,000

District Courts.

No. Dist.	Judge.	Residence.	Term ends.	Salary.
1.	E. C. Palmer,	St. Paul,	Jan. 1, 1865,	$ 2,000
2.	S. J. R. McMillan,	Stillwater,	"	2,000
3.	N. M. Donaldson,	Owatonna,	"	2,000

No. Dist.	Judge.	Residence.	Term ends.	Salary.
4.	C. E. Vandenburgh,	Minneapolis,	Jan 1, 1865,	$2,000
5.	Thomas Wilson,	Winona,	"	2,000
6.	L. Branson,	Mankato,	"	2,000

FINANCES.

State Debt. — The people have voted to lend the credit of the State to various railroads to the amount of $5,000,000. The loans to the roads are made as above stated. Up to October 1, 1858, $250,000 of the eight per cent bonds of the State had been disposed of, and this constituted the debt of the State at that date. Up to December 1, 1859, it is stated that $2,500,000 of the bonds had been issued.

Banks. — There are now four or five banks in existence established under the general banking law. Other banks were started, but have ceased operations.

Common Schools. — Sections 16 and 36, in each township, are reserved and given to the State for School purposes, and a general law of the State prescribes that ½ of one per cent on all taxable property shall be levied for the support of common schools. Common schools are established in all parts of the State where the population is sufficiently compact. Union or High Schools exist in all the large towns and cities. The Union School-House in Minneapolis is a fine brick edifice and was erected at a cost of $14,000.

Charitable Institutions. — A law was passed at the last meeting of the Legislature for the establishment of a deaf and dumb asylum at or near Faribault.

The *State Prison* is located at Stillwater, Washington County. H. N. Setzer, Warden. There are only five or six convicts.

Railroads. — About 250 miles of grading on the four roads are completed (Dec. 1859), ready for the superstructure.

XVIII. MISSISSIPPI.

Capital, Jackson. *Area*, 47,151 sq. m. *Population*, 1850, 606,526.

Government for the Year 1860.

Name	Residence	Office	Term expires.	Salary.
JOHN J. PETTUS,	of Kemper Co.,	*Governor*,	3d Mond. in Nov. 1861,	$4,000
B. R. Webb,	of Pontotoc Co.,	*Sec. of State*,	Jan. 1862,	1,200
M. D. Haynes,	of Yazoo,	*State Treasurer*,	"	1,500
E. R. Burt,	of Knoxubee,	*Auditor of Pub. Ac'ts*,	"	1,500
Charles B. Green,	of Jackson,	*Adjutant-General*,		600
B. W. Sanders,	of Holmes Co.,	*Keeper of Capitol & Librarian*,		500
Dr. Eugene Hilgard,		*State Geologist.*		
A. M. Hardin,		*Keeper of the Penitentiary*,		1,500
E. Barksdale,	of Jackson,	*State Printer*,		1,500
James Drane,	of Choctaw Co.,	*President of the Senate.*		
Fleet T. Cooper,	of Lawrence Co.,	*Clerk of the Senate.*		
J. A. P. Campbell,	of Attala Co.,	*Speaker of the House of Rep.*		
Charles A. Brougher,	of Tippah Co.,	*Clerk.*		

By a recent amendment to the Constitution, the time of electing State officers, &c. was changed from the first Monday and Tuesday of November, to the first Monday in October; and the time of meeting of the Legislature is changed from the first Monday of January to the first Monday of November, *biennially*. The proposed amendment of the Constitution to prohibit suits against the State was not adopted, only 10,170 voting for it.

Judiciary.

High Court of Errors and Appeals.

			Dist.	Term expires.	Salary.
A. H. Handy,	of Canton,	*Judge,*	1st,	Oct. 1860,	$ 3,000
Cotesworth P. Smith,	of Jackson,	*Presid. Judge,*	2d,	" 1862,	3,000
W. L. Harris,	of Lowndes Co.,	*Judge,*	3d,	" 1864,	3,000
Thomas J. Wharton,	of Jackson,	*Attorney-General,*		Jan. 1862,	1,200
George T. Swann,	of Jackson,	*Clerk,*			Fees.
James Z. George,		*Reporter of the Decisions of the Court.*			

Circuit Court.

Dist.	Judge.	Attorney.	Dist.	Judge.	Attorney.
1.	Hiram Cassedy,	J. B. Patton.	6.	J. S. Hamm,	S. M. Meek.
2.	John E. McNair,	G. S. McMillen.	7.	J. W. Thompson,	J. R. Chalmers.
3.	Jacob S. Yerger,	R. S. Buck.	8.	W. M. Hancock,	J. S. Terrill.
4.	John Watts,	Richard D. Cooper.	9.	J. M. Acker,	R. O. Beene.
5.	E. G. Henry,	R. S. Hudson.	10.	Wm. Cothran,	E. C. Walthall.

The jurisdiction of the High Court is appellate exclusively. There are two terms each year in Jackson, commencing on the first Monday of April and of October. The Reporter is elected by the Legislature. The reports are to be called the "Mississippi Reports," and are to be printed, bound, and published in the State of Mississippi. The Circuit Court has original jurisdiction in civil cases in which the sum in controversy exceeds $50. For each of the circuits, ten in number, a judge and attorney are elected, every four years. It has also exclusive criminal jurisdiction. For the counties composing the Judicial Districts, see the American Almanac for 1857, page 298. There is also a Probate Court, with a judge and clerk for each county. The Probate Court in most of the counties has a term of from two to six days each month. The Probate Clerk is also Register of Deeds. The Probate Judges are now paid by salaries instead of fees.

Finances.*

Receipts into the Treasury from November 1, 1857, to October 31, 1858,	$ 632,951.89
Disbursements,	614,659 52
Balance in Treasury,	$ 18,292.37

Chief Source of Income.		Executed slaves,	$ 10,150.00
Taxes,	$ 488,365.65	Chickasaw School Fund,	81,205.29
Principal Items of Expenditure.		Asylum for the Blind,	5,750.00
Judiciary,	$ 139,842.48	Asylum for Lunatics,	34,000.00
Legislative,	17,824.48	Asylum for the Deaf and Dumb,	6,000.00
Executive,	11,216.79	Internal Improvement Fund,	14,323.83
Appropriations,	56,982.80	Two per Cent Fund,	28,536.88
Penitentiary,	19,678.46	Three per Cent Fund,	103,796.28
Commissions for Assessing,	18,978.67	Geological Survey,	2,060.26
Public printing,	9,104.50	Code of Mississippi,	3,902.22
University of Mississippi,	36,410.96	Executive Contingent Fund,	4,061.03

* From Nov. 1, 1858, to Oct. 31, 1859, the receipts were $ 624,020.03; the expenditures, $ 707,015. Excess of expenditures, $ 82,994.97. The excess of expenditures is caused by the settlement and payment of certain funds as follows: 2 per cent fund to S. R. R. Co., $ 34,769.36; 3 per cent do., $ 13,796.79; sinking fund, $ 101,545.25.

Valuation of lands in 1854, $ 90,950,585.17; in 1857, $ 141,747,536.37; increase in value, $ 50,796,951.20. Taxable slaves in 1854, 326,861; in 1857, 368,182; increase, 41,321.

Banks. — For the condition of the bank in this State, Jan. 1858, see the table, *ante*, page 220. The bank there reported is the Northern Bank of Mississippi, at Holly Springs.

An asylum for the blind, one for the deaf and dumb, and a lunatic hospital, are in operation, under the care and support of the State, at Jackson. There were received into the lunatic asylum, from its opening to October, 1858, 219 patients. Dr. W. B. Williamson is Superintendent. October 1, 1857, there were in the asylum 83, — 48 males and 35 females; admitted during the year, 59, — 40 males and 19 females; whole number for the year, 142, — 88 males and 54 females; discharged during the year, 36; leaving under treatment, Oct. 1, 1858, 106. Of those discharged, 21 had recovered, and 7 died. The receipts for the year were $ 39,556.46; expenditures, $ 35,677.74. Excess of receipts, $ 3,878.72.

Common Schools. — There is no uniform common-school system for all the counties. Each township has a school fund arising from the lease of lands granted by Congress for common-school purposes, — every 16th section in each township having been so granted. These lands are leased for various periods, but mostly for ninety-nine years. The money thence arising is loaned annually at not less than 8 nor more than 10 per cent per annum interest. This interest is the amount applied to tuition, &c. annually from the township fund. There is also a county fund, arising from fines, forfeitures, licenses, &c., which is distributed in those townships that are destitute or have but a small school fund. The school sections in some townships are worth many thousand dollars, and in others only a few hundreds. Hence great inequality in the funds of the townships, and the necessity of the above method of distributing the county funds. In all the larger towns, public schools have been established, and there are many flourishing High Schools. In his message to the Legislature in November, 1858, the Governor urgently recommends the appointment of a Superintendent-in-Chief of the Common Schools, and that no further appropriation be made for Common Schools until such office has been created. He recommends also the establishment of a male Normal School in connection with the State University; also one or more Normal Schools for the education of female teachers, for the purpose of supplying home educated teachers for the Common Schools of the State.

State Penitentiary, Jackson. — A. M. Hardin, Superintendent. Oct. 31, 1857, there were in confinement 105 convicts. Admitted during the year, 35. 10 were pardoned in 1857. The wool and cotton factory buildings were destroyed by fire, November 1, 1857. The earnings for 11 months were about $ 27,000, and the expenses about $ 30,000.

XIX. MISSOURI.

Capital, Jefferson City. *Area*, 65,037 sq. m. *Population*, 1850, 682,044.

Government for the Year 1860.

			Term ends.	Salary.
ROBERT M. STEWART,	of Buchanan Co.,	*Governor*,	Dec. 1860,	$ 3,000 [and a furnished house.
Hancock Jackson,	of Randolph Co.,	*Lieut.-Governor*,	Dec. 1860.	
Benj. F. Massey,	of Jasper Co.,	*Secretary of State*,	"	1,000 & f.
Wm. B. Starke,	of Saline Co.,	*Sup. Pub. Schools*,	1860,	1,500
Wm. H. Buffington,	of Jefferson City,	*Aud. of Acc'ts*,	Dec. 1860,	1,850
Alfred W. Morrison,	of Howard Co.,	*Treasurer*,	"	1,850
Jas. Proc. Knott,	of Memphis,	*Attorney-General*,	"	1,600 & f.
George W. Huston,	of Troy,	*Register of Lands*,	Oct. 1860,	1,750 & f.
Wm. H. Lunscomb,	of Jefferson City,	*State Librarian*.		
G. A. Parsons,	"	*Adjutant-General*,		200
James S. Hackney,	"	*Quartermaster-General*,		365

			Salary.
John Loughborough,	of St. Louis,	*Surveyor-General,*	$1,500
James M. Hughes,	"	*President of State Bank,*	1,000
A. S. Robinson,	"	*Cashier* " "	2,000
John T. Coffee,	of Dade Co.,	*Speaker of the House.*	
Wm. S. Mosely,	of New Madrid,	*Clerk.*	
Warwick Hough,	of Jefferson City,	*Secretary of Senate.*	

S. P. Vannoy, George W. Hough, and Henry Overstoltz, constitute the Board of Public Works.

The Governor, Secretary of State, Auditor, Treasurer, Attorney-General, Register of Lands, and Superintendent of Common Schools, are required to live during their term at Jefferson City. The Lieutenant-Governor is *ex officio* President of the Senate, and receives $7 a day while presiding. The pay of the Speaker of the House of Representatives is the same. Senators are chosen every fourth, and Representatives every second year. Their pay is $5 a day during the session. The Legislature meets at the city of Jefferson, biennially, on the last Monday in December. A session will commence in November, 1860.

Judiciary.

Supreme Court.

		Term expires.	Salary.
William Scott,	of Cole Co.,	1863,	$2,500
William B. Napton,	of Saline Co.,	"	2,500
Ephraim B. Ewing,	of Ray Co.,	"	2,500
Wm. E. Dunscomb,	*Clerk* at Jefferson City,		Fees.
W. S. Glanville,	" at St. Louis,		"

The judges of this court are elected for the term of six years by the qualified voters of the State. Two sessions of the Supreme Court are held annually, at Jefferson City and at St. Louis.

Circuit Courts.

Cir.	Judges.	Residence.	Salary.	Attorney.	Residence.	Salary.
1.	George W. Miller,	Boonville,	$1,500	Wm. D. Muir,	Boonville,	$350 & f.
2.	W. A. Hall,	Huntsville,	1,500	John F. Williams,	Fayette,	350 & f.
3.	A. H. Buckner,	Bowling Green,	1,500	N. P. Minor,	Bowling Green,	350 & f.
4.	T. S. Richardson,	Memphis,	1,500	John C. Anderson,	Monticello,	350 & f.
5.	George W. Dunn,	Richmond,	1,500	John W. Bryant,	Marshall,	350 & f.
6.	Robert G. Smart,	Independence,	1,500	Aaron H. Conrow,	Richmond,	350 & f.
7.	Foster P. Wright,	Warsaw,	1,500	Thos. W. Freeman,	Bolivar,	350 & f.
8.	S. M. Breckenridge,	St. Louis,	3,000	Chas. G. Mauro,	St. Louis,	350 & f.
9.	John H. Stone,	Potosi,	1,500	Daniel Q. Gale,	Union,	350 & f.
10.	H. Hough,	Charleston,	1,500	Robert E. Hatcher,	New Madrid,	350 & f.
11.	James A. Clark,	Brunswick,	1,500	John C. Griffin,	Trenton,	350 & f.
12.	Elijah R. Norton,	Platte City,	1,500	James M. Bassett,	St. Joseph,	350 & f.
13.	John R. Chenault,	Carthage,	1,500	Joseph Cravens,	Neosho,	350 & f.
14.	P. H. Edwards,	Marshfield,	1,500	Julian Frazier,	Hartville,	350 & f.
15.	Albert Jackson,	Bloomfield,	1,500	Dana G. Hicks,	Bloomfield,	350 & f.
16.	John T. Redd,	Palmyra,	1,500	W. H. Hatch,	——,	
17.	James McFerran,	Gallatin,	1,500	William J. Lewis,	——,	350 & f.
18.	James H. McBride,	Houston,	1,500	E. Y. Mitchell,	Steelville,	350 & f.
19.	Andrew King,	St. Charles,	1,500			

A Circuit Court is held twice a year in each county. Its jurisdiction extends to all matters of tort and contract over $90, where the demand is liquidated, and over $50 where the agreement is parol. It has exclusive criminal jurisdiction, and a supervision over the County Courts and justices of the peace, subject to the correction of the Supreme Court. The judges of the Circuit Court are elected by the qualified voters of their respective districts, and for the term of six years. The term of the present judges expires in November, 1863; that of the present attorneys in November, 1860.

In addition to the Circuit and County Courts, St. Louis has a Court of Common Pleas, with a jurisdiction very similar to the Circuit Court, a Criminal Court, a distinct Court of Probate, a Recorder's Court, and a Land Court, having sole jurisdiction in St. Louis County in suits respecting lands, actions of ejectment, dower, partition, &c. The judges of the Common Pleas and Criminal Courts are elected in the same manner and for the same term as the circuit judges.

Courts of Common Pleas.

Judge.	Residence.	Salary.	Judge.	Residence.	Salary.
Joseph T. Wyatt,	St. Joseph,	$250 & f.	H. Clay Cockerill,	Weston,	$250 & f.
W. C. Ranney,	Cape Girardeau,	300 "	Sample Orr,	Springfield,	250 "
Jas. K. Sheley,	Kan.&Independence,	500 "	John J. Flood,	Brunswick.	250 "

Courts of St. Louis.

Judge.	Court.	Salary.	Judge.	Court.	Salary.
Samuel Reber,	*Common Pleas,*	$3,000	Charles B. Lord,	*Land Court,*	$3,000
Henry A. Clover,	*Criminal Court,*	3,000	Peter G. Furgusson,	*Probate,*	Fees.

These are local tribunals, exercising jurisdiction only in their counties, except the Recorder's Court, whose jurisdiction is confined to small offences and within the limits of the city. From the Court of Common Pleas and Criminal Court, an appeal lies to the Supreme Court; and the judges of the Common Pleas are appointed like the circuit judges, with like tenures. The probate judge is elected by the people of the county for four years, and the Recorder by the people of the city of St. Louis, for two years.

County Courts.—The jurisdiction of these courts is limited to matters of probate and local county affairs, as roads, &c. A County Court sits in each county, and is composed of three justices, who are elected by the people, and hold their offices for four years. Some are paid $3 and some $2 a day while in session. An appeal lies to the Circuit Court.

FINANCES.

Balance in the treasury, Oct 1, 1856,	$419,931.10
Receipts into the treasury for the two years ending Oct. 1, 1858,	1,795,649.67
Total means,	$2,215,580.77
Expenditures during the same two years,	1,823,344.08
Balance in the Treasury, Oct. 1, 1858,	$392,236.69

The receipts for the two years were from taxes and licenses as given below. There was also received from Road and Canal Fund, $79,030; State School moneys, $248,737; Internal Improvement Fund, $67,764; Interest account of State Interest Fund, $22,819. The chief items of expenditure were,

Civil Officers,	$ 148,872	Institution for the Blind,	$ 26,000
General Assembly and contingencies,	177,829	Taking Census,	10,466
General contingent Fund,	10,412	Geological Survey,	25,157
Printing, &c. Laws and Journals,	37,617	Agriculture and Societies,	9,700
Decisions of Supreme Court,	12,732	Capitol grounds,	42,928
Militia Officers,	908	State School moneys,	491,457
Penitentiary,	25,000	Principal of State Bonds,	180,000
Costs in Criminal Cases,	85,710	Interest on State Bonds,	43,125
Deaf and Dumb Asylum and buildings,	32,259	Road and Canal Fund,	79,630
Lunatic Asylum,	70,037	Internal Improvement Fund,	66,146

Taxable Property and Polls.—In 1858 there were 135,040 polls, taxed at $ 50,635; 26,525,338 acres of land, valued at $ 221,605,767, on which the taxes were $ 443,166.26; 112,337 town lots, valued at $ 14,287,025, and taxed $ 28,571; 101,803 slaves, valued at $ 45,090,028, on which the taxes were $ 89,612; notes and bonds, on which the taxes were $ 74,133; other personal property, $ 39,072,373, taxed $ 77,943; making the total taxes for 1858, $ 762,337. The taxes for 1857, were $ 625,786. The lunatic asylum tax for 1858, was $ 13,824. During the years 1857 and 1858, $ 58,075 were received from licenses.

State Debt.

5½ per cent bonds, due 1862,	$ 63,000	6 per cent bonds, due 1883,	$ 200,000
6 " " " 1862,	100,000	Total,	$ 602,000
6 " " " 1863,	239,000		

Upon which the annual interest (payable semiannually, 1st of January and July, except of $ 100,000 payable 30th of April and October), is $ 35,805. The State has lent its credit to several of its railroads to a large amount. The earlier loans to the roads were thus made. When the directors report that $ 50,000 are subscribed *bonâ fide* by individuals, the State issues its bonds for a similar amount; and so for each similar subscription of $ 50,000, until the appropriation is exhausted. To secure the State, the entire franchise of the roads, their lands, buildings, furniture, and equipment, are mortgaged to the State, and the interest must be paid as it accumulates. The later loans of the State credit were made to the railroads, as follows: for every $ 1,000 reported as subscribed *bonâ fide* by individuals, the State issues its bonds for *double* the amount, payable in thirty years, with six per cent interest. The State takes the roads, their franchises, lands, buildings, furniture, equipments, &c., as security, with the right to take possession and sell in default of payment of the principal or interest of the loan. The condition of these loans to the roads, Oct. 13, 1857, was as follows: Amount of bonds authorized, $ 24,950,000; amount issued, $ 15,930,000; leaving due the roads as above stated, $ 9,020,000. The condition of the loan November 22, 1859, was as follows:—

Name of Road.	Loan.	Issued.	Due.
Pacific Railroad,	$ 7,000,000	$ 700,000	None.
Southwest Branch,	4,500,000	2,800,000	$ 1,700,000
Hannibal and St. Joseph,	3,000,000	3,000,000	None.
North Missouri,	5,500,000	4,350,000	1,150,000
Iron Mountain,	3,600,000	3,501,000	99,000
Cairo and Fulton,	650,000	650,000	None.
Platte Country,	700,000	150,000	550,000
Total,	24,950,000	21,451,000	3,499,000

The North Missouri and Iron Mountain roads did not meet the payment of the semiannual interest due Jan. 1 and July 1, 1859, but it was paid promptly by the State. None of the other roads have failed to pay the interest. The State, Nov. 22, 1859, held stocks for the various funds to the amount of $ 1,017,000.

Banks.—For the condition of the Bank of Missouri and branches, January, 1859, see *ante*, p. 220. For a statement of the condition of the Banks of St. Louis at the dates named, see the Additions and Corrections, at the end of the volume.

Common Schools.—The interest of the Common School Fund is distributed semiannually among the different counties of the State, according to the number of children reported between the ages of 5 and 20, and is disbursed among the teachers therein; and one fourth part of the revenue of the State is appropriated for the support of common schools. Every county of the State has a common school organization. The amount of the school fund, Jan. 1, 1859, was $ 595,663. The amount apportioned in 1857, was $ 242,801; in 1858, $ 248,207. In 1854 there were 1,646 school-houses belonging to the common school system; in 1856, 2,673; and in 1857, 3,332. In 1854 there were 1,780 teachers; in 1856, 2,889; and in 1858, 4,397; 3,545 males, and 862 females. Number of children between 5 and 20 in 1854, 202,658; in 1857, 341,121. Number attending school in 1854, 67,924; in 1855, 74,048; in 1856, 97,907; in 1857, 141,328. The superintendent of schools estimates that there were as many more attending private schools in 1857. The amount of money raised to build and repair school-houses in 1855 was $ 30,437.06; in 1857, $ 130,236.85. Amount paid to teachers in 1854, $ 212,138; in 1857, $ 497,810.

State Lunatic Asylum, Fulton. — The number of patients in the asylum Nov. 24, 1856, 135; 71 males, 64 females; admitted since, 122; 73 males, 49 females. Whole number in the two years, 257; discharged in the same time 86; 47 males, 39 females; of whom 45, 25 males, 20 females were recovered; 12, 6 males and 6 females, were much improved; 5 were stationary; 2 eloped; and 22, 12 males and 10 females, died, leaving Nov. 29, 1858, 171; 97 males, 74 females. Whole number admitted since the opening of the hospital, 426; 240 males, 186 females. Of the 426, 211 were old, and 215 recent cases. Of the 426, some of the probable causes of insanity were, miasmatic fevers, 62; religious anxiety, 22; domestic unhappiness, 16; grief, 25; loss of property, 16; intemperance, 15; puerperal, 29. The disbursements for the two years were $ 77,841.

Deaf and Dumb Asylum, Fulton. — The grounds of this institution contain 16.12 acres, and the new buildings were completed in the fall of 1854. Pupils are received between the ages of 10 and 30. The charge for pay patients is $ 100 per annum. The term of study is for three years only. The first pupil was received November 5, 1851. It receives liberal support from the Legislature.

Asylum for the Blind, St. Louis. — Established in 1851. This institution has been built and supported partly by appropriations from the State, and partly by private contributions.

State Prison, Jefferson City. — Prior to February 23, 1853, the prison and the labor of the convicts were let out. Since that time it has been under State management, with a marked improvement in the cleanliness, health, and comfort of the prisoners. Large improvements have been made in the prison building during the two years 1857 and 1858. The number of convicts, Dec. 1, 1856, was 259; received to Dec. 6, 1858, 340; in all 599. There were discharged during the two years by pardon, 72; by expiration of sentence, 106; by escape, 19; by death, 14; leaving in prison Dec. 6, 1858, 388. Of those pardoned, the terms of the greater number had nearly expired, and the pardon was granted to restore rights of citizenship. Of the 388 in confinement, 46 were committed for murder or for assault with intent to kill; 8 for manslaughter; 225 for grand larceny; 34 for burglary and larceny; 12 for robbery; 18 for forgery; 10 for rape; 6 for decoying slaves; robbing United States mail, 3. 229 were Americans, 155 foreigners, and the nativity of 4 was unknown. None were sentenced for less than 2 years. 147 were sentenced for 5 years and upward. The prison had a library of 603 volumes in Dec. 1858. The number of prisoners Dec. 1856 was 259, Dec. 1857, 344. The cost of feeding each prisoner in 1857 was $ 35.13 per annum, or 9⅔ cents per day. Of clothing, medicine, &c., $ 11.51¼, or $3\frac{34}{365}$ cents per day. The expenses for 1858 were somewhat greater.

XX. NEW HAMPSHIRE.

Capital, Concord. *Area*, 9,280 sq. m. Population, 1850, 317,976.

Government for the Year ending on the 1st Wednesday of June, 1860.

			Term ends.	Salary.
ICHABOD GOODWIN,	of Portsmouth,	*Governor*,	June, 1860,	$ 1,000
Thos. L. Tullock,	of Concord,	*Secretary of State*,	"	800

			Term ends.	Salary.
Allen Tenney,	of Concord,	*Dep. Sec. State*,	June, 1860,	F. & $200
Peter Sanborn,	of Concord,	*Treasurer*,	"	600
John Sullivan,	of Exeter,	*Attorney-General*,	"	1,800
Joseph C. Abbott,	of Manchester,	*Adjutant-General*,	"	400
Joseph A. Gilmore,	of Concord,	*Pres. of the Senate*,		$2.50 per day.
Napoleon B. Bryant,	of Concord,	*Speaker of the House*,	"	"
Greenleaf Cummings,	of Lisbon,	*Clerk of the Senate*,		Fees.
Henry O. Kent,	of Lancaster,	*Clerk of the House*,		Fees.
George G. Fogg,	of Concord,	*State Printer*.		
Thomas J. Whittem,	of Exeter,	*Commissary-General*.		
Jeremy O. Nute,	of Farmington,	*Railroad Commissioners*.		
Greenleaf Cummings,	of Lisbon,			
Arch. H. Dunlap,	of Nashua,			

Executive Council.

	Counties.	Councillors.
1st District,	Rockingham and part of Merrimack,	Reed P. Clark, of Londonderry.
2d "	Strafford, Belknap, and Carroll,	Thos. L. Whitton, of Wolfboro'.
3d "	Hillsborough and part of Merrimack,	John N. Worcester, of Hollis.
4th "	Cheshire and Sullivan,	Robert Elwell, of Langdon.
5th "	Grafton and Coos,	Cyrus Eastman, of Littleton.

Judiciary.

The Legislature, at the June session, 1859, abolished the Court of Common Pleas and added one to the number of the Justices of the Supreme Judicial Court, which now consists of a Chief Justice and five Associate Justices, and is the only State Court, except Justices' and Police Courts. It has jurisdiction in all civil and criminal cases (except those in which justices of the peace and of police courts have jurisdiction) and of appeals, civil and criminal, from justices of the peace and police courts. It has also a limited equity jurisdiction. One or more justices of the Supreme Court hold a trial term twice annually in each county, and in some counties three times annually. Capital cases must be tried by two or more justices. For hearing and deciding law questions, the State is divided into four judicial districts, in each of which two terms are held annually. Four justices constitute a quorum to hold law terms, and the concurrence of three is necessary to the decision of any law question. All legal questions submitted to the court must be decided before the close of the term next succeeding the submission, unless a reargument is ordered; and each justice must, within six months from the time of such decision, prepare for the press and furnish the State Reporter correct reports of such cases only as establish some new, or settle some doubtful point, which has not been adjudicated and reported among the decisions of the State, or of such as are otherwise deemed important to be published.

Supreme Judicial Court.

			Appointed.	Salary.
Samuel D. Bell,	of Manchester,	*Chief Justice,*	1859	$2,000
Ira A. Eastman,*	of Concord,	*Associate Justice,*	1855	1,800
Asa Fowler,	of Concord,	"	1855	1,800
Jonathan E. Sargent,	of Wentworth,	"	1859	1,800
Henry A. Bellows,	of Concord,	"	1859	1,800
Charles Doe,	of Dover,	"	1859	1,800
William E. Chandler,	of Concord,	*Reporter,*	1859	400

Courts of Probate.

Counties.	Judges.	Residence.	Salary.	Registers.	Residence.	Salary.
			$			$
Belknap,	Warren Lovell,	Meredith,	142	Wm. L. Avery,	Gilford,	183
Carroll,	Joel Eastman,	Conway,	150	Daniel G. Beede,	Sandwich,	200
Cheshire,	Larkin D. Baker,	Westmorl'd,	225	Calvin May, Jr.,	Keene,	300
Coos,	Turner Stevenson,	Lancaster,	110	Albro L. Robinson,	Lancaster,	135
Grafton,	Nath. S. Berry,	Hebron,	300	Nath. W. Westgate,	Haverhill,	400
Hillsborough,	David Cross,	Manchester,	425	Wm. Wetherbee,	Amherst,	575
Merrimack,	H. E. Perkins,	Concord,	300	Isaac A. Hill,	Concord,	400
Rockingham,	Wm. W. Stickney,	Exeter,	412	Saml. D. Wingate,	Exeter,	560
Strafford,	Hiram R. Roberts,	Rollinsford,	225	Asa Freeman,	Dover,	300
Sullivan,	Daniel G. Rollins,	Somersw'th,	175	Edward Wyman,	Newport,	225

FINANCES.

[From Treasurer's Report, June 1, 1859.]

Chief Sources of Income.

Railroad tax for 1856 and 1858,	$46,668.02	Loan, temporary, . . .	$22,400 00
Civil commissions (fees), . .	836.00	Balance in treasury, June 1, 1858,	37,372.85
State tax for 1858, and previous years,	69,749.99	Total means, . . .	$177,351.86
State Reporter, ...	325.00		

Principal Items of Expenditure.

Salaries, Executive, Judiciary, &c.	$28,774.26	Railroad tax div'ds paid to towns,	$20,594,27
Legislature, ...	20,234 00	Interest on debt and loan, . .	9,215.54
State printer, ...	5,863.04	Temporary loan repaid, . .	22,400.00
Publishing laws, notices, &c. .	1,130 27	Notes payable, ...	25,820.00
Deaf, dumb, blind, and insane, .	2,514.37	Legislative resolves, . . .	9,174.38
N. H. Reports, ...	2,710.00	Miscellaneous accounts, . .	1,119.13

Total expenditures for the year ending June 1, 1859, ... $149,549.26
Total means for the same period, ... 177,351.86
Balance in the Treasury, June 1, 1859, ... $27,802.60

State of the Treasury, June 1, 1859.

Total indebtedness, June 1, 1859, all floating, ... $113,708.09
Deduct available funds, viz. cash in treasury and taxes outstanding, . . 41.321.62
Amount of indebtedness above available funds, ... $72,386.47

There were besides $15,387.66 of Trust Funds in the Treasury, which are included in the above indebtedness.

Banks. — The condition of the banks, near the first Monday in June, 1859, was substantially as follows:—Capital stock, $4,941.000; deposits, $1,137,889; circulation, $3,245,507; total liabilities, $9,336,409; loans, $8,370,476; deposits in Boston to redeem bills, $790,571;

* Judge Eastman has resigned.

bills of other banks, and checks, $150,966; specie, $253,461; real estate, $67,460; total means, $9,779.938. The whole number of banks in the State was fifty-two. There were also twenty-three savings banks; deposits, $4,133,822; total means, $4,263,660. *Bank Commissioners.* — Daniel P. Wheeler, Orford; Cyrus K. Sanborn, Rochester; George W. Pinkerton, Manchester.

Insurance Companies. — Twenty-three mutual fire-insurance companies made returns, from which it appears that $39,803,796 worth of property was insured under about 32,000 policies, on which the premium notes were $2,007,735. and the cash premiums $32,762. The losses by fire during the year were $72,798. The expenses of the companies for the year were near $24,000. *Insurance Commissioners.* — Otis F. R. Waite, Claremont; Benjamin M. Colby, Sanbornton; Oliver C. Fisher, Henniker.

Common Schools. — A School Commissioner is appointed by the Executive for one year for each county, and the several Commissioners constitute the Board of Education, electing one of their number Chairman, and another, Secretary. The Commissioners for the year ending July 15, 1860, are as follows: —

Rockingham. — Henry L. Boltwood, of Derry.
Strafford. — Daniel Hall, of Barrington.
Belknap. — William N. Blair, of Laconia.
Carroll. — S. D. Quarles, of Ossipee.
Merrimack. — G. W. Gardner, of N. London.
Hillsborough. — Harry Brickett, of Hillsboro'.
Cheshire. — Sullivan H. McCollister, of Westmoreland, *Chairman.*
Sullivan. — Adams Ayer, of Charlestown.
Grafton. — James W. Patterson, of Hanover, *Secretary.*
Coos. — Francis L. Town, of Lancaster.

The school returns for the year ending May, 1859, give the following statistics: — Number of districts, 2,362; number of different scholars 4 years of age and upwards attending public schools not less than two weeks, 86,708; average attendance for the year, 56,606; number between 4 and 14 not attending school anywhere, 1,212; average monthly wages of teachers, males $25.30, females $14.15; number of male teachers employed during the year, 1,104; of female, 3,134. Of the teachers employed 2,556 have attended teachers' institutes. Average length of winter schools, weeks, 10.7; of summer schools, 10.3. Volumes in school district, social, and town libraries, 37,308. Estimated value of school-houses and appurtenances, $704,904; of maps, charts, &c., and school apparatus, $8,743; number of unfit school-houses, 573; amount raised by town tax for schools, $215,465, which is $18,064 more than the law requires; amount contributed in addition to tax, $12,796; income from local funds, $7,928; from surplus revenue, $1,453; from railroad tax, $3,293; amount of literary fund, $23,841; whole amount of money appropriated for public schools, $282,842. Visits of superintending committee, 11,333; of prudential school committee, 4,234; of citizens of the town, 79,516. Number of incorporated academies and permanent schools, in 1858, 84; attendance of different scholars, 8,716. Amount paid for tuition in colleges, academies, &c., $36,298.

Eighteen Teachers' Institutes were held in the ten counties during the year ending May, 1858, at which there was reported the attendance of nearly 1,901 teachers.

State Prison, Concord, for the year ending May 31, 1859. — John Foss, Warden, salary $800; Rev. Samuel Cooke, Chaplain; Timothy Haynes, M. D., Physician. Whole number of convicts in prison, June 1, 1858, 110. Received since, 38. Whole number, 148. There have been discharged during the year, by expiration of sentence, 22; by pardon, 16; by death, 3; sent to Insane Asylum, 1; sent out of the State for trial for murder committed there, 1; and in all 43. Leaving in prison, May 31, 1859, 105. Of those remaining in prison, 103 are males, and 2 are females. 69 convicts are employed in the cabinet-shop, 33 in the shoe-shop, and 2 females are employed in sewing. Of those in prison, 5 were sentenced for murder, 2 for attempts to kill, 8 for burning and attempts to burn, 78 for burglary, larceny, and receiving. 24 are under 20 years of age, 90 were born in this country (54 in New Hampshire), and 15 were of foreign birth. The prison library consists of about 900 volumes. The receipts during the year were $10,578.21; the expenditures $8,247.83. Since the establishment of the prison, in 1812, there have been admitted 1,094; discharged by expiration of sentence, 637; by pardon, 358; removal to insane asylum, 3; by death, 63; by escape, 15.

New Hampshire Asylum for the Insane, Concord. — Jesse P. Bancroft, Superintendent. This institution is under the direction of a board of twelve trustees, three being appointed each year for four years. Rev. Charles Burroughs, D. D., of Portsmouth, is President of the Board, and Joseph B. Walker, of Concord, Secretary. Since the opening of the asylum, in 1843, there have been admitted, to June 1, 1859, 1,650 patients; 182 now remain in the institution. The number of patients admitted during the past year was 98 (55 males and 43 females). 85 (49 males and 36 females) were discharged during the year. Of these, 31 had recovered, 22 had improved, 18 were not relieved, and 14 (8 males and 6 females) died. Causes assigned for the insanity of some of those admitted during the year: — Love affairs, 3; vicious habits, 10; domestic trouble, 6; business perplexities, 2; intemperance, 4; spiritualism, 4. Of those admitted, 45 (23 males and 22 females) were married, 47 (31 males and 16 females) were single, 5 were widows, and 1 was a widower. Of those admitted, 33 were farmers, and 12 were wives of farmers; 9 females were factory operatives, 3 were wives of preachers, and 2 were wives of tailors; 6 males and 9 females had no occupation. Receipts during the year, $28,850.10; expenses, $28,279.28; excess of receipts, $570.72. The crops the last year (1858) from the farm belonging to the institution were valued at $3,327.64. By the aid of the income of the permanent funds of the institution, the trustees are enabled to put the price of board to patients at $2.50 a week. It is estimated that there are, including those in the asylum, 550 insane persons in the State.

House of Reformation for Juvenile and Female Offenders against the Laws. — This institution has a farm of 100 acres, near Manchester. The buildings were dedicated May 12, 1858. The cost of land, buildings, and furniture has been near $50,000. Horton D. Walker, of Portsmouth, N. H., is President of the Board of Trustees. Brooks Shattuck, and his wife, Mary Shattuck, are the Superintendents. The plan is that of the "Family System." The buildings are so arranged as to accommodate several families of children, each family in separate buildings, but all so connected by a narrow corridor as to form externally but one building. The intended classification is such, that not more than 63 children will associate together, and no boy in one family can see those in another, except in the chapel. From its opening to the 30th April, 1859, 40 boys and girls had been received, of whom 2 had escaped. 25 were committed for larceny, 4 for shop breaking, 9 for vagrancy, 1 for horse stealing, and 1 as a common drunkard. Their average age was 13 years and 9 months. 24 were born in New Hampshire; 6 were of foreign birth. The estimated value of the products of the farm for the year was $1,516.05. There is a library of nearly 500 volumes. The Superintendent taught a school of 17 weeks during the winter and spring, and there has been a Sabbath School since October.

XXI. NEW JERSEY.

Capital, Trenton. *Area*, 6,851 sq. m. *Population*, 1850, 489,555.

Government for the Year 1860.

			Term expires.	Salary.
CHARLES S. OLDEN,*	of Princeton,	*Governor*,	January, 1863,	$1,800 & fees.
Thomas S. Allison,	of Trenton,	*Sec. of State*,	Mar. 18, 1861,	500 & fees.
Rescarrick M. Smith,	of Hightstown,	*Treasurer*,	Feb. 21, 1860,	1,000 & fees.
John H. Phillips,	of Pennington,	*Superintendent of Public Schools*,	April 1, 1860,	$500
R. F. Stockton, Jr.,	of Trenton,	*Adjutant-General*,		100
Lewis Perrine,	"	*Quartermaster-General*,		100
C. J. Ihrie,	"	*State Librarian*,		$2 a day.

* William A. Newell is governor until the 3d Tuesday of January, 1860.

			Salary.
Thos. H. Herring,*	of Bergen Co.,	*Pres. of the Senate,*	4.00 a day.
Edwin Salter,*	of Ocean Co.,	*Speaker of the Assembly,*	4.00 a day.
John C. Rafferty,*	of Hunterdon Co.,	*Secretary of the Senate,*	3.50 a day.
John P. Harker,*	of Camden Co.,	*Clerk of the Assembly,*	3.50 a day.

The Governor is elected by a plurality vote for three years. His term commences the 3d Tuesday of January. The Secretary of State is appointed by the Governor with the advice and consent of the Senate. His term of office is five years. The Treasurer is elected by the Legislature on joint ballot for one year, and until his successor is qualified, and the State Librarian is elected for two years. The Superintendent of Schools is appointed by the Trustees of the School Fund for two years. The Adjutant and Quartermaster-General are appointed by the Governor. Senators, 21 in number, are elected for three years, one third every year. Representatives, 60 in number, are elected each year. The pay of members of both branches is $2 a day for the first 40 days, $1.50 a day afterwards. The presiding officers have $4 a day for the first 40 days, and $2 a day afterwards. The Legislature meets annually at Trenton on the second Tuesday of January.

Judiciary.

Court of Errors and Appeals.

This court is composed of the Chancellor, the judges of the Supreme Court, and six other judges appointed by the Governor with the consent of the Senate, who hold office for six years, one judge vacating his seat each year in rotation. The court holds stated terms at Trenton, on the second Tuesday in March, and third Tuesday in June and November. The Governor, Chancellor, and the six judges of the Court of Errors and Appeals, constitute the pardoning power. A major part of them, of whom the Governor shall be one, may remit fines and forfeitures, and grant pardons, after conviction, in all cases except impeachment. All the judges of this court receive $5 a day for each day's attendance. The six judges receive no other salary. This *per diem* is in addition to the salary of the Chancellor and of the judges of the Supreme Court.

			Term expires.
Caleb H. Valentine,	of Warren Co.,	*Judge,*	1860.
John M. Cornelison,	of Hudson Co.,	"	1861.
Joseph L. Risley,	of Salem Co.,	"	1862.
Joshua Swain,	of Cape May Co.,	"	1863.
Joseph E. Combs,	of Monmouth Co.,	"	1864.
William N. Wood,	of Morris Co.,	"	1865.

Court of Chancery.

The Chancellor is appointed by the Governor, with the consent of the Senate, for seven years. This court holds three terms annually at Trenton, on the first Tuesday in February, and third Tuesday in May and October.

* Officers of the session of 1859. A new session commences in January, 1860.

		Term expires.	Salary.
Vacant,*	*Chancellor*,		$2,500
William M. Babbitt, of Trenton,	*Clerk*,	1861,	Fees.

Supreme Court.

This court consists of a chief justice and six associate justices, who are appointed by the Governor, with the consent of the Senate, for seven years; and the State is divided into seven districts, to each of which a justice of this court is assigned. This court holds three terms each year at Trenton, on the fourth Tuesday in February, and the first Tuesday in June and November; and the judges of this court hold Circuit Courts and Courts of Oyer and Terminer three times a year in each county. The judges of the Supreme Court are also *ex officio* judges of the Courts of Common Pleas, Orphans' Court, and Court of General Quarter Sessions of the Peace, of the several counties, and the judge holding the Circuit Court of any county is the presiding judge of said court. Courts of Common Pleas are held three times a year in each county, by judges appointed by the Legislature for five years, who receive fees and $2 *per diem* for each day's attendance, and the number of whom is limited to three in each county.

			Term expires.	Salary.
Henry W. Green,	of Trenton,	*Chief Justice*,	1860,	$2,100
Elias B. D. Ogden,	of Paterson,	*Associate Justice*,	1862,	2,000
Peter Vredenburgh,	of Freehold,	"	1862,	2,000
Daniel Haines,	of Hamburg,	"	1866,	2,000
John Van Dyke,	of New Brunswick,	"	1866,	2,000
Wm. S. Clawson,	of Salem,	"	1866,	2,000
Edw'd W. Whelpley,	of Morristown,	"	1866,	2,000
William L. Dayton,	of Trenton,	*Attorney-General*,	1862,	1,500
Charles P. Smith,	of Trenton,	*Clerk*,	1862,	Fees.
Andrew Dutcher,	of Trenton,	*Reporter*,	1861,	$200

JUDICIAL DISTRICTS.

Dist.	Counties.	Judges.
1.	Cape May, Cumberland, Salem, and Atlantic,	W. S. Clawson.
2.	Gloucester, Camden, and Burlington,	John Van Dyke.
3.	Hunterdon, Mercer, and Somerset,	H. W. Green.
4.	Ocean, Monmouth, and Middlesex,	P. Vredenburgh.
5.	Morris, Sussex, and Warren,	E. W. Whelpley.
6.	Passaic, Bergen, and Hudson,	E. B. D. Ogden.
7.	Essex and Union,	Daniel Haines.

FINANCES.

Balance on hand, January 1, 1858,	$3,058.52	
Whole amount received in 1858,	212,400.04	
		$215,458.46
Ordinary expenditures,	$131,431 86	
Extraordinary expenditures,	70,970.52	
Whole amount expended,		202,412.38
Balance in Treasury, January 1, 1859,		$13,046 08

* Upon the expiration of Chancellor Williamson's term in 1859, nominations for the office were made by the Governor, but not confirmed by the Senate.

Principal Items of Ordinary Expenditure.			
Salaries of Executive & Judiciary,	$24,618.86	Farnum Preparatory School, .	$1,200.00
Legislature,	24,127.95	Lunatic Asylum, Managers, .	8,218.49
State Prison, — salaries,	12,223.92	State Prison repairs, .	6,935.72
Transportation of prisoners, & costs,	14,452.46	Agricultural appropriation, .	1,000.00
Court of Errors and Appeals,	5,103.00	Advertising public laws in newspapers,	1,750.00
Printing,	13,393.85	Arresting fugitives from justice,	1,036.67
Pensions,	700.00	*Chief Sources of Income.*	
Court of Pardons,	1,130.80	Transit duties on railroads and canals,	$111,531.92
Support of deaf, dumb, and blind,	5,399.04	Dividends on stock of railroads and canals,	16,000.00
Lunatic Asylum, salaries,	3,575.00	Taxes on capital stock,	69,969.36
Interest,	6,401.54	Interest on joint bonds,	2,640.00
Library,	1,134.07	Peddlers' licenses, .	1,712.00
State and incidental account,	13,962.79	School Fund for Public Schools,	10,000.00
Extraordinary Expenditures.			
Public Schools,	$39,077.90		
Normal School,	7,800.00		

State Debt. — The whole amount of the absolute debt of the State, January 1, 1859, was . . . $95,000.00
Annual interest upon absolute debt, . . . 5,700.00
The value of the productive property owned by the State in 1859 was . . . 275,528.35
The value of the State property not now productive, consisting of the surplus revenue lent to the counties without interest, . . . 764,670.60
Whole amount of productive School Fund owned by the State, . $437,754.50
There is besides unavailable the sum of . . . 11,169.85
Whole amount of School Fund, available and unavailable, Jan. 1, 1859, . . 448,924.35

Common Schools, Year ending December 15, 1858. — Number of cities and townships in the State, 197; number of townships making returns, 181; number of districts in those townships, 1,455; returns received from 1,370; number of schools in the several townships, 1,651. Children reported between 5 and 18, 184,475; children attending school less than 3 months, 16,645; 3 months and less than 6, 29,705; 6 months and less than 9, 33,617; 9 months and less than 12, 23,974; 12 months, allowing for usual vacations, 28,155; number over 18 years of age who attended school, 1,447; colored children taught, 3,170; whole number of children taught, 133,543. Average length of schools in months, 9.25; average price of tuition per quarter to each pupil, $1.29. Amount raised by tax to support schools, $333,160.06; received from the State, $86,073.31; from other sources, $40,820.17; amount raised in addition for building, repairing, and furnishing school-rooms, $61,518.63; total amount appropriated for common school purposes, $526,572.17. Whole number of teachers, 2,103, — 1,235 males and 868 females. Salary of males per annum, $393; of females, $237. Teachers' Institutes were held in all but two counties (Camden and Monmouth), during the year.

School Fund. — For the amount, see above. The receipts of the fund during the year, including balance of cash, January 1, 1858, were $78,835.72. By the School Act of 1851, $40,000 are appropriated to the use of schools from the School Fund, and $40,000 from the State treasury, which sum of $80,000 is apportioned among the counties upon the basis of population. There is a Board of Trustees of the School Fund, and for the support of Free Schools consisting of the Governor, the Secretary of State, the Attorney-General, the President of the Senate, and the Speaker of the Assembly. The Secretary of State is the secretary of the Board. The State Treasurer is the treasurer of the School Fund.

A Normal School was established by the act of Feb. 9, 1855, for five years, and in 1859 the school was extended for a further term of five years. The school is at Trenton, and was opened in buildings temporarily occupied for the purpose, Oct. 1, 1855. The Principal is William F. Phelps Since then up to January 15, 1859, there have been 264 pupils, 146 of whom had then left and were teachers in the public schools. Connected with the Normal School are, — 1st, the *Model School*, a representative of the district school, and furnishing a school of practice, in which all the pupils of the senior class in the Normal School are required to put in practice the principles they have been taught, and in which there were 300 pupils in attendance in January, 1859; and 2d, the *Farnum Preparatory School*, (established by the liberality of Paul Farnum, of Beverley, N. J.,) designed to prepare pupils for the Normal School. This school was opened September 14, 1857, with 135 pupils. There were 120 in January, 1859.

Banks, January 1, 1859. — Of the 47 banks, 11 are organized under the general banking law. For the detailed condition of the banks, see the table, *ante*, p. 220. A general banking law was passed in 1851. Under its provisions, up to January 1, 1859, 29 banking associations had been organized, but at that date only 11 were in operation. Of the other 18, 6 obtained special acts of incorporation, 7 had closed up their business, 2 were winding up, and 3 were closed by injunction. Of the 11 banks, the circulation at that date was $ 796,908 and the city and State stocks deposited as securities to redeem the same amounted to $ 842,333.

Blind, Deaf, and Dumb. — There are thirty deaf and dumb and blind beneficiary pupils of the State in the respective institutions of Philadelphia and New York.

State Lunatic Asylum, Trenton. — H. A. Buttolph, M. D., Superintendent. The Asylum was opened for the admission of patients, May 15, 1848. January 1, 1858, there were in the Asylum 279 patients (135 males and 144 females). Received during the year, 147 (72 males and 75 females); 133 were discharged; leaving, January 1, 1859, 293 (148 males and 145 females). Of this number 230 are county patients, and 63 private. There were under treatment during the year, 426. Of those discharged, 62 (30 males and 32 females) were recovered; 51 (17 males and 34 females) were improved; 2 were unimproved; and 16 (9 males and 7 females) died. Whole number received at the Asylum 1,377 (660 males and 717 females); discharged recovered, 529 (248 males and 281 females); improved, 334 (151 males and 183 females); unimproved, 35 (16 males and 19 females); escaped, 5 males; died, 180 (91 males and 89 females). The expenses of the Asylum for the year were $ 47,097.46. The receipts, $ 47,097.53. Excess of receipts, $ 0.07. Of the receipts, $ 8,185.49 were from the State.

Terms. — Board per week, for those supported at public charge, $ 2; for those supported by friends, $ 3.50 and upwards, according to the nature of the case and their ability to pay. A bond is required, in the penal sum of $ 500, to pay all charges for board, &c., and also to pay not exceeding $ 50 for such damages to the property of the Asylum as may be done by the patient.

State Prison, Trenton. — Robert P. Stoll, Keeper. Number of prisoners, Dec. 31, 1857, 235; received during the year, 212; total, 447. Discharged during the year, by expiration of sentence, 85; by pardon, 88; died, 4; in all, 177. Remaining in prison, Dec. 31, 1858, 270; white males, 185, and females, 6; colored males, 74, and females, 5. Of those in confinement, 4 were committed for manslaughter, 1 for murder, 8 for murder in the second degree, 7 for rape, 7 for forgery, 24 for burglary, 68 for larceny, 17 for violent or felonious assaults, and 4 for robbery. 117 were natives of New Jersey, 31 of New York, 31 of Pennsylvania, 15 of other States, and 76 were foreigners. The longest sentence is for 30 years, and 1 is under that sentence, the shortest sentence was for 6 months; 2 are fifth-comers, 4 are fourth-comers, 9 are third-comers, and 30 are second-comers. There are near 1,100 volumes in the library of the prison, which are distributed among the prisoners once in two weeks. The expenses of the prison for the year were $ 13,335.45, and the receipts, mostly from the labor of the prisoners, were $ 14,369.90.

Geological Survey of the State. — This was commenced in July, 1854, and was continued during 1855, 1856, and part of 1857. A partial report has been made. The work was suspended in 1857, and has not since been resumed.

Births, Marriages, and Deaths. — The Secretary of State transmitted to the Legislature, in 1859, the abstract of the last annual report upon this subject. Number of births reported, 14,012 (6,895 males and 6,862 females, 255 sex not reported); of marriages, 3,883; of deaths, 7,932, of which 3,208 were under 5 years of age, and 36 over 90 and under 100 years of age, and 2 over 100 years of age.

XXII. NEW YORK.

Capital, Albany. *Area*, 46,000 sq. m. *Population*, 1855, 3,466,212.

		Government for the Year 1860.	Term ends.	Salary.
Edwin D. Morgan,	of New York,	*Governor*,	Dec. 31, 1860,	$4,000
Robert Campbell,	of Bath,	*Lieutenant-Governor*,	"	$6 a day.
David R. Floyd Jones,	of South Oyster Bay,	*Sec. of State*,	Dec. 31, 1861,	2,500
John C. Tucker,	of New York,	*Dep. Sec. of State & Clerk of Comm'rs of the Land-Office*,		1,500
Robert Denniston,	of Salisbury Mills,	*Comptroller*,	Dec. 31, 1861,	2,500
Philip Phelps,	of Albany,	*Dep. Comptroller*,		2,000
Philip Dorsheimer,	of Buffalo,	*Treasurer*,	"	2,500
Joseph Stringham,	of Buffalo,	*Deputy Treasurer*,		1,500
Charles G. Myers,	of Ogdensburg,	*Attorney-General*,	"	2,000
Van R. Richmond,	of Lyons,	*State Eng. and Surveyor*,	"	2,500
George R. Perkins,	of Utica,	*Deputy* " "		2,000
Henry H. Van Dyck,	of Albany,	*Sup't of Pub. Inst.*,	Apr. 4, 1860,	2,500
Emerson W. Keyes,	of Albany,	*Dep. Superintendent*,		1,500
James M. Cook,	of Ballston,	*Sup't of Bank. Dep.*,	Jan. 30, 1862,	5,000
Edward Hand,	of Albany,	*Deputy Superintendent*,		1,500
John M. Jaycox,	of Syracuse,	*Canal Commissioner*,		1,700
Hiram Gardner,	of Lockport,	" "		1,700
William J. Skinner,	of Little Falls,	" "		1,700
W. C. Rhodes,	of Elmira,	*Inspector of State Prisons*,		1,600
Josiah K. Everest,	of Schuyler Falls,	" "		1,600
David P. Forest,	of Schenectady,	" "		1,600
H. H. Hull,	of Albany,	*Canal Appraisers*,		$4 a day, and 5 cents a mile for travel, each.
William Wasson,	of Pt. Byron,			
A. B. Parmelee,	of Malone,			
Nathaniel S. Benton,	of Little Falls,	*Aud. of Canal Dep.*,	Feb. 9, 1862,	2,500
Alfred B. Street,	of Albany,	*State Librarian*,		1,000
Elisha W. Skinner,	of Albany,	*Assist.* "		1,000
Henry A. Homes,	of Albany,	*Assist.* "		1,000
George Bliss, Jr.,	of New York,	*Private Secretary of Governor*,		1,500
Frederick Townsend,	of Albany,	*Adjutant-General*,		1,500
George F. Sherman,	of Cold Spring,	*Inspector-General*,		$5 a day.
James L. Mitchell,	of Albany,	*Quartermaster-General*,		"
J. H. Hobart Ward,	of New York,	*Commissary-General*,		1,500
Clarence A. Seward,	of New York,	*Judge Advocate*,		750
DeWitt C. Littlejohn,*	of Oswego Co.,	*Speaker of the House*,		$6 a day.
Samuel P. Allen,*	of Albany,	*Clerk of the Senate.*		
William Richardson,*	of Albany,	*Clerk of the House.*		

The Governor, Lieutenant Governor, Secretary of State, Comptroller, Treasurer, Attorney-General, State Engineer, and Surveyor are elected by the people by a plurality vote for two years; the Governor and Lieutenant-Governor on one year, and the other officers on alternate years. The Canal Commissioners and Inspectors of the State Prisons are elected

* Officers of the session of 1859. A new session commences January, 1860.

for three years, one each year. The Canal Appraisers are appointed by the Governor for two years, and until their successors are qualified. The Superintendent of Public Instruction is elected by the Legislature for three years. The Superintendent of the Banking Department and the Auditor of the Canal Department are appointed by the Governor for three years, subject to confirmation by the Senate. The several officers appoint their own deputies and clerks. The State Librarian is appointed by the Regents of the University. The Adjutant-General and other officers of the Staff are appointed by the Governor. The Lieutenant-Governor, Speaker of the Assembly, Secretary of State, Comptroller, Treasurer, Attorney-General, and State Engineer and Surveyor constitute the *Commissioners of the Land-Office.* The same officers, except the Speaker and the Engineer and Surveyor, are the *Commissioners of the Canal Fund.* The Commissioners of the Canal Fund, the State Engineer and Surveyor, and the Canal Commissioners compose the *Canal Board.*

Senators, 32 in number, are elected in single districts for two years. They are chosen the same year the Secretary of State is elected. Members of Assembly, 128 in number, are elected annually in single districts. The pay of Senators and Representatives is $3 per day for not over 100 days, and $1 for every 10 miles' travel. The Speaker of the Assembly has $4 a day.

JUDICIARY.

1. *Court for the Trial of Impeachments.*

This court is composed of the President of the Senate (who is president of the court, and when absent the chief judge of the Court of Appeals presides), the Senators, or the major part of them, and the judges of the Court of Appeals, or the greater part of them. It is a court of record, and, when summoned, meets at Albany, and has for its clerk and officers the clerk and officers of the Senate. If the Governor is impeached, the Lieutenant-Governor cannot act as a member of the court. Two thirds of the members present must concur for conviction. The judgment of the court extends only to removals from or disqualifications for office, or both; the party being still liable to indictment.

2. *The Court of Appeals.*

This court has full power to correct and reverse all proceedings and decisions of the Supreme Court, or of the old Supreme Court and Court of Chancery. It is composed of eight judges, of whom four are elected (one every second year) by the people at large, for eight years, and four selected each year from the justices of the Supreme Court having the shortest time to serve. These selections are made alternately from the first, third, fifth, and seventh, and from the second, fourth, sixth, and eighth judicial districts. The judge (of the four chosen at large) whose term first expires presides as chief judge. Six judges constitute a quorum. Every cause must be decided within the year in which it is argued, and, unless reargued, before the close of the term after the argument. Four terms must be held each year, and every two years there must be one term in each judicial district. Each judge has a salary of $3,500 per annum. The court for 1860 is thus constituted: —

	Chosen by the People at Large.		Term expires.
George F. Comstock,	of Syracuse,	*Chief Judge,*	Dec. 31, 1861.
Samuel L. Selden,	of Rochester,	*Judge,*	" 1863.
Hiram Denio,	of Utica,	"	" 1865.
Henry E. Davies,	of New York,	"	" 1867.

Selected from the Justices of the Supreme Court to serve until Dec. 31, 1860

Thomas W. Clerke,	of New York.	William J. Bacon,	of Utica.
William B. Wright,	of Kingston.	Henry Welles,	of Pennyan.

E. Peshine Smith,	of Rochester, *State Reporter.*	Salary, $2,000
Charles Hughes,	of Sandy Hill, *Clerk.*	" 2,000
George E. Baker,	of Albany, *Dep. Clerk.*	" 1,500

3. *Supreme and Circuit Courts.*

The Supreme Court has general jurisdiction in law and equity, and power to review judgments of the County Courts, and of the old Courts of Common Pleas. For the election of the justices, the State is divided into eight judicial districts, each of which elects four to serve eight years, with an annual salary of $3,500. In each district one justice goes out of office every two years. The justice in each district whose term first expires, and who is not a judge of the Court of Appeals, is a presiding justice of the court, and the clerks of the several counties serve as clerks. At least four general terms of the Supreme Court are held in each district every year. Every county has each year at least one special term, and two Circuit Courts. Any three or more of the justices (including one presiding justice) hold the general terms; and any one or more hold the special terms, at which are heard all equity cases, and Circuit Courts, which are held exclusively for the trial of issues of fact.

Justices of the Supreme and Circuit Courts.

Justices.	Residence.	Term expires.
	First District.	
——— ———,	New York,	Dec. 31, 1861.
Thomas W. Clerke,	New York,	" 1861.
Josiah Sutherland,	New York,	" 1863.
Daniel P. Ingraham,	New York,	" 1865.
Wm. H. Leonard,	New York,	" 1867.
	Second District.	
John A. Lott,	Brooklyn,	" 1861.
James Emott,	Poughkeepsie,	" 1863.
John W. Brown,	Newburg,	" 1865.
Wm. W. Scrugham,	Yonkers,	" 1867.
	Third District.	
Wm. B. Wright,	Kingston,	" 1861.
George Gould,	Troy,	" 1863.
Henry Hogeboom,	Hudson,	" 1865
Rufus W. Peckham,	Albany,	" 1867.
	Fourth District.	
Amaziah B. James,	Ogdensburg,	" 1861.
Enoch H. Rosekrans,	Glen's Falls,	" 1863.
Platt Potter,	Schenectady,	" 1865.
Augustus Bockes,	Saratoga Springs,	" 1867.
	Fifth District.	
William J. Bacon,	Utica,	Dec. 31, 1861.
Wm. F. Allen,	Oswego,	" 1863.
Joseph Mullin,	Watertown,	" 1865.
LeRoy Morgan,	Syracuse,	" 1867.
	Sixth District.	
Charles Mason,	Hamilton,	" 1861.
Ransom Balcom,	Binghamton,	" 1863.
Wm. W. Campbell,	Cooperstown,	" 1865.
John M. Parker,	Owego,	" 1867.
	Seventh District.	
Henry Welles,	Pennyan,	" 1861.
E. Darwin Smith,	Rochester,	" 1863.
Thomas A. Johnson,	Corning,	" 1865.
Addison T. Knox,	Waterloo,	" 1867.
	Eighth District.	
Benjamin F. Greene,	Buffalo,	" 1861.
Rich. P. Marvin,	Jamestown,	" 1863.
Noah Davis, Jr.,	Albion,	" 1865.
Martin Grover,	Angelica,	" 1867.

4. *County Courts.*

When the real estate, or all the defendants, or all the parties interested, are in the county, the jurisdiction of the County Courts extends to actions of contract, tort, and replevin, when the debt or damages claimed are not above $500. They have equity jurisdiction for the foreclosure and satisfaction of mortgages; for the sale of the real estate of infants; for partition of lands; for admeasurement of dower; to compel the specific performance of contracts in certain cases, and for the care and custody of lunatics and habitual drunkards, and for various other matters. The Surrogates' Courts have the ordinary jurisdiction of courts of probate. The judges of the courts of New York City and County, named below, are elected for six years.

5. *Criminal Courts.*

These are the Courts of Oyer and Terminer and the Court of Sessions. The Courts of Oyer and Terminer, in each county, except in the city and county of New York, are composed of a justice of the Supreme Court, who presides, the county judge, and the two justices of the peace chosen members of the Court of Sessions. The presiding justice and any two of the others form a quorum. In the city and county of New York, they are composed of a justice of the Supreme Court, who presides, and any two of the following officers: judges of the Court of Common Pleas of the city and county; the mayor, recorder, and aldermen of said city. These courts are all held at the same time and place at which the Circuit Courts are held. Courts of Sessions are composed of the county judge and the two justices of the peace designated as members of the Court of Sessions, and are held at the same time and place as the County Courts.

6. *Courts of New York City and County.*

Superior Court.

Judges.	Salary.	Term expires.	Judges.	Salary.	Term expires.
Murray Hoffman,	$5,000,	Dec. 31, 1861.	Edwards Pierpont,	$5,000,	Dec. 31, 1863.
Lewis B. Woodruff,	"	" 1861.	James Moncrief,	"	" 1865.
Joseph S. Bosworth,	"	" 1863.	A. L. Robertson,	"	" 1865.
Clerk.			*District Attorney.*		
George T. Maxwell,	$2,500.		Nelson J. Waterbury,	$5,000,	Dec. 31, 1860.

Common Pleas.

John R. Brady,	$5,000,	Dec. 31, 1861.	Charles P. Daly,	$5,000,	Dec. 31, 1865.
Henry Hilton,	"	" 1863.	Benj. H. Jarvis, *Clerk*, Salary $2,500.		

Marine Court.

Arba K. Maynard,	$3,000,	Dec. 31, 1861.	Henry Alker,	$3,000,	Dec. 31, 1865.
Florence McCarthy,	"	" 1863.	Moses D. Gale, *Clerk*, Salary $2,500.		
Recorder.			*Surrogate.*		
George G. Barnard,	$5,000,	Dec. 31, 1860.	Edward C. West,	$5,000,	Dec. 31, 1860.
City Judge.			*Register.*		
Abram D. Russell,	$5,000,	Dec. 31, 1860.	William Miner,	Fees,	Dec. 31, 1860.

Education. — The amount of capital and annual revenue of the several funds appropriated to the purposes of education, for the year ending September 30, 1858, was as follows: —

	Capital.	Revenue.
Common School Fund,	$2,551,260.52	$500,384.55
United States Deposit Fund,	4,014,520.71	248,767.52
Literature Fund,	269,952 12	60,034.61
	$6,835,733.35	$809,186.68

Common Schools. — Of the funds devoted to education, what was exclusively the Common School Fund in 1858 may be stated as follows: —

Productive capital of the Common School Fund,	$2,551,260.52
Amount from United States Deposit Fund which will produce $165,000, the sum annually appropriated therefrom, for the support of Common Schools, at six per cent interest,	2,750,000.00
Amount from same fund which will produce at six per cent $25,000 annually, that being the sum reserved by the Constitution to be added annually to the capital of the School Fund,	416,666.67
Making a total of	$5,717,927.19

The annual interest on this sum, at six per cent, is $343,076. The balance of the income of the United States Deposit Fund is appropriated to the support of Colleges, Academies, the Normal School, Indian Schools, Teachers' Institutes, &c. The income of the Literature Fund must, by the Constitution, be applied to the support of Academies.

The whole amount of public money received from all sources by the Commissioners of cities, and town Superintendents, during the year ending January 1, 1858, was $3,792,284.79. Paid for teachers' wages, $2,372,113.86; for libraries, $40,059.86; for purchasing sites for school-houses, for building and hiring school-houses and for repairs, school furniture, &c., was $765,526.59. The amount paid for school apparatus was $96,537.94; for colored schools, $10,729.93; for all other incidental expenses $369,027.15. The amount raised by tax for teachers' wages, besides public money, was $1,420,455.17. Aggregate expenditures for school purposes during the year, $3,653,995.23.

Statistics of the Common Schools. — Whole number of districts for the nine months ending Sept. 30, 1858, the school-houses of which are situated within the town, 11,756. Returns were received from most of the districts. Average length of schools in the rural districts, 7.6 months. Volumes in district libraries, 1,402,253. 757,731 children were taught during the nine months. 1,238,175 were returned between 4 and 21 years of age. 213,032 pupils attended school less than 2 months; 222,328 attended 2 months and less than 4; 175,191, 4 and less than 6; 98,380, 6 and less than 8; 48,750, 8 and less than 10. Number of school-houses, 11,534, of which 9,775 are framed buildings, 861 of brick, 586 of stone, and 292 of logs. Number of teachers employed at the same time for six months during the last 12 months in the State, 14,384. During the year ending September 30, 1858, there were employed 26,153 teachers, — 8,266 males and 17,877 females. Of the 31,787 teachers reported in 1857, 327 had the diploma of the State Normal School, 759 were licensed by the Superintendent of Public Instruction, and the others, 30,661, by local officers. Number of private schools reported in the districts, 1,531; number of pupils therein, 40,186. Number of free schools, 662. There are also 23 Indian schools which it is estimated about 500 pupils attend annually, which is nearly one third of the Indian children in the State between 4 and 21. The "Thomas Asylum for Orphan and Destitute Indian Children," is located on the Cattaraugus Reservation, has about 50 Indian children, and is sustained partly by State appropriations, and partly by contributions from the benevolent. In 1855, 1,803 pupils, and in 1856, 1,745 pupils (569 males, 1,176 females) had their tuition paid by the State at academies, in the expectation that they would become teachers, at an expense in 1855 of $17,850, and in 1856 of $16,550. In 1859 Teachers' Classes were to be organized in 90 academies. In 1858 Teachers' Institutes were held in 48 counties. The appropriation for each county for the purposes of the Institutes is $120. There is a Normal School at Albany. During the 14 years it has been in operation (Sept. 1858) 3,068 pupils have been instructed a longer or shorter time, of whom 1,057, 481 males and 576 females, have received diplomas. The average attendance is about 250. In 1857, 327 of its graduates are reported as teaching in the common schools of the State. There is an Experimental School connected with the Normal School, taught entirely by members of the graduating class in the Normal School.

Finances.

Debt of the State.—The general fund and railroad debt, at the close of the fiscal year ending September 30, 1858, was $ 6,605,654.37; the canal debt, Sept. 30, 1858, was $ 24,307,704.40; total, $ 30,913,258.77. There was also a contingent debt, Sept. 30, 1858, consisting of State stock, of $ 570,000, upon which the State does not pay interest. This makes the total indebtedness of the State at that date $ 31,483,258.17, on which accrues annually about $ 1,960,000 of interest.

The property of the State, in addition to the educational funds mentioned above, consists of the works of internal improvement. The amount of tolls derived from them during the year 1858 was $ 2,072,204.88; the expenses of collection, repairs, and superintendence, were $ 1,078,878.91; making the net revenue $ 993,425.97. The average annual income for the six years 1849 to 1854 inclusive was $ 3,232,094.21, which is equal to a capital of $ 53,868,236, at six per cent interest. Deducting the expenses for repairs as well as for collection, the *net* average revenue for the six years was $ 2,330,049.42, which is equal to a capital of $ 38,834,157, at six per cent interest. The amount of debt incurred for their construction, and yet unpaid, is as stated above, $ 24,307,684.48. There was besides an outstanding indebtedness, paying no interest, of $ 152,330, and what is called a "floating debt," estimated at $ 2,000,000 in September, 1858, making their whole cost $ 26,460,014.48. The taxable property of New York in 1858 was $ 1,404,907,679; being $ 1,095,403,134, the assessed value of 27,696,053 acres of real estate, and $ 307,049,165 of personal estate. The State tax was $ 2,458,538; the county tax $ 9,908,691; the town taxes, $ 2,105,633. Total taxation, $ 15,426,593, of which $ 8,621,091 was in the County of New York,—making the rate of State, county, and town taxes, 10.98 mills on a $ 1 valuation. The highest rate was 27 mills on $ 1, in Hamilton County; the lowest, 4.2 mills, in Orange County. The valuation and taxation as compared with 1857, are as follows:—Valuation of real estate, $ 16,148,496 less; personal estate, $ 12,847,990 less; total diminution, $ 28,996,485. The total taxation was increased $ 260,283.

General Fund, on which are charged the ordinary Expenses of Government.

Receipts for the year ending Sept. 30, 1858,		$ 4,806,418.48
Expenditures during same period,	$ 4,413,176.54	
Deficiency of revenue of General Fund in 1857,	84,702.59	
		4,497,879.13
Balance of revenue in the treasury,		$ 308,539.35

The amount received and expended at the Treasury during the year was as follows:—

Balance, October 1, 1857,	$ 3,301,298.58
Receipts from all sources from October 1, 1857, to September 30, 1858,	13,149,693 62
Total available means,	16,450,992.20
Payments during same period,	14,358,214.81
Balance, September 30, 1858,	$ 2,092,777.39

Chief Sources of Income to General Fund.		Banking Department expenses,	$ 28,497.46
Auction duty,	$ 100,527.95	Railroad Commiss'rs & expenses,	4,977 48
Salt duty,	58,138.18	Commissary's Department,	11,959.34
Fees of public offices,	4,504.93	Fugitives from justice,	10,120.53
Peddlers' licenses,	545.00	Apprehension of criminals,	900.00
State tax,	3,071,331 05	Reformation of juvenile delinquents,	32,400.00
Arrears of county taxes, & interest,	44,598.51	State printing,	124,264.43
Banking Department,	24,607.95	Deaf and dumb,	66,740.84
State Prisons' earnings,	76,880.96	Blind, N. Y. Institution,	20,785.69
Railroad Commissioners,	12,030.76	Agricultural Societies,	7,845.00
Metropolitan Police fund,	1,319,695.02	Onondaga Salt Springs,	89,563.21
Principal Items of Expenditure.		State Prisons, debt, &c.,	311,170 97
Executive,	$ 79,717.94	State Library,	14,975.28
Judiciary,	105,510.96	Postage, official letters,	2,771 09
Legislature,	139,741.62	Hospitals, &c.,	63,700.00

House of Refuge for Western N.Y.,	$25,000.00	Eye and Ear Infirmaries, . .	$1,500.00
Orphan Asylums, ...	44,117.43	Dispensaries, ...	8,700.00
State Lunatic Asylum, ...	81,630.44	Draining Cayuga marshes, .	31,553.99
Asylum for idiots, and building,	24,000.00	Building State Arsenals, . .	137,012.99
Geological survey, ...	4,338.20	Metropolitan Police Fund, .	1,319,595.02

Banks. — There were in the State doing business, September 25, 1858, 32 incorporated banks, 231 banking associations, 34 individual bankers, and 38 closing and insolvent banks. 5 banking associations have deposited securities and commenced the business of banking during the year; 14 banks during the year closed business. The actual increase of bank capital during the year was, — new banks, $520,000; increase of capital of old banks, $1,968,391; total, $2,488,891. For the condition of the banks, Sept. 25, 1858, see *ante*, p. 220.

The New York city banks make their returns weekly. The American Almanac for 1856, p. 263, gave their monthly returns from December 1, 1854, to Nov. 13, 1855, inclusive. The Almanac for 1857, p. 264, gives the returns to November 1, 1856. The Almanac for 1858, p. 265, gives the returns to November, 1857, with the weekly returns during the financial crisis. The Almanac for 1859, p. 260, gives the returns to December, 1858, with the weekly returns during December, 1857, and January and February, 1858. The following table shows their condition monthly, from December 4, 1858, to November, 1859.

Date.	Loans and Discounts.	Specie.	Circulation.	Deposits.
December 4, 1858,	$128,338,324	$27,407,727	$7,838,517	$109,338,334
January 1, 1859,	127,584,319	27,129,725	7,854,090	90,684,193
February 5, "	130,442,176	25,991,441	7,950,855	91,965,256
March 5, "	125,221,067	26,769,965	8,071,693	86,800,028
April 2, "	128,702,192	25,732,161	8,221,758	89,737,138
May 7, "	129,519,905	26,086,632	8,804,697	88,872,043
June 4, "	125,006,766	23,728,311	8,427,642	82,578,836
July 2, "	122,401,773	22,491,665	8,365,790	78,132,611
August 6, "	118,938,069	20,083,877	8,623,050	72,524,855
September 3, "	118,184,258	21,478,299	8,373,318	73,165,700
October 1, "	118,208,752	19,259,126	8,337,702	70,812,105
November 5, "	120,118,037	20,228,342	8,627,421	73,673,898
December 3, "	122,137,034	20,046,667	8,398,819	76,258,722

The amount of circulation issued to individual bankers and banking associations, September 30, 1858, was $24,603,194; decrease during the year, $3,826,328; to redeem which the Superintendent of the Banking Department had securities amounting to $26,393,098 83; made up of bonds and mortgages, $6,427,077.79; New York State stocks, $18,795,185.93; Illinois State stocks, $537,429.40; Arkansas do. $162,000; Michigan do. $412,000; United States stocks, $339,100; cash, $91,305.71. The circulation of the incorporated banks was reduced during the year $1,810,414, making the total reduction of circulation $5,636,742. The Savings Banks, January 1, 1859, had $48,194.847, due 230,074 depositors; the assets exceeded the liabilities $2,472,658; amount deposited during the year 1858, $26,514,144; amount withdrawn, $21,789,493; amount of interest placed to the credit of depositors during the year 1858, $2,197,787.

State Prisons. — There are three State Prisons, one at Auburn, one at Sing Sing, and one at Clinton. The whole number of convicts in these prisons, Oct. 1, 1857, was 1,890. Received during the year, 922. Discharged during the year, by expiration of sentence, 506; by death, 39; by process of law, 2; by transfer, 15; by escape, 8; by pardon, 116; in all, 686. Remaining in prison, Sept. 30, 1858, 2,120, — at Auburn, 696; Sing Sing, 1,072; Clinton, 358. There is at Sing Sing a female prison. The expenses and earnings of the several prisons were as follows: — Auburn, expenses, $77,674 13; earnings, $59,840.67. Sing Sing, expenses, $119,900.14; earnings, $75,916.48. Clinton, expenses, $55,781.76; earnings, $21,420.88. In all the prisons, expenses, $253,356 03; earnings, $157,178.03. The average yearly number of prisoners for the nine years ending in 1858 was 1,728. The yearly average increase in all the prisons for the seven years ending in 1854 was 86.

The average daily earnings of each convict for the same seven years were nearly 38.1 cents. The number of punishments in all the prisons in 1856 was 998. The punishments were the shower-bath, cropping the hair, confinement in a dark cell, yoking, bucking, and wearing ball and chain. Average hours of labor for convicts per day for the year 1857, at Auburn, 10 hours 23 minutes; at Sing Sing, 9 hours 47 minutes; at Clinton, 10 hours 30 minutes.

Institution for the Deaf and Dumb, New York. — Harvey P. Peet, President. Number of teachers, 15; number of pupils, Dec. 31, 1857, 302, — 168 males and 134 females; left during the year, 49, and 4 died; admitted, 56; whole number, Dec. 31, 1858, 305, — 162 males and 143 females. Of these 234 were supported by New York; 16 by the city of New York; 15 by New Jersey; 36 by their friends; and 4 by the Institution. The time of admission is the first Wednesday in September; terms, $150 *per annum* for each pupil, clothing and travelling expenses excepted, to be paid semiannually in advance, and satisfactory security for punctual payment of bills and clothing, which, if desired, is furnished by the Institution at an additional charge of $30 a year. Those educated at the public expense must be between 12 and 25 years of age. The receipts of the Institution from all sources for the year 1858 were $59,633.04. Expenditures, $63,201.18. Excess of expenditures, $3,568.14. The Legislature at its session in 1854 authorized the admission, with the sanction of the Superintendent of Public Instruction in each case, to whom application should be made, of all deaf-mute children residents of the State, whose circumstances entitle them to share in the legislative provisions for their education.

New York Institution for the Blind. — The number of pupils Dec. 31, 1857, was 181. Dec. 31, 1858, there were 200. Eleven blind persons are employed as teachers or assistants. The employments taught are the manufacture of brooms, mats, bandboxes, and mattresses. Basket-making, being found unprofitable, is discontinued. The young women use the needle with facility. Receipts during the year, $62,966.19; expenditures, $60,430.01.

State Lunatic Asylum, Utica. — John P. Gray, M. D., Superintendent. The number of patients at the commencement of the year (Dec. 1, 1857) was 451; admitted during the year, 333, 172 males and 161 females; whole number treated during the year, 784, 410 males and 374 females. Discharged during the year, 282; remaining Nov. 30, 1858, 502, 260 males and 242 females. Of those discharged, 114 were recovered, 33 were improved, 99 unimproved, 5 were not insane, and 31 died. Total admissions since Asylum was opened, January 16, 1843, 5,516. Discharged, 4,896, of whom 2,226 were recovered, 801 improved, 1,194 unimproved, and 636 died, and 39 were not insane. The form of mental disease of those admitted was *mania*, 172, 85 males and 87 females; *melancholia*, 24, 8 males, 16 females; *dementia*, 123, 67 males, 56 females. Drunkards, 5; paralysis, 5; imbecile, 2; not insane, 2. Of those admitted, 97 were housekeepers, 58 farmers and 17 farm laborers, 15 laborers, 42 employed in housework, 10 seamstresses, 7 carpenters, 6 merchants, 3 lawyers, and 3 teachers. 210 were natives of New York; 26 of other of the United States; 97 were of foreign birth, among whom were 44 natives of Ireland, 19 of England, and 16 of Germany. The receipts for the year were $116,520.40; The payments $103,864.05. There are accommodations at this Asylum, at the New York City Asylum, at the Asylum at Flatbush, and at Bloomingdale, for nearly 1,360 insane, which leaves nearly one half of the insane unprovided for.

Pauperism. — (Albany County is not included in the returns.) Paupers relieved or supported during the year ending Dec. 1, 1858, 261,155; of which there were county paupers, 103,499; town paupers, 23,205; temporarily relieved, 207,207; number received into poorhouses, 38,582. Of those supported or relieved, 58,700 were foreigners, 2,408 were lunatics, 595 idiots, and 52 mutes. 849 paupers were born in the poorhouses during the year, and 2,584 died. Number in poorhouses, Dec. 1, 1858, 13,422, of whom 7,203 were males and 6,219 females. 3,219 children under 16 years were taught in poorhouses about 7.9 months each The total poorhouse expenses were $884,119.78; do. of temporary relief, $607,271.50; total expenses, $1,491,391.28. Value of labor of paupers, $29,484.66. Average expense of each pauper beyond earnings per week, 90½ cents. Some of the assigned causes of pauperism were, — intemperance, 29,733; idleness, 9,662. The number of acres of land attached to poorhouses was 7,208.

The number of alien emigrants that arrived in New York in 1858, for whom commutation was paid, or special bonds required, was 78,589, — being 105,186 less than in 1857, — of whom 31,874 were from Germany, 25,075 from Ireland, and 12.324 from England.

Western House of Refuge, Rochester, New York, Samuel S. Wood, Superintendent. — This institution was opened August 11th, 1849, and the completed buildings accommodate 360 inmates, besides the officers, &c. From August, 1849, to January 1, 1858, there had been received 1,105 boys. Number remaining January 1, 1859, 386. 164 were received during the year; average age, nearly 13¼; 60 were Americans, 93 foreigners, and 11 colored. 102 were committed for petit larceny, 10 for grand larceny, 31 for burglary, 15 for vagrancy. Of those who left during the year, 54 were indentured, 55 discharged to parents and guardians, 3 died, and 9 escaped. The boys work seven hours a day, and are at school three and a half hours. The institution has a library of 1,657 volumes. The expenses for the year were $31,601.54. There are 42¼ acres of land connected with the institution. Of these, 4¼ acres are surrounded with a stone wall 20 feet high, within which are the playgrounds and all the buildings except the barns. 22 acres designed for cultivation are enclosed by a stockade fence 10 feet high, formed of cedar posts connected together by iron rods. Ten acres are pasture land.

Asylum for Idiots, Syracuse, New York, Dr. Hervey B. Wilbur, Superintendent. — This institution was opened at Albany, in October, 1851, and was removed to Syracuse in August, 1855. There were in the institution, Oct. 1, 1857, 112 pupils, 92 of whom were State beneficiaries. During the year, 20 were admitted, 16 discharged, and 4 died, leaving Oct. 1, 1858, 112. The average number was 110. Children between the ages of 7 and 14, so deficient in intelligence as to be incapable of being educated at any ordinary school, and who are not *epileptic, insane*, or *greatly deformed*, may be admitted. Applications on behalf of others are acted on by the trustees. All pupils are received for a month on trial.

Statistics of Crime. — The following table is compiled from the returns of the Clerks of Court and the sheriffs, prepared by the Secretary of State. The returns are not complete, and are more full for some years than others. They, however, show substantially the history of convictions for crime in the State for 29 years.

Classification of Crimes for which Convictions were had in Courts of Record during 29 Years.

[1. Offences against the person. 2. Offences against property with violence. 3. Offences against property without violence. 4. Offences against the currency. Other offences not enumerated above. 6. Total.]

	1830	1831.	1832.	1833.	1834.	1835.	1836.	1837.	1838.	1839.	1840.	1841.	1842.	1843.	1844.
1.	237	242	289	362	214	287	316	393	296	287	463	458	484	408	394
2.	102	93	79	75	99	92	86	124	112	115	120	121	175	244	172
3.	502	461	440	462	355	426	379	477	472	479	437	460	504	504	489
4.	74	63	60	61	53	34	32	52	42	51	49	49	63	78	60
5.	144	94	98	163	148	237	150	145	164	186	274	427	376	336	312
6.	1,039	956	966	1,113	869	1,076	963	1,191	1,086	1,118	1,343	1,515	1,602	1,570	1,427

	1845.	1846	1847.	1848.	1849.	1850.	1851.	1852.	1853.	1854.	1855.	1856	1857.	1858
1.	471	334	335	437	397	397	409	411	484	432	395	425	375	436
2.	177	135	132	120	150	199	148	228	185	189	268	248	340	332
3.	467	471	396	512	545	521	475	480	573	580	574	573	607	607
4.	54	38	24	33	43	36	49	50	52	75	37	49	63	90
5.	520	440	408	425	404	410	401	434	653	853	556	212	168	247
6.	1,689	1.471	1,295	1,527	1.539	1,563	1,482	1.603	1,847	2.129	1,830	1.507	1,554	1.712

Among the non-enumerated offences, the largest number of convictions was for selling liquor without a license and for keeping a noisy and disorderly house. The whole number of convictions, as above, is 41,602.

State Inebriate Asylum. — This institution was definitely located May 19, 1857, in Binghamton, the citizens of which town had given 252 acres of land to the institution. The corner-stone of the building, which is to be of brick and stone, was laid Sept. 24, 1857. The Asylum will have capacity for 300 patients. It is divided into 8 wards, each ward containing 23 rooms, varying in size from 12 feet by 18 to 18 feet by 24, thus giving ample opportunity for the classification of patients.

XXIII. NORTH CAROLINA.

Capital, Raleigh. *Area*, 45,500 sq. m. *Population*, 1850, 869,039.

Government for the Year 1860.

			Salary.
John W. Ellis, of Salisbury County, *Governor* (term of office, from Jan. 1, 1859, to Jan. 1, 1861),			A furnished house and $3,000
Rufus H. Page,	of Wake Co.,	*Secretary of State*,	$800 and fees.
Daniel W. Courts,	of Rockingham Co.,	*Treasurer*,	2,000
Wm. H. Richardson,	of Raleigh,	*Clerk of the Treas. Dep.*,	750
Curtis H. Brogden,	of Wayne Co.,	*Comptroller*,	$1,000 and fees.
Calvin H. Wiley,	of Guilford Co.,	*Supt. Common Schools*,	1,500
Oliver H. Perry,	of Raleigh,	*State Librarian*,	300
William W. Holden,	of Raleigh,	*Public Printer.*	
Ebenezer Emmons,		*State Geologist*,	2,500
Henry T. Clarke,	of Edgecombe Co.,	*Speaker of the Senate*,	$4 per diem.
Thomas Settle,	of Rockingham Co.,	*Speaker of House of Com.*	"
John Hill,	of Stokes Co.,	*Clerk of the Senate*,	$6 per diem.
Edward Cantwell,	of Raleigh,	*Clerk of the House*,	"

The Governor is elected by the people by a plurality vote for two years. The General Assembly elect, on joint ballot, every two years, the Secretary of State, Treasurer, Comptroller, Superintendent of Common Schools, Public Printer, and Council of State. The term of the present incumbents expires in 1860. The State Librarian is appointed by the Governor and Judges of the Supreme Court. The Literary Board are appointed by the Governor and Council of State for two years. The Board fill their own vacancies.

Literary Board.—The Governor is *ex officio* President. ***Members***, Archibald Henderson of Rowan Co., J. B. Gordon of Wiekes Co., Wm. P. Ward of Jones. Pay, $3 per diem and travelling expenses.

Council of State.—Josiah T. Granberry of Perquimons Co., President; John L. Bridgers of Edgecombe Co.; John A. Avirett of Onslow Co.; Jesse A. Waugh of Forsythe Co.; Columbus Mills of Polk Co.; William J. Yates of Mecklenburg Co.; P. M. Powell of Richmond Co. Pay, $3 per diem while in service, and $3 for every 30 miles' travel.

The sessions of the Legislature are biennial. The next session will commence on the third Monday (19th) of November, 1860.

Judiciary.

Supreme Court.

			Salary.
Rich. M. Pearson,	of Surry Co.,	*Chief Justice*,	$2,500
William H. Battle,	of Chapel Hill,	*Associate Justice*,	2,500

			Salary.
Thomas Ruffin,	of Alamance,	*Associate Justice,*	$2,500
Wm. A. Jenkins,	of Warrenton,	*Attorney-General.*	
Hamilton C. Jones,	of Rowan Co.,	*Reporter,*	$600 and copyright.
Edm. B. Freeman,	of Raleigh,	*Clerk at Raleigh,*	$300 and fees.
James R. Dodge,	of Morganton,	*Clerk at Morganton.*	"

Superior or Circuit Courts.

Judges. — Salary, $1,950 each.*		*Circuit Solicitors.*†	
Jesse G. Shepherd,	of Fayetteville.	Elias C. Hines,	of Edenton.
John M. Dick,	of Greensboro'.	W. J. Houston,	of Kenansville.
D. F. Caldwell,	of Salisbury.	Wm. A. Jenkins,	of Warrenton.
R. R. Heath,	of Edenton.	Thomas Ruffin, jr.,	of Wentworth.
John L. Bailey,	of Hillsborough.	Robert Strange,	of Wilmington.
M. E. Manly,	of Newbern.	William Lander,	of Lincoln Co.
R. M. Saunders,	of Raleigh.	Marcus Erwin,	of Buncombe.

The Supreme Court holds three sessions in each year; two in the city of Raleigh, — to wit, on the second Monday in June and the last Monday in December, — and one at Morganton, on the first Monday of August, for the western part of the State; and continues to sit at each term until all the business on the docket is determined, or continued upon good cause shown. It has original and appellate jurisdiction in law and equity. The judges of the Supreme and the Superior Courts are elected by joint ballot of both houses of the General Assembly, to hold office during good behavior. Their salaries cannot be diminished during continuance in office.

The Attorney-General is Solicitor for the Third Circuit, and receives, in addition to his pay as solicitor, $100 for each term of the Supreme Court which he attends.

The Superior Courts of Law, and the Courts of Equity, are held twice each year in every county of the State. There are seven circuits, of about ten counties each, which the judges ride alternately, never visiting, however, the same circuit twice in succession. The judges of these courts have complete equity jurisdiction.

Finances,

For the two Years ending November 1, 1858.

Amount in hands of State Treasurer, November 1, 1856,	$256,456.28
Receipts into the Treasury during the year 1857,	512,205.02
" " " " " 1858,	507,450.35
Total,	$1,276,111.65

The receipts and expenditures are on account of the Public Fund and the Literary Fund. The receipts of the Literary Fund are from entries of vacant lands, bank and railroad dividends, and retail license and auction taxes. Some of the disbursements are for common schools, and the deaf, dumb, and blind.

The sources of income of the Public Fund are, besides sales of bonds and loans, dividends and interest, public taxes, taxes on bank stocks, and attorney's licenses. The principal items

* $90 additional for each court they hold on a circuit over twelve.

† Salary $20 each court, and fees.

of expenditure annually are, for the Executive and Council of State, about $ 10,000; for the Judiciary, about $ 30,000; for interest, about $ 300,000; for printing and advertising, about $ 5,000; for Agricultural Societies, about $ 2,500.

State Debt. — On the 1st of November, 1858, the bond debt was $ 6,879,505, upon which the annual interest is $ 412,770. The State has also a floating debt amounting to $ 302,418. Total debt, $ 7,181,923. Of this, $ 210,000 became due in 1859, and $ 500,000, January 1, 1860. $ 40,000 becomes due in 1861. Under existing laws the State must besides issue bonds to the amount of $ 640,000, which would increase the indebtedness to $ 7,821,923. The State had also indorsed bonds at the same date to the amount of $ 550,000. The State has productive property to the amount of $ 4,616,274.28, and is secured for its loans to the roads by mortgages of the roads.

Sinking Fund. — By the act of February 2, 1857, a Sinking Fund was established, to be made up of all funds derived from the State stock in the various Railroads and Plank Roads, Turnpike and Navigation Companies, whether from dividends or the sale of stocks. Three commissioners were authorized, at first elected by the General Assembly, but vacancies to be filled by the Governor and Council. Their pay is $ 3 a day for actual service. They elect a Secretary. The commissioners are Thomas Ruffin, Senior, of Alamance, Weldon N. Edwards of Warren, David L. Swain of Orange. Secretary, Quentin Busbee. Up to December 18, 1858, from the income of the fund, the commissioners had purchased State Bonds to the amount of $ 63,285.

Taxation in 1859. — The following are some of the taxes levied. Polls, white and black, 80 cents each; land, on each $ 100 value, 20 cents; attorney's licenses, each, $ 15; bank agencies, each county, $ 500; insurance companies, do., $ 100; brokers, do., $ 300; express companies, do., $ 10; peddlers, do., $ 40; fortune-tellers, do., $ 100; stage-players, do., $ 20; itinerant singers, do., $ 10; circus riders, do., $ 75; billiard-tables, public, $ 125, private, $ 25; bowling-alleys, public, $ 50, private, $ 10; livery stables, $ 25; retailers, $ 30; marriages, $ 1; mortgages, $ 1; other deeds, 50 cents; corporation charters, $ 25; stud horses, $ 6; harps, $ 2.50; pianos, $ 1.50; pistols, dirks, &c., $ 1.25; cards, 35 cents a pack; ferries, 1 per cent on receipts; toll-gates, 5 per cent do., slave dealers ½ per cent; carriages, &c., 1 per cent; watches and plate, 1 per cent; bank profits, ½ to 1 per cent; auctioneers, 1 per cent on sales; merchants, ½ per cent on purchases; dentists, doctors, lawyers, 1 per cent on income over $ 500. The taxes are paid into the Treasury by the sheriffs each year, between June 30 and October 1. Sheriffs are allowed $ 3 a day, $ 2 for every 30 miles travel to and from Raleigh, and 5 per cent commission. The revenue collected from taxes for the year 1859 was, Oct. 1, 1859, $ 638,503.01. For the year 1859 New Hanover County pays the highest tax, $ 29,988.70; Alleghany the lowest, $ 700.

Banks. — For the number and condition of the banks in this State, January, 1859, see the table, *ante*, page 220.

Common Schools for the year ending September 31, 1858. — The present common-school system went into operation in 1840, and is now growing rapidly in usefulness and efficiency, and in few States have the schools a more energetic superintendence. The State is divided into school districts, with local committees, and the districts in each county are under the direction of a board of county superintendents, the chairman of which is the treasurer of the school fund for the county. This board appoints committees of examination, not more than three to a county, who examine applicants for the office of teacher, and give or refuse a license. In 1853, a General Superintendent, the present incumbent, was appointed, and reappointed in 1855, and again in 1858, who is responsible to the Board of Literature and to the Legislature. There is also a committee of examination in each county, whose special duty is to examine teachers. The county board report the condition of the schools to the State Superintendent. There are 85 counties. Returns were received from 77. Number of districts in the 77 counties, 3,237; districts in 77 counties in which schools were taught, 2,602; whole number of white children in the State between 6 and 21 years of age (estimate), 225,000; number attending school in 75 counties, 102,287, being 57,700 males, and 44,587 females; number of teachers licensed in 72 counties, 2,199, — 1,994 males, and 205 females teachers. Average length of schools, 3.7 months. Average wages of teachers per month, $ 23.62.

The receipts for school purposes for the year are reported to have been $371,320.07: the expenditures, $221,132 60.

School Fund.—There was a fund invested in December, 1858, of the nominal value of $2,181,850. Besides the income of this fund, the proceeds of sales of swamp lands, and of vacant lands other than swamp lands, and the taxes upon retail licenses and auctioneers are distributed. The amount apportioned for common schools for each of the years 1857 and 1858 was $180,850.18, and $10,000 each year was appropriated for the institution for the deaf and dumb and the blind. The counties raise by taxation about $60,000 more, making the amount devoted to schools annually about $240,000.

Deaf, Dumb, and Blind.—The North Carolina Institution for the Deaf and Dumb and the Blind is in Raleigh, Wm. D. Cooke, Principal. It was established by the act of 1845, and its 13th session closed June 31, 1858. At that time there were in the Institution 57 pupils, 39 being deaf-mutes, and 18 in the department for the blind. The expenditures are about $12,500 a year. In 1857, the manufacturing brooms was established for the blind. The expenses have exceeded the receipts $548.44. The deaf mutes are taught printing. The charges for the session of ten months are, for deaf mutes, $130; for the blind, $175. This is only for board and tuition. Pupils should be present at the beginning of the session in September.

Insane Asylum.—The Insane Asylum of North Carolina is in Raleigh, Dr. Edward C. Fisher, Superintendent. October 31, 1857, there were in the asylum 138 patients; 80 males and 58 females. During the year 57,—41 males and 16 females,—have been admitted; whole number during the year, 195. During the year there have been discharged 48, of whom 24,—14 males and 10 females, were restored; 4,—2 males and 2 females, were much improved; 2 females were improved; 9,—3 males and 6 females, were unimproved; and 9 died, leaving in the asylum, Nov. 1, 1858, 147,—95 males and 52 females. The annual expenses of the institution are about $30,000, met by State appropriations.

The State has no State Prison.

XXIV. OHIO.

Capital, Columbus. *Area*, 39,964 sq. m. *Population*, 1850, 1,980,329.

Government for the Year 1860.

			Term expires.	Salary.
WILLIAM DENISON, JR.,	of Columbus,	*Governor*,	Jan. 1862,	$1,800
Robert C. Kirk,	of Mt Vernon,	*Lt.-Gov. & Pres. Sen.*,	1863,	$5 a day [during the session of the Legislature.
Addison P. Russell,	of Wilmington,	*Secretary of State*,	1862,	$1,400
Robert W. Taylor,	of Youngstown,	*Auditor of State*,	1862,	1,600
Alfred P. Stone,	of Columbus,	*Treasurer of State*,	1862,	1,500
William B. Thrall,	of Columbus,	*Comptroller of Treas.*,	1862,	1,200
Chris. P. Wolcott,	of Akron,	*Attorney-General*,	1861,	1,400
Anson Smyth,	of Toledo,	*Commissioner of Schools*,	1863,	1,500
Edw. D. Mansfield,	of Cincinnati,	*Com. of Statistics*,	April, 1861,	1,500
James M. Ashley,	of Toledo,	*Commissary-General.*		
David L. Wood,	of Cleveland,	*Quartermaster-General*,		200
Robert M. Moore,	of Cincinnati,	*Paymaster-General.*		
H. B. Carrington,	of Columbus,	*Adjutant-General*,		300
Wm. L. McMillen,	of Columbus,	*Surgeon-General.*		
W. T. Coggeshall,	of Cincinnati,	*Librarian of the State Library*,		600
L. G. Van Slyke,	of Columbus,	*Warden of the State Penitentiary*,		1,200

*Commissioners of the Board of Public Works.**

			Salary.
John Waddle,	of Ross Co.,	Term expires Feb. 1860,	$1,500
Abner L. Backus,	of Lucas Co.,	" " 1861,	1,500
John L. Martin,	of Middletown,	" " 1862,	1,500

JUDICIARY.

Supreme Court.

The Supreme Court consists of five judges, a majority of whom form a quorum; they are chosen by the people for five years, and their terms are so arranged that one goes out of office, and a successor is elected, each year. The judge having the shortest time to serve is Chief Justice. This court has original jurisdiction in *quo warranto*, *mandamus*, *habeas corpus*, and *procedendo*, and appellate jurisdiction in other matters. It holds at least one term in each year, at the seat of government, and such other terms as may be provided for by law.

			Term expires.	Salary.
Jacob Brinkerhoff,	of Mansfield,	*Chief Justice*,	Feb. 1861,	$1,700
Josiah Scott,	of Hamilton,	*Judge*,	" 1862,	1,700
Milton Sutliff,	of Warren,	"	" 1863,	1,700
William V. Peck,	of Portsmouth,	"	" 1864,	1,700
William Y. Gholson,†	of Cincinnati,	"	" 1865,	1,700
James H. Smith,	of Columbus,	*Clk. of Supreme Ct., and Sup. Ct. Franklin Co.*		
L. J. Critchfield,	of Delaware,	*Reporter*,		300

Courts of Common Pleas.

The State is divided into ten Common Pleas districts, each of which is subdivided into three or more parts, from each of which parts one judge, to reside while in office in his district, is chosen by the electors of each subdivision for five years. In several districts some of the subdivisions each elect two or more judges. Courts of Common Pleas are held by one or more of the judges in every county, and more than one court may be held at the same time, in each district. District Courts composed of the judges of the Courts of Common Pleas of the respective districts, and of one of the judges of the Supreme Court, any three of whom form a quorum, are held in each county at least once in each year. The District Courts have the same original jurisdiction with the Supreme Court, and appellate jurisdiction. There is a Probate Court, with the usual probate jurisdiction, in each county, open at all times, holden by one judge, who is chosen by the voters of each county, for three years. Justices of the peace are elected in each township, for three years. Clerks of the Common Pleas are chosen in each county, by the people, for three years.

* John B. Gregory of Portsmouth is elected a Commissioner, and his term commences February, 1860, and expires February, 1863.

† Judge Gholson is appointed to fill the unexpired term of Judge Swan, resigned, and his own full term commences February, 1860, to expire February, 1865.

Dist.	Sub-Dist.	Judges.	Residence.
1.	1.	A. G W. Carter,	Cincinnati.
	2.	Patrick Mallon,	Cincinnati.
	3.	Isaac C. Collins,	Cincinnati.
2.	1.	William J. Gilmore,	Eaton.
	1.	James Clark,*	Hamilton.
	2.	E. Parsons,	Troy.
	3.	George J. Smith,	Lebanon.
	3.	William White,*	Springfield.
3.	1.	William Lawrence,	Bellefontaine.
	2.	A. Sanky Latty,	Paulding.
	2.	Benj. F. Metcalf,*	Lima.
	3	M. C. Whiteley,	Findlay.
	3.	George E. Seney,*	Tiffin.
4.	1.	S. F. Taylor,	Milan.
	1.	J. Fitch,*	Toledo,
	1.	Saml T. Worcester,*	Norwalk.
	2.	James S. Carpenter,	Akron.
	2.	William H. Canfield,*	Medina.
	3.	Thomas Bolton,	Cleveland.
	3.	Jesse P Bishop,*	Cleveland.
	3.	Horace Foot,*	Cleveland.
5.	1.	Shepherd F. Norris,	Batavia.
	2.	Alfred S. Dickey,	Greenfield.
	2	Robert M. Briggs,*	Washington.
	3.	James L. Bates,	Columbus.

Dist.	Sub-Dist.	Judges.	Residence.
6.	1.	S. Finch,	Mt. Vernon.
	2.	G W. Geddis,	Mansfield.
	3.	William Sample,	Coshocton.
		William Given,†	Wooster.
7.	1.	Henry C. Whitman,	Lancaster.
	2.	John P. Plyley,	Vinton Co.
	2.	W. W. Johnson,*	Ironton.
	3.	Simeon Nash,	Gallipolis.
8.	1.	Lucius P. Marsh,	Zanesville.
	2.	John W. Okey,	Woodsfield.
	3.	Saml. W. Bostwick,	Cadiz.
		Nathan Evans,†	Cambridge.
9.	1.	Jacob A Ambler,	Salem.
	1.	John W. Church,*	Massillon.
	2.	B F. Hoffman,	Warren.
	3.	H. Wilder,	Conneaut.
10.	1.	George E. Seney.	Tiffin.
	2.	J. S. Plants,	Bucyrus.
	2.	Vacant.	
	3.	M C. Whiteley,	Findlay.

The salaries of these judges are $1,500 each. Their term of office commences on the 2d Tuesday of February after their election.

Superior Court of Cincinnati.

		Term ends.	Salary.
Bellamy Storer,	*Judge,*	May 5, 1862,	$ 3,500
Oliver M. Spencer,	"	" 1863,	3,500
George T. Hoadley,	"	" 1864,	3,500

Superior Court of Montgomery County.

Daniel A. Haynes, of Dayton, *Judge,* July 1, 1861, $1,500

Superior Court of Franklin County.

Fitch J. Matthews, of Columbus, *Judge,* May 1, 1862, $1,500

Finances,

For the Fiscal Year ending November 15th, 1858.

The total receipts for the year ending Nov. 15th, 1858, were		$3,758,721.57
Balance which should have been in Treasury, Nov. 15th, 1857,		726,939.66
Total means,		$4,485,661.23
Total disbursements for all purposes during the year,	3,515,458.77	
Amount of defalcation,	744,083.51	
Total,		4,259,542 28
Balance in Treasury, Nov. 15th, 1858,		$226,118.96

State Debt. — The Constitution provides that "the State shall never contract any debt for purposes of internal improvement. It may contract debts to meet casual deficits in the revenue, or expenses not otherwise provided for, but the aggregate of such debts shall never exceed $750,000. It may further contract debts to repel invasion, &c., or redeem the present outstanding debt, but the money arising therefrom shall be applied to the purposes for which it was raised, and to none other. The credit of the State shall not be lent to any individual or corporation, nor shall the State become a stockholder in any association, or assume any debt, except such as may have been incurred in repelling invasion, suppressing insurrection, or

* Additional judge for the subdivision. † Additional judge for the whole district.

defending the State in war. The Secretary of State, Auditor, and Attorney-General shall be the Commissioners of the Sinking Fund, which shall consist of the net annual income of the public works and stocks, and of such funds raised by taxation or otherwise as may be provided by law, which shall be made sufficient to pay the accruing interest on the public debt, and annually not less than $ 100,000. A Board of Public Works, to consist of three members, shall be elected, and so classified that one member shall be elected annually, and for three years."

State Debt, January 1, 1859.	Principal.	Interest.
Foreign debt payable in New York:—		
5 per cent stocks, payable at will of State, after 1865,	$ 1,025,000 00	$ 51,250.00
6 " " " Jan. 1, 1860,	6,413,325.27	384,799 52
6 " " " July 1, 1860,	350,000.00	21,000.00
6 " " " March 1, 1861,	350,000.00	21,000.00
6 " " " Jan. 1, 1870,	2,183,531 93	131,011.92
6 " " " " 1875,	1,600,000.00	96,000.00
6 " " " " 1886,	2,400.000.00	144,000.00
Total foreign debt and interest, (int. payable in N. York,)	$ 14,321,857.20	$ 849,161.44
Domestic State debt, payable at Columbus (6 per cent), .	275.385.00	16.523.10
Total foreign and domestic debt, ...	$ 14,597,242 20	$ 865,684.54
Irreducible State debt, being school and trust funds, . .	2,534,076.95	152,044.61
Total debt, ...	$ 17,131,319.15	$ 1,017,629.15

In addition to the public works, the State owns $ 2,807,796.44 of turnpike, railway, and canal stock. The total value of taxable property, real and personal, in the State, for the year 1858 was $ 840,800,031 (being $ 590,285,947 real, and $ 250,514,084 personal), upon which the State tax was $ 2,978,122, and the total taxes were $ 9,756,650.30. The increase in the valuation of real estate in 1858 over that of 1857 was $ 4,664,265. The decrease of personal property was $ 13,279,813. Decrease in the total of property, $ 8,614,548. The increase in the aggregate of the State tax was $ 363,727; of the total taxes, $ 1,083,352. In 1847 the valuation was, real estate, $ 326,793,730; personal, $ 83,964,430; total, $ 410,763,160. Increase in 11 years, $ 430,036,871.

Chief Sources of Income.		*Principal Items of Expenditure.*	
State taxes, ...	$ 2,509,807.29	Expenses of State government,	$ 788,268.88
Canal tolls, water rents, &c., .	283,366.29	Common schools, ...	1,189,479.67
Dividends on stocks and sales of lands, &c., ...	125,632 90	Interest on foreign debt, . .	967,650 53
		Int. special school and trust funds,	149.205.66
Ohio Penitentiary, convict labor,	61,739.05	Interest on domestic bonds, .	16,757.85
Auction duties, Licenses, &c., .	8,714.23	Superintendence and repairs on public works, ...	383,009 92
Bank taxes, ...	793.04		

Banks. — For the condition of the banks in Ohio in November, 1858, see *ante*, page 220. Their condition on November 7, 1859, was as follows: —

Name.	Capital.	Circulation.	Deposits.	Specie.	Exchange.	Loans.
Independent Banks,	650.000	541,237	863,012	121,545	166,905	1,453,756
Free Banks, . .	719 615	665,678	982,272	117.445	257,481	1,403,036
State Banks, .	4,005,500	6.362,705	2,156,433	1,423,363	784,575	8,206,434

Common Schools. — The Constitution of Ohio makes ample provision for the education of all the youth in the State, and the Legislature has liberally carried into effect the injunctions of the Constitution. A general fund is raised by levying a tax of one and a half mills on the dollar on the duplicate, which on the duplicate of 1858 is $ 1,259,092 50. A tax of one tenth of a mill for libraries was suspended in 1857, but it was renewed in 1858, and amounted to $ 83,920 76. There was received in 1858 from the State tax, $ 1,212,855.52; from irreducible school funds, $ 164,946.24. Total, $ 1,377,801.76. The receipts are applied exclusively to the payment of teachers. In addition to this, townships and districts may levy additional taxes to continue their schools, and are required to procure sites, erect school-houses, provide fuel, &c. The amount received for these purposes in 1858 was $ 1,436,268 81. The whole amount of school money received from all sources during the year, including the balance of the previous year, was $ 3,357,678.12. The total number of townships in the year 1857 was 1,357. Each township is a district divided into sub-districts; cities and towns form special districts. The whole number of sub-districts within the townships in 1858 was 9,027; parts of sub-districts, 1,761; total, 10,788; number of sub-districts with school-houses within the townships, 9,902. The number of youth in the State between the ages of 5 and 21 was 843,227. Of these 12,562 were colored. They have separate schools. The whole number enrolled in all the schools was 611,720; white males, 326,132, females, 280,700; colored males, 2,493, females, 2,395. The average daily attendance in all the schools was 352,145. 10,628 male, and 9,612 female teachers have been employed, and $ 1,995,775.04 paid in wages. Amount paid for sites, buildings, and repairs, $ 510,079 84; for fuel and all other contingent expenses, $ 233,982.14; total expenditures, $ 2,739,837.02. Whole number of common schools, 12,224. The average wages per month in common schools were, males, $ 27.89; females, $ 12.95. Average length of common schools, 6 23 months. Number of school-houses built during the year 1857, 589; cost, $ 391,306; number of school-houses heretofore erected in the State, 9,795; value, $ 3,905,495. Number of school-libraries, 6,437; value, $ 135,958; number of volumes in libraries, 245,887; value of school apparatus, $ 37,198. 18 teachers' institutes were held in 1858, lasting in the aggregate 35 weeks, at which were present 116 instructors and 1,829 members.

High Schools. — Number, 139; number of teachers, male, 170, female, 93; average daily attendance, males, 3,156, females, 3,531; average length in months, 8.54. Teachers' wages per month, males, $ 61.81; females, $ 32.82.

Colored Schools. — Number, 129. Number of scholars during the year, males, 2,493; females, 2,395. Average attendance, males, 1,354; females, 1,292. Number of teachers, males, 92; females, 45. Monthly pay of teachers, males, $ 27.24; females, $ 21.88. Average length of school, 5.06 months.

German and English Schools. — Number, 110. Number of scholars during the year, males, 5,727; females, 2,010. Average daily attendance, males, 1,357; females, 1,168. Average length of school, 6.3 months. Number of teachers, 70 males, and 47 females. Average wages per month, males, $ 31.72; females, $ 21.88.

Lunatic Asylums. — There are three Lunatic Asylums. *The Central Ohio*, at Columbus, opened for patients November, 1838, R. Hills, M. D., Superintendent; *The Northern Ohio*, at Newburg, opened March 6, 1855, Oscar C. Kendrick, M. D., Superintendent; and *The Southern Ohio*, at Dayton, opened September 5, 1855, John McIlhenny, M. D., Superintendent. The number of patients in the three asylums, Nov. 1, 1857, was 568. Received to Nov. 1, 1858, 414; males, 209, females, 205. Discharged during the same period, 412; males, 180, females, 232. Remaining, Nov. 1, 1858, 570. Of those discharged, 240 were recovered, 34 were improved, 94 unimproved, 1 escaped, and 43 died. Their current expenses for the year were $ 100,638.21.

Ohio Penitentiary, Columbus. — Lewis G. Van Slyke, Warden. The number of prisoners, November 1, 1857, was 608; received during the year, 305; total, 913. Discharged, 220; by expiration of sentence, 161; by pardon, 37; process of law, 1; escaped, 1; removed to Reform Farm School, 9; died, 11. Remaining, Nov. 1, 1858, 693. Of those received, 266 were white males, 5 white females; 28 colored males. Of those committed during the year, 6 were for arson, 32 for assault with felonious intent; 2 for bigamy; 73 for burglary; 6 for forgery; 69 for grand larceny; 29 for horse stealing; 22 for counterfeiting or passing counterfeit money; 24 for manslaughter; 5 for murder; 1 for perjury. 91 were foreigners, 214 natives. The expenses for the year to Nov. 1, 1858, were $ 79,850.90; the receipts for the same period were $ 62,700.76; balance against the State, $ 17,150.14. The labor of the prisoners is let out on contracts at prices varying from 35 to 48 cents a day. The contractors employ the convicts in manufacturing different articles. By the act of 1856 it is provided that each prisoner under the age of 21, and without a common English education, shall have *three* hours' instruction per day; and all over 21, who cannot read and write, one hour's teaching. By the act of 1856 corporal punishment and the shower-bath, &c. give place to solitary imprisonment on bread and water. The change works well. Punishments have diminished one fifth. The convicts are paid *for* extra work. Regular good conduct shortens the term of imprisonment, and when continued during the whole term of imprisonment entitles the prisoner on his discharge to restoration to his civil rights forfeited by conviction.

Deaf and Dumb Asylum, Columbus. — Collins Stone, Superintendent. The Asylum was opened October 16, 1829, in a private house, and from that time to November 1, 1858, there have been 725 pupils. The number present, November 1, 1857, was 150; 35 were discharged during the year, and 35 were admitted, leaving in the institution, November 1, 1858, 150, — 84 males and 66 females. The current expenses for 1858 were $ 21,432. Pupils are admitted between the ages of 12 and 20; terms, $ 100 for session of ten months, payable quarterly in advance, which covers all expenses but clothing and travelling. Pupils from Ohio pay nothing except for travelling expenses and clothing. Session commences second Wednesday in September, and ends first Wednesday in July. Regular course of instruction 6 years. During vacation, board at the Asylum is $ 1.50 per week.

Institution for the Blind, Columbus. — Asa D. Lord, M. D., Superintendent. Opened July 4th, 1837. Since its opening, 332 pupils have been admitted. The number of pupils in this institution, November 1, 1858, was 100. During the year there were 105 pupils instructed in the institution, 55 males and 50 females; 22 were admitted during the year. The current expenses for the year were near $ 16,000. Applicants for admission must be between the ages of 6 and 21. If able to pay, the charges to those out of the State are $ 100 for the 10 months' session, payable half yearly in advance, exclusive of clothing and travelling expenses. To residents of the State no charge is made for board or tuition. The session is from the second Wednesday of September to the first Wednesday of July. The regular course of instruction is 5 years.

Statistics of Crime. — From the report of the Commissioner of Statistics, it appears that, during the year ending July 1, 1858, 3,553 indictments were found; that 807 were for offences against the person; 987 for offences against property; and 1,759 for offences against society. Number of convictions, 1,272.

Asylum for the Education of Idiotic and Imbecile Youth. — This institution is established at Columbus. R. J. Patterson, M. D., is Superintendent. Children between 6 and 15 years of age, who are idiotic, or so peculiar or deficient in intellect that they cannot be educated at any ordinary school, and who are not epileptic, insane, or greatly deformed, may be admitted by the Superintendent, with the advice of the Executive Committee. A bond is in all cases required to insure the removal of the pupil free of expense to the asylum, when required by the Superintendent. The first pupil was admitted August 3, 1857, and 26 were under treatment to November 1, 1858. Of these, 18 are supported at the expense of the State. It is estimated that there are 2,000 idiotic persons in Ohio, about 500 of whom are under 15 years of age, and susceptible of a greater or less degree of improvement.

Reform Schools. — A board of commissioners was appointed in April, 1857, under the Act "to provide for the establishment of Reform Schools." They purchased a farm in Lancaster, Fairfield County, of about 1,170 acres, and, January 30, 1858, one of their "Family Buildings" was opened for inmates, and 9 boys were received. There were received to November 30, 1859, 48; of whom 14 were honorably discharged, 1 escaped, and 33 remained in the institution. In November, 1859, five of the "Family Buildings" were completed, and there were then about 120 boys in the schools. The experiment has thus far succeeded beyond the expectations of its friends.

State Statistics. By the act of 15 April, 1857, the office of Commissioner of Statistics was created. Edward D. Mansfield is appointed Commissioner, and February 1, 1859, made his second report, which includes the time from November 1, 1857, to November 1, 1858. The second report avoids a repetition of the permanent statistics of the State, and seeks to give the *movement* in the business, social, and productive relations. His summary of the statistics of Ohio in his first report was divided into eight series, as follows: — I. Physics; II. Population; III. Agriculture; IV. Manufactures; V. Mining; VI. Commerce and Navigation; VII. Property, Debt, and Taxation; VIII. Social Statistics. Some of the statistics under each head are as follows: — I. *Physics.* Mean annual temperature, 52°; in 1858, 53°; average fall of rain and melted snow, 50 inches; highest elevation above the sea, 1,250 feet; lowest, 425 feet. II. *Population.* July, 1857, (estimated,) 2,363,000; born in Ohio, 1,335,000; in other States, 640,000; in foreign countries, 393,000. III *Agriculture.* Land occupied by or attached to farms, 19,800,000 acres; actually cultivated, 10,836,000; by the plough, 5,225,000 acres; in grass 4,811,000 acres; in gardens, &c, 800,000 acres. Number of land-owners, 277,000. Average size of farm, 90.82 acres. Average corn crop, 67,000,000 bushels; largest in 8 years, 87,587,000 bushels; smallest in 8 years, 52,171,000 bushels; average crop of corn per acre, 35 bushels. Average wheat crop, 20,000,000 bushels; largest in 8 years, 31,403,000 bushels; smallest, 4,819,110 bushels; average per acre, 14 bushels. Average price of farm labor per year, $150 and board; per month, $15 and board; per day, $1 without board. Fuel, per cord of wood, average, $2. Aggregate value of agricultural products, $132,700,000. IV. *Manufactures.* Number of grist mills, 2,200; saw-mills, 3,740; planing-mills, 175; oil mills, 70. Value of products of manufactures, $79,300,000; of mechanical labor in trade, $40,000,000. V. *Mining.* Value of mining products, $9,483,500. VI. *Commerce and Navigation.* Miles of canals, 849; turnpikes, 2,400; railroads, 2,834; cost of railroads, $95,000,000; debt, $55,000,000. VII. *Property Debt and Taxation.* Aggregate debt, (mortgage, railroad, judgment, &c. debt,) $282,809,547. VIII. *Social Statistics.* Number of marriages, 24,500; in 1858, 21,044. Paupers, including out-door poor, 14,146; in 1858, 14,616; ratio to population in 1857, 1 in 167. — The first report of the Commissioner gives (as the statute requires) the plan of a Statistical Bureau, to consist of a commissioner of statistics and one clerk and providing that the various State, county, and town authorities, and officers of corporations, shall make reports to this bureau. The second report states the number of persons naturalized for the year ending July 1, 1858, to be 4,601; of which 379 were from England, 595 from Ireland, 372 from Scotland, 263 from Prussia, 2,050 from Germany, and 431 from other countries.

XXV. OREGON.

Capital, Salem. *Area*, 185,030 sq. m. *Estimated Population*, 1857, 43,000.

For the act admitting Oregon into the Union and the boundaries of the State, see "Public Laws," *ante*, pp. 133, 134. A constitution was adopted in convention Sept. 18, 1857, after a session of thirty-two days, and was ratified by the people Nov. 9, 1857, by a vote of 7,195 for, to 3,215 against it. Some of its provisions are as follows: — *Voters.* — White male citizens of the United States, aged twenty-one years and residents in the State six months next preceding the election, and white males of foreign birth, aged twenty-one years, residents in the United States one year and in the State six months next preceding the election, and who have declared their intention to become citizens one year preceding the election, may vote. Idiots, insane persons, those convicted of any crime punishable by imprisonment in the penitentiary, negroes, Chinamen, and mulattoes, cannot vote. Fighting a duel, or sending or carrying a challenge, or agreeing to go out of the State to fight a duel, makes a person ineligible to any office of trust or profit. General election shall be on the first Monday of June *biennially.* In all elections by the people, or by the legislative assembly, votes shall be given *vivâ voce*, and not by ballot. A plurality of votes elects.

Executive — The Governor must be a citizen of the United States, thirty years of age, and three years next before his election a resident of the State. His term of office is four years. In case of disability, the Secretary of State, and after him the President of the Senate, shall act as Governor. He shall for the first five years be Superintendent of Public Instruction, after which a separate Superintendent may be elected. The Governor may pardon, after conviction, any offence except treason. He must report to the Legislature all cases of pardons and the reasons therefor. He may veto a bill, but two thirds of the members present in each house, by yea and nay vote, with their names entered on the journal, may pass it over the veto. Any bill retained by him five days, when the Legislature is in session, becomes a law. In case of adjournment, a bill retained by the Governor becomes a law unless the Governor, within five days, files the bill with his objections in the office of the Secretary of State. A Secretary of State — to be *ex officio* Auditor of Public Accounts — and Treasurer of State are elected by the people for four years, but neither of these officers, nor the Governor is eligible, more than eight years in any twelve. A State printer is elected for four years.

Legislative. — A Senate and House of Representatives constitute the legislative assembly. Senators, sixteen in number, are elected for four years, one half every two years, and Representatives, thirty-four in number, for two years. The number may be increased, but there shall never be more than thirty Senators or sixty Representatives. Senators and Representatives must be twenty-one years of age, citizens of the United States, and one year inhabitants of their election districts. They are privileged from arrest in criminal cases, except for treason, felony, or breach of the peace, and cannot be served with civil process, during the session, or fifteen days before its commencement. In 1865, and every ten years thereafter, there shall be a State census, and a new apportionment after such census or any federal census. The sessions are *biennial.* The pay of members shall be $3 a day, and $3 for every twenty miles of travel, but the *per diem* of any member shall not exceed $120. The presiding officers have additional compensation, equal to two thirds *per diem* allowance. If a quorum is present, and either house fail to organize in five days, the members shall have no pay after the five days until the organization. Any member may protest, and have his protest and reasons entered on the journal. Any two members may have the yeas and nays called, except on motions to adjourn, when one tenth of those present shall be necessary. The provisions for the expulsion of members and punishment for contempt, for the appointment of members to offices created by the Legislature, are similar to those in Minnesota. See *ante*, p. 287. Provision may be made for suits against the State for liabilities existing after or at the adoption of the constitution. The Legislature cannot grant divorces by special law. A majority of all members elected is necessary to pass any bill or resolution. Extra sessions shall not last over twenty days.

Judiciary. — The Supreme Court consists of four justices, chosen in districts for six years, those first elected to be so arranged that afterwards one or more shall be elected every two years. The judge having the shortest time to serve, or the oldest of such judges, shall be Chief Justice. They must be citizens of the United States, residents in the State three years next before their election, and after their election be residents of their districts. The number of justices and districts may be increased, but shall not exceed five until the white population of the State exceeds 100,000, and shall never exceed seven. The boundaries of districts may be changed, but the change shall not have the effect to remove a judge from office or require him to change his residence without his consent. The Supreme Court shall have appellate jurisdiction only. Circuit Courts shall be held twice a year in each county, by a justice of the Supreme Court. They have original jurisdiction, and appellate from the county courts and other inferior tribunals. When the white population of the State amounts to 200,000, the legislative assembly may provide for the election of Supreme and Circuit Judges in distinct classes, one of which shall consist of three justices of the Supreme Court, who shall not perform circuit duty, and the other of the necessary number of Circuit Judges, who shall hold full terms without allotment. Each county shall elect one judge for four years. He shall have probate jurisdiction, and as County Commissioner, and civil jurisdiction to the amount of $500, and limited criminal jurisdiction. Sheriffs and clerks are elected for each county, and prosecuting attorneys in districts. Of the jurors in attendance on any court, seven shall be drawn by lot as grand jurors, five of whom must concur to find an indictment. The Legislature may modify or abolish grand juries. The Governor may remove from office, for specified causes, any judge of the Supreme Court or prosecuting attorney, upon joint resolution passed by a two-thirds vote of all the members elected to each house. Public officers shall not be impeached; but incompetency, corruption, &c.,

may be tried as criminal offences, and judgment be given for dismissal from office, and such further punishment as may be prescribed by law.

Education. — The proceeds of lands granted to the State for educational purposes except those granted for a university, all escheats, forfeitures, moneys paid as exemption from military duty, all gifts or devises for common school purposes, all grants by the State when the purpose of the grant is not stated, the proceeds of the 500,000 acres grant, and the five per cent net proceeds of sales of public lands, if Congress consents, shall be set apart as a separate and irreducible fund, called the Common School Fund, the interest of which "shall be exclusively applied to the support and maintenance of common schools in each school district, and the purchase of suitable libraries and apparatus therefor." The division shall be made among the counties in proportion to the number of children therein between the ages of four and twenty years. The Governor, Secretary of State, and State Treasurer constitute a Board of Commissioners for the sale of school and university lands.

Finance. — Neither the State nor any county or town shall in any way be interested in the stock of any company or corporation. The State shall not loan its credit, nor incur any debt of over $ 50,000, except to repel invasion, &c., and any contract or assumption of indebtedness, when the existing debts and liabilities of the State amount to that sum, shall be void. Nor shall any county incur or assume any debt, except as aforesaid, of over $ 5,000. No bank or moneyed institution shall be incorporated in the State, nor shall it exist with power to circulate paper as money. Corporations may be formed under general laws, but shall not be created by special acts, and the stockholders shall be individually liable to the amount of their stock subscribed and unpaid, and no more.

The salary of the State officers and judges is established as given below. The people are to vote upon the establishing a permanent seat of government, and when established it shall not be removed for twenty years. All officers except members of the Legislature shall hold office until their successors are qualified. The Legislature shall not create an office whose tenure is over four years. Lotteries and the sale of lottery tickets are prohibited. The property of married women shall be secured to them. Chinamen, not resident in the State at the adoption of the constitution, shall not hold any real estate or mining claim, or work any mining claim therein. Opinions upon religious matters shall not make a person an incompetent witness. Imprisonment for debt, except in cases of fraud or absconding debtors, is abolished.

Proposed amendments, passed by a majority of all the members elect to each house, entered on the journals, and referred to the next legislative assembly, passed in such assembly by the like majority, and then submitted to the people, shall, if adopted by them, become part of the constitution. While an amendment, or amendments, agreed upon by one legislative assembly, shall be waiting the action of the legislative assembly or the electors, no additional amendment shall be proposed.

When the constitution is submitted to the people (the vote being *vivâ voce*), these questions shall also be submitted: "Do you vote for slavery in Oregon?" "Do you vote for free negroes in Oregon?" and each shall be answered "Yes," or "No." If the constitution is accepted, and the vote is for slavery, this section shall be added to the Bill of Rights: — "Persons lawfully held as slaves in any State, Territory, or District of the United States, under the laws thereof, may be brought into this State, and such slaves and their descendants may be held as slaves within this State, and shall not be emancipated without the consent of their owners." If a majority of votes is given against slavery, the above section shall not be added, but this section shall be added: — "There shall be neither slavery nor involuntary servitude in this State, otherwise than as a punishment for crime, whereof the party shall have been duly convicted."

If a majority of votes are given against free negroes, the following section shall be added to the Bill of Rights: — "No free negro or mulatto, not residing in this State at the time of the adoption of this constitution, shall come, reside, or be within this State, or hold any real estate, or make any contracts, or maintain any suit therein; and the legislative assembly shall provide, by penal laws, for the removal by public officers of all such negroes and mulattoes, and for their effectual exclusion from this State, and for the punishment of persons who shall bring them into the State, or employ or harbor them therein."

The official vote on these questions was: — For Slavery, 2,645; against Slavery, 7,727; majority against, 5,082. For Free Negroes, 1,081; against Free Negroes, 8,640; majority against, 7,559.

Government for the Year 1860.

			Term ends.	Salary.
JOHN WHITEAKER,	of Eugene City,	*Governor and ex officio Supt. of Pub. Instruction,*	1862,	$1,500
Lucien Heath,	of Salem,	*Sec'y of State and Auditor of Pub. Accounts,*	"	1,500
John D. Boon,	of Salem,	*Treasurer of State,*	"	800
Asahel Bush,	of Salem,	*State Printer,*	"	

JUDICIARY.

Supreme Court.

			Term ends.	Salary.
Reuben P. Boise,	of Salem,	*Chief Justice,*	1860,	$2,000
Aaron E. Wait,	of Oregon City,	*Associate Justice,*	1862,	2,000
Matthew P. Deady,	of Winchester,	"	1864,	2,000
Riley E. Stratton,	of Scottsburg,	"	"	2,000

XXVI. PENNSYLVANIA.

Capital, Harrisburg. *Area,* 47,000 sq. m. *Population,* 1850, 2,311,786.

Government for the Year 1860.

			Term expires.	Salary.
WM. F. PACKER,	of Lycoming Co.,	*Governor,*	Jan., 1861,	$4,000
Wm. M. Hiester,	of Berks Co.,	*Secretary of State,*	" "	1,700
H. L. Dieffenbach,	of Clinton Co.,	*Deputy Secretary of State,*	"	1,500
Henry S. Magraw,	of Lancaster Co.,	*State Treasurer,*	May, 1860,	1,700
Jacob Fry, Jr.,*	of Montgomery Co.,	*Auditor-Gen.,*	" 1860,	1,700
John Rowe,*	of Franklin Co.,	*Surveyor-General,*	"	1,600
Thomas J. Rehrer,	of Berks Co.,	*Dep'y Surveyor-General,*	"	1,000
Henry C. Hickok,	of Union Co.,	*Supt. Com. Schools,*	June, 1860,	1,500
John M. Sullivan,	of Butler Co.,	*Dep. Supt., C. S.*	"	1,400
Wm. R. DeWitt,	of Harrisburg,	*State Librarian,*	Feb., 1860,	800
Edwin C. Wilson,	of Venango Co.,	*Adj.-General,*	April 21, 1861,	1,200
John Creswell, Jr.,		*Speaker of the Senate.*†		
Wm. C. A. Lawrence,		*Speaker of the House.*†		

The Governor is elected by the people for three years by a plurality vote. He appoints the Secretary of State and the Attorney-General, who hold

* Thomas E. Cochran of York Co. is elected *Auditor-General,* and William H. Keim of Berks Co., *Surveyor-General.* Their terms commence the 1st Monday of May, 1860, and continue for 3 years.

† These were officers at the session of 1859. A new session commences in January, 1860.

office during his pleasure, and the Adjutant-General who holds office for three years. The State Treasurer is elected each year by the Legislature in joint ballot. The Auditor-General and Surveyor-General are elected by the people, by plurality vote, for three years. The Governor, with the advice and consent of the Senate, appoints the Superintendent of Common Schools and State Librarian for three years. The Canal Board was abolished at the last session of the Legislature, the public works having been sold. Senators, 33 in number, are elected for three years, one third (11) each year. Representatives, 100 in number, are elected annually. The pay of Senators and Representatives is $ 700 each per annum, and 15 cents per mile for necessary travel in going and returning.

Judiciary.

All judges are elected by the people. The judges of the Supreme Court are chosen at large, and for a term of fifteen years. The one having the shortest term to serve is chief justice. The president judges of the several Courts of Common Pleas and other courts of record, and all other judges required to be learned in the law, are elected by the electors of the districts over which they are to preside, and for a term of ten years. The associate justices of the Common Pleas hold their offices for five years. All judges hold office for their term during good behavior. For reasonable cause, though not sufficient grounds for impeachment, the Governor may remove them, upon the address of two thirds of each branch of the Legislature. Any vacancy among the judges arising from any cause is filled by appointment by the Governor, the incumbent holding office until the first Monday in December succeeding the next subsequent general election. During their continuance in office the judges of the Supreme Court must reside within the Commonwealth, and the other judges in the district or county for which they were elected.

The District Courts are invested with the civil jurisdiction of the Common Pleas in their respective districts, in all cases exceeding a certain amount.

Supreme Court.

			Term expires.	Salary.
Walter H. Lowrie,	of Allegheny,	*Chief Justice,*	1st Mond. Dec. 1863,	$3,000
G. W. Woodward,	of Luzerne Co.,	*Associate Justice,*	" " 1867,	2,800
William Strong,	of Berks Co.,	" "	" " 1872,	2,800
James Thompson,	of Erie Co.,	" "	" " 1872,	2,800
John M. Read,	of Philadelphia,	" "	" " 1873,	2,800
John C. Knox,	of Tioga Co.,	*Attorney-General,*		3,000 [and $500 for clerk hire.
Joseph Casey,	of Dauphin Co.,	*Reporter of Supreme Court Decisions,*	July, 1860,	Fees.
Robert Tyler,	of Phila.,	*Prothonotary for the Eastern District,*		"
John Coyle,	of Pittsburg,	" " *Western* "		"
William H. Miller,	of Harrisburg,	" " *Middle* "		"
Chas. P. Pleasants,	of Sunbury,	" " *Northern* "		"

District Court for the City and County of Philadelphia.

George Sharswood,	*President,*	Dec., 1861,	$2,800
George M. Stroud,	*Associate,*	"	2,800
J. J. Clark Hare,	"	"	2,800

District Court for the County of Allegheny.

Moses Hampton,	*President,*	Dec., 1861,	$2,500
Henry W. Williams,	*Associate,*	"	2,500

Courts of Common Pleas.

For the sessions of this court, the State is divided into 26 districts. The following is a list of the judges: —

Districts.	President Judges.	Salary.	Term ends.
1. Philadelphia, ...	Oswald Thompson,	$2,500	1861
Associate Judges, Joseph Allison,	Jas. R. Ludlow, each	2,500	
2. Lancaster, ...	Henry G. Long,	2,000	1861
3. Northampton and Lehigh, . .	John K. Findlay,	2,000	1867
4. Tioga, Potter, McKean, and Elk,	Robert G. White,	2,000	1861
5. Allegheny, ...	Wm. B. McClure,	2,000	1861
	*Thomas Mellon,	2,000	1869
6. Erie, Crawford, and Warren, .	J. Galbraith,	2,000	1861
Associate Judge,	David Derrickson,	1,600	1866
7. Bucks and Montgomery, . .	Daniel M. Smyser,	2,000	1861
8. Northumberland, Lycoming, and Montour, ...	Alexander Jordan,	2,000	1861
9. Cumberland, Perry, and Juniata,	James H. Graham,	2,000	1861
10. Westmoreland, Indiana, and Armstrong, ...	Joseph Buffington,	2,000	1866
11. Luzerne, ...	John N. Conyngham,	2,000	1861
12. Dauphin and Lebanon, . .	John J. Pearson,	2,200	1861
13. Bradford and Susquehanna, . .	David Wilmot,	2,000	1868
14. Washington, Fayette, and Greene,	Samuel A. Gilmore,	2,000	1861
15. Chester and Delaware, . .	Townsend Haines,	2,000	1861
16. Franklin, Bedford, Somerset, and Fulton, ...	F. M. Kimmell,	2,000	1861
17. Beaver, Butler, and Lawrence, .	Daniel Agnew,	2,000	1861
18. Venango, Clarion, Jefferson, Forest, and Mercer, ...	John S. McCalmont,	2,000	1861
19. York and Adams, ...	Robert J. Fisher,	2,000	1861
20. Mifflin, Union, and Snyder, .	Abraham S. Wilson,	2,000	1861
21. Schuylkill, ...	Charles W. Hegins,	2,000	1861
22. Monroe, Pike, Wayne, and Carbon,	George R. Barrett,	2,000	1865
23. Berks, ...	J. Pringle Jones,	2,000	1861
24. Huntingdon, Blair, and Cambria, .	George Taylor,	2,000	1861
25. Centre, Clearfield, and Clinton,	Samuel Linn,	2,000	1869
26. Columbia, Sullivan, and Wyoming,	Warren J. Woodward,	2,000	1866

* Associate Law Judge of the Common Pleas under an act of the last session.

Finances.

The debt of the State was, January 5, 1859, as follows: —

Funded.		*Unfunded.*	
Six per cent loans,	$445,180.00	Relief notes in circulation,	$106,360.00
Five per cent loans,	38,200,773 16	Interest certificates outstanding,	23,357.12
Four and a half per cent loans,	388,200.00	" " unclaimed,	4,448.38
Four per cent loans,	100.000 00	Domestic creditors,	802.50
Total funded debt,	$39,134,153.16	Total unfunded debt,	$133,958.00

Total public debt, January 5, 1869,	$39,268,111.16
Regular annual interest on loans, nearly	$1,958,218.46
Add guaranteed interest on internal improvement companies,	18.500 00
Total interest each year, nearly	$1,976,718.46

The loans, January 1, 1859, were payable as follows: —

Am't over due,	$17,245,245.69	Due in 1863,	$188,200.00	Due in 1877,	$5,000,000.00
Due in 1859,	1,123,083.70	" 1864,	3,020,968.63	" 1878,	426,000.00
" 1860,	2,398,450.94	" 1865,	1,640,015 95	" 1879,	400,000.00
" 1861,	79,900 00	" 1868,	2,466,365.33	" 1882,	850,000.00
" 1862,	2,047,875.82	" 1870,	1,819,720.70		

The productive property owned by the State at the same date was: —

Stock in incorporated companies,	$1,752,996.62
Proceeds of sale of main line public works, being the bonds of the companies making the purchases,	10,900,000.00
Total productive property,	$12,933,996.62
The State has depreciated funds in the treasury, unavailable, to the amount of	41,032.00
Total receipts during the year ending November 30, 1858,	$4,139,778.35
Balance in Treasury, November 30, 1857,	528,106.47
Total available means,	$4,067,884.82
Total expenditures during the same period,	3,775,857.06
Available balance in treasury, November 30, 1858,	$692,027.76

Principal Items of Expenditure.		*Chief Sources of Income.*	
Public improvements,	$202,665.62	Tax on real and personal estate,	$1,610,229.19
Expenses of government,	399,888.36	Canal and railroad tolls,	95,070.06
Militia expenses,	2,854.96	Collateral inheritance tax,	92,318.69
Pensions and gratuities,	9,482.70	Tax on bank dividends,	260,740 31
Charitable institutions,	111,908.49	Tax on corporation stocks,	408,406.37
Common Schools,	277,590 18	Retailers' licenses,	190,664.24
Farmer's High School (Phil.),	6,000.00	Tavern licenses,	190,440.67
New State Arsenal (Phil.),	10,000.00	Other licenses,	38,153.95
Commissioners of Sinking Fund,	422,277.85	Tax on loans,	148,363.11
Interest on loans,	1,989,243.82	Premiums on charters,	97,066 20
Guaranteed interest,	18,517.50	Auction duties,	42,253.10
Domestic creditors,	153.50	Auction commissions,	28,350.00
Old claims and damages on pub. wks,	138,370.96	Tax on writs, wills, deeds, &c.,	78,556.97
Penitentiaries,	27,950.20	Tax on certain offices,	12,018.33
Amendments to the constitution,	7,345.17	Militia tax,	12,329.05
Abatement of State tax,	51,093.78	Lands,	12,948.51
Counsel fees and commissions,	1,312.71	Tax on enrolment of laws,	8,840.00
Houses of Refuge,	57,500.00	Tax on tonnage and passengers,	224,535.62
Penn. archives, &c.,	1,266.50	Escheats,	3,666.17
State Library,	3,593.50	Foreign insurance agencies,	9,189.85
Public buildings and grounds,	15,352 60	Interest on loans,	411,043.24
State Agricultural Society,	2,000.00	Sales of public property,	1,994.27
State Colonization Society,	240 00	Fees of the public offices,	3,324.41
Geological Surveys,	7,183 45	Millers' tax,	2,773.63
Special Commissioners,	377.43	Loans,	28,000.00
		Pa. R R. Co., bond No. 1, redeemed,	100,000 00

The total valuation of the real and personal estate of Pennsylvania taxable for State purposes for the year 1851 was $492,898,829; tax assessed in 1853, $1,685,691.76. The valuation in 1854 was $531,731,304, and the tax assessed thereon for that year was $1,649,967.76, and in 1855 and 1856 the valuation and assessment were the same. In 1857 the valuation was $563,770,234; and the assessment $1,762,839.13. In 1858 the valuation was $568,770.234, and the assessment $1,484,816.23. Number of taxable inhabitants in the State in 1853, 547,191; in 1854, 558,236; in 1855, 565,156; in 1856, 582,185; in 1857, 597,652. in 1858, 613,509. The whole main line of the public works of the State between Philadelphia and Pittsburg was transferred and delivered to the Pennsylvania Railroad Company, July 31 and August 1, 1857, for $7,500,000 of the 5 per cent bonds of the company, which bonds are in the State Treasury, and pledged to the payment of the funded debt, except the first for $100,000 which has been paid. The several divisions of the canals belonging to the State have been sold to the Sunbury and Erie Railroad Company for $3,500,000, and their bonds to that amount were deposited in the Treasury. Portions of these have been sold by the railroad company, and from such sale there has been realized to the State, $281,000.00, which amount has been paid into the Treasury in bonds of the purchasing corporations, and bonds of the same corporations have been substituted for portions of the Sunbury and Erie bonds.

Banks. — There are no returns of the banks in the State, later than those in the table on page 220 of this volume. The newspapers give the condition of the Philadelphia Banks in the following items, at the dates named: —

1859.	Capital Stock.	Loans.	Specie.	Due from other Banks.	Due to other Banks.	Deposits.	Circulation.
Jan. 17,	11,668,065	26,365,335	6,060,743	1,040,765	3,258,315	17,323,908	2,830,384
Mar. 7,	11,589,485	26,719,383	5,926,714	1,650,946	3,854,990	16,372,368	2,901,337
April 4,	11,596,350	27,637,429	6,363,043	1,862,562	4,329,343	17,154,770	3,425,196
May 2,	11,597,515	27,747,339	6,630,813	2,016,015	4,217,834	17,781,229	3,081,102
June 6,	11,586,365	26,177,875	5,415,587	1,817,914	3,367,146	16,386,995	2,992,198
July 5,	11,616,265	24,446,440	4,897,063	1,907,454	2,855,312	15,491,064	2,808,208
Aug. 1,	11,619,005	25,007,875	4,942,313	1,731,183	2,789,266	14,354,543	2,775,043
Sept. 5,	11,632,295	24,640,746	5,435,090	1,537,902	2,843,855	14,901,572	2,702,837
Oct. 3,	11,638,120	25,479,419	5,321,153	1,696,161	2,732,862	15,550,755	2,742,446
Nov. 7,	11,645,185	25,658,185	5,017,936	1,465,965	2,742,790	15,480,452	2,737,150
Dec. 5,	11,617,645	24,963,565	4,564,453	1,334,491	2,398,251	14,852,018	2,648,226

Common Schools in 1858. — A system of popular education was attempted in Pennsylvania, and a common school fund established, in 1831. The State was not divided into districts for school purposes until 1834, and the act of April 1st of that year is generally considered the first common school law. The act of May 8, 1854, revised the school laws of the State. There is a County Superintendent elected by the school directors of the several districts in the county for three years, who attends specially to the schools in the county, and examines and gives certificates to teachers. The school districts are under the immediate care of the school directors, who report to the county superintendent. Teachers are required to report monthly to the directors, and can have no pay until such report is made. The directors are required to establish in their districts separate schools for mulatto and negro children, when they can be located so as to accommodate twenty pupils; and when so established, and kept open four months in any year, the directors shall not be compelled to admit such pupils into other schools of the district. No district can receive its share of the State appropriation for any year, until its schools have been kept four months in such year. The directors and teachers in each district meet annually before the schools are opened, and determine the school-books to be used during the year, and no others than those thus selected can be used. The county superintendents report to the State Superintendent in June of each year. The effect of this law is visible in the improved condition of the teachers and schools, and in the increased attendance of pupils. By the act of April 18, 1857, the State and school departments were separated, and the appointment by the Governor of a Superintendent of Common Schools to hold office for three years, at a salary of

$1,400, was authorized. By the act of May 20, 1857, the State was divided into twelve Normal School Districts of about 200.000 population each, and provision was made for establishing, by private subscription, a Normal School in each district. Several (8 or 10) Normal Schools have been established, and one, the Lancaster County Normal School at Millersville, has (Dec. 1859) become a State Institution. The legislature appropriates annually $ 260,000 for the Common Schools. Of this, $ 43,285 is the pro rata share of Philadelphia; $ 38,870 is the amount of the salaries of the 64 County Superintendents, and the residue goes to the schools of the rest of the State. The whole number of school districts reported, exclusive of the city and county of Philadelphia, for the year ending June 7th, 1858, was 1,722. The whole number of schools was 11,281. The average number of months that schools were taught was 5.25. Number of male teachers, 8,191; number of female teachers, 4,637. Average wages per month of male teachers, $ 24.25; of female teachers, $ 17.22. Number of male scholars, 310,937; number of female scholars, 258,943; number learning German, 7,523. The average number of scholars attending school was 387,139; and the cost of teaching each scholar per month, 53 cents; average number of scholars in each school, 50 5. Of the teachers, 10,946 were born in Pennsylvania; 3,889 had taught less than one year; 4,833 intend making teaching their permanent business; 5,087 give full satisfaction; 5,387 are "medium" teachers, and the services of 2,213 should be dispensed with. Of the school-houses, 1,627 are of brick; 1,280 of stone; 5,751 are frame, and 1,381 are log. In 1,942 schools there is no grading nor any classification of the pupils. The amount of tax levied for school purposes, $ 1,636,317 21; for building purposes, $ 370.909.24; total amount levied, $ 2,009,437.07. Received from the State appropriation, $ 188,646.41; from the collector of school tax, $ 1,554,780.64. The cost of instruction was $ 1,325,992.65; fuel and contingencies, $ 162,670.98; of school-houses, repairs, &c., $ 454,343.53. The number of taxables was 603,407. Teachers' Institutes, District Institutes, and Teachers' Libraries are established in the various counties or districts.

Common Schools in Philadelphia in 1858. — Robert J. Hemphill, Secretary of Board of Controllers of Public Schools. The city and county of Philadelphia constitute the first school district, but are not subject to the general school law. The grades of schools are a high school, a normal school, and school of practice, grammar schools, secondary schools, and primary schools. The whole number of schools in operation for the year ending December 31, 1858, was 314, — 1 high, 1 normal, 1 school of practice, 55 grammar, 48 secondary, 1C2 primary, and 47 unclassified. Number of teachers, 1,013, 79 males and 934 females. Number of male scholars, 30,312; number of females, 29,088: in all, 59,400. $ 476,781.49 was expended during the year for the purpose of education, of which $ 308,618.23 was paid to teachers. $ 11,270 36 was expended for night schools. Average annual cost per pupil in the grammar, secondary, and primary schools, $ 6.24; in High School, $ 35 03; in Normal School, $ 26.65. There were 200 normal-school, average attendance, 186, and 545 high-school pupils, average attendance, 511.

Farmer's High School. — A school with this title has been established in Centre County. There are 400 acres of land connected with the institution, and during the years 1857 and 1858 buildings to accommodate 300 students were constructed. The school was opened for pupils February 16, 1859. The school opens on the 3d Wednesday of February and closes the 3d Wednesday in December in each year. Students must be not under 16 years of age, must have good knowledge of reading, writing, geography, arithmetic, and grammar, and an acquaintance with the elements of natural philosophy, algebra, and geometry, and be of good moral character and of industrious habits. They will be required to work 3 hours each day in every description of labor necessary at the institution. The charge for tuition is $ 100, to be paid in advance.

State Lunatic Hospital, Harrisburg.—John Curwen, M. D., Superintendent. On the 31st of December, 1857, there were 250 patients, — 130 males and 120 females. Admitted during the year, 151, — males, 97, females, 54; discharged, 134, — males, 77, females, 57; leaving in the Hospital, December 31, 1858, 267, — 150 males and 117 females. Of those discharged, 36 were restored, 30 were improved, 54 stationary, and 14 died. Of 1,049 admissions since the opening, 430 were married, 82 widowed, 537 single. The forms of insanity were, acute mania 273, chronic do. 273, epileptic do. 41, puerperal do. 15, monomania 27, melancholy,

294, dementia 104, imbecility 13, idiocy 3, delirium 8. 543 had been insane one year and less before admission; 157, 2 years; 81, 3 years; 81, 5 years; 45, 10 years; 18, 20 years; 3, 35 years; and 1, 50 years. 199 were farmers, and 73 wives and 30 daughters of farmers; 156 laborers, and 34 wives of laborers; 53 males and 179 females were of no occupation. The disbursements during the year were $ 62,241.31; receipts, $ 59,738.62. The State appropriates $ 25,000 per annum to the Hospital. There are apartments for 300 patients, a farm of 130 acres, and a garden.

Western Pennsylvania Hospital, Pittsburg. — This institution has medical and surgical wards and an insane department. Nearly two thirds of the admissions are free patients. 141 persons have been admitted since April 6, 1856, the date of the first admission under the act of 1855. December 31, 1857, there were 74, — 48 males, 26 females; admitted during the year, 83, — 48 males and 35 females; discharged, 67; remaining in the hospital December 31, 1858, 90, — 52 males and 38 females. Of the 67 discharged, 34 were restored, 13 much improved, 8 not improved, and 12 died. Of the 224 patients admitted since the opening of the Hospital, the forms of insanity were, mania, 101; melancholy, 66; monomania, 34; dementia, 15; general paralysis, 1; imbecility, 7. Of those remaining, 37 are supported by their friends, 29 by the authorities having charge of the poor, and 23 were committed by the court. The expenses of the institution for the year were $ 23,733.73. The greater part of the cost of establishing this institution was contributed by private individuals. A farm of about 100 acres has been purchased on the Ohio River about 7 miles from Pittsburg, and preparations have been made for the erection of hospital buildings on these grounds.

Institution for the Instruction of the Blind, Philadelphia. —Wm. Chapin, Principal. 2 principal teachers, 3 assistants, 4 teachers of music, 1 prefect, 4 teachers of handicraft, 2 matrons, 1 salesman. The school was opened in March, 1833. Number of pupils, January 1, 1858, 150; discharged or left during the year, 17; received, 19; remaining, January 1, 1859, 152. Of this number there are from Pennsylvania 122, Maryland 5, New Jersey 14, Delaware 5, all other places 6. Value of goods manufactured during the year 1858, $ 10,565.89. Expenses of the Institution, about $ 40,000. No sectarian faith is inculcated. School, music, and work alternately occupy 8¼ hours daily. The terms for pay pupils are $ 200 a year, including board, instruction, and medical attendance. Blind children in indigent circumstances from Pennsylvania, New Jersey, and Delaware are provided for by those States for from 5 to 8 years. Pupils are not usually received under 10, nor over 17, except for a shorter time than the regular course of 8 years, except for a more limited period to learn some useful handicraft. Pupils should commence in September. The institution has had in operation for several years a department called the "Home," which is intended to shelter and give occupation to those adults who have graduated with honor. Jan. 1, 1859, there were 6 graduates in the home, who are employed part of their time as teachers in the institution.

House of Refuge, Philadelphia. — Jesse K. M'Keever and Elisha Swinney, Superintendents. This institution has been in existence thirty years. Number of inmates, Jan. 1, 1858, 451. Admissions during 1858, 287 boys and 105 girls in the white, and 82 boys and 48 girls in the colored department; total, 522. Discharges, 284 boys and 99 girls in the white department, and 83 boys and 33 girls in the colored; total, 479. Remaining, Jan. 1, 1859, 269 boys and 74 girls in the white, and 101 boys and 49 girls in the colored department; total, 493 Average number during the year, 419. The institution is a school designed for the reform of juvenile delinquents. They are kept at work at various manufacturing operations a portion of the time, and are instructed in the elementary branches of a good English education. Most of the inmates are committed by magistrates, and a few by the county courts. Of the whites, 153, 101 boys and 52 girls, were committed on complaint of their parents or nearest friends, and of the colored, 55 were committed at the request of their parents or nearest friends, and 25 for want of friends. The work done by white boys amounted to $ 3,085.44. The ordinary expenses of the year are about $ 40,000, which are met by appropriations from the city and State. During the year, 76, 66 boys and 10 girls were indentured in Illinois and other Western States. Heretofore, those bound out have been sent mainly to Delaware, Maryland, and New Jersey.

State Prisons. Eastern Penitentiary, Philadelphia. — John S. Halloway, Warden; Thomas Newbold, Physician; Thomas Larcombe, Moral Instructor. January 1, 1858, there were in the prison 376 convicts; received during the year, 207: in all, 583. Discharged by expiration of sentence, 173; by pardon, 22; by habeas corpus, 1; by death, 8; in all, 205; leaving in prison, January 1, 1859, 378. Of these 277 were natives of the United States, and 101 were foreigners. 314 were white males, 7 white females; 54 colored males and 3 colored females. Of the 207 admitted during the year, 109 were natives of Pennsylvania, and 43 of other States, and 55 were foreigners; 175 were whites, 172 males and 3 females; 32 colored, 29 males and 3 females. Of the 207, 36 were abstainers, 74 were moderate drinkers, 60 sometimes intoxicated, 37 often intoxicated; 36 were illiterate, 27 could read only, 144 could read and write. 102 were convicted of larceny, 15 of burglary, 6 of passing counterfeit money, 6 of forgery, 2 of felonious assaults, 9 of arson, 12 of manslaughter, 3 of murder in second degree, and 2 of rape. 1 was sentenced for 10 years, 19 for 5 and not over 9 years, 42 for 3 and not over 5 years, 145 for 2 years and under. The shortest sentence was for three months. Since the opening of the prison, Oct. 25, 1829, there have been admitted 3,949 convicts, and discharged 3,577, of whom 2,725 were by expiration of sentence, 541 by pardons. 245 by death, 9 by suicide, 14 by writ of error, 9 by removal to lunatic hospital. Of the 3.949 convicts, 2,960 were first convictions in any prison. 585 had served a term elsewhere, but were first convictions here, 325 were second-comers here, 52 third-comers, 10 fourth-comers, and 2 came for the fifth time. Of the 541 pardoned, 31 have been again returned to this prison for crime. During the year 1858, 95 prisoners were taught to read and write The library of the prison now numbers over 2,300 volumes, of which 500 are in the German language.

Western Penitentiary, Pittsburg. — John Birmingham, Warden. January 1, 1858, there were in the prison 187 convicts; received during the year, 119; in all, 306. Discharged during the year, by expiration of sentence, 70; by pardon, 11; by death, 4; by suicide, 1; by escape, 2 In prison January 1, 1859, 218, — 216 males and 2 females. Whole number received since the opening of the prison, July 1, 1826, 2,155; being white males, 1,813, females, 35; colored males, 267, females, 40. 1,937 were discharged; 1,449 by expiration of sentence, 372 by pardon, 98 by death, 19 by escape, 4 by process of law. Of the 318 remaining in prison, 18 were convicted of arson, 22 of murder in the second degree, 14 of manslaughter, 78 of larceny, 21 of burglary, 1 of robbery, 9 of counterfeiting, 12 of horse-stealing, 14 of felonious assaults, and 2 of perjury. 24 were received for second offence, 6 for third, and 2 for fourth.

House of Refuge of Western Pennsylvania, Pittsburg. — The charter of this institution was granted in April, 1850. The site was purchased and the buildings erected partly from appropriations from the State, partly by contributions from the five western counties of the State, and partly by individual subscriptions. The site (eleven acres) and the buildings have cost $100,000. The institution was opened for the admission of inmates Dec. 13, 1854, and up to Dec. 31, 1858, 583 were received, of whom 409 were boys and 174 girls, and 94 were of foreign birth. During the year ending Dec. 28, 1858, 139 boys and 59 girls were received, and 119 boys and 55 girls were discharged, and there remained on that date 163 boys and 62 girls, in all 225. The average age of those admitted was, boys 14.25 years, girls 15 years. The inmates are taught daily for four hours. The expenses for the year were about $63,000. The Refuge is intended, not only for those youth of the western counties of Pennsylvania who have been convicted of crime or misdemeanor, but for those who, from their incorrigible or vicious conduct, are beyond the control of their parents or guardians.

Pennsylvania Institution for the Deaf and Dumb, Philadelphia. — January 1, 1858, there were in the institution 174 pupils; 97 boys and 77 girls. Admitted during the year, 29; 12 boys and 17 girls. Discharged, 25; 13 boys and 12 girls. Remaining January 1, 1859, 178; 95 boys and 83 girls. Of these, 125 are supported by the State of Pennsylvania, 19 by Maryland, 9 by New Jersey, 4 by Delaware, and 21 by the institution or friends. Children are not admitted under 10 years of age. The annual charge is $160, or $140 if pupils find their own clothing. The best time for admission is the 1st of October. The term for State pupils is 6 years; those from Maryland are allowed to remain 7 years. The building will conveniently contain about 200 pupils. About 6 hours each day are spent by the pupils in the schools, and 3 hours by the males in the tailor's or shoemaker's shop. The females are instructed in sewing, and other branches of domestic economy. The expenses for the year were about $40,000.

Pennsylvania Hospital for the Insane, Philadelphia. — Thomas S. Kirkbride, M. D., Physician. Number of patients, Dec. 31, 1857, 230, — 117 males and 113 females. Admitted during the year, 131, — 63 males and 68 females; discharged, 131, leaving in the hospital Dec. 31, 1858, 230, — 115 males and 115 females. Of those discharged, 63 were cured, 12 much improved, 29 improved, 9 stationary, and 18 died. Expenses for the year, $62,008; receipts, $62,056. Since the opening of the hospital, Jan. 1, 1841, there have been admitted 1,671 males and 1,518 females, in all, 3,189. 1,562 have been discharged cured, 274 much improved, 461 improved, 313 stationary, and 349 died. Of the 3,068 admitted, 4 were under 10 years of age, 15 between 10 and 15, 202 between 15 and 20, 466 between 20 and 25, 505 between 25 and 30, 420 between 30 and 35, 431 between 35 and 40, 345 between 40 and 45, 278 between 45 and 50, 203 between 50 and 55, 113 between 55 and 60, 91 between 60 and 65, 50 between 65 and 70, 40 between 70 and 75, 20 between 75 and 80, 2 between 80 and 85, and 1 between 90 and 95.

Pennsylvania Training-School for Feeble-Minded Children, Germantown. — Joseph Parrish, M. D., Superintendent. Originally, it was a school for the training of idiots simply; it now proposes to provide a department for epileptics and such children as are not yet qualified for school training. There were, January, 1858, 35 pupils in the institution, 22 males and 13 females. Admitted during the year, 21; removed, 5; died, 4; leaving Jan. 1, 1859, 47, — 32 males, 15 females. 35 are from Pennsylvania, 3 from New Jersey, 3 from Virginia, 2 from Maryland, and 1 each from Louisiana, Mississippi, and Florida. Of those remaining, 4 are mutes, 15 semi-mutes, 15 with defective articulation, and 13 with correct articulation, 9 are epileptics, and 33 are scrofulous. The current expenses of the institution for the year were near $10,000. Of those removed, 9 were improved. A farm of 60 acres has been purchased in Media, the county seat of Delaware County, and the corner-stone of a building for the use of the institution was laid Dec. 8, 1857.

Internal Improvements. — For railroads, see *ante*, p. 224. There are in the State 1,293 miles of canal; of which 921 miles are east, and 372 are west, of the Alleghany Mountains.

XXVII. RHODE ISLAND.

Capitals, Providence and Newport. *Area*, 1,200 sq. m. *Population*, 1850, 147,545.

Government for the Year ending last Tuesday in May, 1860.

			Salary.
Thomas G. Turner,	of Warren,	*Governor*,	$1,000
Isaac Saunders,	of Scituate,	*Lieutenant-Governor*,	250
John R. Bartlett,	of Providence,	*Sec. of State*,	Fees & 1,000
Samuel A. Parker,	of Newport,	*General Treasurer*,	800
William R. Watson,	of Providence,	*Auditor*,	1,000
Jerome B. Kimball,	of Providence,	*Attorney-General*,	1,200
J. B. Chapin,	of Providence,	*Comm'r of Public Schools*,	1,200
E. C. Mauran,	of Providence,	*Adjutant-General.*	
Wingate Hayes,	of Providence,	*Speaker of the House.*	

The Governor, Lieutenant-Governor, Secretary of State, Treasurer, and Attorney-General are elected annually on the 1st Wednesday of April, for the year commencing the last Tuesday of May. The Auditor is elected by the Assembly. The Commissioner of Schools is appointed by the Governor, subject to confirmation by the Senate. The Senate consists of the Governor, who presides, the Lieutenant-Governor, and one Senator from each of the thirty-two towns in the State. The House of Representatives consists of 72 members. The Legislature holds its regular session at Newport on the last Tuesday of May, and a session, by adjournment, at Providence in January following. The pardoning power, except in cases of impeachment, is taken from the Legislature, and vested exclusively in the Governor, with the advice and consent of the Senate.

Judiciary.

Supreme Court.

			Elected.	Salary.
Samuel Ames,	of Providence,	*Chief Justice,*	1856	$2,500
George A. Brayton,	of Warwick,	*Associate Justice,*	1843	1,800
Alfred Bosworth,	of Warren,	"	1854	1,800
Sylvester G. Sherman,	of North Kingston,	"	1854	1,800
Samuel Ames,	of Providence,	*Reporter,*		500

The judges of the Supreme Court hold office until they are removed by a resolution passed by both houses of the Assembly, and voted for by a majority of the members elected to each house. The Court of Common Pleas in each of the five counties is held by a single judge of the Supreme Court. The associate judges of the Supreme Court divide this duty among themselves.

Clerks of the Supreme and Common Pleas Courts.

County.	Post-Office.	Clerk of Supreme Court.	Clerk of Common Pleas.
Newport,	Newport,	John W. Davis,	John W. Davis.
Providence,	Providence,	John A. Gardner,	Amasa S. Westcott.
Washington,	Kingston,	Powell Helme,	John G. Clarke, jr.
Bristol,	Bristol,	Massadore T. Bennett,	Massadore T. Bennett.
Kent,	E.Greenwich,	Elisha R. Potter,	Elisha R. Potter.

Sheriffs.

Newport County, Wm. D. Lake, Newport; Providence County, Elias Nickerson, Providence; Washington County, George H. Olney, Brand's Iron-Works; Bristol County, Stephen Johnson, Bristol; Kent County, Jonathan C. Taylor.

Finances.

For the Year ending April 30, 1850.

Chief Receipts.		*Principal Expenses.*	
State direct tax,	$55,559.95	Salaries,	$19,250.55
Banks, tax,	70,996.49	General Assembly,	10,476.90
Peddlers and Auctioneers,	4,732.10	Courts,	33,190.23
Insurance Companies,	6,629.26	Printing,	6,209.21
From Courts,	15,880.75	Public Schools,	49,996.85
Dividend on School Fund,	$4,770.50	Militia,	$7,641.22
Interest on Deposit Fund stock,	10,036.66	Normal School,	2,999.97
Jailers,	3,690.82	Providence Reform School,	9,250.71
Town Councils,	1,160.67	Butler Hospital for the Insane	8,787.52

The total receipts during this period were,	$189,988.89
Total payments,	195,769.30
Excess of payments,	$5,780.41

The repairs of State Prison, Court-Houses, and various other expenses, are included in accounts allowed by Legislature. The State has no debt. There are about $ 40,000 of disputed Revolutionary claims, which are sometimes called the old State debt. The Public Deposit Fund amounts to $ 336,611.26, the Permanent School Fund to $ 229,435.65, and the Touro Jewish Synagogue Fund to $ 17,488.91. The valuation of the State by a committee of the Legislature appointed therefor in May, 1855, was, — Providence County, $ 78,534,807; Newport County, $ 14,329,548; Washington County, $ 6,402,496; Kent County, $ 6,168,630; Bristol County, $ 5,739,693. Total, $ 111,175,174.

Banks in Rhode Island. — The condition of the 53 banks out of Providence, December 5, 1859, was as follows, to wit: — Capital, $ 5,654,419. Circulation, $ 1,560,045.25. Deposits, $ 873,163 10. Due other banks, $ 56,927.09. Loans, $ 7,566,568.16. Specie, $ 141,003 95. Bills of other banks, $ 150,866 83. Deposits in other banks, $ 350,629 78. The 39 banks in Providence make their returns weekly. Their Capital Stock was, Dec. 5, $ 15,179,750. The following table indicates their movements for seven months.

Date.		Circulation.	Deposits.	Due other Banks.	Loans.	Specie.	Bills of other Banks.	Deposits in other Banks.
1859.		$	$	$	$	$	$	$
June	6,	2,009,163	2,421,901	946,691	18,697,814	378,196	814,763	660,869
July	4,	2,407,141	2,392,843	1,076,323	19,124,155	336,393	1,023,680	650,334
August	1,	2,108,775	2,331,067	1,327,874	18,927,737	315,809	812,144	492,674
September	5,	1,991,193	2,394,917	956,545	18,900,466	321,487	753,133	462,840
October	3,	1,914,490	2,602,946	807,826	19,019,690	312,658	850,695	604,535
November	7,	2,098,610	2,732,380	1,043,439	19,322,775	334,249	925,401	669,502
December	5,	2,074,874	2,585,794	990,100	19,087,115	328,582	993,874	686,855

Savings Banks. — In the 20 institutions for savings, Nov. 22, 1858, there were: — Depositors, 27,613; amount of deposits, $ 6,349,621.75. These institutions divide on an average 6 per cent per annum. The largest amount due any one depositor was $ 13,385.08. The increase since May, 1858, is as follows; in number of depositors, 1,182; in amount of deposits, $ 311,906.42.

Public Schools.—The State has a permanent School Fund, actually invested, of $ 299,435.65. The interest of the State's part of the United States surplus revenue (commonly called the Deposit Fund), and the proceeds of the militia commutation tax in each town, are appropriated to the public schools. $ 50,000 are annually paid from the State treasury for schools. Number of school districts in the State, April 30, 1858, the date of the last published report, 336; number of school-houses, 400; expended on school-houses during the year, $ 43,035.16; number of scholars attending summer schools, 25,682; average attendance, 19,240; number attending winter schools, 29,081; average attendance, 21,506. Number of male teachers in summer schools, 86; of female, 466; in winter schools, — males, 273; females, 336. Amount apportioned from the State to towns, $ 49,996 82; amount raised by towns, $ 107,121 18; whole amount from all sources, $ 195,512.74. Expended, exclusive of school-houses, $ 112,177 33; expended on school-houses, $ 48,085.16. A State Normal School was established at Providence in May, 1854. Number of pupils to December 31, 1856, 286 Average attendance, 66. A Teachers' Institute was held at Newport in October, 1858. More than 200 teachers were present.

State Prison, Providence — S. L. Blaisdell, Warden; salary, $ 1,050. The number of prisoners, January 1, 1858, was 67; committed to December 31, 1858, 26; whole number during the year, 93; average, 66. Discharged by expiration of sentence, 20; by pardon, none; died, 3; escaped, 1; leaving in prison, December 31, 1858, 70. The whole number of convicts since the establishment of the institution, in 1838, to January 1, 1859, was 325. Discharged by expiration of sentence, 166; by pardon, 69; 16 died, and 7 escaped. Of this whole number 137 were natives of Rhode Island, and 92 of foreign places. 315 were males, 10 females; 287 whites, 38 blacks. The State prison now more than supports itself. The jail is an expense to the State of about $ 2,000 yearly. The convicts in the State prison are principally employed at cabinet-work; those in the Providence County jail in shoemaking. The average number of persons in Providence jail at the suit of the State is 64; at the suit of the city, 32; debtors, 3; U. S. witness, 1. During the year, 237 were committed on sentence by the State, of whom 5 (1 male and 4 females) were for drunkenness, 99 for assault, and 71 for theft. 574 were committed to jail for debt during the year.

Butler Hospital for the Insane, Providence, R. I. — Dr. Isaac Ray, Superintendent. On the 31st of December, 1857, there were in the Hospital 140 patients, — 67 males and 73 females. Admitted during the year, 47, — 29 males, 18 females; whole number during the year, 187. Discharged, 52, — 29 males, 23 females; leaving in the Hospital, December 31, 1858, 135 patients, — 67 males, 68 females. Of those discharged, 22 had recovered, 7 were improved, 14 were unimproved, and 12 died. The disbursements during the year were $25,972.39; the receipts were $27,726.54. The amount charged for board of the patients was $27,576.82. The other receipts are from the permanent funds of the Hospital. The minimum price of board for patients is $3 per week. An obligation, signed by two responsible persons, must be given the Treasurer of the Hospital to pay the board and other expenses quarterly, to furnish suitable clothing, &c. The Hospital can accommodate about 145 patients. The State now makes an appropriation of $1,500 per annum to enable the Governor to aid the poor insane persons at the Butler Hospital, and it also pays a portion of the expenses of such poor insane as the towns may choose to send there. Since the opening of the institution in 1848, 861 have been admitted and 726 discharged, of whom 282 were recovered, 218 improved, 59 unimproved, and 170 died.

Deaf, Dumb, &c. — The sum of $2,500 is appropriated annually to the deaf, dumb, and blind, and idiots are included in its benefits. The State beneficiaries among the deaf and dumb, 12 in number, are sent to the American Asylum at Hartford; those of the blind, 6 in number, are sent to the Perkins Institution at South Boston; 6 indigent idiots, at other places out of the State; indigent insane (exclusive of those at the Butler Hospital) at Brattleboro', Vt., 23.

Providence Reform School. — Eleazer M. Cushman, Superintendent. This School was established in 1850, and was opened to receive inmates, Nov. 1, 1850. From that date to Nov. 30, 1857, there were committed, 608, — 489 boys, 119 girls. Number in the school Dec. 1, 1857, 181, — 133 boys and 48 girls. 7½ hours in each day except Sundays, are devoted to labor; 5 to school exercises; 2½ to meals and recreation; 1 to religious exercises, and 8 to sleep. Their labor has been employed in making such articles as are needed in the institution, and in housework. An arrangement is made by the State by which all juvenile delinquents may be sent to this school.

Births, Marriages, and Deaths. — According to the Sixth Registration Report for the year ending December 31, 1858, which has been carefully prepared by Dr. Charles W. Parsons of Providence, the number of *births* was 4,263 (males 2,200, females 2,053, 10 sex unknown). 2,234 were of American parentage, 1,723 of foreign, and 267 of mixed. Number of *marriages* 1,438, of which 872 were between Americans, 422 between foreigners, and 140 between Americans and foreigners. Whole number of *deaths* 2,616 (1,293 males and 1,319 females). Of these 1,428 were Americans, and 978 were foreigners. The average age of all the deaths was 26.44 years, — of the males 23.95 years, of the females 28.87 years.

The City Registrar of Providence, Edwin M. Snow, M. D., has prepared the Third Annual Report on the Births, Marriages, and Deaths in the City of Providence for the year 1858, with his usual care, clearness, and system. The statistics for Providence are included among those of the State given above, and only a few items are here given. There were 1,724 births (890 males and 824 females, — 712 of American parentage, 886 of foreign, and 126 of mixed). Number of marriages, 560. Number of deaths, 1,017 (502 males, 515 females, — 512 of American parentage, 505 of foreign). Estimated total population in 1856, 49,152; in 1857, 50,000; population in July, 1855, 47,785.

XXVIII. SOUTH CAROLINA.

Capital, Columbia. *Area*, 34,000 sq. m. *Population*, 1850, 668,507.

Government for the Year 1860.

			Salary.
Wm. H. Gist,	of Union Dist.,	*Governor* (term ends December, 1860), House-rent and	$3,800
M. E. Carn,	of Colleton Dist.,	*Lieutenant-Governor.*	
Isaac H. Means,	of Fairfield Dist.,	*Secretary of State,*	Fees.
Thos. J. Pickens,	of Pickens Dist.,	*Comptroller-General,*	2,000
William J. Laval,	of Charleston,	*Treasurer, Lower Division,*	2,000
H. G. Charles,	of Darlington,	*Treasurer, Upper Division,*	1,600
W. M. Hunt,	of Columbia,	*Surveyor-General,*	Fees.
R. G. M. Dunovant,	of Chester Dist.,	*Adjutant and Inspector-General.*	
C. M. Furman,	of Charleston,	*Pres. Bank of the State of S. C.,*	3,000
John G. Bowman,	of Columbia,	*State Librarian.*	
Wm. D. Porter,	of Charleston,	*President of the Senate.*	
Wm. E. Martin,	of Charleston,	*Clerk.*	
James Simons,	of Charleston,	*Speaker of the House.*	
J. T. Sloan,	of Anderson Dist.,	*Clerk.*	
Theodore Starke,	of Columbia,	*Keeper of the State-House and State-House Grounds.*	

The Governor is elected by the Senate and House of Representatives jointly, to serve for two years, and is not re-eligible until after the expiration of four years. In case of his death, or removal from office, the Lieutenant-Governor acts as Governor.

Legislature. — Assembles at Columbia, on the fourth Monday in November, annually. Representatives (124 in number) are chosen for two years, on a mixed basis of population and taxation. Pay, $3 a day, and 10 cents for every mile of travel. The Senate consists of 46 members, who are elected for four years; one half chosen every second year. Pay of Senators the same as that of Representatives.

Judiciary.

The judges and chancellors, elected by joint ballot of both houses, hold their commissions during good behavior, and receive a compensation which can neither be increased nor diminished during their continuance in office. A judge or chancellor may order a special court, and a chancellor may hear cases, by consent, at chambers.

Chancellors in Equity.

		Elected.	Salary.
Job Johnston,	of Newberry,	1830,	$3,000
Benjamin Faneuil Dunkin,	of Charleston,	1837,	3,000
F. H. Wardlaw,	of Edgefield,	1851,	3,000
James P. Carroll,	of Columbia,	1859,	3,000

Judges of the General Sessions and Common Pleas.

		Elected	Salary.
J. B. O'Neall,	of Newberry,	1828,	$ 3,000
D. L. Wardlaw,	of Abbeville,	1841,	3,000
T. J. Withers,	of Camden,	1847,	3,000
J. N. Whitner,	of Anderson,	1851,	3,000
T. W. Glover,	of Orangeburg,	1853,	3,000
Robert Munro,	of Charleston,	1853,	3,000

Isaac W. Hayne, of Charleston,	*Attorney-General,*		$ 1,100 and fees.
Henry McIver,	*Solicitor for Eastern Circuit,*		900 and fees.
J. P. Reid, of Anderson Dist.,	" *Western* "		900 and fees.
Simeon Fair, of Newberry Dist.,	" *Middle* "		900 and fees.
C. D. Melton, of Chester,	" *Northern Circuit*		900 and fees.
W. A. Owens, of Barnwell,	" *Southern* "		900 and fees.
J. S. G. Richardson, of Sumter,	*State Reporter,*	1854,	1,500

Law Court of Appeals, and *Equity Court of Appeals.* — The former, consisting of all the law judges, for hearing appeals from the courts of law, and the latter, of all the chancellors, for hearing appeals from the courts of equity, are held in Columbia on the first Monday in May and fourth Monday in November. These courts are also held in Charleston on the second Monday in January, for hearing and determining appeals for the Districts of Georgetown, Horry, Beaufort, Colleton, and Charleston.

Clerks. — At Charleston, T. J. Gantt. At Columbia, John Waities.

Courts for the Correction of Errors, consisting of all the judges in law and equity, to try constitutional questions, or questions where the law and equity courts are divided, and which are referred thereto by either of the courts, are held at such times, during the sitting of the Court of Appeals, as the chancellors and judges may appoint.

Courts of Common Pleas and General Sessions. — These courts have original jurisdiction in all civil cases where *legal* rights are involved (except in matters of contract where the amount is $20 or under), and in all criminal cases affecting free white men; and appellate jurisdiction in all appeals from Magistrates' Courts, and in appeals from the Court of Ordinary in all cases except in matters of account. They are held in each and every district of the State twice in each year. The times of holding the court for Charleston District are the first Monday in May, to sit six weeks, and the fourth Monday in October, to sit four weeks. Daniel Horlbeck, *Clerk for Charleston District.*

Courts of Equity take cognizance of all matters belonging to a court of equity, as contradistinguished from a court of law. A term is held by one chancellor, annually, in each district, except Charleston District, where two terms are held; viz. on the first Monday in February, to sit six weeks, and on the second Monday in June, to sit four weeks. James Tupper, *Master in Equity*, for Charleston.

City Court of Charleston. — An inferior court of limited jurisdiction both in civil and criminal causes. Alston Pringle, *Recorder.*

Ordinary's Court. — Each district has its own Ordinary. The principal duties of the Ordinary are to grant letters of administration; probate of wills; examine executors and administrators' accounts, &c. His office is the proper depository of wills and other papers relative to the administration of estates. An appeal lies from his determination, in matters of account, to the Court of Equity, and, in all other cases, to the Court of Common Pleas.

Magistrates' Courts have exclusive jurisdiction in matters of contract of and under twenty dollars.

Court of Magistrates and Freeholders, for the trial of slaves and free persons of color for criminal offences.

Finances.

Total receipts during the year ending September 30th, 1856,	$ 593,962.00
Balance, October 1, 1855,	136,809.64
Total means,	730,771.64
Total expenditures for same period,	591,145.98
Balance, October 1st, 1856,	$ 139,625.66

Chief Sources of Income.		Jurors and constables,	$ 30,906.00
General Taxes,	$ 501,771.87	Legislative certificates,	15,988.10
Dividends on railroad shares,	14,582.00	Libraries,	3,015.00
New State Capitol,	73,375.86	Paupers at Lunatic Asylum,	1,080.00
		Public buildings,	53,164.83
Principal Items of Expenditure.		Public printing,	13,465.62
Artillery expenses,	$ 1,612.50	Quarantine Regulations,	1,000.00
Military Academies,	30,010.00	Salaries of public officers,	60,090.00
New State Capitol,	71,514.48	Transient poor,	7,800.00
Deaf, dumb, and blind,	5,036.60	Orphans at College,	800.00
Free schools,	77,538.87	Charleston Harbor,	42,196.00
Indemnity for slaves executed,	1,000.00	State Agricultural Society,	5,000.00

State Debt. — The debt of the State, October 1, 1858, was as follows: —

Three, five, and six per cent State stocks and bonds,	$ 3,192,742.96
Annual interest thereon,	184,200.00

The State is liable for its subscription to the Blue Ridge Railroad Company, yet to be called for, which will increase its indebtedness. The State has also agreed to indorse its 7 per cent bonds for $ 1,000,000, and has guaranteed the bonds of the South Carolina Railroad Company for $ 2,000,000, making a contingent liability of the State of $ 3,000,000, in addition to the $ 1,051,422.09 of surplus revenue. To meet this indebtedness, the State has the surplus assets of the State Bank, and stock in various railroads, amounting to nearly $ 6,000,000.

State Bank. — From the annual income of the bank for the year ending September 30, 1856, there was paid $ 50,602.63, for interest on the debt in Europe; also the interest on the 6 per cents (fire loan), amounting to $ 44,807.51; and the sum of $ 184,919.18 was transferred to the sinking fund. It also paid $ 103,739.31 of the public debt during the year. It also made advances on account of the new State Capitol to the amount of $ 124,613 05.

During the year ending September 30, 1858, the bank redeemed of the 5 per cent sterling bonds (fire loan), $ 406,666.67, and of the 6 per cent stock (fire loan), $ 22,574 98; in all, $ 429,241.65.

The aggregate funds of the bank on the 1st of October, 1856, were $ 7,682,359.99. It was liable at that time for its issues, $ 2,421,658.12; its capital, $ 1,104,367.25; to the State treasury for sinking fund, &c., $ 1,630,018.21; rebuilding of Charleston, $ 1,640,017.80; deposits, $ 741,324.25; miscellaneous, $ 144,975.08; total, $ 7,682,359.99.

For the condition of the banks in this State in Dec., 1858, see the table, *ante*, page 220.

The taxes for the year 1856 were as follows: — Upon 387,318 slaves, $ 290,488.50; on 2,931 free negroes, $ 5,863 00; on sales of merchandise, $ 58,841.99; on faculties, professions, &c., $ 10,794 49; on bank, &c. stocks, $ 25,678 60; on premiums received by agents of insurance companies, $ 3,936.47; on town lots, $ 73,681.52; on 17,443,791 acres of land, valued at $ 10,284,001, $ 61,702.99; arrears, &c., $ 947.08. Total, $ 532,744.41.

Free Schools. — The Legislature appropriates $ 74,400 annually to free schools, and applies it at the rate of $ 600 to each representative in the popular branch of the Legislature. The Legislature of 1855 provided for the making of annual returns of the condition of the free schools, and for a compilation of the acts and resolutions in relation to free schools. Academies are established, called the Arsenal and Citadel Academies, in which the youth are practically educated in military tactics, and in engineering and surveying. The State provides annually for the education at the South Carolina College of one youth from the Charleston Orphan House, to be selected as a reward of merit by the Commissioners.

State Lunatic Asylum, Columbia. — J. W. Parker, Superintendent. The number of patients, Nov. 5, 1855, was 171. Received during the year, 67; whole number, 238. Discharged during the year, cured, 22; removed, 11; and 18 died; leaving in the Asylum, November 5, 1856, 187, of whom 100 were males and 87 were females. 89 were paupers and 98 pay patients. The receipts during the year were $ 39,230.99; the expenditures, $ 38,037.67.

XXIX. TENNESSEE.

Capital, Nashville. *Area*, 44,000 sq. m. *Population*, 1850, 1,002,717.

Government for the Year 1860.

			Term ends.	Salary.
Isham G. Harris,	of Memphis,	*Governor*,	Oct. 1861,	$ 3,000
J. E. R. Ray,	of "	*Sec'y of State*,	March, 1864,	800 & f.
Wm. F. McGregor,	of McMinnville,	*Treasurer*,	March, 1862,	1,500 & f.
James T. Dunlap,	of Paris,	*Compt. of Treas.*,	"	2,750 & f.
John W. Head,	of Gallatin,	*Att'y-Gen. & Rep.*,	Aug. 1865,	1,500 & f.
J. M. Safford,	of Lebanon,	*State Geologist*,		1,500
E. G. Eastman,	of Nashville,	*Sec. Agricult. Bureau*,		600
T. W. Newman,	of Winchester,	*Speaker of the Senate*,		$ 6 per diem
W. C. Whitthorne,	of Columbia,	*Speaker of the House*,		and travel.
John McClarin,	of Carthage,	*1st Clerk of the Senate*,		$ 6 per diem.
T. E. S. Russwurm,	of Murfreesboro',	*1st Clerk of the House.*	"	"

The Governor is elected by the people, by a plurality vote, for two years. The Secretary of State, Treasurer, Comptroller, and Attorney-General, are chosen by the Legislature on joint ballot, the Secretary of State for four years, the others for two years. The sessions of the Legislature are biennial. The last session commenced on the first Monday in October, (October 3,) 1859.

Judiciary.

Supreme Court.

				Salary.
Archibald Wright,	of Memphis,	*Judge*,	*Western Division*,	$ 2,500
Robert J. McKinney,	of Greenville,	"	*Eastern* "	2,500
R. L. Caruthers,	of Lebanon,	"	*Middle* "	2,500
M. D. Welch,	of Memphis,	*Clerk*,	*Western Division*,	Fees.
Carrick W. Nelson,	of Knoxville,	"	*Eastern* "	"
James P. Clark,	of Nashville,	"	*Middle* "	"

The judges of the Supreme Court are elected by the people, for the term of 8 years. The judges of the inferior courts are elected in the same manner, for 8 years. There are 15 Circuit Courts. Salary of each judge, $2,000. Each circuit has an attorney, paid by fees, who is also elected by the people for 6 years.

Court of Chancery.

					Salary.
Isaac B. Williams,	of Paris,	*Chancellor,*	*Western*	*Division,*	$2,000
S. J. W. Luckey,	of Jonesborough,	"	*Eastern*	"	2,000
S. D. Frierson,	of Columbia,	"	*Middle*	"	2,000
Bromfield L. Ridley,	of Jefferson,	"	*Fourth*	"	2,000
T. Nixon Vandyke,	of Athens,	"	*Fifth*	"	2,000
Stephen C. Pavatt,	of Camden,	"	*Sixth*	"	2.000

Circuit Courts.

Judge.	Residence.	Attorney-General.	Residence.
1. David T. Patterson,	Greenville.	Samuel Powell,	Rogersville.
2. George Brown,	Madisonville.	W. G. McAdoo,	Knoxville.
3. J. C. Gaut,	Cleveland.	George W. Bridges,	Athens.
4. Samuel L. Fite,	Carthage.	T. H. Williams,	Carthage.
5. E. L. Gardenhire,	Shelbyville.	W. C. Payne,	Sparta.
6. Nathaniel Baxter,	Nashville.	W. B. Bate,	Gallatin.
7. W. W. Pepper,	Springfield.	W. E. Lowe,	Dover.
8. W. P. Martin,	Pulaski.	Nathan Adams,	Pulaski.
9. Wm. Fitzgerald,	Paris.	John A. Rogers,	Dresden.
10. John Read,	Jackson.	T. P. Scurlock,	Jackson.
11. J. C. Humphreys,	Somerville,	W. P. Finnie,	Somerville.
12. Thos. J. Turly,	Rutledge.	M. Thornburg,	New Market.
13. A. J. Marchbanks,	M'Minnville.	G. J. Stubblefield,	M'Minnville.
14. Elijah Walker,	Waynesboro'.	L. M. Bentley,	Lawrenceburg.
15. Samuel Williams,	Trenton.	Robert P. Caldwell,	Trenton.

Criminal Court of Davidson County.

			Salary.
William K. Turner,	of Nashville,	*Judge,*	$1,500

Common Law and Chancery Court of the City of Memphis.

John P. Caruthers,	of Memphis,	*Judge,*	$1,800

Criminal Court of the City of Memphis.

Judge.	Residence.	Salary.	Attorney-General.	Residence.	Salary.
B. F. McKiernan,	Memphis,	$2,000	John F. Sale,	Memphis,	$2,000

Finances

For the Two Years ending October 1, 1859.

Total amount received,	$1,848,094.88
Whole amount expended,	1,704,287.61
Excess of receipts,	$143,807.27
Balance in the treasury, Oct. 1st, 1857,	36,496.06
Balance in the treasury, Oct. 1st, 1859,	$180,303.33

The assessed value in 1856 of 25,362,726 acres of land was $139,378,342; of town lots, $27,039,565; of 119,283 slaves, $82,319,723; other taxables, $11,581,981. Total taxable property, $ 280,319,611. Total tax, $ 406,025.40. Average value of land per acre, $ 5 49; average value of slaves, $ 639. The number of polls was 104,727. The State tax was 10 cents on $ 100. Poll tax 25 cents. The aggregate taxable property of the State in 1859 was $ 377,208,641, an increase in two years of $ 76,849,830. During the fiscal year 1858 a beginning was made in establishing a Sinking Fund for the payment of the State bonds loaned to, or indorsed for, railroad companies. The fund, Oct., 1859, was $ 109,750.

State Debt. — The total absolute liabilities of the State, October 1, 1859, were $ 3,844,606 66, on which accrue annually $ 209,388.25 of interest. The average rate of interest is between 5 and 5½ per cent. Of this liability $ 2,063,606 66 are internal improvement bonds, $ 1,125,000 are bank bonds, $ 608,000 are bonds for building the State Capitol, and $ 48,000 for bonds for the purchase of the Hermitage. The State has, in addition, indorsed the bonds of, or lent its own bonds to, certain rail and plank roads, to the amount of $ 12,799,000, thus creating a contingent liability of the State for this amount. Total absolute and contingent debt, $ 16,643,606.66.

The State, in 1857, owned stocks, chiefly productive, which cost $ 3,292,717; and their estimated value was $ 2,244,827.

Common Schools. — There was in 1853 a school fund of $ 584,060.39 invested in bank stock. In 1857 the disbursements by the State Treasurer on account of school funds were $ 199,328. The sums received for distribution were $ 203,177.92. The scholastic population was 288,538. Amount distributed per scholar, 70 cents.

Banks. — For the condition of the banks in January, 1859, see *ante*, page 220.

Hospital for the Insane, near Nashville, William A. Cheatham, M. D., *Superintendent.* — The building has accommodations for 250 patients. There are 455 acres of land connected with the hospital. The buildings are warmed by steam and ventilated with the "fan." The whole number of patients from March 1, 1852, (the date of the opening of the hospital,) to October 1, 1857, was 390, 251 males and 139 females; discharged, 232, 155 males and 77 females. Remaining, 158, 96 males and 62 females. Indigent patients are boarded, clothed, &c. at the institution at the expense of the State.

School for the Deaf and Dumb, Knoxville. — It is estimated that there are at least 250 deaf mutes in the State, proper subjects for instruction in this institution. The institution provides board, &c., and the average cost is nearly $ 1.91 a week for each pupil. Pupils from other States are charged $ 130 a year, and everything but clothing and travelling expenses is furnished for that sum. Regular time of admission, October 1st. For the two years ending July 15, 1857, the number of pupils under instruction was 80; 40 males and 40 females. Receipts for the same period, $ 28,295.68. Expenditures, $ 25,547.13.

Institution for the Instruction of the Blind, Nashville. — The seventh biennial report of this institution was made to the General Assembly at its last session in 1857. During the two years ending October 1, 1857, 26 pupils were taught therein, as large a number, says the Superintendent, "as the means at our disposal will warrant us in taking." The receipts for the two years were $ 9,031.50; the expenditures, $ 9,367.06.

Tennessee Penitentiary, Nashville. — There were received during the two years, ending Sept. 30, 1857, 197. Discharged by expiration of sentence, 29; by pardon, 105; by death, 16; by escape, 1; in all 151. In prison, Sept. 30, 1857, 286. Of these, 138 were natives of Tennessee, and 31 were foreigners; 13 were sentenced for life, and 64 for 10 years and upwards. Since the prison went into operation, in 1831, there have been (1857) 1,761 convicts. Of which 182 were for murder in the 1st or 2d degree, or manslaughter, 52 for assault with intent to kill, 41 for stabbing, 18 for shooting, 6 for maiming, 23 for burglary, 21 for rape, 23 for arson, 44 for negro-stealing, 194 for horse-stealing, 22 for receiving stolen goods, 45 for forgery, 74 for counterfeiting, 11 for robbing mail, 33 for bigamy, 805 for grand and petit larceny, 19 for perjury.

Agriculture. — In 1854 a State Agricultural Bureau was established by law, and County and District Societies were authorized to receive annually from the State a bounty on certain conditions. The first meeting of the Bureau was held in April, 1854. The Governor is, *ex officio*, President, and a Secretary is elected. State and County Fairs are held each year, and premiums are given and awards made. The establishment of the Bureau has done much to promote the intelligent culture of the soil. Forty-two county societies have been chartered in the State.

Geological Survey. — In February, 1851, the office of "Geologist and Mineralogist of the State" was created, and J. M. Safford was elected to fill it. In October, 1857, he made his second biennial report, in which he states that the groundwork of the survey is sufficiently completed, and that the final report can be prepared by the next session of the Legislature, in 1859.

XXX. TEXAS.

Capital, Austin. *Area*, 274,356 sq. m. *Population*, 1850, 212,592.

Government for the Year 1860.

			Term ends.	Salary.
Samuel Houston,	of Bowie Co.,	*Governor,*	Dec. 21, 1861,	$3,000*
Edward Clark,	of Marshall,	*Lieut.-Gov. & Pres. of Sen.,*	"	$5 a day
[during session of Legislature, and $5 for every 25 miles' travel.				
Thos. S. Anderson,	of Austin,†	*Secretary of State,*		$1,800
Malcolm D. Graham,	of Henderson,	*Attorney-General,*		1,800
Cyrus H. Randolph,	of Austin,	*Treasurer & ex offic. Supt. Schools,*		1,800
Clement R. Johns,	of San Marcos,	*Comptroller,*		1,800
Francis M. White,	of Texana,	*Comm. of Land-Office,*		2,000
E. Fairfax Gray,	of Houston,	*State Engineer,*		3,000
——— Shumard,		*State Geologist.*		
——— ———,		*Superintendent of Penitentiary,*		1,500

The sessions of the Legislature are biennial, and are held at Austin, beginning on the first Monday in November. Members receive $5 a day, and $5 for every twenty-five miles' travel. The eighth biennial session met at Austin, in November, 1859.

Judiciary.

The Supreme Court consists of a chief justice and two associates, who are chosen by the people for six years. Sessions are held once a year, at Austin, on the 3d Monday of October; at Galveston, on the last Monday of January; and at Tyler, on the 4th Monday in April. The court has appellate jurisdiction only coextensive with the limits of the State; but in criminal cases, and appeals from interlocutory judgments, it is under legislative regulations. The judges of the District Court are elected for six years, and hold a court twice a year in each county. The District Courts have original jurisdiction in all criminal cases, and in all suits, both in law and equity, in which $100, exclusive of interest, is at stake. In criminal cases, if the punishment be not specifically determined by law, the jury shall determine it. In equity causes, either party may demand a jury.

---

* And a furnished house.

† The Secretary of State is appointed by the Governor for two years. The Attorney-General, Treasurer, Comptroller, and Commissioner of Land-Office are elected by the people biennially. The State Engineer is elected by a joint vote of the two houses of the Legislature. The Superintendent of the Penitentiary is appointed by the Governor. The office of Commissioner of Claims has expired by the limitation of the law creating it.

The judges of both courts may be removed by the Governor on the address of two thirds of each house; or upon impeachment, to be tried by the Senate. There is also in each county a County Court, sitting once a month as a Court of Ordinary, and once in three months for the transaction of county business. Justices of the Peace, with jurisdiction to the amount of $100, are elected in precincts for two years.

Supreme Court.

			Term ends.	Salary.
Royall T. Wheeler,	of Independence,	*Chief Justice,*	1864,	$3,000
Orin M. Roberts,	of Tyler Co.,	*Associate Justice,*	1863,	3,000
James H. Bell,	of Columbia,	"	1864,	3,000
Thomas Green,	of Austin,	*Clerk,*		Fees.
George F. Moore, Richard S. Walker,	of Nacogdoches,	*Reporters,*		Sale of Reports.

District Courts.

Judge.	Residence.	Salary.	Attorney.	Residence.	Salary.
1. George W. Smith,	Columbia,	$2,250	W. B. Wilson,	Wharton,	$500 & fees.
2. Alex. W. Terrell,	Austin,	2,250	George W. Jones,	Bastrop,	500 "
3. R. E. B. Baylor,	Independence,	2,250	C. B. Jarver,		500 "
4. T. J. Devine,	San Antonio,	2,250	Frank Egan,	San Antonio,	500 "
5. A. W. O. Hicks,	Shelbyville,	2,250	L. F. Casey,	Shelbyville,	500 "
6. C. A. Frazer,	Marshall,	2,250	J. M. Clough,	Marshall,	500 "
7. Peter W. Gray,	Houston,	2,250	Jas. G. McDonald,	Anderson,	500 "
8. W. S. Todd,	Clarksville,	2,250	S. R. G. Mills,	Paris,	500 "
9. R. A. Reeves,	Palestine,	2,250	Geo. Rosenbaum,	Van Zandt Co.,	500 "
10. Fielding Jones,	Victoria,	2,250	William Tate,	Lavuca Co.,	500 "
11. Josiah F. Crosby,	El Paso,	2,250	Vacant,		500 "
12. Edmund J. Davis,	Loredo,	2,250	Edw. Dougherty,	Brownsville,	500 "
13. John Gregg,	Fairfield,	2,250	Charles Stewart,	Marlin,	500 "
14. M. P. Norton,	Corpus Christi,	2,250	J. B. Murphy,		500 "
15. James M. Maxey,	Livingston,	2,250	Saml. A. Wilson,		500 "
16. N. M. Burford,	Dallas,	2,250	James S. Robinson,	McKinney,	500 "
17. E. H. Vontress,	Georgetown,	2,250	R. T. Posey,	Burnett,	500 "
18. E. F. Buckner,	Castroville,	2,250	James Paul,	Castroville,	500 "
19. N. W. Battle,		2,250	J. L. L. McCall,		500 "

Finances.

Receipts for the Year ending Oct. 31, 1857.

Balance on hand, Oct. 31, 1856:—		
In United States 5 per cent bonds,	$1,263,000.00	
In specie,	154,148.34	$1,417,148.34
Receipts from dues of late Republic, taxes assessed by the State prior to 1852, interest on United States bonds, and Miscellaneous sources,		127,546.16
		$1,544,694.50
The expenditures were:—		
Paid on the debt of the late Republic,	$9,271.34	
Paid on Treasury warrants,	271,301.49	
Paid to School Fund,	1,105.51	
United States bonds transferred to School Fund in lieu of specie received from said fund,	33,000.00	314,678.34
Balance on hand in United States bonds,	1,230,000.00	
In specie,	16.16	1,230,016.16
		$1,544,694.50

From November 1, 1857, to August 31, 1858, the receipts were $ 424,770.83, and the disbursements, $ 1,005,868.26.

The State is entirely free from debt. The expenses of the State have been paid, since the year 1851, from the general fund in the treasury, consisting of United States five per cent bonds, which were obtained in the settlement of the northwestern boundary of the State. The State taxes are now (with the exception of one tenth thereof, which is appropriated by the Constitution to the School Fund) paid into the State Treasury to meet the expenses of the State Government.

The State taxes upon property are 12½ cents on each $ 100.00. For 1858 they amounted to $ 268,883.05. They were derived from the following sources, viz.: —

47,237,537 acres of land, value $ 73,677,316; 43,690 town lots, value $12,861,990; 134,201 slaves, value $71,912,496; 238,203 horses, value $11,583,247; 2,220,433 cattle, value $ 13,259,537; miscellaneous property, $ 6,347,298. There were 2,638 money-lenders, with property valued at $ 2,745,493, on which the tax was at the rate of 20 cents the $ 100. The above includes returns from 88 counties. Those not returned are estimated.

For the condition of the debt of the late Republic of Texas, and the legislation of the United States concerning it, see the volumes of the American Almanac for 1854, p. 287; for 1855, p. 284; and for 1856, pp. 145 and 306.

Education. — The State has a permanent School Fund, amounting to $ 2,192,000, $ 150,000 of which is invested in 6 per cent bonds of railroad companies of this State, and the residue in United States 5 per cent bonds. This fund is increased each year by the addition of one tenth of the annual revenue of the State derived from taxation. The income of this fund is annually disbursed for the support of schools. The number of scholars between the ages of 6 and 18 years returned for the year 1856, was 72,826. The number returned for 1857 was 86,782. Besides this fund, each of the 116 counties in the State has four leagues, or 17,712 acres, of land set apart for the support of schools. These lands amount altogether to 2,054,592 acres; but no provision has been made for their sale, and they are not available at present.

State University. — 221,400 acres of land were set apart some years since for a State University.

Lunatic Asylum. — The Legislature, at its session in 1855, appropriated $ 50,000 for the erection of a lunatic asylum, and $ 10,000 a year for its support. 100,000 acres of land were also appropriated for this object. It is established at Austin.

Deaf and Dumb Asylum. — This institution is under the control of five trustees, appointed by the Governor. It was opened in September, 1856, and had (Oct. 1, 1857) 11 pupils. Buildings are rented at Austin for its use. The State pays $ 5,000 a year for its support, and has endowed it with 100,000 acres of land.

Blind Asylum. — This institution is under the control of five trustees, appointed by the Governor. It was opened in November, 1856, and had, Oct. 1, 1857, 7 pupils. Buildings are rented at Austin for its use. The State pays $ 500,000 a year for its support, and has endowed it with 100,000 acres of land.

Orphan Asylum. — 100,000 acres of land have been appropriated by the State for an Orphan Asylum, but no provision has yet been made for its erection.

State Penitentiary, Huntsville. — From 1850 to 1857, both years inclusive, 281 convicts were received. During that time 114 were discharged by expiration of term, 30 were pardoned, 17 died, 1 was discharged by Supreme Court, and 23 escaped, of whom 6 were retaken, leaving in prison September 30, 1857, 102. Of this whole number, 104 were married, 5 were widowers, 1 was a widow, and 171 were single. All were males but 3. 27 were under 20 years of age, 149 were between 20 and 30, 66 were between 30 and 40, 30 were between 40 and 50, 5 were between 50 and 60, 3 were between 60 and 70, and 1 was over 70. 29 were sent for murder, 14 for manslaughter, 29 for assault with intent to kill, 89 for larceny, 51 for horse-stealing, 14 for burglary, 2 for robbery, 7 for stealing cattle, 1 for stealing hogs, 11 for stealing slaves, 1 for enticing away a slave, 5 for forgery, 1 for arson, 5 for assault with intent to commit rape, 2 for rape, 1 for receiving stolen goods, 2 for perjury, 1 for infanticide, 1 for counterfeiting, 21 whose offences were not stated in the commitment. 6 of this number were sent for two offences. 13 were natives of Texas, 148 of other States and Territories in the United States, 64 of Mexico, and 56 of other foreign countries.

Public Lands. — The estimated quantity of vacant public lands of the State, after satisfying all claims upon it, is about one hundred millions of acres.

XXXI. VERMONT.

Capital, Montpelier. *Area*, 8,000 sq. m. Population, 1850, 314,120.

Government for the Year ending October, 1860.

			Salary.
Hiland Hall,	of Bennington,	*Governor,*	$1,000
Burnham Martin,	of Chelsea,	*Lieut.-Gov. & Pres. Sen.,*	$4 a day.
Henry M. Bates,	of Northfield,	*Treasurer,*	500
Benj. W. Dean,	of Grafton,	*Secretary of State,*	400
Wilbur F. Davis,	of Woodstock,	*Sec. Civil and Military Affairs,*	225
William M. Pingry,	of Bethel,	*Auditor of Accounts,*	500
John S. Adams,	of Burlington,	*Sec. of Board of Education,*	1,000
Edward Hitchcock,	of Massachusetts,	*State Geologist,*	1,000
Carlisle J. Gleason,	of Montpelier,	*Secretary of the Senate,*	250
Geo. F. Edmunds,	of Burlington,	*Speaker of the House,*	$4 a day.
Charles Cummings,	of Brattleboro',	*Clerk of the House,*	700
Harvey Webster,	of Brookfield,	*State Librarian,*	125
Erastus S. Camp,	of Montpelier,	*Sergeant at Arms.*	
Hiram Harlow,	of Windsor,	*Superintendent of State Prison,*	500
H. Henry Baxter,	of Rutland,	*Adjutant and Insp.-General,*	150
George F. Davis,	of Cavendish,	*Quartermaster-General.*	
Hiram F. Stevens,	of St. Albans,	*Commissioner of the Insane.*	
A. B. Gardner,	of Bennington,	*Bank Commissioner.*	
Ambrose L. Brown,	of Rutland,	*Railroad Commissioner.*	

The Senate was established in 1836. It now consists of thirty members. The House of Representatives is composed of about 230 members, one member from each town. Pay of the members of each house, $2.00 a day during the session of the Legislature.

Judiciary.

The Supreme Court consists of six judges, elected annually by the Legislature. The County Court is held by one of the judges of the Supreme Court, and two county judges, who are elected annually as assistant judges of the county courts by the people of their respective counties. One term of the Supreme Court and two terms of the County Court are held annually in each county, and a *General Term* is held, at such place and time as the Court shall designate, on the east side of the mountain, for the eastern counties; and on the west side of the mountain for the western counties. The General Terms are held annually. Questions of law may be carried from the County Court to the Supreme Court for revision. No judge can sit in the Supreme Court in the trial of any cause tried before him in the County Court.

The Court of Chancery has two stated sessions annually, in each county, and is always in session, except for the final hearing of a cause. Each judge of the Supreme Court is a Chancellor, and an appeal from his decree lies to the Supreme Court.

Supreme Court.

			Elected.	Salary.
Isaac F. Redfield,	of Windsor,	*Chief Judge*,	Nov. 1859,	$1,500
Luke P. Poland,	of St. Johnsbury,	*Assistant Judge*,	"	1,500
Asa Owen Aldis,	of St. Albans,	"	"	1,500
John Pierpoint,	of Vergennes,	"	"	1,500
James Barrett,	of Woodstock,	"	"	1,500
Loyal C. Kellogg,	of Benson,	"	"	1,500
William G. Shaw,	of Burlington,	*Reporter*,	"	450

Assistant Judges of the County Courts. — Term of Office Expires Nov. 1860.

Salary a per diem allowance.

County.	Assistant Judges.	County.	Assistant Judges.
Addison,	Harrison O. Smith. S. E. Cook.	Lamoille,	Sam'l M. Pennock, Norman Atwood.
Bennington,	Stephen C. Millard, Thomas S. Bebee.	Orange,	James M. George, John Wait.
Caledonia,	William Chase, Thomas Wasson.	Orleans,	Henry Richardson, Durkee Cole.
Chittenden,	David Fish, John Work.	Rutland,	Rollin C. Hunter, Morris H. Cook.
Essex,	William Trask, Milton Cutler.	Washington,	Alvin Braley, Edwin C. Watson.
Franklin,	Seth Oakes, Samuel Kendall.	Windham,	Marshal Newton, Ira Goodhue.
Grand Isle,	Buel Landon, Calvin S. Robinson.	Windsor,	John S. Marcy, Joseph W. Colburn.

Clerks of the Supreme and County Courts.

Counties.	Clerks.	Residence.	Counties.	Clerks.	Residence.
Bennington,	Sam. H. Blackmer,	Bennington.	Washington,	Luther Newcomb,	Montpelier.
Windham,	Royall Tyler,	Brattleboro'.	Caledonia,	Charles S. Dana,	Danville.
Rutland,	Fred. W. Hopkins,	Rutland.	Lamoille,	Edward B. Sawyer,	Hydepark.
Windsor,	Norman Williams,	Woodstock.	Grand Isle,	Jed. P. Ladd,	North Hero.
Addison,	Dugald Stewart,	Middlebury.	Franklin,	Jos. H. Brainerd,	St. Albans.
Orange,	Samuel B. Hebard,	Chelsea.	Orleans,	Norman W. Bingham,	Irasburg.
Chittenden,	John S. Adams,	Burlington.	Essex,	Wm. H. Hartshorn,	Guildhall.

Common Schools. — The school fund was abolished in 1845, to pay the State debt. There was no State Superintendent of Schools from 1851 to 1856. In 1856 a Board of Education was established, consisting of the Governor and Lieutenant-Governor, *ex officio*, and three members appointed by the Governor with the advice and consent of the Senate. The Board appoint a Secretary for a year, to whom the town superintendents report on or before the 1st of September in each year. The salary of the Secretary is $1,000 and expenses of postage and stationery. The pay of the members is $3 a day and mileage. The Secretary is

John S. Adams, of Burlington. The third annual report of the Secretary was made to the board in September, 1859, and is published. It contains no statistics of the schools, as sufficient returns were not received. The Legislature, in 1858 (Nov. 23, 1858), passed a school law, providing among other things, that the Board of Education should select and publish before Jan. 1, 1859, a list of certain classes of school-books to be used in the schools, and that this list when published should be binding until Jan. 1, 1864. It also provided for the election in each town of a Superintendent of Common Schools for the town, who receives a small compensation, and has the general supervision of the schools and examines teachers in some public place, after due notice given, and an invitation to all citizens to attend. He also has the power to dismiss teachers for sufficient cause.

The Legislature of 1856 made provision for the "Registry and Return of Births, Marriages, and Deaths," and for the appointment of a State Geologist to complete the geological survey of the State. A report of Prof. Hitchcock was presented to the Legislature in Oct., 1859.

State Prison, Windsor. — *Year ending September* 1, 1859. — Hiram Harlow, Superintendent, salary $500. Number of convicts, September 1, 1858, 78; committed during the year, 38; total, 116. 34 were discharged during the year; 22 by expiration of sentence; 9 by pardon; 2 sent to lunatic asylum; 1 escaped; leaving in confinement, September 1, 1859, 82; 77 white males, 3 black males, and 2 white females. The services of the convicts are let out to contractors. The contract per-diem charge per convict is two shillings. There is a library of 675 volumes for the use of the prisoners. Since 1809 there have been 1,625 committed, 626 pardoned, 6 sent to Insane Hospital, 23 escaped, 61 died. The income for the year was $13,792 66, the expenditures $13,568.21. Excess of receipts, $224.45.

Vermont Asylum for the Insane, Brattleboro'. — William H. Rockwell, M.D., Superintendent. Since the opening of the Asylum, December 12, 1836, there have been admitted, to August 1, 1859, 3,025 patients; 2,594 have been discharged, and 431 remain in the institution. Of the 2,594 patients discharged, 1,433 have recovered, equal to 55.2 per cent. Of those placed at the Asylum within six months from the attack, nearly nine tenths have recovered. During the year ending August 1, 1859, the whole number of patients was 571 (287 males and 284 females). Admitted, 156 (80 males and 76 females); discharged, 140 (75 males and 65 females); remaining in the institution, 431. Of those discharged, 67 were recovered; 40 died; improved, 17; not improved, 16. There have been 166 State beneficiaries in the Asylum during the year, and 124 remained, August 1, 1859. Income during the year, $59,433.70; expenditures, $60,408.76; balance against the Asylum, $975.06. There is connected with the Asylum a library of over 1,200 volumes, and a large number of newspapers and periodicals are taken.

Terms of admission, $2 per week. No charge is made for damages. When the insanity is connected with epilepsy or paralysis, $3.00 per week. No patient received for less than three months. Extra accommodations can be had by paying for them.

Banks. — From Bank Commissioners' Report, dated September 19, 1859. — Number of banks in the State, 41; capital paid in, $4,081,500; circulation, $3,560,501. Total liabilities, $8,498,939. Notes and bills discounted, $6,402,215; deposits in city banks, $932,049; specie, $207,184; total resources $8,636,975. The average dividend has been nearly 7 per cent upon the capital. The net decrease of bank capital during the year was $135,000.

In the session of the Legislature of 1851 a General Banking Law was adopted, under which the Bank of Castleton went into operation. It is now closing its affairs.

Savings Banks. — September 17, 1859, there were 14 savings banks; 2 were in the hands of receivers in chancery, 2 were winding up their affairs, and 10 were doing business. Deposits in the 12 banks, $971,159.81; increase during the year, $116,367.51.

FINANCES

For Fiscal Year ending August 31, 1859.

Amount received into the Treasury, including former balance,	$175,853.04
" expended,	179,163.30
Balance due the Treasurer, Aug. 31, 1859,	$3,310.26

Principal Items of Expenditure.		Infirm poor, insane, deaf and dumb,	$12,149.43
Expenses of the Legislature,	$30,058.00	Agricultural Societies, &c.,	2,346 38
Stationery,	700.50	Financial disbursements,	15,008.24
Newspapers,	1,042.50	State Geologist,	1,021.88
Legislative Printing,	966.39	Regist. births, marriages, &c ,	359.75
New State-House,	12,773.15	Ethan Allen monument,	1,500.00
Executive expenses, — salaries, &c.,	3,362 46		
Special grants by Assembly,	4,241.09	*Principal Sources of Revenue.*	
Salaries of Judges,	9,950.00	From taxes,	122,589.64
Vermont Reports,	1,020.36	State Attorneys,	4,114.34
Other Court expenses, including prosecution of crime,	62,468.32	Court fees by Clerks,	6,015.48
		Peddlers' license-money,	936.00
Military expenses,	2,699.61	For State-House,	5,000.00

State Liabilities, Sept. 1, 1859.

Indebted to Safety Fund,	$13,012.50	To meet which, it has, —	
Due towns for U. S. surplus revenue, over notes on hand,	4,322.18	Taxes not collected,	$67,002.96
		Due from clerks and attorneys,	4,706.08
Add orders unpresented,	7,348.22		
Loan of 1857,	100,000.00		
Loans from banks,	20,000 00	Total,	$71,708.04
Due Treasurer,	3,310.26	Liabilities,	147,993 16
Total,	$147,993.16	Balance against the State,	$76,285.12

Taxable Property and Taxation. — Aggregate of Grand List of 1857.

53,668 polls at $2,	$107,336.00	Polls and one per cent are,	$976,161.50
Real estate (4,629,436 acres),	69,274,600 00	Deduct for Fire Companies,	1,808.00
Personal estate, over debts owed,	17,607,949.46	Balance list for State taxes,	$974,353.50
Total real and personal,	$86,882,549 46		

New State Capitol. — The new State-House was first occupied at the session of the Legislature commencing October, 1859. For the first thirty years of its existence as a State, Vermont had no permanent seat of government. In 1805 Montpelier was made the seat of government, on condition that it should give the land and build the Capitol by Sept. 1, 1808. These conditions were performed. In 1832 the Legislature made provision for erecting a new State-House at Montpelier, if Montpelier would pay $15,000 towards the expense; and the second State-House was erected and used until January 6, 1857, when it was burned. At an extra session of the Legislature, in February, 1857, a sum was appropriated for rebuilding the State-House, on condition that Montpelier would give security to pay a part of the expense This was done, and the present enlarged structure was erected, consisting of a central building, surmounted by a dome, and two wings. The central building is 72 feet front and 95 feet deep; the wings are 52 feet front and 50 feet deep. The centre and wings are three stories high. It is said that the whole cost, including finishing and furnishing, will fall within $150,000.

XXXII. VIRGINIA.

Capital, Richmond. *Area*, 61,352 sq. m. *Population*, 1850, 1,421,661.

Government for the Year 1860.

			Term ends.	Salary.
John Letcher,	of Rockbridge Co.,	*Governor*,	Jan. 1, 1864,	$5,000
R. L. Montague,	of Essex Co.,	*Lt.-Gov. & Pres. Sen.*,	"	$8 per day [during the session of the Legislature.

			Term ends.	Salary.
J. Randolph Tucker,	of Frederick Co.,	*Att'y-General,*	Jan. 1. 1864,	* $ 1,500
Geo. W. Munford,	of Richmond,	*Sec. State & Libr.,*	Jan. 1, 1859,	*1,620
John S. Calvert,	of Shenandoah Co.,	*Treasurer,*	"	2,000
Jonath. M. Bennett,	of Lewis Co.,	*Auditor of Public Accts.,*	"	2,000
Wm. A. Moncure,	of Caroline Co.,	*2d Aud. & Sup. Lit. Fund,*	"	2,000
Stafford H Parker,	of Richmond,	*Register of Land-Office,*	"	2,000
William Munford,	of Richmond,	*Sup't of Weights and Measures,*		300
James F. Pendleton,	of Smyth Co.,	*Sup't of Penitentiary,*		2,000
Robert M. Nimms,	of Richmond,	*Gen'l Ag't & Storekeeper of do.*		

The Legislature of 1857-8 failed to elect the above officers, whose term expired Jan. 1, 1859, and they continue by law in office until their successors are appointed.

Board of Public Works.

		Term ends.	Salary.
Alex. R. Holladay, *President,*	of Henrico Co.,	July 1, 1861,	$1,500 per annum, and travelling expenses, not to exceed $250 per annum.
Zedekiah Kidwell,	of Marion Co.,	" 1863,	
Oden G. Clay,	of Campbell Co.,	" 1865,	
Thos. H. DeWitt,	of Richmond, *Secretary,*		$ 1,300 per annum.

The Secretary of the Commonwealth, the Auditor of Public Accounts, and Register of the Land-Office are, *ex officio*, members of the Board of Commissioners of the Sinking Fund. Thos. H. DeWitt of Richmond, Va., Secretary of the Board.

The Governor, Lieutenant-Governor, and Attorney-General are elected by the people for four years. The Secretary, Treasurer, Auditor, Second Auditor, Register of the Land-Office, and Superintendent of the Penitentiary, are elected by joint vote of the General Assembly for two years, and until their successors are elected and qualified. They are all obliged to reside at Richmond during their term of service. The members of the Board of Public Works are elected by the people for six years, one every two years. The House of Delegates consists of 152 members, elected biennially from single districts, apportioned upon the basis of the white population. The Senate, apportioned upon the basis of population and taxation combined, consists of 50 members elected for four years, one half every two years, from single districts. The sessions of the Legislature are *biennial;* no session can last more than 90 days, except by a vote of three fifths of all the members; and then it shall not be extended more than 30 days. The last session commenced the 1st Monday in December, 1859. The pay of senators and members is $ 4 a day and mileage.

Judiciary.

For the administration of justice there are established County Courts, Circuit Courts, District Courts, and a Supreme Court of Appeals. The County Courts are held monthly in each county, by not less than three

* And fees.

nor more than five justices. These justices are thus chosen by the people. Each county is divided into districts, and each district elects four justices for the term of four years. These justices elect one of their own number to attend each term of the court.

The State is divided into 21 circuits. The voters in each circuit elect a judge for eight years, who must be 30 years old and reside in the circuit. Two Circuit Courts are held annually in each county by each judge. These 21 circuits form 10 districts, and these 10 districts form 5 sections. The voters of each section elect a judge of the Court of Appeals, who must be 35 years old and reside in his section. The judges of these five sections constitute the Court of Appeals; any three of whom may hold the court, which has jurisdiction, except in certain specified cases, where the matter in controversy is not less than $ 500 in value. This court sits at *Richmond* from January 5th to March 5th, from April 1st to May 14th, from October 15th to December 15th, and at *Lewisburg* on the 2d Monday in July, the term to last ninety days if necessary.

District Courts are held once every year in each district, by the judges of the circuits constituting the section and the judge of the Supreme Court for the section, any three of whom may hold the court.

The Court of Appeals and the District Courts appoint their officers, but in the Circuit and County Courts the officers of the court are elected by the people. For the prevention of crime, each county in the several circuits elects a prosecuting attorney.

Court of Appeals.

Section.	Name.	Residence.	Term began.	Term ends.	Salary.
1.	William Daniel,	of Lynchburg,	July 1, 1852,	July 1, 1864,	$ 3,000
2.	R. C. L. Moncure,	of Fredericksburg,	"	"	3,000
3.	Wm. J. Robertson,	of Charlottesville,	" 1859,	"	3,000
4.	John J. Allen,	of Pattonsburg,	" 1852,	"	3,000
5.	George Hay Lee,	of Clarksburg,	"	"	3,000

Circuit Courts.

Cir.	Name of Judge.	Post-office.	Salary.	Cir.	Name of Judge.	Post-office.	Salary.
1.	Richard H. Baker,	Norfolk,	$ 2,000	12.	John Kenney,	Harrisonburg,	$ 2,000
2.	Thomas S. Gholson,	Petersburg,	2,000	13.	Richard Parker,	Winchester,	2,000
3.	H. H. Marshall,	Halifax C. H.,	2,000	14.	Robert M. Hudson,	Fincastle,	2,000
4.	George H. Gilmer,	Pittsylvania C.H.,	2,000	15.	Edward B. Bailey,	Fayette C. H.,	2,000
5.	Edward P. Pitts,	Accomac C. H.,	1,500	16.	Andrew S. Fulton,	Wytheville,	2,000
6.	John B. Clopton,	Richmond,	2,000	17.	Saml. V. Fulkerson,	Abingdon,	2,000
7.	John A. Meredith,	"	2,300	18.	David McComas,	Kanawha C. H.	2,000
8.	Rich. H. Coleman,	Bowling-Green,	2,000	19.	Matthew Edmiston,	Wiston,	2,000
9.	John W. Tyler,	Warrenton,	2,000	20.	Geo. W. Thompson,	Wheeling,	2,000
10.	Richard H. Field,	Culpeper C. H.,	2,000	21.	Gideon D. Camden,	Clarksburg,	2,000
11.	Lucas P. Thompson,	Staunton,	2,000				

The term of office of all these judges ends July 1, 1860.

Finances.

Public Debt, October 1, 1859.

By the last Constitution, and by the Act creating the Sinking Fund, it becomes necessary to divide the debt of the State into two parts, that created previously to January 1, 1852, which is called the old debt, and that created since that time to the present as new debt. There is an annual charge upon the Treasury of the State of the sum of $838,028.68 to pay the interest due to holders of the same, and for the purposes of redemption, until the debt due January 1, 1852, is paid. Upon the debt created since Jan. 1, 1852, there is an annual charge of 7 per cent, or 1 per cent over the interest due, for the purpose of investment, to redeem the debt after 34 years from the time of its issue.

Old debt, outstanding Jan. 1, 1852,	$10,709,995.30
New debt, created since Jan. 1, 1852,	19,480,321.33
	$30,190,316.63
Of which the State has for investment,	1,083,657.20
Actual outstanding debt,	$29,106,659.43

Operation of the Sinking Fund for 1860.

Annual appropriation for debt, January 1, 1852,	$838,028.68
6 and 7 per cent on new debt (part being 5's),	1,344,972.48
	$2,183,001.16
Deduct the interest to be paid to holders,	1,782,164.66
Applicable for redemption and investment,	$400,836.40

Which will give $206,033.29 for redemption, and $194,808.21 for investment.

Funds and Resources of the Commonwealth, Sept. 30, 1857.

1. *Productive Funds.*	
Banks of the State,	$3,346,950 00
Railroad companies' stock and bonds,	1,137,741.33
Turnpike companies,	323,664 46
Navigation "	66,500.00
Bridge "	16,000.00
Total,	$4,885,856.79

2. *Funds unproductive,*	
But more or less available and secured by mortgages, &c.; bonds of, and loans to, railroad and navigation companies and loans to towns,	$4,958,339.33

3. *Stocks in Improvements not completed.*	
Railroad companies,	$5,975,867.75
Navigation "	3,691,367.37
Plank-road "	165,563 41
Turnpike "	577,926.49
Bridge "	26,892.00
Total,	$10,437,617.02

4. *Stocks in Improvements completed, but unproductive.*	
Railroad companies,	$7,207,659.75
Navigation "	1,001,798.93
Plank-road "	230,893.03
Turnpike "	1,393,123.18
Bridge "	84.182 60
Total,	$9,917,657.39

Total productive and unproductive property of the Commonwealth, $30,199,469.53

These investments are here stated at their par value. It is impossible to ascertain the intrinsic, or even the true market value. Many could not be sold at all. Others, which are quoted in the market at various rates, could be sold only in small quantities, and would command very little if offered for sale at once. There are yet others, which might be sold at fair rates, if the sales were gradually and judiciously made.

Receipts and Expenditures on Account of the Commonwealth for the Year ending September 30, 1859.

Total receipts for the year on account of this fund from all sources,	$4,326,549.67
Total disbursements,	4,222,536 81
Excess of receipts,	$104,012.86

The entire movements of the treasury in 1857 were, receipts, $5,114,089.52; disbursements, $4,734,117.60. Balance, $379,971.92.

In regard to taxation and the contracting of debts and the payment of the State debt, the Constitution provides as follows:—

"The yeas and nays shall be taken on all tax and appropriation bills. No incorporated company shall be released from its liability to the State, nor shall the faith of the State be pledged for the debts of any company. Seven per cent of the State debt existing January 1, 1852, shall be annually set apart as a sinking fund to redeem said debt. No loans shall be contracted irredeemable for a period of over 31 years. Whenever a debt is contracted, there shall be set apart, annually, for 34 years, a sum exceeding by one per cent the aggregate amount of the annual interest agreed to be paid thereon at the time of its contraction, which sum shall be a part of the sinking fund. Stocks held by the Commonwealth may be sold, but the proceeds must be applied to the payment of the public debt."

Banks. — For the number and condition of the banks in Virginia, in January, 1859, see the table, *ante*, page 220.

Schools. — The returns are imperfect. Those for the year ending September 30, 1857, give the number of School Commissioners in 121 counties and 2 towns, 1,475; schools in 99 counties, 3,523; poor children in 81 counties, 55,446; poor children sent to school in 123 counties and 1 town, 49,547. Expended for tuition of poor children at the common schools, including all their school expenses, in 125 counties and 3 towns, $ 136,589.50; average attendance of each poor child at school, 53 days, 10.6 scholastic weeks; average cost per annum of each poor child sent to school, $ 2.77. In addition to the above there was expended for tuition, &c. at the free schools in 6 counties and 1 town, $ 40,066.11. The Governor, Treasurer, Auditors, and Registers are, *ex officio*, the Board of the Literary Fund.

The available capital of the literary fund, October 1, 1857, was $ 1,677,651.67.

Taxation in 1859. — The items of taxation and amount of taxes thereon were lots, improved and unimproved, $ 238,255; lands, do., $ 1,262,436; other property, exclusive of slaves, $ 493,239. The rate of taxation on the foregoing was 40 cents on each $ 100. 207,195 white males, at 80 cents, $ 165,756; 9,334 free negroes, between 21 and 55 years, at $ 1 each, $ 9,334; 273,170 slaves, of and over 12 years of age, at $ 1.20 each, $ 327,804; fees of office, $ 5,594; income, $ 31,028; interest or profits, $ 56,430; dividends, $ 10,454; toll-bridges and ferries, $ 3,515; collateral inheritance tax, $ 3,224; licenses, $ 509,647; total taxation, $ 3,120,922. Of which it is estimated that $ 2,778,332 were applicable to the ordinary expenses of government. In 1858 the amount so applicable was $ 2,740,970; in 1757, $ 2,790,613.

Eastern Lunatic Asylum, Williamsburg. — The number of patients in the asylum, October 1, 1855, was 232, 128 males and 104 females; admitted during the two years ending September 30, 1857, 161, 100 males and 61 females. Discharged, 65, 35 males and 30 females. Died, 69, 44 males and 25 females. Escaped 2. Leaving in the Asylum, October 1, 1857, 257, 147 males and 110 females. Receipts for the two years, $ 119,329. Expenses, $ 123,419.

Western Lunatic Asylum, Staunton. — Patients in the Asylum, October 1, 1855, 388, 226 males and 162 females; admitted during the two years ending September 30, 1857, 136. 81 males and 55 females; discharged, 135, 79 males and 56 females; leaving, October 1, 1857, 389, 228 males and 161 females. Of the 135 discharged, 62 were recovered, 12 much improved, 7 improved, 5 unimproved, 3 eloped, and 46 died. The expenditures for the "support account" of the Asylum for the two years, were $ 128,284.

Institution for the Deaf and Dumb and the Blind, Staunton. — The number of pupils in the institution, September 30, 1857, was 112, being 75 deaf mutes, 42 boys and 33 girls; and 37 blind pupils, 23 boys and 14 girls. The expenses for the two years for the "support account" were $ 24,459.

Penitentiary, Richmond. — October 1, 1856, there were in the prison, 312, 219 white males, 79 colored males, and 14 colored females. Admitted during the year, 111; 76 white men and 3 white women, 29 colored men and 3 colored women. Discharged, 110; by expiration of sentence, 80; by pardon, 12; and 18 died. Remaining September 30, 1857, 313; 218 white males and 2 white females; 84 colored males and 9 colored females. Of these, 226, 136 white and 90 colored, were natives of Virginia, and 42 were foreigners. Since the year 1800, there have been received 3,434 prisoners; 2.546 white males, 44 white females; 748 colored males, 96 colored females. 545 were pardoned; 15 escaped; and 585 died.

Births, Marriages, and Deaths. — In 1855 there were reported 5,792 marriages; 35.912 births, 18,173 males and 17,739 females; and deaths, 17,885, 8,848 males and 9,037 females. In 1856, the Auditor's report gives 5,806 marriages; 31,096 births, 15,629 males and 15,467 females; and 12,410 deaths, 6,072 males and 6,338 females. In 1857 there were reported 6,797 marriages, 38,764 births, 16,575 deaths; in 1858, 6,359 marriages, 37,949 births 14,792 deaths. The increase of reported births over reported deaths in nine years, was 189,519. The report is prepared by the Auditor of Public Accounts. The present population of the State is thus stated by the auditor, — white, 1,087,918; free negroes, 59,118; slaves, 511,154; total, 1,658,190.

XXXIII. WISCONSIN.

Capital, Madison. *Area*, 53,924 sq. m. *Population*, 1855, 552,451.

Government for the Year 1860.

			Term expires.	Salary.
ALEX. W. RANDALL,	of Milwaukee,	*Governor*,	Dec. 31, 1861,	$1,250
Butler G. Noble,	of Whitewater,	*Lieut.-Governor*,	"	$5 per [diem while Legislature is in session.
Louis P. Harvey,	of Shopiere,	*Sec. of State & Auditor*,	1861,	$1,200
Samuel D. Hastings,	of Trempeleau,	*Treasurer*,	"	800
James H. Howe,	of Green Bay,	*Attorney-General*,	"	800
J. L. Pickard,	of Plattville,	*Sup't of Public Instruc.*,	"	1,000
G. Van Steenwyk,	of Kilbourn City,	*Bank Comptroller*,	April, 1860,	2,000
Hans C. Heg,	of Racine,	*State Prison Commiss.*	"	
Horace Rublee,	of Madison,	*Librarian*,	"	1,000
Wm. H. Watson,	of Milwaukee,	*Private Secretary to Governor.*		

All the above-named officers except the Librarian and Governor's private secretary are elected by the people by a plurality vote for two years. The office of comptroller was established in 1858. It has been declared unconstitutional by the Supreme Court of the State, and Horace A. Tenney, of Madison, who had been chosen comptroller, has ceased to act as such officer. Senators, 30 in number are elected for two years. Members of Assembly, 97 in number are elected annually. The Legislature meets each year on the second Wednesday in January.

JUDICIARY.

Supreme Court.

			Term expires.	Salary.
Luther S. Dixon,	of ——,	*Chief Justice*,	1863,	$2,500
Orsamus Cole,	of Madison,	*Assistant Justice*,	1861,	2,000
Byron Paine,	of Milwaukee,	"	1865,	2,000
Lafayette Kellogg,	of Madison,	*Clerk*,		Fees.
Abram D. Smith,	of Milwaukee,	*Reporter*,	Sale of Reports, &	1,000

Circuit Courts.

Circuit.	Judge.	Residence.	Term expires.	Salary.
1.	David Noggle,	of Janesville,	1865,	$2,500
2.	Arthur McArthur,	of Milwaukee,	1863,	2,500
3.	John M. Mann,	of West Bend,	1860,	2,500
4.	David Taylor,	of ——,	1865,	2,500
5.	Montgomery M. Cothren,	of Mineral Point,	1864,	2,500
6.	George Gale,	of Galesville,	1862,	1,500

Circuit.	Judge.	Residence.	Term expires.	Salary.
7.	George W. Cate,	of Plover,	1860,	1,500
8.	S. S. N. Fuller,	of St. Croix,	1860,	1,500
9.	Harlow S. Orton,	of Madison,	1860,	2,500
10.	S. R. Cotton,	of Green Bay,	1861,	1,500

The judicial power of the State, as to matters both of law and equity, is vested in a Supreme Court, in Circuit Courts, in County Courts with probate powers and jurisdiction, and in justices of the peace. The Supreme Court, except the power of issuing writs of *habeas corpus*, *mandamus*, and the like, has appellate jurisdiction only, and in no case holds jury trials. It consists of one chief justice and two associate justices, who are elected by the people, and whose term of office is six years. At present, two terms of the court are held annually, at the seat of government. The State is divided into ten judicial circuits. The judges are elected by the voters of each circuit respectively, and hold their office for six years. The salary of the judges of the Supreme and Circuit Courts was raised to $2,500, in March, 1857, to apply to all judges elected after that date. The Circuit Courts have original jurisdiction in all matters civil and criminal within the State (except in a few specified cases), and an appellate jurisdiction from all inferior courts. They have also power to issue writs of *habeas corpus*, *quo warranto*, and the like. Terms of the Circuit Courts are held at least twice in each year in every county. A clerk of the Circuit Court is elected by the people in each county. The District Attorneys, elected by the people in each county, are the prosecuting officers in the Circuit Courts held in their respective counties.

The County Court, except as a Probate Court, is abolished in all the counties but Milwaukee, La Crosse, St. Croix, Douglass, and La Pointe, where it has concurrent civil jurisdiction in law-cases with the Circuit Court, to the amount of $5,000.

Justices of the peace are elected in the several towns, hold office for two years, and have jurisdiction throughout their counties in civil matters when the debt or damages claimed do not exceed $100.

Finances.

Total receipts into the Treasury for the year ending October, 1859, . . .	$1,119,407.76
The disbursements during the same period were, ...	994,733.84
Balance in the Treasury, October, 1859, ...	$124,673.92

The receipts and disbursements on account of particular funds were as follows: —

	Receipts.	Disbursem'ts.	Balance.
General Fund, ...	$559,113.47	$547,908.36	$11,205.11
School Fund, (including bal. on hand, Oct. 1, 1858,) .	128,330.42	95,682.47	32,647.95
School Fund Income, ...	237,508.20	191,742.01	45,508.20
University Fund, ...	6,179.66	2,981.28	3,198.38
University Fund Income, ...	21,247.06	20,746.02	501.04
Swamp Land Fund, ...	14,502.37	22,526.24	* 8,023.87
Swamp Land Fund Income, ...	62,256.17	35,384.64	26,871.53

* This amount, being an overdraft, is deducted from the general balance.

	Receipts.	Disbursements.	Balance.
Normal School Fund,	$14,090.91	$12,109.92	$1,980.99
Drainage Fund,	8,275.70	7,123.75	1,151.95
Drainage Fund income,	26,775.12	23,372.48	3,402.64
Deposit Fund,	8,840.28	3,469.83	5,370.45
Capitol Land Fund,	288.40		288.40
Madison City Bonds (bal. from last year),*	32,000.00	31,686.84	313 16
Totals,	$1,119,407.76	$994,733.84	$124,673.92

The ordinary expenses of the State, for salaries of the Executive and Judiciary, and permanent appropriations, are near $63,000; for the Legislature and legislative expenses, $52,000; for benevolent institutions, $85,000; State Prison, $25,000; other miscellaneous expenses, not including debt or schools, $60,000; total, $285,000.

Taxable Property in 1859. — Acres of land, 17,411,319; average equalized value per acre, $6.78; assessed value, $118,178,829; value of village and city lots, $36,833,511; personal property, deducting debts, $13,607,893; aggregate assessed value, $152,537,700; total *equalized* value, $169,620,234. The State taxes on this amount for 1859 were, — State tax of nearly .89 of a mill, $150,000; .4 mill for interest on State indebtedness, $67,448.09; .1 mill for town libraries, $16,862.02; making the total tax, $238,310.11. The balance of the .4 mill tax, after paying the interest on the State debt, goes into the general fund.

Banks. — For the condition of the banks in Wisconsin, January, 1859, see *ante*, p. 220.

Common Schools. — The capital of the School Fund, Oct. 1, 1858, was $3,107,484.88, which bears interest at 7 per cent, which is $217,523.94. Deducting the amount set apart for Normal School purposes, the School Fund proper is $2,845,846.34, on which the interest is $199,209.24. From this fund there was disbursed during the year for schools, near $150,000. The capital is constantly increased by the sale of school lands, of 25 per cent net of sales of swamp lands, and from other sources. There was, besides, the University Fund, of $316,365.83, the income of which, at 7 per cent, is applied for the benefit of the State University. For the year ending August 31, 1858, returns were received from all but two counties. In the State there were 3,181 districts and 1,566 parts of districts, in which there were 3,482 school-houses. Average length of schools, 5.6 months. Number of children in the State between 4 and 20 years, 264,078, of whom 167,110 attended school. Average monthly wages of male teachers, $27.02; of female, $14.92. $334,000 was raised by tax and expended for teachers' wages. Number of volumes reported in libraries, 38,755, of which number 34,104 were loaned during the year. There were, in 1856, 141 select and private schools, with an average attendance of 4,632 pupils, and 3 incorporated academies. The total valuation of school-houses in 1858 was $1,127,191.69. The highest valuation of any school-house is $28,000, and the lowest $0.01. A Normal department, for the instruction of teachers, is established in the State University. A Board of Regents of Normal Schools has been established by law, who are authorized to distribute one fourth of the net income of the Swamp Land Fund among such institutions as maintain under certain regulations a Department of Normal Instruction.

Wisconsin State Lunatic Asylum. — The site, containing 104 acres, for an asylum for the insane, authorized by the Legislature to be erected, was selected in 1854, and a contract was entered into for the necessary buildings, in accordance with the plans adopted by the Commissioners in charge; but the Legislature of 1855 repealed the act. The Legislature has since authorized the completion of the buildings, and the last report of the Commissioners states that they hope the buildings will be ready for occupancy in January, 1860. The Governor states in his message that the number of the insane in the State requiring treatment is between 300 and 400. The Asylum, by the act of 1859, is placed in charge of seven trustees, three of whom must reside in Dane County. Those first appointed shall be classified so that one holds office for one year, two for two years, and three for three years, and afterward the vacancies are filled by appointments for three years.

Wisconsin Institute for the Education of the Blind, Janesville. — W. H. Churchman,

* Bonds given by city of Madison towards expense of enlarging the Capitol.

Superintendent. This institution is now supported by legislative appropriations. It was opened August 1, 1850. The number of pupils received, to June 30, 1858, was 53, 27 boys and 26 girls, of whom 18 remained at that date. The buildings were not then entirely completed. To pupils from Wisconsin board and tuition are free, but they must supply themselves with good comfortable clothing. The session of the Institute is from the first Monday in September to the last Wednesday in June. The females are employed in sewing, knitting, braiding, and fancy bead-work; the males in broom-making.

Deaf and Dumb Institute, Delavan, Walworth Co. — J. S. Officer, Principal. The institution was established in 1852. Buildings have been erected to accommodate 60 pupils. There were during the nine months ending September 1, 1858, 52 pupils in attendance, 37 males and 15 females. To pupils from Wisconsin board and tuition are free. The charge to pupils from other States is $100 per annum for tuition and board. The sessions commence on the first Wednesday in September, and last ten months. The care of the Institute is put into the charge of nine trustees, who are divided into three classes of three each. They hold office for three years, and their terms are so arranged that those of one class go out of office each year. It is made the duty of the Governor to visit annually and inspect the State prisons and the charitable institutions of the State, and public institutions in other States, and he is required to report annually to the Legislature, in writing, the condition of all the State institutions.

State Prison, at Waupun, Fond du Lac Co. — Number of convicts, January 1, 1858, 160; received to Jan. 1, 1859, 127; in all, 287. Discharged, 85. In prison, Jan. 1, 1859, 202. Of those discharged, 67 were by expiration of sentence, 16 by pardon, 1 by habeas corpus, and 1 died. Of the 287 in prison, 25 were convicted of murder, 21 being convicted of murder in the first degree; 11 of manslaughter; 5 of rape; 28 of burglary; 164 of larceny; 7 of arson; 2 of perjury; 7 of counterfeiting. Of the 202, 96 were natives of the United States, and 106 were foreign-born. The labor of the convicts is let out by contract. Since the opening of the prison there have been admitted 472 prisoners, and 270 discharged, 152 by expiration of sentence, 108 by pardon, 4 by order of court, 1 escaped, and 5 died. Of the 472, 30 were convicted of murder, 20 of manslaughter, 21 of assaults with felonious intent, 8 of rape, 3 of perjury, 17 of counterfeiting, 39 of burglary, 272 of larceny. 210 were natives of other countries, and 262 of the United States.

State Reform School for Juvenile Delinquents. — The Commissioners appointed to locate and erect the House of Refuge purchased a site of nearly eleven acres, in Waukesha, about twenty miles west of Milwaukee. The citizens of Waukesha gave, in addition, sixty acres of contiguous land. The plan consists of three independent buildings, fifty feet apart, parallel to each other, all united by a corridor nine feet wide, passing through and between the buildings, dividing each in the centre. The front of each building is designed for the officers and their families, and the rear for the inmates. Portions of the building are under contract. A portion of one wing is completed. The name of the institution was changed in 1859 from House of Refuge to its present name.

State Debt. — The constitution provides that the State debt in the aggregate shall never exceed $ 100,000. The permanent debt of the State is $ 100,000, on which the annual interest is $ 7,000.

Population by the State Census of 1855. — For details of the State Census of 1855, see the American Almanac for 1857, page 336.

Geological Survey. — A survey of the State has been in progress for the past 18 months, under the law of 1857, which provided for $ 6,000 per annum to be expended for 6 years, if necessary, and created a commission for the work, consisting of Professors James Hall, Ezra S. Carr, and Edward Daniels. Professors Charles Whittlesey and J. D. Whitney have been engaged in the work during a portion of the time.

XXXIV. UTAH TERRITORY.*

Area, 187,923 sq. m. *Population*, 1850, 11,380.

			Term ends.	Salary.
ALFRED CUMMINGS,	of Salt Lake City,	*Governor*,	1861,	$2,500
Almon W. Babbitt,	"	*Secretary*,		2,000

JUDICIARY.

Delana R. Eckles,	of Salt Lake City,	*Chief Justice*,	1862,	2,500
Charles E. Sinclair,	"	*Associate Justice*,	"	2,500
John Cradlebaugh,	"	"	"	2,500
Alexander Wilson,	"	*Attorney*,	Fees and 250	
P. K. Dotson,	"	*Marshal*,	Fees and 200	

XXXV. NEW MEXICO TERRITORY.

Area, 210,774 sq. m. *Population*, 1850, 61,547.

			Term ends.	Salary.
ABRAHAM RENCHER,	of Santa Fé,	*Governor*,	1861,	$3,000
William W. H. Davis,	"	*Secretary of State*,		2,000

JUDICIARY.

Kirby Benedict,	of Albuquerque,	*Chief Justice*,	1862,	2,500
W. F. Boone,	of Santa Fé,	*Associate Justice*,	"	2,500
Wm. G. Blackwood,	"	"	1863,	2,500
R. H. Tompkins,	"	*Attorney*,	Fees and 250	
C. P. Clever,	"	*Marshal*,	Fees and 200	

XXXVI. WASHINGTON TERRITORY.

Area, 123,022 sq. m. *Estimated Population*, 1857, 10,000.

			Term ends.	Salary.
RICHARD D. GHOLSON,	of Olympia,	*Governor*,	1861,	$3,000
Charles H. Mason,	"	*Secretary*,		2,000

JUDICIARY.

Obadiah B. McFadden,	of Vancouver,	*Chief Justice*,	1862,	2,500
William Strong,	of Cathlamet,	*Associate Justice*,	"	2,500
E. C. Fitzhugh,	of Whatcomy,	"	"	2,500
——,	of Olympia,	*Attorney*,	Fees and 250	
Geo. W. Corliss,	"	*Marshal*,	Fees and 200	

XXXVII. KANSAS TERRITORY.

Area, 114,798 sq. m. *Estimated Population*, August, 1858, 75,000.

			Term ends.	Salary.
SAMUEL MEDARY,	of Leavenworth,	*Governor*,	1862,	$2,500
Hugh S. Walsh,	"	*Secretary*,		2,000

JUDICIARY.

John Pettit,	of Leavenworth,	*Chief Justice*,	1863,	2,000
Joseph Williams,	of Fort Scott,	*Associate Justice*,	1862,	2,000
Rush Elmore,	of Lecompton,	"	1862,	2,000
A. C. Davis,	of Wyandotte,	*Attorney*,	Fees and 250	
P. T. Colby,	of Leavenworth,	*Marshal*,	Fees and 200	

* For something relative to the proposed new Territories of Arizona, Dacotah, and Jefferson, see the Additions and Corrections, at the end of the volume.

XXXVIII. NEBRASKA TERRITORY.

Area, 335,866 sq. m. *Population*, 1856, 10,716.

			Term ends.	Salary.
Samuel W. Black,	of Omaha City,	*Governor*,	1863,	$ 2,500
Thomas B. Cuming,	"	*Secretary*,	1861,	2,000
	Judiciary			
Augustus Hall,	of Omaha City,	*Chief Justice*,	1861,	2,000
Joseph Miller,	"	*Associate Justice*,	1863,	2,000
Eleazer Wakeley,	"	"	1861,	2,000
L. L. Bowen,	"	*Attorney*,		Fees and 250
William A. West,	"	*Marshal*,		Fees and 200

XXXIX. DISTRICT OF COLUMBIA.

Area, 50 sq. m. *Population*, 1850, 51,687.

The District of Columbia is under the immediate government of Congress.

Judiciary.

			Salary.
	Circuit Court of the District.		
James Dunlop,	of Georgetown,	*Chief Justice*,	$2,700
James S. Morsell,	of Georgetown,	*Associate Justice*,	2,500
William M. Merrick,	of Washington,	"	2,500
Robert Ould,	"	*Attorney*,	Fees and 200
William Selden,	"	*Marshal*,	Fees.
John A. Smith,	"	*Clerk*,	Fees.*
	Criminal Court for the District.		
Thomas H. Crawford,	of Washington,	*Judge*,	$2,000
John A. Smith,	"	*Clerk*,	Fees.*
	Orphans' Court.		
W. F. Purcell,	of Washington,	*Judge*,	$1,500
Edward N. Roach,	"	*Register*,	Fees.

AMERICAN STATES.

1. *Governments of North America.*

Governments.		Area in Square Miles.	Population.	Capitals.	Governors, &c.
Danish America (Greenland),		390,000	9,400	Lichtenfels,	C. S. M. Olrick, *Insp.*†
French Possess'ns (St. Pierre, &c.)		118	200	St. Pierre,	E. de la Ronciere, *Com't.*
Russian America,		394,000	66,000	N. Archangel,	——— ———, *Gov.*
New Britain,	British,	1,800,000	180,000	York Factory,	Sir Geo. Simpson, *Mana.*
Canada West,	British,	147,832	999,847	Toronto,	Sir E. W. Head, Bt., *Gov.-Gen. of Brit. N. Amer.*
Canada East,	British,	201,989	890,261	Quebec,	
New Brunswick,	British,	27,700	200,000	Frederickton,	J. H. T. M. Sutton, *Lt.-G.*
Nova Scotia, &c.,	British,	18,746	300,000	Halifax,	Earl of Mulgrave, *do.*
Prince Edward's Island,	British,	2,134	62,348	CharlotteT'n,	George Dundas, *do.*
Newfoundland,	British,	57,000	120,000	St. John's,	Sir A. Bannerman, *Gov.*
British Columbia,		213,500	7,500	Ft. Langley,	Sir James Douglas, *do.*
United States of America,		3,306,934	23,191,876	Washington,	James Buchanan, *Pr.*
United States of Mexico,		1,033,865	7,200,000	Mexico,	Benito Juarez,¶ *do.*
San Salvador,		9,500	450,000	Cojutepeque,	Gen. G. Barrios, *do.*
Nicaragua,		141,000	400,000	Granada,	Gen. T. Martinez, *do.*
Honduras,		153,000	380,000	Comagagua,	Don Santos Guardiolado.
Guatemala,		59,000	1,100,000	N. Guatemala,	Don Rafael Carrera, *do.*
Costa Rica,		§23,000	200,000	San José,	J. M. Montealgre, *do.*
Mosquitia, ‖			6,000	Blewfields,	Jamaso (Indian), *King.*
Honduras (British Colony),			11,066	Balize	Fred. Seymour, *Supt.*
Total,		7,779,218	35,774,498		

* Fees limited to $3,500.

‡ These two include the area of Mosquitia.

‖ Annexed in 1846 to Nicaragua.

† Dr. H. Rink is Inspector of South Greenland.

§ Including area of Guanacaste.

¶ Gen. M. Miramon also claims to be President.

2. *West Indian Governments.*

Governments.	Area in Square Miles.	Population.	Capitals.	Governors, &c.
Hayti, San Domingo, *Em.*	11,000	800,000	Cape Hayt'n,	Fabre Geffrard, *Pres't.*
Dominica, *Rep.*	18,000	200,000	San Domingo,	J D. Valverde, *Pres't.*
Cuba, Spanish,	42,383	1,007,624	Havana,	Francis Gerrano, *Ct. G.*
Porto Rico,	3,865	500,000	San Juan,	F. Coton y Chacon, *do.*
Jamaica, British,	5,468	379,690	Spanish Town	C. H. Darling *Gov. Gen.*
Trinidad,	2,000	60,319	Puerta d'Esp.	Robt. W. Keate, *Gov.*
Windward Islands,			Bridgetown,	—— ——,
Barbadoes,	166	135,939	"	Francis Hincks, *Lt.-G.*
Grenada, &c.,	155	28,923		Cornelius Kortright, *do.*
St. Vincent,	131	27,248	Kingston,	W. C. Sergeaunt, *do.*
Tobago,	187	13,208	Scarboro',	Jas. V. Drysdale, *do.*
St. Lucia,	225	24,500	Castries,	—— ——, *do.*
Leeward Islands,			St. John's,	Edward J. Eyre, *Gov.*
Antigua,	168	36,178	"	[*and Com. in Chief.*
Montserrat,	49	7,365		E. Rushworth, *Pres't.*
St. Christopher and Anguilla,	103	24,508	Basseterre,	Sir B. C. Pine, *Lt. G.*
Nevis,	30	10,200	Charlestown,	A. H. Rumbold, *Pres't.*
Virgin Islands,	137	4,027		Thomas Price, *do.*
Dominica,	291	22,469	Rosseau,	H St. G. Ord, *Lt.-Gov.*
Bahama Islands,	5,422	27,519	Nassau,	Chas J. Bayley, *Gov.*
Turk's Island,	400	3,400		W. R. Inglis, *Pres't.*
Bermuda Islands,	47	14,000	Hamilton,	Col. F. Murray, *Gov.*
Guadalupe, &c.,	534	134,514	Basseterre,	P. V. Touchard, *do.*
Martinique, French,	322	121,145	Port Royal,	M. de Candé, *do.*
St. Martin's, N. Side,	21	2,200		—— ——, *do.*
St. Martin's, S. Side, — Dutch,	11	3,500		—— ——, *do.*
Curaçoa, &c., — Dutch,	580	26,311	Wilhemstadt,	J. D. Crol, *do.*
Santa Cruz, &c.,	81	35,000	Christ'nstadt,	J. F. Schlegel, *Gov. of*
St. Thomas, Danish,	37	8,000		*the Danish W. India*
St. John's,	72	3,000		*Islands.*
St. Bartholomew's, — Swedish,	25	9,000	La Carenage,	—— ——, *Gov.*
Total,	94,910	3,669,817		

3. *Governments of South America.*

Governments.	Area in Square Miles.	Population.	Capitals.	Governors, &c.
Venezuela, *Republic,*	416,600	1,356,000	Caraccas,	M. F. Tovar, *Pres.*
Ecuador, *do.*	325,000	665,000	Quito,	Francisco Robles, *do.*
Bolivia, *do.*	374,480	1,650,000	Chuquisaca,	J. M. Linares, *Pr. Pr.*
Peru, *do.*	580,000	2,400,000	Lima,	Ramon Castilla, *Pres.*
Chili, *do.*	170,000	1,439,120	Santiago,	Manuel Montt, *do.*
Granadian Confederation,	380,000	2,363,000	Sta Fé de Bog.	M. Ospina, *do.*
Argentine Confederation,	927,000	874,000	Parana,	J. J. Urquiza, *do.*
Buenos Ayres, *Republic,*	60,000	350,000	Buenos Ayres,	Don Valen. Alsina, *Gov.*
Uruguay, The Oriental Repub. of,	120,000	250,000	Montevideo,	Gab. Ant. Pereyra, *Pres.*
Paraguay, *Republic,*	74,000	600,000	Asunçion,	Carlos Ant. Lopez, *do.*
Brazil, *Empire of,*	2,300,000	7,677,800	Rio de Janeiro	Pedro II., *Emperor.**
Guiana (*British*),	76,000	127,695	Georgetown,	P. E. Woodhouse, *Lt. G.*
Guiana (*Dutch*),	38,500	64,270	Paramaribo,	C. J. M. Nagtglas, *Gov.*
Guiana (*French*),	21,500	30,000	Cayenne,	Tardy de Montravel, *do.*
Patagonia,	380,000	120,000		(Native Chiefs.)
Falkland Islands,	16,000	500	Port Louis,	T. E. L. Moore.
Total,	6,259,080	19,967,385		
Grand Total of America,	14,130,208	59,411,700		

POPULATION OF THE GLOBE.

Africa, variously estimated from 60,000,000 to	200,000,000
America (as above), ...	59,411,700
Asia, including Islands, ...	755,000,000
Australia and Australian group of Islands, ...	1,445,000
Europe (as on p. 363), ...	277,932,296
Polynesia (a mere estimate, as there are few or no data), ...	1,500,000
Total population of the Globe, ...	1,295,288,996

* Born Dec 2, 1825; ascended the throne April 7, 1831.

31

EUROPE.

REIGNING SOVEREIGNS OF EUROPE.

September 15, 1859.

State.	Name.	Title.	Date of Birth.	Date of Accession.	Age at Accession.	Religion.
Anhalt-Bernburg	Alexander	Duke	Mar. 2, 1805	Mar. 24, 1834	29	Evangelical
Anhalt-Dessau	Leopold	"	Oct. 1, 1794	Aug. 9, 1817	22	"
Austria	Francis Joseph	Emperor	Aug. 18, 1830	Dec. 2, 1848	18	Catholic
Baden	Frederic	Grand Duke	Sept. 9, 1826	Apr. 24, 1852	26	Evangelical
Bavaria	Maximilian II.	King	Nov. 28, 1811	Mar. 21, 1848	36	Catholic
Belgium	Leopold	"	Dec. 16, 1790	July 21, 1831	40	Lutheran†
Brunswick	William	Duke	Apr. 25, 1806	Apr. 25, 1831	25	"
Denmark	Frederic VII.	King	Oct. 6, 1808	Jan. 20, 1846	39	"
France	Napoleon III.	Emperor	Apr. 20, 1808	Dec. 2, 1852	44	Catholic
Great Britain	Victoria	Queen	May 24, 1819	June 20, 1837	18	Prot. Episc.
Greece	Otho	King	June 1, 1815	May 7, 1832	17	Catholic†
Hanover	George V.	"	May 27, 1819	Nov. 18, 1851	33	Evangelical
Hesse-Cassel	Frederic Wm.	Elector	Aug. 20, 1802	Nov. 20, 1847	45	Reformed
Hesse-Darmstadt	Louis III.	Grand Duke	June 9, 1806	June 16, 1848	42	Lutheran
Hesse-Homburg	Ferdinand	Landgrave	Apr. 26, 1783	Sept. 8, 1848	65	Reformed
Holland or Netherlands	William III.	King	Feb. 19, 1817	Mar. 17, 1849	32	"
Leichtenstein	John	Prince	Oct. 5, 1840	Nov. 12, 1858	18	Catholic
Lippe	Leopold	"	Sept. 1, 1821	Jan. 1, 1851	30	Reformed
Lippe-Schaumburg	George	"	Dec. 20, 1784	Feb. 13, 1787	2	"
Mecklenburg-Schwer.	Fred. Francis	Grand Duke	Feb. 28, 1823	Mar. 7, 1842	19	Lutheran
Mecklenburg-Strelitz	George	"	Aug. 12, 1779	Nov. 6, 1816	37	"
Modena and Massa	*					Catholic
Monaco	Chas. Honoré	Prince	Dec. 8, 1818	June 20, 1856	37	"
Nassau	Adolphus	Duke	July 24, 1817	Aug. 20, 1839	22	Evangelical
Oldenburg	Peter	Grand Duke	July 8, 1827	Feb. 27, 1853	26	Lutheran
Parma	*					Catholic
Portugal	Pedro V.‡	King	Sept. 16, 1837	Nov. 15, 1853	16	"
Prussia	Fred. Wm. IV.	"	Oct. 15, 1795	June 7, 1840	45	Evangelical
Reuss, Elder Line,	Henry XX.	Prince	June 29, 1794	Oct. 31, 1836	42	Lutheran
Reuss, Younger Line,	Henry LXVII.	"	Oct. 20, 1789	June 19, 1854	64	"
Russia	Alexander II.	Emperor	Apr. 29, 1818	Mar. 2, 1855	37	Greek Church
Sardinia	Vict. Eman. II.	King	Mar. 14, 1820	Mar. 23, 1849	29	Catholic
Saxe-Altenburg	Ernest	Duke	Sept. 16, 1826	Aug. 3, 1853	26	Lutheran
Saxe-Coburg-Gotha	Ernest II.	"	June 21, 1818	Jan. 29, 1844	25	"
Saxe-Meiningen	Bernard	"	Dec. 17, 1800	Dec. 24, 1803	3	"
Saxe-Weim.-Eisenach	Chs. Alexander	Grand Duke	June 24, 1818	July 8, 1853	35	"
Saxony	John	King	Dec. 12, 1801	Aug. 9, 1854	52	Catholic†
Schwarzburg-Rudolst.	Fred. Gunther.	Prince	Nov. 6, 1793	Apr. 28, 1807	13	Lutheran
Schwarz'g-Sonder'n,	Gunther	"	Sept. 24, 1801	Aug. 19, 1835	35	"
Spain	Isabella II.	Queen	Oct. 10, 1830	Sept. 29, 1833	3	Catholic
States of the Church	Pius IX.	Pope	May 13, 1792	June 16, 1846	54	"
Sweden and Norway	Charles XV.	King	May 3, 1826	July 8, 1859	33	Lutheran
Turkey	Abdul Medjid	Sultan	Apr. 20, 1823	July 1, 1839	16	Mahometan†
Tuscany	*					Catholic
Two Sicilies	Francis II.	King	Jan 16, 1836	May 22, 1859	23	"
Waldeck	George Victor	Prince	Jan. 14, 1831	May 15, 1845	14	Evangelical
Wurtemberg	William I.	King	Sept. 27, 1781	Oct. 30, 1816	35	Lutheran

* Chevalier Buoncompagni is Governor-General of the League of the Provinces of Central Italy.

† The King of Belgium is a *Protestant*, though his subjects are chiefly *Catholics*; the King of Saxony is a *Catholic*, though the greater part of his subjects are *Protestants*; and the King of Greece is a *Catholic*, though most of his subjects are of the *Greek Church*. Of the 16,440,000 European subjects of the Sultan of Turkey, 10,435,079 are Christians, and 6,004,921 are Mahometans.

‡ His father, Ferdinand, husband of the late queen, was regent until Sept. 16, 1855.

STATES OF EUROPE,§

With the Form of Government, and Square Miles, according to McCulloch's Geographical Dictionary, with Corrections; and the Population (chiefly) from the Almanach de Gotha for 1860.

States and Titles.	Form of Government.	Square Miles.	Population.	Date of Enum'n.
Andorra, Pyrenees, *Repub.*	With two syndics and a council,	190	7,000	
*Anhalt-Bernburg, *Duchy,*	States having limited powers,	339	56,031	1859
*Anhalt-Dessau-Cöthen,	" "	678	119,515	1859
*Austria, *Empire,*	Absolute monarchy,	255,226	39,411,309	1854
*Baden, *Grand Duchy,*	Limited sovereignty; two chambers,	5,712	1,389,952	1858
*Bavaria, *Kingdom,*	Limited monarchy; "	28,435	4,615,748	1858
Belgium, "	" "	11,313	4,623,089	1859
*Bremen, *Free City,*	Republic; senate and assembly,	112	88,856	1855
*Brunswick, *Duchy,*	Limited sovereignty; one chamber,	1,525	273,394	1858
Church, States of, *Popedom,*	Absolute sovereignty,	17,048	3,124,668	1853
Denmark, *Kingdom,*	Limited monarchy; with prov. states,	21,856	2,915,000	*a* 1859
France, *Empire,*	Const. mon.; senate and legislat. body,	203,736	36,039,364	*b* 1856
*Frankfort, *Free City,*	Republic; senate and assembly,	91	79,278	1859
Great Britain, *Kingdom,*	Limited monarchy; lords and commons,	116,700	28,416,506	*c* 1857
Greece, "	Limited monarchy; two chambers,	18,244	1,067,216	1856
*Hamburg, *Free City,*	Republic; senate and assembly,	149	222,379	1859
*Hanover, *Kingdom,*	Limited monarchy; two chambers,	14,600	1,843,978	1859
*Hesse-Cassel, *Electorate,*	Limited sovereignty; two chambers,	4,430	726,739	1859
*Hesse-Darmstadt, *G. Duch.,*	Limited sovereignty; two chambers,	3,761	845,571	1858
*Hesse-Homb'g, *Landg'v'te,*	Absolute sovereignty; one chamber,	206	25,746	1858
Holland, with Luxemburg,	Limited monarchy; two chambers,	13,890	3,543,775	*c* 1859
Ionian Islands, *Republic,*	Under Brit. protec.; council and chamb.	1,097	246,483	1858
*Lichtenstein, *Principal.,*	Limited monarchy; with one chamber,	52	7,150	1857
*Lippe, "	" "	445	106,086	1858
*Lippe-Schaumburg, "	" "	205	30,144	1858
*Lubec, *Free City,*	Republic; senate and assembly,	142	55,423	1857
*Mecklen.-Schwerin, *G. Du.*	Limited sovereignty; with one chamber,	4,701	542,148	1859
*Mecklenburg-Strelitz, "	" "	997	99,628	1851
Modena and Massa, *Duchy,*		2,073	604,512	1857
Monaco, *Principality,*	Absolute sovereignty,	50	7,000	
*Nassau, *Duchy,*	Limited sovereignty; two chambers,	1,736	439,454	1859
*Oldenburg, *Grand Duchy,*	" "	2,470	294,359	1858
Parma, *Duchy,*		2,184	499,835	1857
Portugal, *Kingdom,*	Limited monarchy; two chambers,	34,500	3,568,895	*c* 1857
*Prussia, "	" "	107,300	17,739,913	1858
*Reuss, *Principalities of,*	Limited sovereignty; one chamber,	588	120,203	1859
†Russia (in Europe), *Empire,*	Absolute monarchy,	2,120,397	63,472,706	*c* 1856
San Marino, *Republic,*	Senate and council of ancients,	21	8,000	1858
Sardinia, *Kingdom,*	Limited monarchy; two chambers,	28,830	5,167,542	1857
*Saxony, "	Limited monarchy; two chambers,	5,705	2,122,148	1858
*Saxe-Altenburg, *Duchy,*	Limited sovereignty; one chamber,	491	134,659	1859
*Saxe-Coburg & Gotha, "	Lim. sov.; one chamb. for each duchy,	790	153,879	1859
*Saxe-Mein.-Hildburgh. "	Limited sovereignty; one chamber,	968	168,816	1858
*Saxe-Weim.-Eisenach, "	" "	1,403	267,112	1859
*Schwarzburg-Rudolst., *Pr.*	" "	405	70,036	1859
*Schwarzburg-Sondersh., "	" "	358	82,974	1859
Sicilies, The Two, *Kingdom,*	Absolute monarchy,	41,521	9,117,050	1856
Spain, "	Limited monarchy; with a legislature,	176,480	15,867,753	*c* 1855
Sweden, } "	Limited monarchy; with a legislature,	170,715	3,639,332	1857
Norway, }		121,725	1,490,047	1855
Switzerland, *Republic.*	Confederation of republics; a diet,	15,261	2,391,478	1850
‡Turkey (in Europe), *Emp.*	Absolute monarchy,	189,920	16,440,000	1845
Tuscany, *Grand Duchy,*		8,712	1,793,967	1858
*Waldeck, *Principality,*	Limited sovereignty; one chamber,	455	57,550	1858
*Wurtemberg, *Kingdom,*	Limited monarchy; two chambers,	7,568	1,690,898	1858
	Total,	3,768,506	277,932,296	

* Member of the Confederation of Germany.

† Including Poland (4,696,919) and Finland (1,632,977).

‡ Including Wallachia, Moldavia, and Servia, containing respectively 1,800,000, 1,200,000, and 1,100,000 inhabitants. Including Turkey in Asia and African possessions, the population in 1844 was 36,600,000.

a Exclusive of Iceland, with a population in 1855 of 64,603, and an area of 32,000 square miles, and other colonies with a population of 55,680, but including the Duchies of Schleswig, Holstein, and Lauenburg.

b Exclusive of the colonies, with a population (in 1858) of 4,070,124.

c The colonies and dependencies of Great Britain have, besides, a population stated at 187,661,739; those of Holland, 20,080,536; of Portugal, 2,759,412; of Russia, 7,771,910; and of Spain, 5,022,731.

§ Important changes have since been made by the peace of Villafranca (July 11, 1859). "The

GREAT BRITAIN.

The Royal Family.

The Queen. Alexandrina Victoria, born May 24, 1819; succeeded her uncle, William IV., June 20, 1837; was crowned, June 28, 1838; married, Feb. 10, 1840, to Albert Francis Augustus Charles Emanuel, Duke of Saxe-Coburg and Gotha, Prince Consort, born Aug. 26, 1819. *Issue*, Victoria Adelaide Mary Louisa, Princess Royal, born Nov. 21, 1840; married to Prince Frederic William of Prussia, Jan. 25, 1858; Albert Edward, Prince of Wales, born Nov. 9, 1841; Alice Maud Mary, born April 25, 1843; Alfred Ernest Albert, born Aug 6, 1844; Helena Augusta Victoria, born May 25, 1846; Louisa Caroline Alberta, born March 18, 1848; Arthur William Patrick Albert, born May 1, 1850; Leopold George Duncan Albert, born April 7, 1853; Beatrice Mary Victoria Feodore, born April 14, 1857.

Ministry. — *Formed June, 1859.*

		Salary.
Viscount Palmerston,	*First Lord of the Treasury,*	£5,000
W. E. Gladstone,	*Chancellor of the Exchequer,*	5,000
Sir G. Cornwall Lewis,	*Secretary of State, — Home Dep.,*	5,000
Lord John Russell,	*Secretary of State, — Foreign Dep.,*	5,000
Duke of Newcastle,	*Secretary of State, — Colonial Dep.,*	5,000
Sidney Herbert,	*Secretary of State, — War Dep.,*	5,000
Sir C. Wood,	*Secretary of State, — for India,*	5,000
Duke of Somerset,	*First Lord of the Admiralty,*	4,500
Lord Campbell,	*Lord High Chancellor,*	10,000
Earl of Granville,	*Lord President of the Council,*	2,000
Duke of Argyll,	*Lord Privy Seal,*	2,000
Earl of Elgin,	*Postmaster-General,*	2,500
Charles P. Villiers,	*President of the Poor-Law Board,*	2,000
Thomas Milner Gibson,	*President of the Board of Trade,*	2,000
Sir George Grey,	*Chancellor of the Duchy of Lancaster,*	2,000
E. Cardwell,	*Chief Secretary for Ireland,*	5,500

*** *The above form the Cabinet.*

Duke of Cambridge,	*Commander-in-Chief of the Forces,*	3,460
Earl of Carlisle,	*Lord Lieutenant of Ireland,*	20,000
Sir R. Bethell,	*Attorney-General,*	5,500
William Atherton,	*Solicitor-General,*	2,580
T. E. Headlam,	*Judge-Advocate-General.*	
Robert Lowe,	*Vice-President of the Committee of the Privy Council on Education.*	
Viscount Sydney,	*Lord Chamberlain.*	
Duchess of Sutherland,	*Mistress of the Robes.*	
Earl St. Germans,	*Lord Steward.*	
Henry Fitzroy,	*First Commissioner of Public Works,*	2,000

Judiciary.

England.

High Court of Chancery. — Lord Campbell (b. 1779, ap. 1859), *Lord High Chancellor*, salary, £10,000; Sir John Romilly (ap. 1851), *Master of the*

Emperor of Austria cedes to the Emperor of the French his rights over Lombardy, with the exception of the fortresses of Peschiera and Mantua, so that the frontier of the Austrian possessions shall start from the extreme range of the fortress of Peschiera, and shall extend in a direct line along the Mincio as far as Grazio, thence by Scorzarolo and Luzzera to the Po, whence the actual frontiers shall continue to form the limits of Austria. The Emperor of the French will hand over (*remettra*) the ceded territory to the King of Sardinia." Tuscany, Modena, Parma, and the Roman Legations have by elective votes and formal decrees annexed themselves to Sardinia, and Victor Emanuel has accepted the annexations subject to the decision of a Congress

Rolls, £7,000; Sir R. T. Kindersley (b. 1792, ap. 1851), Sir John Stuart (b. 1793, ap. 1852), Sir William Page Wood (b. 1801, ap. 1853), *Vice-Chancellors*, £6,000 each.

Court of Appeal in Chancery. — Rt. Hon. Sir James L. Knight Bruce (b. 1791, ap. 1851), Rt. Hon. Sir George James Turner (b. 1798, ap. 1851), *Lords Justices*, £6,000 each.

Court of Queen's Bench. — Sir Alexander J. E. Cockburn (ap. 1859), *Lord Chief Justice*, £8,000; Sir Wm. Wightman (ap. 1841), Sir Charles Crompton (b. 1797, ap. 1852), Sir Hugh Hill (ap. 1858), and Colin Blackburn (ap. 1859), *Judges*, £5,500 each.

Court of Common Pleas. — Sir William Erle (b. 1793, ap. 1859), *Lord Chief Justice*, £7,000; Sir Edw. Vaughan Williams (ap. 1847), Sir James Shaw Willes (ap. 1855), Sir John Barnard Byles (ap. 1858), and Sir H. S. Keating (ap. 1859), *Judges*, £5,500 each.

Court of Exchequer. — Rt. Hon. Sir Frederic J. Pollock (b. 1783, ap. 1844), *Lord Chief Baron*, £7,000; Sir Samuel Martin (ap. 1850), Sir George W. W. Bramwell (ap. 1856), Sir W. H. Watson (ap. 1856), and Sir William Fry Channell (ap. 1857), *Barons*, £5,500 each.

Court of Probate, and Court of Divorce and Matrimonial Causes. — Rt. Hon. Sir Creswell Creswell, *Judge Ordinary*.

Admiralty Court. — *Judge*, Rt. Hon. S. Lushington (b. 1782, ap. 1838); *Queen's Advocate*, Sir J. D. Harding; *Admiralty Advocate*, Dr. J. Phillimore.

Court of Bankruptcy. — *Lords Justices of Appeal*, Sir J. L. Knight Bruce, Sir George J. Turner; *Chief Registrar*, W. H. Whitehead.

Insolvent Debtors' Court. — *Chief Commissioner*, William James Law; *Commissioner*, J. S. Murphy; *Chief Clerk*, H. Simpson.

Scotland.

Court of Session: Inner House. — *1st Division*. Duncan McNeill, *Lord* Colonsay (b. 1794, ap. 1852), *Lord President*, £4,800. James Ivory, *Lord* Ivory; John Marshall, *Lord* Curriehill (ap. 1855); Sir George Deas, *Lord* Deas (ap. 1855), *Judges*, £3,000 each.

Inner House: 2d Division. — Rt. Hon. John Inglis, *Lord* Glencoe, *Lord Justice Clerk*, £4,500. Alexander Wood, *Lord* Wood; John Cowan, *Lord* Cowan; Hercules J. Robertson, *Lord* Benholme, *Judges*; £3,000 each.

Outer House: Permanent Lords Ordinary. — Charles Neaves, *Lord* Neaves; James Craufurd, *Lord* Ardmillan; Thomas Mackenzie, *Lord* Mackenzie (ap. 1855); William Penney, *Lord* Kinloch (ap. 1858); Charles Baillie, *Lord* Jerviswoode (ap. 1859); £3,000 each. James Moncrieff, *Lord Advocate*, £2,500 and fees. Edward Francis Maitland, *Solicitor-General*, £1,000.

Court of Justiciary. — *Lord Justice General*, Duncan McNeill; *Lord Justice Clerk*, Rt. Hon. John Inglis; *Commissioners*, Lords Cowan, Ivory, Deas, Ardmillan, and Neaves.

There is no division of common law, equity, civil law, or admiralty; but the whole business, civil and criminal, original and appellate, is discharged by the Court of Session.

Ireland.

Court of Chancery. — Rt. Hon. Maziere Brady (ap. 1859), *Lord Chancellor*, £8,000; Rt. Hon. T. B. C. Smith (ap. 1846), *Master of the Rolls*, £4,300.

Court of Queen's Bench. — Rt. Hon. Thos. Lefroy, *Lord Chief Justice*, £5,074. Rt. Hon. Louis Perrin (ap. 1836), Rt. Hon. John O'Brien (ap. 1858), Rt. Hon. Edm. Hayes, *Judges*, £3,688 each.

Court of Common Pleas. — Rt. Hon. James Henry Monahan (ap. 1850), *Lord Chief Justice*, £4,615; Rt. Hon. Nicholas Ball (b. 1791, ap. 1839), Rt. Hon. William Keogh (ap. 1856), and Rt. Hon. Jonathan Christian (ap.

1858), *Judges*, £3,688 each. *Attorney-General*, Rt. Hon. John David Fitzgerald. *Solicitor-General*, Sergeant Deasy.

Court of Exchequer. — Rt. Hon. David R. Pigott (ap. 1846), *Lord Chief Baron;* Rt. Hon. F. Fitzgerald, Rt. Hon. H. G. Hughes, Rt. Hon. Richard W. Greene (ap. 1852), *Barons*, £3,688 each.

Ecclesiastical Courts. — Rt. Hon. R. Keatinge, *Judge of Court of Probate.* Joseph Radcliff, *Vicar-General.*

Court of Admiralty. — T. F. Kelly, *Judge.* Joseph Radcliff, *Surrogate.*

Court of Appeal. — Rt. Hon. Francis Blackburne, *Lord Justice*, ap. 1856.

Parliament.

The Parliament of Great Britain consists of a House of Lords and a House of Commons. The present is the 18th Imperial or 8th Reformed Parliament. The House of Lords has 462 members.

The present House of Commons, John Evelyn Denison, Speaker, was elected in June, 1859. It numbers 654 members.

MINISTRY OF FRANCE.

State. M. Achille Fould.
Justice. M. Delangle.
Foreign Affairs. Count Walewski.
Interior. Duc de Padoue.
Finance. M. Magne.
War. Maréchal Randon.
Marine. Admiral Hamelin.
Public Instruction. M. Rouland.
Agriculture, Commerce, and Public Works. M. Rouher.
Algeria and the Colonies. Count Prosper de Chasseloup-Laubat.
President of the Council of State. M. Baroche.

AMERICAN OBITUARY.

1858.

Sept. 3. — In Winchester, Ky., *Hon. Chilton Allen*, aged 73. He was born in Albemarle County, Virginia, and moved while a lad to Kentucky. In 1807 he removed to Winchester, first teaching school, then studying law, and afterwards practising his profession there. In 1811 he was elected a member of the State Legislature, and subsequently served in both branches for many years. He was elected to Congress in 1831, and was a member of the House from 1831 to 1837. In 1837 and 1838 he was President of the Board of Internal Improvement in Kentucky.

Nov. 29. — In New York City, *Cornelius V. Anderson*, formerly Chief Engineer of the Fire Department in that city, and at the time of his death one of the Board of Ten Governors.

Dec. 6. — In Alexandria, Va., *Thomas C. Atkinson*, a native of Baltimore, but for nine years a resident of Alexandria. He was the Chief Engineer of the Orange and Alexandria Railroad from the beginning of the work.

Sept. 15. — In Boston, Mass., *Samuel Austin*, aged 65. He was born in Boston, and here passed his whole life. In 1816 he entered mercantile business and continued in it until his death. He was extensively engaged in the Calcutta trade and amassed a large fortune. He was elected a State Representative in 1827, and was re-elected for the six following years. He was a member of the Common Council of Boston in 1829 and 1830. He was a Director in the State Bank from 1824 to the time of his death.

Nov. 4. — In Rochester, N. Y., *Dr. Frederic F. Backus*, aged 64. He was a native of Connecticut. He had been in the active practice of medicine in Rochester since 1815. He was State Senator in 1842, and in 1846 was a member of the Constitutional Convention. At his death he was President of the Board of Managers of the Western House of Refuge. While in the Senate he was conspicuous for his intelligent and earnest advocacy of liberal aid to asylums and hospitals, and his able report on the Education of Idiots gave an impulse to the movement in this country in behalf of that class of unfortunates.

Sept. 21. — In Mobile, Ala., *Hon. Arthur P. Bagby*, aged 64. He was born in Virginia in 1794, and studied law. He settled in Alabama in 1818. He was a member of the Alabama Legislature in 1820 and 1822, and was Speaker of the House. He was Governor of Alabama from 1837 to 1841, and was Senator in Congress from that State from 1843 to 1849. He was appointed Minister to Russia in 1849, and held that mission for four years.

Nov. 20. — In Boston, Mass., *Adams Bailey*, aged 69. He was a native of Scituate, Mass. With an interval of two years, he held office in the Boston Custom-House for a period of forty-two years, and was for near half of the time Deputy Collector. He was for many years Secretary of the Massachusetts Society of Cincinnati.

Oct. 1. — In Boston, Mass., *Joseph A. Ballard*, aged 53. He had been connected with the shipping department of the Boston Daily Advertiser for many years, and by his industry and exactness had gained an excellent reputation; and he was exemplary in his private and social relations.

Dec. 15. — In Baltimore County, Md., *Samuel Barnes, Esq.*, aged 72, for many years the editor of a paper at Frederick, Maryland, and more recently editor of the Baltimore Clipper.

Nov. 26. — Near Shephardstown, Va., *Hon. Henry Bedinger*. He was a Representative in Congress from Virginia from 1845 to 1849, and had but recently returned home from five years' service (from 1853 to 1858) as Minister to Denmark, where he negotiated the treaty settling the vexed question of the Sound dues.

Sept. 22. — In New Haven, Conn., *Timothy P. Beers, M. D.*, aged 69. He was born in New Haven, December 25, 1789, graduated at Yale College in 1808, and there resided occupied with his duties as medical practitioner. In 1830 he was appointed a Professor in the Medical Department of Yale College, and continued in that office until his resignation in 1846.

Sept. 10. — In Pittsburg, Pa., *Rev. A. W. Black, D. D.*, an eminent divine of the Reformed Presbyterian Church. He had been recently appointed Professor of Biblical Literature in the theological seminary of that denomination in Philadelphia.

Nov. 26. — In Indianapolis, Ind., *Nathaniel P. Bolton*, late United States Consul in Geneva, and for a long time connected with the press in Indiana.

Dec. 26. — In Georgetown, Mass., *Rev. Isaac Braman*, aged 88. He was born in Norton, Massachusetts, July 5, 1770; graduated at Harvard College in 1794; studied theology, and was settled in 1797 in New Rowley, now Georgetown. The parish had been destitute of a minister nine years, and he was the last of sixty-four candidates who preached there on probation. He continued their pastor for sixty-one years, until his death, having latterly a colleague.

Nov. 8. — In Paris, France. *Hon. Benjamin F. Butler*, of New York City, aged 62. He was born in Kinderhook, New York, Dec. 15, 1795; studied law with Martin Van Buren, and on being admitted to the bar became his partner, and at once took rank as an able practitioner and intelligent lawyer. He served in the State Assembly, and with John Duer and John C. Spencer, he revised the Statutes of New York. He was Attorney-General of the United States during part of General Jackson's administration, and was afterwards for a time United States District Attorney for the Southern District of New York. Worn out by overwork in his profession, he sailed for Europe, October 15th, to attempt to recover his health. Distinguished honors are paid to his memory by the New York bar.

Oct. 15. — In Brunswick, Me., *Parker Cleaveland, LL. D.*, aged 78. He was born in Rowley (Byfield Parish), Massachusetts, January 15, 1780, graduated at Harvard College in 1799, taught school and studied law until 1803, when he was appointed Tutor in Mathematics in Harvard College. He was made Professor of Mathematics and Natural Philosophy, Chemistry, and Mineralogy in Bowdoin College in 1805, and discharged with distinguished ability the extended duties of that professorship until 1828, when a Professor of Mathematics was appointed, and he was relieved from that part of his labor. He continued to be the Professor in the other departments until his death. He became widely known in the United States, and in Europe, by his early and successful treatise on Mineralogy and Geology published in 1816, and in a second edition in 1822. A third edition was called for, and he labored in its preparation more or less for thirty-five years, leaving it nearly ready for the press. His high reputation as a lecturer was spread through the country by a succession of graduates of Bowdoin College of more than fifty years. He was a member of the American Academy of Arts and Sciences, and of many literary and scientific societies in this country and in Europe. In 1824, the honorary degree of Doctor of Laws was conferred upon him by Bowdoin College. In private life he was universally respected for his unblemished moral character, and his genial and affable disposition. His death called forth unusual and remarkable demonstrations of respect to his character and memory.

Nov. 21. — In Hartford, Conn., *Dr. John L. Comstock*, widely known as the author of valuable text-books in Natural History, Chemistry, &c.

Aug. 18. — In Hartford, Conn., *Dr. Abiel A. Cooley*, aged 76, said to be the inventor of friction matches.

Near Nov. 1. — In New York City, *Rev. Frederic Crowe*. He was born in Belgium, and was the son of a British subject. He labored for thirteen years in the dissemination of the Scriptures in Spanish America, and was the author of a valuable historical work on Central America. He was expelled from San Salvador, as is said by the Catholics, because he circulated the Bible, and intended to open a school in San Miguel.

Oct. 20. — In New London, Conn., *Constans F. Daniels*, aged 69. He was educated for the legal profession, and was for many years connected with the press in South Carolina, in the city of New York, and afterwards in New London, where he edited the New London Chronicle.

Oct. 4. — In Philadelphia, Pa., *Aaron Ogden Dayton, Esq.*, of Washington, D. C., for twenty years Fourth Auditor of the Treasury Department.

Sept. 28. — In Charleston, S. C., *Rev. Henry Mandeville Denison*, Rector of St. Peter's Church in that city. He was a native of Pennsylvania, and was educated at the Episcopal seminary in Virginia. He was first settled in Greenville, South Carolina, then in Brooklyn, New York, and then as Rector in Louisville, Kentucky.

Aug. 9. — In the Island of Mackinac, *William Draper* of Pontiac, Michigan, aged 78. Mr. Draper was born in Dedham, Massachusetts, and graduated at Harvard College in 1803. After completing his legal studies he opened an office in Marlborough, Massachusetts. In 1832 he went to Nashua, New Hampshire, and in 1833 he removed to Michigan, and established himself at Pontiac, where he remained during the rest of his life.

Nov. — In Morrisania, N. Y., *Mary Anne Dwight*, aged 52. She was a native of Northampton, Massachusetts, and was a woman of literary capacity and cultivation. She published in 1849 a work on Grecian and Roman mythology, and had prepared for the press an abridgment of Lauzi's History of Painting.

Dec. 27. — In New Haven, Conn., *Henry L. Ellsworth*, aged 67. He was son of Hon. Oliver Ellsworth, of Windsor, Connecticut, and was born November 10, 1791. He graduated at Yale College in 1810, studied law and practised in Windsor and in Hartford, Connecticut. He was appointed by General Jackson Commissioner among the Indian Tribes south and west of Arkansas. About two years later he was appointed Commissioner of Patents of the United States. While in this office he gave special attention to the agricultural interests of the country, and published valuable reports on these subjects. After about ten years he left the Patent Office, and established himself at Lafayette, Indiana, in the settlement and cultivation of extensive tracts of land. He gave a great impulse to the agricultural enterprise of that State. His health failing under the burden of his numerous labors, he determined to return to his native State, and removed to the village of Fair Haven, in the town of New Haven, a few months before his decease.

Dec. 22. — In New Orleans, La., *Hon. George Eustis*, aged 62. He was born in Boston in 1796, graduated at Harvard College in 1815, was soon after private secretary to his uncle, Governor William Eustis, then Minister to the Hague, where he commenced his legal studies, and laid the foundation of his remarkable proficiency in the civil law. In 1817 he went to New Orleans, completed the study of his profession, and was admitted to the bar. He was several times elected to the State Legislature, was Secretary of State for Louisiana, and as a leading commissioner of the Board of Currency he instituted reforms which added stability to the currency of the State. He was also Attorney-General of

Louisiana, and a Justice and afterwards a Chief Justice of the Supreme Court of the State. He was a member of the constitutional convention of 1845. When the present constitution was adopted in 1852, he withdrew to private life, being entirely opposed to the principle of an elective judiciary. He had a high reputation as a jurist. The Bar of New Orleans paid a warm tribute of respect to his memory.

Sept. — In Genoa, *E. Felice Foresti*, United States Consul at that place. He was arrested January 7, 1819, with other youthful adherents of Carbonarism, by the Chief of Police of Venice, and committed to prison, in November, 1821; he was condemned to death December 25, 1821; — the condemned were led to the scaffold, when the sentence was commuted to imprisonment, and he was imprisoned in Spielberg until 1836, when he was released and transported to America.

Sept. 21. — In Boston, Mass., *Ebenezer Francis*, aged 82. He was born in Beverly, Massachusetts, October 15, 1775. His father, Colonel Ebenezer Francis, was an officer in the Revolutionary army, and was killed in battle in 1777. Mr. Francis came to Boston while quite young, and engaged in mercantile pursuits. He was eminently successful, and for some years had been the wealthiest man in Boston, if not in New England. He left a fortune of not less than three and a half millions of dollars. He was President of the Suffolk Bank from 1818 to 1825, and Director for nine years afterwards. While President he originated what is known as the "Suffolk Bank System," requiring other banks in the State and New England to redeem their bills in Boston. He was an efficient agent in establishing the Massachusetts General Hospital, and was for several years its President and Chairman of its Trustees. He was Treasurer of Harvard College from 1827 to 1830, and established order in the financial affairs of that institution. In 1843 he received from the College the honorary degree of Master of Arts. In his business transactions he was distinguished for his strict integrity, and in private life was social and affable.

Dec. 8. — In Concord, Mass., *Rev. Barzillai Frost*, aged 54. He was born in Effingham, New Hampshire; graduated at Harvard College in 1830; studied theology at the Divinity School in Cambridge; was instructor in mathematics to the undergraduates for two years; was settled in 1837 in Concord, and continued to be pastor there until October, 1857, when his failing health compelled him to give up his professional duties.

Dec. 26. — In Charleston, S. C., *Hon. James Gadsden*, aged 70. He was born in Charleston, May 15, 1788, was graduated at Yale College in 1806, and entered public life at an early age. He served in the war of 1812, and at its close was confidential aid-de-camp of General Jackson, and accompanied him in the Seminole war. In 1853 President Pierce appointed him Minister to Mexico. Through his agency was made from Mexico the celebrated "Gadsden Purchase" for ten millions of dollars.

Sept. 21. — In New York City, *José de Garay*, aged 57. He was born in Mexico, September 21, 1801. He was well known in the United States as the projector of the Tehuantepec Transit route, for which he obtained the grant from Santa Anna in 1841, and had it renewed in 1846.

Nov. 19. — In Indianapolis, Ind., *General Robert Hanna*, a member of the Indiana Constitutional Convention of 1816.

Nov. 24. — In Petersburg, Ill., *Hon. Thomas L. Harris*, aged 42. He was born in Norwich, Connecticut, October 29, 1816; graduated at Trinity College, Hartford, in 1841; studied law in Connecticut with Governor Isaac Toucey, and was admitted to the bar in Virginia in 1842, and subsequently commenced the practice of his profession in Menard County, Illinois. He served in the late war with Mexico as Major of the Illinois regiment of volunteers. While absent in Mexico he was elected a Senator in the Illinois Legislature, and in 1848 was chosen a Representative in Congress. He served through the thirty-first Congress, was elected to the thirty-fifth Congress, and had just been re-elected to the thirty-sixth Congress.

Oct — In Freetown, Mass., *Elnathan P. Hathaway*, a graduate of Brown University in 1818, and a lawyer. He had represented his town in the State Legislature, his County in the Senate, and was a Member of the Convention of 1853 for revising the Constitution.

Sept. 19. — In East Bridgewater, Mass., *Hon Aaron Hobart*, aged 71. He was born in Abington, Massachusetts, June 26, 1787; graduated at Brown University in 1805; studied law and practised his profession in his native county, in which he was highly esteemed, and repeatedly elected to offices of honor and responsibility. He was in the State Senate in 1820; was Representative in Congress from 1825 to 1827; and from 1828 to 1831 he was a member of the Executive Council. He was a Member of the Constitutional Convention of 1853. He was for many years Judge of Probate for the County.

Oct. 28. — In Brooklyn, N. Y., *Alvah Hunt*, aged 60. He was for many years an enterprising merchant in Greene County, New York, but removed some four years ago to Brooklyn. He was for five years State Senator, and for two years State Treasurer.

Sept. 4. — In Hartford, Conn., *William H. Imlay*, aged 78, a merchant distinguished for his enterprise and success.

Oct. 14. — In Bedford, West Chester County, N. Y., *William Jay*, aged 69. He was the second son of John Jay, and was born at New York, June 16, 1789. He entered Yale College in 1804, graduated there in 1807; studied law in Albany with John B. Henry, Esquire; was admitted to the bar, but his health failing him, he returned to Bedford and aided in the management of his father's estate, which, at his death in 1839, he inherited. Soon after 1812 he was appointed first Judge in West Chester County, which office he held until 1843. He was an early and efficient advocate of the American Bible Society, and was one of its Vice-Presidents. He was also a warm advocate of the Sabbath, Sunday Schools, Peace (being President of the American Peace Society), Temperance, and African Colonization, and wrote and published much on all these subjects. He was also in correspondence with the leaders of the antislavery movement in the United States. In 1833 he published the life and writings of his father.

Sept. 4. — In Basle, Switzerland, *General James J. Jones*, of New York City. His services in the financial and charitable institutions of that city were constant and important.

Sept. 12. — In Accomac County, Va., *Thomas R. Joynes, Senior, Esq.*, aged 69, a distinguished lawyer, and a member of the State Convention in 1829 – 30.

Nov. 22. — In Washington County, Pa., *Hon. Jonathan Knight*, aged 69. He was eminent as a civil engineer, and was engaged for many years upon the Baltimore and Ohio Railroad. He was a Member of Congress from Pennsylvania from 1855 to 1857.

Oct. 27. — In San Francisco, Cal., *Thomas O. Larkin*, aged 56. He was a native of New England, and emigrated to California as early as 1832. He was appointed United States Consul in Monterey in 1844, and was a prominent man in the new State of California.

Nov. 14. — In Detroit, Mich., *Aaron Larkin Leland*, aged 45. He was born in Sherborn, Massachusetts, in 1813; graduated at Harvard College in 1835, studied medicine; settled in Pontiac, Michigan, in 1839 as a physician; removed to Detroit in 1847, where he continued in practice until his death.

Sept. 10. — In Fredonia, N. Y., *Hon James Mullett*, one of the Justices of the Supreme Court for the Eighth Judicial District of New York.

Dec. 4. — In Hillsborough, N. C., *Hon. Frederic Nash*, aged 77. He was born in Newbern, North Carolina, in 1781, studied law; represented Newbern in the State Legislature in 1804 and 1805. He was appointed to the Bench of the Superior Court of his native State in 1836; in 1844 was transferred to the Supreme Court, of which tribunal in 1853 he was made Chief Justice.

Sept. 8. — In Philadelphia, *George Newbold*, aged near 76, the President of the Bank of America in New York.

Nov. 22. — In New York City, *Isaac Newton*, aged 64, long associated with the most extensive enterprises of North River navigation.

Aug. 21. — In Middletown, Conn., *Francis Johonnot Oliver*, aged 80. He was born in Boston, October 10, 1777; graduated at Harvard College in 1795; became a merchant; was elected the first ensign of the Boston Light Infantry; was the first President of the American Insurance Company, and held the office from 1818 to 1835; was President of the City Bank, Boston, from 1835 to 1840, when he removed to Middletown. He was a representative in the State Legislature from Boston in 1822 and 1823; was for several years a member of the Common Council in Boston, and its President in 1824 and 1825.

Sept. 22. — In Charleston, S. C., *Rev. Reuben Post*, aged 66. He was a native of Vermont, graduated in 1814, studied theology at Princeton, New Jersey, was ordained pastor of the First Presbyterian Church in Washington, D. C., where he remained until 1836, when he was called to Charleston, and settled as pastor of the Circular Church in that city, in which he labored until his death.

Oct. 24. — In Beverly, Mass., *Hon. Robert Rantoul*, aged 79. He was born in Salem, November 23, 1778, and was for the most of his life a druggist in Beverly. He was elected a Representative to the State Legislature in 1809, and held this office by successive re-elections until 1820, when he was chosen Senator from Essex district, and was re-elected in 1821 and 1822. In 1823 he was again chosen Representative, and was re-elected every year until 1833, with the exception of the year 1827. He was also a member of the Conventions of 1820 and 1853 for amending the Constitution. He was an ardent friend of education, temperance, and peace. He lived a life of great usefulness and of unblemished integrity.

Dec. 3. — In Boston, Mass., *Rev. John T. Roddan*. He was a graduate of the College of the Propaganda, in Rome, and had been for two years pastor of the Catholic Church in Purchase Street, in that city.

Oct. 14. — In Bangor, Me., *Rev. John Sawyer*, aged 103 years and five days.

Near Oct. 10. — In Schenectady, N. Y., *Madame Amelia Schoppe*, a German novelist and poetess, aged 67. She followed her son to this country soon after the European revolutions in 1848.

Nov. 21. — In Augusta, Ga., *Hon. William Schley*, aged 73. He was born in Maryland, December 10, 1786; was admitted to the bar in Augusta, Georgia, in 1812; was elected Judge of the Superior Court, Middle Circuit, in 1825, and held the office for three years. In 1830 he was a member of the Legislature, was a Representative in Congress from 1833 to 1835, and from 1835 to 1837 was Governor of Georgia. He advocated the Internal Improvements in Georgia, and especially the construction of the Western and Atlantic Railroad. He was President of the Medical College of Georgia at the time of his death.

Oct. 26. — In New Haven, Conn., *Aaron Nichols Skinner*, aged 58. He was born in Woodstock, Connecticut, in 1800, and graduated at Yale College in 1823. He was Tutor in that college from 1825 to 1829. He studied law; was admitted to the bar, but did not engage in practice, preferring to engage in the work of instruction. He established in New Haven a classical school of a high order, which he continued to the close of life. He was occasionally called into public service, and was distinguished for his generous public spirit. The enclosure and adornment of the New Haven Burial-Ground, and various other improvements in that city, bear witness to his devotion to the public interests.

Nov. 20. — In St. Albans, Vt., *Hon. John Smith*, aged 68. He was an active, enterprising, and influential citizen. He was one of the originators of railroads in Vermont. He was member of Congress from that State from 1839 to 1841.

Sept. 29. — In Washington, D. C., *George Thomas*, aged 67. He was born in St. Mary's County, Maryland, but for forty years had resided in Washington. He was distinguished as an able cashier in the Bank of the Metropolis for many years, and was one of the oldest and worthiest of the citizens of that city.

Sept. 28. — In Kinderhook, N. Y., *Lucas J. Van Alen*, aged 81, a highly respected citizen of Columbia County, New York.

Sept. 1. — In Boston, Mass., *Dr. William Wesselhoeft*, aged 65, Homœopathic physician and formerly President of the Massachusetts Homœopathic Medical Society. He was born in Chemintz, Saxony, but spent the last thirty-four years of his life in the United States.

Sept. 5. — At his residence on Trinity River, Texas, *Hon. George T. Wood*, Colonel of a regiment of Texas volunteers at the storming of Monterey; a Representative in the Congress of Texas, and Governor of Texas from 1847 to 1849.

Nov. 5. — In Lowell, Mass., *Hon. Nathaniel Wright*, aged 73. He was born in Sterling, Massachusetts, graduated at Harvard College in 1808; studied law, and was admitted to the bar in 1811. When Lowell was organized as a town he was made chairman of the selectmen, and held the office for five years. He was the first Representative of the new town in the State Legislature, was Senator from Middlesex County, and was Mayor of Lowell in 1841-1842, and was for more than thirty years President of the Lowell Bank.

Sept. 14. — In Hanover, N. H., *Ira Young*, Professor of Mathematics and Natural Philosophy in Dartmouth College, New Hampshire.

1859.

Jan. 31. — In West Cambridge, Mass., *Rev. Abiel Abbot, D. D.*, aged 93. He was born in Wilton, New Hampshire, in 1765; graduated at Harvard College in 1787; was Teacher at Phillips Academy, Exeter; Tutor in Harvard College 1794 – 1795; settled in Coventry, Connecticut, from 1795 to 1811; Principal of Dummer Academy, Newbury, from 1811 to 1819, and a minister at Peterborough, New Hampshire, from 1827 until near 1854, after which he resided in West Cambridge. The degree of D. D. was conferred on him by Harvard College in 1838. He had been for several years her oldest surviving graduate. In 1811 he published a statement of the proceedings which led to his dismission from Coventry, and in 1829 a history of Andover, Massachusetts.

March 30. — Near Cairo, Egypt, *Dr. Abbott*, aged near 47, the collector of the valuable gallery of the Egyptian antiquities in New York. He was a native of London, England; had been surgeon in the British navy, and for a long time practised his profession in Cairo.

July 31. — At the Virginia Springs, *Rev. James W. Alexander, D. D.*, a distinguished preacher of New York city, and formerly Professor of Belles-lettres and Rhetoric in the College of New Jersey.

Jan. 23. — In Brooklyn, Ohio, *Quintus F. Atkins*, aged 77 years. He emigrated to Ohio from Connecticut, and was one of the most hardy and enterprising of the Reserve pioneers. He served as lieutenant under General Harrison.

June 21. — In Boston, Mass., *John Augustus*, aged 74. He was a boot-maker by trade, but for many years he spent much of his time in the criminal courts of the city, in attempting to reform and save those who were willing to try to save themselves.

June 5. — On board the Steamer Arago, on his passage to Havre, *Dr. Gamaliel Bailey*, aged 52. He was born in New Jersey in 1807, studied medicine in Philadelphia, and took his degree in 1828. He began his career in journalism as editor in Baltimore of the Methodist Protestant. In 1831 he removed to Cincinnati, and was appointed physician to the Cholera Hospital during the cholera season. In 1836 he was associated with James G. Birney in the Philanthropist. In 1837 Mr. Birney withdrew, and Mr. Bailey continued its publication until it was merged in the National Era, published at Washington, D. C., which he edited and afterwards owned. He was a man of great cultivation and refinement, moderation, firmness, and courage. The many threats and attempts made to destroy his paper never intimidated him or drove him from his post.

Jan. 16. — In Montgomery, Ala., *Hon. James E. Belser*, Member of Congress from Alabama from 1845 to 1847.

April 14. — In Georgetown, D. C., *George M. Bibb*, aged near 87. He was a native of Virginia, graduated at Princeton College, and removed to Kentucky. He served in the Legislature of that State, was for three successive terms its Chief Justice; was Chancellor of the Chancery Court of Louisville; was Senator in Congress from 1811 to 1814, and again from 1829 to 1835, and in 1844 was appointed Secretary of the Treasury by President Tyler upon the resignation of John C. Spencer.

Jan. 29. — In Cambridge, Mass., *William Cranch Bond*, aged 69. He was born in Portland, Maine, in 1789. He early devoted himself with much industry, talent, and success to astronomical observations, and to the improvement and construction of optical instruments, in every detail of which he was well informed and practically skilful. He had gained a reputation as an observer at his private observatory at Dorchester, and had been employed in astronomical observations by the United States government, when he was made Director of the Observatory at Cambridge in 1839, before any buildings were erected. His labors there in connection with his sons have added largely to our knowledge of Astronomy in most important particulars, and observers are indebted to his practical skill for several inventions of the greatest value to the mechanism and recording of observations. His successful experiments in stellar photography have been recorded in our volumes. His talents and acquirements as a skilful astronomer were duly appreciated, not only in this country, but in Europe. In 1842, the honorary degree of Master of Arts was conferred upon him by Harvard College, and he was a member of the American Academy of Arts and Sciences, of the American Philosophical Society, and of the Royal Astronomical Society of London.

April 19. — In Schoharie County, N. Y., *Hon. William C. Bouck*, aged 73. He was born in Schoharie County in 1786. He was early elected to town offices, was appointed Sheriff of the County in 1812; was Member of the State Assembly in 1813 and 1815, and again in 1817; was elected State Senator in 1820; was chosen Canal Commissioner in 1821, and continued in office for nineteen years; was elected Governor of the State in 1842; was a member of the Constitutional Convention in 1846, and was from 1846 for three years Assistant-Treasurer in New York city, until removed by President Taylor. The last ten years of his life were devoted to agriculture.

March 8. — In Washington, D. C., *Hon. Aaron Vail Brown*, aged 63. He was born in Virginia in 1795, graduated at the University of North Carolina in 1814; removed to Tennessee in 1815, where he studied law, and commenced practice in Nashville, and was at one time a law partner of James K. Polk. He was from 1821 to 1832 a member of the Legislature of Tennessee; from 1839 to 1845 a representative in Congress, and from 1845 to 1847 Governor of Tennessee. He was a delegate to the Southern Convention at Nashville in 1850, and was the author of the report known as the "Tennessee Platform." His congressional and political speeches were published in Nashville in 1854 in a volume of some seven hundred pages.

Jan. 3. — In Richmond, Va., *James Brown, Jr.*, for a long time Second Auditor of Virginia.

March 19. — In Abingdon, Va., *David Campbell*, aged 80. He was a Major of infantry in the war of 1812, and was Governor of Virginia from 1836 to 1839.

July 3. — In Nahant, Mass., *Hon. Thomas Greaves Cary*, of Boston, aged 67. He was born in Chelsea, Massachusetts, in 1791, graduated at Harvard College in 1811; studied law and began to practise his profession in Boston, but soon removed to Brattleborough, Vermont. In 1821 he went to New York and engaged in business in the Canton trade, and afterwards was engaged in business in Boston. He was for many years the Treasurer of the Hamilton and Appleton manufacturing companies in Lowell. He was State Senator from Suffolk for several years. He was a member and officer of many charitable institutions, and took a great interest in education and questions of social reform. He contributed frequently to the standard magazines and reviews, and published occasional essays on subjects connected with the fine arts, finance, and political economy. He also published a memoir of his father-in-law, Thomas Handasyd Perkins. In 1847 he delivered the Fourth of July oration before the city authorities. He was a member of the American Academy of Arts and Sciences, and of the Massachusetts Historical Society.

March 2. — In Newark, N. J., *Rev. James Carnahan, D. D.*, aged 78. President of the College of New Jersey from 1823 to 1853. At the time of his death he was one of the Trustees of the College, and President of the Board of Trustees of Princeton Theological Seminary.

July 15. — In Halifax, N. S., *Hon. Rufus Choate*, of Boston, Massachusetts, aged 59. He was born in Essex, Massachusetts, graduated at Dartmouth College in 1819; was at the college as a tutor for a year; was at the Law School in Cambridge, and afterwards for a year at the office of William Wirt at Washington, D. C., was admitted to the bar in 1824, and began to practise law in Danvers, Massachusetts, but soon removed to Salem. He was for two years in the State Legislature, one year as Representative, and one as Senator. He was chosen a Member of Congress in 1832, and served one term. He came to Boston in 1834, and became at once the leader of the bar. In 1841 he was elected to the United States Senate to succeed Mr. Webster who was in the Cabinet of President Harrison, and remained there until March, 1845. He was for three or four years one of the Regents of the Smithsonian Institution, and was a member of the State Constitutional Convention in 1853. He was the acknowledged head of the New England bar, and had no superior as an able, eloquent, and successful advocate; and few men equalled him in his knowledge, love, and appreciation of literature and all useful learning.

Aug. 15. — In Franklin County, Va., *Hon. Nathaniel H. Claiborne*, aged 82, from 1825 to 1837 a Member of Congress from Virginia.

May 18. — In Greenesboro', Ga., *Francis H. Cone*, aged 61. He was a native of Connecticut; a graduate of Yale College in 1818; studied law and settled in Greenesboro', in 1824. He was Judge of the Ocmulgee Circuit from 1841 to

1845, and State Senator in 1855-56. He was an eminent and successful lawyer.

May 17. — In Natchez, Miss., E. J. Cornish, aged 37. He was born in Connecticut in 1841; graduated at Amherst College in 1845, and since 1856 had been President of Jefferson College, Mississippi.

March 4. — In New Haven, Conn., *Sherman Croswell*, aged 56. He was born in Hudson, New York, and graduated at Yale College in 1822. He studied law, and was admitted to the bar in 1825. In 1831 he removed to Albany, New York, where he was connected with Edwin Croswell, Esq., in the editorial management of the Albany Argus, from which he finally retired in 1855. Soon after this he removed to New Haven.

Feb. 20. — In Boston, Mass., *Edward Augustus Crowninshield*, aged 41. He was born in Salem, Massachusetts, in 1817; graduated at Cambridge in 1838, read law, but never practised his profession. He had great taste in bibliography, and had collected a rare and choice private library.

Jan. 29. — By the burning of the Steamer North Carolina, in Chesapeake Bay, *Dr. Thomas Curtis*, of Limestone Springs, South Carolina, aged 71. He was the projector and editor of the Encyclopædia Metropolitania, and sole editor of Mr. Teigg's London Encyclopædia.

Aug. 26. — In Newburyport, Mass., *Rev. Daniel Dana, D. D.*, aged 88. He was the son of Rev. Dr. Joseph Dana of Ipswich, and was born in 1771; graduated at Dartmouth College in 1788; was settled as pastor of the First Presbyterian Church in Newburyport in 1794; was President of Dartmouth College in 1820-21, and in 1825 was settled over the Second Presbyterian Church in Newburyport, where he remained until 1845, when he was released from his pastoral duties at his own request.

June 12. — In Columbia, S. C., *Hon. George W. Dargan*, aged 58. He was for a time Commissioner in Equity for the Charleston District; was State Senator, and was one of the Chancellors of the State from 1847 to his death.

Aug. 22. — In Carlisle, Ind., *John W. Davis*, aged 60. He was a member of the House of Representatives of Indiana for many years, and also Speaker; was a Member of Congress from Indiana from 1835 to 1837, from 1839 to 1841, and from 1843 to 1847, and was Speaker during his last term. He was appointed Commissioner to China by President Polk, and Governor of Oregon by President Pierce. He was President of the Convention in Baltimore in 1852, that nominated General Pierce for the Presidency.

April 26. — In Lockport N. Y., *Nathan Dayton*, aged 63, formerly Judge of the Supreme Court of that State, and one of the eminent citizens and lawyers of Western New York.

April 23. — In Bristol, R. I., *Francis M. Dimond*, aged 63. He was for several years United States Consul at Vera Cruz, and afterwards Lieutenant-Governor of Rhode Island.

Jan. 14. — In Williamstown, Mass., *Daniel Noble Dewey*, aged 59. He was born in Williamstown, and graduated at Yale College in 1820. He studied law, and was extensively engaged in the practice. He held numerous offices of trust, civil and judicial, and for about fifteen years past he had been Secretary and Treasurer of Williams College.

April 27. — In Burlington, N. J., *Rt. Rev. George Washington Doane, D. D.*, since 1832 Protestant Episcopal Bishop of New Jersey, aged 59. He was a native of New Jersey, and graduated at Union College, Schenectady, in 1822. He was assistant minister and rector in New York and Boston, and was for a time Professor of Rhetoric in Trinity College, Hartford, Connecticut. He was devoted to education in connection with Episcopal colleges, and was a person of scholarly attainments and literary taste.

July. — In Louisiana, *Major A. J. Donelson*, formerly private secretary of General Jackson, and editor of the Washington Globe, and in 1856 a candidate of the American party for Vice-President.

April 23. — In Baltimore, Md., *Wyndham D. M. Dyer*, the British Consul in that city.

March 24. — In Detroit, Mich., *John W. Farmer*, well known as the compiler of several valuable maps of Michigan and Wisconsin.

May 11. — In Milledgeville, Ga., *Dr. Tomlinson Fort*, aged 72. He studied medicine; had been a member of the State Legislature, and was Member of Congress from Georgia from 1827 to 1829. He was President of the Central Bank of Georgia from 1832 until his death.

July 21. — In Mobile, Ala., *John Gayle*, aged 66. He was Governor of Alabama from 1831 to 1835, Member of Congress from 1847 to 1849, and since 1849 Judge of the United States District Court for the District of Alabama.

March 5. — In St. Louis, Mo., *Hon. Henry S. Geyer*. He was an eminent lawyer, and was Senator in Congress from Missouri, from 1851 to 1857.

May 12. — In Newark, N. J., *Archer Gifford*, aged 64, a highly respected citizen, and member of the bar of New Jersey.

July 3. — In Mecklenberg County, Va., *Hon. William O. Goode*. He was for many years a member of the Virginia House of Delegates, and at one time its Speaker; a member of the Constitutional Convention of 1829, and since 1855 Member of Congress for Virginia, and member elect to the thirty-sixth Congress.

Feb. 25. — In St. Louis, Mo., *Hon. Edward A. Hannegan*. He was a native of Ohio, spent his boyhood in Kentucky, and studied law and commenced practice in Indiana. He was frequently a member of the State Legislature of Indiana, was Representative in Congress from that State from 1833 to 1837, and Senator from 1843 to 1849, and Minister to Prussia from 1849 to 1853.

March 15. — In Hopkinsville, Ky., *William T. Haskell*, Colonel of a regiment of Tennessee volunteers in the Mexican war, and member of Congress from Tennessee from 1847 to 1849.

Aug. 28. — In Boston, Mass., *Prince Hawes*, aged 69, an upright and honorable merchant, and a charitable and religious man.

Jan. 7. — In Washington, D. C., *Brevet Brigadier-General Archibald Henderson*, Commandant of the U. S. Marine Corps, aged 75.

April 29. — In Utica, N. Y., *Joshua Sidney Henshaw*, aged 47. His original name was Joshua Belcher, and was changed by the Pennsylvania Legislature in 1845. He was born in Boston in 1811, was Professor of Mathematics in the Navy until 1848, when he settled in Utica in the practice of the law. He published four or five volumes, among which are "Around the World," "Life of Father Matthew," "and United States Manual of Consuls," and had a work, called "Bible Ethics," nearly completed at the time of his death.

May 3. — In Albany, N. Y., *Nicholas Hill*, aged 53. He was a distinguished lawyer, was from 1840 to 1845 a State Reporter, and, with Sydney Cowen, prepared Cowen & Hill's Notes to Phillips's Evidence.

March 14. — Near Paris, France, *Augustus Lucas Hillhouse*, aged 67. He was the youngest son of Hon. James Hillhouse, and was born in New Haven, Conn., Dec. 9, 1791. He graduated at Yale College in 1810, and, his health being infirm, he went to France in 1815, and there resided, engaged in literary pursuits. He was the author of the English translation of Michaux's North American Sylva, and has left a large collection of manuscripts on political and social philosophy.

March 31. — In Columbus, Ga., *Hon. Hopkins Holsey*, aged 59. He was well known as editor of the Athens Banner, and was a member of Congress from Georgia from 1836 to 1839.

July 17. — In Charleston, S. C., *Hon. Jacob Bond Ion*, aged 77. He was a native of South Carolina, and a graduate of Yale College in the class of 1803. In 1811 he entered the United States Army as Captain of First Regiment of Artillery, and served until 1815. At the reorganization of the army on the close of the war, he was retained. The fortifications at Charleston, S. C., and Savannah, Ga., were intrusted to his command. He was conspicuous for his devotion to the interests of his native State. For many years he was President of the State Senate, and he was an influential member of the Convention which in 1832 put the State upon her sovereignty, and passed the ordinance of nullification.

March 27. — In Somerville, Mass., *Col. Samuel Jacques*, aged 82, a well-known agriculturist and gentleman of the old school.

April 20. — In Baltimore, Md., *Rev. Henry V. Johns*, aged 56, Rector of the Church of the Emmanuel, a talented and influential minister of the Gospel.

March 17. — In Plymouth, Mass., *Rev. James Kendall, D. D.*, aged 89. He was born in Sterling, Mass., in 1769, graduated at Harvard College in 1796, was a teacher in Phillips Academy in Andover, studied theology, was Tutor in Greek in Harvard College in 1798–99, was ordained in Plymouth in 1800, and was the sole pastor of the society for thirty-eight years, when a colleague was settled with him. The degree of D. D. was conferred upon him in 1825 by Harvard College. He published fifteen sermons at different times. He was a man of exemplary piety and purity of life, and beloved by all.

Aug. 6.—In Roxbury, Mass., *Rev. Benjamin Kent*, aged 65. He was born in what is now Somerville, Mass., in 1794, graduated at Harvard College in 1820; studied theology, and was settled in Duxbury, Mass., in 1826. In 1833 he removed to Roxbury, where he taught a private school for young ladies for several years, and was afterward Librarian of the Roxbury Athenæum.

June 6.—In Somerville, Mass., *Edward L. Keyes*. He edited for many years a paper in Dedham, Mass., and served in the State Senate, and as a member of the Executive Council. He was a man of great natural talents.

March 18.—In Brandon, Miss., *Hon. John W. King*, aged 49. In 1838 and 1839 he was Speaker of the House of Representatives of the Mississippi Legislature.

May 5.—In Greencastle, Ind., *William C. Larrabee*, aged 59, a native of Maine, and formerly Superintendent of Public Instruction in Indiana.

Aug. 28.—In Concord, N. H., *Gen. Joseph Lowe*, aged 70, a well-known and public-spirited citizen.

April 9.—In Shanghai, China, *Rev. William Allen Macy*, aged 35. He was born in New York City, Jan. 29, 1825, was graduated at Yale College in 1849, and devoted his life to labors as a teacher and missionary in China. He was an excellent scholar, and eminent for his zeal and devotion to the cause of missions.

Aug. 2.—In Yellow Springs, O., *Hon. Horace Mann, LL. D.*, aged 63. He was born in Franklin, Mass., May 4, 1796, graduated at Brown University in 1819, and was for a time Tutor and Librarian there. He studied law, and practised first in Norfolk County, Mass., and afterwards in Boston. He was a member of the State Senate, and by his labors the system of education and charitable institutions was matured. In 1835 he was appointed one of the Commissioners to superintend the publication of the Revised Statutes of the State. He was for twelve years Secretary of the Board of Education of Massachusetts, and his Annual Reports are an enduring monument to his fame. The great cause of common school education in the United States is indebted to no man more than to him. In 1848 he was elected to succeed John Quincy Adams in Congress, and served as Representative there until 1853, when he was appointed President of Antioch College. To the best interests of this institution he devoted his maturest thoughts and energies.

March 3.—In Washington, D. C., *John Marron*, Third Assistant Postmaster-General, aged near 60.

Feb. 26.—In Columbus, O., *W. W. Mather*, a geologist, and heretofore State Geologist in New York, Ohio, and Kentucky.

Feb. 26.—In New York, *Col. Thomas L. McKenney*, aged 76. He was an officer of volunteers in the District of Columbia in the war of 1812, and afterwards was joint Commissioner with General Cass in negotiating treaties with the Indians of the Northwest.

May 2.—In Montpelier, Vt., *Hon. Ferrand F. Merrill*, aged 47. He was born in 1811, and from 1835 was almost constantly in public life. He was then elected Clerk of the Vermont House of Representatives, and was re-elected for eleven successive years. In 1849 he was chosen Secretary of State, and re-elected for five successive years. He was subsequently State Attorney for the County, and a Representative in the State Legislature.

May 19.—In Fleming Co., Ky., *General Daniel Morgan*, aged 68. He was from 1831 to 1843, with the exception of one session, a member of the State Legislature.

Feb. 16.—In Vicksburg, Miss., *Hon. John M. Moore*, one of the prominent citizens of Mississippi.

July 17.—In Powhatan, Va., *John W. Nash*, for some years a member of the State Legislature, and for the last ten years one of the Circuit Judges of Virginia.

Jan. 2.—In Cambridge, Mass., *Rev. Ichabod Nichols, D. D.*, aged 74. He was born in Portsmouth, N. H., in 1784, graduated at Harvard College with the highest honors of his class in 1802, was from 1805 to 1809 Tutor in Mathematics in the College, studied theology and was settled in 1809 in Portland, Me., where he continued until Jan., 1855, when a colleague was settled with him, and he removed to Cambridge. He published a work on Natural Theology in 1830, and left nearly ready for publication a work entitled "Hours with the Evangelists." In 1821 Bowdoin College, and in 1831 Harvard College, conferred upon him the degree of Doctor of Divinity. He was a member, and had been Vice-President, of the American Academy of Arts and Sciences.

April. — In Holly Springs, Miss., *Col. J. R. Norfleet*, a highly respected citizen, and a member of the Mississippi Legislature.

May 13. — In New Haven, Conn., *Prof. Denison Olmsted*, aged 68. He was born in East Hartford, Conn., June 18, 1791, and graduated at Yale College in 1813, in which College he was for two years a Tutor. In 1817 he was appointed Professor of Chemistry in the University of North Carolina, — the sciences of Mineralogy and Geology being also included in his department. While in this office he made a survey of the geological and mineral resources of the State of North Carolina, which is worthy of special mention as the first enterprise of the kind in this country undertaken by State authority. In 1825 he accepted the appointment of Professor of Mathematics and Natural Philosophy in Yale College. In 1836 the Professorship was divided, and he retained the chair of Natural Philosophy and Astronomy. The duties of these offices he discharged with distinguished usefulness to the close of life. He was the author of valuable text-books on Natural Philosophy and Astronomy, which are extensively used. He contributed a large amount of important matter to the literary and scientific journals of his time. His elaborate articles on the great meteoric shower of November, 1833, attracted great attention, and gave him much celebrity both at home and abroad. A Discourse commemorative of his life and services was delivered by President Woolsey, May 20th, 1859, and has been published.

Jan. 28. — In New York City, *Rev. Benjamin Clark Cutler Parker*, aged 62. He was born in Boston in 1796, and graduated at Cambridge in 1822. For the last fifteen years he was pastor of the "Floating Chapel for Seamen" in New York City.

Jan. 12. — In Havana, Cuba, *Jacob Perkins*, of Cleveland, Ohio, aged 38. He was a native of Ohio, and graduated at Yale College. He was a member of the State Convention to form the Constitution.

May 14. — In Mobile, Ala., *Right Rev. Michael Portier*, aged 64, Roman Catholic Bishop of the diocese of Alabama and Florida. He was a native of France.

April 23. — In Louisville, Ky., *James Porter*, the Kentucky giant. He was seven feet nine inches high, and weighed three hundred pounds.

May 4. — In New York City, *Hon. J. Phillips Phœnix.* He was a native of New Jersey, but was a merchant for the most of his life in New York. He was member of Congress from New York City from 1843 to 1845 and from 1849 to 1851, and was a member of the State Assembly in 1848.

Jan. 28. — In Boston, Mass., *William Hickling Prescott*, aged 62. He was born in Salem, Mass., in 1796, graduated at Harvard College in 1814, and devoted himself to literary pursuits. During his Junior year in College, he lost the sight of one of his eyes by an accident, and that of the other became impaired. He spent two years in Europe after his graduation, and returned with his general health improved, but with his sight permanently injured, so that he was obliged to pursue his studies chiefly with the eyes of others. By quiet perseverance and continuous industry he triumphed over all difficulties, and achieved a vast amount of literary labor. He made frequent contributions to the North American Review. A volume of his articles from this Review was published in 1845 in Boston and London. He wrote the memoir of Charles Brockden Brown, published in Sparks's American Biography in 1834. He published his "Ferdinand and Isabella" in 1838, and the seventh, revised edition of this work appeared in 1854. His "Conquest of Mexico" was first published in 1843, and the "Conquest of Peru" in 1847. Two volumes of "Philip the Second" appeared in 1855; and the third volume shortly before his death. In 1856 he published an edition of Robertson's "Charles the Fifth." Literary honors were heaped upon him from nearly all countries. He was made an honorary member of a large number of societies in this country and Europe. In his private life, "the man was more than his books. His character was loftier than all his reputation."

July 30. — In Philadelphia, Pa., *Hon. Richard Rush*, aged 78. He was born in 1780; was Attorney-General of Pennsylvania in 1811; of the United States from 1814 to 1817; edited an edition of the Laws of the United States in 1815; was temporary Secretary of State in 1817; was Minister to England from 1817 to 1825; was Secretary of the Treasury in the administration of John Quincy Adams; was candidate for Vice-President with Mr. Adams in 1829. In 1829 he went to Holland to obtain a loan; in 1837, to England, to obtain the Smithson legacy; and in 1847 was appointed Minister to France by President Polk. During the latter part of his life he did not participate actively in public affairs.

Jan. 5.—In Richmond, Va., *Hon. Green B. Samuels*, aged near 65, for eleven years Judge of the Supreme Court of Appeals of that State.

April 18.—In Boston, Mass., *Dr. William Sawyer*, aged 88, a graduate of Harvard College in 1788, and, after the death of Dr. Abbot (Jan. 31, 1859), he was the oldest graduate of the College. He studied medicine and practised his profession for a few years, but, finding it distasteful, entered into mercantile business, and acquired a fortune. He withdrew from active business twenty-five years since.

Jan. 17.—In Boston, Mass., *Lemuel Shattuck*, aged 65, a well-known statistician, and the author of the census of Boston in 1845.

April 28.—In Westchester County, N. Y., *Frederic Sheldon*, aged 76. He occupied for forty years a leading position in the commercial, educational, and religious movements of the times. He was one of the founders of the United States Life Insurance Company and of the United States Trust Company, and for many years a Director in the Bank of America.

Jan. 16.—In Middlebury, Vt., *Hon. William Slade*. He was born in Vermont, graduated at Middlebury College, was Representative in Congress from his native State from 1831 to 1843, was Governor of Vermont from 1844 to 1846, and since has been Secretary of the National Board of Popular Education.

March 19.—In Indianapolis, Ind., *Hon. Oliver Hampton Smith*, aged 64. He was born in New Jersey in 1794, and emigrated to Indiana in 1817, and began to practise law. In 1824 he was chosen Prosecuting Attorney, in 1826 was elected Representative in Congress, and in 1836 to the United States Senate. After his retirement from the Senate, he devoted himself to the practice of his profession, and made great efforts in behalf of railroads.

May 31.—In Wooster, O., *Cyrus Spink*, aged 66. He was born in Berkshire County, Mass., in 1793, emigrated to Ohio in 1815, and was successively County Surveyor, County Auditor, State Representative, Land Register, Presidential Elector, member of the State Board of Equalization, and Director of the Ohio Penitentiary. He was at the time of his death Member elect to the Thirty-sixth Congress from the Fourteenth Congressional District of Ohio.

March 30.—In Swedesboro', N. J., *Hon. Charles C. Stratton*, aged 63. He was Representative in Congress from New Jersey from 1837 to 1839 and from 1841 to 1843, and was Governor of New Jersey from 1845 to 1848.

———.—In Hornitas, Cal., *Dr. Edward Alexander Theller*. He was an active participant in the Canadian disturbances in 1837, for which he was convicted and sentenced to death, but made his escape. He published in 1841 a work in two volumes, upon the attempted revolution in Canada in 1837–38. He went to California in 1853, was connected with the "Public Ledger" and "Argus" in San Francisco, and was for a time Superintendent of Public Schools in that city.

April 3.—In Alabama, *Tilghman M. Tucker*. He lived for a great part of his life in Mississippi, where he was for many years a member of the State Senate, was Governor from 1841 to 1843, and member of Congress from 1843 to 1845.

February 28.—In Springfield, Mass., *William Tully, M. D.*, aged 72. He was born in Saybrook, Conn., Nov. 18, 1785, and was graduated at Yale College in 1806. He studied the profession of medicine, and became eminent as a practitioner and a teacher. He was for many years President of the Medical School at Castleton, Vermont, and was Professor there of the Theory and Practice of Medicine. He was also Professor of Materia Medica and Therapeutics in the Medical Institution of Yale College from 1829 to 1842. He was a man of varied and excellent scholarship, and published several learned papers in the medical and other journals, besides the first volume of an extended Treatise on the Materia Medica.

Feb.—*Dionysius Walker*, of Yazoo, Miss., while on his way as Consul to Genoa. He was formerly editor of the Vicksburg Sentinel, subsequently practised law, and was highly esteemed for his character and talents.

March 17.—In New York City, *Mike Walsh*, a native of New York, at one time the editor of a paper in that city, an active member of the State Assembly, and from 1853 to 1855 Representative in Congress.

Feb. 7.—In Paris, France, *Robert Walsh*, aged 76, formerly United States Consul in Paris, and well known as a correspondent of the National Intelligencer and other American papers.

June 7.—In Coventry, R. I., *Thomas Whipple*, aged 71, frequently a Representative in the State Legislature, a Judge of the Court of Common Pleas from 1820 to 1822, and Lieutenant-Governor in 1849.

April. — In Janesville, Wisc., *Hon. Edward V. Whiton*, Chief Justice of the Supreme Court of Wisconsin, aged 51. He was a native of Massachusetts, emigrated to Wisconsin in 1825, and had been Circuit Judge.

June 11. — In Ohio, *Rev. P. B. Wilber*, aged 52, since 1842 Principal of the Wesleyan Female College.

April 14. — In New York, *Rev. Bird Wilson, D. D.*, aged 83, a Professor in the General Theological Seminary of the Episcopal Church.

FOREIGN OBITUARY.

1858.

May 8. — In London, Eng., *William Ayrton*, aged 81. He was editor of the Harmonicon from 1823 to 1833; wrote the musical articles and biography in the Penny Cyclopædia from 1833 to 1844; edited the "Sacred Minstrelsy," and the "Musical Library," and wrote some of the musical notices in "Knight's Pictorial Edition of Shakespeare"

Dec. — In Scotland, *Isabella Beggs*, aged 87. She was born in 1771, and was the sister of Robert Burns, and the youngest child of the family. Her husband was killed in 1813, leaving her a widow with nine children.

Dec. 16. — In Saville Row, London, Eng., *Dr. Richard Bright*, the well-known physician, aged 69.

Sept. 16. — *Cassaduco*, the Emperor of Japan, aged 36.

Sept. 1. — Near Exeter, Eng., *Richard Ford*, aged 61, an author of some note, particularly of works relating to Spain. His "Hand-Book for Spain" is one of the best books of its class.

Nov. 9 — In England, *Rev. John Hickling*, aged 93. He was said to be the oldest Methodist preacher in the world, and the last survivor of the "Helpers of John Wesley."

Nov. 23. — In Arundel Castle, Eng., *Lord Edmund Lyons*, aged 68. He was born in 1790, entered the navy in 1802, and was made Commander in 1812. He was appointed in 1835 Minister at Athens, and from 1851 to 1853 he was Minister at Stockholm. During the Crimean war he rendered most important services as commander of the fleet.

Sept. 15. — In Bradfield, Berks, Eng., *Rev. Charles Marriot, B. D.*, aged 47. He was the author of several theological works, published many sermons, and was for ten years associated with Dr. Pusey and Mr. Keble as joint editor of "The Library of the Fathers." He was also the first editor of the "Literary Churchman," and was one of its most valuable contributors.

Nov. 16. — In Eywood, Herefordshire, England, *Lazarus Mészáros*, aged 62, a distinguished Hungarian general and patriot. He was a member of the Hungarian Academy of Sciences; was Hungarian Minister of War in 1848; was confined in Kutaia from August, 1849, to May, 1851, when he went to England; remained there two years, then went to America and became a naturalized citizen of the United States. He returned to England in October, 1858.

Oct. 31. — In Milan, *Charles Mozart*, aged 79, second and only surviving son of the great composer.

Nov. 17. — In Newtown, Wales, *Robert Owen*, aged 80, founder of what is called Socialism. He was born in Newtown; was teacher in a school at the age of seven, and under-master at nine. At the age of eighteen he became a partner in a cotton-mill, and rose from one lucrative position to another until he became head of the New Lanark establishment, which included a farm of 150 acres, and supported two thousand inhabitants. He carried out here his peculiar plans and theories, and his social and educational success was so great that in spite of his infidelity and liberalism many prelates and statesmen went to him to inspect his schools, and to learn his method. Metternich had many interviews with him, and employed government clerks for several days to register conversations. In 1828 the English government sanctioned his going to Mexico. In 1824 he formed the group of communities in America at Harmony, Indiana, but the experiment was a short one. As early as 1816 he founded Infant schools. During the latter years of his life his mind was much employed with spirit-rappings.

Nov. 11. — In Gateshead, Eng., *Hugh Lee Pattinson, Esq., F. R. S.*, aged 60. He was in early life a tradesman, but soon discovered a taste for mineralogy, and was employed as assayer to the Commissioners of Greenwich Hospital. He was afterwards engaged at some lead-works, and while there discovered a process of extracting silver from lead. He made many valuable improvements in the industrial arts, one of the most important of which was his substitute for white lead. He was a member of many learned societies.

Nov. 8. — In Ely, Eng., *Rev. George Peacock, D. D.*, Dean of Ely, aged 67. For twenty-five years he filled the offices of tutor and professor in the University at Cambridge, during which time he did much to promote mathematical learning by lectures and by writings. He was made Dean of Ely in 1839.

Dec. 31. — In London, Eng., *Charles Phillips*, aged 70, the eminent Irish Barrister, and at the time of his death Commissioner of the Insolvent Debtor's Court. He was the author of a "Life of Curran."

Oct. 25. — In Manchester, Eng., *Sir John Potter*, aged 43. He was at the head of a mercantile house in that city, and had been for three years Mayor of the city, during which time he took the chief part in founding the Manchester Free Library. Near the expiration of his mayoralty, he was knighted by Queen Victoria, who was then visiting Manchester. His father while Mayor of Manchester had been knighted by the same sovereign.

Oct. 21. — In England, *Major-General Sir William Reid, K. C. B.* He served in the Peninsular War. In 1832 he was employed at Barbadoes in rebuilding the Government buildings which had been destroyed by a hurricane, and then conceived the idea of his well-known work on the "Law of Storms." He was subsequently Governor of Bermuda, Barbadoes, and Malta, and was chairman of the Executive Committee of the Great Exhibition of 1851.

Sept. 1. — In Dresden, Prussia, *Moritz Steinla*, aged 66, Professor of Engraving at the Dresden Academy. His best work is the engraving of the "Madonna" of Holbein.

Dec. 1. — In Richmond, Eng., *Richard Taylor*, aged 77. He learned the printer's trade, and during his leisure hours made himself acquainted with several languages, especially of those of the mediæval age. In 1808 he established himself as a printer, and his press soon became the favorite one for all classical and scientific publications. He was made member of various literary and scientific societies; and was from 1822 to his death co-editor of the Philosophical Magazine. He established the "Annals of Natural History," published several volumes of "Taylor's Scientific Memoirs," and in 1829 prepared a new edition of Horne Tooke's "Diversions of Purley."

Sept. 16. — In London, Eng., *Henry Warburton, Esq.*, aged 73. He was in early life engaged in trade, but his taste for letters, science, and politics led him to abandon commerce. He was a co-laborer with Lord Brougham in the cause of education, and in many of the reform measures.

Near Sept. — In Vienna, *Baron Ward*, the famous Yorkshire groom. He was born in Yorkshire, England, and was employed when a boy as a jockey at Vienna for four years, when he became employed by the Duke of Lucca. He was there promoted from the stable to be the valet to his Royal Highness until 1846. Eventually he became Minister of the Household, and Minister of Finance until 1848, when he became an active agent of Austria during the revolution. He returned to Parma as Prime Minister, negotiated the abdication of Charles II. and placed Charles III. on the throne. He represented Parma at the Court of Vienna until the death of Charles in 1854, when he retired from public life and engaged in agricultural pursuits. He was able to write and speak German, French, and Italian.

Sept. 15. — In London, Eng., *William Weir*, aged 56. Since 1854 the principal editor of the "Daily News." He was born in North Britain in 1802, and called to the Scottish bar in 1826.

1859.

March 28. — In Southampton, Eng., *Alderman R. Andrews*, aged 60. He was originally a journeyman blacksmith, and then became the largest coach-maker in the South of England, and accumulated a fortune. He was three times Mayor of Southampton, and it was at his residence while he was Mayor that M. Kossuth made his first great oration in England.

April 9. — In Gibraltar, on his passage home from India, *William Delafield Arnold, Esq.*, Director of Public Instruction in the Punjaub; fourth son of the late Dr. Arnold of Rugby, aged 31.

Feb 27. — In London, Eng, *William John Broderip.* He studied law and was called to the bar in 1817. He aided in the publication of several volumes of Law Reports (Broderip and Bingham), and edited a work on "Sewers." He was appointed Police Magistrate, and held the office for thirty-four years, when a tendency to deafness caused him to resign. He then devoted himself to Natural History. He wrote the articles on Zoölogy in the Penny Cyclopædia, and published many articles on subjects connected with Natural History.

July 17. — In London, Eng., *General Earl Cathcart*, a distinguised officer, and in 1846 Governor and Commander-in-chief of Canada, Nova Scotia, and New Brunswick.

June 9. — In Harborne, near Birmingham, Eng., *David Cox*, aged 76, the greatest of the English water-color landscape painters.

Near Feb. 20. — In Milan, *Count Emilio Dandolo*, a young man of unimpeachable probity, an ardent patriot, a soldier, and a man of letters. His later works are travels in Egypt, in Soudan, and in Palestine.

Jan. 28. — In Port au Prince, Hayti, *Charles Clodomir Fabre Geffrard*, a colonel in the Haytien army, and son of the President of the Republic.

April 27. — In England, *Sir Isaac Lyon Goldsmid*, aged 81. He was born in London in 1788; was created baronet in 1841, and was the first Jew on whom the title was conferred. He was a Fellow of many scientific societies, and was the first who attempted to remove the Jewish disabilities.

July 16. — In Ireland, *Henry Grattan*, the only surviving son of the distinguished Henry Grattan.

Aug. 18. — In France, *Charles Hardwick, M. A.*, Archdeacon of Ely, aged 39, author of a "History of the Articles of Religion," and of a History of the Christian Church in the Middle Ages, and, since 1855 Divinity Lecturer in King's College, Cambridge. He was accidentally killed by falling from a precipice in the Pyrenees.

Feb. 17. — In Kentish Town, Eng., *Thomas Kibble Hervey*, aged 60. He was the author of several poetical works, among which were "Australia," and "The Devil's Progress." He was a leading contributor for more than twenty years to the "Athenæum," and from 1846 to 1854 its sole editor.

May 6. — In Berlin, *Frederick Henry Alexander von Humboldt*, aged 89, known generally as Alexander von Humboldt. He was born in Berlin, September 14, 1769. From 1783 to 1786 he studied the classics, botany, philosophy, and political economy under the private direction of the professors of the University. The years 1786 to 1788 were passed at the University of Frankfort. He went in 1788 to Göttingen, and here it is said he made his first literary effort in an essay read in 1789, but never published, on the textile fabrics of the Grecians. He made geological exploring expeditions, and published their results in his first work in 1790. To make himself familiar with foreign languages, he went from Göttingen to Hamburg, and thence to the Academy of Freiberg to study under Werner, where he fitted himself to hold office in the administration of mines in Baireuth and Anspach. While holding this office he collected the materials for his works on the Fossil Flora. The death of his mother in 1796 left him free to indulge his wish, long entertained, of a great exploring voyage, for which he prepared himself by a careful study of meteorology. For this purpose he visited Paris, and here met his fellow-traveller Bonpland. They went to Spain, to Egypt, returned to Spain, and sailed from Corunna in 1799, and after visiting the Peak of Teneriffe reached Cumana July 16 of the same year. From that time until 1804 he explored the equatorial regions of South America, Central America, and Mexico, ascending Chimborazo June 23, 1802, and visiting Cuba and the United States. In 1804 he returned to Europe, reaching Bordeaux August 3, and remained in Paris arranging his materials for publication, and engaged in investigating with Gay-Lussac the composition of the atmosphere. In 1827 "The Voyage to the Equinoctial Regions of the New Continent" was published. In 1829 he commenced his second great journey of scientific exploration in the Russian Possessions in Asia, and published its results from 1837 to 1842. From 1830 to 1847 he resided alternately in Berlin and Paris; after 1847 he lived in Berlin in close intimacy with the King of Prussia. He published numerous scientific volumes and papers, but is more generally known by his

"Aspects of Nature" and "Cosmos." As a man, he was beloved and venerated throughout the civilized world.

Aug. 28. — In London, *James Henry Leigh Hunt,* the eminent poet and journalist, aged 74. He was born in England in 1784; was educated at Christ's Hospital, London; commenced his career as a journalist as theatrical critic to the "News," and afterwards established with his brother the "Examiner." While conducting that paper they were prosecuted, and were imprisoned for two years and forced to pay fines amounting to ten thousand dollars. Among his published works are "The Story of Rimini," "Lord Byron and some of his Contemporaries," "Feasts of the Poets," "Imagination and Fancy," "Wit and Humor," with numerous others, including his beautiful allegory of "Abou Ben Adhem and the Angel."

April 14. — In Bombay, *Sir Jamsetjee Jejeebhoy,* aged 76. He was at the head of the native mercantile body of India, and had been within a few years created a baronet by the British Government.

June. — In Agram, *Jellachich,* the celebrated Ban of Croatia, aged 58.

Feb. 28. — In Oxford, Eng., *Manuel John Johnson,* aged 54. In 1821 he entered the army, and during a ten years' military residence at St. Helena his taste for Astronomy was developed. The St. Helena Observatory was completed under his direction in 1829. In 1835 he published a "Catalogue of 606 Principal Fixed Stars of the Southern Hemisphere." Upon his return to England he entered Oxford, and upon taking his degree was appointed Radcliffe Observer. Of late years he gave much attention to Meteorology.

March 23. — In Paris, France, *Count Sigismund Krasinski,* a Polish noble, hero, and poet.

April 29. — In Paris, France, *Dr. Dionysius Lardner,* aged 66. He was born in Wexford, Ireland, and in 1817 graduated at Trinity College, Dublin. He remained at the University ten years and published treatises on Mathematics, and on the Steam-engine, and wrote scientific articles for the Encyclopædia. In 1827 he was elected Professor of Natural Philosophy and Astronomy in the London University. He held the office only a short period, and then devoted himself to the publication of the Cabinet Cyclopædia. In 1840 he visited the United States, where he lectured with great success. He returned to Europe in 1845. His last important work was the "Museum of Science and Art."

May 5. — Near London, Eng., *Charles Robert Leslie,* an eminent artist, aged 65. He was born in London in 1794 of American parents, but came while young to Philadelphia, where he was educated. He soon displayed a fondness for painting, and in 1811 returned to England to study the art. He was for a few months Professor of Drawing in the Military Academy at West Point.

April 27. — In Benhall, Suffolk, *Rev. John Mitford,* aged 77. He was the author of several poems, and known as the editor of the works of Gray, Milton, Dryden, and other poets.

April 13. — In London, Eng., *Lady Sydney Morgan,* aged 76. She was known in early life as Miss Owenson, the authoress of "The Wild Irish Girl," and other fictions, and in later years by her "Sketches of France, Italy, and Ireland."

March 7. — In Edinburgh, Scotland, *Sir John Archibald Murray,* aged 80. He was called to the bar in 1799. In 1834 and again in 1835 he was Lord Advocate, and in 1839 was raised to the bench.

Near April 16. — In Auteuil, near Paris, France, *Musard,* the originator of the Promenade Concerts, aged 67.

May 10. — Near Liverpool, Eng., *Susan Cushman Muspratt,* aged 37, wife of Dr. Sheridan Muspratt, known before her marriage as the accomplished actress, Susan Cushman.

May 29. — In London, Eng., *Robert Pashley,* aged 54, a distinguished scholar and lawyer, and assistant judge of the Middlesex sessions.

Aug. 7. — In Clonmel, Ireland, *Richard Pennefather,* aged 90, for thirty years a Baron of the Court of Exchequer.

Aug. 27. — In Cheltenham, Eng., *Rev. J. E. Riddle,* aged 55, known as the author of a complete English-Latin and Latin-English Dictionary, and other school and literary works.

Jan. 28. — In Putney-Heath, *Frederick John Robinson, first Earl of Ripon,* aged 76, for many years one of the prominent public men of England.

Aug. 10. — In London, Eng., *Sir George Thomas Staunton,* aged 79, author of a translation of the penal code of China, and of several works of authority on that country.

May 14. — Near Birmingham, Eng., *Joseph Sturge*, aged 65, a well-known member of the Society of Friends. He was born near Bristol in 1793. He was a corn merchant first at Bewdley, and at Birmingham from 1822 until his death. He actively participated in the various philanthropic movements of the day, and especially devoted himself to the Antislavery cause, and to the Anti-Corn-Law League, and visited America. In 1845 he attended the Peace Congress at Brussels, and had a principal share in the guidance of their proceedings until 1852. In 1854 he with two Friends went to Russia and presented to the Emperor a remonstrance against the war on religious grounds.

April. — In France, *Alexis C. H. Clarel de Tocqueville*, aged 53. He was appointed in 1831 to visit the United States and report upon the Penitentiary systems of the States. The result of his journey was his book "Democracy in America." He was member of the Chamber of Deputies from 1839 to 1848, and was Minister of Foreign Affairs under Napoleon when President.

May 1. — In Stockton-upon-Tees, Eng., *John Walker*, aged 78, a chemist, and said to be the inventor, in 1827, of lucifer or friction matches.

June 11. — Near Vienna, *Clement Wenceslas*, Prince Metternich, Duke of Portella, aged 86. He was born in 1773. At the age of 15 he entered the University of Strasbourg, but completed his studies at Mayence. In 1790 he made his first public appearance as Master of Ceremonies at the coronation of the Emperor Leopold II., and in 1794 was attached to the Austrian Embassy at the Hague. In 1801 he was appointed Minister at the Court of Dresden, and afterwards in 1803-4, as Ambassador to Berlin, he took a leading part in the arrangement of the coalition which was dissolved by the battle of Austerlitz. After the peace of Presburg he was Austrian Minister at the Court of Napoleon, where he remained until the war broke out in 1809, when he returned to the Austrian Court, and was appointed Minister of Foreign Affairs. He suggested the marriage between Napoleon and an Austrian Archduchess; conducted the negotiations, and after Napoleon was divorced from Josephine escorted Marie Louise to Paris. In 1813, on the field of Leipsic, he was raised to the dignity of a Prince of the Empire. He took a prominent part in the subsequent conferences and treaties, and signed the Treaty of Paris in behalf of Austria. At the age of forty-two he was chosen to preside at the Congress of Vienna, and subsequently exerted a powerful influence in the affairs of Europe.

April 9. — In Calcutta, *Yeh*, the well-known Chinese mandarin.

CHRONICLE OF EVENTS.

1858.

Sept. 1. — There is a grand celebration in New York, and many other cities in this country and the Provinces, in honor of the successful laying of the Atlantic Telegraph cable.

Sept. 1. — Yesterday and to-day there is a trial of steam fire-engines, under the direction of the City Government of Boston, for the prizes offered by the Insurance Companies.

Sept. 1. — The East India Company ceases to exist, and its vast possessions pass into the hands of the English Government.

Sept. 1. — There is a battle at Four Lakes, Oregon, between the U. S. troops under Col. Wright, numbering 300, and 500 Indians, in which the latter are routed, with the loss of 17 killed.

Sept. 1. — An attack is made on the State Quarantine buildings on Staten Island, New York, by an organized band of 1,000 armed men, who break in the gates, overpower all resistance, remove the sick from the hospitals, and set the buildings on fire. The Board of Health of Castleton had declared and published it to be a nuisance. The attack is renewed the night of Sept. 2.

Sept. 3. — Paul Morphy, in Paris, at the Café de la Regence, plays blindfolded eight games of chess at the same time, and in ten hours; wins six games and two were drawn.

Sept. 7. — A public debate on the subject of Slavery between Rev. Mr. Brownlow of Tennessee and Rev. Mr. Pryne of New York commences in Philadelphia.

Sept. 7. — Governor King of New York by proclamation declares, in consequence of the burning of the Quarantine buildings and hospitals at Staten Island, the County of Richmond in a state of insurrection, and that a military force shall be stationed at Quarantine.

Sept. 9. — There is a firemen's muster at Worcester, Mass.; 55 engine companies are present, besides delegations from other companies and numerous spectators. The city throughout the day and evening is in great confusion.

Sept. 13. — The steamship Austria, Capt. Heydtman, from Hamburg Sept. 2, and Southampton Sept. 4, for New York, is found to be on fire at 2 P. M. in lat. 45° 01′ N., long. 41° 30′, and is consumed. There are from 500 to 550 persons on board; only 67 are saved.

Sept. 13. — The slave "Little John" is arrested in Oberlin, Ohio, by a United States Deputy Marshal; he is rescued at Wellington, a few miles from Oberlin. In December, 37 of the principal persons connected with the affair are indicted in the U. S. Court.

Sept. 14. — The third National Exhibition of horses is opened in Springfield, Mass., and continues four days. There are 361 horses on exhibition.

Sept. 15. — The Board of Health in Mobile, Ala., declare the yellow fever epidemic in that city.

Sept. 15. — The Custom-House at Baltimore, Md., is damaged by fire to the amount of about $ 40,000.

Sept. 15. — The steamship Hammonia from Hamburg for Southampton and New York, this day explodes her magazine and puts back. Five persons are wounded.

Sept. 15. — The new Constitution of Nicaragua is promulgated and inaugurated.

Sept. 16. — The first overland mail for California leaves St. Louis, Mo., at 7 A. M., and reaches San Francisco Oct. 10.

Sept. 17. — The Boston Public Library is opened for the first time in the new building in Boylston Street, erected and fitted at a cost of nearly $ 450,000.

Sept. 19. — The temporary buildings erected by the Health Commissioners outside of Quarantine for the sick islanders from the infected district are burned.

Sept. 20. — The U. S. steamship the Niagara sails from Charleston, S. C., for Liberia with the Africans captured from the Echo. Number 271, originally 306; mortality 35.

Sept. 21. — The Russian steam frigate General Admiral is successfully launched in New York from the ship-yard of William H. Webb.

Sept. 23. — This day, appointed by the Mayor, is observed in Charleston, S. C. as a day of public fasting, on account of the yellow fever.

Sept. 24. — The corner-stone of the New York State Asylum for Inebriates is laid at Binghampton with appropriate ceremonies.

Sept. 27. — The order requiring the Police of Boston to be uniformed passes the Board of Aldermen by a vote of 8 to 4.

Sept. 29. — A magazine explodes in Havana, filled with powder, shells, and rockets, killing 28 persons and wounding 105. Ninety sugar-houses were wholly destroyed, the gas-works rendered useless, and the whole city is affected by the shock.

Oct. 4. — The corner-stone of the lighthouse to be erected on Minot's Ledge is laid by the Master of the Grand Lodge of Massachusetts, in presence of the City Government of Boston and invited guests.

Oct. 5. — A fire in the basement story of the Ohio State-House, used by the Secretary of State as a storeroom, consumes some public State documents of great value.

Oct. 5. — The Crystal Palace in New York City is destroyed by fire, with a large amount of valuable property on exhibition.

Oct. 8. — There is a violent gale in Northern New York. Snow falls in many places to the depth of several inches.

Oct. 9. — The first overland mail from California arrives at St. Louis at 8 45 P. M. in 24 days 18½ hours from San Francisco, and is received with great rejoicings. Oct. 11. There is similar rejoicing in San Francisco on the arrival of the mail there from St. Louis.

Oct. 9. — Governor Denver of Kansas issues from Lecompton a farewell address to the people of that Territory.

Oct. 16. — The Presidents of the Boston Banks issue a Circular to the New

England Banks, urging the continuance and preservation of the Suffolk Bank system.

Oct. 16.—The Suffolk Bank notifies the Boston Banks that their foreign money department will be given up November 30, 1858.

Oct. 16.—It is announced in the newspapers that George Peabody of London has added $ 200,000 to the Peabody Institute of Baltimore, his donations thereto now reaching a half-million.

Oct. 17.—The "Appleton Chapel," the new house of worship for Harvard College, so called in honor of its founder, Samuel Appleton, is dedicated at Cambridge.

Oct. 20.—There is a prize-fight between Morissey and Heenan at Long Point, Canada, for the championship. After eleven rounds Morissey is declared the victor.

Oct. 20.—The bark Isla de Cuba is brought to the port of Boston from St. Michael's, in the Western Islands, where she was abandoned by her master, who had endeavored to persuade the crew to go for slaves, and is delivered into the hands of the U. S. Marshal.

Oct. 20.—Piccolomini, the Italian opera singer, sings for the first time at the Academy of Music, New York.

Oct. 21.—The steamer Ben Franklin, with 3,000 bales of cotton on board, is destroyed by fire on the Mississippi River, near Lake Providence. The passengers and their luggage are saved.

Oct. 25.—The United States Agricultural Fair at Richmond, Va., is opened to exhibitors and (26) to the public, and is kept open through the week.

Oct. 26.—The Grand Jury in New York indict several of the city officials for conspiracy and obtaining goods under false pretences.

Oct. 30.—President Buchanan issues his proclamation, warning all persons against joining in a third attempt to set on foot a military expedition against Nicaragua.

Oct. 30—The barque Parmelia Flood, built at Green Bay, Wisconsin, arrives in New York from Green Bay Sept. 11, via Quebec Oct. 15.

Nov.—With the publication for this month, Emerson's Magazine and Putnam's Monthly is discontinued. Putnam's Monthly ceased to exist in Sept. 1857.

Nov. 1.—Queen Victoria's proclamation, announcing her assuming the government of the British Territories in India, is read to the people in Bombay.

Nov. 3.—A convention of slaveholders on the eastern shore of Maryland meets at Cambridge, Md., and discusses the subject of protecting slave property. It continues in session two days.

Nov. 3.—The Grand Jury of New York City indict ex-Mayor Wood, and a majority of the Boards of Aldermen and Councilmen of 1857, for violation of the City Charter and conspiring to defraud the City.

Nov. 5.—Police-officer Rigdon of Baltimore is shot dead while on duty. He had been a witness for the government in the trial of a man for the murder of a police-officer.

Nov. 11.—The formal opening of the Detroit and Milwaukee Railroad is celebrated at Milwaukee.

Nov. 13.—A fire at Valparaiso, Chili, destroys property to the amount of $ 3,000,000.

Nov. 16.—108 Banks of New England out of Boston meet in convention in Boston, and vote that it is the duty of New England Banks to redeem their bills in Boston.

Nov. 25.—The centennial anniversary of the settlement of Pittsburg, Pa., is celebrated with much enthusiasm.

Nov. 26.—The House of Representatives of Indiana, by a vote of 51 to 45, pass the joint resolution which had previously passed the Senate, that the election of Mr. Bright and Mr. Fitch to the Federal Senate was illegal, unconstitutional, and void.

Nov. 28.—The yacht Wanderer lands more than 300 Africans near Brunswick, Ga.

Nov. 30.—The Grand Jury in Columbia, S. C., return "no bill" on all three indictments against the crew of the slaver Echo.

Dec. 2.—General Paez leaves New York for Venezuela. A demonstration is made in his honor.

Dec. 3. — The first through train on the Suez Railroad crosses the Isthmus in eleven hours from Suez to Alexandria.

Dec. 6. — A large mass-meeting is held in New Orleans in honor of Senator Douglas now visiting that city.

Dec. 8. — A fire in Cairo, Ill., destroys a building in which are the offices of the Clerk of the Common Pleas, City Clerk, and Register of Deeds. All the books and papers are destroyed. The post-office building is also destroyed.

Dec. 16. — The schooner Susan is wrecked near Balize, British Honduras. She has on board a large number of fillibusters for Nicaragua, who are brought to Mobile (Jan. 2) by the British war-steamer Basilisk.

Dec. 18. — There is an affray in Washington, D. C. between Mr. Montgomery, member of Congress from Pennsylvania, and Mr. English, member from Indiana.

Dec. 20. — The Public Library of Boston is open in its new building for the general distribution of books.

Dec. 21. — The Imperial Court of Appeal in Paris find Count de Montalembert guilty in publishing certain statements contrasting English liberty of speech with French repression of opinion, in his pamphlet entitled "India and England," and pass sentence upon him, which (Dec. 25) the Emperor Napoleon remits.

Dec. 22. — Gen. Geffrard initiates a revolution in Hayti, which results in his being proclaimed President and the overthrow and banishment of Faustin.

Dec. 22. — The legislature of Indiana, by concurrent resolution, elect Henry S. Lane and William M. McCarty to the United States Senate in place of Messrs. Bright and Fitch.

Dec. 23. — There is a violent shock of earthquake at Kingston, Jamaica.

Dec. 23. — The two houses of the Arkansas disagreeing about the day of their adjournment, Gov. Conway adjourns the Legislature to a given day.

Dec. 26. — From its first appearance in New Orleans, during the week ending June 27, to the week ending this day, there have been in that city 4,852 deaths from yellow-fever.

1859.

Jan. 1. — A two-story brick engine-house in Worcester, Mass., is nearly demolished by the explosion of illuminating-gas.

Jan. 1. — The speech of Napoleon III. to M. Hübner, the Austrian Minister, at the annual reception at the Tuileries this day, causes great sensation. It is said to have been as follows: "I regret that our relations with your government are not so good as they were; but I request you to tell the Emperor that my personal feelings for him have not changed."

Jan. 3. — The new Roman Catholic church in Montreal, Canada, is destroyed by fire.

Jan. 3. — The Trustees of the Dudley Observatory, Albany, take possession of the Observatory building, held against them by the Scientific Council.

Jan. 3. — A convention of agriculturists from all parts of the Union assembles in Washington, D. C., as an advisory board of the Patent-Office, at the invitation of Mr. Holt, the Commissioner of Patents. Marshal P. Wilder, of Mass., is chosen President, and B. Perley Poore, of Mass., Secretary. Congress refuses to appropriate money for their pay. It adjourns, Jan. 12.

Jan. 4. — The Emperor of Austria, at Vienna, in reply to the French Ambassador, expresses the profoundest personal esteem for the French Emperor, "notwithstanding the dissidences occasioned by political necessities."

Jan. 4. — The Senate of the United States abandon their old senate-chamber, and move into their new hall.

Jan. 7. — M. Couza, the new Hospodar of Moldavia, is elected to the Hospodarship of Wallachia, and the two principalities are thus practically united.

Jan. 10. — Senator Slidell introduces a bill into the United States Senate, appropriating $ 30,000,000 "to facilitate the acquisition of the island of Cuba."

Jan. 23. — Geffrard is inaugurated President of Hayti.

Jan. 23. — There is a volcanic eruption in the Hawaian Islands. The lava bursts forth about three thousand feet from the summit of Mauna Loa and flows into the sea, Jan. 31, a distance of forty miles from the place of the eruption.

Jan. 26. — Commissioner Bowlin is received in Paraguay by President Lopez and delivers his credentials. Jan. 27, negotiations are commenced which, Feb. 10, terminate favorably in the signing of the treaty.

Jan. 29. — Prince Napoleon marries Princess Clotilde, at Turin.

Feb. 1. — The new standard of weight for the sale of corn in Liverpool, Eng., and other markets, founded on the decimal principle, comes into operation.

Feb. 5. — Mr. Russell's steam mechanical bakery in Boston, Mass., is burned with its contents. It had just commenced operations.

Feb. 8. — The buildings of William and Mary College at Williamsburg, Va., are destroyed by fire.

Feb. 12. — The Prussian government issue a circular despatch, expressing the hope that peace will not be interrupted.

Feb. 17. — A public ball is given in Washington, D. C., in honor of Lord and Lady Napier.

Feb. 20. — By continued rains, the Ohio and other Western rivers overflow their banks. Railroad trains are stopped.

Feb. 22-24. — A national convention of Sunday-school Teachers is held in Philadelphia.

Feb. 22. — The Hannibal and St. Joseph Railroad, Mo., is completed and formally opened.

Feb. 22. — The birthday of Washington is very generally celebrated in the United States, and the Americans in London have a banquet, and in Paris they give a ball.

Feb. 23. — Lord Cowley, the British Minister, leaves Paris on a mission to Vienna, where he arrives Feb. 27, and leaves March 5.

Feb. 26. — President Buchanan vetoes the bill donating public lands to the States providing colleges for agriculture and the mechanic arts. He calls an extra session of the Senate for March 4th.

Feb. 26. — Mr. Slidell withdraws his bill to purchase Cuba.

Feb. 27. — The steamboat Princess, from Vicksburg for New Orleans, explodes her boiler and is burned near Baton Rouge. Of her passengers, 25 are killed and 35 wounded, mostly residents of Louisiana and Mississippi.

Feb. 27. — In Washington, D. C., Daniel E Sickles, Representative in Congress from New York, kills Philip Barton Key, United States District Attorney for the District, for an alleged intrigue with the wife of Mr. Sickles. Mr. Sickles is indicted for the murder, but the jury, April 26, on the twentieth day of the trial, acquit him.

Feb. 28. — Mr. Disraeli presents to the House of Commons his new Reform Bill.

March 1. — Many leading members of Congress of different political parties tender a public dinner to Hon. A. H. Stephens, of Georgia, as a mark of their personal respect on his retirement from Congress; which he, March 2, declines.

March 1. — A fire in Memphis, Tenn., consumes a portion of one of the principal squares on Main Street, destroying several newspaper offices, and property to the amount of $ 150,000.

March 5-25. — Public meetings in favor of the Reform movement are held from time to time in London and in the principal places in England.

March 5. — The Boston Post-Office is removed from State Street to the new building in Summer Street. June 4th, it goes back to State Street.

March 5. — The Federal Council unanimously decide to defend and uphold by every means the integrity and neutrality of the Swiss territory.

March 5. — The Emperor Napoleon explains, as is said, in the Moniteur, his intentions in regard to Sardinia and Austria.

March 8. — Poerio and his companions, who had been liberated from prison by the king of Naples, arrive in Cork, Ireland.

March 9. — Joseph Holt, Commissioner of Patents, is confirmed as Postmaster-General.

March 10. — The special session of the United States Senate adjourns.

March 16. — Forty-six railroads are represented in convention at Buffalo.

March 18. — General Miramon appears with his troops before Vera Cruz, and, March 27, commences his retreat from that city. There is no fighting.

March 19. — Thirty-five fillibusters, some of them escaped convicts from Cuba, sail from New York to invade Cuba. They attempt to land (April 7th), but fail, and sail for Port au Prince, where they arrive April 12th.

March 19. — There is a terrible accident on the Great Western Railway, Canada, between Copetown and Dundas. The embankment was washed away to the depth of twenty feet, and the cars are precipitated together into this hole. Six persons are killed, and many are wounded.

March 19.—The English papers announce that Russia proposes a Congress of the Five Powers. March 23, Count Buol informs the Russian Minister at Vienna that the Austrian Emperor accepts the proposition.

March 22.—There is a violent earthquake in the city of Quito and the surrounding country. A large part of the city is destroyed.

March 26.—The Governor-General of Canada gives his assent to the new tariff bill, which goes into immediate operation.

March 27.—Governor Cumming, of Utah Territory, protests against the United States troops being stationed around the court-house at Provo during the session of the Federal Court; and, March 30, Judge Cradlebaugh denounces in court the protest of the Governor.

March 28.—Thirty vessels are detained on the bar below New Orleans, with cargoes of cotton amounting to over 100,000 bales.

March 29.—Quito is much injured by an earthquake. Churches, monasteries, and government buildings are thrown down. It is said that 5,000 persons were killed, and $ 3,000,000 of property were destroyed.

March 29.—The Cochituate aqueduct gives way at Newton Lower Falls, at the crossing of Charles River. Before the water could be shut off, it had made a ravine 60 feet wide at the top, about 80 feet deep, and 200 feet in length. The breach is repaired in a few days.

March 31.—The Derby ministry are defeated on the Reform Bill, by a vote of 291 to 330.

April 2.—A beautiful exhibition of the phenomena of "Parhelia" or "mock suns" is witnessed this afternoon throughout Massachusetts and other of the New England States.

April 4.—Mr. McLane, the minister in Mexico, recognizes the Juarez government, and presents his credentials to Juarez at Vera Cruz.

April 6.—The lower Levee Press in New Orleans, La., with a large amount of cotton, is burned. The loss is stated at $ 1,000,000.

April 12.—Lord Lyons, the new British minister at Washington, presents his credentials to President Buchanan.

April 13.—A fearful storm sweeps the southern coast of Brazil. Many vessels are destroyed, and a Brazilian frigate is lost and all but 40 of her officers and crew.

April 14.—The reactionary Mexican Government (of Zuloaga and Miramon) protest against the recognition of Juarez, a Constitutional Government by Mr. McLane, and against all treaties, &c., made by the same. They deliver his passports to Mr. Black, the American Consul, and withdraw the exequature from all the American consular offices in Mexico.

April 15.—Bushnell, one of the alleged rescuers of the slave Little John, is found guilty in the Federal Court at Cleveland, Ohio.

April 16.—In the United States Circuit Court for South Carolina, the jury find the crew of the slaver Echo not guilty.

April 16.—The corner-stone of the Peabody Institute in Baltimore, Md., is laid.

April 17.—There is a riot at Panama between the natives within the city and the blacks without the walls. At the request of the U. S. Consul, Commodore Long sends on shore three hundred men to protect the American residents.

April 18.—Tantia Topee, the last of the principal rebel chiefs in India, is hanged.

April 18-23.—During these days it is said that 3,500 volunteers arrived at Genoa, and 2,000 at Turin.

April 19.—The Sardinian ministry decide to yield to the demand of England and France, and accepts the principle of disarmament.

April 19.—The Austrian Government notify Sardinia to place its army on a peace footing and to disband the Italian volunteers, and to answer within three days from the delivery of the summons "Yes" or "No." The summons is presented at Turin, April 23.

April 21.—The English Cabinet transmit a telegram to the Court of Vienna, protesting most strongly against this "hasty and haughty menace."

April 23.—The English papers announce that an "intimate understanding" exists between France and Russia.

April 23.—The Sardinian Parliament is convoked, and confers on the King full powers to meet the exigencies of the times; and the army is placed on a war footing.

April 23 - 25. — The French troops leave Paris for the frontier on their march to Piedmont. April 26. Some arrive at Genoa; and April 30, they reach Turin.

April 24. — The steamer St. Nicholas, from St Louis to New Orleans, explodes her boilers near 10 o'clock, P. M. 30 or 40 persons are said to be killed or missing The boat and cargo are a total loss.

April 26. — The King of Sardinia refuses to comply with the summons of Austria to disarm.

April 26. — The French Chargé d'Affaires at Vienna announces to the Austrian Government that the French Emperor would consider the crossing of the Ticino by the Austrian troops as a declaration of war.

April 27. — The troops in Tuscany fraternize with the revolutionists, and the Grand Duke abdicates.

April 28. — Señor Mata is presented to the President as minister from Mexico to the United States.

April 28. — The Supreme Court of Ohio refuse Bushnell's (one of the Oberlin rescuers) application for a *habeas corpus*, the proceedings against him in the Federal District Court not yet being terminated.

April 28. — The emigrant ship Pomona is lost off the coast of Wexford, Ireland. Of 380 passengers only 23 are saved.

April 29. — The Emperor of Austria publishes his declaration of war, and his troops cross the Ticino.

April 29. — The opening of the Brooklyn (N. Y) water-works is celebrated.

April 30. — The English government offer a large bounty for seamen.

May 2. — The steamship Edinburgh, from New York for Glasgow, strikes an iceberg, and (May 3) puts into St. Johns, N. F., with two compartments full of water.

May 3. — The French Emperor publishes his declaration of war.

May 3. — The St. Petersburg papers announce that there is no treaty of alliance offensive and defensive between Russia and any other country.

May 7. — The subscription to the French Loan of 500,000,000 francs opens, and is closed May 17. The number of subscribers exceeds 525,000; the amount subscribed, 2,307,000,000 francs.

May 8. — The brig Rolerson, from Pensacola (Fla.) for Boston, stops at Hyannis, Mass., with a fugitive slave (Columbus Jones) on board, who (May 9) is sent to Norfolk in the schooner Elizabeth. The parties concerned in sending him back are arrested for kidnapping and held to bail.

May 10. — The Emperor Napoleon leaves Paris for the seat of war, and arrives in Genoa May 12. The Empress Eugenie is made Regent.

May 11. — The Archduke of Austria, father of the present Emperor, dies at Vienna.

May 11. — A Southern Convention assembles at Vicksburg, Miss. Eight States are represented. Resolutions in favor of reopening the slave-trade are introduced.

May 13. — Brevet-Major Van Dorn, with United States troops, attacks a party of from 90 to 100 Camanche Indians near old Fort Atkinson, and kills 49, wounds 5, and captures 36.

May 16. — The Knight Templars from Boston and Providence arrive in Richmond, Va.

May 16. — The Grand Jury in Charleston, S. C., refuse to indict Capt. Corrie, of the Wanderer.

May 16. — A destructive fire at Key West. An area of twenty acres is burned over, 110 houses are destroyed, and property destroyed to the amount of $ 2,750,000.

May 19 — A reciprocal money-order system has been adopted between Great Britain and Canada.

May 20. — The battle of Montebello is fought between the Austrians and the allies. The latter are successful. The French general estimates his loss at 700 killed and wounded; Austrian (official) killed 290, wounded 718, missing 283.

May 22. — Ferdinand II., the King of the Two Sicilies, dies, aged 49. His successor is Francis II. The English court go into mourning from June 5 to June 19.

May 23. — Garibaldi, with his volunteers, is at the foot of the Lago Maggiore; 24th, he compels the Austrians to retreat from Varese; May 27th, he is in possession of Como.

May 24. — A tornado near Jacksonville, Illinois; and near Iowa City, Iowa, there is a water-spout.

May 26. — The post-office, land-office, and other buildings at Dubuque, Iowa, are burned.

May 30. — The battle of Palæstro is fought. The Austrians are defeated.

May 30. — President Buchanan leaves Washington on a visit to the University of North Carolina.

May 31. — The new English Parliament assemble. In the House of Commons, John Evelyn Dennison is re-elected Speaker.

June 3. — Mr. Joseph Charless, President of the Mechanics' Bank in St. Louis, Mo., and one of the most esteemed citizens of that place, is shot dead in the street by Joseph W. Thornton.

June 3–5. — There is a great flood in the Upper Mississippi. Great damage is done at St. Paul and St. Anthony.

June 4. — The battle of Magenta is fought. The loss of the Austrians (official) is 1,365 killed, 4,348 wounded, and 4,000 missing. French 223 killed, 2,165 wounded, 470 missing. June 8, the French Emperor and the King of Sardinia enter Milan.

June 4. — There are severe frosts throughout Ohio, Indiana, Western New York, and the New England States.

June 8. — A fire at Salem, Mass., destroys a large amount of property, $ 100,000.

June 8. — A Slaveholder's Convention assembles at Baltimore, Md. Each County in the State is represented, except Alleghany and Baltimore City. Delegates subsequently attend from the city.

June 8. — Telegrams between England and India are accelerated about seven days by the submarine telegraph cable laid down in the Red Sea.

June 9. — The Duchess of Parma leaves Parma.

June 9. — Kossuth warns his exiled fellow-countrymen in America that it is not yet time for them to move.

June 10. — The Derby Ministry are defeated on the motion to amend the Address, the vote being 323 for the amendment to 310 against it.

June 14. — The bark Orion is brought into New York from the coast of Africa, where she was seized by the United States officers as a slaver.

June 16. — A public meeting is held in Boston to devise means to help the starving inhabitants of Fayal.

June 20 to July 1. — Unusually excessive heat prevails in California, the mercury ranging in some places from 102o to 113o in the shade.

June 20. — Perugia, which had revolted from the authority of the Pope, is captured by a body of his Swiss troops. Extraordinary cruelties are committed upon the inhabitants. The Pope promotes the commanding officer.

June 20. — The Emperor of Austria assumes the sole command of his army.

June 22. — Kossuth arrives at Genoa, and 23, at Turin.

June 24. — The battle of Solferino is fought. The Austrians are defeated with a loss of 2,352 killed, 10,645 wounded. 9,289 missing. The loss of the French in killed and wounded is stated to be 12,000 rank and file, and 720 officers.

June 25. — The English and French attempt to force the passage of the Peiho, but are repulsed by the Chinese with a total of 634 killed and wounded, and the loss of three gunboats and others greatly injured. The American squadron render assistance to the sufferers.

June 27. — A fearful railroad accident occurs on the Michigan Southern Railroad, near South Bend. A culvert is washed away, and the cars are thrown into the chasm. 38 are killed, and over 50 wounded.

June 27. — Forty-two prisoners escape from the State Prison in California in open day. The remaining prisoners, 160 in number, preparing to follow, are fired upon, and return to the yard. Of those escaping, several are killed, and the most of the others are brought back.

June 30. — M. Blondin walks across Niagara River on a tight rope. He repeats the feat afterwards several times.

June and July. — There is a remarkable religious revival in Ireland.

June. — "Gold placers" are said to be discovered at Plymouth, Vt., and 300 miners are there at work.

July. — Excessive heat prevails in Europe. July 6th is said to have been the hottest day ever known in Paris.

July 1. — Mr. Wise, the balloonist, with three companions, leaves St. Louis in the "Airship Atlantic," at 7.20 P. M. They land, July 2, near Henderson, Jefferson Co., New York, at 2.20 P. M., having travelled 1,200 miles in 19 hours.

July 4. — The first national banquet in honor of the day is given by the Americans in Paris.

July 9. — The island of San Juan, near Vancouver's Island, is taken possession of by General Harney with United States troops. Governor Douglass of British Columbia protests.

July 5. — The Kansas Constitutional Convention assembles at Wyandotte.

July 8. — An armistice is concluded between the French and Austrians, to extend to August 15th.

July 11. — A treaty of peace is signed by the Emperors of France and Austria at Villafranca.

July 12. — The Tuscan Council of State unanimously vote the union of Tuscany with the new kingdom of Northern Italy, under the House of Savoy.

July 12. — The Juarez government in Mexico decree the secularization of the Church property and the abolition of the religious orders.

July 17. — A tornado passes over the city of Memphis, destroying property to a considerable amount.

July 22. — A steam-boiler in the wire-factory of Messrs. J. Washburn & Co., at Worcester, Mass., 30 feet long, 4 feet in diameter, and weighing about 5 tons, explodes, shatters the brick engine-house, and a portion of it, weighing nearly 3 tons, is thrown into the air 200 feet high, and strikes the ground three eighths of a mile from the factory. Of more than 100 persons at work in the factory, only five are injured.

July 24. — Dr. Doy, under sentence in the jail of St. Joseph, Mo., for kidnapping, is rescued.

July 25. — The builders' strike in London (to make the working day *nine* hours) commences by 470 workmen leaving the employment of Messrs. Trollope & Sons.

July 27. — The Emperor Napoleon returns to St. Cloud.

July 30. — The Grand Duke of Tuscany abdicates in favor of his son, Archduke Ferdinand, born June 10, 1835.

July. — The Panama papers announce the discovery of gold images to a large amount in the Indian graves at Chiriqui.

August. — Vigilance Committees have been formed in Louisiana, and the Governor issued his proclamation ordering them to disband.

Aug. 2. — A convention of colored persons is held in Boston, Mass., to consider their political and social condition.

Aug. 8. — The conference at Zurich meets for the first time.

Aug. 8. — The first trial of the paddles and screws of the Great Eastern is made with great success.

Aug. 13. — The State Reform School at Westboro', Mass., is nearly destroyed by fire, set by one of the inmates.

Aug. 14. — Napoleon and the army of Italy make their triumphal entry into Paris. The "fêtes Napoleon" continue through Monday, the 15th.

Aug. 17. — The Moniteur announces "a full and entire amnesty to all persons sentenced for political crimes and offences, and to those who have been the object of any measures taken for public security." Louis Blanc and Victor Hugo, among others, decline to accept it.

Aug. 21. — The City House of Reformation, at Deer Island in Boston Harbor, is set on fire by one of the boy inmates, and is nearly destroyed.

Aug. 24. — A destructive conflagration in New Bedford, Mass., destroys property, it is said, to the value of $ 300,000.

Aug 28. — There is a beautiful exhibition of the Aurora Borealis. See *ante*, pp. 65, 66.

Aug. 31. — The National Assembly of Tuscany unanimously vote that Tuscany shall form part of an Italian kingdom under Victor Emmanuel; and a deputation, Sept. 3, present this action to the king of Sardinia.

ADDITIONS AND CORRECTIONS.

Page 86.—FLOWERING OF FRUIT-TREES IN 1859.

Places.	Plum.	Pear.	Peach.	Cherry.	Apple.
Naples, Me., near Portland,		May 26			May 26
Montpelier, Vt.,	May 15				May 28
Cambridge, Mass.,	May 13	May 8	May 12*	May 8	May 25
Lambertville, N. J.,	April 18	April 18	April 19	April 18	April 24
Perth Amboy, N. J.,	April 26	April 30		April 23	May 5
Powhatan Hill, King George Co., Va.,	March 23-26	April 4	March 18-23	March 28	April 12
Savannah, Ga.,	March 1		Feb. 20		
Columbus, Ohio,	April 14	April 17	April 9	April 15	May 3

Page 97.—The land-office at Helena, Arkansas, is to be discontinued from Jan. 1, 1859.

Page 99.—The residence of Ward B. Burnett is said to be Nebraska City, Neb. T.

Page 108.—Captain Thomas Paine died November 9, at Washington, D. C.

Page 112.—The residence of Judge Grier is Philadelphia, Pa.

Page 114.—James J. Roosevelt is District Attorney of the Southern District, New York, *vice* Sedgwick, deceased.

Page 122.—M. Theodore Mercier is French Minister, *vice* M. le Comte de Sartiges.

Page 144.—The Public Debt, July 1, 1859, was $ 58,821,777.66, being, permanent debt, $ 43,775,977.66, and Treasury-notes, $ 15,046,800. The permanent debt had been increased, to Dec. 1, 1859, $ 1,380,000, the balance of the $ 20,000,000 loan.

Page 152.—The imports for the year ending June 30, 1859, were $ 338,768,130; the exports for the same period were $ 356,789,462.

Page 167.—The *gross revenue* of the Post-office Department from all sources, for the year ending June 30, 1859, was $ 7,968,484.07. Actual paid *expenditures*, $ 11,458,083.63; additional *liabilities*, $ 4,296,009.26; total expenditures and liabilities, $ 15,754,092.89. Deficit, $ 7,785,608.82.

Page 189.—Morton S. Wilkinson is elected Senator from Minnesota, and Louis T. Wigfall from Texas.

Page 204.—Rev. George W. Samson, D. D., is President of Columbian College, Washington, D. C.

Page 211.—The salary of the Governor of Indiana is $ 3,000.

Page 258.—The receipts of the *Sinking Fund*, including the balance, were $ 614,041.17, and not $ 572,877.29. The balance of *Ordinary Revenue* in 1858 was $ 36,727.58.

Page 295.—The statement of the condition of the Banks of St. Louis, at the dates named, is as follows:—

1859.	Exchange maturing.	Circulation.	Specie.
January 8,	$ 3,297,559	$ 2,030,608	$ 1,705,962
February 5,	2,480,693	2,032,235	1,599,203
March 5,	3,545,202	1,808,100	1,575,362
April 2,	3,337,296	1,566,380	1,542,211
May 7,	3,435,940	1,300,835	1,549,133
June 4,	3,678,049	1,267,675	1,367,181
July 2,	3,331,027	1,028,760	1,353,069
August 6,	3,265,140	919,460	1,190,829
September 3,	3,306,732	684,745	894,908
October 1,	3,190,900	550,810	820,574
November 5,	2,960,496	537,720	816,334
December 3,	3,256,203	497,890	683,496

Pages 323, 326.—The estimated population of Oregon in 1859 is 60,000. P. P. Prim, of Jackson Co., is Judge, *vice* Matthew P. Deady. Judge Prim is Judge of the 1st Circuit, Judge Stratton of the 2d, Judge Boise of the 3d, and Judge Wait of the 4th. The Supreme Court has a session annually at Salem, on the 2d Monday in December, and at Portland, on the 2d Monday of July.

Pages 359, 360.—The proposed Territory of *Arizona* is bounded *west* by the Rio Colorado; *south* by Sonora and Chihuahua, on the boundary line between the United States and Mexico, and from the Rio Grande on the 32d parallel of latitude in Texas to the 104° of longitude; *east* by a line on the 104° of longitude to the 34th parallel of latitude, thence *north* on the 34th parallel to the Colorado River. It has an area of about 100,000 square miles. The population is from 8,000 to 10,000. Nine tenths are Mexicans, and they are chiefly in the valley of the Rio Grande. There is an abundance of mineral wealth, but very little agricultural land.

Decotah is bounded *east* by Minnesota and Iowa; *south* and *west* by the Missouri River and Nebraska Territory, and *north* by the British possessions;—being that portion of *Minnesota* not included in her *State* boundary. It has an area of about 65,000 square miles, and an estimated population (which is rapidly increasing) of from 6,000 to 8,000 inhabitants. It has a large quantity of fertile agricultural land. The products are those of the Northwestern States. There are numerous salt lakes. Some coal has been found. Timber is scarce, but there is said to be enough for all building purposes.

There are two other proposed Territories,—that of *Jefferson*, embracing the Pike's Peak gold country, and that of *Nevada*.

* Hardly any blossoms. The peach crop of New England was mostly cut off.

Penmanship and Book-keeping.

THE UNRIVALLED SYSTEM OF PENMANSHIP.

The most successful series of Copy-Books ever published. In use throughout the United States, from Maine to California.

Payson, Dunton, and Scribner's Combined System of Rapid Penmanship. In eleven parts. With copies at the head of each page, executed in the most beautiful manner, and in a style exactly resembling a copy written by the authors with pen.

The history of this Series of Copy-Books is unprecedented in the annals of Chirography, and its wonderful success is only to be accounted for by its unequalled merit, and its peculiar adaptation to the wants of our schools. Commenced in the year 1851, the novel features of the system at once attracted the attention of teachers, and commended it to the use of those desirous of advancing their pupils in this branch of education. The old and laborious plan of requiring the teacher to set the copies for each scholar was at once superseded by a plan which furnished a copy at the head of every page, in exact imitation of a finished handwriting, and far more beautiful than could be written by any but a most accomplished penman. A marked improvement was at once visible in the schools where this system was introduced, and so manifest was the fact of its superiority to any previous publication, that it at once took the lead of all others, and acquired a reputation as extensive as our country. The authors of this System, being all practical teachers devoted to their profession, have, from time to time, improved the Series, by incorporating into it the results acquired by so many years' experience; and have thus, with the assistance of the publishers, who have spared neither labor nor expense, been able to present the public the most valuable and popular Series of Copy-Books ever published.

Payson, Dunton, and Scribner's Chirographic Chart. Comprising the Elements of the Letters, both large and small, with full and systematic directions for their formation and combination. Illustrated by Polygrams on an entirely new plan. The whole on a large sheet, executed in the most beautiful manner, and designed for illustration in the school-room.

Hanaford and Payson's Book-keeping. For Schools and Academies. Adapted to Payson, Dunton, and Scribner's Combined System of Penmanship. Issued in three different editions.

The most complete and elegant work of the kind ever published. Some of the leading peculiarities of these books are: 1. The engraved ACCOUNT BOOKS, which are *fac-similes* of handwriting so much admired in the Copy-Books, which serve as models for Book-keeping and copies for Penmanship. 2. The rules and explanations are very plain and simple, at the same time very full. 3. The size and forms are such as are most convenient for the school-room. 4. The price is moderate, bringing it within the reach of all who have use for it.

Book-keeping by Single and Double Entry. For High Schools and Academies.

*** These works are designed to follow the System of Penmanship so well known and so deservedly popular throughout the United States. They combine instruction in both Book-keeping and Penmanship, the exercises being fac-similes of the beautiful style of writing taught in the Copy-Books. The Chart, Copy-Books, and Book-keeping, are more full and complete than any before published. The master of one of the largest schools in Boston says: "I have just introduced Hanaford and Payson's 'Book-keeping by Single and Double Entry' into my school. It appeared to me to possess several points of excellence, which determined my choice. Its copies are excellent, and the whole book is 'got up' in a beautiful style. Its teachings are simple, intelligible, to the point, and very concise; while it presents all the facts necessary to be learned by an ordinary student of the subject."

All interested in Education

Are respectfully requested to examine the above works, which comprise a complete course of instruction in the important branches of Penmanship and Book-keeping. The publishers would also respectfully call attention to the fact that these books contain ideas entirely original, and have therefore served as models for imitation, which unprincipled parties have not hesitated to follow.

TOWER'S NEW GRAMMAR.

TOWER'S COMMON-SCHOOL GRAMMAR;

With Models of Clausal, Phrasal, and Verbal Analysis, and Parsing; gradually developing the Construction of the English Sentence. By DAVID B. TOWER, A.M., Author of "Gradual Lessons in Grammar" and "Sequel," "Elements of Grammar," "Grammar of Composition," "Oral Algebra," "Readers," etc. 12mo. Price, 42c.

This work is designed to follow TOWER'S ELEMENTS OF GRAMMAR, OR FIRST LESSONS IN LANGUAGE; being a continuation and further development of the system which has given that book such widely extended popularity.

The ELEMENTS OF GRAMMAR, OR FIRST LESSONS IN LANGUAGE, so favorably received, so strongly commended, and so extensively used, at the very start, has steadily increased in circulation and popularity, till, it is said, no text-book on this subject is so successful, or gives such universal satisfaction.

Out of this popular use of the ELEMENTS has grown an urgent demand for another Grammar, on the *same plan*, more full in particulars, and more extended in application, to meet the wants of advanced pupils, and to complete a preparatory course to Composition.

In complying with this request, urged from every quarter, we have thought it best to have such a text-book prepared as would meet the expressed wish of teachers on this point, and at the same time furnish a preliminary course.

The book, then, is intended as a School Grammar, complete in itself; yet so far a further development and continuance of the plan adopted in the ELEMENTS, that it will most advantageously *follow* that book. The GRADUAL LESSONS IN GRAMMAR, which was the *first System of Analysis* published in this country, has been highly praised by the most prominent educators; but it is not on the plan of the ELEMENTS, and therefore does not well follow it. Hence the call for a new book.

These Grammars, with the GRAMMAR OF COMPOSITION, make a full course in the study of written language, and the application of the principles of grammar to *Composition*. School committees and teachers are invited to examine them.

The following extract from a letter of D. P. GALLOUP, Esq., Principal of the Varnum School, Lowell, is the unsolicited opinion of a gentleman well known as a prominent and most successful teacher, and one whose judgment is entitled to great weight: —

"Tower's Common-School Grammar I have examined with much interest. This, with his "Elements," is all we want in our Grammar Schools. I like its definitions, and the inverted form of some of them in the introduction. No matter in how many different ways the same idea is expressed, I believe, with the author, that 'a thought should have several suits of clothing,' and that they should be changed so often, that it may be recognized in spite of its dress.

"This book does not do all the work for the pupil, or require it to be done for him during recitation, but leaves something for him to do himself, by way of preparation. Those books, and those teachers, are always best for the scholar that lead him to do his own thinking, instead of doing it for him."

The Board of Education of the State of Vermont has directed the introduction of TOWER'S ELEMENTS OF GRAMMAR into all the District Schools of the State; and has also recommended the introduction of the Grammar of Composition; Payson, Dunton, and Scribner's Penmanship; and Hanaford and Payson's Book-keeping.

HON. THOMAS H. BENTON, jun., *Secretary of the Board of Education of Iowa*, recommends the introduction of Tower's Elements, Grammar of Composition, Algebra; Payson, Dunton, and Scribner's Penmanship; and Hanaford and Payson's Book-keeping.

The New Hampshire Board of Education adopts Tower's Elements, and Hanaford and Payson's Book-keeping. The Penmanship is already widely introduced into the Schools.

THE BOSTON TRAVELLER
FOR 1860.

Encouraged by the commendation they have received from intelligent newspaper readers, and business men in every part of the country, as also from a steady increase of circulation, and enlarged advertising in its columns, the proprietors present with strong and renewed confidence the programme of the

DAILY, SEMI-WEEKLY, AND WEEKLY TRAVELLER,

FOR THE COMING YEAR.

These journals are now edited by gentlemen who have had many years' experience in editorial life, and were early educated to the profession. They are aided by a large and efficient corps of Assistants, Reporters, and Correspondents in the various departments, so as to be able to furnish to the public some of the cheapest and at the same time most valuable papers in the country.

The TRAVELLER aims to be a complete Family Newspaper, always maintaining a high moral tone; instructive and interesting; embracing all the tastes and interests of the Domestic Circle, — Literary, Scientific, Religious, and Industrial, generally. It is a paper specially designed for introduction to the Family Fireside, and a paper the good influence of which upon every relation of life, in such a circle, has long been appreciated by the most intelligent and worthy in the community, as of great and inestimable value. It is also largely devoted to **NEWS**, and will give in a compendious and intelligible manner a full history of all the events of the times, separating, as far as possible, the true and valuable grain from the great mass of chaff and rubbish, with which much of the actual news of the times comes encumbered, since the great increase of journalism and the introduction of the Magnetic Telegraph.

THE DAILY EVENING TRAVELLER is rapidly increasing in circulation, and the increase is going on at this time at the rate of *one thousand copies a week*, — but the proprietors are disposed to avoid boasting, and work on quietly to deserve the appreciation of the public.

SEMI-WEEKLY TRAVELLER,

Published TUESDAY and FRIDAY MORNINGS, at Three Dollars a year, and as follows:

TO CLUBS.

Five Copies one year.................$12.50	Ten Copies one year.................$20.00

To all men engaged in commerce and manufactures, and who desire a newspaper which gives the best epitome of business affairs of every description, divested of the great mass of matter and advertisements of a local character which necessarily fills a large space in the columns of the *daily* press, confidently recommend the SEMI-WEEKLY TRAVELLER as one of the most useful papers in the country.

WEEKLY TRAVELLER.

The best Family Paper in New England.

THE WEEKLY TRAVELLER is one of the best and cheapest papers in the country. Each number contains, in addition to much other interesting reading, a comprehensive review of all the news of the week, a choice selected Sermon of Henry Ward Beecher's, and a good moral story.

PRICE OF THE WEEKLY TRAVELLER.

One copy, one year,....................$2.00	Five copies, one year, to one address, $6.00
Two copies, one year, to one address,..3.00	Ten copies, one year, to one address, 10.00

And to the getter up and paymaster of the club, one copy for each ten copies paid for.

PAYMENT INVARIABLY IN ADVANCE, and the paper will always be stopped when the time is out, so that no one may run the risk of having the paper forced upon him.

To Advertisers.

The TRAVELLER is among the papers of largest circulation in the country, and though it is exceeded in number by a few of the more cheaply printed journals, yet the high character of its contents, and its beauty of typography, printed as it is with new type, and on a superior quality of paper, gives it a wide circulation among the comfortable, intelligent, and wealthy classes, who have money to spend, and are the best customers of advertising parties.

WORTHINGTON, FLANDERS, & CO., Publishers,
31 State Street, Boston.

DR. HUNTINGTON'S NEW VOLUME.

CHRISTIAN BELIEVING AND LIVING.

A SERIES OF DISCOURSES,

BY REV. F. D. HUNTINGTON, D.D.,

Preacher to the University, and Plummer Professor of Christian Morals in Harvard College.

12mo. . . . . Price, $1.25.

The Publishers request particular attention to this volume, which, for obvious reasons, m[ay] excite great interest in the religious world.

THE TEACHER'S ASSISTANT; or, Hints and Methods [in] School Discipline and Instruction; being a Series of Familiar Letters to o[ne] entering upon the Teacher's Work. By CHARLES NORTHEND, A.M., Auth[or] of "The Teacher and Parent," &c. 12mo. Price, $1.00.

From the numerous commendatory notices of this work we select the following from gentlem[en] whose opinions upon the subject of education are entitled to universal respect.

From the Superintendent of Public Schools, Boston:

"MESSRS. CROSBY, NICHOLS, & CO.

"Gentlemen: I desire to say to you, and to all whom it may concern, that I consider your [re]cent publication, entitled the 'Teacher's Assistant,' by Charles Northend, A. M., one of the [ve]*best* books ever written for teachers and parents. It is the result of long and varied experie[nce] and extensive observation. By no other means could such a book be produced. Like its auth[or], it is sensible, sound, and practical. I would say to all teachers, whether experienced or [not], *buy it*, and *read it*, — you cannot afford to do without it. The cost is not worth mentioning [in] comparison with the benefit you may derive from it.

"Very truly yours,

"JOHN D. PHILBRICK."

From George B. Emerson, Esq.:

"Gentlemen: I have read with much pleasure the 'Teacher's Assistant' which you sent [me]. Please to accept my thanks. It is a very valuable work, and ought to be in the hands of [all] teachers, and especially of those persons who are just entering upon the work of teaching. It [is] full of important suggestions, and breathes throughout an elevated and earnest moral spirit.

"Respectfully yours,

"GEO. B. EMERSON."

HOURS WITH THE EVANGELISTS. By ICHABOD NICHO[LS], D.D. Vol. I. 8vo. Price, $2.50.

CROSBY, NICHOLS, AND COMPANY

PUBLISH

The Great American Quarterly,

THE NORTH AMERICAN REVIEW,

which they would commend to the attention of the American public, as a work which, dati[ng al]most from the commencement of the literature of our country, has always sustained its high [repu]tation wherever our language is known.

It is to America what the Edinburgh and London Quarterlies are to Great Britain, and [it] rank with them both in Europe and America.

Nearly all the great authors of our country were first brought before the public through [the] Review. WEBSTER, EVERETT, SPARKS, PRESCOTT, BANCROFT, with scores of other [em]men, of whom our literature is proud, have been among its contributors; and its pages con[tinue] to reflect the best talent of our times.

The NORTH AMERICAN REVIEW is published Quarterly, in numbers of nearly *three [hun]dred pages each*, at Five Dollars a year.

THE BOSTON TRANSCRIPT,
DAILY AND WEEKLY,
FOR 1860.

THE DAILY EVENING TRANSCRIPT

was established in **1830,** and ever since that period (thirty years) has enjoyed a larger circulation in Boston and vicinity than any other Journal. It contains all the FOREIGN, DOMESTIC, AND LOCAL NEWS received by Ocean Steamers, Electric Telegraphs, and Special Reporters up to 3 o'clock, P. M.; besides which, its columns are enriched by the **Original Contributions** of a host of talented Writers at home and intelligent Correspondents abroad, comprising the more varied and interesting topics of general discussion upon National Subjects, Literary Matters, Commercial Affairs, the Arts, Sciences, &c.

While in view of the approaching Presidential election, the coming year promises to be one of intense political heat, which is liable to engender partisan strife and sectional jealousies highly detrimental to the common welfare, we intend that the TRANSCRIPT shall continue its endeavors to cordially maintain that "era of good feeling" which ought never to be broken in a land so highly favored as our own.

No pains nor expense will be spared to make its Editorial and Reportorial departments, and its correspondence equal in all respects to the demands of the age. The aim of all those connected with the paper will be to make it a first-class high-toned newspaper, that shall ever be a welcome, genial, and trusted visitor to the homes of men of all creeds and parties. While the news of the day will have due prominence, the columns of the paper will contain a great variety of articles on current topics of general interest, and all public questions will be discussed in an independent manner. The Transcript has many literary friends who make it their chosen vehicle of communication with the public, and whose contributions add much to its other attractions. We shall continue to publish a liberal and independent newspaper, which will "cherish the interests of literature and the sciences; countenance and inculcate the principles of humanity and general benevolence, public and private charity, good humor and all social affections and generous sentiments among the people."

Early in the Spring we shall remove to our

New Office on Washington Street,

in the granite building at Nos. 90 and 92, extending through to Devonshire street, now being erected specially for the publication of the TRANSCRIPT, and to be furnished with all requisite conveniences in the different departments of the establishment. With improved facilities wherever needed, and with the employment of a twenty horse-power Corlis engine in driving Hoe's Lightning Press, and other machinery, we hope to be able to supply the constantly increasing demands of our Daily, Weekly, and California editions.

Terms, Five Dollars per annum,

Or one Dollar less than any other Subscription Daily published in Boston.

THE BOSTON WEEKLY TRANSCRIPT

Is a good-sized, handsomely printed paper, completely filled with twenty-eight columns of Reading Matter, having *no Advertisements.* Its miscellaneous contents are varied, interesting, and useful, and the sheet altogether is prepared with a view to its being a most WELCOME WEEKLY VISITANT in the Family Circle. With the current News of the Day are given the latest reports of the Cattle and other Markets, Prices Current, and other matters specially adapted to the wants of residents throughout the New England States, and New England men at the West and South.

Published every Wednesday Morning, at $1.50 per annum,

and to Clubs to one address, at the following rates:—Two copies, $2.50; Three copies, $3.50; Five copies, $5.00. And one copy *free* to the getter-up of all Clubs of over five. Terms, INVARIABLY IN ADVANCE.

TRANSCRIPT FOR CALIFORNIA.

A large, thirty-two column paper, one fourth larger than the *Daily Transcript,* is issued on the 4th and 19th of each month, to go by the regular mail to California, containing the Latest News, Prices Current, Births, Marriages, and Deaths, and other intelligence interesting to all Emigrants from New England.

Advertisements inserted at twelve cents a line for each insertion.

☞ Orders for either of the above—accompanied with the cash—should be addressed to the Publishers,

HENRY W. DUTTON & SON,
TRANSCRIPT BUILDING, CONGRESS STREET, BOSTON.

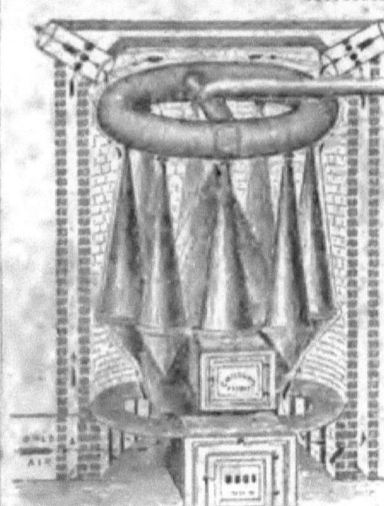

www.ingramcontent.com/pod-product-compliance
Lightning Source LLC
Chambersburg PA
CBHW030552300426
44111CB00009B/951
9783337217327